30 great cities to start out in

SANDRA GURVIS

MACMILLAN • USA

T o my daughter Amy, who will soon be taking her place in the world, and my son Alex, whose time will come.

Macmillan General Reference USA
A Simon & Schuster Macmillan Company
1633 Broadway
New York, NY 10019-6785

An Arco Book

ARCO, MACMILLAN and colophons are registered trademarks of Simon & Schuster Inc.

Manufactured in the United States of America
10 9 8 7 6 5 4 3 2 1

Note: Please be advised that travel information is subject to change at any time. Neither the author nor the publisher can be held responsible for the experiences of readers while traveling.

Library of Congress Catalog Card Number: 96-078702
ISBN: 0-02-861522-0

Book design by Scott Meola
Cover design by George Berrian

CONTENTS

ACKNOWLEDGMENTS

30 Great Cities to Start Out In took over a year to write, much longer than anyone anticipated. I felt compelled to provide the most thorough (and fun) information possible: a time-consuming, complex, sometimes frustrating, but ultimately rewarding task. However, no project, particularly one of this depth and magnitude, is accomplished alone.

My agent, Bert Holtje, and editor, Barbara Gilson, were essential in the beginning stages, while editor Jennifer Perillo was more than helpful and understanding throughout the various throes of creation and deadline extensions. Convention and Visitors Bureau and Chamber of Commerce personnel were invariably friendly and accommodating, providing me with many trees' worth of information. Likewise for the cities' residents quoted throughout the book. They were generous with their time and their thoughts.

Linda Deitch, my right-hand researcher, was always there with the needed facts and figures, and sometimes more, which, if not always applicable, were at least interesting. The staff at Macmillan was flexible and compassionate, particularly production editor Michael Thomas, who put up with the delays in scheduling.

And finally, thanks to my patient and long-suffering husband, Ron: maybe the next one will be easier. But perhaps not. You never know what you're getting into until you're up to it in alligators.

INTRODUCTION

Young professionals today have an advantage over Baby Boomers. In the '60s and '70s people who wanted to move around stuck out their thumbs and hitchhiked, bumming around the country (or Europe) for a few weeks or months. Then reality would hit (money would run out) and they'd get a job, most likely near family or a significant other.

In the '70s, when I graduated from college and moved to Columbus, I didn't know a soul, except for my cousin (who was married at the time) and some aunts. The first few months, I'd come home from my job (which I hated, but it was the only one that paid enough so I could leave Dayton and my parents' house), plop down on the bed of my lonely apartment, and brood. I spent evenings by myself, because it was winter and everyone in our complex stayed inside.

Things have changed for young people living on their own. Options for college graduates and those fairly new to the workforce include a wide-ranging network of arts, sport, social, and charitable organizations. Any man or woman, regardless of religion or color, can feel comfortable going alone to a gallery walk, concert, or fund-raiser.

Having endured their parents' or friends divorce, more people in their twenties and thirties are waiting to settle down in a serious relationship. This opens up even more possibilities for folks wanting to relocate in the nation's large cities. They're faced with such decisions as "If I take this job, will I be happy with the locale?" Or, "If I can't find employment, where do I look for work?" Ethnic and religious factors are also a consideration; for instance, an Orthodox Jew might feel uncomfortable in Salt Lake City.

Young professionals today are often told they have the freedom to settle anywhere they want. However, preferences can be dictated, just as they were in the past, by an offer of a high-paying job or the location of relatives or a paramour. When you get there you may find it wasn't what you expected at all. Wouldn't it be nice to know what's out there in advance?

30 Great Cities to Start Out In attempts to cover all aspects of living in a metropolis, from nightlife to vital statistics to livability to the top employers. Chamber of Commerce information, demographic data, tour guides and books, research on the World Wide Web (a hotbed of hip info), and interviews with people who have lived in the area for years help provide a comprehensive picture. In effect, once you unpack your things (or even before, if you so choose), you can plug right into restaurants, nightlife, and recreational activities, getting around by using the local lingo.

Of course, adjusting to a new place is rarely that simple. However, *30 Great Cities to Start Out In* aims to give you a sense of what the city is like and whether you'll feel comfortable there. Each chapter is designed to be user-friendly, with subject headings that enable you to zero in on a specific topic. This also allows for comparisons among cities, as no one city is "best" or "worst." It's more a question of what's right for you.

As for me, things got better when the weather warmed up and I switched jobs. My cousin got a divorce and introduced me to my husband. After twenty-some years of marriage, I got to write this book and vicariously experience some of the really neat alternatives open to young professionals today.

A GUIDE TO USING THIS GUIDE

Sometimes people skip over the introductory material, but a review of this section will help you use this book to its fullest advantage. The chapters are laid out according to a specific format for easy reference. Twenty cities are given "full treatment" chapters; the remaining ten chapters offer a more general overview of cities. Both long and short chapters provide a wealth of in-depth information.

Full-treatment chapters are organized as follows:

City at a Glance

This statistical list is meant to provide a "snapshot" and general overview of the city. The numbers have been culled from references such as *America's Top-Rated Cities,* Mobile guides, *Moving & Relocation Sourcebook, City Profiles USA, World Book Encyclopedia, ACCRA Cost of Living Index,* the U.S. Census, and many others. They vary from year to year and source to source, and sometimes measure different things, so statistics alone might not be the best course for making a decision.

Certain terms and abbreviations used in this section include the following:

- *MSA:* Metropolitan Statistical Area. The city itself and surrounding area, including (possibly) nearby counties. Not available for all cities; if only one number is given for size, it's the city proper.

- *Per capita income:* The amount of money available (through income, Social Security, government assistance, property and other assets, and other sources) for each individual in the city. Because it encompasses everyone, including the unemployed or retired, it's usually a low figure.

- *Average household income:* The total salary reported by each family member age 15 or older. This number is generally higher than per capita income and is based on an average number of people per household.

- *ACCRA cost of living:* An estimate utilizing a scale of 100 against which most large American cities are measured. A city with an overall ACCRA rating below 100 is considered less expensive; those over 100 are costlier. These statistics are published quarterly by ACCRA, an organization that gathers cost-of-living information on various U.S. cities and regions, and are subject to change.

- *Medical costs:* ACCRA also averages U.S. medical costs. Each city's hospital, doctor, and dentist costs (in the "Community Services" section) can be measured against the following U.S. average: $378.71/day for a hospital stay; $45.16 for a doctor's visit; and $57.12 for a dentist's visit.

After the "At A Glance" section, an overview/essay offers a brief history of the city and a discussion of its quality of life and general opportunities. If you like what you're reading, then continue on to...

Major Breadwinning

A discussion of the job opportunities and leading industries, including their financial impact on the community at large.

Social and Recreational Scene

How...Plays
Arts and Sciences
The Sporting Life
After-Hours Diversions
Culinary and Shopping Haunts
Ethnic and Religious Prospects

Gets down and dirty with info on attitudes, the dating scene, and the best places to get acquainted when you first arrive. Includes a roundup of local music, arts, and sports; nightlife as well as other leisure-time pursuits; a discussion of popular restaurants and stores/malls; and resources for finding members of your religious/racial persuasion, if available. "Where It's At" sidebar indexes contain the addresses and phone numbers of establishments that appear in boldface.

Crib Sheet

Housing and the most appropriate neighborhoods for the 20–30 age group, as well as brief information on schools.

Navigating...

The best ways to get around and other transportation news.

Mini-chapters are set up similarly, except they contain condensed descriptions of the following sections:

> A Brief Glance (statistical information)
> General Opportunities
> How... Works and Plays
> Major Breadwinning
> Crib Sheet

If you need more information on either these or the full-treatment chapters, contact the resources listed in Appendix B.

A Brief Glance

Size and Growth: 480,000 (city). Percent change, 1980–1990: +16.0%. Percent change, 1990–1995: +8.3%.

Money Matters: *Unemployment rate—* 4.4%.
Per capita income—$14,013.
Average cost of a home—$131,500.
Average rent for an apartment— $656/month.
ACCRA Cost of Living Index (based on 100)—101.2.
*ACCRA Housing Index—*103.4.

People Profile: *Crime rate* (per 100,000 population)—9,581.7 (city), 7,547.8 (MSA).

*Racial and ethnic characteristics—*White: 78.5% (city), 77.1% (MSA); Black: 3.0% (city), 2.7% (MSA); American Indian/Eskimo/Aleut: 3.0% (city), 3.3% (MSA); Asian/Pacific Islander: 1.8% (city), 1.5% (MSA); Hispanic Origin: 34.2% (city), 36.9% (MSA); Other: 13.8% (city), 15.3% (MSA).
*Gender ratio—*94.3 males per 100 females (all ages); 91.1 males per 100 females (18 years old+).
*Age characteristics—*18–24 (10.4%); 25–44 (35.4%). Median age: 32.4.

Major Players: Services, retail/ wholesale trade, government, manu- facturing. Also opportunities in research.

Photo by Ron Behrman, courtesy of ACVB

Steeped in ancient history and modern technology, Albuquerque seems full of contradictions. Home to the ancestors of the Pueblo Indians dating as far back as A.D. 500, the city was a Spanish outpost and is quite old by U.S. standards (it will be 300 in the year 2006). Reflected here is a mix of mostly Hispanic, Native American, and Anglo cultures, with some African-American and Asian influences thrown in. Monikered after the Spanish Duke of Alburquerque, the city name got mangled to its present incarnation and is also known as Duke City and the much-easier-to-spell ABQ.

A railroad stopover in the 1880s, the city developed a reputation for a pleasant physical and ethnically tolerant climate, and drew thousands of tuberculosis patients looking for "the cure." During World War II, the military moved in, most notably through Sandia Laboratories, a highly restricted munitions research facility, and the Manhattan Project, where the first atomic bomb was developed. The latter evolved into Kirtland Air Force Base, a major player in the subsequent Cold War (and in UFO cover-ups mentioned in "The X-Files" and elsewhere).

You'd think that a smallish metropolis in such a big state (density: a mere 12.8 people per square mile) would manufacture tortilla and cow chips rather than those of the silicon variety. But Albuquerque produces a whopping 9.2 percent of the world's market for silicon chips; its reputation as a technology, medical research, and high-tech manufacturing leader has earned it yet another nickname: Silicon Mesa. (The first personal computer, the Altair, had its debut here in the 1970s.)

Yet Old Town, the original settlement, looks much as it did in the early 1700s—except when you browse inside its more than 100 shops, galleries, and restaurants. The rest of the city's budding skyscrapers are surrounded by the ancient Sandia Mountains. You have the world's largest hot-air ballooning event (the Kodak Albuquerque International Balloon Fiesta), side by side with ancient Indian pueblos that still abide by tribal law, and an incredible array of Native American art, culture, and architecture. And the Sandia Peak Tram (at 2.7 miles, it's the longest ever) provides views of forests, canyons, extinct volcanoes, and mountains. With squirrels and granite at the base and eagles and limestone at the peak (elevation: 10,378 feet), the tram spans four different ecological zones and is the environmental equivalent of traveling from Mexico to Alaska.

With a technologically savvy population, Albuquerque might be a nerd haven, yet its rugged setting makes it a training ground for runners and other athletic types from around the globe. Folks here are friendly; at 5,314 feet above sea level (the highest metropolitan elevation in the Lower 48), ABQ is so spread out that people can't get on your nerves.

Altitude and temperatures vary from neighborhood to neighborhood, so if you don't like the climate in one section of town, you can always move. And four moderate seasons, a minimum of humidity, and a preponderance of sunshine more than make up for two disadvantages: The area is slightly water-impaired, and public transportation is, at best, minimal. Much of Albuquerque is laid out on a logical grid pattern, so getting around is pretty easy in a car. And the local government is working on the H_2O problem. Besides, where else can you get a rebate for having the right kind of toilet?

General Opportunities

Some might consider Albuquerque to be in the middle of nowhere, but it has been noticed. Its business atmosphere has been praised by *The Wall Street Journal* and by *Kiplinger's Personal Finance* and *Entrepreneur* magazines, and *U.S. News & World Report* has complimented ABQ's home-buying market and health care delivery systems. Companies can also bloom in the desert with lower-than-average tax burdens and salaries, especially in the service sector, although folks with an electronic or computer chip background can start out at about $30,000 a year.

Although hit fairly hard by military reductions, the economy has managed to bounce back through diversification. And many developments pioneered by the defense industries have been shifted profitably to private enterprise.

With an annual job increase of between 5 and 6 percent, employment is well below the national average, although a slowdown of construction may reduce the number of new jobs.

Still, nearly 20 percent of all positions can be found near the University of New Mexico (UNM) and other knowledge factories, including Albuquerque Public Schools, Albuquerque Technical Vocational Institute (TVI), and several hospitals. Other major employment centers consist of the uptown area near the malls, the north I-25 corridor, and downtown. Job location is particularly important: Some commutes stretch as long as 30 minutes. Interstates are basically limited to I-25 (north-south) and I-40 (east-west), although state Route 66 (really!) sort of meanders through the center of town. A link between the population centers on the east and west sides of the Rio Grande is being worked on, although PDQ doesn't seem to be an ABQ concept.

HOW ALBUQUERQUE WORKS AND PLAYS

Major Breadwinning

Top employers in the public and private sectors are Albuquerque Public Schools (10,596 employees), Sandia National Laboratories (7,488), Kirtland Air Force Base (civilians, 6,865; military, 5,742), and Intel Corporation (about 5,000). Other local biggies consist of Lovelace Medical Center, Motorola Ceramic Products, Wal-Mart, Furr's Supermarket, and US WEST Communications. MCI, Citicorp, America Online, Southwest Airlines, Intel (again!), and Radisson Hotels have recently expanded or relocated here.

Many of Albuquerque's businesses are on the smallish side and employ fewer than 20 people. Yet not only are they prospering to the extent that many have added more workers, but their numbers have also increased 8.4 percent in a recent year—about 2 percent above the national average. Major growth occurred in holding and investment companies, electrical equipment manufacturing, engineering firms, and social services. Various incentives and groups such as the Albuquerque Economic Development (AED) provide support and training.

Albuquerque's proximity to Mexico makes it a natural export hub during these times of NAFTA, although products go to Japan and South Korea as well. Items such as semiconductors, tractors and parts, jewelry, computers and software, and more are shipped abroad to the tune of an overall increase of 34 percent between 1991 and 1995. Bilingualism and a background in international trade are pluses in this rapidly growing field.

With a recent annual increase of 8.7 percent, the service sector shows no sign of slowing down. Although many positions (such as customer service and travel reservation agents) don't require degrees, others (such as technical support technician for America Online) require a computer background. Taco Bell is also making a run for the border by expanding its accounting division. And, with an employment upswing of 7.9 percent, health care is thriving: Along with the highly regarded Cancer Center at UNM, the area has 1,500 physicians and numerous private and public systems and hospitals, including the federal Indian Health Service. Biomedical firms, such as InVivo Medics, which tests "noninvasive" drugs and procedures on animals (an oxymoron?), are relatively new transplants also.

Employment in construction, which accelerated a whopping 20 percent from 1992 to 1994, makes use of those handy with a hammer and saw, as well as architects and engineers. Many stores, malls, hotels, and luxury apartments have sprung up in the past few years, although the activity is expected to level off somewhat. Trade employment, including retail sales and food service, remains fairly stable, as does the finance, insurance, and real estate

(FIRE) industry. Banking prospects have moderately improved as many smaller, local institutions merge with nationwide systems, resulting in a more stable job base.

But the real action is in the manufacturing sector, where places such as (you guessed it!) Intel, Motorola, and Philips Semiconductors helped boost employment levels by 3.9 percent. New companies include the alliterative Sumitomo Sitix Silicon and Silimax, which specializes in silicon production and recycling; the icky-sounding Tissue Technologies, which makes lasers for skin resurfacing; and Cycle Plastics, creator of polyethylene bags.

> **The Sandia Peak Tram provides views of forests, canyons, extinct volcanoes, and mountains. With squirrels and granite at the base and eagles and limestone at the peak, the tram spans four different ecological zones and is the environmental equivalent of traveling from Mexico to Alaska.**

And nearly 20 percent of Albuquerqueans work in some sort of civil service capacity. A recent threatened closing of Kirtland Air Force Base (it didn't) gave a few thousand employees the heebie-jeebies, and even Sandia Labs is scaling down through attrition. Most jobs in this area can be found in public schools or with the city and state.

 ## ARTS AND SCIENCES

Entertainment in area code 505 includes much more than attending September's ever-popular New Mexico State Fair, which draws over one million people (a humongous horde in this sparsely populated state), or watching floating "gas bags" in the sky, although colorful hot air balloons are often associated with Albuquerque. The city's rich performing arts scene has nearly a dozen theaters, including the Albuquerque Civic Light Opera; the Albuquerque Little Theater, which offers excellent amateur versions of comedies, mysteries, and classics; the Adobe Theater, winner of the Theater New Mexico Actfest; the Matchbox Theater, with its innovative performances; and La Compania de Teatro de Albuquerque, one of the few major Hispanic troupes in the U.S.

For music, you can enjoy the New Mexico Symphony Orchestra, the Chamber Orchestra of Albuquerque, and Musica Antigua de Albuquerque. And there are several singing groups: the New Mexico Gay Men's Chorus, the New Mexico Women's Chorus, the Enchanted Mesa Chorus of Sweet Adelines, and the New Mexi-Chords (a barbershop quartet in this, the most unlikely of places). Dance boasts the New Mexico Ballet Company, the eclectic Lane Lucas and Drop Dead Dance productions, and others, while Albuquerque's 100 or so galleries are highlighted at monthly arts crawls. Folks wanting to get involved in the community can do so through the Albuquerque Arts Alliance, the Albuquerque Public Arts Program, or the Harwood Arts Center. Albuquerque United Artists, the New Mexico Art League, and the South Broadway Cultural Center and Library provide performance spaces, classes, and support.

Many Native American communities and activities are located in or near Albuquerque, and the city's Indian Pueblo Cultural Center serves as an overall introduction. The city of ABQ observes Indian life, feast days, and other rituals—and respects their regulations and traditions on their homelands. ABQ also offers a number of other historical sites: the Spanish History Museum, the National Atomic Museum, and the Albuquerque Museum in Old Town, which traces local art and history. More art can be explored at the Maxwell Museum of Anthropology, the University Art Museum, and the Jonson Gallery.

There's plenty of science at the New Mexico Museum of Natural History, Explora! Science Center, and the Museum of Southwestern Biology. The recently opened Albuquerque Biological Park combines a new aquarium and botanical garden with the existing Rio Grande Zoo, whose sea lion and giraffe exhibits stand out above the crowd. Real stargazing can be found at the UNM Campus Observatory or the more down-to-earth Institute of Meteoritics, Geology and Meteoritic Museum (which has the world's second-largest stone meteorite, among other space debris). You can find a world o' collectibles at the Tinkertown Museum, including 48,000 bottles. Then there are snakes alive and dead at the American International Rattlesnake Institute. No, thank you.

THE SPORTING LIFE

Albuquerque offers 240 sites encompassing 2,205 acres of land, including Rio Grande State Park, a natural habitat in the middle of the city. But the biggest sports draw is the Sandia Mountains, with picnicking in the foothills, wildlife in the Cibola Forest, and hiking at the 5.3-mile Piedra Lisa trail. The mountains also offer biking at the Tramway Mountain Path and skiing in designated areas. Other natural wonders: the Petroglyph National Monument (its five prehistoric volcanoes are still considered by the Pueblo Indians to be a sort of spiritual uplink to their gods); Coronado State Park and Monument, an ancient pueblo and temporary residence of its namesake explorer; Apache Trails, which covers everything from Billy the Kid's stomping grounds to the snowlike White Sands; and the Turquoise Trail, the "scenic route" to Santa Fe, dotted with ghost towns.

Other recreational pastimes include swimming, golfing, tennis, ballooning, horseback riding, llama treks, and rafting. The state is chock-full of casinos. Horse racing is available at the Downs at Albuquerque, and there's a speedway at Albuquerque National Dragway. Spectator sports are limited to the AAA Dukes, the L.A. Dodgers farm team, the New Mexico Chiles (soccer), the New Mexico Scorpions hockey club in San Pedro, and whatever's available at UNM. Oh well, you can't have everything.

AFTER-HOURS DIVERSIONS

Central Avenue (and environs) is the place to be for club crawling 'round these parts, drawing everybody from gentrified suits to blue jeans casuals to college kids. You'll find musical acts at the El Ray, a sophisticated crowd at the Z-Pub, homemade brews at the Rio Bravo Brewpub, and TV sports at the Time Out Restaurant. There's dancing (and more) at Daqz, Dingo Bar, and Zone. Brewster's, the University Draft House, and Anodyne offer pool tables, a college-y atmosphere, and beer, although not necessarily in any order. A stop at Java Joe's, Cafe Au Lait, or Albuquerque Coffee Roasting Company finishes off the evening.

The University–Nob Hill area is another popular hangout, with O'Neills Pub, the Outpost Performance Space, Marble Cow, Double Rainbow Bakery and Cafe, and Cafe Intermezzo. Other hot spots in and around ABQ: the Gulf Coast Eatery for crawfish and jazz; Midnight Rodeo for day and evening country-western dancing; Conrad's Downtown, which has a flamenco guitarist; and the Lloyd Shaw Dance Studio, with its Friday night "pickup" lessons (a double meaning?) and homemade snacks.

 ## CULINARY AND SHOPPING HAUNTS

Albuquerque is the place for Mexican/New Mexican/Native American food and steaks. Not only are many offerings in the under-$15 range, but you can choose from upscale dining in various hotels to noisy cantinas to unassuming family fare. Southwestern standouts include the top-rated Tio Tito's and Rio Grande Cantina as well as Casa de Ruiz, Monica's El Portal, and Montoya's in Old Town. The Rancher's Club in the Albuquerque Hilton, the Tumbleweed Steak House, Great American Land & Cattle Company, and Copper Creek provide plenty to "beef" about. There are a number of American (65 Diner, Yester-Dave's Grill), barbecue (Ribs Hickory Smoked Pit, Sweet Mesquite), and ethnic (New Chinatown Restaurant, La Crepe Michel) offerings as well.

Local goods—silver, turquoise, and Southwestern and Native American art and furnishings—are not only plentiful but reasonably priced, particularly if you purchase them from the original artists, many of whom work and live in pueblos and reservations. Places such as Old Town, the Indoor Mercado, and the New Mexico State Fairgrounds offer a wide selection as well, with the latter being the largest open-air flea market around. Traditional malls like the Coronado Center, Cottonwood Mall, and Winrock Shopping Center complement the eclectic Nob Hill and discount New Mexico Outlet Center and Santa Fe Factory Stores, making for a well-rounded shopping experience.

 ## ETHNIC AND RELIGIOUS PROSPECTS

Rated as one of the top cities for Latinos by *Hispanic* magazine, ABQ boasts a Hispanic mayor (Martin Chavez), a great deal of Hispanic representation in city government, and an influential Hispano Chamber of Commerce. None of this should be a surprise, considering that the population is more than one-third Latino and the culture was there long before the Anglos moved in. New Mexico has more Hispanic-owned businesses per capita than any other state. The other original occupants, the Native Americans, also seem to garner their fair share of honor and respect in addition to having more festivals, museums, and monuments here than in many other places.

Women and other minorities have found success as well. New Mexico ranks second in the nation in the percentage of businesses owned by females. Albuquerque has an Urban League, Jewish Federation, and Catholic Archdiocese of Santa Fe, as well as several dozen churches.

CRIB SHEET

Although housing costs are slightly above the national average, the diversity of settings—from pastoral to quasi-urban, Victorian to modern, mountainous to almost desertlike—helps make up the difference. With artists, poetry readings, and plenty of unique shops, the Nob Hill–University area has become a favorite choice for the up-and-coming and for others who like the "quirky" last two syllables of their city. Older neighborhoods like Ridgecrest and Near Heights are within walking distance of many attractions, with Altura Park in Near Heights providing a rare touch of greenery. Huning Highlands is chock-full of turn-of-the-century homes waiting to be renovated, while bustling Old Town is undergoing a resurgence of its own. Nearby South Valley and Barelas offer meandering streets and some of the area's oldest dwellings, along with little family-owned restaurants, Spanish haciendas, and local attractions. Prices vary greatly, although the average cost of a home in these areas is about $145,000.

> You'd think that a smallish metropolis in such a big state would manufacture tortilla and cow chips rather than those of the silicon variety.... But Albuquerque's reputation as a technology leader has earned it the nickname "Silicon Mesa."

A bit farther away is the horsey, country-clubbish Four Hills (average cost: don't ask) with its mansions and resident coyotes who know a good thing when they see it. The North Valley (around $220,000) and Corrales ($275,000) reflect a quiet, rural life, albeit a somewhat dusty and pricey one. Those looking for newer, more urban communities will find them in Northeast Heights ($150,000) and Far Northeast Heights ($210,000), some of which border the foothills. The fastest-growing areas in the region, they offer privacy, security, and increasing property values.

South Valley ($115,000), Rio Rancho ($135,000), and the Near Northeast Heights ($140,000) are for the more budget-minded; while Tijeras ($255,000), Sandia Heights ($305,000), and North Albuquerque Acres ($350,000) command a more dukely sum.

With year-round programs, extended and after-school care for working parents, and bilingual classes at the elementary level (including Spanish and Native American dialects), Albuquerque's public schools seem to be slightly ahead of the curve. There are also a number of religious and private institutions, such as Albuquerque Academy and Sandia Preparatory.

Postsecondary offerings include technical schools focusing on masonry, electrical engineering, and construction (TVI, others); massage and holistic schools (New Mexico School of Natural Therapeutics); cooking schools (Jane Butel's Southwestern Cooking School, programs in TVI and UNM); and the Tamarind Institute, which teaches lithography. Along with medical and law programs, UNM offers degrees in over 150 disciplines and has an excellent faculty as well as low student-teacher ratios.

ATLANTA, GEORGIA

Atlanta at a Glance

Birthdate and Present Size: 1837.
Metropolitan Statistical Area—
1980: 2,138,231; 1990: 2,833,511.
1/1/95 (estimate): 3,383,500.
Percent change, 1980–1990: +32.5%.
Percent change, 1990–1995: +19.4%.

Weather Report: *Average annual temperature—*61° F. In January: 51/33° F. In July: 88/69° F.
*Average annual precipitation—*48".
*Average annual snowfall—*2".

Money Matters: *Unemployment rate—* 4.5%.
Per capita income—$15,279.
Average household income—$37,882 (city); $44,968 (MSA).
Average cost of a home—$128,500.
Average rent for an apartment— $561/month.
ACCRA cost of living indexes (based on 100)—Composite Index: 100.9; Utilities Index: 106.2; Housing Index: 100.1.
*Sales and use tax—*4.0% (state); 2.0% (local).
*Personal income tax—*1.0 to 6.0%.

People Profile: *Crime rate* (Per 100,000 population)—16,118.5 (city); 7,333 (MSA).
Racial and ethnic characteristics— White: 31.1% (city), 71.3% (MSA); Black: 67.1% (city), 26.0% (MSA); American Indian/Eskimo/Aleut: 0.2% (city), 0.2% (MSA); Asian/Pacific Islander: 0.8% (city), 1.8% (MSA); Hispanic

Origin: 1.9% (city), 1.9% (MSA); Other: 0.9% (city), 0.7% (MSA).
*Gender ratio—*91 males per 100 females (all ages); 87.8 males per 100 females (18 years old+).
*Age characteristics—*18–24 (13.2%); 25–44 (34.7%). Median age: 31.4.
*Educational attainment—*percent having completed high school: 69.9%; percent having completed college: 26.6%.

Major Players: Services; retail/wholesale trade; government; manufacturing, especially transportation equipment and textiles.
*Largest employers—*BellSouth Telecommunications, Coca-Cola, Delta Air Lines, Equifax (credit investigations), Food Services Mgmt. by MGR, Fulton DeKalb Hospital Authority, Georgia Baptist Medical Center, Georgia-Pacific Corp., Georgia Power Co., National Service Industries, Piedmont Hospital, St. Joseph's Hospital of Atlanta, SunTrust Banks, Turner Broadcasting System.

Community Services: *Average hospital cost—*$316.40/day.
Average doctor visit—$47.00.
Average dentist visit—$66.40.
Newspapers—The Atlanta Constitution, The Atlanta Journal, Atlanta Business Chronicle, Business Atlanta, The Georgia Bulletin (Catholic), *Creative Loafing* (alternative). The following serve the black community: *Atlanta Daily World, The Atlanta Inquirer, Atlanta Tribune, The Atlanta Voice.*

Photo courtesy of the Metro Atlanta Chamber of Commerce

With a metropolitan area of 6,150 square miles, Atlanta is one big mother of a city. Although downtown has been not-so-flatteringly compared to a strip mall—albeit a verdant and well-tended one—this city *was* chosen to host the 1996 Summer Olympics. And it has gathered enough kudos to win a gold, silver, and bronze in several categories: one of the "Best U.S. Cities for Business" (#2, *Fortune*, several years); "Best Airport in North America" (#1, *Business Traveller International*); "America's friendliest city" (*Roper*); one of the "Top Cities for Relocation" (#3, the PHH Relocation company); and many others, including one of the best places for African-Americans to live and work (*Black Enterprise* magazine), one of the most viable for foreign investors (Association of Foreign Investors), and a terrific big burg for small businesses (*Entrepreneur* magazine).

Plaudits have been given for Atlanta's commercial real estate, convention accommodations, trade shows, retail sales, and ability to create jobs. Plus, it's incredibly inexpensive for its size, has the world's largest toll-free calling zone, and has a great climate, except when it occasionally snows or sleets. It's enough to make you rent a U-Haul and move there, as more people did in 1993 than to any other U.S. city.

Not bad for a town that was originally—and rather pessimistically—named Terminus, the southernmost crossroads for the Western & Atlantic railway. In 1843, it was changed to Marthasville, after the then-Governor's daughter, and two years later to Atlanta in honor of the train company that helped drive those annoying Cherokees and Creek Indians away from the lands they'd lived on for several hundred years. By the outbreak of the Civil War, the city had become a major transportation hub, manufacturing center, and supply depot. General William T. Sherman made a point of stopping by in 1864 during his infamous "March to the Sea," burning down businesses and homes, and providing dramatic impetus for the novel *Gone With the Wind*.

Four years later, however, Atlanta was back on its feet, doubling its population to 20,000 and serving as military and federal headquarters for reconstructing the South. The city became the state capital as well as a mecca for new jobs, transportation, and manufacturing. Soon, higher institutions of learning were established, among them Atlanta University, the largest black educational complex in the country. Telephones and trolleys were introduced, as was a new soft drink, Coca-Cola™. In the 1920s, William B. Hartsfield convinced the city to turn an empty racetrack into an airport. They elected him mayor and named the airport after him. Equivalent to over 45 football fields in length, the Hartsfield Atlanta International Airport is the largest in the world and the second busiest.

Race relations in Atlanta haven't always been as smooth as a Georgia peach. The year 1906 saw a serious riot, and in the '20s the city served as headquarters for the Ku Klux Klan. But later, leaders such as Atlanta native Dr. Martin Luther King and others helped effect political and civil rights reforms, including changes in voter registration and the integration of high schools. Atlanta was the only metropolis in the South to support the Civil Rights Bill and the first major Southern city to elect an African-American mayor.

New high-rises, stadiums and convention centers, and an underground entertainment plaza brought prosperity to Atlanta. City planners hope that Centennial Olympic Park, Georgia International Plaza, and other Olympic-themed improvements will do the same to impoverished and crime-ridden downtown sections. And if having more cellular phones per capita and the longest freestanding escalator in the world (8 stories, at CNN Center) are any indication of success, then Atlanta certainly seems capable of going the distance.

Quality of Life

Atlantans just love their town. Although it can get cold, dreary, and rainy for a couple of months in the winter, "there's very little to dislike about this place," enthuses marketing manager Brent Bridges.

Even the occasional snowfall is regarded as a blessing, "because businesses close and you get the day off," adds Kristi Burnham, who works for a nonprofit organization. Summers can be hot and humid, but "when you live and work in air-conditioning, it's comfortable. Atlanta has the full four seasons, but it can be nice enough in February and March to open windows."

Except for parts of downtown that are inhabited by vagrants and the poor, "most places are secure, especially where there are lots of folks," observes public relations executive Chester Jacinto. "And during the daytime, you can go just about anywhere."

> Atlanta has "the benefits of the big city combined with the advantages of a small town," says one resident. "Neighborhoods are distinctive and friendly, and the pace is slow and Southern. And there's always something to do."

With lower prices for food, rent, and utilities, "you can choose from a studio apartment in a neat old house to a brand-new condo with all the amenities," continues Bridges. Salaries can be smaller than in other major cities, but the reduced cost of living helps make up the difference. Restaurants and shopping opportunities are as abundant as the local greenery.

But perhaps the most outstanding characteristic of Atlanta is its friendliness. "There are a lot of transplants," comments Jacinto. The city is a combination of the "best of the progressive South and the top people from all over the U.S. who come to live here. So it's a very tolerant environment" towards minorities and gays, who have a strong community here as well.

And, although it's not New York or Los Angeles, local thespians, a popular arts festival, and opera, ballet, and symphony provide live entertainment. With nine "good" months for games of the non-Olympic kind, there are golf and tennis courses, parks galore, and lakes and mountains for outdoor activity. And although the national baseball, basketball, football, and hockey franchises fire up the usual fans, individual sports are really big. No wonder so many carry a torch for Atlanta.

General Opportunities

Atlanta can be the land of opportunity for everyone wanting to flee the impersonal bustle of Yankee (or La-La) land for a kinder, gentler climate. "If you're enterprising and ambitious, you can mix with people who are movers and shakers," remarks Jacinto, who recently found himself organizing a party for baseball great Hank Aaron.

The Olympics alone created nearly 170,000 new jobs, almost half of which are permanent. With 16.5 million visitors a year, "Atlanta is primarily a service-industry town, although we have one of the best fiber-optic networks in the U.S.," points out Bridges. Along with being the font for Coca-Cola—more than 8,000 soft drinks are consumed every second of every day—the first cable satellite connection was developed here. In 1977, Bell Labs provided the first commercial fiber optics application; Cox, CNN, and dozens of others have made use of Atlanta's 29 fiber-optic pathways (compared to a mere nine in New York). Nearly two-thirds of the Fortune 1000 companies have offices in this city. Its advantages—as the crossroads of major highways and railroads; as a hub for many large transportation companies; with an airport that processes well over 50 million passengers annually—are legion. The city's global presence includes more than 1,200 businesses and representation from nearly 55 countries.

The unemployment rate is lower than the national average, so there's no excuse not to find a job. According to one transplant, "people here can get ahead if they're willing to work." Or, you can just hang out downtown and let folks wonder whether or not you're dangerous.

MAJOR BREADWINNING

CNN. Coca-Cola. Delta Air Lines. Georgia Pacific. Holiday Inn. UPS. Scientific-Atlanta. These are but a smattering of the companies headquartered in this city, whose Capitol Dome is tellingly layered in 23-carat gold. But with great opportunities comes responsibility. Although Atlantans certainly know how to relax, "work is a priority here," comments Jacinto. "You see lots of younger folks putting in extra hours to get the job done." They are educated as well: More than one-fourth of people age 25 and over have a college degree.

New businesses have attracted even more migrants, making Atlanta the nation's leader in metropolitan population growth as well as number of jobs created. Companies such as Magellan Health Services, digital Electronics, Ryder, Ball Container, and Vanity Fair Mills recently joined Atlanta's approximately 85,000 enterprises; international corporations include Kyodo NewsService, AECSolutions architectural design, Liuski International computers, Mitsubushi, and others. Foreign-based facilities increased almost 50 percent from 1990–1994, with their employment doubling concurrently.

But service is the name of the game, taking a healthy chunk (28 percent) of Atlanta's 1.7 million employee pie. Tourism, telemarketing, law, health care, and even the airport (which alone employs 40,000) contribute to the job base. Retail outlets, such as building materials, general merchandise, food, automotive, apparel, furniture, restaurants, and others, make up another 18 percent. Remaining jobs can be found in government (14 percent); manufacturing (12 percent); wholesale trade (8 percent); transportation, communications, and utilities (8 percent); finance, insurance, and real estate (7 percent); construction (4 percent), and mining (1 percent).

With a 60 percent growth since the early '90s, and with an annual economic impact of more than $15 billion, technology keeps this city wired. AT&T, MCI, and Sprint as well as BellSouth provide thousands of computer, research, and support positions. Forty-five of the globe's top 50 electronics companies have a presence in the state. Many, such as AT&T Atlantaworks, the world's largest fiber-optic manufacturing facility, are located in and around Atlanta. And with the recent merging of Turner/Time Warner, Atlanta is now co-headquarters of that media empire (CNN, HBO, TBS, TNT, and others can be found in the city). There are also over 10 daily newspapers and TV stations, 50 radio stations, and 30 regional bureaus for broadcasting and print news. Even the climate is right for the Weather Channel. Those with a communications background and skills might find themselves royally employed.

The city is also a nucleus for research, training, and nonprofit organizations. Along with Emory University, which has graduate programs in medicine, law, and business, and other highly rated private schools, there's Georgia State University, the Georgia Institute of Technology, and the primarily African-American Atlanta University System. The American Cancer Society, Arthritis Foundation, Yerkes Regional Primate Center, Georgia Biomedical

Partnership, and the U.S. Centers for Disease Control and Prevention provide fundraising, scientific, social service, and related positions.

Atlanta is home to the Sixth District Federal Reserve Bank as well as more than 25 international financial institutions and dozens of local banks. And even though there's been a resurgence in commercial real estate, office space in Atlanta, particularly in some outlying areas, is still inexpensive enough to attract small business owners, whose presence is also encouraged by city planners.

A strong African-American business community can provide support to black entrepreneurs, too. "The opportunities are excellent here," observes Caesar Ramirez, a record store manager and disc jockey. "If you put your mind to it, everything's pretty much open-ended."

SOCIAL AND RECREATIONAL SCENE

How Atlanta Plays

With 100,000 college students and tons of newcomers just off the boat (so to speak), folks who don't meet others in area code 404 may need to re-evaluate their own social skills. And contacts certainly aren't limited to a certain age group: "This city is definitely a mixed bag," comments Bridges. "It has straights, gays, blacks, whites, old, and young. And everyone likes to help," he adds, citing as an example a dry cleaner who arranged to give out the phone number of a woman to a man who thought her attractive (with both parties' consent, of course). "You can strike up a conversation at work, in your neighborhood, even at the gym."

"Atlanta has to be the nicest city in the world," adds Ramirez. "There's a sense of pride you don't find in other cities. Rather than pointing to their respective nationalities, people say they're from Atlanta, even if they weren't born here."

Still, it helps to know what everyone's talking about. "Peachtree" could be one of 55 different streets with that name or "the Peachtree," the nation's largest 10K footrace. "Spaghetti Junction" refers to the crazy-making freeway system. Or you might choose "to Marta" (as in "to Marta, or not to Marta?") and utilize Atlanta's mass transit system. It may not be nobler, but it's certainly less confusing. Food has its own lingo as well. All soft drinks are called Coke; those who don't want sugar in their tea had better ask for "unsweet"; and a plain hot dog to go is a rather unappetizing sounding "nekked dog running."

 ### ARTS AND SCIENCES

Despite the "good 'ol boy"–isms, the Atlanta scene is pretty durn erudite. One way to become involved (along with volunteering) is to contact **Individual Visual Arts Coalition (IVAC),** a statewide organization of about 300 creative souls. Another cultural nucleus would be the **Robert W. Woodruff Arts Center,** where you'll find the **Atlanta Symphony,** which holds over 200 concerts, performs in area parks and has several specialized series, always a good way to mix and mingle. The **Alliance Theatre Company,** one of the country's largest, provides entertainment ranging from classics to premieres. Housed in an award-winning structure that

Where It's At

 Unless otherwise noted, all area codes are 404.

African-American Panoramic Experience, 135 Auburn Ave. NE, 521-2739

Agatha's Mystery Dinner Theatre, 693 Peachtree St. NE, 875-1610

Alliance Theatre Company, 1280 Peachtree St. NW, 733-5000

American Adventures & White Water Park, 250 N. Cobb Pkwy., Marietta, 770/424-9283

Where It's At

(continued)

Arts Exchange, 750 Kalb St., 624-1572 or 624-4211

Arts Festival, Piedmont Park

Atlanta Artist Gallery, 2300 Peachtree St. NW, 355-8231

Atlanta Botanical Garden, Piedmont Ave., at the Prado, 876-5859

Atlanta College of Art, 733-5100

Atlanta Cyclorama, 800 Cherokee Ave., 658-7625

Atlanta History Center, 130 W. Paces Ferry Rd., 814-4000

Atlanta International Museum of Art and Design, 285 Peachtree Center Ave., 688-2467

Atlanta Opera, 355-3311

Atlanta Shakespeare Company, 874-5299

Atlanta Symphony, 1280 Peachtree St. NW, 733-5000

Callanwolde Fine Arts Center, 980 Briarcliff Rd., 872-5338

Carter Presidential Center, One Copenhill Ave., 331-3942

Center for Puppetry Arts, Spring & 18th, 873-3089 or 873-3391

Christine Sibley's Urban Nirvana, 15 Waddell St. NE, 688-3329

Confederate Cemetery, Goss St. and Powder Springs Rd., Marietta, no phone (for obvious reasons)

Department of Cultural Affairs, 817-6815

Ebenezer Baptist Church, 407 Auburn Ave.

Fernbank Compound, 767 Clifton Rd., 378-0127; 156 Heaton Park Dr. NE, 378-4311

Fox Theatre, 660 Peachtree St. NE, 881-2100

Georgia Department of Industry, Trade, and Tourism, 656-3590

Hammonds House, 503 Peeples St. SW, 752-8730

High Museum of Art at Georgia-Pacific Center, 30 John Wesley Dobbs Ave., 577-6940

High Museum of Art, 1280 Peachtree St. NW, 733-4400

Individual Visual Arts Coalition (IVAC), 876-4745

resembles whitewashed Legos morphed during an acid trip, the **High Museum of Art** has 135,000 square feet of special exhibitions and permanent collections. Folk art, photography, and related forms are highlighted at its 4,500-square-foot "branch office," the rather redundantly named **High Museum of Art at Georgia-Pacific Center.** Lowbrows and novices can make a stab at creative greatness at the **Atlanta College of Art,** also part of the Woodruff complex.

The **Callanwolde Fine Arts Center** focuses on specialized exhibits and classes, while the **Atlanta Artist Gallery** showcases primarily Southern efforts. The eclectic is celebrated at the **Nexus Contemporary Arts Center;** African-American and multicultural works can be found at **Hammonds House** and the **Atlanta International Museum of Art and Design.** Local colleges have their own spaces, and galleries abound, such as the **Arts Exchange,** which coordinates displays at its Municipal Gallery. A bit of an anomaly, the **Michael C. Carlos Museum** offers 45,000 square feet of Egyptian, pre-Columbian, Greek, and other ancient relics.

Theater can be had for as cheap as five dollars a ticket and usually not more than $30, with more than 20 different performances on any given night. Offerings range from **Agatha's Mystery Dinner Theatre** to the **Atlanta Shakespeare Company** to **Jomandi,** which portrays the African-American experience. Other media range from puppetry (**Center for Puppetry Arts**) to Celtic works (**Theatre Gael**) to chamber music (**Pandean Players**) and more.

The historic **Fox Theatre** hosts a wide range of entertainment in a so-called Moorish/Egyptian/Art Deco vision (or nightmare, depending on your decorating preferences), including performances by the **Atlanta Opera.** A much newer venue is the **Rialto Center for the Performing Arts.**

Kingfest celebrates music, dance, poetry, and other art forms all summer long, while fall brings the **Arts Festival** (September), **Montreaux Atlanta International Music Festival** (September), and **Renaissance Festival** (October/November). (For information on these and other celebrations, contact the **Department of Cultural Affairs** or the **Georgia Department of Industry, Trade, and Tourism.**)

Atlanta has almost as many museums as "Peachtrees." Standouts include the **African-American Panoramic Experience,** which concentrates on local lore; the **Atlanta**

History Center, an in-depth re-creation of the city's tribulations and triumphs; and the **Carter Presidential Center,** which showcases the 39th President's personal papers and memorabilia. The world's largest collection of information on the civil rights movement can be found at the **Martin Luther King Jr. Center for Nonviolent Change,** and the **Martin Luther King Historic District** features King's birthplace as well as the **Ebenezer Baptist Church,** the spiritual center of the civil rights movement. A warm (especially in the summer) and fizzy experience can be found at the **World of Coca-Cola,** which has all kinds of Coke memorabilia; while *Gone With the Wind* fans can swoon at the **Road to Tara Museum.** The **Margaret Mitchell House,** where Mitchell wrote her famous novel, is currently being restored by a group that gives a damn.

Civil War buffs can satisfy their cravings at **Atlanta Cyclorama,** a 100-year-old circular painting of the Battle of Atlanta. The **Confederate Cemetery** has 3,000 graves, while the **Kennesaw Mountain National Battlefield Park** allows for immersion into the total experience through trails and memorabilia. The pinnacle, as it were, can be found at **Stone Mountain Park,** an 800-foot granite monolith that honors Southern leaders Robert E. Lee, Jefferson Davis, and Stonewall Jackson.

Atlanta has plenty of recreational parks (**American Adventures & White Water Park, Mountasia Family Funcenter, Six Flags Over Georgia,** and others) to provide a break from serious stuff. You can commune with tropical, desert, and endangered plants at the **Atlanta Botanical Garden;** buffalo, deer, and 600 other critters at the **Yellow River Wildlife Ranch;** and 1,000 more representing 250 species at **Zoo Atlanta. SciTrek** houses dozens of interactive exhibits, while the **Fernbank** compounds boast a natural history museum and 70-foot planetarium. Home improvement buffs might find bright ideas at the **Southface Energy and Environmental Resource Center. Christine Sibley's Urban Nirvana** has a little bit of everything, including artworks, birds, animals, and plants. Heavenly.

 ## THE SPORTING LIFE

Not only can you hit the golf course practically year 'round—the city hosts half-a-dozen major annual tournaments, and boasts over 100 courses—"but Atlanta has an amazing amount of amateur sports," remarks Bridges. The

Where It's At

 Unless otherwise noted, all area codes are 404.

Atlanta Amateur Hockey League, 973-0753

Atlanta Braves, 249-6400

Atlanta Club Sport, 842-0317

Atlanta Falcons, 223-8000

Atlanta Hawks, 249-6400

Atlanta Knights, 525-8900

Atlanta Lawn Tennis Association, 770/399-5788

Atlanta Ruckus, 770/645-6655

Atlanta Sport and Social Club, 262-7665

Atlanta Sports Council, 586-8510

Atlanta Thunder, 770/246-0300

Atlanta Track Club, 231-9064

Atlanta-Fulton County Stadium, 521 Capitol Ave. SW, 522-7630 or 522-1967

Chattahoochee Outdoor Center, 1990 Island Ford Pkwy., 770/952-4419

City Parks & Recreation Department, 817-6766

Georgia Balloon Association, 770/330-JOIN

Georgia Dome, One Georgia Dr. NE

Georgia State, 651-2772

Georgia State Soccer Association, 770/452-0505

Georgia Tech, 894-5400

Georgia Wildlife Federation, 950 Cochran Rd., 770/929-3350

Georgia World Congress Center, 285 International Blvd. NW, 223-4200

Gridiron Classic, 220-0367

Identified Flying Objects, 524-4628

Lake Allatoona, P.O. Box 487, Cartersville, 770/386-0549

Lake Lanier, P.O. Box 567, Buford, 770/945-9531

Lanier Sailing Academy Passport Sailing Club, 770/945-8810

Metro Atlanta Street Hockey, 770/923-0697

Metropolitan Cricket Club, 241-1348

Olympic Stadium, corner of Ralph David Abernathy Blvd. and Capitol Ave., 522-1967

OMNI Coliseum, 100 Techwood Dr. NW

Peachtree Road Race, Piedmont Park

Appalachians, Gulf Coast, Atlantic shore, and dozens of parks practically beg for outdoor activities. Even better, there's no sweat to getting involved: There are over 100 organized clubs and associations (call the **Atlanta Sports Council** for more information). Two biggies include the **Atlanta Lawn Tennis Association,** with over 70,000 members and 200 courts (not all grass, of course), and the **Atlanta Track Club,** which hosts more than 200 dashes a year, including the previously mentioned **Peachtree Road Race.**

The **Southern Bicycle League, Atlanta Amateur Hockey League, Lanier Sailing Academy Passport Sailing Club,** and **Georgia State Soccer Association** offer training and programs. Other options: cricket (**Metropolitan Cricket Club,** many others), frisbee (**Identified Flying Objects,** others), hot air ballooning (**Georgia Balloon Association**), even street hockey (**Metro Atlanta Street Hockey**), and dozens more. Part-time and aspiring jocks and jockettes might appreciate **Atlanta Club Sport, Single Outdoor Adventures, Weekend Escape Club,** and **Atlanta Sport and Social Club.**

Atlanta's national, state, and local parks are varied as well, with over 1,000 in the metro area alone (call the **City Parks & Recreation Department** for more information). There's "shooting the hooch" (rafting) at the **Chattahoochee Outdoor Center;** hiking, beach, and water opportunities at the previously mentioned Stone Mountain Park; and even more beach and water action at lakes **Lanier** and **Allatoona.** Tree huggers can make sure these resources remain pristine through affiliation with the **Wilderness Society, Sierra Club,** or **Georgia Wildlife Federation.**

Even the tepidly enthused might find themselves gaping at the state-of-the-art **Olympic Stadium,** where the 1996 games were held, now the new hunting grounds for the **Atlanta Braves** baseball team; the **OMNI Coliseum,** where the **Atlanta Hawks** (basketball) fly and **Atlanta Knights** (hockey) joust; and the **Georgia Dome,** with the helmet-crashing NFL **Atlanta Falcons.** The second largest convention site in the U.S., the **Georgia World Congress Center** hosts a variety of sporting events, as does **Atlanta-Fulton County Stadium.** In addition, there's the **Atlanta Thunder** (tennis) and the **Atlanta Ruckus** (soccer), as well as collegiate leagues at **Georgia Tech, Georgia State,** the **University of Georgia,** and private colleges (**Gridiron Classic**).

AFTER-HOURS DIVERSIONS

"Atlanta is a great city just to hang out in," observes Ramirez. Venues offer "acid jazz, hip hop, alternative, blues," along with good old rock 'n' roll. Plus, "there's lots of terrific local talent and many interesting bands" that play hot spots such as **Eddie's Attic,** the **Cotton Club,** and **Dark Horse Tavern.**

Like the Holiday Inn, Atlanta claims few surprises—usually you know what you're getting into before you arrive. According to one native, the area of Buckhead "is where you'll find all the decked-out, former-fraternity-and-sorority-types turned yuppie, while Little Five Points is definitely alternative," with multiple body piercings, obvious dye jobs, and tattoos being acceptable, if not the norm. Virginia Highlands offers up an infestation of trendies and college students, while Midtown has "lots of gay men." The suburb of Decatur attracts gay women, as in the "Digging Dykes of Decatur" a local (really!) garden club. So you can dress and act accordingly, although "no one really cares whether you're a prep, lesbian, or punk." That's in Atlanta, folks, not the outskirts.

Certain places are destinations in themselves. **Pomp, Duck, and Circumstance** is a three-hour lunacy of music, circus acts, and food. The improvisational comedy at **Dad's Garage,** a sort of millennial "What's My Line?," is "a really cheap and fun way to spend an evening," adds Kristi Burnham, while **Laughing Matters** is another favorite. The **CNN Center** offers studio tours, a chance to be "live" (as opposed to pre-taped) on TV, and Ted Turner's horde of networks, movies, and related memorabilia. **Underground Atlanta** provides restaurants, shopping, and nightclubs amidst the few remaining buildings that survived the Civil War.

Clubs have themes as well. Bradys and other bunches will appreciate the atmosphere at **Bell Bottoms** and **Have a Nice Day Cafe.** The woven-hair-and-Rogaine set (read: divorced, 30s, 40s) may find **Otto's, e.s.s.o.,** and **Tongue & Groove** in good taste. (Asking someone you've just met to go to the latter might be misinterpreted, however.) Perhaps a safer first-date bet would be **Bar,** which has a variety of music, dancing on the countertops, and drinks served on an ice carving.

You can pick other shots from pool tables and additional games at **Dave & Buster's, Champions,** and the **Cue Club.** Abundant TV sports, drinks, and munchies can be found in

---

Where It's At

(continued)

Sierra Club, 1447 Peachtree St., 607-1262 or 898-9778

Single Outdoor Adventures, 770/242-2338

Southern Bicycle League, 770/594-8350

University of Georgia, 542-1621

Weekend Escape Club, 332-0970

Wilderness Society, 1447 Peachtree St., 872-9453

Where It's At

Unless otherwise noted, all area codes are 404.

Bar, 250 E. Paces Ferry Rd., 841-0033

Bell Bottoms, 225 Pharr Rd., 816-9669

Blind Willie's, 828 N. Highland Ave. NW, 873-2583

Cafe 290, 290 Hilderbrand, 256-3942

Champions, Marriott, 265 Peachtree Center Ave., 586-6017

Cheetah, 887 Spring St. NE, 892-3037

CNN Center, Marietta St. at Techwood Dr., 827-2491 or 827-2300

Cotton Club, 816 N. Highland Ave. NE, 783-3607

Cue Club, 247 Buckhead Ave., 261-0660

Dad's Garage, 280 Elizabeth St., 523-3141

Dante's Down the Hatch, several locations

Dark Horse Tavern, 1021 Peachtree St. NE, 874-9524

Dave & Buster's, 2215 D&B Dr., 770/951-5554

e.s.s.o., 489 Courtland St., 872-3776

Eddie's Attic, 515 N. McDonough St., Decatur, 377-4976

Frankie's, 5600 Roswell Rd., 843-9444

Have a Nice Day Cafe, 857 Coller Rd., 351-1401

Jock's & Jill's, several locations

Johnny's Hideaway, 3771 Roswell Rd., 233-8026

Where It's At

(continued)

Kaya, 1068 Peachtree St., 874-4460

Laughing Matters, 710 Peachtree St., 523-4459

Lodge, 248 Buckhead Ave., 233-3345

Otto's, 65 E. Paces Ferry Rd., 233-1133

Pomp, Duck, and Circumstance, 84 Peachtree St. SW, 222-0000

Tongue & Groove, 3055 Peachtree Rd., 251-2365

Two Steps West, 3535 Chamblee Tucker Rd., 770/458-WEST

Underground Atlanta, Peachtree St., Central Ave. and Alabama St., 523-2311

Yin Yang, 64 3rd St., 607-0682

Where It's At

Unless otherwise noted, all area codes are 404.

2300 Peachtree Rd., 355-1288

Abbay, 3375 Buford Hwy., 321-5808

Anis, 2976 Grandview, 233-9889

Atlanta Antique Center & Marketplace, 5360 Peachtree Industrial Blvd., Chamblee, 770/458-0456

Atlanta Bread Co., several locations

Atlanta Fish Market, 265 Pharr Rd., 262-3165

Azio Pizza and Pasta, several locations

Bardi's, 182 Courtland St., 659-4848

Bones, 3130 Piedmont Rd., 237-2663

Boston Sea Party, 3820 Roswell Rd., 233-1776

Brasserie Le Coze, 3393 Peachtree Rd., 266-1440

Buckhead Diner, 3073 Piedmont Rd., 262-3336

Cafe Diem, 640 N. Highland Ave., 607-7008

Cajun Crabhouse, 5495 Old National Highway, 209-9432

Calhoun Outlet Center, 455 Belwood Rd., 866-5900

Frankie's, Jock's & Jill's, and the **Lodge.** Or cool down with jazz at the well-patroned **Kaya, Cafe 290,** and **Yin Yang.** In addition to a fondue menu and an 18th-century sailing ship decor, there's also jazz at **Dante's Down the Hatch.** So much ambiance, so little time. **Johnny's Hideaway** (big band), **Blind Willie's** (blues), **Two Steps West** (country & western), and among many others, **Cheetah** (so-called adult entertainment) round out the scene.

CULINARY AND SHOPPING HAUNTS

Atlanta's food chain is so lengthy you could probably write a book on eateries alone. Plus, you can get by for less than $10 in many places. One notable exception is the four-star **Pablo & Paul's,** where prices start at $16. At the other end of the culinary and economic spectrum is the **Varsity,** the world's largest and arguably one of the oldest fast-food drive-ins. Being able to dine al fresco most of the year makes things taste even better.

Along with standard Southern fare and the inevitable culinary faves du jour, the city has a variety of African-American eateries. Highlights include the New Orleans-inspired **Cajun Crabhouse,** the **Caribbean Restaurant,** where the menu is more original than the title, **Catfish Station,** the final stop for all manner of seafood, **Daddy D'z,** which was tapped by *The New York Times* as having the town's best BBQ 'n' blues, and **Patti Hut,** West Indian food in a homey Jamaican atmosphere.

Local steak houses such as **Bones, Chops,** and **Kobe** join standbys like **Morton's** and **Ruth's Chris.** Surf can be found at the **Atlanta Fish Market, Boston Sea Party,** and **Crab House,** while the **Palm** offers the best of both worlds. Many have won local and national awards and high ratings.

A bounty of bistros can be found as well. **Chow,** the **Buckhead Diner, Atlanta Bread Co.,** the **Cheesecake Factory, Einstein's, South City Kitchen,** and **Murphy's** serve up cornucopious options and often portions. Buckhead and Virginia Highlands in particular are peppered with such places.

Ethnic options include such rarities as Ethiopian (**Abbay**), Cuban (**Mambo**), Moroccan (**Imperial Fez**), Peruvian (**Machu Picchu**), and non-feline Persian (**Salar**). But of course there are many French (**Anis, Brasserie Le Coze,** and **Ciboulette**) and Italian (**Azio Pizza and**

Pasta, Bardi's, Veni Vidi Vici) selections, too. Asia is represented by **Chin Chin, Hong Kong Delight,** and **Nickiemotos's,** and Mexico by **Neuvo Laredo** and **Rio Bravo Grill.**

Atlantans often top their meals with dessert and coffee at a separate site. **Cafe Diem, Java Jive, San Francisco Coffee, Cascade Java,** and **Urban Coffee Bungalow** provide the requisite caffeine, sugar, and face time fix.

With 130 retail centers and the largest mall in the Southeast (**Lenox Square,** 1.6 million square feet), shopping in Atlanta, and particularly the suburb of Buckhead, is prime. Two of the area's finest malls, Lenox Square and **Phipps Plaza,** can be found there. Along with a multiscreen cinema and a food court, Phipps Plaza serves up Saks, Gianni Versace, Nike Town, and more than 100 other stores in a marble-and-brass Georgian mansion atmosphere. One of the most affluent spots in the U.S., Buckhead is studded with scores of places selling antiques, vintage clothing, books, sports equipment and more, and even offers a Web site (www.buckhead.org) for online browsers. **Virginia Highlands** and **Little Five Points** also provide distinctive, pedestrian-friendly boutiques, galleries, and spas.

Underground Atlanta is another novel option, covering six city blocks of specialty shops, while **CNN Center** offers up a few dozen more, including the Turner Store and Studio, yet another satellite in the Ted orbit. If malls were considered a first line of defense, Atlanta would be practically impenetrable—the city is ringed with such places as **Cumberland Mall,** the **Galleria, Gwinnet Place, Greenbriar Mall,** and many more. There's even a **Health and Fitness Mall** and a turquoise-and-gold-leaf Art Deco extravaganza (**Rio Mall**).

According to Bridges, Atlanta's numerous antique shops and flea markets are not always mutually exclusive. "If you look, you can find items from each in both." The **Atlanta Antique Center & Marketplace, Georgia Antique Center and International Market, Cheshire Bridge Road Antique Shops, Historic Roswell Antique Market,** and **2300 Peachtree Rd.** have odds and ends mixed with treasures. Those looking for deals on something new might want to stop at **Stone Mountain Handbag Outlet** in Stone Mountain Village, **Forsyth Fabrics,** and **Shoemaker's Warehouse.** Discount malls include **Calhoun Outlet Center, Tanger Factory Outlet Center,** and more in the northern part of the state.

Where It's At

(continued)

Caribbean Restaurant, 180 Auburn Ave., 658-9829

Cascade Java, 2345 Cascade Rd., 752-JAVA

Catfish Station, 618-A Ponce de Leon Ave., 875-2454

Cheesecake Factory, 3024 Peachtree Rd., 816-2555

Cheshire Bridge Road Antique Shops, street addresses 1845–1927, various phones

Chin Chin, several locations

Chops, 70 W. Paces Ferry Rd., 262-2675

Chow, several locations

Ciboulette, 1529 Piedmont Rd. NE, 874-7600

CNN Center, 1 CNN Center Plaza, 827-4711

Crab House, several locations

Cumberland Mall, 100 Cumberland Mall, 770/435-2206

Daddy D'z, 264 Memorial Dr., 222-0206

Einstein's, 1077 Jupiter St., 876-7925

Forsyth Fabrics, 1190 Foster St., 351-6050

Galleria, One Galleria Pkwy., 770/955-9100

Georgia Antique Center and International Market, 6624 I-85 NE., 446-9292

Greenbriar Mall, 2841 Greenbriar Pkwy. SW, 344-6611

Gwinnet Place, 2100 Pleasant Hill Rd., 770/476-5160

Health and Fitness Mall, 5675 Jimmy Carter Blvd., 770/416-1111

Historic Roswell Antique Market, 1207-C Alpharetta St., 770/587-5259

Hong Kong Delight, 5920 Roswell Rd., 255-3388

Imperial Fez, 2285 Peachtree Rd., 351-0874

Java Jive, 790 Ponce de Leon Ave., 876-6161

Kobe, 5600 Roswell Rd., 256-0810

Where It's At

(continued)

Lenox Square, 3393 Peachtree Rd., 233-6767

Little Five Points, Moreland and Euclid aves.

Machu Picchu, 3375 Buford Hwy., 320-3226

Mambo, 1402 N. Highland Ave., 876-2626

Morton's, several locations

Murphy's, 997 Virginia Ave. NE, 872-0904

Neuvo Laredo, 1495 Chattahoochee, 352-9009

Nickiemotos's, 247 Buckhead Ave., 842-0334

Pablo & Paul's, 1232 W. Paces Ferry Rd., 261-3662

Palm, 3391 Peachtree Rd., 814-1955

Patti Hut, Rio Mall, 595 Piedmont Ave., 892-5133

Phipps Plaza, 3500 Peachtree Rd., 261-7910

Rio Bravo Grill, 240 Peachtree St., 524-9224

Rio Mall, 595 Piedmont Ave., 874-6688

Ruth's Chris, several locations

Salar, 5920 Roswell Rd., 252-8181

San Francisco Coffee, several locations

Shoemaker's Warehouse, Amsterdam Ave. at Monroe Dr., 881-9301

South City Kitchen, 1144 Crescent Ave., 873-7358

Stone Mountain Handbag Outlet, 963 Main St., 770/498-1316

Tanger Factory Outlet Center, 1000 Tanger Dr., 770/957-0238

Urban Coffee Bungalow, 1425 Piedmont Rd., 892-8212

Varsity, 61 North Ave., 881-1706

Veni Vidi Vici, 41 14th St., 875-8424

Virginia Highlands, 1038 N. Highland Ave., 876-7728

 ## ETHNIC AND RELIGIOUS PROSPECTS

Atlanta's African-American population is so large that "you're meeting people all the time," observes singer Sonya Tinsley. "People are constantly moving here, so there are always different faces." Services that assist newcomers range from **Diversity Marketing Group,** which publishes restaurant and travel guides, to the **Black Pages** to **Black Atlanta Transplants,** a relocation service. Organizations such as the **Minority Business Development Agency, Atlanta Business League, Sweet Auburn Area Business Association,** and other professional groups provide assistance and contacts. In addition, "interracial dating is accepted, particularly within the city."

The tolerance has carried over into all aspects of life, from the workplace to Atlanta's many neighborhoods. "I've been around good old boys whose views were shaped before the Civil Rights movement, and have seen their capacity for change," remarks one man. "You may not see an abundance of a minority, but as a member of such a group, I've not felt out of place or threatened."

Atlanta's diversity is carried over into its multitudinous churches. The variation includes the **AME Sixth District Headquarters; CME Sixth District Headquarters; Episcopal Diocese of Atlanta; Georgia Baptist Convention; Evangelical Lutheran Church in America; United Church of Christ, Southeast;** two Presbyterian organizations (**Presbyterian Church in America; Presbytery of Greater Atlanta**); and many others. These are just the Protestants; Catholics and Greek Orthodox have the **Archdiocese of Atlanta** and **Diocese of Atlanta,** respectively. Atlanta's large Jewish community is represented by the **Jewish Community Center** and the **Atlanta Jewish Federation,** along with several synagogues. Although religion may not have as high a profile as in smaller or more conservative cities, Atlanta's strong religious community is easily accessible.

CRIB SHEET

Atlanta's unique blend of big-city sophistication and Southern charm is nowhere more evident than in its real estate. Although residents have 20—count 'em—20 counties to choose from, nearly two-thirds live in Cobb, DeKalb, Fulton (which includes the city proper), and Gwinnett. Much wealth and industry is concentrated there as well.

Although rent's usually higher and you get less for your dollar, newcomers and singles often choose to live in Fulton county. Not only are many apartments and smaller homes located here, but it's where the action is, and includes Buckhead, Virginia Highlands, Little Five Points, and Midtown, areas heavily populated by young people. Buckhead is now considered Atlanta's most prestigious address. Along with having the homes of the second and third wealthiest women in the world (Anne Cox Chambers and her sister) and other historic and/or opulent residences, this area's a vortex for conspicuous consumption.

Less ostentatious but certainly with as much character, the restored Virginia Highland/Little Five Points/Morningside districts offer 1920s brick bungalows and larger Tudor revival homes amid plenty of trees. Another laid-back spot is Midtown, which has many fine renovated neighborhoods and an eclectic mix of people and manors, condos, and duplexes.

Close to downtown (10 minutes) and practically in the lap of the airport is South Fulton. Although it's loaded with industrial parks, hotels, and highways, several smaller municipalities boast state-of-the-art public and private schools as well as many parks and recreational opportunities. Jefferson Park in particular has a nice selection of older, well-kept homes, modern high-rises, and single and multifamily domiciles, all within a reasonable price range. Farther (30 minutes) from the city, the area known as North Fulton County offers rolling hills, excellent schools and health care, and a low crime rate. Wooded lots in swim-and-tennis communities start in the $130,000s; the area also has numerous apartments and townhouses. Golfcentric neighborhoods include St. Ives, Windward, and the Country Club of the South, where homes begin in the low $100,000s and range upward to $5 million. More of the good life can be found in Sandy Springs, another high-ticket area with residences set among trees and thriving businesses.

About 10 minutes northeast of the metro area, Cobb County is one of the fastest-growing spots in the nation. Home of the Galleria, Six Flags Over Georgia, several lakes, and the Chattahoochee River, it also enjoys a diverse and healthy local arts scene. Neighborhoods include luxurious Charington ($260,000+) and Glenbrook (custom builds starting at $220,000) in exclusive Upper East Cobb and Legacy Park. Less pocketbook-intensive are Fairway Station, a private swim-and-tennis neighborhood where houses average about $155,000, and Waterstone, a wooded district with smaller residences beginning in the $140,000s.

DeKalb county (25 minutes from city center) offers not only an ethnically mixed population—about half the total residents are African-American, Hispanic, Asian, and "other"—but

Where It's At

 Unless otherwise noted, all area codes are 404.

AME Sixth District Headquarters, 524-8279

Archdiocese of Atlanta, 888-7801

Atlanta Business League, 127 Peachtree St. NE, 584-8125

Atlanta Jewish Federation, 873-1661

Black Atlanta Transplants, 219 Hermer Circle NW, 696-3571

Black Pages, 3711 College St., 766-1692

CME Sixth District Headquarters, 752-7800

Diocese of Atlanta, 634-9345

Diversity Marketing Group, 2426 Glenwood Ave. SE, 243-8070

Episcopal Diocese of Atlanta, 365-1010

Evangelical Lutheran Church in America, 873-1977

Georgia Baptist Convention, 455-0404

Jewish Community Center, 875-7881

Minority Business Development Agency, 730-3300

Presbyterian Church in America, 320-3366

Presbytery of Greater Atlanta, 633-8061

Sweet Auburn Area Business Association, 236 Auburn Ave. NE., 525-0205

United Church of Christ, Southeast, 607-1993

is home to many of Georgia's international firms. It also has the advantages of being connected to Atlanta's mass transit system. The proximity of Stone Mountain Park, a variety of cultural activities and festivals, and the lowest dropout rate in the state make DeKalb even more attractive. Some selections include Deer Creek, a picturesque spot at the base of Stone Mountain ($140,000s–190,000s); Druid Hills, an estate-filled (read: expensive) neighborhood that's on the National Register; Mills Creek Place, a new cluster community priced from the high $200,000s; and Water's Edge, which features new, custom builds starting around $140,000.

> The unemployment rate is lower than the national average, so there's no excuse not to get a job. According to one transplant, "People here can get ahead if they're willing to work."

Also less than a half-hour away and experiencing phenomenal expansion is Gwinnett County. This well-organized community is noted for its schools (top in the state), public services, and shopping and recreational opportunities, and includes Lake Lanier, the so-called houseboat capital of the world. Plus it's the best deal in town, with the average price of a home in the $125,000 range. Options vary from the close-knit Madison Place, with its clubhouse and various athletic courts, to Oaktree Meadows (brick and stucco homes starting in the $120,000s), to the upscale, wooded Russell's Pond.

Unlike some Southern states, Georgia has a strong school system. The different counties are strong in different areas; for more information, contact the Georgia Department of Education (656-2800). Private options range from parochial to Afrocentric (mostly black students) to boarding schools to preparatory curriculums. The Atlanta Association of Independent Schools (923-9230) has a detailed directory.

Atlanta's 36 colleges, universities, and seminaries provide over 350 programs of study; the largest schools are Atlanta University, Emory, Georgia State, and Georgia Tech. Vocational/technical institutions include DeKalb, the Institute of Paper and Science Technology, and many others.

NAVIGATING ATLANTA

Driving in Atlanta can be harrowing, even for people who've lived there for years. The city's labyrinthine freeway system—I-75, I-85, and I-20—merging and looping around in four- to seven-lane variations, surrounded by I-285's enormous traffic jams and roads quickly made treacherous by freezing rain or snow, can result in frustration and accidents.

"It can take an hour to get 20 miles," points out Burnham. And once you're off the freeway, there's no guarantee you'll find your destination. "The streets don't run on a grid, so it can get confusing." Parking is also a problem in areas such as Buckhead, where you can spend hours cruising for an available spot, particularly during evenings and weekends. Recent implementation of High Occupancy Vehicle (HOV)/carpool lanes will hopefully alleviate some difficulties.

A more immediate solution, however, can be found in the form of Marta (848-5000), the city's train and bus system. Not only does it provide access to all the major districts, Hartsfield International, and some outlying areas, but the $1.25 rate includes transfers. Cobb County Transit (770/427-4444) also connects from smaller towns into MARTA at various points.

Along with massive Hartsfield International (off I-85, 530-6600), Atlanta has DeKalb-Peachtree Airport (936-5440), for general aviation and charter flights; Fulton County Airport (699-4200), for corporations; and McCollum Airport (770/422-4382), a private field. Amtrak (800/872-7245) provides train service, while over 200 buses arrive and depart daily from the Greyhound Terminal (522-6300). Too bad getting around in Atlanta isn't half as easy as leaving it.

Boston at a Glance

Birthdate and Present Size: 1630 (incorporated as a city in 1822). *Metropolitan Statistical Area*— 1980: 2,805,911; 1990: 2,870,650. 1/1/95 (estimate): 3,550,300. Percent change, 1980–1990: +2.3%. Percent change, 1990–1995: +23.7%.

Weather Report: *Average annual temperature*—51.5° F. In January: 36/23° F. In July: 82/65° F. *Average annual precipitation*—43.81". *Average annual snowfall*—41.5".

Money Matters: *Unemployment rate*— 4.6%. *Per capita income*—$15,581 (city); $19,288 (MSA). *Average household income*—$37,907 (city); $50,478 (MSA). *Average cost of a home*—$242,240. *Average rent for an apartment*— $1,057/month. *ACCRA cost of living indexes* (based on 100)—Composite Index: 139.8; Utilities Index: 130.1; Housing Index: 194.5. *Sales and use tax*—5.0% (state); none (local). *Personal income tax*—5.95% to 12.0%.

People Profile: *Crime rate* (Per 100,000 population)—9,534.0 (city); 3,469.1 (suburbs); 4,459.4 (MSA). *Racial and ethnic characteristics*— White: 63.0% (city), 87.2% (MSA); Black: 25.5% (city), 7.2% (MSA);

Hispanic Origin: 10.4% (city), 4.3% (MSA); American Indian/Eskimo/Aleut: 0.3% (city), 0.2% (MSA); Asian/Pacific Islander: 5.3% (city), 3.3% (MSA); Other: 5.9% (city), 2.1% (MSA). *Gender ratio*—91.4 males per 100 females (all ages); 90.3 males per 100 females (18 years old+). *Age characteristics*—18–24 (17.3%); 25–44 (36.8%). Median age: 30.2 (city); 33.3 (MSA). *Educational attainment*—percent having completed high school: 75.7% (city), 83.7% (MSA); percent having completed college: 30.0% (city), 33.1% (MSA).

Major Players: Services, retail/wholesale trade, manufacturing, government, finance/insurance/real estate. A leading educational, cultural, and medical center, as well as high-tech and electronics research and tourism hot spot. *Largest employers*—Bank of Boston, Blue Cross & Blue Shield of Mass., Brigham and Women's Hospital, Children's Medical Center, General Hospital Corp., Globe Newspapers, John Hancock Mutual Life.

Community Services: *Average hospital cost*—$607.00/day. *Average doctor visit*—$60.33. *Average dentist visit*—$72.00. *Newspapers*—Boston Globe, Boston Herald, Christian Science Monitor, Boston Jewish Times, Massachusetts Lawyers Weekly, The Pilot (Catholic), Boston Phoenix (alternative), others.

BOSTON: SPACE JAM

Boston is a city of contrasts. On one hand, the city is full of narrow streets, crazy drivers (called "Massholes" by locals), segregated neighborhoods, and housing where you pay twice the rent for half the square footage. On the other, Boston boasts the latest in technology, education, health care, and research, along with powerhouse financial institutions and an extraordinarily rich cultural life that doesn't skimp on the ingredients. All this is set in a state that still refers to itself as the Commonwealth, the country's most historical (and arguably picturesque) area, which has been lovingly preserved. Plus, the region is as diverse as the city itself, offering recreational opportunities galore. With the nation's highest percentage of college-educated 24- to 34-year-olds, Boston is not for Beavii and Butt-heads.

Anyone with a basic knowledge of American history is familiar with the story of the Pilgrims, the Massachusetts Bay Colony, and the fact that Boston was declared a town in 1630 and named for Boston, England (where?).

> "The social part of Boston is great," says a local. "Bars are always packed with young professionals" and there are loads of cybercafes, coffeeshops, and bookstores, as well as cultural, volunteer, and sporting options.

Boston served as a flashpoint for the rebellions leading to the Revolutionary War. However, British troops had withdrawn by early 1776, leaving most of the buildings untouched. The surrounding towns have had their brush with destiny as well: The Pilgrims landed in Plymouth; the American Revolution started in Lexington and Concord; Quincy is the birthplace of two presidents (John Adams and John Quincy Adams); Concord was home to Nathaniel Hawthorne, Ralph Waldo Emerson, Henry David Thoreau, and other literary lions; and Lowell was the home of the American labor movement. Boston itself offers a taste of every era, from the Freedom Trail, where the founding fathers walked, to the Bull & Finch Pub, inspiration for the TV show "Cheers."

Boston has endured and prospered, despite the decline of the textile and leather industries that fueled its growth during the 1800s, a fire in 1872 that destroyed a part of downtown, and, 100 years later, interracial fighting over court-ordered school desegregation. Extensive restoration and remodeling of rundown neighborhoods and office buildings, a continual supply of new industries as well as the best and brightest young minds, and the political fortunes of a family named Kennedy have added a patina of glamour, romance, and excitement to the region.

Quality of Life

Especially for those in their 20s, "the social part of Boston is great," observes media coordinator John Caprio. "Even people who didn't go to college here have no problem making friends." Boston has more outlets than an appliance store: "Bars are always packed with young professionals and there are loads of dating services," in addition to multitudinous cybercafes, coffeeshops, and bookstores as well as cultural, volunteer, and sporting options. The work of the area's 16,000 artists can be found in galleries, bookstores, and at dance and musical events. And professional sports teams inspire a loyalty that can be frightening to non-devotees (but can also result in a major bonding experience for those of like mind).

Although cost of living can be steep, particularly in housing and utilities, salaries "are fairly equitable and there are many restaurants where you can get a great but inexpensive meal," adds marketing director Jennifer Storey. Known as America's Walking City, downtown is a mere two square miles. Boston's efficient, safe, and cheap subway system (the "T") can take you just about anywhere else. Those who live inside the city might want to make other arrangements for their cars: Not only is parking astronomical and scarce, but driving can result in excessive agitation, as with the case of one newcomer who abandoned his rental in the middle of downtown (definition of a "U-ey": The official turn of Boston drivers).

More than 65 colleges and universities, including Boston (which has one of each), Northeastern, Wellesley, Tufts, Brandeis, MIT, and Harvard help give the region an international flavor. Cambridge, the home of the latter two, draws more than 28,000 students from more than 100 countries. Known as the birthplace of higher education (Harvard was founded here in 1636), Cambridge is a colorful melange of street performers, different languages, and vociferous public discourse, a definite change of pace from serious, sometimes stodgy Boston.

With 11 of America's best hospitals (according to *U.S. News & World Report*), if one must get sick, then this is the place to do it. Beth Israel, Brigham and Women's Hospital, Mass General, and more than 20 other hospitals have provided the impetus for health care undertakings. If you've got more than gas from the Boston baked beans, you're in good hands.

General Opportunities

Slackers, take note: Jobwise, "Boston is a tough city, but it respects hard workers," points out corporate relations specialist Suzanne Maddocks. With all that competition and brainpower, "you have to prove yourself professionally. If you sit back, you can easily be replaced by another young person of quality." But there's also a great tolerance for individuality, she continues. "You can be whatever you want to be" and pursue your goals. "Boston's pretty laid back in the sense that you can go to a party and talk to just about anyone." It's getting invited to the gathering that can be the challenge.

With an "A" bond rating, the region has traditionally been financially stout—Appleton Farms, a livestock and sawmill enterprise, has been around since 1638 and the Bank of Boston was established in 1784. A recent *Fortune* magazine survey ranked Boston among the top 10 U.S. cities for business. MIT alone has given birth to nearly 650 businesses since 1867, while research at other universities has created even more enterprises.

Boston's highly developed transportation system encompasses land, air, sea, and rail. Along with being the center for the area's train and truck service, the Port of Boston handles about 16 million tons of cargo a year. A mere three miles away, Logan Airport handles nearly 25 million passengers and 770 million pounds of cargo annually, creating a $4.4 billion impact on the economies of Boston, Massachusetts, and New England.

Despite the Yankee sensibility, however, "Boston is still an ethnic society," remarks one man. "The Italians live on the North End; the South End is Irish; Chinatown is mostly Asians; and Roxbury is primarily African-American, although the composition of that neighborhood is changing." In fact, an influx of Asians, Hispanics, and blacks moved into the city for the first time in decades, although the outlying areas remain primarily white.

According to another woman, discrimination on the job still exists, although "we're educating corporations by getting them involved with minorities. A lot of immigrants who go to college here want to stay, so conscience-raising benefits everyone."

MAJOR BREADWINNING

You don't have to talk like a native (Hahvuhd, cah, Cuber, regula, etc.) to fit in professionally. Despite numerous comedy acts and parodies, most Bostonians are easily understood, giving rise to the thought that perhaps all those colloquialisms and missing "r's" are for the benefit of stumping visitors (nine million of whom generate more than $7.1 billion a year).

But tourism is only one slice of Boston's $2.4 million job pie. "This area has an incredible amount of opportunity," remarks Ron Kelner, a computer expert and marketer. "You can look in the paper and see hundreds of openings in programming and engineering, while other cities are just climbing out of a recession. The financial sectors are also strong and there are dozens of software start-up companies" in addition to health care positions.

Between 1960 and 1990, the white-collar labor force grew 23 percent and service industry jobs increased four percent; manufacturing and blue-collar workers declined 18 percent, and the once-important fishing industry has gone south as well. Still, Boston remains strong in the production of precision tools, aerospace instruments/systems, and electronic components, in addition to the production of books, magazines, and other printed materials.

Boston is still considered a major publishing center, utilizing white-collar workers with related skills. Another 16 percent of the workforce is employed by some form of government, making it the dominating factor in the service sector. Small businesses have a presence too, even though office space in Boston proper can be stratospheric (it's about $10 a square foot less in the suburbs).

> "This area has an incredible amount of opportunity," remarks a local computer marketer. "You can look in the paper and see hundreds of openings in programming and engineering. The financial sectors are strong and there are dozens of software start-up companies, too."

Much employment can be found within Boston's "big four" economic drivers: financial services, health care, high technology, and higher education. Combined, they make up over 25 percent of the area's total employment, and support almost the same number of positions in the legal, accounting, transportation, printing, and business and service firms.

Boston is one of the nation's leading financial centers, and area institutions such as Fidelity and State Street Bank manage more than 25 percent of all mutual fund assets in the U.S. Employment can also be found in venture capital, life and property insurance, commercial banking, and savings and loans; major players include the First National Bank of Boston, Fleet National Bank, BayBank, and a couple of dozen others. Some 100,000 jobs, with an average salary of around $40,000, are primarily located in Boston and the South Shore area.

With medical manufacturing and research on the upswing, health care jobs total nearly 200,000, including positions for doctors, nurses, scientists, and other support personnel. Those in general health services earn an average of $30,000+ a year, while biotech jobs pull in approximately $10,000 more.

Research has also spawned biotechnology companies such as Genzyme and Cambridge Neuroscience. Other enterprises develop medical supplies, instruments, drugs, and products and have future-shock sounding names like Biopure, Immunotech, and Repligen. With total sales of $1.6 billion, Boston is the second largest producer of revenue in biotechnology in the U.S., as well as the third biggest employer.

With the rise of companies like Digital Equipment Corporation, Wang, and Raytheon, Boston has been a leader in high technology since the late 1970s. Although Raytheon survived the recent recession, both Wang and DEC have dwindled. What remains, however, are more than 700 firms that develop information technologies in computer hardware, software, and peripherals; information retrieval services; communications equipment and services; precision instruments; and electronics components. Companies like Powersoft and Parametric Technologies utilize the talents of programmers and others with computer training in creating products. Many of these enterprises are located west and north of Boston and employ almost 115,000 people in computer services (average salary: about $47,000) and telecommunications ($42,000). Prepackaged software, another growing area, retains another 35,000 souls and consists of companies like the MIT-bred Viewlogic.

With a never-ending supply of students and their funds (almost a billion dollars a year), the knowledge industry is a perpetual incubator for new ideas and talent. Along with educators and administrators in all fields, the skills of computer specialists, publishers, electronics experts, consultants, engineers, and other support businesses are put to use. The more than 150,000 people in college/university positions are primarily employed in Boston and the Metro North area; salaries average about $32,000 per annum, while general professional positions in the field earn approximately $9,000 more.

Boston likes to claim the world's largest concentration of higher-education institutions, whose R&D laboratories provide the foundation for new businesses. MIT's Technology Licensing Office has helped develop more than 60 companies since 1986, and has produced hundreds of inventions, patents, and licensing agreements. Independent researchers such as Draper, MITRE, and Lincoln Laboratories test many new products and keep another 11,000 employed.

With projected gains in legal services (48.1 percent), engineering (32.1 percent), research and testing (49 percent), management and public relations (37.6 percent), and computers/data processing services (a whopping 90.3 percent) by 2005, it's no wonder qualified folks revere Boston. "Although this area's pretty conservative, those who pursue strategic goals will be successful, no matter who they are," emphasizes Maddocks. "It's up to each person to make things happen."

SOCIAL AND RECREATIONAL SCENE

How Boston Plays

Let's face it: A place that jokingly calls itself the "hub" (as in Hub of the Universe) and has an actual plaque commemorating that name on the sidewalk in front of Filene's downtown has got to be brimming with confidence (and a sense of humor). Which is why area code 617 is great for beginners: "You run into a lot of people in their 20s along with old, established families," observes Storey.

But all ages can flourish, despite the sometimes rocky New England reserve. "It can be tough to build friendships, so you've got to hang in there," remarks Kelner. "There's so much to do that there's no excuse to sit home."

Adds Maddocks: "Don't get discouraged if people don't immediately fall all over you." Most agree that the best way to get involved is to get involved: Popular charities include chestnuts like the Boston Jaycees (Greater Boston Chamber of Commerce, One Beacon St., 557-7307), Boston Junior League (117 Newbury St., 247-4078), and Easter Seals (20 Park Plaza, 482-3370); the youth-focused City Year (235 Dudley St., 427-8301); or "gimmee shelters," including Project Place Homeless Resource Center (32 Rutland St., 262-3740), Boston Night Center (Bulker St., 521-7113), and many more.

Sports activities are another point of entry. "You can meet a ton of nice people at different events," continues Kelner. And the chances of forming meaningful relationships are better than at, say, a bar "because people behave more normally and act like themselves."

ARTS AND SCIENCES

Before venturing into Boston life, take a walk along the **Freedom Trail,** which includes stops at 16 sites seminal to American history, including the Boston Common, King's Chapel, Faneuil Hall, and the Bunker Hill Monument (if you have to ask, you really need to go). Just look for the painted red line on sidewalks and streets.

Another good way to familiarize yourself with the city would be through the Black Heritage Trail (at the **Boston African-American National Historic Site**), which covers the development of the black community on Beacon Hill between 1800 and 1900. Highlights consist of the **African Meeting House,** the oldest standing black church in the U.S. and a focal point for social, educational, political, and religious activity, and the **54th Regiment Memorial,** which honors the first black battalion to serve in that war. The former also houses the Museum of Afro-American History.

Boston's plentiful African-American museums, monuments, and cultural centers provide excellent meeting grounds. The **Dillaway-Thomas House** offers events, lectures, and special exhibits. The **John D. O'Bryant African-American Institute** houses reference materials and is the home for the Uhuru Dance Theatre and Unity Ensemble and Nia, a drama and literary group, among other

Where It's At

Unless otherwise noted, all area codes are 617.

A.B.D.M., P.O. Box 362, Somerville, 666-1859

African Meeting House, 46 Joy St., 742-1854

American Repertory, 64 Brattle St., 495-2668

Bank of Boston Celebrity Series, 20 Park Plaza, Suite 832, 482-2595

Ben Franklin Alive, 182 Westminster Ave., Arlington, 648-0628

Blue Hills Trailside Museum, 1904 Canton Ave., Milton, 333-0690

Boston African-American National Historic Site, 46 Joy St., 742-5415

Boston Ballet, 19 Clarendon St., 695-6950

Boston Center for the Arts, 539 Tremont St., 426-5000

Boston Conservatory, 8 The Fenway, 536-6340

Boston Massacre Monument, Boston Common, Tremont St.

Boston Tea Party Ship and Museum, Congress St. Bridge, 338-1771

Broadmoor Wildlife Sanctuary, 280 Eliot St., Natick, 235-3929

Cape Ann Whale Watch, P.O. Box 345, Gloucester, 508/283-9550

Captain Bill and Sons, 9 Traverse St., Gloucester, 800/33-WHALE

Colonial Theatre, 106 Boylston St., 426-9366

things. The internationally recognized **Museum of the National Center of Afro-American Artists** provides courses and displays the work of blacks from all over the world. And the **Boston Massacre Monument** honors escaped slave Crispus Attucks and others who were murdered in 1770 when British troops opened fire on their gathering. Old news, but it comes alive in the retelling.

Some other wickedly good collections include the self-explanatory **Boston Tea Party Ship & Museum;** the **Harvard University Art Museums,** whose three clusters include more than 150,000 works; the **John F. Kennedy Library and Museum,** a vivid re-creation of modern-day Camelot; the **MIT Museum,** which offers exhibitions on holography, architecture, and the interplay between art and science; the **Museum of Fine Arts,** whose more than 200 galleries draw works from the world over; and the **Isabella Stewart Gardener Museum,** a Venetian palace which displays art. The **USS _Constitution_ Museum** offers a chance to get up close and personal with Old Ironsides. And that's not even mentioning the dozens of other historical spots studding the outer perimeter.

The area's vivid cultural life is brought into focus at the **Boston Center for the Arts,** which in addition to rotating exhibits has theaters and studio space for artists. The **Boston Ballet, Lyric Opera,** and **Symphony Orchestra/Pops** provide some of the best in their genre, while the **Handel and Hayden Society** drums up baroque and classical works, and the **Boston** and **New England Conservatories** utilize the considerable talents of their students and faculty. African-American culture is celebrated in music and dance through the **A.B.D.M.** group and the **Impulse Company.**

All brands of live theater are here: **The American Repertory,** which mounts classics as well as the newest works; the **Huntington Theatre Company,** the area's leading professional thespians; and the **Colonial Theatre,** host to touring shows. The **Bank of Boston Celebrity Series** brings in class acts and plays of renown (no Dead Kennedys, please). The area has also given birth to uniquely Boston entertainment: **Ben Franklin Alive,** a one-man re-creation of that wild and creative guy; **Late Night Catechism,** likely to produce guilty laughs even from non-Catholics; and **Mass Hysteria,** a satirical look at the state's disunion. The **Tsai Performance Center,** the **Wang Center for the Performing Arts,** the **Shubert Theatre,** the **Wilbur Theatre,** and others host traveling troupes.

Where It's At

(continued)

Computer Museum, 300 Congress St., 800/370-CHIP, http://www.tcm.org

Cranberry World, 225 Water St., Plymouth, 508/747-2340

Cybersmith, 42 Church St., 492-5857, http://www.cybersmith.com

Dillaway-Thomas House, 184 Roxbury St., Roxbury, 445-3399

54th Regiment Memorial, corner of Park and Beacon sts.

Franklin Park Zoo, Franklin Park, Dorchester, 442-4896

Freedom Trail, 15 State St., 242-5695

Handel and Hayden Society, 300 Massachusetts Ave., 266-3605

Harvard University Art Museums, 32 Quincy St., Cambridge, 495-9400

Huntington Theatre Company, 264 Huntington Ave., 266-0800

Impulse Company, 129 Massachusetts Ave., South End, 536-6989

Isabella Stewart Gardener Museum, 280 The Fenway, 566-1401

John D. O'Bryant African-American Institute, 40 Leon St., Roxbury, 373-3141

John F. Kennedy Library and Museum, Columbia Point, 929-4523

Late Night Catechism, 333 Tremont St., 338-8606

Lyric Opera, 114 State St., 248-8811

Mass Hysteria, 11 Green St., 524-2500

MIT Museum, 265 Massachusetts Ave., 253-4422

Museum of Afro-American History, 46 Joy St., 742-1854

Museum of Fine Arts, 465 Huntington Ave., 267-9300

Museum of Science, Science Park, 723-2500

Museum of the National Center of Afro-American Artists, 300 Walnut Ave., Roxbury, 442-8614

New England Aquarium, Central Wharf, 973-5200

New England Conservatory, Jordan Hall, 30 Gainsborough St., 262-1120

Seven Seas, 7 Seas Wharf on Rt. 127, Gloucester, 508/283-1776

Shubert Theatre, 265 Tremont St., 426-4520

Where It's At

(continued)

South Shore Natural Science Center, Jacobs Ln., Norwell, 659-2559

Symphony Orchestra/Pops, Symphony Hall, 301 Massachusetts Ave., 266-1492

Tsai Performance Center, 685 Commonwealth Ave., 353-6467

USS Constitution Museum, Charlestown Navy Yard, 426-1812

Virtually Wired Education Foundation, 55 Temple Pl., 542-5555

Wang Center for the Performing Arts, 270 Tremont St., 482-9393

Wilbur Theatre, 246 Tremont St., 423-4008

Where It's At

 Unless otherwise noted, all area codes are 617.

Acres Country Club, 58 Randall Rd., Stow, 508/568-1100

Basketball Hall of Fame, 1150 W. Columbus Ave., Springfield, 413/781-6500 or 413/781-5759

Blue Hills, 4001 Washington St., Canton, 828-7490, 828-5090, or 828-8171

Boston Athletic Association/Boston Marathon, 131 Clarendon St., 236-1652

Boston Bruins, 150 Causeway St., 227-3223

Boston Celtics, 151 Merrimac St., 523-6050

Boston Common, 522-1966

Boston Parks and Recreation Department, 1010 Massachusetts Ave., 635-4505

Boston Red Sox, 4 Yawkey Way, 267-8661

Boston Ski and Sports Club, 214 Lincoln St., 789-4040

Community Boating, 21 Embankment Rd., 523-1038

Earth Bikes 'n' Blades Rentals, 35 Huntington Ave., 257-4733

Glen Ellen Country Club, 84 Orchard St., Millis, 508/376-2978

Technophobics might want to avoid the **Computer Museum,** which has the world's largest desktop; **Cybersmith,** with over 50 workstations, Net access, and food, too; and the hands-on virtual reality **Virtually Wired Education Foundation.** The more than 400 participatory exhibits, including the Theatre of Electricity, at the **Museum of Science** can be another future shock, while a different kind of wildlife can be found at the **Franklin Park Zoo, South Shore Natural Science Center, Broadmoor Wildlife Sanctuary,** and the **Blue Hills Trailside Museum.** The **New England Aquarium** is home to more than 8,000 species of sea creatures and a penguin colony; it also offers whale-watching voyages. Other excursions that might deliver Moby Dick's cousins: the **Cape Ann Whale Watch, Captain Bill and Sons, Seven Seas,** and more. Those wanting a break from the heavy mental might want to visit **Cranberry World,** which offers free samples and cooking demonstrations.

 ## THE SPORTING LIFE

Even professional sports 'round these parts have a historical and commemorative bent. Fenway Park, home of the Major League **Boston Red Sox,** is one of the oldest baseball fields in the country. However, this did not discourage the NBA **Boston Celtics** and the **Boston Bruins** (professional hockey) from making Fleet Center their new digs a couple of years ago. A few miles away in Foxboro are the NFL **New England Patriots,** while Cambridge boasts the **Sports Museum of New England.** Springfield has the **Basketball Hall of Fame.**

However, real-time opportunities abound. You can log on through the **Boston Ski and Sports Club,** the **Sport and Social Club of Boston,** and the **Boston Athletic Association/Boston Marathon** (which has been held since 1897, way before running was considered cool). The **Boston Parks and Recreation Department** organizes clinics and serves as contact for various leagues.

During the warm months, serious beaches range from Concord's Walden Pond to the shores of Massachusetts Bay, Cape Cod, Martha's Vineyard, and Nantucket. The Charles River (Massachusetts' longest) and other waterways offer canoeing and kayaking (contact **Community Boating** for more information). The Charles is also the site of the 17.7-mile Paul Dudley White Bike Path, just one of several trails (for rentals, contact **Pro-Motion** or **Earth Bikes 'N' Blades**

Rentals), as well as many touch football games, a sport popularized by an earlier generation of Kennedys.

Rivers and more than 2,800 lakes, ponds, and reservoirs attract freshwater and saltwater fish enthusiasts (**Sport Fishing Information Line**). Golfers will find dozens of public courses around the area, including the **Glen Ellen** and **Stow Acres Country Clubs.**

State forests and parks are a major source of recreation with biking, camping, boating, fishing, hiking, picnicking, swimming, and cross-country skiing (contact **Massachusetts State Parks** for more information). The **Trustees of Reservations** also maintains a number of areas interlaced with trails, while Boston proper has Emerald Necklace, a strand of Frederick Law Olmsted–designed green spaces that encircle the city. The 48-acre **Boston Common,** with its flower-filled public garden, pond, and swan paddle boats, is considered a local crown jewel.

Skiing is another favorite pastime. Popular resorts include **Jiminy Peak, Wachusett,** and the closer and smaller **Blue Hills.** Ski skills or a reasonable facsimile thereof can be socially helpful: "It's a great way to meet people, if a friend invites you to the mountains for a weekend," adds Kelner.

AFTER-HOURS DIVERSIONS

In Boston and Cambridge it's not which club to go to, but where to begin. "There are so many to choose from," remarks Storey. And it's not about putting on an attitude and clothes to fit the scene: "People are pretty easy-going. Mostly they go out in groups, rather than on formal dates. It's more of a trial run while you're getting acquainted." Keep in mind that many of the town's finer restaurants and bars require a jacket and tie.

With dozens of offerings, Lansdowne Street is an obvious point of entry. Here, you'll find the Aerosmith-owned **Mama Kin,** a multi-stage hot spot which offers a menu of music that changes nightly; the Eurohaus-style **Avalon,** with Top 40 dancing and a state-of-the-art light and sound system; **Venus De Milo,** a Roman Gothic fantasy and favorite of *Boston Magazine;* **Bill's Bar,** alliterative '60s retro with a quieter atmosphere; **Axis,** which features an '80s alternative/techno night, and others. With even more alternative offerings at **Avenue C,** popular spin doctors at **Quest,** a Caribbean getaway at **Zanzibar,** serious blues at **Sticky Mike's,** and dancing at the **Mercury Bar,** Boylston Place/Street are other hubs, although not of the universe.

Where It's At

(continued)

Jiminy Peak, Hancock, 413/738-5500

Massachusetts State Parks, 100 Cambridge St., 727-3180

New England Patriots, Sullivan Stadium, 800/543-1776

Pro-Motion, 111 South St., Bedford, 275-1113

Sport and Social Club of Boston, 203 Newbury St., 262-8990

Sport Fishing Information Line, 800/ASK-FISH

Sports Museum of New England, 100 CambridgeSide Place, Cambridge, 57-SPORT

Trustees of Reservations, Hingham, 740-7233, several other locations

Wachusett, 499 Mountain Rd., Princeton, 800/SKI-1234

Where It's At

Unless otherwise noted, all area codes are 617.

African Source, 48 Fairmont St., 868-0267

August Moon Festival, Chinatown, 536-4100

Avalon, No. 15 Lansdowne St., 262-2424

Avenue C, No. 25 Lansdowne Pl., 423-3832

Axis, No. 13 Lansdowne St., 262-3437

Bill's Bar, No. 5 Lansdowne St., 421-9678

Black History Month, various locations, 742-1854

Boston Harbor Mystery Cruise, 800/697-CLUE

Boston Kite Festival, Franklin Park, May, 635-4505

Boston Pops Summer Season, Symphony Hall, 536-4100

Brewskeller Pub in the Faneuil Hall Marketplace, 227-9663

Bull & Finch, 84 Beacon St., 227-9600

Where It's At

Across the river in Cambridge is a different atmosphere. Not only are the crowds funkier and more multicultural, but they tend to be younger. There's plenty to choose from: the New Orleans–based **House of Blues,** the not-so-quiet **Western Front,** the Irish-themed **Finnegan's Wake,** and the oh-so-clubby **John Harvard's Brew House. Sculler's Grille** is known for dependable jazz, while the **Middle East** has poetry along with well-known acts. Those looking for something different might find it at **Man Ray,** which has something called "Bondage Night." Central and Harvard squares are loaded with other clubs. The latter is also said to have the highest concentration of bookstores in the solar system (for another kind of adventure between the covers). Cambridge offerings range from **African Source** to **Cambridge Architectural Books** to **Global Village Books** to **New England Comics** to **Revolution Books,** and more.

Other magnets in and around Boston include **M-80,** yet another European-style club with eclectic decor; **Jillian's Boston,** which has everything from hi-tech games to billiards; and a smorgasbord of music at **Trattoria Il Panino, Midway Café,** and **Wonder Bar.** Or you can do the tourist thing at the **Bull & Finch** pub of "Cheers" fame; visit the olde English **Brewskeller Pub** in the Faneuil Hall Marketplace; or take in **Boston Harbor Mystery Cruise** (at least the meat isn't) or comedy "knight" at the **Medieval Manor.** Those needing a coffee fix will find multiple Starbucks, as well as other shops in Cambridge (like **Gloria Jean's Coffee Bean**).

Boston has a calendar full of annual events, undeterred by snow, hail, freezing rain, or extraterrestrial visitors who might take offense at its calling itself the Hub. January marks the start of a five-month–long **Jazz Festival** in Cambridge, while **Black History Month** consists of four weeks of events in February. Spring brings the previously mentioned Marathon and the **Boston Kite Festival,** while June blossoms into a bouquet of outdoor entertainment (**Boston Pops Summer Season, Summer Music Series, Summer Stage,** and **Harborfest**). There's an **August Moon Festival** as well as a **Caribbean Carnival** (same month, August), while October brings a **Harvest Moon Festival** and a pumpkinful of scary events in the bewitched town of Salem (**Salem Haunted Happenings**). **"Holiday Happenings"** in December and the African celebration of **Kwanzaa** round out the year.

CULINARY AND SHOPPING HAUNTS

Although famous for its baked beans and fresh fish, Boston's global array of restaurants ranges from Afghan (**The Helmund**) to Jewish (**S&S Deli, Rubin's, Johnny's Luncheonette**) to Vietnamese (**Ba Dat, Pho Bang**) and just about everyplace else. A good meal can run well over $40; no wonder "Cheap Eats" are a hot topic of conversation. Still, "there's a lot available for under $20," observes Storey, who considers a $16 or $17 tab getting off easy. "The city itself doesn't have a lot of grocery stores, so people eat out constantly." Although Chinese food is particularly abundant and generally more on the economical side, "there's a real shortage of decent Mexican." A few exceptions: the **Border Cafe, Casa Romero, Sol Azteca,** and **Casa Mexico.**

Woe to the person who dislikes seafood, because Boston has a netful of great restaurants, particularly in the Waterfront area. Many places offer a selection of fresh-caught, live lobsters, for those with no qualms about eating something they've met personally. Often lobsters are served whole on the plate, so it's best to know how to dissect one before coming face to face with those dead, beady eyes. Crab legs can also be problematic, requiring dexterity in ejecting the meat without squirting everyone at the table with juice (crab cakes might be better for the unskilled). Local favorites include, but are hardly limited to, the **Capital Grille, Library Grill,** the **Charles Restaurant, Jeannie's, Michael's Waterfront,** and **Grillfish. Barrett's** offers a view of Old Ironsides and the Boston Harbor, while **Cornucopia** shows a skyline panorama. **Legal Seafoods** has won kudos from NBC News and *Travel/Holiday* magazine, and the chowder at **Turner Fisheries** has been inducted into a local hall of fame. Although short on fancy decor, the **Barking Crab** and the **No-Name Restaurant** combine a wide assortment with reasonable prices.

Each section of Boston has its own flavor. Heavy dough can be dropped into chic Back Bay spots like **Aujourd'hui** (American), **Bernard's** (Chinese cuisine), **Grill 23** (steaks), **L'Espalier** (French-American), and **Morton's** (more steaks). Less pricey (around $20–25) but face-time intensive places include **Biba, Mirabelle,** and **Sonsie,** while the politically and gastronomically correct **Small Planet** offers eclectic fare in an atmosphere equal to the menu. Downtown eateries range from the **Blue Diner** (yuppiefied comfort food) to the Zagat-rated, decorous **Julien** to Thai dishes in the

Where It's At

(continued)

Venus De Milo, No. 11 Lansdowne St., 421-9595

Western Front, 343 Western Ave., 492-7772

Wonder Bar, 186 Harvard Ave., Allston, 351-COOL

Zanzibar, No. 1 Lansdowne Pl., 451-1955

Where It's At

 Unless otherwise noted, all area codes are 617.

Accento, S. Market, 723-8114

Atrium Mall, 55 Boylston St.

Aujourd'hui, 200 Boylston St., 451-1392

Ba Dat, 28 Harrison Ave., 426-8838

Barking Crab, 88 Sleeper St., 426-CRAB

Barrett's, 2 Constitution Plaza, Charlestown, 242-9600

Bartley's Burger Cottage, 1246 Massachusetts Ave., 354-6559

Bernard's, 545 Boylston St., 236-4040

Biba, 272 Boylston St., 426-7878

Black Rose, 160 State St., 742-2286

Blue Diner, 150 Kneeland St., 695-0087

Blue Room, 1 Kendall Sq., 494-9034

Border Cafe, 819 Broadway, Saugus, 233-5308

Cambridge Antique Market, 201 Msg. O'Brien Highway, 868-9655

Cambridge Artists Cooperative, 59A Church St., 868-4434

CambridgeSide Galleria, 100 CambridgeSide Pl., 621-8666

Capital Grille, 359 Newbury St., 262-8900

Carl's Pagoda, 23 Tyler St.

Casa Mexico, 75 Winthrop St., Cambridge, 491-4552

Casa Romero, 30 Gloucester, 536-4341

Charles Restaurant, 75 Chestnut St., 523-4477

Where It's At

French-sounding **Montien.** The **Locke-Ober Cafe** is a favorite with Brahmins and their "hopers" (wannabees), while the **Black Rose** and **Harp at the Garden** provide a bit o' the Irish.

Although less restaurant-intensive, Beacon Hill boasts **Ristorante Toscano,** an Italian eatery popular with the pedigreed neighbors, while Charlestown has **Olives,** whose Mediterranean menu reads like a novel, according to one local. At the other end of the spectrum are Brookline and Faneuil Hall, whose numerous culinary hangouts probably merit their own ZIP code. Those looking for ethnic cuisine will find it at Chinatown (**Imperial Seafood, Carl's Pagoda, Chau Chow,** and many more) and the Italian North End (**Dom's, Felicia's, Pomodoro,** and others).

And then there's Cambridge, which has everything from the self-descriptive **Bartley's Burger Cottage** (under $15) to the elegant **Salamander** (over $40). But most places fit the moderate price range and include the **Blue Room** (ethnic), **Elephant Walk** (Cambodian/French), **Green Street Grill** (Caribbean), **Sunset Cafe** (Portugese), and many more. You'd be hard pressed to find chains like Hooter's 'round these parts.

Many Bostonians think their town is the center of the shopping universe. You'll find things here you'd never see in neighborhood malls, and prices reflect this.

Those who have the money or just enjoy window-gazing will find hours of amusement in died-and-gone-to-heaven spots like **Copley Place,** which offers restaurants, a theater, and 100 stores; and the **Prudential Center,** which has the rarest of big-city offerings—a 24-hour supermarket—in addition to emporiums like Saks. Nearby Boylston Street serves up everything from exclusive apparel at **Escada** to the **Women's Educational and Industrial Union,** which has been selling gifts, antiques, and needlework since 1877 and whose profits go toward women's causes. Downtown has clusters of stores and discount places, with **Filene's Basement, Jordan Marsh, Lerner New York,** and **Macy's** on Washington Street. **Newbury Street** boasts over 300 stores, antique shops, and jewelers set in 19th-century townhouses. Dueling Armanis (**Emporio** and **Giorgio**), art galleries featuring dolls at **Mann,** paintings at **Vose,** oldies-but-goodies at the **Nostalgia Factory,** and sports apparel at **Reebok** and **St. Moritz** make this a dangerous place to be alone with a credit card.

But with over 14 million annual visitors, the most well-trod shopping territory is **Faneuil Hall.** A Mall of America

with character, its 6.5 acres along the historic waterfront include upwards of 125 stores and 20 restaurants, as well as the outdoor entertainment of street performers and push-cart vendors. Offerings range from South American women's apparel at **Accento** to novelty boxer shorts at **Wise Guys.** Other rarities can be found at **Kites of Boston, Purple Pizazz, Scribes Delight,** and **Christmas Dove.**

Across the river are some bargains. Cambridge has "the Coop" (a.k.a. the **Harvard Cooperative Society Department Store**), the **Cambridge Artists Cooperative,** and the **Cambridge Antique Market,** which consists of approximately 150 dealers. With more than 100 outlets, including Polo, Ann Taylor, London Fog, and Dansk, the **Cambridge-Side Galleria** caters to more conventional tastes, as do two clusters in Chestnut Hill: the **Atrium Mall** and the **Mall at Chestnut Hill.** Those willing to meander can find additional deals at **Howland Place, Kittery Outlet Association, Lakes Region Factory Stores, Tanger Outlet Centers,** and **Worcester Common Fashion Outlets.**

ETHNIC AND RELIGIOUS PROSPECTS

Although Boston has a viable and highly educated African-American community, "you really have to work to make contacts," observes one woman. Afrocentric businesses such as **A Nubian Notion, Treasured Legacy,** and **Ujamaa Mart,** and specialized programs for blacks at the **Sportsman's Tennis Club,** show that "there's been some progress, but not enough," she continues. Groups such as the **Coalition of 100 Black Women** and the **Black Community Information Center,** as well as churches like **Charles St. A.M.E., Concord Baptist, St. Cyprian Episcopal,** the nondenominational **New Christian Covenant Center, Muhammed's Mosque #11** (founded by Malcolm X), and many more can be places to start. Newcomers to America might want to get in touch with their country's **Consulate General.**

In general, "religion's pretty important around here," observes Maddocks. "Even though there's a strong Catholic population, it's pretty diverse." In addition to dozens of churches, professional Catholic singles can hook up with the **Catholic Alumni Club of Boston,** while those of the Hebrew persuasion can get in touch with **Jewish Boston Online** or various synagogues (**Temple Beth Shalom, Beth El Temple Center**). Religious freedom is alive and well in the region and includes the mother church of **Christian Science,** the headquarters for the **Unitarian Universalist Association,** the

Where It's At

(continued)

Macy's, 357-3000

Mall at Chestnut Hill, 199 Boylston St., 965-3037

Mann, 39 Newbury St., 696-6666

Michael's Waterfront, 85 Atlantic Ave., 367-6425

Mirabelle, 85 Newbury St., 859-4848

Montien, 63 Stuart St., 338-5600

Morton's, 1 Exeter Plaza, 266-5858

Newbury Street, 267-7961

No-Name Restaurant, Boston Fish Pier, Northern Ave., 423-2705

Nostalgia Factory, 336 Newbury St., 236-8754

Olives, 10 City Square, 242-1999

Pho Bang, 7 Beach St., 422-0501

Pomodoro, 319 Hanover St., 367-4348

Prudential Center, 800 Boylston St.

Purple Pizazz, N. Market, 742-6500

Reebok, 344 Newbury St., 266-2440

Ristorante Toscano, 47 Charles St., 723-4090

Rubin's, 500 Harvard St., Brookline, 566-8761

S&S Deli, 1334 Cambridge St., Cambridge, 354-0620

Salamander, 1 Atheneum St., 225-2121

Scribes Delight, S. Market, 800/ 866-PENS

Small Planet, 565 Boylston St., 536-4477

Sol Azteca, 914 Beacon St., 262-0909

Sonsie, 327 Newbury St., 351-2500

St. Moritz, 145 Newbury St., 236-1212

Sunset Cafe, 851 Cambridge St., 547-2938

Tanger Outlet Centers, 100 Commercial St., Portland, ME, 800-4-TANGER

Turner Fisheries, 10 Huntington Ave., 424-7425

Vose, 238 Newbury St., 536-6176

Wise Guys, N. Market, 367-9192

Women's Educational and Industrial Union, 356 Boylston St., 536-5651

Worcester Common Fashion Outlets, 100 Front St., Worcester, 508/798-2581

Where It's At

Unless otherwise noted, all area codes are 617.

A Nubian Notion, 146 Dudley St., Roxbury, 442-2622

Beth El Temple Center, 2 Concord Ave., Belmont, 484-6668

Black Community Information Center, 466 Blue Hill Ave., Dorchester, 445-3098

Catholic Alumni Club of Boston, P.O. Box 131, Belmont, 397-8811

Charles St. A.M.E., 551 Warren St., Roxbury, 427-1298

Christian Science, 175 Huntington Ave., 450-3790

Coalition of 100 Black Women, 499-4876

Concord Baptist, 190 Warren Ave., 266-8062

Consulate General, several locations

Jewish Boston Online, http://www.shamash.nysernet.org

Massachusetts Council of Churches, 523-2771

Muhammed's Mosque #11, P.O. Box 123, 10 Washington St., Dorchester, 442-6082

New Christian Covenant Center, 1500 Blue Hill Ave., Dorchester, 445-0636

Old North Church, 193 Salem St., 523-6676

Sportsman's Tennis Club, 930 Blue Hill Ave., 288-9092

St. Cyprian Episcopal, 1073 Tremont St., 427-6175

Temple Beth Shalom, 8 Tremont St., Cambridge, 864-6388

Treasured Legacy, Copley Place, 424-8717

Ujamaa Mart, 62 Warren St., Roxbury, 445-9446

Unitarian Universalist Association, 25 Beacon St., 742-2100

Witches League of Public Awareness, P.O. Box 8736, Salem

Witches League of Public Awareness, and more. Other institutions, including historical landmarks such as the **Old North Church,** where the signal was given for Paul Revere's ride back in '75 (17, that is), are still operational and can be located through the **Massachusetts Council of Churches.**

CRIB SHEET

Although Boston is small, real estate can be mighty confusing *and* expensive. Although there are almost 130 areas to choose from, some are obviously more desirable than others. "Nobody lives downtown or in the really scary neighborhoods, such as the border between South Boston and Roxbury," explains Storey. The cost of a studio apartment in town or in one of the more exclusive suburbs starts around $900 and quickly escalates with each additional square foot (three bedrooms can run upwards of $2,500 a month). However, it's also possible to get cheaper digs in Cambridge or a less gentrified locale.

Roommates are another solution for those wanting to live close to the action; referral services include Roommate Works (247 Newbury St., 859-9777 or 859-7711) as well as several Web sites (such as http://www.boston.com and http://www.roommateconnection.com).

Beacon Hill and Back Bay are among the most desirable addresses in the city. With gaslights and narrow, cobblestone streets, Beacon Hill has traditionally been a stronghold of local bluebloods; however, certain spots (most notably the "Flats" section toward the Charles River and apartments on the hill's northern slope) are popular with those starting out.

Originally a mud basin, the brownstone townhouses of Back Bay have become newly chic, thanks to renovation efforts by their largely gay tenants, many of whom have departed since the rents went up. With tree-lined streets, lots of great shops, and high-rise apartments with terrific views, it's become a magnet "for affluent yuppies who don't mind spending a couple of hundred dollars a month extra for a parking space for their Beamers," adds one man.

Both the self-descriptive Midtown Cultural District and The Fenway (home of the Boston Red Sox as well as several museums, hospitals, and universities) have small pockets of streets and green spaces, making dwellings in these areas especially prized. Those who can afford it can also opt for the Waterfront, whose condos are among the most luxurious in the city.

After years of deterioration, the less expensive South End "has become popular with the artsy crowd," according to Storey, as well as young professionals, Hispanics, and gays. Built in the mid-1800s, most dwellings are brick bow-front townhouses with hidden backyards and overhanging balconies. A flourishing cultural and club scene adds to the area's cachet.

Many of Boston's neighborhoods offer a lively cultural mix. These include Allston, whose denizens can just as easily hail from New Jersey as from Russia or Brazil. Inexpensive rent with many brownstones and triple-deckers that need renovation make this an ideal place for those passing through to something bigger and better (or worse and more dangerous).

Sometimes accused of being crunchy-granola or a refuge for aging hippies, Jamaica Plain consists of blacks, whites, yuppies, gays, Hispanics, and all religions living in relative harmony in an area full of unabashed greenery and macrobiotic restaurants. The heavily African-American Mattapan and Roxbury offer a wide range of housing.

There's an even wider variety in the area known as Greater Boston. Jokingly called the People's Republic of Cambridge (median selling price of a house: $241,000; commute time: 29 minutes), that community has a reputation as an ivory tower, where driving down the street with a deer carcass strapped to the back of your pickup is definitely uncool. Still, all incomes, races, and ages make for a lively cosmopolitan atmosphere not duplicated even in many big cities. A less rarified clone, Somerville ($152,000; 31 minutes) consists of professors, computer specialists, and other intelligentsia looking for a lower rent and nice eateries. Once the poorest city in the Commonwealth, Chelsea ($81,000; 33 minutes) is now a deal for the adventuresome.

The more traditional suburbs of Braintree ($155,000; 50 minutes) and Quincy ($137,000; 43 minutes) offer entry-level homes, inexpensive townhouses, tree-lined streets, and good schools as well as a view of the Boston skyline. Towns along what's known as the 128 belt are popular choices, mostly because of the easy commute, wide variety of dwellings, and proximity to suburban shopping centers and restaurants. These include Burlington ($180,000; 48 minutes), Malden ($129,000; 39 minutes), Revere ($110,000; 36 minutes), Waltham ($165,000; 39 minutes), and Woburn ($150,000; 43 minutes).

Knee-deep in WASP country, Lexington ($283,000; 46 minutes) and Concord ($350,000; 55 minutes) (sound familiar?) offer a more upscale selection as well as an emphasis on skis, sails, and country clubs. Other exclusive (read: few Hispanics, blacks, and immigrants) enclaves include Brookline ($375,000; 31 minutes), which is known for its good schools close to the city; Wellesley ($374,000; 43 minutes), where nouveau riche meets old money; Sharon ($214,000; 63 minutes) described by *Boston* magazine as a "premillennium Beaver Cleaverville"; and Cohasset ($300,000; 72 minutes), a wooded retreat where $800,000 homes are as common as stock portfolios and trust funds.

Although few places beat Boston in terms of higher education, primary and secondary schools suffer from a wide variation. "Unfortunately, it's mostly caused by race and money," admits one man. The best and worst are within a few miles of each other; for instance, Boston and Chelsea have some of the state's lowest test scores and numbers of students going to college, while Lexington, Newton, and Weston regularly rank among the nation's top systems.

Still, "many people are working to bridge this gap," points out Maddocks. Recent innovations include a big brother/big sister mentor program with local companies, alternative "charter" schools, and newly legislated standards. Recently, Boston schools realized a reduced dropout and suspension rate, with an increase in grade-level promotions.

Those looking at public schools "need to examine each district carefully," states the man. The Parent Information Center (800/297-0002) publishes a profile of all districts; more information can be obtained from the Boston Public Schools (635-9000) or the Massachusetts Department of Education (770-7500). Folks opting for the 60+ private and parochial schools can contact the New England Association of Schools and Colleges (729-6762) or their local church.

NAVIGATING BOSTON

Everything you've heard about Boston drivers is true. Not only are they impatient but "he who hesitates gets killed," observes Maddocks. While denizens in other cities may carry guns, maps and public transportation are the survival tools of choice around here.

Complicating the situation even more is the fact that at least in the city "there are no street names, so when you try to give someone directions, you have to go by landmarks or what's in the area," explains Storey.

However, there is a proverbial—albeit expensive—light at the end of the Third Harbor Tunnel. Known as the Central Artery Project (the "Big Dig"), this $1-billion-a-mile (and climbing) venture will basically replace the overcrowded elevated road and streets below it with an eight- to ten-lane underground expressway. Looks like gahkablahka (definition: traffic tie-up caused by people looking at an accident on the other side of the road) might become a thing of the past.

Boston is served by three interstate highways—I-90 (the Massachusetts Turnpike, which goes west to New York), and I-93 and I-95 (both north-south), which sort of encircle the city. (If you go east, you'll end up in Massachusetts Bay.) Route 128/95 runs about ten miles out of the city, while 495 is an extremely loose outerbelt connecting the surrounding areas.

Bostonians love their MBTA (Massachusetts Bay Transportation Authority, the "T," 10 Park Plaza, general information, 722-5000; route information, 722-3200). One of the most comprehensive services in the country, it provides commuter rail, subway, local bus, and express bus service to 78 cities and towns. With 680,000 riders and more than one million passenger trips a day, it's safe, cheap, and convenient. Expanded service is planned for Worcester and additional South Shore suburbs.

Although Boston is supposedly the only large city with a downtown international airport, finding your way around Logan (567-5400) may require a map as well. One of the world's biggest and busiest airports, it's easily reached by subway and even boat, although driving or taking a taxi there can make it seem a whole lot farther. The airport is undergoing a modernization project (Logan 2000) and even has its own Web site (www.massport.com) for information on flights.

About 20 miles northwest of Boston in Bedford, the Lawrence G. Hanscom Field (274-7200) serves corporations and smaller aircraft. Along with Amtrak (482-3660; for Back Bay, South, and North Station commuters, 722-3200), the wide array of bus options includes Greyhound (526-1810), Plymouth and Brockton St. Railway (508/746-0378), and Peter Pan Trailways (426-8554). However, once you leave Boston proper, driving becomes almost civilized again.

CHARLESTON, SOUTH CAROLINA

Charleston at a Glance

Birthdate and Present Size: 1670 (settled); 1783 (incorporated). *Metropolitan Statistical Area—* 1980: 430,346; 1990: 506,875. 1/1/95 (estimate): 535,000. Percent change, 1980–1990: +17.8%. Percent change, 1990–1995: +5.5%.

Weather Report: *Average annual temperature—*65° F. In January: 58/38° F. In July: 90/73° F. *Average annual precipitation—*52". *Average annual snowfall—*very infrequent (0.5").

Money Matters: *Unemployment rate—* 6.1%. *Per capita income—*N/A. *Average household income—*$41,324. *Average cost of a home—*$114,702. *Average rent for an apartment—* $557/month. *ACCRA cost of living indexes* (based on 100)—Composite Index: 97.5; Utilities Index: 124.2; Housing Index: 87.1. *Sales and use tax—*6%. *Personal income tax—*2% to 7%.

People Profile: *Crime rate* (Per 100,000 population)—6,663. *Racial and ethnic characteristics—* White: 67.8%; Black: 30.2%; Hispanic Origin: 1.5%; Other: 2.0%. *Gender ratio—*Male 49.9%; Female 50.1%. *Age characteristics—*18–24 (N/A); 25–44 (34.7%). Median age: 29.5. *Educational attainment—*N/A.

Major Players: Government, retail trade, services, manufacturing. *Largest employers—*U.S. Navy, Medical University of South Carolina, U.S. Air Force, Charleston County Schools, Berkeley County Schools, Roper Hospital, Westvaco Corporation, U.S. Postal Service, Robert Bosch Corporation, Piggly Wiggly Carolina, Santee Cooper.

Community Services: *Average hospital cost—*$369.75/day. *Average doctor visit—*$47.00. *Average dentist visit—*$57.71. *Newspapers—The Post and Courier, Charleston Chronicle* (black community), *Upwith Herald* (alternative).

Forget power ties, high heels, and fast living. In a city as steeped in tradition as Charleston, they're about as appropriate as a nose ring on Wall Street. Besides, even slightly tight shoes will kill your feet in this town where nearly everyone walks to their destination. And although well-established names have an edge here, newcomers and lesser-knowns with ambition and savvy can also prosper.

Founded in 1670, Charles Towne (named after King Charles II of England) started out as a colony on the Carolina Coast. By 1762, settlers recognized the advantages of relocating across the river to a peninsula between the Ashley and Cooper Rivers. A wise move, since Charleston soon became known as the "little London" of the New World, with international trade, elegant mansions, and continental-style streets that flourish to this day.

Deerskins, rice, indigo, hemp, and slaves provided income to the burgeoning community. The first African was described by local records as a "lusty Negro" who arrived in 1670. The sheer number of slaves corralled and sold in Charleston has garnered a rather unsavory comparison to Ellis Island. But not all blacks remained indentured; some bought their freedom and became business owners and artisans.

A groundbreaking (for the 17th century) charter also guaranteed religious liberty. This attracted French Huguenots, Baptists, Congregationalists, Presbyterians, Jews, Lutherans, Methodists, and Catholics. Along with red-light districts near the wharf where drunken sailors could stumble back to their ships, Charleston's narrow, storied streets eventually became dotted with 350 churches of varying denominations.

You can't make a move without stepping in someone's saga. Charleston has a tradition rich with framers of the Constitution (as opposed to the Declaration of Independence, because Charleston was under British rule until after the Revolutionary War), pirates (including a "gentleman bandit" who ingratiated himself with the city's finest families, escaped, and was hanged in a city square by the angry populace), and a genteel resistance to the Civil War symbolized by continuous Confederate occupation of Fort Sumter. But underneath this thick coat of history beats the heart of a town tuned in to the times.

Quality of Life

Like a true Southerner, Charleston draws you in with its mannerly charm. Although the quaint streets, tangy breeze—courtesy of horse-drawn carriages and the sea—and lack of big-city glitter may not immediately inspire a gee-whiz attitude, the friendly people and relaxed pace have a major tranquilizing effect. Even strangers will tell you how proud they are of their city and offer to help should you look the least bit confused or upset. With an annual tourism industry of $1.5 billion and over 5 million visitors, newcomers are treated with the respect accorded to a major account. A pity Paris isn't populated with Charlestonians.

With 234 days of sunshine, there's lots for inhabitants to smile about. Plentiful beaches, gardens, and plantations; festivals such as the world-renowned Spoleto USA; outstanding golf, sailing, and other sports; excellent shopping and dining; the ubiquitous historical distractions and more have earned Charleston a top spot in *Condé Nast Traveler's* annual ranking of best places to visit as well as in other publications, like *50 Fabulous Places to Raise Your Family*.

Six major universities give the town a charge of youthful energy. The most well-known is The Citadel, a military college whose students can be spotted striding about in their impeccably starched uniforms. With nine hospitals, the Medical University of South Carolina, and 1,400 local physicians, the question "Is there a doctor in the house?" would likely be answered with the latest in research and care. And the locals brag about Reuben Greenberg, Charleston's black, Jewish police chief, who has helped reduce crime and homelessness.

General Opportunities

With a generally below-average cost of living and a relatively cushy average household income, Charlestonians "can get a lot for their money, if they know where to look," observes banker Craig Goldberg. Although state and local per capita taxes are well below the national average, utilities and miscellaneous services such as eating out and entertainment can be more expensive than normal. "It's easy to spend a mint here, if you're not careful."

Still, "Charleston is an easy sell," comments Doug Warner, who works with relocating companies. "The international trade community makes it very appealing." There's also a personal element: "Business is often conducted in a social manner, over a meal or through the development of relationships." He cites as an example one large company's choice between relocating to Charleston or another Southern city. "[The owners] got invited to someone's house for dinner. They went sailing on the host's boat and that clinched the deal."

Charlestonians readily tell you that having an old family name helps in taking care of business. "Frankly, people here are almost too complacent," states one native. "You see the same names over and over again in certain dealings."

But "things are changing," emphasizes Kathy Boles, marketing director for a local resort. "A lot depends on the industry you're in." There's definitely room for entrepreneurs and service industries; *Money* magazine cited the Charleston area as one of the top places in the U.S. for running a small company.

It may take a little longer to establish yourself here, but the extra effort is worth it. "Charleston is a jewel in the U.S.," remarks Warner. "There's nothing like it. It has the intimacy and friendliness of a small town, yet it's cosmopolitan and attracts people from all over. It's nothing to go out to dinner and have, say, Kelly McGillis sitting at the next table."

MAJOR BREADWINNING

For years, the military dominated employment and the economy. But current downsizing in defense cut several thousand jobs, and might have had folks worrying, "What next?" Not Charleston, the city that refers to the Civil War as "the late unpleasantness" and treated Hurricane Hugo as a minor interruption in the pursuit of civic and leisure activities. Although the Charleston Navy Base has phased out more than 19,000 positions since the announcement in 1993 that it would close—it currently employs about 7,800—the city has rebounded with efforts to recruit more industry, and recently attracted such enterprises as NuCor Steel and Amoco Chemicals.

The Port of Charleston remains a main asset, moving over 9 million tons of cargo a year, supplying nearly 14,000 jobs, and generating $1.6 billion annually. Expansion of a terminal and a sophisticated electronic system have resulted in a 20 percent increase in capacity and a ranking as one of the world's most (if not *the* most) efficient transportation networks. And the military is still a presence; along with an existing Air Force base, the transfer of three naval electronic engineering facilities added 3,000 new positions. The state and local government accounts for over one-fourth of employment.

But diversification is the name of the game in Charleston. The hospitality industry provides a whopping 34,000 positions. Old homes, picturesque shops, eateries, and beaches help keep unemployment fairly low, although it's somewhat higher than the national average, thanks to the influx of college students and recent graduates. Those wishing to work in tourism might get their foot in the door by attending the Johnson & Wales Culinary University.

Medicine comprises another big chunk of the employment pie. With an estimated 22,000 positions, 16,000 of which are directly related to area hospitals, qualified health care workers may find easy pickings. However, the local medical establishment and colleges also supply a steady stream of doctors, nurses, dentists, pharmacists, and others.

More and more companies are making Charleston their home, or at least their branch office. Doug Warner is hesitant to reveal who might be moving into town, but "potential clients are almost always wowed by the quality of life and the attitude of the locals. Since the naval base closed, we've taken a more aggressive approach, and it's beginning to pay off." One recent year saw the addition of 63 new businesses and the expansion of 21 existing firms. Companies such as Piggly Wiggly, Westvaco, Santee Cooper, and Oneita Industries supply thousands of positions.

> **Forget power ties, high heels, and fast living. In a city as steeped in tradition as Charleston, they're about as appropriate as a nose ring on Wall Street.**

"People usually want to stay in Charleston, even if they don't have a job," says Craig Goldberg. But those with an entrepreneurial spirit will put their ears to the ground and start making appointments to do lunch.

SOCIAL AND RECREATIONAL SCENE

How Charleston Plays

Despite its surface cordiality, "it can be harder to make friends here if you're a newcomer," admits Craig Goldberg. "There needs to be a common element in meeting someone."

Still, avenues are open in area code 803 for those willing to put forth the effort. The Charitable Society of Charleston (P.O. Box 211334, 577-0702) raises tens of thousands of dollars a year for local foundations and community centers. "The young people here want to make a difference," observes Doug Warner. "They care about the community."

Some may wrinkle their noses at the conventionality of it—this isn't San Francisco, folks— but the Junior League (51 Folly Rd., 763-5284) and the Preservation Society of Charleston (Box 251, 722-4630) are very strong, as are private social and sporting organizations. "You almost always have to know someone to be invited to join" the first two, admits one native.

But for those who can get over the Groucho Marx philosophy that they wouldn't belong to any club that wants them as a member, more than 1,000 additional civic, professional, support, and other groups address just about every interest. And they welcome participants.

ARTS AND SCIENCES

Among the more receptive organizations is a wide-ranging array of arts associations and events. These consist of, but are hardly limited to, the **Gibbes Museum of Art,** which has one of the finest colonial portrait collections in the U.S. and offers a number of special exhibitions. Membership includes special previews and tours. As the oldest (dating from 1773) continuing collection in North America, the **Charleston Museum** has artifacts from the first settlers to the current residents. Museum buffs can also choose from the **Citadel Museum, Confederate Museum,** and even **Herbie's Antique Car Museum,** among many others.

Forts **Moultrie** and **Sumter** feature more front row tickets to history, while the plantations at **Boone Hall, Drayton Hall,** and

Where It's At

 Unless otherwise noted, all area codes are 803.

Afro American History Tours, 853-2500

Boone Hall, Hwy. 17, East of the Cooper, 884-4371

Charleston Area Arts Council, 207 E. Bay St., 577-7137

Charleston Ballet Theatre, 723 Meeting St., 723-7334

Charleston Museum, 360 Meeting St., 722-2996

Where It's At

(continued)

Charleston Stage Company, 133 Church St., 577-5967

Charleston Symphony, 14 George St., 723-7528

Citadel Museum, 171 Moultrie St., 800/868-DAWG

Confederate Museum, 188 Meeting St., 723-1541

Drayton Hall, 3380 Ashley River Rd., 766-0188

Fort Moultrie, West Middle St., Sullivan's Island, 883-3123

Fort Sumter, Fort Sumter Tours Inc., 505 King St., 722-1691

Gaillard Auditorium, 77 Calhoun St., 577-7400

Gibbes Museum of Art, 135 Meeting St., 722-2706

Herbie's Antique Car Museum, Mt. Pleasant, 176 L.O. Darby Blvd., 884-9700

Middleton Place, Ashley River Rd., 556-6020

MOJA Arts Festival, Dock Street Theatre, 724-7305

North Charleston Coliseum, 5001 Coliseum Dr., 529-5000

Original Charleston Walks, 334 E. Bay St., 577-3800

Southwestern Wildlife Exposition, Meeting St., 800/221-5273

Spoleto USA, P.O. Box 157, 722-2764

Where It's At

 Unless otherwise noted, all area codes are 803.

Charleston County Parks and Recreation Commission, 861 Riverland Dr., 762-2172

Charleston River Dogs, 701 Rutledge Ave., 723-7241

Charleston Southern University, 863-7000

Citadel, 171 Moultrie St., 792-6552

College of Charleston, 9 Chelsea Way, 792-5613

South Carolina Wildlife and Marine Resources, P.O. Box 12559, Charleston, SC, 29422, 795-6350

Stingrays, 3107 Firestone Rd., 744-2248

Middleton Place and others provide intimate glimpses of antebellum and pre-Revolutionary War life. The construction, artifacts, and written and verbal narrative are so authentic you can almost feel the pain in George Washington's false teeth as he posed for his formal portrait. Another way of getting to know Charleston is through tours such as the **Original Charleston Walks** and **Afro-American History Tours.**

Founded in 1877 as the American counterpart to an Italian festival whose town it's named after, **Spoleto USA** draws thousands of artists and aficionados. With over two weeks of opera, dance, theater, and music in May and June, "it's an ideal way to get involved," points out Kathy Boles. The annual **MOJA Arts Festival** in September highlights African and Caribbean arts, and each February, the **Southwestern Wildlife Exposition** honors our four-, six-, and eight-legged friends via a unique celebration of crafts and collectibles.

In conjunction with the **Charleston Area Arts Council,** the **Charleston Ballet Theatre,** the **Charleston Symphony,** and the **Charleston Stage Company** offer classes, exhibitions, and shows. The **Gaillard Auditorium** and the relatively new 14,000-seat **North Charleston Coliseum** draw such varied acts as Billy Joel, the Eagles, and World Cup figure skating.

 ## THE SPORTING LIFE

Along with more conventional water sports (boating, skiing, and fishing), horseback riding, golf, and tennis, a number of alternative diversions are available. "Rock climbing, kayaking, and mountain biking have become increasingly popular," observes Charleston native and tour guide John Venable. "People are looking for something different."

Charleston has more than 50 parks. Two of the most well known, Waterfront Park by the harbor and White Point Gardens at the Battery, offer a pier, picnic tables, and other amenities in addition to a gorgeous view. Other parks have campgrounds, meeting facilities, and lakes (contact the **Charleston County Parks and Recreation Commission**).

Beach resorts or time-share accommodations provide easy access to such prime locations as Kiawah Island, Seabrook, Wild Dunes, the Isle of Palms, and Sullivan's Island. "It's not uncommon to take long weekends around here," he goes on. Outstanding golf and tennis facilities;

some of the most pristine beaches in the country; and plentiful fish in the lakes, rivers, and Atlantic Ocean make the area a leisure-time mecca.

Another sort of game—white-tailed deer, feral hogs, wild turkeys, ducks, and other native critters—can be found in nature preserves at the 250,000-acre Francis Marion National Forest. Those who feel compelled to *really* check them out can contact the **South Carolina Wildlife and Marine Resources** for seasonal hunting and fishing permits.

Spectator sports at colleges, particularly NCAA action at the **Citadel,** the **College of Charleston,** and **Charleston Southern University** are another hot ticket, particularly among young professionals. The city even has its own minor league baseball team—the rather undignified-sounding **Charleston River Dogs**—and the **Stingrays,** a professional hockey team that draws capacity crowds.

AFTER-HOURS DIVERSIONS

Although there are slightly more females than males, "it's fairly easy to meet men here," observes Kathy Boles. Charleston's colleges churn out a constant supply of military graduates as well as other professionals.

Both sexes are "young, single, and have usually just completed a postgraduate degree," remarks marketing coordinator Victoria Bryant. Once you get plugged into the social scene, "it's simple to meet friends of friends. You find yourself encountering lots of familiar faces."

John Venable, who also performs at various clubs, finds the music scene "incredibly supportive, like Seattle a few years ago. Charleston has a big-city atmosphere without the gridlock." Pubs such as **Level 2** and the **Music Farm** rock into the wee hours, while **Louie's Jazz Lounge Grill** and **Sports Rock Cafe/The Comedy Zone** feature more specialized entertainments.

Numerous bars line the Market Street area. "People just walk around and listen to music outside," adds Boles. "It's more like visiting with friends than actual bar hopping."

> # Where It's At
>
> **Unless otherwise noted, all area codes are 803.**
>
> *Level 2,* 36 N. Market St., 577-4454
>
> *Louie's Jazz Lounge Grill,* Omni Hotel, 722-4900
>
> *Music Farm,* 32 Ann St., 853-FARM
>
> *Sports Rock Cafe/The Comedy Zone,* 3025 W. Montague St., 566-9000

CULINARY AND SHOPPING HAUNTS

Charleston stacks up against the biggest in terms of quality cuisine. Choices range from fine dining (**Blossom Cafe, Carolina's**) to grease 'n grits and other down-home goodies (**Sticky's, Squeaky's Tavern & Grill**). Local specialties include she crab soup, pea cakes and collard greens, deviled crab and raw oysters, fresh seafood, and barbecued anything.

Although pricey ($15 and up) restaurants like **Louis's Charleston Grill** and **Magnolia's** have won raves from *Travel and Leisure* and *Town and Country,* the city is loaded with less expensive options. Locally owned eateries such as **T-Bonz** and **Arizona Bar & Grill** usually cost less than $10.

> # Where It's At
>
> **Unless otherwise noted, all area codes are 803.**
>
> *Aaron's Deli,* 215 Meeting St., 723-0233
>
> *Alice's Fine Foods and Southern Cooking,* 468–470 King St., 853-9366
>
> *Applebee's,* 24 N. Market St., 723-3531
>
> *Arizona Bar & Grill,* 14 Chapel St., 577-5090
>
> *Audubon Shop and Gallery,* 245 King St., 723-6171
>
> *Blossom Cafe,* 171 E. Bay St., 722-9200
>
> *Carolina's,* 10 Exchange St., 724-3800

Where It's At

(continued)

Charleston Chocolates, 90 E. Bay St., 577-4491

Citadel Mall, Hwy. 7 and 17 at I-526, 766-8511

Festival Centre, 5101 Ashley Phosphate Rd., 552-3345

Home, 268 King St., 723-9063

Hyman's Seafood Co., 212 Meeting St., 723-6000

Louis's Charleston Grill, 224 King St., 577-4522

Magnolia's, 185 E. Bay St., 577-7771

Omni Charleston Place, 130 Market St., 722-4900

Scents Unlimited, 92 N. Market St., 800-854-8804

Squeaky's Tavern & Grill, 5 Cumberland St., 722-1541

Sticky's, 235 Meeting St., 835-RIBS

Where It's At

 Unless otherwise noted, all area codes are 803.

Avery Institute, 125 Bull St., 727-2009

Boone Hall Plantation, 125 Bull St., 727-2009

Congregation Beth Elohim, 90 Hassell St., 723-1090

Diocese of Charleston, 119 Broad St., 723-3488

Emanuel A.M.E. Church, 110 Calhoun, 722-2561

First Baptist Church, 48 Meeting St., 722-3896

First (Scots) Presbyterian Church, 53 Meeting St., 722-8882

French Protestant (Huguenot) Church, 136 Church St., 722-4385

Jewish Community Center, 1645 Raoul Wallenberg Blvd., 571-6565

Old Slave Mart, 6 Chalmers St.

St. Mary's, 89 Hassell St., 722-7696

Trident Urban League, P.O. Box 20249, 720-2780

Charleston offers the usual chains and ethnic choices as well. For every **Alice's Fine Foods and Southern Cooking,** there's an **Applebee's** or **Aaron's Deli.**

However, no visit to the city would be complete without a stop at **Hyman's Seafood Co.** A tourist attraction also frequented by natives, it offers mostly fish for under $10. An added bonus: tables at which famous people have eaten are marked with plaques. So you may be chowing down at a booth once frequented by David Lee Roth.

Shopping is another way to wear out your feet and your bank account. The fare at the **Citadel Mall, Festival Centre,** and others, and a score of exclusive emporiums at the **Omni Charleston Place** suit a wide array of needs and pocketbooks.

King, East Bay, and Market streets might tempt even the most spending-impaired. The **Audubon Shop and Gallery** sells bird-watching accouterments, prints, and other wildlife art. **Home** consists of state-of-the-art kitchen gadgets in a circa 1800s building. **Scents Unlimited** and **Charleston Chocolates** entice the senses. And there are scores of antique shops on King and Meeting streets.

With its jewelry, leather goods, and assortment of knickknacks, the Market Street area can be a bargain-hunter's dream.

 ### ETHNIC AND RELIGIOUS PROSPECTS

Charleston is rich in African-American history and presence, particularly in the areas of visual arts, architecture, music, and cooking. Locals eagerly point out the work of wrought-iron craftsman Phillip Simmons, whose creations have gained worldwide admiration. Many Charlestonians feel their shared past gives them an appreciation of black culture not found in Northern metropolises.

Anyone serious about understanding Charleston would do well to explore its African-American heritage. Places such as the **Avery Institute** serve as a clearinghouse for information and offer exhibits relating to local and "Gullah" history and culture. Other sights include "Slave Street" at **Boone Hall Plantation;** the **Old Slave Mart,** where slaves were bought and sold; and the **Emanuel A.M.E. Church,** the site of an unsuccessful 1822 uprising, to mention a few.

However, "compared to larger cities, the pool of African-American professionals remains small," comments entrepreneur Stacy Vanderhorst. Although in recent years opportunities have gradually begun to unfold, "many of the quality people don't want to wait, so they move on to bigger arenas."

Still, organizations such as the **Trident Urban League** provide a chance to network with other young professionals. "We work on leadership development, fund-raising, and youth service projects for minorities and the disadvantaged," explains Vanderhorst, who is also the group coordinator.

> Like a true Southerner, Charleston draws you in with its mannerly charm. "Charleston is a jewel in the U.S.," remarks a local. "There's nothing like it—it has the intimacy and friendliness of a small town, yet it's cosmopolitan and attracts people from all over."

Charleston's dizzying array of historical denominations range from the second oldest synagogue in the United States and the birthplace of American Reform Judaism (**Congregation Beth Elohim**) to its neighbor **St. Mary's,** the oldest Roman Catholic Church in the state. The **First Baptist Church, First (Scots) Presbyterian Church, French Protestant (Huguenot) Church,** and a score of others add to this sacred mix.

Still, prospects can be limited for Jews and Catholics. "Charleston has a fairly large population for a town of its size," observes Craig Goldberg. "But there are even more in other cities. So natives move away, get married, and come back here to raise their families." The **Jewish Community Center** and **Diocese of Charleston** can provide points of contact.

CRIB SHEET

Consisting of 90 miles of Atlantic coastline and reaching 50 miles inland, the Charleston metropolitan area includes the cities of Charleston and the less-costly North Charleston, villages such as Jamestown (population: 84), and beach locales like the Isle of Palms.

With its plethora of styles from different eras, downtown Charleston can produce a state of architectural ecstasy. The lovingly preserved Colonial, Georgian, Federal, Classical and Gothic Revival, Italianate, Victorian, and Art Deco homes are a point of pride and frequent display. "In certain circles, it's not about how many square feet you have, but how old your house is and who owned it before you," remarks John Venable.

A residence in the historic district *can* be had—for a price. Mansions start at around $300,000 and can move easily upwards to $1,000,000 or more. Plus, home buyers must deal with city rules and regulations regarding preservation and upkeep. "Frankly, people get tired of the constant renovation and move out after a few years," he adds.

However, a wide choice of apartments, condominiums, beach houses, and starter and executive homes can also be found in the metro and surrounding locale. Apartment rents average around $600 a month for a two-bedroom with washer/dryer hookup. And a basic three-bedroom, two-bath home in a middle-class neighborhood is available for around $119,000.

Traditional suburban communities such as West of the Ashley and Summerville provide options at a reasonable price. West Ashley's apartments, starter homes, 1960s-style neighborhoods, and country club communities suit many lifestyles, while being convenient to downtown. Summerville also boasts moss-draped streets and Victorian homes, elegant shops and restaurants, and nearby recreational facilities.

East Cooper encompasses the town of Mount Pleasant, as well as Sullivan's Island and the Isle of Palms; seclusion amid outstanding recreational facilities makes the latter two highly desirable. Now that the I-526 connector bridge is complete, resulting in an easy and quick commute to Charleston, "East Cooper has become one of the fastest-growing districts, and property values have risen accordingly," observes Victoria Bryant. Once again, there's great diversity, from beachfront cottages to country-club estates.

North Charleston is a booming area that might appeal to the budget-conscious. Along with being home to the Charleston Coliseum, airport, Amtrak station, and port facilities, its central location and reasonably priced selection of dwellings make it attractive to new residents.

However, few Charlestonians brag about the public school system (566-8100), although class sizes are reasonable. With SAT scores being lower than the national average and slightly more than half of the high school graduates going on to college, the public schools "are just adequate," states one local. "Most people who want a quality education either move to Mt. Pleasant or Summerville or send their kids to Ashley Hall or a parochial school." Approximately 10 percent of the total student population opts for one of the area's twenty-five private institutions (Independent School Association, 736-0346).

NAVIGATING CHARLESTON

Parking in the historical district is at a premium, so the best way to get around is either by foot or via the downtown area shuttle (DASH, 724-7420). The problem with the DASH, however, is that you may actually have to do so in order to catch the tram. They only run every 20 minutes or so and are sometimes late. But they're a bargain at 75 cents a ride and $2 a day for an unlimited pass.

Bus service, the odd-sounding South Carolina Electric & Gas (SCE&G, 747-0922), also operates within the city, the Isle of Palms, Mt. Pleasant, and Sullivan's Island. Cabs are supposedly available, but sightings of these are as rare as a glaring neon mini-mart.

Those who wish to wander farther can do so via I-26, I-95, and I-526. Although it's fairly easy to learn your way around, the stunning sunsets and glimmering water may distract you into making a wrong turn.

Charleston's rail system extends to more major cities than any other Southern port and connects through Amtrak (744-8623). Over a million passengers a year fly through Charleston International (767-7009); its quaint charm adds weight to the hypothesis that you can tell a lot about a place by spending a few minutes in its airport. The Greyhound bus service (747-5341) is another option for getting out of town.

Charlotte at a Glance

Birthdate and Present Size: 1750 (settled); 1768 (chartered). *Metropolitan Statistical Area—* 1980: 971,391; 1990: 1,162,093. 1/1/95 (estimate): 1,279,000. Percent change, 1980–1990: +19.6%. Percent change, 1990–1995: +10.1%.

Weather Report: *Average annual temperature*—60° F. In January: 50/30° F. In July: 88/68° F. *Average annual precipitation*—43.16". *Average annual snowfall*—6".

Money Matters: *Unemployment rate*— 3.9%. *Per capita income*—$16,793 (city); $14,611 (MSA). *Average household income*—$41,578 (city); $38,214 (MSA). *Average cost of a home*—$128,700. *Average rent for an apartment*— $484/month. *ACCRA cost of living indexes* (based on 100)—Composite Index: 97.2; Utilities Index: 103.4; Housing Index: 94.0. *Sales and use tax*—4.0% (state); + 2.0% (local). *Personal income tax*—6.0% to 7.75%.

People Profile: *Crime rate* (Per 100,000 population)—9,686 (city); 6,886.5 (MSA).

Racial and ethnic characteristics— White: 65.6%; Black: 31.9%; Asian/Pacific Islander: 1.7%; Native American/Eskimo/Aleut: 0.4%; Hispanic Origin: 1.3%; Other: 0.5%. *Gender ratio*—90.2 males per 100 females (all ages); 86.7 males per 100 females (18 years old+). *Age characteristics*—18–24 (10.16%); 25–44 (37.3 percent). Median age: 32.0. *Educational attainment*—percent having completed high school: 81.0% (city), 72.5% (MSA); percent having completed college: 28.4% (city), 19.6% (MSA).

Major Players: Retail/wholesale trade, services, manufacturing, government. *Largest employers*—Charlotte Mecklenburg Housing Authority, Duke Power Co., First Union Corp., First Union National Bank, Homelite Inc., Knight Publishing, Lance (cookies), Mercy Health Services, NB Holdings Corp., Royal Group (insurance), Sandoz Chemicals.

Community Services: *Average hospital cost*—$338.00/day. *Average doctor visit*—$45.40. *Average dentist visit*—$59.60. *Newspapers—The Charlotte Observer, Business Journal of Charlotte, The Charlotte Post* (black), *Creative Loafing* (alternative).

CHARLOTTE: TRULY ROYAL

This gleaming heartthrob of a city seems to offer almost every promise of the American dream: prosperity, jobs, and clean, quiet suburbs.

Although what is now uptown Charlotte was used as a trading center by the Catawba Indians, the first white settlers, Scotch-Irish immigrants who arrived in the 1740s, built a farming community there. They named the area after Charlotte, the 17-year-old bride of King George III. The city didn't remain in royal favor for long: During the Revolutionary War, General Cornwallis labeled Charlotte "a veritable nest of hornets," unwittingly providing the moniker for what would become the town's championship basketball team (and it's not "Veritable Nest"). No army has invaded the city since, although an NFL franchise, the Carolina Panthers, was recently added, much to the delight of sports fans.

Charlotte also has the distinction of being the site of America's first gold rush. The discovery of a 17-pound nugget in 1799 set the stage for the next 50 years, when the city became a leading producer of gold. The town established itself as a financial presence in 1836, when the government built the first branch of the U.S. Mint there.

Charlotte also prospered from the invention of the cotton gin; railroads provided the necessary distribution of processed cotton and other products to other Southern cities and the East Coast. By the turn of the 19th century, the city was renowned for its quick and efficient ability to move commodities.

> **Everything in this city seems shiny and new—the executive-style homes; the shopping malls, art galleries, and specialty stores; and the burgeoning arts scene heavily supported by local businesses.**

Charlotte understates its role in the Civil War—most of it was built after that time, anyway—but what it loses in history, it makes up for in civic pride. The population has almost quadrupled since 1940, as the town has gathered steam as a center for transportation, commerce, and finance.

Quality of Life

Now the fifth-largest urban area in the U.S. (with about six million people living in a 100-mile radius) and the largest city between Washington, D.C. and Atlanta, Charlotte is within easy access of much of the U.S. Yet "it has the friendliness of a small town but the sophistication" of a major metropolis, according to marketing specialist Wendy Morefield. "The city is on the brink of spectacular growth. It's exciting to see everything come together."

Skyscrapers—such as the 871-foot-high glass-and-steel NationsBank Corporate Center—share space with scrupulously restored buildings like Founder's Hall, which boasts a two-story enclosed "winter garden" with retail stores, restaurants, and the adjacent Blumenthal Performing Arts Center. Spotless walkways, pavements, sculptures, and water fountains are accented by trees and flowers that bloom even in colder weather. Charlotte's uptown may be smaller than many major cities', but it's mighty.

With an average annual temperature of 60 degrees and a winter that rarely gets below freezing, the pace of life is distinctly slower. "There are many different Charlottes," observes reporter Bob Meadows. "You can drive down the street and see a beautiful old home with a perfectly tended lawn, another with a pickup truck and Confederate flag, and still another with goats and chickens in the front yard."

General Opportunities

Cynics might label Charlotte a yuppie mecca, but with a median age of 32, the town seems to have missed the migration of baby boomers. Along with being ranked by *Newsweek* as one of the most desirable cities to live in the U.S., it has also been hailed as an outstanding place to do business by *The New York Times* and *Fortune* magazine.

Over 18,000 new jobs were created in 1995 in this, the country's second-largest banking center. Institutions such as NationsBank, First Union, and a branch of the Federal Reserve account for $310 billion in assets. Charlotte's major employers range from the public schools to USAirways to IBM. And since 1991, the rate of joblessness has dropped almost 2 percent, thanks to the juxtaposition of corporations, government, and service industries.

With $10.9 billion in annual retail sales, this town is booming. Everything seems shiny and new—from the executive-style ($250,000 and up) homes that seem to be popping up everywhere; to the shopping malls, art galleries, and specialty stores at nearly every major intersection; to the burgeoning arts scene, heavily supported by local businesses. An 850,000-square-foot Convention Center built in 1995 and a recently completed 72,302-seat football stadium are the latest sparklers in the Queen City's crown.

MAJOR BREADWINNING

Don't be fooled by the plethora of suits in uptown Charlotte; it is, after all, a primary employer of bank, accounting, and insurance professionals. But along with companies like the aforementioned financial institutions, the Charlotte-Mecklenburg Hospital Authority, Presbyterian Health Services Corporation, and branches of the "Big Six" accounting firms, the area serves as the national headquarters for Belk department stores, Continental General Tire, Family Dollar stores, and others. Over one-third of the country's largest enterprises have a local presence, with IBM, Wal-Mart Stores/Sam's, and AT&T providing thousands of jobs. Charlotte's approximately 3,800 manufacturers supply textiles, furniture, and electronics. Products move through here as well, as Charlotte is the center of the country's largest consolidated rail system and has over 235 trucking firms.

Charlotte also prides itself on attracting international corporations. Three hundred–plus foreign-owned enterprises from 35 countries have facilities here, and it's an international port of entry. "The Chamber and the local government try to make it convenient for these folks to do business here," remarks Morefield. In contrast to a few years ago, "the town has become a melting pot. It's not uncommon to walk down the street and overhear a conversation in a foreign language."

Over the past decade, nearly 5,500 new firms have started new businesses in Charlotte or have moved to the area, infusing $3.2 billion into the economy. Recent relocations and expansions include TransAmerica Insurance, Sea-Land Corporation, and Stanley Tools. "Many people request a transfer to the Charlotte branch," observes banker Ameil Goldberg. "Life is much less complicated here. You get more for your money in terms of housing, food, and clothing without losing the cultural variety and excitement of a big city. Many times people I know have turned down promotions to stay in Charlotte."

Entrepreneurs can thrive as well. "The increased population creates a demand for service businesses," adds lawyer Charles "Chet" Rabon. "People who are willing to work hard can find success that's not as easily gained in more established or large urban areas where there's lots of competition." The growth is also reflected in the nearly four million square feet of available office space. At least two more skyscrapers are planned for uptown in the next decade.

For many young, college-educated professionals, Charlotte symbolizes a new type of promised land. "Along with escaping from the rat race of, say, a Washington or Los Angeles, newcomers find it easy to become engaged in the community," adds Goldberg. "There's a synergy at work here that makes the whole bigger than the sum of its parts." And if you don't like your job, chances are you'll find another.

SOCIAL AND RECREATIONAL SCENE

How Charlotte Plays

Area code 704 lacks the exclusiveness that can characterize more entrenched Southern towns. "It's easy to meet people here," observes Morefield. "Many come from other cities so everyone's accepting of newcomers." It's also a great place to meet guys: "The city has a lot of bankers, accountants, and lawyers, which are traditionally male occupations. They come here in droves," and since many are starting out, are often unattached.

One of the best and easiest ways to get involved is through the arts scene. The Charlotte Arts and Science Council (227 W. Trade St, 372-9667) raises over $3 million annually for organizations such as the Afro-American Children's Theatre, Discovery Place, and Opera Carolina.

Another visible group is the Young Affiliates of the Mint Museum of Art (2730 Randolph Rd., 337-2000). Noted for its collections of American and European paintings, pre-Columbian art, pottery, and ceramics, the former home of the U.S. Mint is an easy-to-navigate and user-friendly place. Along with presenting an annual series highlighting various crafts (hors d'oeuvres included), the Young Affiliates hold several fund raising events. "Without exception, it's the best and most fulfilling way to meet people," remarks Realtor Paige Gunter. They can also plug you into other worthy causes, such as Second String Santa, which provides thousands of dollars' worth of toys at Christmastime. Folks with specialized interests can get involved with hundreds of local clubs and associations, which range from saving the animals to astrology to square dancing to tree climbing.

 ### ARTS AND SCIENCES

Culture vultures wishing to circle Charlotte have plenty to choose from. Along with hosting the local ballet, symphony, and opera, the **Blumenthal Performing Arts Center** attracts national touring shows. Located in a former Baptist church, the **Spirit Square Center for Arts and Education** provides another venue as well as an excellent gallery and classrooms. Even NationsBank gets into the act with an 800-seat performance place. (It's in the tallest building in the Southeast, so you can't miss it.) Also not to be overlooked is the **Afro-American Cultural Center.** This lively spot celebrates African-American and other cultures' histories through a variety of exhibitions, performances, and hands-on activities.

Science enthusiasts will find a mecca at **Discovery Place.** A tropical rain forest, North American Wildlife collection, aquarium touch pool, and more complement a unique combination of an OMNIMAX big-screen-and-sound theater system and Space Voyager Planetarium, the latter of which is the largest in the U.S.

Where It's At

 Unless otherwise noted, all area codes are 704.

Afro-American Cultural Center, 401 N. Myers St., 374-1565

Blumenthal Performing Arts Center, Founder's Hall, 130 N. Tryon St., 372-1000

Charlotte Arts and Science Council, 227 W. Trade St., 372-9667

Discovery Place, 301 N. Tryon St., 800/935-0553

Spirit Square Center for Arts and Education, 345 N. College St., 800/922-6431

Young Affiliates of the Mint Museum of Art, 2730 Randolph Rd., 337-2000

Where It's At

Unless otherwise noted, all area codes are 704.

Carolina Panthers, 337 W. Trade St., 358-7000

Charlotte Checkers, 2700 East Independence Blvd., 342-4423

Charlotte Hornets, 100 Hive Dr., 357-0252

Charlotte Knights, 2280 Deerfield Dr., 357-8071

Charlotte Motor Speedway, P.O. Box 600, 455-3200

Charlotte Sport and Social Club, 1409 E. Blvd., 442-1655

Mecklenburg County and Recreation Department, 5841 Brookshire Blvd., 336-3854

Morrow Mountain State Park, 49107 Morrow Mtn. Rd., Albemarle, 982-0601

Paramount Carowinds, off exit 90 at I-77, 14523 Carowinds Boulevard, 800/888-4386

THE SPORTING LIFE

Charlotte is a great place for sports, both spectator and participatory. Its (mostly) year-round temperance allows for plentiful golf, tennis, hiking, and water activities. The Charlotte-Mecklenburg area has nearly 150 parks scattered over 10,000 acres and over a dozen recreational centers (contact the **Mecklenburg County and Recreation Department**). And the **Charlotte Sport and Social Club** organizes baseball, basketball, and volleyball tournaments. According to former director Katy Hosmer, "we have plenty of guys for the teams, but never enough women," yet another golden opportunity for females.

Proximity to the beach and mountains is another plus. "On summer weekends, people flock to Hilton Head, the Outer Banks, and other beaches," comments Morefield. **Morrow Mountain State Park** (about an hour away in Albemarle) is a favorite with ski and nature enthusiasts, and several preserves and historical attractions are an easy two- to three-hour drive. The research triangle area of Raleigh-Durham and the college town of Chapel Hill are also popular day trips.

Everything from professional basketball (**Charlotte Hornets**) to NFL football (**Carolina Panthers**) to AAA baseball (**Charlotte Knights**) to minor league hockey (**Charlotte Checkers**) can be found here. The city has hosted the NCAA Men's Final Four, the PGA World Seniors Invitational, men's marathon Olympic Trials, and dozens of other special events. Adds Ameil Goldberg, "People around here take their sports seriously, and support the teams both financially and in terms of attendance," particularly since the Panthers advanced all the way to the NFC Championship in only their second year.

Approximately 10 miles from town is **Paramount Carowinds,** a 92-acre amusement complex with six roller coasters, a water park, racing simulators, and other attractions. With expanded seating and the addition of boxes and other amenities, the **Charlotte Motor Speedway** offers "real" racing excitement with the Coca-Cola 600 and other NASCAR events.

AFTER-HOURS DIVERSIONS

Charlotte nightlife is more collegiate than what's-your-sign. Bars such as **Atlantic Beer and Ice Company** and **Southend Brewery and Smokehouse** draw a sophisticated crowd, and **Mythos** features alternative dance music, from house to techno to European. Jazz performers appear at some of the clubs, while others provide entertainment ranging from poetry readings (the **Moon Room**) to any major televised sporting event (**Champions Sports Bar, Coach's Sports Bar & Grill**).

Where It's At

Unless otherwise noted, all area codes are 704.

600 Festival, Charlotte Motor Speedway, 455-3200

Atlantic Beer and Ice Company, 330 N. Tryon, 339-0566

Carolina Renaissance Festival, Davidson, 896-5555

Champions Sports Bar, Marriott City Center, 333-9000

Coach's Sports Bar & Grill, 10403 Park Rd., 544-0607

Loch Norman Highland Games, Rural Hill on Neck Rd., 875-3113

Moon Room, 433 S. Tryon, 342-2003

Mythos, 300 N. College St., 375-8765

Festivals present another outlet for meeting and mingling. They vary from **New Plays in America,** held in January, to the Scottish-themed **Loch Norman Highland Games** in April to SpringFest, also in April, to the 16th-century **Carolina Renaissance Festival** in the fall. The **600 Festival,** a late May event honoring the Winston Select and Coca-Cola 600 races, drags in enthusiasts from all over the country.

 ## CULINARY AND SHOPPING HAUNTS

Charlotte serves up the whole spectrum of food, from the ultraexpensive **Morton's of Chicago** to **Bubba's Barbecue,** where traditional Southern barbecue with all the hush puppies you can handle can be had for well under a ten-spot. Restaurants favored by locals include **Bistro 100,** which offers French and American dishes; the **Lamplighter,** whose award-winning American and Continental cuisine is served in a historic home and complemented by an excellent wine list; and the much less pricey **Gus' Sir Beef,** whose bragging rights include home-cooked meals and cornbread.

This town literally caters to every taste. Along with typical Low Country fare—shrimp and grits, deviled crab, and collard greens at the moderately priced **Blue Marlin**—you can choose from a wide array of Italian, Mexican, and Chinese/Japanese places along with Vietnamese, Thai, and Jamaican exotica. Retro fodder is dished up in fine fondue form at the **Melting Pot.** The no-surprise crowd may delight in the local **Ben & Jerry's, Spaghetti Warehouse,** and the "Delightfully Tacky Yet Unrefined" **Hooters** among others.

North Carolina has a reputation for superb furniture. The **Hickory Furniture Mart** in Hickory lures folks from all over, while closer to Charlotte, **Boyles Furniture** and **Mecklenburg Furniture Shop** also offer discounts. Antiques can be found in the **Brem House,** the **Crescent Collection,** and lots of other places in addition to the towns of Pineville, Matthews, and Waxhaw.

Southpark and **Eastland** malls in Charlotte and **Carolina Place** in nearby Pineville have the selection of stores that mall mavens know and love. Discount divas (and their male counterparts) may find heaven and great towels, sheets, and other goodies at **Cannon Village** in nearby Kannapolis, and the **Outlet Marketplace,** just over the South Carolina border in Ft. Mill. Those with a weakness for high-quality shoes at incredible discounts should probably avoid the **Off-Broadway Shoe Warehouse** in uptown Charlotte.

The **Specialty Shops on the Park** and the older neighborhoods of Dilworth and Myers Park sell everything from futons

Where It's At

(continued)

Southpark, 4400 Sharon Rd.,
364-4411

Spaghetti Warehouse, 101 W.
Worthington Ave., 376-8686

Specialty Shops on the Park,
6401 Morrison Blvd., 366-9841

Where It's At

 **Unless otherwise noted,
all area codes are 704.**

Catholic Center, 1524 E. Morehead St.,
377-6871

Jewish Center, 5007 Providence Rd.,
366-5007

Young Black Professionals, 581-2365

to jewelry to books to what one Charlottean described as "very granola" groceries and supplies. Eclectics and meanderers would do well here.

 ## ETHNIC AND RELIGIOUS PROSPECTS

One might expect a predominately white, Christian mentality from the birthplace of evangelist Billy Graham. (In fact, the Billy Graham Parkway, linking interstates 77 and 85 at the airport, serves as a sort of informal welcome to the Bible Belt.) Charlotte's 600 well-attended churches include a sizable representation of Southern Baptist, United Methodist, and Presbyterian congregations.

Still, over a third of Mecklenburg County's population is African-American. Educated blacks are attracted to the area, "particularly in the past few years, as more executive-level positions have become available to minorities," observes writer Angela Shannon. "Several groups have formed around a particular interest"—for example, accountants or lawyers and the more generalized **Young Black Professionals.** A recent gathering of an informal coalition of these organizations was a huge success. "It spoke to a need to network. There's more of us out there than even we realize."

However, many African-Americans feel there's room for improvement. "Because Charlotte has less poverty than most big cities, people tend to be complacent and not as motivated to alleviate social problems," remarks Meadows. "Charlotte is no different from any other city in terms of racism."

The "other" (about 2.5 percent) piece of the population pie is served by local Hindu, Islamic, and other houses of worship and support groups. Along with a **Catholic Center,** Charlotte has eleven Roman Catholic parishes as well as several Jewish synagogues. According to Ameil Goldberg, the Jewish population is one of the largest in the South, after Washington D.C. and Atlanta. The **Jewish Center** is "a magnificent facility. The entire Jewish community pulled together to consolidate all activities in one location."

CRIB SHEET

North Carolina ranks among the least expensive states to buy property in. So although newcomers might want to rent an apartment, condominium, or home, buying "is the best way to go," observes one Realtor. Also, because brick and lumber are more readily available, new builds tend to be less costly. And there are plenty of scenic neighborhoods to choose from.

Uptown is a popular area, particularly with singles and young marrieds. The Victorian Fourth Ward offers a potpourri of reasonably priced architecture, from early 19th century to Art Deco. The Salvation Army and welfare homes abutting this recently revitalized neighborhood have hardly discouraged buyers. With policemen on bicycles and a minimum of crime, "the entire district is very safe," adds Morefield.

The suburbs of Myers Park and Eastover have some of the loveliest and most expensive homes in Charlotte. Eastover in particular is noted for its impressive estates. Like Myers Park, the neighborhood of Dilworth was designed by the same architects who laid out New York's Central Park, with a closeness to uptown that makes it attractive to young professionals.

Those who prefer new might appreciate the Southpark area. Along with the area's biggest shopping mall and many large businesses, this locale offers a wide selection of upscale homes, apartments, and condominiums. Others on a budget might want to consider the Cotswald Mall area. Although land is at a premium here, most of the dwellings are 30 years old or less.

> **"Life is much less complicated here," says a local. "You get more for your money in terms of housing, food, and clothing without losing the cultural variety and excitement of a big city."**

Longtime residents will tell you that North Carolina's reputation for public education isn't exactly tops in the U.S., although the Charlotte-Mecklenburg area has the 28th largest school system in the nation (375-6000). Still, "it is improving," remarks writer C.J. Clemmons. The addition of "magnet schools," with programs tailored to special interests, has become popular. "The influx of sophisticated professionals has created a demand for quality education."

With more than 80 percent of high school graduates furthering their studies, Charlotte is on par nationally with College Boards and slightly below average on SATs. Excellent child care programs along with a wide selection of private/parochial schools (Department of Non-Public Education, 919/733-4276) and local universities (UNCC/Charlotte, Central Piedmont Community College, many others) cover kids from cradle to college.

NAVIGATING CHARLOTTE

Getting uptown may be a hassle, what with road construction and a rather confusing freeway system. Along with I-77 (north-south) and I-85 (east-west), there's I-277, a connector belt; I-485, which meanders west off of 77; and I-74 (southeast), which isn't quite hooked up with the rest of the network. Initially, the best way to get around may be on the main roads, although the city's not laid out on a grid pattern and the same street can change names several times. But people are friendly and willing to give directions.

This is a car town (lots of shiny new ones) and it's quite compact and logical in a Southern sort of way. Even rush hour traffic seems laid-back. Although bus service has been somewhat expanded (Charlotte Transit System, 336-2420 or 336-3366), public transportation hasn't quite evolved to where you can easily get to any destination. However, there is a spanking new bus station, with Greyhound (372-0456) and Trailways (342-2506) offices.

A hub for USAirways, the pristine Charlotte-Douglas International Airport (359-4027) has about 500 direct/nonstop flights to nearly 150 cities worldwide. The airport is the 14th busiest in the nation and it's a good bet that most travelers will stop there at least once. Amtrak (376-4416) is another transportation option, albeit a less speedy one.

Chicago at a Glance

Birthdate and Present Size: 1803 (incorporated as a city in 1837).
Metropolitan Statistical Area—
1980: 6,060,387; 1990: 6,069,974.
1/1/95 (estimate): 7,737,200.
Percent change, 1980–1990: +0.2%.
Percent change, 1990–1995: +27.5%.

Weather Report: *Average annual temperature*—49.2° F. In January: 29/13° F. In July: 84/63° F.
Average annual precipitation—33.34".
Average annual snowfall—40".

Money Matters: *Unemployment rate*—5.5%.
Per capita income—$12,899 (city); $16,447 (MSA).
Average household income—$34,682 (city); $44,583 (MSA).
Average cost of a home—$169,640.
Average rent for an apartment—$827/month.
ACCRA cost of living indexes (based on 100)—Composite Index: 123.3; Utilities Index: 122.9; Housing Index: 138.0.
Sales and use tax—6.25% (state); + 1.25% (local).
Personal income tax—Chicago/Illinois: 3%.

People Profile: *Crime rate*—N/A.
Racial and ethnic characteristics—White: 45.5% (city), 67.6% (MSA); Black: 39.0% (city), 21.9% (MSA); American Indian/Eskimo/Aleut: 0.2% (city), 0.2% (MSA); Asian/Pacific Islander: 3.7% (city),
3.8% (MSA); Hispanic Origin: 19.2% (city), 11.8% (MSA); Other: 11.5% (city), 6.5% (MSA).
Gender ratio—91.8 males per 100 females (all ages); 88.4 males per 100 females (18 years old+).
Age characteristics—18–24 (11.3%); 25–44 (33.3%). Median age: 31.1.
Educational attainment—percent having completed high school: 66.0% (city), 75.7% (MSA); percent having completed college: 19.5% (city), 24.4% (MSA).

Major Players: Services, wholesale and retail trade, manufacturing, government.
Largest employers—Allstate Corp., Arthur Andersen & Co., Continental Casualty, Elite Labor Services, First National Bank of Chicago, Heatherton Ltd.
Major Business Headquarters—Ameritech, Amoco, Fruit of the Loom, Illinois Central, Montgomery Ward, Morton International, Sara Lee, Sears, Unicom, USG.

Community Services: *Average hospital cost*—$639.00/day.
Average doctor visit—$51.25.
Average dentist visit—$69.75.
Newspapers—*Chicago Sun-Times, Chicago Tribune, Crain's Chicago Business, Chicago Reader* (alternative), several neighborhood weeklies and publications for the Black, Spanish, Catholic, and Jewish communities.

CHICAGO:
SECOND TO FEW

Photo by Peter J. Schulz/City of Chicago

Chicago's reputation as a "windy city" is well-deserved. Not only do gusts literally whip around the skyscrapers thanks to air movement from Lake Michigan, but it always seems to be in a frenzy, albeit a mostly thriving and fun one. And it's hard to resist a place that produces 16 billion Oreos a year.

Things began hopping in 1779 with the arrival of fur trader and former Haitian slave Jean Baptist Point du Sable. A proximity to various rivers and the Great Lakes made the locale an ideal trading post as well as a garrison for fighting off those pesky Indians, who wanted their land back. They didn't have a chance; settlers kept coming and, by 1837, when the town was incorporated, it was Palefaces: 4,170, Native Americans: zilch. However, Chicago is named after an Illinois tribe word meaning "strong" or "great."

> "Chicago's a great place if you're just starting out," comments a local PR manager. "There are lots of job openings, and if you're good at what you do, you can go far." Although the city is expensive, salaries can be commensurate with costs, and housing is rather reasonable.

And indeed the sum is bigger than its parts, for Chicago is no stranger to adversity. In October 1871, Mrs. Patrick O'Leary's cow allegedly knocked over a lantern in a barn, starting a fire that spread rapidly. It wiped out downtown and most of the North Side and left 90,000 people homeless.

Within a year, however, everything was rebuilt, creating a prosperity that's seemingly made Chicago impervious to budgetary whims. In 1893, the World Columbian Exposition celebrated the 400th anniversary of Christopher Columbus's arrival in the New World in the "second city" in size after the Big Apple. Chicago was also recognized as the nation's architectural capital and home of that uniquely American invention, the skyscraper. And during the Great Depression, another World's Fair attracted 39 million visitors and bolstered the economy.

But Chicago has suffered through gangster and bootlegging wars (1920s and '30s), uprisings (race riots and Vietnam War protesters in the '60s), and flooding in 1992 when the polluted Chicago River poured through downtown tunnels, causing the city to be declared a disaster area. Yet this "city of big shoulders" has soldiered on and its residents keep smiling.

Quality of Life

Living in Chicago is like being a member of a large, noisy family. You may not always get what you want, but it's rarely dull and there's usually someone around to listen and help. Now the third largest metropolis in the country, Chicago is the only inland urban area considered equal to that of New York. And, along with being a national transportation, industrial, and financial center, it also offers tremendous ethnic diversity and cultural activity.

Sports, shopping, and food are impressive enough to double the population with tourists, who make an average of 26 million leisure trips a year. And as a mecca for college graduates from Indiana, Ohio, Wisconsin, and of course Illinois, it's Midwestern friendly. "It's easy to meet people," observes writer Kelly Williams. It's nothing to strike up a conversation "in your apartment building, in the health club, or just walking the dog. Many people are from someplace else, so they're anxious to make friends." Even the cab drivers are amicable.

But Chicago's high-crime and danger zones are particularly tricky. "You can be walking around in a perfectly respectable neighborhood and accidentally wander into a place like Cabrini Green," points out public relations manager Pam Tvrdy. Certain areas in the South Side are especially unsafe. Or you can get on the wrong train and suddenly be surrounded by individuals who know a good handout when they see one. "You really need to pay attention to where you're going and ask questions beforehand. Chicago's so pleasant it's easy to forget."

This isn't, however, always the case with the weather. Because of the lake effect, the city can suffer from extremely hot and humid summers and bitterly cold winters. During certain months, "temperatures vary as much as 90 degrees," points out Tvrdy. "January and February are particularly isolating if you're single."

But "after the first year or so, people adjust," counters marketing manager Robert Mills. "There's lots going on year-round, even festivals." So buck up and buy a fur coat, fake or otherwise. If Chicago were the perfect city, everyone would want to live there.

General Opportunities

Any place that produced the first roller skates (1884), elevated railway (1892), window envelope (1902), and Hostess Twinkie (1930) has to have interesting prospects. Beginning in the early 1800s, scores of young men arrived from Germany and Ireland to help dig a shipping canal, while many from other nations flocked to work in factories, steel mills, and the docks. Not only did this make Chicago an industrial force, but it also established distinct ethnic neighborhoods, from German to Swedish to Polish to African-American to Greek to Jewish and others.

With an estimated annual production of $154 billion worth of goods and services, Chicago has been named by *Fortune* magazine as a top city in the nation for doing business. In addition to manufacturing, printing and publishing, and finance and insurance, Chicago is considered the nation's candy capital (a more appetizing and politically correct image than its previous incarnation as "Hog Butcher of the World"). It ranks second (again) to New York in the production of nationally distributed magazines, books, and other printed material, and is headquarters for nearly 50 Fortune 500 companies, including McDonald's and Kraft. But Chicago has three of the four largest futures exchanges in the U.S. and the world's largest stock option exchange. So *there*, Big Apple.

The city is also a gold mine for researchers. Along with several universities—Northwestern, the University of Chicago, Loyola, and others—it has an immense number of industrial research laboratories as well as several high-technology industries. The $175 million Harold Washington Library Center, named for the city's first black mayor, is equipped with over 2 million books and up-to-the-minute facilities. The Center for Research has 3.2 million books and studies various cultures and war crimes, while the National Opinion Research Centers collects data for governments, industries, and professional pollsters. And that's just a thimbleful of the knowledge factories.

Chicago is a city of superlatives. You have the world's tallest building (Sears Tower, 110 stories); the most enormous structure in America, not counting the Pentagon (Merchandise Mart, with 90 acres of floor space); the largest free food festival in the known universe (Taste of Chicago, 3 million attendees); the busiest airport (O'Hare); even the biggest post office in the world (Main Post Office, downtown). And the Chicago River flows backwards (reversed in 1900 for sanitary purposes) and is always dyed green for St. Patrick's Day. What more could you ask for?

MAJOR BREADWINNING

In many professions (notable exception: law), "Chicago's a great place if you're just starting out," comments Tvrdy. "There are lots of job openings, and if you're good at what you do, you can go far." Although the city is expensive, salaries can be commensurate with costs, particularly in professional fields, and housing is rather reasonable, especially in certain areas.

In the recent past Chicago has nearly doubled its new businesses, generating more employment than any other city except for L.A. And, according to the Northeastern Illinois Planning Commission, the good times will keep on coming. Some 200,000 new jobs—particularly in finance, insurance, and lower-level service—are projected by 2010. (The population is estimated to increase by 1.3 million as well.)

Traditionally, Chicago's bulwark has been its transportation network. A vital link between the Great Lakes and the Mississippi, the port at Lake Michigan processes hundreds of overseas and domestic ship arrivals. As the leading transportation center in America in terms of volume of freight handled, the city transports more than 100 million tons a year via train, plane, and truck.

Chicago's financial prowess remains awesome. With the second largest center of finance in the world (LaSalle Street) and with a banking community that controls 78 percent of the state's assets, it can be a gold mine for stockbrokers, bankers, accountants, and others of their ilk. Most of the nation's largest financial institutions are found here, and downtown alone boasts nearly 40 foreign branches and 50 representatives from international banks. Consulates from over 40 countries have permanent offices here. The Chicago Stock Options Exchange, the Chicago Stock Exchange, the Federal Reserve Bank of Chicago, and the Chicago Board of Trade (CBT) offer prime opportunities.

And even those who aren't trained in finance, particularly educators, marketers, software programmers, and systems analysts, can break in. All you need is a little chutzpah and a willingness to start on the trading floor and work your way up. "Chicago is where the action is," adds Tvrdy.

> **Living in Chicago is like being a member of a large, noisy family. You may not always get what you want, but it's rarely dull and there's usually someone around to listen and help.**

Although downsizing has taken its toll—Chicago is, after all, a corporate kinda town—technology has borne much of the slack. The metropolitan area now has more than 2,000 computer and software programming firms and has enjoyed immense growth in desktop publishing, which is good news for professionals in related jobs like writing, editing, design, marketing, management, and others. Increased manufacturing of electronics communication equipment has spurred growth in companies ranging from Ameritech to Unicom. Even the former backbone of the economy—wholesale trade and the movement and storage of goods—now utilizes automated systems. "If you're in computers, you can basically write your own ticket," adds Mark Koegler, a lawyer.

Those with a bent for science or engineering will find plenty of padding in Chicago's big shoulders. Giants such as Archer Daniels and USG (heating and plumbing contractors), Amoco (petroleum), and hundreds of smaller and related enterprises have attracted the largest number of chemists and the second biggest pool of engineers in the United States.

Over half (about 1.5 million) of Chicago's labor force is in service industries. Tourism (which brings in billions of green bucks annually), wholesale and retail trade, and general-type positions can be found in community, social, and personal markets. Although teachers, social workers, and support people do well, "the city is inundated with lawyers and even medicine is becoming more competitive," he goes on. Nurses and lab technicians in particular may have a difficult time, although there's still growth potential for physical and occupational therapists and those in psychology-related fields.

"Chicago is progressive, so a woman can do well," says legal secretary Cathy Gurvis. The city's cultural diversity encourages opportunity: "Most of my female friends are professionals, making a lot of money, either from their own businesses or a high-level job." Regardless of race, creed, color, or sex, even babes in the woods can find their way in Chicagoland.

SOCIAL AND RECREATIONAL SCENE

How Chicago Plays

Chicagoans are big on brevity, commonly shortening names of things to one word, such as "Comiskey" (as in baseball park, home of the White Sox), the "L" (as in the elevated train that runs through downtown and some outlying areas), and "Stadium" (as in the place where the Bulls [basketball] and Hawks [hockey] play). "Ike" or "Ryan" usually refer to the Eisenhower or Dan Ryan Expressways. And more often than not, they'll give the name of the two streets nearest their home when asked where they live.

This terseness can carry over into relationships as well. "People here don't mess around," comments one woman. "They'll let you know right away where you stand. In fact, they're almost too blunt," she says, alluding to an example of a man who walked out of a restaurant after a quarrel, leaving his longtime girlfriend without transportation. "That sort of thing happens a lot."

Another man recalled a blind person's having to stand while riding the subway. "No one bothered to offer him a seat. People are so concerned with what they need to do they sometimes don't slow down and think of others."

Overall, however, folks in area code 312 "are incredibly outgoing and helpful. You never have to dig to make friends," remarks Tvrdy. Those looking for love in all the obvious places will find bars galore. "And someone's always giving a party."

Even if you have neither the time nor inclination for the usual meat, er, *meet* markets, there are numerous networking opportunities. "Many single young professionals are approached by dating clubs," observes Mills. Sports organizations are very big here, as are arts functions like a recent event at the Art Institute, which drew almost 10,000 people. There are dozens of career-related organizations, book groups, and, for those who can afford it, "Country clubs are booming. People can make a lot of money here and aren't afraid to spend it."

Where It's At

Unless otherwise noted, all area codes are 312.

Adler Planetarium & Astronomy Museum, 1300 S. Lake Shore Dr., 922-STAR

American Police Museum, 1705-25 S. State St., 431-0005

Annoyance Theatre, 3747 N. Clark St., 773/929-6200

Arie Crown Theatre, 2300 Lakeshore Plaza, 791-6004

Art Institute of Chicago, 111 S. Michigan Ave., 443-3600

Auditorium Theatre, 50 E. Congress Pkwy., 922-4046

Bicycle Museum, 435 E. Illinois St., 225-0500

Capone's Chicago, 605 N. Clark St.

Chicago's Gangstertown, 9351 W. Irving Park Rd., 800/GANGSTER

Chicago Academy of Sciences, N. Pier, 435 E. Illinois, 549-0343

Chicago Athenaeum: Museum of Architecture and Design, 6 N. Michigan Ave., 251-0175

Chicago Botanic Garden, Glencoe, Lake Cook Rd., 847/835-5440

Chicago Cultural Center, 78 E. Washington St., 346-3278

Chicago Historical Society, Clark St. and North Ave., 642-4600

Chicago Opera Theatre, 60 E. Balbo St., 392-7578

Chicago Symphony Orchestra, Orchestra Hall, 220 S. Michigan Ave., 435-6666

DuSable Museum of African-American History, 740 E. 56th Pl., 947-0600

Field Museum, Roosevelt Rd. at Lake Shore Dr., 922-9410

Grant Park Music Festival, Petrillo Bandshell

Hellenic Museum, 168 N. Michigan Ave., 726-1234

Improv Olympic, 3541 N. Clark St., 880-0199

International Museum of Surgical Science, 1524 N. Lake Shore Dr., 642-6502

Lincoln Park Zoo, 2200 N. Stockton, 742-2000

Lyric Opera, 20 N. Wacker Dr., 332-2244

Mayfair, 636 S. Michigan Ave., 786-9120

 ## ARTS AND SCIENCES

The decision here isn't what to do, but where to go first. An easier choice might be to start with the latest: Of Chicago's more than 40 museums, the newest is the **Museum of Contemporary Art,** the first constructed in the city in over 60 years. Here you will find 125,000 square feet of sculpture, painting, film, and other media. The previously mentioned **Art Institute of Chicago** not only has masterpieces, but a wide range of Impressionist and Post-Impressionist paintings, decorative arts and sculpture from around the world, and traveling exhibitions.

Another art must-see is the **Chicago Cultural Center,** if only to catch the world's largest Tiffany stained-glass dome, marble staircases, and brilliant mosaics. The Center is also home to the **Museum of Broadcast Communications,** one of many collections around town that delve into various media, including the **Museum of Contemporary Photography,** the **Chicago Athenaeum, Museum of Architecture and Design,** the **Terra Museum of American Art,** and the **Museum of Holography,** a truly three-dimensional experience. For the less aesthetically inclined, there's the **American Police Museum,** the **Bicycle Museum, Capone's Chicago,** and the **International Museum of Surgical Science.**

Just about every ethnic group has its own space, the most famous of which is the **DuSable Museum of African-American History,** which offers exhibits and books as well as youth-oriented activities, music and dance performances, and seminars. Chicago has the largest Polish population outside of Warsaw, so the **Polish Museum of America** is no joke, encompassing art, costumes, and a 30,000-volume library. The Judaism-based **Spertus Museum, Mexican Fine Arts Center Museum** (the only in the Midwest), **Swedish American Museum Center,** and **Hellenic** (Greek, not Satanic) **Museum** are but a few more. The world's first **Vietnam Veterans Art Museum** and a **Peace Museum** round things out. Groovy.

The oldest cultural institution is the **Chicago Historical Society,** which tells the city's story from frontier days to the present. **Lincoln Park Zoo** is not only free but a bit more in your face with its collections of big cats and apes. Those who prefer quieter (as in non-living) displays might enjoy the **Field Museum** with its four-story Brachiosaurus. Like the **Shedd Aquarium** and the **Adler Planetarium & Astronomy Museum,** which has a *really* far-out Sky Theatre and special-effects escalator, it's part of a planned lakefront complex at Grant Park. With the largest indoor fish tank in the world, the Shedd's massive holdings include the Oceanarium, which houses beluga whales, dolphins, seals, penguins, and others a long way from home. Those who like their science straight up might also appreciate the **Museum of Science and Industry,** noted for its innovative, hands-on approach, and the **Chicago Academy of Sciences,** which focuses on the local environment.

The dozens of performances on any given week in Chicago's more than 150 theaters range from "Co-ed Prison Sluts," now in its umpteenth year at the **Annoyance Theatre,** to traditional fare such as "Showboat" at the sumptuous **Auditorium Theatre** to touring Broadway shows at the **Schubert.** In between you'll find such staples as "Shear Madness" (**Mayfair**); "**Chicago's Gangstertown,**" a dinner club where cement shoes are optional; and other ever-changing offerings with a heavy emphasis on comedy. This is likely due to the influence of the now-famous **Second City,** a starting point for many actors, directors, and writers, and its improvisational partner in crime, **The Second City E.T.C.,** the **Improv Olympic,** and others.

There's plenty of classical stuff as well. The **Chicago Opera Theatre, Lyric Opera, Chicago Symphony Orchestra,** and **Grant Park Music Festival** (June–August) provide year-round entertainment. Ballet, concerts, and major performers can be found at the **Arie Crown Theatre,** and **Performing Arts Chicago** roams the city doing same. The 27,000-seat **World Music Theatre** is the largest outdoor performance venue in North America.

And most of this is just downtown. The outskirts offer everything from the renowned 20-garden, 385-acre **Chicago Botanic Garden** to the **Ravinia Festival,** a nonstop summer event that draws world-famous acts. You could be here a month of Sundays and still not do everything.

THE SPORTING LIFE

With nearly 100 miles of hiking and biking trails and 131 forest preserves in the Chicagoland area, "once the winter's over, everyone comes out to take advantage of the warm weather," observes Gurvis. Parks and public areas are clogged with joggers, roller bladers, and bike riders. The **Chicago Park District** offers an array of activities, as do the conservatories at **Garfield Park, Lincoln Park,** and (somewhat farther away) **Oak Park.** Those who like their sports organized

Where It's At

(continued)

Mexican Fine Arts Center Museum, 1852 W. 19th St., 738-1053

Museum of Broadcast Communications, 629-6000

Museum of Contemporary Art, 220 E. Chicago Ave., 280-2660

Museum of Contemporary Photography, 600 S. Michigan, 663-5554

Museum of Holography, 1134 W. Washington Blvd., 226-1007

Museum of Science and Industry, 57th St. at Lake Shore, 684-1414

Peace Museum, 314 W. Institute Pl., 440-1860

Performing Arts Chicago, 663-1628

Polish Museum of America, 984 N. Milwaukee, 384-3352

Ravinia Festival, 1575 Oakwood Ave., Highland Park, RAV-INIA

Schubert, 22 W. Monroe, 902-1500

Second City E.T.C., 1608 N. Wells, 642-8189

Second City, 1616 N. Wells, 227-3992

Shedd Aquarium, 1200 S. Lake Shore Dr., 939-2426

Spertus Museum, 618 S. Michigan, 922-9012

Swedish American Museum Center, 5211 N. Clark St., 728-8111

Terra Museum of American Art, 664 N. Michigan Ave., 664-3939

Vietnam Veterans Art Museum, 1801 S. Indiana Ave., 913-9117

World Music Theatre, Ridgeland Ave. and Flossmoor Rd., 368-0606

Where It's At

Unless otherwise noted, all area codes are 312.

Bike Chicago, 800/915-BIKE

Chicago's First Lady, southwest corner of Michigan Ave. bridge, 847/358-1330

Chicago Architecture Foundation River Cruise, Michigan and Wacker, 902-1500

Chicago Area Runners Association, 357-0303

can contact **Chicago Sport and Social Club, Command Performance, Bike Chicago,** the **Chicago Area Runners Association,** and **PPT In-Line Skate Instruction. Hoops the Gym** can provide a full-fledged basketball and volleyball court in (almost) a moment's notice, and those looking for a quick golf game can contact **Linksource** or **Kemper Golf Management.**

The warm months wash up loads of fishing and boating opportunities (**Cook County Forest Preserve**) at dozens of public and private beaches and pools in and around Lake Michigan and the Chicago River. Boat tours, another option, range from the "tall ship" **Windy of Chicago** to the luxurious dining of the **Odyssey** and **Spirit of Chicago** to the **Chicago Architecture Foundation River Cruise** and **Chicago's First Lady.**

In winter, ponds freeze over as ice skating rinks for those hardy enough to brave the bracing blasts. Cross-country skiing is available in such year-round recreation areas as **River Trail Nature Center** and the **Fox Valley River Trail.**

Everybody knows about spectator sports in Chicago. Or, as Koegler puts it, "There's no better place in the world to watch a game than in Wrigley Field." No wonder Chicago fans are among the most loyal (some would say fanatical) around. The city claims such high-visibility sports celebrities as Michael Jordan, Mike Ditka, and Ryne Sandberg. Not only that, but the excitement never seems to stop: fall offers the **Chicago Bears** football team, and winter the **Chicago Blackhawks** (hockey) and the NBA champion **Chicago Bulls.**

Spring sprouts two baseball options—the beloved **Chicago Cubs** at Wrigley Field or the **Chicago White Sox** at the newer (but not as popular with locals) Comiskey Park. "People around here like tradition, and besides, the seats at Comiskey aren't nearly as comfortable," remarks one native.

AFTER-HOURS DIVERSIONS

Chicagoans love fads, but "once a place becomes well-known, it's not as cool," observes Tvrdy. Along with single/divorcee institutions like **P.J. Clark's** and **Butch McGuire's,** where according to local legend over 3,000 couples have met their match, the inner circle smorgasbord of clubs range from the rapper-oriented **Elbo Room** to the post-industrial starkness of **Crobar** to the salsa-flavored dressiness of **Salsero.** Even avid trendies may have a hard time keeping up with **Chris's Billiards,** the quintessential pool hall; **Waveland Bowl,** where you can get a 24-7 kegling fix; **Lola's Club Roulette,** a haunt of the rich and physically attractive (men in mid-life crisis and models); and **Red Dog** and **Berlin,** a favorite with gays and drag queens, not always mutually exclusive categories.

Certain areas of Chicago almost seem to cater to specific groups, and get nicknamed accordingly. For instance, "north of Lakeview is unofficially called Boy's Town," points out Williams. A nifty little neighborhood of artsy bookstores, cafes, and shops amidst a predominately homosexual community, it's a popular destination for all persuasions.

"Chicago is a pretty gay-friendly town," adds Koegler. "It has a large population, which is politically active. And people are tolerant."

Koegler and his friends avoid the bars on Division Street, condemning them to the "cheesy, loud, what's-your-sign" slot. Rush Street and "Wrigleyville" (near Wrigley Field) are hangouts for mostly 25-and-unders, while the clubs in Lincoln Park cater to a more sophisticated crowd. Bucktown and Wicker Park are two more hot districts for the mature club-goer.

Some bars are integral to the Chicago experience, especially those that dish up blues (**B.L.U.E.S., Kingston Mines,** many others), jazz (**Andy's Jazz Club, Jay's Swing'n Door Lounge, Milt Trenier's Nite Club**), oldies (**America's Bar,** the **Hangge-Uppe**), and seeing is believing (**Baja Beach Club, Drink, House of Beer**). Sports bars galore include the **Hunt Club, Timothy O'Toole's Public House & Victuals,** and others. No perusal would be complete without a turn around the floor at **The Original Mother's** (the location for the movie *About Last Night*) or after-dinner liquors at the **Redhead Piano Bar,** which has a dress code.

Those saturated with bars might want to check out Chicago's architecture, a generally cheaper and often healthier form of entertainment. Along with the aforementioned **Sears Tower,** there are the **Amoco** and **John Hancock** buildings. Chicago's edifices (edifi?) are impressive enough to merit specialized free Loop Tour Trains (**Chicago Cultural Center**), previously mentioned boat tours, or assorted other options through the **Chicago Architecture Foundation.** Literal standouts include Art Deco ornamentation at the **Chicago Board of Trade;** the **Home Insurance Building,** the world's first skyscraper, constructed in 1885; the **Harold Washington Library Center,** a mini-microcosm of local styles; and the new

Arlington, Euclid and Wilke, Arlington Heights, 847/255-4300

B.L.U.E.S., 2519 N. Halsted, 528-1012

Baja Beach Club, 401 E. Illinois, 222-1993

Balmoral Park, 26435 S. Dixie Hwy., Crete, 708/672-7544

Berlin, 954 W. Belmont Ave., 348-4975

Butch McGuire's, 20 W. Division St., 337-9080

Chicago Architecture Foundation, 224 S. Michigan, 421-8151

Chicago Board of Trade, La Salle St. and Jackson Blvd.

Chicago Cultural Center, 744-2400

Chris's Billiards, 4802 N. Broadway, 878-5522

Crobar, 1543 N. Kingsbury St., 413-7000

Drink, 541 W. Fulton, 441-0818

Elbo Room, 2781 N. Lincoln Ave., 549-5549

Empress, Rt. 6 and Empress Dr., Joliet, 888/4-EMPRESS

Ernest Hemingway residence, 200 N. Oak Park Ave., 708/848-2222

Ferrari Fantasia, Oak St. between Michigan and State, 563-0495

First National Plaza, Dearborn and Monroe sts.

Frank Lloyd Wright Home and Studio, 951 Chicago Ave., 708/848-1976

Grant Park, 744-3370

Hangge-Uppe, 14 W. Elm St., 337-0561

Harold Washington Library Center, 400 S. State St.

Harrah's, Joliet and Cass sts., Joliet, 800/HAR-RAHS

Hawthorne, 3501 S. Laramie, Cicero, 708/780-3700

Hollywood, Aurora, 49 W. Galena Blvd., 800/888-7777

Home Insurance Building, LaSalle and Adams sts.

House of Beer, 16 W. Division St., 642-2344

Where It's At

(continued)

Hunt Club, 1100 N. State St., 988-7887

James R. Thompson Building, 100 W. Randolph St.

Jay's Swing'n Door Lounge, 933 N. State St., 649-9188

Jenny Jones, 454 N. Columbus Dr., 836-9485

Jerry Springer, 454 N. Columbus Dr., 321-5350

John Hancock Building, #10, 875 N. Michigan Ave.

Kingston Mines, 2548 N. Halsted, 477-4646

Lola's Club Roulette, 711 N. Wells St., 787-5111

Milt Trenier's Nite Club, 610 N. Fairbanks, 266-6226

Oprah Winfrey, 1058 W. Washington St., 591-9222

P.J. Clark's, 1204 N. State, 664-1650

Red Dog, 1958 West North Ave., 278-5138

Redhead Piano Bar, 16 W. Ontario St., 640-1000

Salsero, 1860 N. Elston Ave., 276-4846

Sears Tower, 233 S. Wacker Dr., 875-9400 (number for Skydeck)

Social Security building, 600 W. Madison St.

The Original Mother's, 26 W. Division St., 642-7251

Timothy O'Toole's Public House & Victuals, 622 N. Fairbanks Ct., 642-0700

Waveland Bowl, 3700 N. Western Ave., 773/472-5902

Where It's At

 Unless otherwise noted, all area codes are 312.

65 Restaurant, 2414 S. Wentworth, 842-6500

900 N. Michigan Shops, 915-3935

Atrium Mall, James R. Thompson Center, 346-0777

and controversial glass and granite atrium-shrouded **James R. Thompson Building.**

The city is also rich in public sculpture, such as a 100-foot tall bat in front of the **Social Security building** (a not-so-subliminal message?) and a mosaic by Marc Chagall at the **First National Plaza,** a favorite lunching spot for office workers and picnickers.

With the **Frank Lloyd Wright Home and Studio** and the greatest concentration of Wright-designed homes in the U.S., Oak Park can practically claim its own architectural ZIP code and as an added bonus includes the **Ernest Hemingway** residence. You can explore the structure of human relationships by being a victim—er, *participant*—or audience member in nationally televised talk shows (**Oprah Winfrey, Jenny Jones, Jerry Springer**).

Another type of parade (of which Chicago has 200 a year) can be found in festivals, the most prominent of which take place in "Chicago's front yard," **Grant Park.** The commanding, multicolored (at night) Buckingham Fountain and formal gardens make it a perfect lakefront setting for the Blues Festival (May/June), Taste of Chicago (June/July), Chicago Air and Water Show (August), and the Jazz Festival (August/September), among others. Neighborhoods, ethnic and interest groups, artisans, and even car lovers (**Ferrari Fantasia,** June) host gatherings as well.

Bored yet? Well, there's always a half-dozen casinos and the ponies, the former of which include **Hollywood, Empress,** and **Harrah's.** Only the toll call is free. Tracks can be made to **Balmoral Park, Hawthorne,** and **Arlington.** Before peeling off the roll, however, it might be wise to check out the next section.

CULINARY AND SHOPPING HAUNTS

With over 6,000 restaurants (and considering that many change hands or themes every few months), you could probably eat at a different place for the rest of your life and never leave the Chicagoland area. Pizza, steak, and Italian cuisine are this city's prime specialties.

It's hard to butcher a steak in Chicago, the originator of **Morton's.** Few customers beef about the **Butcher Shop,** where you can grill your own; the **Chop House,** with its three-week dry-aged steaks; **Gene & Georgetti,** voted best on the Zagat survey; and others. Some (but not all) tend to be a bit pricey ($20 and up). Those not minding the separation from greenbacks can also indulge in such classy joints as the

Signature Room at the top of the John Hancock Building, **Charlie Trotter's,** the **Pump Room, Brasserie Jo,** and the **Dining Room** at the Ritz-Carlton, all of which serve a variety of fare.

If you don't care for Italian food, you'll likely be missing a hearty portion of the city's culinary offerings. According to Williams, "Just about any place is good," particularly those in the Italian section in the Near West Side. This includes one-room holes-in-the wall with a few tables and chairs (the people lined up outside are a dead giveaway). Many times you'll have to bring your own booze: "It's hard to get and keep a liquor license in Chicago, because basically it's controlled by the Mob." Just a few Italian landmarks include **Bacchanalia,** known for its large portions; **Grappa,** chosen as one of the best by *Chicago* magazine; **Nick & Tony's,** outstanding homestyle dining; **Orso's,** which specializes in Northern Italian cuisine; the **New Rosebud Cafe,** whose pasta has won national raves; **Vinny's,** with linoleum floors and storefront windows; and **VIVO,** which has attracted the likes of Michelle Pfeiffer and Harrison Ford. Best of all, most are in the inexpensive to moderate range ($10 or under to $20).

Good eating in Chicago is often a catch-as-catch-can affair. Any number of places in Chinatown, Greektown, West Rogers Park (Jewish), Pilson (Mexican), West Town (Polish, Ukranian), and Devon St. (Indian) attract droves from all over the city. "If you see the natives dining there, then you know it's a winner," observes Koegler. **Penny's Noodle Shop** (Thai), **Bando Restaurant** (Korean), **65 Restaurant** (Chinese), **Three Happiness** (Cantonese, Szechwan), and **Raj Dabar** (Indian) represent Asia and India. A taste of France can be found at **Everest** and **Marche;** Germany at **Berghoff Restaurant, Weinkeller Brewery,** and **Zum Deutschen Eck;** and Mexico at **El Jardin** and **Hat Dance. Manny's** and **Chalfin's** serve up authentic Jewish delicacies.

The city has its share of eclectic dining experiences where the atmosphere is (sometimes) more interesting than the food. Be prepared for insults—along with burgers, fries, and other '50s fare—at **Ed Debevic's** diner. Along with horse-riding knights and jousting, the **Medieval Times Dinner & Tournament** features a four-course meal in the modern comfort of a climate-controlled castle (hmm….). Sports giants get their day in the kitchen with namesake restaurants by **Michael Jordan, Walter Payton,** and Cubs announcer **Harry Caray.**

Where It's At

(continued)

Bacchanalia, 2413 S. Oakley, 254-6555

Bando Restaurant, 2200 W. Lawrence, 728-7400

Berghoff Restaurant, 17 W. Adams St., 427-3170

Brasserie Jo, 59 W. Hubbard, 595-0800

Butcher Shop, 358 W. Ontario., 440-4900

Carson Pirie Scott, 1 S. State St., 641-7000

Century Shopping Center, 2828 N. Clark, 929-8100

Chalfin's, 200 E. Chestnut St., Arcade level, 943-0034

Charlie Trotter's, 816 W. Armitage, 248-6228

Chicago Music Mart, 333 S. State St., 362-6700

Chicago Place, 700 N. Michigan, 266-7710

Chinatown, 2169B S. China Pl., 326-5320

Chop House, 60 W. Ontario, 787-7100

Crate & Barrel, 646 N. Michigan, 787-5900

Devon Northtown, 2535 W. Devon, 743-6022

Dining Room, 160 E. Pearson, Ritz-Carlton, 266-1000

Ed Debevic's, 640 N. Wells, 664-1707

El Jardin, 3335 N. Clark St., 773/528-6775

Everest, Chicago Stock Exchange, 663-8920

Gene & Georgetti, 500 N. Franklin St., 527-3718

Grappa, 200 E. Chestnut St., 337-4500

Gurnee Mills, I-94 and Rt. 32, 800/YES-SHOP

Harry Caray (restaurant), 33 W. Kinzie St., 828-0966

Hat Dance, 325 W. Huron, 649-0066

Kane County Flea Market, Rt. 64 and Randall Rd., 708/377-2252

Where It's At

(continued)

Little Mexico, 3610 W. 26th, 521-5387

Manny's, 1141 S. Jefferson St., 939-2855

Marche, 833 W. Randolph St., 226-8399

Marshall Field's, 111 N. State St., 781-1000

Medieval Times Dinner & Tournament, 2001 N. Roselle Rd., Schaumberg, 847/843-3900

Merchandise Mart, 222 Merchandise Mart Plaza, 446-2666

Michael Jordan (restaurant), 500 N. LaSalle St., 644-3865

Morton's, several locations

Navy Pier, 700 E. Grand Ave., 595-3030

New Rosebud Cafe, 1500 W. Taylor St., 942-1117

Nick & Tony's, 1 E. Wacker Dr., 467-9499

Niketown, 669 N. Michigan, 642-6363

North Pier Festival Markets, 455 E. Illinois St., 836-4300

Oakbrook Center, Rt. 83 and 22nd St., 708/573-1300

Old Orchard Shopping Center, 34 Old Orchard Center, 847/673-6800

Orso's, 1401 N. Wells, 787-6604

Penny's Noodle Shop, several locations

Pump Room, 1301 N. State Pkwy., 266-0360

Raj Dabar, 2350 N. Clark St., 348-1010

Signature Room (at the top of the John Hancock Building), 875 N. Michigan, 787-9596

T.H.E. A.V.E.N.U.E., 730 Lake St., 708/383-1911

Three Happiness, 209 W. Cermak Rd., 842-1964

Vinny's, 2901 N. Sheffield Ave., 871-0900

VIVO, 838 W. Randolph St., 733-3379

Walter Payton (restaurant), Roundhouse Complex, 205 N. Broadway, Aurora, 708/892-0034

Water Tower Place, 835 N. Michigan, 440-3165

Although Chicago has more prime shopping haunts than a deep-dish pizza has ingredients, "the areas are laid out so well, it's easy to get around," remarks Williams. "Even my mom, who's intimidated by big cities, feels comfortable by herself."

State Street is a major pulse point. Here you'll find the mothership for retailing giant **Marshall Field's** and **Carson Pirie Scott.** On the opposite side of State St. are Filene's Basement, T.J. Maxx, Group USA, and others.

A high-priced stretch along Michigan Avenue from Oak Street to the Chicago River, the "Magnificent Mile" is its own mecca, with three vertical shopping malls, and two more in the throes of final completion. **Chicago Place** is anchored by Saks and buoyed by Talbot's, Louis Vuitton, and Ann Taylor, to mention a few. Bloomingdale's is the star of the **900 N. Michigan Shops,** with Gucci, Henri Bendel, and others in supporting roles. The shopping firmament at **Water Tower Place** includes another Marshall Field's, Lord & Taylor, et al. Peppered among the malls are exclusive boutiques and specialty stores like **Crate & Barrel** and **Niketown.** No trip would be fully realized without a gander at Oak Street, where Ultimo rubs shoulders with Versace, Armani, and others of that ilk. Even if you don't have money, pretend you do.

Places for "just folks" can be found elsewhere at the **Navy Pier** and **North Pier Festival Markets.** The renovated waterfront buildings are loaded with fun and unusual shops, restaurants, and even museums. North of the Chicago River is River North (get it?), an exclusive neighborhood with mostly art galleries, furniture, and specialty stores. And the **Merchandise Mart** has several retailers, as does the **Atrium Mall** in the previously mentioned James R. Thompson Center. The **Chicago Music Mart** presents a score of music stores as well as related greeting cards and apparel. Had enough yet?

Oh, but there's more. The **Century Shopping Center** has seven levels of primarily fashion stores. Belmont Avenue offers lots of antiques and vintage apparel, while the Hyde Park district is the place for new and used books. Chicago's ethnic neighborhoods have their own specialties, such as herb and tea and exotic groceries in **Chinatown,** Mexican blankets and clothing in **Little Mexico,** and, for those who like one-stop offerings, **Devon Northtown,** two miles of international discount bazaar.

The 'burbs provide their share of shopping escapades as well. The **Woodfield Shopping Center** is a mallrat's

Valhalla, with 300+ shops and five anchors in a 2.7 million-square-foot complex. The same can be said for the discount stores at **Gurnee Mills. Oakbrook Center** and **Old Orchard Shopping Center** are delightful (when the weather is the same) outdoor experiences; the 150 or so places in each are set among fountains, flowers, and ponds. Oak Park boasts **T.H.E. A.V.E.N.U.E.,** which has local and international designer clothing, art, and other items. And although it's a bit of a drive, tube socks (and other garb, furniture, and accessories) don't come much cheaper than at the **Kane County Flea Market.** Now *that's* a bargain.

 ### ETHNIC AND RELIGIOUS PROSPECTS

"Chicago is still a segregated city," points out Williams. "If you stand near Michigan Avenue during rush hour, you'll see whites going north and African-Americans going south." Still, every census tract in Chicago has African-American residents, resulting in one of the largest populations of black homeowners in the nation. "Interracial dating and marriage are also on the rise," adds Mills.

Equality has carried over into the workforce as well. High-ranking and middle-management African-Americans can be found in nearly every occupation and company, from engineer to researcher to politician. In fact, there are more so-called middle-class blacks (whose overall average income has increased steadily since 1980) than economically disadvantaged blacks.

Newcomers can contact their respective chambers of commerce ("there are about 350"), the several previously mentioned cultural centers/museums, and the **Minority Enterprise Growth Assistance Center** for guidance and information.

Although church doesn't seem to play as much of a role here as it does in other cities, there are plenty to choose from. They range from **Lawndale Community,** an integrated congregation on the Southwest Side; to the **Ashburn Baptist Church,** which concentrates on Bible study; to the **Hyde Park Christian & Missionary Alliance Church,** which focuses on contemporary worship. There's even a **Chinese Christian Unitarian Church** and a **First Korean United Methodist Church** as well as mosques and temples. Catholics can contact the **Archdiocese of Chicago,** and Jews, the **Jewish Federation,** for information on nearby houses of worship.

CRIB SHEET

Any discussion of Chicago real estate must of necessity (and space) be limited to the city and a few close suburbs. Homes in the Aurora, Lake County, DuPage County, Schaumberg, and

Where It's At

(continued)

Weinkeller Brewery, several locations

Woodfield Shopping Center, Golf Rd. and Rt. 53, Schaumberg, 847/330-1537

Zum Deutschen Eck, 2924 N. Southport Ave., 773/525-8121

Where It's At

 Unless otherwise noted, all area codes are 312.

Archdiocese of Chicago, 155 E. Superior St., 751-8200

Ashburn Baptist Church, 153rd Rd., 708/403-1363

Chinese Christian Unitarian Church, 3000 S. Wallace St., 225-5564

First Korean United Methodist Church, 4850 N. Bernard St., 773/463-2742

Hyde Park Christian & Missionary Alliance Church, 5144 S. Cornell Rd., 288-2677

Jewish Federation, One S. Franklin, 346-6700

Lawndale Community, 3825 W. Ogden Ave., 762-5772

Minority Enterprise Growth Assistance Center, 105 W. Adams

Joliet areas have their own median price range ($130,000–180,000) and styles, from wide-open spaces to exclusive country club communities to "treeless wonder"–type new developments to small towns. All have enjoyed increased construction in recent years.

Apartments and condos are the domicile of choice in the Chicago metro area. "The standby neighborhoods are Lincoln Park, and for those just out of college, Wrigleyville," points out Williams. With a median rent (or a monthly mortgage) in the mid-$600s, Lincoln Park offers all the shopping amenities, grocery stores, and bars you could want within a few yuppiefied blocks. Those comfortable with social and economic (although not necessarily racial) homogeneity will like it here. Not far away are the renovated brownstones, eclectic boutiques, and open-air cafes of Old Town ($650). "You used to be able to find a place to rehab for less, but now that it's hip, they're pretty scarce."

Those not quite ready to say sayonara to the beer-guzzling, party-hearty atmosphere of college might prefer Wrigleyville. There are tons of unattached folks and rent is about $100 a month cheaper than Lincoln Park. Your time there may be finite, however: "The oldest person I know there is 27, and he just moved out," Williams continues. Wrigleyville tends to be a bit farther away, so you may need to rely on public transportation or a car.

For many years, Bucktown/Wicker Park was a well-kept secret. Rent was also inexpensive ($400, Wicker Park; $500, Bucktown), attracting "more of an artsy crowd, although even these people are starting to get priced out," according to Koegler. Reminiscent of San Francisco's North Beach (in clement weather), this neighborhood is chock full of coffeehouses, art galleries, jazz clubs, and other cultural hobnobs.

Those who like diversity might appreciate Rogers Park ($640), Dearborn Park (varying prices), and the older neighborhoods around the University of Chicago, University of Illinois, and DePaul. Rents differ as well (for instance, Hyde Park in the University of Chicago area is about $730, while the DePaul area is about $646). The streets are full of 19th- and early 20th-century homes, many of which have been maintained and restored. You'll find a variety of ages, cultures, and races along with museums and other attractions.

If you're willing to spend $1,500 or so a month, you can choose from districts closer to downtown and the Magnificent Mile. The Gold Coast, River North, River West, the Loop, South Loop, Burnham Park, and Cityfront Center offer the best of big-city living and excitement. (Too much for some: "I always felt like I was underdressed when I lived near the Gold Coast," observes Koegler.) Renovated factories and warehouses, brownstones, and new highrises are a few options. There's nothing quite like looking out your window at the brilliant cityscape at night or watching the first fingers of dawn touch the gleaming skyscrapers.

At the other end of the rent spectrum are Chicago's ethnic neighborhoods, such as Chinatown (about $300), which is closer to Comisky Park. Things are also less pricey (about $325) as you move westward to Little Italy, Greektown, and the Mexican district.

"Cityburbs" include Riverside ($500), one of the country's first planned communities; Andersonville ($500), a favorite with young families; and Ravenswood (about $450), a quieter, treed neighborhood. Although you get more for your money and choices can range from bungalows to ranches to elegant Victorians, "you need to be careful in lower rent districts, particularly if you're a woman," remarks a longtime resident. Although many represent the best of both worlds, "some streets are prone to gang graffiti and muggings."

A bit farther away but with easy access to the city and less crime are Oak Park and River Forest (both about $675). Along with newer and historical homes and Frank Lloyd Wright prairie-style architecture, they offer cultural attractions, restaurants, and shops, as well as district schools.

Chicago city schools (Chicago Board of Education, 535-8000) are primarily African-American (55 percent) and Hispanic (30 percent), with Caucasians making up a mere 11 percent of the student population. Pupil/teacher ratios are about 21 to 1. Many people opt for private or parochial schools (Cook County Superintendent, 443-6350; Catholic School Board, 751-5200; others) or move to the suburbs (Illinois Board of Education, 814-2220).

With 95 institutes of higher learning, Chicago's colleges range from the Nobel Laureate–laden University of Chicago (also one of the top 10 medical schools in the U.S.) to the medical, dental, and law schools of Northwestern to several mostly African-American community and junior colleges (Olive-Harvey and others) to the very Catholic St. Xavier.

NAVIGATING CHICAGO

Everything you've heard about traffic in Chicago is true. "Getting around can be a nightmare, especially if you have a car," remarks Koegler. You may find yourself moving it at 6 a.m. to avoid being towed, and unless you have fabulous parking karma or lots of free time, open meters are almost impossible to find.

It's a hung jury on whether or not an auto is even necessary; some feel that the bus and trains are undependable and dangerous after dark, while others are very comfortable using public transportation. "A lot really depends on where you live," he adds. The Chicago Transit Authority (CTA) operates surface bus routes and elevated and subway trains in Chicago and the closest suburbs. Metra offers rail services to many suburban areas within a 40-mile radius of the downtown Loop. Pace buses provide access to commuter stations from locations not covered by Metra, as well as some express and direct routes downtown. All three are under the aegis of the Regional Transportation Authority (836-7000).

Although streets in Chicago form a logical grid running either north/south (with Madison Street as the divider) or east/west (separated by State Street), once you get out of the city, you can't tell the players without a program. The eight interstate highways (I-55, I-57, I-80, I-90, I-94, I-294, I-355, and I-394) and various parts thereof have specific names (e.g., Kingery Expressway, JFK Expressway, etc.) and are constantly being upgraded and added to. Contact the Illinois Department of Transportation (800-452-IDOT) for specific instructions; otherwise you might feel like an extra "I" between the D and the O if you end up in Midway Airport (767-0500) instead of O'Hare (686-2200). The third airport, Meigs Field (744-4787) is mostly limited to private, corporate, and charter planes. There's always Amtrak (800/USA-RAIL), Greyhound/Trailways (408-5971), and Indian Trails (service to Indiana and Michigan, 928-8606 or 744-0996) for those not wanting to chance total confusion.

Cleveland at a Glance

Birthdate and Present Size: 1796.
Metropolitan Statistical Area—
1980: 1,898,825; 1990: 1,831,122.
1/1/95 (estimate): 2,232,600.
Percent change, 1980–1990: –3.6%.
Percent change, 1990–1995: +21.9%.

Weather Report: *Average annual temperature*—49.6° F. In January:
33/19° F. In July: 82/61° F.
Average annual precipitation—35.4".
Average annual snowfall—54".

Money Matters: *Unemployment rate*—
5.3%.
Per capita income: $9,258 (city),
$15,092 (MSA).
Average household income—$22,921 (city),
$38,413 (MSA).
Average cost of a home—$135,333.
Average rent for an apartment—
$647/month.
ACCRA cost of living indexes (based on
100)—Composite Index: 103.8; Utilities
Index: 113.05; Housing Index: 105.8.
Sales and use tax—5.0% (state); 2.0%
(local).
Personal income tax—0.743 to 7.5%.

People Profile: *Crime rate* (Per 100,000
population)—7,456.1.
Racial and ethnic characteristics—
White: 49.6% (city), 78.4% (MSA);
Black: 46.5% (city), 19.4% (MSA);
American Indian/Eskimo/Aleut: 0.3%
(city), 0.2% (MSA); Asian/Pacific Islander:

1.0% (city), 1.1% (MSA);
Hispanic Origin: 4.4% (city),
1.8% (MSA); Other: 2.7% (city),
0.9% (MSA).
Gender ratio—90.1 males per 100 females
(all ages); 85.9 males per 100 females
(18 years old+).
Age characteristics—18–24 (10.4%);
25–44 (31.7%). Median age: 31.8 (city),
34.7 (MSA).
Educational attainment—percent having
completed high school: 58.8% (city),
75.7% (MSA); percent having completed
college: 8.1% (city), 19.9% (MSA).

Major Players: Services, retail/wholesale
trade, manufacturing, government,
transportation. Known also for its
wealth of educational institutions,
medical facilities, and arts groups.
Largest employers—American Greetings,
Cleveland Clinic, East Ohio Gas,
Fairview General Hospital, Health
Cleveland, Keycorp, Lincoln Electric Co.,
Metrohealth System, Mt. Sinai Medical
Center, Nestle's Frozen Foods.

Community Services: *Average hospital
cost*—$644.40/day.
Average doctor visit—$44.40.
Average dentist visit—$58.80.
Newspapers—*The Plain Dealer, Crain's
Cleveland Business, Daily Legal News, Call
and Post* (black), *Cleveland Jewish News,
Catholic Universe Bulletin, Cleveland Free
Times* (alternative).

Photo by Joan Tiefel /CVB of Greater Cleveland

CLEVELAND: THE COMEBACK KID

O y vey, did Cleveland have problems. Pollution from steel mills and other heavy manufacturing and industrial fires on the Cuyahoga River during the '50s and '60s earned it the nickname "Mistake On the Lake," making it the butt of comedy monologues from New York to Los Angeles. Bleak economic opportunities, racial discrimination, and ghetto conditions resulted in riots in the 1960s. Companies moved out and the city's population began to recede faster than a Baby Boomer's hairline. Things couldn't get worse, but they did—in 1978, Cleveland was the first American metropolis to default on its loans since the Great Depression.

Another city might have turned its back on such urban decay. But not the hardy folks who originally hailed from Germany, Italy, and other parts of Eastern Europe, including healthy assortments of African-Americans, Catholics, and Jews. Under the guidance of former mayor George Voinovich, the public and private sectors combined forces to form a partnership, injecting millions of dollars into rebuilding neighborhoods, encouraging tourism and new businesses, and revitalizing manufacturing. And it worked: Since 1990, the number of residents has increased by more than one-fifth, and Cleveland is now touted as a preferred place for African-Americans and Latinos to do business and live, according to both *Black Enterprise* and *Hispanic* magazines. The city got a major facelift, to the tune of a total of $9.2 billion. Of the almost 100 large corporations headquartered here, fourteen are Fortune 500 companies, and more are moving in every year. Should they open a lemonade stand, or what?

Even the Indians' baseball record (bottom of the league for several years, then the American League Championship in 1995) hints at the kind of attitude that drives this city. Originally founded by Moses Cleaveland in 1796, the half-million-acre piece of land at the mouth of the Cuyahoga River was abandoned a few months later when dysentery and insects forced the settlers back to New England. Even the name is a typo, the result of trying to fit "Cleaveland" onto a newspaper masthead.

By 1813, however, Cleveland began emerging as a port, thanks to the efforts of Lorenzo Carter, who developed friendly relations with the natives. The completion of canal systems and railroads before the Civil War, as well as the discovery of soft coal for steel and iron during and after, brought wealth to locals and investors. John D. Rockefeller's establishment of the Standard Oil Company and the empowerment of the Brotherhood of Locomotive Engineers (which bettered conditions for many workers) cemented it into the industrial landscape. The city enjoyed unparalleled growth between 1850 and 1910, when the population soared from slightly over 17,000 to half a million.

> Another city might have turned its back on the urban decay that Cleveland once faced. But the hardy people of Cleveland injected millions of dollars into neighborhoods, tourism, new businesses, and manufacturing. Today the city atrracts thousands of new residents and is a powerful mecca for business.

Cleveland has always had strong ties with African-Americans. Many citizens opposed slavery during the Civil War and helped with the Underground Railroad. After World War I and during World War II, the prospect of blue-collar jobs attracted large numbers of blacks. And in 1967, Cleveland was the first major city to elect an African-American mayor, Carl Stokes, and has had another, Michael White, for several years.

Quality of Life

Cleveland could be the best-kept secret in the Midwest. "I've visited lots of other cities, but people have roots here," asserts native Cheryl Strom, an account executive. "And there's just about everything you'd want, from culture to shopping to restaurants to sports. You can live anywhere and be downtown in a few minutes. Traffic is manageable—rush hour here is like Chicago on a Saturday afternoon."

One local returned to Cleveland after a four-year hiatus and was amazed at what he saw: "It had totally changed, particularly downtown. There was so much to do and so many things had been added. You can get involved through museums or other organizations or just go to art galleries or coffee shops."

Okay, so the only palm trees are at the Zoo's Rain Forest, but "even in winter months, people still go out and do things," says magazine editor Anton Zuiker, who moved back from Honolulu. "This isn't a hibernating community—you can participate in the arts, go to football games, even hike in the parks all year round." Lakefront State Park has more shoreline than any metropolitan green space in the world. And 100 miles of one of the nation's largest district park systems circles the city's neck. (Just don't break yours on the snow and ice.) During the warm season, nearby Lake Erie also provides boating, sailing, and fishing.

In Cleveland, the venerable Art Museum mixes well with the raucous new Rock and Roll Hall of Fame. Lots of additions and innovations have increased this town's appeal—museums, theaters, and entertainment centers; sports arenas and a football stadium under construction; the renovation of downtown neighborhoods; and the addition of a light rail system that enables citizens to get around more easily and safely.

Plus, Cleveland has location, location, location. Not only can you choose from about any type of house or apartment in a variety of settings, but the city is situated midway between Chicago and New York. And with loads of excellent colleges and universities as well as the Cleveland Clinic and Mt. Sinai Medical Center, health care, while expensive, is considered among the best in the world. No wonder the natives, while friendly, would rather fight than switch.

General Opportunities

The cost of living in Cleveland is slightly above the national average, with utilities being particularly expensive. However, salaries are comparable to paychecks in many of the pricier cities. And work is plentiful: "When I moved back from Baltimore, within a month, I'd landed a full-time job in a bookstore," recalls social worker Joe Cimperman. Before long he had three offers from as many agencies in his profession.

People are also helpful, "especially to newcomers," adds Zuiker. "They know what it's like to go through tough times. They'll tell you to call this person, or go talk to that person" who can provide leads "and make the job search easy."

The fastest-growing segments of the economy include international trade; health care, including biotechnology and research/development; polymer studies, especially plastics; and service industries like insurance, accounting, and law. Small businesses thrive here as well. Tourism has become a major economic player in the past few years, with Cleveland being ranked the second most popular new vacation destination by AAA. "Now when I go to the bars in the Flats on a Friday night, I meet people from different states or even countries," observes Strom.

Even the less fortunate have benefited from the boom. Along with civic pride and aesthetic improvements, Cleveland's recent 200-year anniversary spurred the development of Bicentennial Village, a project that included renovating existing homes and constructing several new houses, some for Habitat for Humanity. Federal and private funds have also been allocated for inner city rehabilitation as well as a $13 million shopping center in Church Square, one of Cleveland's poorest neighborhoods.

MAJOR BREADWINNING

It's almost too good to be true: Cleveland has approximately 1.2 million jobs in about 70,000 firms, with another 78,000 new positions anticipated by the year 2000. Brand names such as Nestle, American Greetings, Revco, Sherwin-Williams, B.F. Goodrich, and others have their headquarters here. Although much of the economy still depends on manufacturing, from such companies as Eaton and TRW (motor vehicle parts), LTV (metals), and Lubrizol (chemicals), there's been a steady shift towards service and other sectors. But the economy is as robust as a year-old puppy—nearly 100 of Cleveland's top corporations enjoy a revenue of $100 million or more. "With so many large companies, people with even basic skills have a wide choice" of employment opportunities, adds Strom.

Declared a foreign trade zone in 1990, the Port of Cleveland serves over 50 countries, shipping and receiving iron ore, coal, grain, and other cargo from 120 ports around the world. Tonnage actually *doubled* to 870,000 in the three-year period from 1992–1995. In addition, 70 foreign-owned firms have their headquarters here.

With about 7,000 start-ups a year, small businesses greatly increase their chances for success through the Council of Smaller Enterprises, which provides management consulting, government advocacy, and health care/insurance discounts, saving local entrepreneurs millions of dollars. Cleveland is particularly ripe for new undertakings in the biotechnology, computer, and legal sectors.

More than 125,000 people are utilized in the health care field, one of the region's top five employers. Cleveland's 100 biotechnology companies and 300 research and development centers focus on corneal transplants, geriatrics, infant disorders, and high-risk pregnancy, as well as cancer, heart disease, and other ailments. The partnership of Case Western Reserve and University Hospitals of Cleveland has resulted in one of the nation's largest biomedical research centers, with the Cleveland Clinic being another major force.

These days, Ohio and particularly Cleveland are even more "plastic" than California, leading that state in polymer production. More than half of Ohio's plastic processors are located in the Cleveland area, providing employment for those with a chemical or technical background. The 1,500 local polymer firms work with Case Western Reserve and the nearby University of Akron in research and training, resulting in two of the country's top programs.

The increased prosperity has reflected well on Cleveland's financial scene, with a steady accumulation of assets each year. Cleveland is the hometown for such heavy hitters as Key Bank, National City Bank, and Bank One as well as a number of smaller institutions.

And for those in certain specialties, it's a seller's market. To wit: the legal profession (projected gain of 32 percent by the year 2000); engineering and management (28 percent); and health care, including registered nurses and aides (combined total: 42.5 percent), social services (21 percent), and private health services (21 percent). Other desirable skills: banking and investment (37 percent), paralegals (45 percent), computer scientists and analysts (combined total: 85 percent), and all manner of salespersons, clerks, receptionists, and "Would you like fries with that?" types. The last three in particular are expected to expand. Cleveland is bursting with copious possibilities—for instance, the fastest-growing local occupation (67.6 percent) is that of strippers—for printing presses, that is. Folks who move here with no prospects may be pleasantly surprised.

SOCIAL AND RECREATIONAL SCENE

How Cleveland Plays

"There's no getting around it—the winters are terrible," admits one local. Thanks to Lake Erie, Cleveland gets more snow than just about anywhere else in the state. And "the springs aren't always great, either, cold and rainy, and then you go right into summer's humidity."

Those who can get over the above-average number of bad hair days will find not only lots to do but plenty of willing companions—even "newcomers who make even a minimal effort," remarks Strom. Meeting people "is like anything else. You can sit back and watch or go out and get involved."

Still, certain organizations make it easy to get acquainted in area code 216. Playhouse Square Partners (1501 Euclid, Suite 810, 348-5265) pairs new members with longtime residents to help them get acclimated. "This is particularly great for folks interested in theater and the arts," she continues. The Cleveland Sport and Social Club (1322 Old River Rd., 696-3770) has a particularly active branch, which in addition to the usual baseball/basketball/volleyball tournaments sponsors ski trips.

Just about any gathering can be turned into a social opportunity. Magazine editor Melanie Payne attends the Wednesday night program at the Cleveland Museum of Art, which features a casual, year-round dinner, movies, and/or music. "You can go by yourself and feel comfortable." And it's natural to strike up a conversation over a piece of art.

As for dating, "it's a challenge in any city," comments Strom. "Cleveland may have a smaller pool, but it attracts quality people in a diverse number of professions" from musicians to medical workers. And with a few exceptions, Clevelanders are notoriously outgoing. "Everyone is nice," whether you're a newcomer or a native.

Where It's At

Unless otherwise noted, all area codes are 216.

African-American Museum, 1765 Crawford Rd., 791-1700

Blossom Music Center, 1145 W. Steels Corners Rd., 330/920-8040

Children's Museum, 10703 Euclid Ave., 791-KIDS

Cleveland Ballet, 621-2260

Cleveland Botanical Garden, 11030 East Blvd., 721-1600

Cleveland Center for Contemporary Art, 8501 Carnegie Ave., 421-8671

Cleveland Film Society, 1621 Euclid Ave., #428, 623-0400

Cleveland Metroparks Zoo and Rain Forest, 3900 Brookside Park Dr., 661-6500

Cleveland Museum of Art, 11150 East Blvd., 421-7340

Cleveland Museum of Natural History, 10600 Wade Oval, 231-4600

Cleveland Opera, 575-0903

Cleveland Orchestra, 231-1111

Cleveland Play House, 8500 Euclid Ave., 795-7000

DANCECleveland, 861-2213

Dittrick Museum, 11000 Euclid Ave., 368-3648

Great Lakes Science Center, North Coast Harbor, 736-7900

Great Lakes Theatre Festival, 241-5490

Health Museum, 8911 Euclid Ave., 231-5010

Holden Arboretum, 9500 Sperry Rd., 946-4400

Hoyts Tower City Cinema, 623-0400

Karamu House, 2355 E. 89th St., 795-7070

Lyric Opera Cleveland, P.O. Box 016198, 231-2910

NASA Lewis Research Center, 21000 Brookpark Rd., 433-4000

Playhouse Square Center, Euclid at E. 17th, 241-6000

Rock and Roll Hall of Fame and Museum, 1 Key Plaza, 781-7625

Severance Hall, 1101 Euclid Ave., 231-1111

ARTS AND SCIENCES

With the country's largest concentration of cultural/educational institutions, the University Circle area might be considered a sort of Stonehenge for the arts. A centerpiece is the previously mentioned **Cleveland Museum of Art,** one of the top in the U.S., which not only represents all civilizations and periods (particularly Asian and Medieval European), but, with the exception of traveling exhibits, is free. Other nearby collections include the **Western Reserve Historical Society,** noted for its local and genealogical records as well as its "auto-aviation" array; the **African-American Museum;** the **Children's Museum,** with its multi-sensory, hands-on exhibits; the **Cleveland Center for Contemporary Art;** and others.

The place that spawned pepsin chewing gum, the submachine gun, and the first successful separation of Siamese twins can be expected to have lots of science, weird and otherwise. In University Circle alone: The **Cleveland Museum of Natural History,** the state's largest, offers everything from dinosaur fossils to live animals. The first of its kind in the U.S., the **Health Museum** has Juno the transparent talking woman, among other exhibits. A few blocks away, the **Dittrick Museum** unearths early medical instruments and diaries. And the **Cleveland Botanical Garden** offers classes on horticulture, environmental design, and cultivation.

Severance Hall is the University Circle winter home to the world-renowned **Cleveland Orchestra,** with performances at **Blossom Music Center** in nearby Cuyahoga Falls during the warm months. The oldest regional theater in the country, the **Cleveland Play House** has three theaters and serves up dramas, comedies, and musicals. As a multicultural venue founded in 1915, **Karamu House** is another "first." And the adventuresome **Lyric Opera Cleveland** provides picnics during intermission.

But there's more. Go a few miles west downtown and the **Playhouse Square Center,** a 16-acre, four-theater complex, is home to the **Cleveland Ballet, DANCE-Cleveland,** the **Cleveland Opera,** and the **Great Lakes Theatre Festival,** as well as various touring national and international productions. The **Cleveland Film Society** exhibits movies from around the world and holds a festival (March, **Hoyts Tower City Cinema**).

The North Coast Harbor provides a couple of recent additions to the local constellation. The subject of much controversy and many delays, the **Rock and Roll Hall of Fame and Museum** flaunts its I.M. Pei told-ya-I-could-do-it architecture and unique multimedia exhibits and memorabilia, drawing droves from all over the world. The **Great Lakes Science Center** focuses 165,000 square feet on science, the environment, and technology via virtual reality, OMNIMAX, and other innovations. While there, you might as well check out the massive **Steamship William G. Mather Museum,** a gen-u-ine Great Lakes freighter now restored to its former glory.

Scattered around the city are **NASA Lewis Research Center,** an aerospace archive; the **Cleveland Metroparks Zoo and Rain Forest,** which houses 3,300 animals and a two-story atrium with "tropical" thunderstorms and a waterfall; and the **Holden Arboretum,** another huge preserve of natural woodlands and horticultural wonders. And that's not even mentioning the suburbs or the outlying areas.

THE SPORTING LIFE

Professional sports are near and dear to many local hearts and have inspired major pocketbook digging. Along with having a brand-new, natural grass **Jacobs Field,** the **Cleveland Indians** made recent baseball history by being the first team to sell out its season within days. NFL football will again rear its helmeted head once the replacement Browns and their soon-to-be-built new stadium are in place. The NBA **Cleveland Cavaliers** and **Cleveland Lumberjacks** hockey team have *their* freshly minted **Gund Arena.** Another relatively recent addition, the **Cleveland Crunch** soccer team, can be found at the **Convocation Center.**

When not at various contests, Clevelanders enjoy walking, biking, swimming, and nature- (and people-) watching in the "Emerald Necklace"—19,000 acres worth of **Metroparks** surrounding the city. And—surprise!—there are many beaches, including East 55th, Edgewater, Euclid Beach, Wildwood, and others, all part of Lakefront State Park.

Ohio is a great state for golfers—for at least three months, anyway. Its 600 courses are on par with the nation's best; over half of these are in the Cleveland area. Courses vary from the six at the Metroparks to **Manakiki** and **Sleepy Hollow,** two of the most challenging public courses, to almost 190 private clubs, including **Canterbury,** host of the U.S. Senior Open.

A major summertime passion for 400,000 registered boaters is Lake Erie. Walleye, bass, and perch fishing and sailing opportunities abound, with the latter culminating in Cleveland Race week (July, **Edgewater Yacht Club**). Fishing licenses can be purchased at local bait stores and marinas. Those who prefer to let others do the navigating can charter a

Where It's At

(continued)

Steamship William G. Mather Museum, E. Ninth St. Pier, 572-6262

Western Reserve Historical Society, 10825 East Blvd., 721-5722

Where It's At

 Unless otherwise noted, all area codes are 216.

Canterbury, 22000 S. Woodland Rd., 561-1021

Cleveland Cavaliers, 420-2000

Cleveland Crunch, 349-2090

Cleveland Indians, 2401 Ontario Ave., 420-4200

Cleveland Lumberjacks, 420-0000

Cleveland Race, Edgewater Yacht Club, 281-6470

Convocation Center, 500 Lakeside Ave.

Edgewater Yacht Club, 281-6470

Geagua Lake, 1060 N. Aurora Rd., 562-7131

Goodtime III, 825 E. 9th St., 861-5110

Gund Arena, 400 Huron Rd.

Jacobs Field, 2401 Ontario Ave., 420-4200

Manakiki, 35501 Eddy Rd., 942-2500

Metroparks, 351-6300

Nautica Queen, 1153 Main Ave., 696-8888

Sea World, 1100 Sea World Dr., 562-8101

Sleepy Hollow, 374 Homeworth Rd., 330-823-0186

Wave Walker, P.O. Box 27382, 641-2549

Zephyr, 6500 W. Memorial Shoreway, 694-FISH

Where It's At

 Unless otherwise noted, all area codes are 216.

Basement, 1078 Old River Rd., 344-0001

Black Nativity, Karamu House, 795-7070

Cabaret Dada, 1210 W. 6th St., 696-4242

Cleveland Indians Winterfest, CSU Convocation Center, 420-4200

Cleveland Performance Art Festival, Cleveland State University, 221-6017

Club 1148, 575-0600

Club Isabella, 2025 Abingdon Rd., 229-1177

Club Visions, 1229 W. 6th St., 522-0060

Downtown Holiday Lighting Program, Public Square, 621-3300

Euclid Tavern, 11629 Euclid Ave., 229-7788

Expresso Express, Lakeside Pl. Lobby, 241-8835

Great American Rib Cook-off, Burke Lakefront Airport, 247-2722

Greater Cleveland Auto Show, 328-1500

Grid, 1281 W. 9th St., 623-0113

Hilarities, 1230 W. 6th St., 781-7333

Howl at the Moon Saloon, 861-HOWL

Improv Comedy Club, 696-4677

I-X Center, 6200 Riverside Dr., 676-6000

Jullian's Billiard Club, 575-0300

Kwanza Celebrations, Tri-C, 987-4801

Medieval Feasts and Spectacles, Trinity Cathedral, 579-9475

Mickey's Diamond Club, 1628 Fall St., 621-1840

Mid-America Boat Show, 621-3618

Mirage on the Water, 2510 Elm Ave., 348-1135

Moondog Coronation Ball, Cleveland Convention Center, 348-2200

Music Hall at Cleveland Convention Center, 500 Lakeside Ave. E., 348-2200

National Home & Garden Show, 529-1300

vessel (**Wave Walker, Zephyr**) or sail aboard the *Goodtime III* and *Nautica Queen,* which offer sightseeing and entertainment cruises.

Other watery amusements include **Sea World,** a 90-acre marine park, and **Geagua Lake,** which features dry diversions as well. Due to open in 1998, the Great Waters Aquarium in the Flats will have $100 million worth of dramatic fish and tank tableaux.

 ## AFTER-HOURS DIVERSIONS

In 1951, Cleveland rocked the world when local disc jockey Alan "Moondog" Freed and record store owner Leo Mintz termed a new sound "rock 'n' roll." Today, rock, jazz, and pop tours make regular stops at the previously mentioned Gund Arena and Blossom Center, the **Music Hall at Cleveland Convention Center,** and **Nautica Stage.**

The latter is part of the **Nautica Entertainment Complex** in the Flats, 28 acres including two major enclosed structures, apartments, and a boardwalk. Clubs cater to every whim, age group, and taste, ranging—in the glassed-in Sugar Warehouse—from **Shooter's,** whose name says it all, to the gussied-up pool hall at **Jullian's Billiard Club** to a 5,000-foot dance floor and colossal video wall at **Club 1148.** The Powerhouse, the other major building, is not only a historical landmark but also offers the **Improv Comedy Club,** which attracts national as well as local comedians; **Powerplay,** consisting of 100 video games and two bars to help ease the headache-inducing clamor; and **Howl at the Moon Saloon,** with dueling baby grand pianos. **Rockbottom Brewery** and **Tommy's,** respectively, provide a traditional brew pub and a variety of live acts. Speaking of which, "adult entertainment" (a misnomer?) can be found in the Flats (im)proper at **Mickey's Diamond Club** and **Tiffany's Cabaret,** which offers docking facilities as well as free peeks between the wooden slats. The area also boasts a boatload of other bars: The self-descriptive **Basement, Whiskey in the Flats** (a perennial with hipsters), and **Peabody's Downunder,** the state's oldest concert venue, to mention a very few.

The recently revived Warehouse District has become another magnet. **Hilarities** and **Cabaret Dada** cover the spectrum of humor, while great jazz can be found at **Sixth Street Under** and **Sammy's. Club Visions,** the **Grid,** and **Numbers** feature alternative music, while alcohol levels can be lowered at **Expresso Express** and the **Phoenix Coffee Shoppe.** Other popular choices around the Ohio City, Tremont, and other areas include (but are hardly limited to) **Wilbert's Bar and Grill, Euclid Tavern, Club Isabella,** and **Mirage on the Water.**

At certain times of the year, newcomers may find themselves relying more heavily on clubs or other distractions than they'd like. "Cleveland is much more of a family town than, say, Chicago or D.C.," observes Payne. "In larger cities, it's common to spend the holidays with friends. Here, people have their folks."

However, festivals and other gatherings provide a constant source of options. Along with having the world's largest exposition building/park with a Ferris wheel, golf course, and petting zoo, the **I-X Center** hosts events such as the **Mid-America Boat Show** (January), the **National Home & Garden Show** (February), the **Greater Cleveland Auto Show** (March), and others. The colder months also bring arts, crafts, and sports: the **Winter Expo** (January); the **Cleveland Indians Winterfest** (February); and the **Cleveland Performance Art Festival** (March). Also in March is the **Moondog Coronation Ball,** a concert commemorating the birth of rock 'n' roll. There's a huge assortment of fetes for the other three seasons—the **Great American Rib Cook-off** (May), the **Ohio Derby** (June), the **Off-Shore Power Boat Races** (August), *two* **Oktoberfests,** and countless ethnic and church celebrations. Holiday blues can be warded off at the **Downtown Holiday Lighting Program,** various programs at **Stan Hywet Hall, Medieval Feasts and Spectacles,** and, for African-Americans, the **Black Nativity** or the **Kwanza Celebrations.** And if all else fails, there's always the **Thanksgiving Polka Weekend.**

CULINARY AND SHOPPING HAUNTS

Cleveland's main culinary distinctions are: a) recognition as the "Pirogi Capital of the World"—and even preeminence in these large Russian pastries crammed with meat, vegetables, fish, or other goodies is in dispute with another city (see "Pittsburgh")—and b) outstanding kielbasa, a spicy smoked Polish sausage. Still, there's plenty of fine dining ($15–30 and over): for steaks, **Hyde Park Grille, Morton's,** and **Nighttown;** seafood, **Watermark Restaurant;** continental, **Classics in the Omni Hotel;** and French, **Sans Souci** in the Stouffer Renaissance Hotel.

Cleveland also has lots of great cheap eats. The average meal runs under $15, and even pricier places rarely charge more than $30. "For about three dollars, you can stuff

Where It's At

(continued)

Nautica Entertainment Complex, Main Ave. east to the river, 460-4545

Nautica Stage, 621-3000

Numbers, 620 Frankfort Ave., 621-6900

Off-Shore Power Boat Races, Nautica Entertainment Complex, 247-2722

Ohio Derby, Thistledown Race Track, 662-8600

Oktoberfest, Lake County Fairgrounds, 881-7773; Geagua Lake, 562-7131

Peabody's Downunder, 1059 Old River Rd., 241-0792

Phoenix Coffee Shoppe, 1373 W. 3rd St., 579-1910

Powerplay, 696-7664

Rockbottom Brewery, 623-1551

Sammy's, 1400 W. 10th St., 523-5560

Shooter's, 861-6900

Sixth Street Under, 1266 W. 6th St., 589-9313

Stan Hywet Hall, Akron, 714 N. Portage Path, 836-5533

Thanksgiving Polka Weekend, Marriott Society Center, 692-2225

Tiffany's Cabaret, 1180 Main St., 574-6222

Tommy's, 861-0534

Whiskey in the Flats, 1575 Merwin Ave., 522-1575

Wilbert's Bar and Grill, 1360 W. 9th St., 771-2583

Winter Expo, Cleveland Winterparks Chalet, 572-9990

Where It's At

 Unless otherwise noted, all area codes are 216.

Antigoni's, 2405 W. Erie Ave., 244-1880

Arcade, 401 Euclid Ave., 621-6644

Aurora Farms Factory Outlet, 549 S. Chillicothe Rd., 562-2000

Where It's At

(continued)

Balaton, 12521 Buckeye Rd., 921-9691

Beachwood Place, 26300 Cedar Pl., 464-5294

Big Egg, 5107 Detroit Ave., 961-8000

Cafe Tandoor, 2096 S. Taylor Rd., 371-8500

City Bike, 1392 W. 6th St., 771-2489

Classics in the Omni Hotel, Carnegie and E. 96th St., 791-1300

Cleveland Cutlery Company, 1296 W. 6th St., 781-5088

Colonial Arcade, 530 Euclid Ave., #206, 621-0057

Corky & Lenny's, 27091 Chagrin Blvd., 464-3838

Cravings, 2366 W. 11th St., 621-3838

Czech Inn, 9729 Granger Rd., 587-1158

Dillards, 579-2580, several locations

Dubrovnik Gardens, 34900 Lake Shore Blvd., 946-3366

Empress Taytu, 6125 Saint Clair Ave., 391-9400

Euclid Square, Babbitt Rd. and E. 260th, 731-6899

Galleria at Erieview, E. 9th and St. Clair, 621-9999

Great Lakes, Ridge Rd. and Mentor Ave., 255-6900

Great Northern Mall, Great Northern Blvd. at I-480, 734-6304

Greek Isles, 500 W. St. Clair, 861-1919

Ho Wah, 2101 Richmond Rd., 831-2327

Hofbrau House, 1400 E. 55th St., 881-7773

Hyde Park Grille, 123 W. Prospect, 321-6444

Jack's Deli, 2175 S. Green Rd., 382-5350

Kluck's, 1313 W. 117th St., 226-9765

Korea House, 3700 Superior Ave., 431-0462

La Place Fashion Center, 2101 Richmond Rd., 831-3198

Lake Erie Factory Outlet Center, I-90 and 250N in Sandusky, 419/499-2528

Li Wah, 2999 Payne Ave., 696-6566

yourself at a greasy spoon," observes Cimperman. Popular diners include the **Big Egg** and **Ruthie and Moe's.** Those wanting to really splurge can go to Little Italy and visit **Mama Santa's** for less than $10 or, for a little more, enjoy gourmet heaven at **Porcelli's.** "Just about any place in Little Italy is good," Cimperman adds. Plus, you get the experience of eating in an Old World atmosphere, possibly among Mafiosos (It's not New York, but still…). Speaking of the Big Apple, downtown has the **New York Spaghetti House,** which has been owned by the same family since 1927.

The city has a number of Asian restaurants. *Cleveland Magazine* flagged **Li Wah** as a local favorite; other well-known Far East eateries include **Ho Wah, Lu Cuisine,** and **Pearl of the Orient.** Korea, India, and Ethiopia weigh in with **Korea House, Cafe Tandoor,** and **Empress Taytu,** respectively. Among the several Greek places are the **Greek Isles** and **Theo's.** Other restaurants of Middle Eastern descent include **Antigoni's, Yacov's, Petra Cafe,** and more.

Eastern Europe is particularly well-represented. Delis such as **Corky & Lenny's** and **Jack's Deli** abound, as do German (**Hofbrau House**), Hungarian (**Balaton**), and Czech (**Czech Inn** [really!]) eateries. **Dubrovnik Gardens, Kluck's,** and **Zosia's** further widen the ethnic gamut. Although it isn't run by aliens, **Pete & Dewey's Planet** serves "out of this world" pastas, soups, and salads.

Cleveland has some of the best shopping in the Midwest, with the added bonus of competitive prices. The best way to "do" the city is to start downtown and work your way to the outskirts, starting with the deluxe Avenue at **Tower City Center,** a 52-story landmark located in Public Square. Along with having more than 100 stores, including Liz Claiborne, J. Crew, and 9 West, the Avenue is connected to the rapid transit system and has a multiscreen cinema in case you need something else to do.

Close by is **Dillards,** an upscale department store and local institution of spending. The **Galleria at Erieview** has another 50 shops and a food court. Downtown also provides the **Arcade,** America's first mall (built in 1890), restored to its former rococo glory with dozens of shops/restaurants, and the **Colonial Arcade,** a smaller version with a variety of boutiques and cafes.

The 'burbs are riddled with centers, squares, and plazas, including **Beachwood Place,** an easy spot to drop a few hundred (or thou), having such emporiums as Saks, Lillie Rubin, and their ilk. Nearby are **La Place Fashion Center** and **Pavilion Mall** in case you have money or credit left. **Euclid Square, Great Lakes,** and **Randall Park** are three more options. And that's just some of what's on the East Side. Other area malls include **Westgate, Parmatown, Great Northern,** and many more.

Cleveland has lots of eclectic offerings, too, particularly at **Shaker Square**—restaurants, shops, and other entertainments in a restored 1920s setting. Nearby Larchmere Boulevard provides 10 blocks of antiques, art galleries, and more. The previously mentioned Flats, Warehouse District, and Little Italy boast a wide selection of stores, such as the **Cleveland Cutlery Company** (costume jewelry, watches, and housewares), **City Bike** (for pedal pushers), and **Mainstreet Easyriders** (for the other kind of biker) to mention a few.

No experience would be complete without a visit to the **West Side Market.** More than 100 merchants peddle ethnic delights in an indoor/outdoor setting established at the turn of the century. Lorain Avenue and West 65th Street is another spot in the same general area loaded with unusual stuff, including the coffee shops/food emporiums **Uncommon Grounds** and **Cravings.** Those who have exhausted their resources (or don't care to) would do well at the **Aurora Farms Factory Outlet** or, a bit farther west, at the **Lake Erie Factory Outlet Center** in Sandusky.

ETHNIC AND RELIGIOUS PROSPECTS

Despite the mass migrations of strong-minded ethnic and religious groups in Cleveland's past, things have generally remained harmonious. The Italians arrived first (around 1850), carrying on their heritage today in Little Italy and through Catholic churches such as **Our Lady of Mount Carmel** and **Holy Rosary.** Likewise, the extremely large Polish community gravitates towards Slavic Village with its many Catholic churches such as **St. John Cantius.** Greek Orthodox and Germans have a presence as well, and Cleveland boasts one of the largest Jewish communities in the U.S., which is serviced by an active **JCC** and several synagogues. "People are concerned with the overall welfare of the city, rather than their particular skin color or background," adds Cimperman.

Cleveland's black population has also prospered. The city draws several major conventions (NAACP, National Conference of Black Mayors, etc.) and has countless African-American–owned businesses and landmarks.

Where It's At

(continued)

Lu Cuisine, 1228 Euclid Ave., 241-8488

Mainstreet Easyriders, 1275 Main Ave., 241-7800

Mama Santa's, 12305 Mayfield Rd., 231-9567

Morton's, W. 2nd and Prospect, 621-6200

New York Spaghetti House, 2173 E. 9th St., 696-6624

Nighttown, 12387 Cedar Rd., 795-0550

Parmatown, W. Wedgewood Dr. and Ridge Rd.

Pavilion Mall, 24055 Chagrin Blvd., 464-5900

Pearl of the Orient, 20121 Van Aken Blvd., 751-8181

Pete & Dewey's Planet, 812 Huron Rd., 552-1500

Petra Cafe, 1026 Euclid Ave., 696-7667

Porcelli's, 12022 Mayfield Rd., 791-9900

Randall Park, Warrensville Center and Miles rds., 663-1250

Ruthie and Moe's, 4002 Prospect Ave., 431-8063

Sans Souci, Stouffer Renaissance Hotel, 24 Public Square, 696-5600

Shaker Square, 3221 Shaker Square, 991-8700

Theo's, 4250 Pearl Rd., 459-1555

Tower City Center, Terminal Tower, 771-0033

Uncommon Grounds, 3408 Bridge Ave., 631-3010

Watermark Restaurant, 1250 Old River Rd., 241-1600

West Side Market, 1995 W. 25th St., 664-3386

Westgate Mall, W. 210th and Center Ridge Rd., 333-8333

Yacov's, 13969 Cedar Rd., 932-8848

Zosia's, 7801 Broadway Ave., 641-1863

Where It's At

Unless otherwise noted, all area codes are 216.

Antioch Baptist Church, 8869 Cedar Ave., 421-1516

First Methodist Church, Euclid and E. 30th St.

Holy Rosary, 12015 Mayfield Rd., 421-0700

JCC, 3505 Mayfield Rd., 382-4000

Mohamed's Temple No. 18, 2746 E. 40th St., 391-8052

Old Stone Church, 91 Public Square, 241-6145

Our Lady of Mount Carmel, 6928 Detroit, 281-7146

St. John's Cathedral, 1007 Superior Ave., 771-6666

St. John Cantius, 906 College Ave., 781-9095

Zion Lutheran Church, 2062 E. 30th St., 861-2179

However, "although you do see some black faces in places like the Flats," there's not as much mixing as there could be, according to Payne, who is African-American. "Interracial dating is not that prevalent. Compared to other cities, Cleveland still has a way to go." But she noticed an improvement when she moved back here a few years ago. "Opportunities are pretty good here."

Newcomers wanting to become acquainted with the community have plenty of churches to choose from, such as the **Antioch Baptist Church, Mohamed's Temple No. 18,** and others. In fact, Cleveland has a variety of denominations for everybody, including the **Old Stone Church, St. John's Cathedral, First Methodist Church,** and **Zion Lutheran Church.**

CRIB SHEET

If variety is the spice of life, then Cleveland is a highly seasoned kielbasa. Apartments are plentiful and reasonable, with average monthly rent ranging from around $350 for an efficiency to about $700 for a three-bedroom, with the latter being higher in demand and somewhat harder to find.

One of Cleveland's biggest assets is its neighborhoods. Each community has its own character, although "all kinds of people live there," states Cimperman. Just because a neighborhood's in Little Italy or the predominantly Jewish east end of town doesn't preclude a diverse racial and ethnic mix. Homes start as low as $40,000 and go to upwards of $800,000. And with all the attendant growth, the investment value can only increase.

Certain areas, particularly in and around downtown, are considered "hot." The Flats, with their high-rise apartments and nonstop action; the converted lofts and one-floors of the Warehouse District; and Tremont and Ohio City, formerly working-class areas with distinctive architecture and an assortment of residences, have all enjoyed a renaissance, particularly among young professional singles and marrieds. "It used to be that you wouldn't consider going downtown after dark," remarks one woman. "Now people actually want to live there." Best of all, it's affordable: the average sale price still hovers around $50,000. Although they're more expensive ($98,000–190,000), Cleveland Heights and University Heights offer an even wider number of housing choices in a mostly urban environment.

There are plenty of suburbs as well, ranging from the exclusive Gates Mills (homes on 2.5 acre lots, average cost, $417,000), Hunting Valley (estates for a measly $700,000 or so), and Pepper Pike (outstanding school system and colleges set amid a mostly built-up area, $310,000 average cost). There's lots of upper middle ground—Shaker Heights, Beachwood, and Mayfield on the east side ($150,000–300,000) and even more of a bargain in the western 'burbs of Lakewood, Rocky River, and Fairview Park ($70,000–160,000). Parma, Berea, and Euclid ($75,000–150,000) offer small-town living within an easy commute, while those willing to drive a bit farther can find even better deals amid the picturesque beauty of Chagrin

Falls, the New England–style Hudson, and the architecturally different Medina. The reasonable prices ($100,000–220,000) and newer developments in Solon and Twinsburg are hard to duplicate, especially for young families.

With a low pupil-to-teacher ratio (even the city's is 18–1) and loads of classes for slow learners, honors students, and those with special talents, local public school systems boast a high percentage of merit scholarship winners and graduates; 51 percent from the city high schools go on to college (Cleveland Public Schools, 574-8000).

The area has more than a dozen accredited institutions of higher learning (Case Western, Oberlin, Cleveland State, John Carroll), community colleges (Cuyahoga, Lakeland), and outstanding specialty schools (Cleveland Institute of Music, Cleveland Institute of Art, Cleveland College of Jewish Studies). Along with the usual assortment of private and parochial schools, there are an above-average number of educational options for the physically and mentally challenged (Cuyahoga County Special Education and Resource Center, 587-5960). For more information on local suburban and private schools, contact the Greater Cleveland Growth Association (621-3300).

NAVIGATING CLEVELAND

Cleveland has had a leg up on transportation since 1914, when the first electric traffic signal made its debut at the corner of Euclid Avenue & East 105th Street. So, along with a reasonably logical city layout and mostly courteous (but sometimes slow) motorists, driving is relatively painless. Prudence, however, is wise: Local police and state troopers constantly lurk on side streets and behind turnarounds on freeways, waiting for the unsuspecting to fly by or make a "U-ey" (illegal in Ohio).

The city's freeway system is among the most compact in the country. Locations in the metropolitan-suburban area are no more than an hour's drive from downtown, with I-71 and I-77 running north and south and I-90 going east-west, all of which are connected by the too-easily-confused I-480 and I-490. But once you get your bearings, it shouldn't take more than an average of 23 minutes to get to work.

Although many people drive, public transportation is also an option, particularly if you work downtown, where parking is at a premium. Most of the 98 Regional Transit Authority (621-9500) bus routes go there, and the light rail rapid transit system also makes for convenient egress to the Hopkins International Airport (265-6000) and selected parts of the city.

Hopkins is undergoing a $206 million, long-term renovation to accommodate an increased number of flights and passengers, and a secondary airport, Burke Lakefront (781-6411) provides commuter service to regional cities, a heliport, and facilities for business jets. Another way of getting out of town is through Amtrak (800/872-7245), which has service to places such as Boston and Chicago. If you really want to save money and don't mind the fumes, try the Greyhound bus station (781-0520).

Denver at a Glance

Birthdate and Present Size: Founded in 1858; incorporated as a city in 1861. *Metropolitan Statistical Area*—1980: 1,428,836; 1990: 1,622,980. 1/1/95 (estimate): 1,829,400. Percent change, 1980–1990: +13.6%. Percent change, 1990–1995: +12.7%.

Weather Report: *Average annual temperature*—50.3° F. In January, 43/16° F. ·In July, 88/59° F. *Average annual precipitation*—15.31". *Average annual snowfall*—60".

Money Matters: *Unemployment rate*—3.4%. *Per capita income*—$15,590. *Average household income*—$33,983. *Average cost of a home*—$153,160. *Average rent for an apartment*—$698/month. *ACCRA cost of living indexes* (based on 100)—Composite Index: 103.1; Utilities Index: 75.4; Housing Index: 114.7. *Sales and use tax:* 3.0% (state); +4.3% (local). *Personal income tax*—5.0%.

People Profile: *Crime rate* (per 100,000 population)—6,933.1. *Racial and ethnic characteristics*—White: 72.2%; Hispanic Origin: 22.8%; Black: 12.9%; American Indian/Eskimo/Aleut: 1.1%; Asian/Pacific Islander: 2.3%; Other: 11.5%.

Gender ratio—95.1 males per 100 females (all ages); 92 males per 100 females (18 years old+). *Age characteristics*—18–24 (9.5%); 25–44 (37.6%). Median age: 33.8. *Educational attainment*—percent having completed high school: 79.2%; percent having completed college: 29.0%.

Major Players: Services, retail/wholesale trade, government, manufacturing. Manufacturing activities include food processing, defense, high technology, and transportation equipment. *Largest employers*—Federal and state government, U.S. West, Columbia/HealthONE, AT&T, United Airlines, Children's Hospital Association, Cobe Laboratories (medical instruments), Colorado National Bank, Gates Corp. (rubber and plastics), Northwest Bank Colorado, Provenant Health Partners, Public Service Company of Colorado.

Community Services: *Average hospital cost*—$477.40/day. *Average doctor visit*—$58.71. *Average dentist visit*—$65.71. *Newspapers*—Two major dailies, *The Denver Post* and *The Rocky Mountain News; The Denver Business Journal; Denver Catholic Register; Intermountain Jewish News; The Colorado Leader* (community); *Westword* (alternative).

DENVER: ALTITUDE ADJUSTMENT

With more sunshine than San Diego, Honolulu, and Miami Beach, a population that's doubled since 1960, an airport that's twice the size of Manhattan, and the largest single brewery on earth (Coors), it's no wonder Denverites think their city's pretty phat. "I wouldn't live anywhere else," asserts account executive Michelle Snyder, who's "been there, done that" in half-a-dozen other big metropoli. Add the facts that Denver is the smallest city to have four professional sports; that its Performing Arts Complex is the second largest after the Lincoln Center; that both *World Trade* and *Forbes* magazines have ranked Denver among the top ten places to do business; and that all manner of outdoor activities are available year-round, and it's understandable why Denver has become a mecca. It's California without the earthquakes and Venice Beach (folks attracted to the latter generally head to Boulder).

Denver's early history reads like a mini-comedy of errors. Although the local Native Americans warned settlers not to build there, no one listened. When gold flakes were discovered in 1858, thousands of would-be prospectors rushed to the rolling plains along the South Platte River, filling the area with saloons, gambling halls, and crude log cabins. Although not much was found, at least one person, Major General William H. Larimer, got rich quick by claim-jumping the land. Hoping to gain political favors, he named it after then-territorial governor James Denver, unaware that Denver had already resigned.

Not only did Denver have to contend with a flood, two major fires, several Indian attacks, and a Civil War skirmish (a volunteer army drove the Rebels back to Texas), but it was almost deserted when a large quantity of the glittery stuff was later found in the mountain town of Central City. But folks returned when they realized the Rockies acted as a shield from the severe weather conditions, creating a temperate climate a mile high along rolling plains. Along with cowboys (almost a third of whom were African-American) and Hispanic and Asian immigrants, Denver attracted desperadoes, lawmen, and fortune seekers as the discovery of silver and the development of a railroad brought trade and prosperity.

By the turn of the century, Denver was actually respectable, with elegant theaters, fountain- and statue-filled parks, tree-lined streets, and mansions. As home to the finest stores and restaurants between San Francisco and St. Louis, it earned the moniker "Queen City of the Plains." Although growth was kind of pokey until around the end of World War II, word got out about Denver's natural resources and a new rush was on. By the early '90s, the population was growing by as much as 2,000 people a week—many of whom were from the West Coast—prompting an onslaught of hostile bumper stickers and anti-California jokes.

Quality of Life

With over 200 parks and 130 miles of paved, off-street bike paths, including a mile-long pedestrian mall through the heart of downtown, Denver is a city where people "walk, jog, rollerblade, and bike everywhere, including work," notes Kyle Snyder, who is employed in member relations for a local association. "Plus, you get very accustomed to the open spaces and the big sky. Other places feel claustrophobic…. There's nothing better than a good sunset." Ponds, lakes, and streams offer prime fishing, while dozens of nearby mountain parks make it easy to disappear for a few days. Those with any thought of building a road or other obstruction near the trails had better get a good lawyer: "People are very protective of the outdoors."

To some, the Rockies and clean air are almost a religion. "People find God in hiking, skiing, being outside, and in appreciation for environment and life," adds Snyder's wife Michelle. Rugged sports such as downhill skiing, ice and rock climbing, wilderness backpacking, and more are extremely common, and in some circles, the more risk you take (as in scaling a "fourteener," a 14,000-foot mountain), the more highly you're regarded.

But Denver also has a lively arts and social scene for those inhibited by a lack of guard rails. "There's plenty of theater and art," observes accounting specialist Sandra Salih. Museums, theaters, and even the library are well-supported. (Denver has the highest number of library card holders—over 52 percent of the population—than any other major urban area.)

With the addition of several malls and anchor stores, even shopping has expanded. "Denver gets things a little later than either coast," continues Salih. "But people here dress differently anyway. It's more casual." Although cowboy boots are admissible just about everywhere, chaps and whips may raise a few eyebrows in this mostly moderate town. Chains are acceptable as long as they remain around tires.

Of course, being about a mile above sea level can require some altitude adjustment, such as slowing down physical activities, cutting alcohol consumption by half (you get twice the effect anyway), and increasing intake of other liquids, as well as utilizing sunscreen and sunglasses, as the rays are more intense here. Although snow doesn't usually hang around for long, Denver falls prey to some pretty unusual weather phenomena, such as thundersnow (clouds that produce thunder, lightening, and snow), hailstorms that are hell on a car's finish, and wide variations in temperature that may call for shorts during the day but heavy coats by nightfall. Layering's a minor inconvenience for a climate that remains mostly warm and dry, with little humidity, cool summer evenings, and infrequent heat waves.

> To some, the Rockies and clean air are almost a religion. "You get very accustomed to the open spaces and the big sky. Other places feel claustrophobic. . . . There's nothing better than a good sunset," says a local.

On the downside, traffic has gotten so bad that the junction of I-70 and I-25 is not so affectionately known as the Mousetrap, home and condo prices have gone the way of the mountains, and "the pay isn't always great because this is such a desirable place to live," notes Dr. Chris Fleming, an emergency room physician. However, costs "are cheaper than, say, San Francisco. And it's easy to meet people; Colorado's a very friendly state." Unless, of course, your dog encounters a mountain lion or bear.

General Opportunities

"Jobs can be very competitive," continues Fleming. Even her brother and his wife, who are in law and optometry respectively, "are having a hard time finding employment" in Denver.

Still, those who are affiliated with or know about the plenitude of specific companies relocating here or with computer, engineering, or technology skills will likely have better prospects. And the city's overall business picture appears favorable as well: according to the U.S. Department of Commerce, Denver will outpace the rest of the country until well after the year 2000 with a steady increase of over one-half percent above the national average in both personal income and employment. The Mile High City has consistently registered positive job growth since 1988; it's one of the few cities in the country to do so.

Small businesses find it a mecca as well. Harking back from the "Pike's Peak or Bust!" days, Colorado in general (and Denver in particular) has been a hotbed for new ventures. In 1996, Colorado was home to 20 percent of the fastest-growing companies in the 10 western U.S. states (excluding California).

Unlike well-tenured Northern and Southern cities, Denver's relative newness works in its favor, at least racially. "You really don't hear much about discrimination or feuding," observes

Realtor Dan Tessmer. "Denver's not like some towns, where Italians strictly live in one neighborhood and Asians in another."

Although the various groups do tend to congregate in certain areas and participate in certain activities, "people pretty much hang out with whomever they please," adds Salih. "I've seen a lot more interracial dating here than anyplace else and plenty of churches draw from several different communities. They're moving from all over." Except for the buffalo, who were around before anyone else and still can be seen along I-70.

MAJOR BREADWINNING

In Denver, people work so they can play. "It's pretty casual, both in dress and attitude," observes Kyle Snyder. "People are more concerned about happiness, not making big bucks or maintaining an image. They understand it if you want to take a couple of days off and go into the mountains."

Things aren't so laid back in the economic sector, however. With 350 companies that have more than 250 employees—and countless other smaller enterprises—Denver currently ranks as the nation's most diversified economy, according to studies by the Corporation for Enterprise Development. The new airport has also helped augment the city's role in international distribution and trade.

Along with being a hub for oil and gas companies, the economy is also anchored by telecommunications, biotech, hi-tech, cable, and aerospace firms. Major private employers present a varied menu, ranging from U.S. West communications (15,400 workers) to Columbia HealthONE medical services (10,500) to United Airlines (7,700) to King Soopers grocery store (7,000) to Lockheed-Martin aerospace (7,000) to Coors Brewing Company (5,300) to Kaiser-Hill cleanup and waste management (4,500). The job pie is fairly evenly distributed as well, with professional (22 percent), blue-collar (21 percent), clerical (18 percent) and services (16 percent) getting the biggest pieces, followed by sales (13 percent), managerial (9 percent), and agricultural (1 percent).

But statistics don't tell the whole story. Jobs showing the greatest potential growth include sales positions and all levels of managerial and administrative personnel, including top executives. Nurses, janitors and cleaners, office clerks, cashiers, servers, and truck drivers are in a seller's market as well. And while oil, gas, and mining represents only 1 percent of Denver's overall employment base, Denver is still considered a leader in these fields. Construction is another huge growth industry, requiring the skills of engineers, architects, and others in meeting the needs of expanding communities.

But the bulk of the jobs—and the money, about $15 billion for the state each year—can be found in manufacturing, which employs 121,000 souls in the Denver area. Much of it is light industrial, but it also includes a rapidly growing contingent of biotech and medical technology companies. Although it's recently slowed down, finance, insurance, and real estate still provide many positions. Claims adjusters, bankers, and those with expertise in managing and selling properties should continue to have happy prospecting. With commerce outdistancing the national average, wholesale and retail trade is another viable outlet, requiring sales and marketing skills, although many jobs are clerical.

The service industry, the fastest-growing segment in Denver, accounts for about 30 percent of all nonfarm work, with increased employment expected in lodging, personal and business services, automotive, and amusement and recreation, including jobs in accounting, hospitality, and communications/marketing.

Health care, another expanding field, encompasses positions in such recognized facilities as University Hospital, the Children's Hospital, and the National Jewish Center for Immunology and Respiratory Medicine. Emergency and trauma specialists might find a livelihood at the Denver General Hospital and St. Anthony's Hospital, which pioneered Flight for Life, the country's first emergency air ambulance service.

Thousands of jobs can also be found in Denver's highly rated elementary and secondary public and private schools, as well as its colleges. With 50 percent more college graduates than the U.S. average, it's a safe bet that the knowledge industry will continue to boom. Related employment in tourism, another burgeoning field, is available in Denver (as well as in the ski resorts and recreation areas in the Rocky Mountains). Denver pulls in almost a third of the 7 billion tourist dollars that flow Colorado's way each year.

Transportation, communications, and public utilities have also been buffaloing up the economic ladder. Tele-Communications, Inc., the world's largest cable company, has laid their groundwork (so to speak) in the area. Folks with computer, engineering, and related technical skills might find themselves readily plugged in.

> The Mile High City has consistently registered positive job growth; Denver currently ranks as having the nation's most diversified economy, and several sources rank Denver among the top ten places to do business.

Although those on the fast track might not find their dream job, Denver has some high-altitude career opportunities. "People place a lot more emphasis on education here," points out Salih. "A good degree or special training can carry more weight than even experience." There are some pretty unique prospects as well. Along with Coors, Denver has two of the largest brewpubs in the nation, which provide a chance to be part of the world's largest beer-making machine. Or you can opt to be among the 15 or so percent of Denverites working for the government, at such sites as the Federal Center in Lakewood or research facilities in Boulder or Golden. Denver houses national and/or regional headquarters for more federal agencies than any other U.S. city except D.C. The U.S. Mint, which creates 5 billion coins a year, literally provides a chance to make a fortune.

SOCIAL AND RECREATIONAL SCENE

How Denver Plays

Area code 303 "has lots of pep," according to Michelle Snyder. "People here are energetic, healthy, and very much in shape." With one of the lowest percentages of obesity in the U.S., "Colorado doesn't have too many couch potatoes."

Those wanting trendy should perhaps look elsewhere. "This is a real easygoing atmosphere," comments Salih. "Not many people wear fur or dressy shorts. There's a general lack of stuffiness, even at work." You don't see much in the way of green hair or pierced body parts, either, although there is a limited alternative scene. She recommends checking a local publication, the *Westword,* for the latest in what's going on. "It covers just about every activity, including those organized by minority and religious groups."

With a relatively low (or at least low-key), crime rate, "Denver's pretty safe, so you're not constantly worried about wandering into a bad area or getting mugged," notes one woman.

Even male-female relations are relatively unceremonious. "If a guy talks to a girl in a bar, it's doesn't necessarily mean he's picking her up, although the dating scene here is especially good for younger people," observes Kyle Snyder. "However by the time you're in your late 20s and early 30s, the pool gets a bit smaller."

Still, few are in a hurry to settle down. "People around here place a premium on personal well-being," notes one woman. "I'm into my 30s and have no shortage of dates, although divorcees with children might find it more difficult."

ARTS AND SCIENCES

Along with being well-supported, local arts cut a wide and varied swath throughout the city, which in fact had 12 theaters before its first hospital was built.

A 9,000-seat arena carved out of massive red sandstone boulders, Denver's **Red Rock Amphitheater** has hosted everyone from the Beatles to symphony orchestras. The nine theaters in the previously mentioned **Denver Performing Arts Complex** include the up-to-date Buell, which mounts national tours of Broadway productions; and the Boettcher Concert Hall, the nation's first such venue in the round and home to the **Colorado Symphony Orchestra** and **Opera Colorado.** The Plex also features the **Denver Center Theater Company,** the largest of its kind between Chicago and Los Angeles, the **Colorado Ballet,** and other cabaret theater and guest productions.

Additional venues include the century-old **Central City Opera House;** the **Arvada Center for the Arts and Humanities,** which along with an outdoor amphitheater and professional companies offers classes in music, dance theater, and visual arts; and **Fiddler's Green Amphitheater,** providing both fixed and hillside seating for concerts ranging from classical to rock. The Bard is performed in Boulder at the **Colorado Shakespeare Festival. Theater on Broadway** specializes in premieres of new Broadway/Off-Broadway productions, while the **Heritage Square Music Hall** serves up family fare—both in terms of food and entertainment. More dinner theaters include the not-so-originally monikered **Boulder Dinner Theater** and the **Country Dinner Playhouse.**

More than 200 galleries highlight the works of local and national artists and provide an excellent opportunity to meet and

Where It's At

Unless otherwise noted, all area codes are 303.

Arvada Center for the Arts and Humanities, 6901 Wadsworth Blvd., Arvada, 431-3080

Black American West Museum, 3091 California St., 292-2566

Boulder Dinner Theater, 5501 Arapahoe, 449-6000

Buffalo Bill Memorial Museum and Grave, Exit 256 off of I-70, 526-0747

Butterfly Pavilion and Insect Center, 6252 W. 104th Ave., Westminster, 469-5441

Byers-Evans House Museum, 1310 Bannock St., 620-4933

Central City Opera House, 200 Eureka, Central City, 582-5202

Cherry Creek Arts Association, 333-2879

Children's Museum of Denver, 2121 Children's Museum Dr., 433-7444

Colorado Ballet, 1278 Lincoln St., 837-TUTU

Colorado History Museum, 13th and Broadway, 866-3682

Colorado Shakespeare Festival, University of Colorado, 492-1527

Colorado Symphony Orchestra, 1031 13th St., 98-MUSIC

Country Dinner Playhouse, 6875 S. Clinton, Englewood, 799-1410

Denver Art Museum, 14th Ave. and Bannock St., 640-2793

mingle. **"Gallery Strolls"** include one-on-one chats with artists (**Cherry Creek Arts Association**). Approximately 40 galleries in the LoDo district are featured in their **"First Friday"** self-guided walking tours.

Denver's no slouch in the museum department, either. Along with one of the world's greatest assemblages of Native American works, the **Denver Art Museum** boasts pre-Columbian, Spanish, and Asian exhibits. Nearby, in a former bordello and gambling hall, is a collection of good repute: 125 classic paintings and sculptures at the **Museum of Western Art.** The spanking new $64 million **Denver Public Library** boasts originals by Remington, and the **Denver International Airport** flies high with the largest public art program in the country. With 55 pieces of sculpture, the **Museum of Outdoor Arts** is another walkabout-type exhibition, while the **Trianaon Museum and Art Gallery** offers an outstanding accumulation of 18th-century paintings, furniture, crystal, and more. The **Turner Museum** makes for a good Impression(ist), so to speak, of A.M. Turner.

Covered wagons, Native American dances and more are brought to life at the **Colorado History Museum.** Other Wild West stuff can be found at the **Buffalo Bill Memorial Museum and Grave,** the **Byers-Evans House Museum,** the **Golden DAR Pioneer Museum,** and others in addition to a Titanic collection at the unsinkable **Molly Brown House Museum.** The **Black American West Museum** re-creates the often overlooked contributions of African-American cowboys. More ethnic information can be found at the **Mizel Museum of Judaica** and the **Museo De Las Americas,** which also serves as the center of the Latino community. Although it's not affiliated with any group, the **Rocky Mountain Quilt Museum** blankets that entire subject with a variety of rotating exhibits.

Those wanting to go way back in time—as in 3.5 billion years—can take a Prehistoric Journey at the **Denver Museum of Natural History,** which also has an IMAX theater and a planetarium. Folks hoping to actually follow in Dino's footsteps will find 300 prints at **Dinosaur Ridge National Natural Landmark,** along with fossils and bones encased in rock. More knowledge is on tap at the **Children's Museum of Denver,** which also boasts the only year-round ski slope in North America. Ecology is taken a step further at the **Denver Botanic Gardens** which, along with an oasis of plants and Japanese designs, has an educational exhibit about water conservation. Along with over 100 flower-filled public gardens scattered around Denver, the new **Hudson Gardens in**

Where It's At

(continued)

Denver Botanic Gardens, 1005 York St., 331-4000

Denver Center Theater Company, 950 13th St., 640-PLEX

Denver International Airport, 8500 Rosemary St., Commerce City, 289-7845

Denver Museum of Natural History, 2001 Colorado Blvd., 322-7009

Denver Performing Arts Complex, the Plex, 950 13th St., 640-PLEX

Denver Public Library, 1357 Broadway, 640-6200 or 640-8800

Denver Zoo, 2300 Steele St., 331-4110

Dinosaur Ridge National Natural Landmark, 16831 W. Alameda Pkwy., Morrison, 697-3466

Fiddler's Green Amphitheater, 6350 Greenwood Plaza Blvd., Englewood, 220-7000

First Friday, Lower Downtown Arts District, 321-1510

Gallery Strolls, 3003 E. 3rd Ave., 394-2903

Golden DAR Pioneer Museum, 911 10th St., Golden, 278-7151

Heritage Square Music Hall, 18301 W. Colfax Ave., Golden, 279-7800

Hudson Gardens in Littleton, 2888 W. Maplewood Ave., 797-8565

Mizel Museum of Judaica, 560 S. Monaco Pkwy., 333-4156

Molly Brown House Museum, 1340 Pennsylvania, 832-4092

Museo De Las Americas, 861 Santa Fe Dr., 571-4401

Museum of Outdoor Arts, 7600 E. Orchid Rd., Englewood, 741-3609

Museum of Western Art, 1727 Tremont Pl., 296-1880

National Renewable Energy Laboratory, 14869 Denver West Pkwy., Golden, 384-6565

Opera Colorado, 695 S. Colorado Blvd., No. 20, 778-1500

Red Rock Amphitheater, N. of Hogback Rd., Morrison, 694-1234

Rocky Mountain Arsenal National Wildlife Refuge, U.S. Fish & Wildlife Service, Bldg. 613, Commerce City, 289-0232

Where It's At

(continued)

Rocky Mountain Quilt Museum, 1111 Washington Ave., Golden, 277-0377

Theater on Broadway, 13 S. Broadway, 860-9360

Tiny Town, 6249 S. Turkey Creek Rd., 697-6829

Trianaon Museum and Art Gallery, 335 14th St., 623-0739

Turner Museum, 773 Downing St., 832-0924

U.S. Mint, W. Colfax Ave. at Cherokee St., 844-3582

Where It's At

 Unless otherwise noted, all area codes are 303.

Adventure/Lost Continent Golf, 9650 N. Sheridan Blvd., Westminster, 650-7587

Adventures Out West, 800/755-0935

Aurora, several locations, 397-1818

Black Hawk, Gilpin Co. Chamber of Commerce, P.O. Box 343, Black Hawk, 331-LUCK

Blue Quill, 1532 Colorado Hwy. 74, Evergreen, 674-7400

Canyon Marine, P.O. Box, Salida, 800/643-0707

Central City, Central City Casino Association, P.O. Box 773, 800/542-2999

Cloud Base, 5535 Independence Rd., Boulder, 530-2208

Colorado Avalanche, 1635 Clay St., 893-6700

Colorado Division of Wildlife, 6060 Broadway, 297-1192

Colorado Foxes, 6735 Stroh Rd., Parker, 840-1111

Colorado Rockies, 2001 Blake St., 292-0200

Colorado State Parks, 1313 Sherman St., 866-8437

Colorado State University, 970/491-5714

Confluence Kayaks, 1537 Platte St., 433-3676

Coors Field, 2001 Blake St., 292-0200

Copper Mountain, P.O. Box 3001, Frisco, 800/458-8386

Littleton provide 16 more on a 30-acre riverside site. Other environmental awareness programs can be found at the **Rocky Mountain Arsenal National Wildlife Refuge,** where you can view bald eagles via closed-circuit TV, and the **National Renewable Energy Laboratory,** which explores alternative forms of energy, such as the sun. How very Colorado.

The highly rated **Denver Zoo** has mammals, birds, and a re-created tropical rain forest. Buggy personalities might appreciate the self-descriptive **Butterfly Pavilion and Insect Center,** where cans of Raid will likely be checked at the door. You can learn about money at the **U.S. Mint** (although the only "free" thing is admission), or miniatures at **Tiny Town,** where everything's built to 1/6 scale.

THE SPORTING LIFE

Although famous ski resorts such as Aspen, Telluride, and Vail are several hours away, others are less than 100 miles from Denver, including **Copper Mountain, Eldora, Loveland, Winter Park,** and more. With some of the best skiing in the world, it's no wonder Denver's highways are jammed with folks eager to hit the slopes. Along with joining various church- and work-related ski clubs, those wanting to avoid the traffic can take the **Rio Grande Ski Train** to Winter Park, a scenic and relaxing ride that practically drops you off at the lifts. The **Regional Transportation District** (RTD) also offers light rail and bus service to sporting events and to Eldora.

Within a 90-mile radius (give or take a few) of the city center are opportunities for hiking (**Crow Canyon Archaeological Center**), kayaking (**Confluence Kayaks**), hot air ballooning (**Adventures Out West, Life Cycle**), fishing (**Blue Quill**), and horseback riding (**Stockton's Plum Creek Stables**). You can earn macho points by gliding/soaring (the **Cloud Base**), rock climbing (**Paradise Rock Gym**), rafting/river running (**Canyon Marine, River Runners,** more) and mountain biking (**Roads Less Traveled, Two Wheel Tours**). Those interested in hunting, fishing, or critter-watching can contact the **Colorado Division of Wildlife** for more information.

Many outdoor activities take place at the approximately 40 **Colorado State Parks** or in one of the state's 11 national forests (**U.S. Forest Service**) as well as in Denver's many city or mountain parks (contact **Denver Parks & Recreation** for more information). Thirty recreation centers offer outdoor and indoor pools, fitness classes, boating, drop-in gyms, and other organized activities. "If you want to meet people, join a health club," advises Dan Tessmer. The **Denver Sport and Social Club** and **Slippers and Sliders,** an African-American ski group, are just a couple of launching points.

The area's more than 40 golf courses consist of several open to the public (**Aurora, Eagle, Thorncreek**). Those not quite ready for the real thing can visit **Adventure/Lost Continent Golf** or **Riverside.**

Those looking for not-so-cheap thrills can find them at **Lakeside Amusement Park, Water World,** and more, and also at numerous casinos within spittin' distance at **Central City, Black Hawk,** and **Cripple Creek.** But with nearly $98 million worth of rides, entertainment, and natural attractions set against a mountainous backdrop, **Elitch Gardens,** has the markings of a winner.

Other stellar neighbors include **Mile High Stadium,** home of the NFL **Denver Broncos,** who have gone to four Super Bowls, and the relatively new **Coors Field,** a 50,000 seater that's drawn record crowds for the major league baseball **Colorado Rockies.** Also recently transplanted, the **Colorado Avalanche** hockey team recently won the Stanley Cup, giving Denver its first major sports championship, while the **Colorado Foxes** have captured several American Professional Soccer League Championships.

"Everyone here is into the teams, making it almost impossible to get tickets," states Michelle Snyder. (The Broncos have allegedly been sold out for the past 20 years.) Except, perhaps for the hapless (for now) NBA **Denver Nuggets,** "who've been doing so poorly that they're making people purchase tickets to basketball games along with hockey." Those looking for more up-and-coming talent can patronize collegiate competitions at the **University of Colorado** in Boulder or **Colorado State University** in Fort Collins.

AFTER-HOURS DIVERSIONS

Much of Denver's after-hours action can be found in LoDo, a conglomeration of over 60 sports bars, brew pubs, saloons, restaurants, and cafes. With an open-air design and tons of people milling around the area, "it's a natural place to meet others," continues Michelle Snyder. As ground zero for the brewing industry, LoDo surely has the largest accumulation of microbreweries in the galaxy, including the nation's biggest brew pub, **Wynkoop,** the modestly monikered **Sandlot**

Where It's At
(continued)

Cripple Creek, City of Cripple Creek, P.O. Box 430, 800/526-8777

Crow Canyon Archaeological Center, 233990 County Rd. K, Cortez, 800/422-8975

Denver Broncos, 13655 Broncos Pkwy., Englewood, 649-9000

Denver Nuggets, 1635 Clay St., 893-6700

Denver Parks & Recreation, 964-2500

Denver Sport and Social Club, 5303 E. Evans Ave., Suite 107, 639-8466

Eagle, 1200 Clubhouse Rd., Broomfield, 466-3322

Eldora, P.O. Box 1697, 440-8700

Elitch Gardens, I-25 and Speer Blvd., 595-4FUN

Lakeside Amusement Park, I-70 and Sheridan Blvd., 466-1631

Life Cycle, 2540 S. Steele St., 759-3907

Loveland, P.O. Box 899, Georgetown, 571-5580

Mile High Stadium, 2755 W. 17th, 458-4848

Paradise Rock Gym, 6260 N. Washington St., 286-8168

Regional Transportation District, RTD, 1600 Blake St., 299-6700

Rio Grande Ski Train, 555 17th St., 296-4754

River Runners, 11150 U.S. Hwy. 50, Salida, 800/525-2081

Riverside, 2201 W. Oxford, Englewood, 762-9873

Roads Less Traveled, P.O. Box 8187, Longmont, 678-8750

Slippers and Sliders, 758-8149

Stockton's Plum Creek Stables, 7479 W. Titan Rd., Littleton, 791-1966

Thorncreek, 13555 N. Washington St., 450-7055

Two Wheel Tours, P.O. Box 2655, Littleton, 798-4601

U.S. Forest Service, 275-5350

University of Colorado in Boulder, 1333 Grandview Ave., 492-5547

Water World, 88th Ave. at Pecos St., 427-SURF

Winter Park, P.O. Box 36, 800/453-2525

Where It's At

 Unless otherwise noted, all area codes are 303.

1082 Broadway, 11th and Broadway, 831-1082

15th St. Tavern, 623 15th St., 572-0822

Anheuser-Busch, 2431 Busch Dr., Ft. Collins, 490-4691

Aunt Evelyn's, 2648 S. Parker Rd., 750-7897

Blossoms of Light, Denver Botanic Gardens, 331-4000

Blue Hair, 2703 Iris, Boulder, 443-2583

Blue Room, 2040 Larimer, 269-0969

Breckenridge Brewery, 2220 Blake St., 295-BREW

Brendan's, 1624 Market St., 595-0609

Brendan's Pub, 1624 Market, 595-0609

Bullfrog's, 1709 Pearl St., Boulder, 442-2542

Bump & Grind Cardio Cafe, 439 E. 17th Ave., 861-4841

Cactus Moon, 10001 Grant St., 451-5200

Cafe@Netherworld, 1278 Pennsylvania, 861-8638

Celestial Seasonings, 4600 Sleepytime Dr., Boulder, 581-1250

Champion Brewing Company, 1442 Larimer St., 534-5444

Cinco de Mayo, Santa Fe Blvd., 534-8342

Club 156, Broadway and Euclid, Boulder, 800/444-SEAT

Club Synergy, 3240 Larimer, 575-5680

Colorado Performing Arts Festival, Denver PLEX, 640-2678

Colorado Scottish Festival, 238-6524

Colorado State Fair, State Fairgrounds, Pueblo, 800/876-4567

Columbine Cellars, 2401 Blake St., 299-WINE

Comedy Works, 1226 15th St., 595-3637

Common Grounds, 3483 W. 32nd Ave., 458-5248

Coors, 13th and Ford sts., Golden, 277-BEER

Cricket on the Hill, 1209 E. 13th Ave., 830-9020

Deadbeat/40th Chapel, 4040 E. Evans, 758-6853

(which is actually located in Coors Stadium), **Rock Bottom Brewery, Breckenridge Brewery, Champion Brewing Company,** and sports bars like **Sluggers,** which has three—count 'em—three batting cages. With 60 different wines by the glass and 150 by the bottle, **Enoteca** also offers jazz and (cough, cough) a cigar room. The **Tattered Cover Bookstore** provides 600,000 reasons to just say no: 225,000 different titles on four floors.

LoDo's hottest disco would be **I-Beam,** while other jazz/blues favorites include **Brendan's** and **El Chapultepec.** Increasing the area's buzz is the fact that Ahnold (yes, *that* Arnold) has purchased almost a complete square block, with plans for yet another Planet Hollywood. On the northern end of the district, Union Station (still a working passenger railroad) is next on the revitalization hit list, with **Flat Pennies,** a pub/restaurant, already in place. Other clusters of night spots can be found in Larimer Square and in the somewhat ritzier suburb of Cherry Creek.

Folks pretty much hang out at whatever suits their fancy, regardless of fashion, ethnic, or political persuasion. "Different crowds congregate in one place," notes Kyle Snyder. "People are mostly attracted to a theme, such as the **Purple Martini**"—which only serves one kind of drink that isn't beer—"or **Tommy Sunami's,**" upscale sushi and other Asian offerings in a unique, clublike atmosphere.

Live music is a popular pastime, with many clubs offering, say, jazz one night and punk rock the next. **Ziggie's** specializes in blues and all brands of rock 'n' roll. **Cricket on the Hill** showcases local bands, as does **Herman's Hideaway,** which includes some national acts. More rock (in the broadest sense of the word) is heard at **Club 156,** the **Zone,** and others. The conservative might want to think twice, however, before frequenting the **15th St. Tavern;** several bands there have the "F" word in their titles. (Perhaps visitors should wash their mouths out at **Soapy Smith's.**)

Additional jazz/blues offerings can be found at the **Blue Room, Brendan's Pub, Top Hat Tavern, Vartan Jazz,** and others. Dance aficionados will love **Proof of** (in?) **the Pudding,** which offers up hits from the '70s and '80s, as well as **Club Synergy,** The **Edge, Modeans,** and the **Yardie Lounge,** to mention a few.

There's acoustic in unusual places like **Aunt Evelyn's, Blue Hair,** and **Bullfrog's**—hopefully the music doesn't sound that way—as well as Denver's multitudinous coffeehouses (**Cafe@Netherworld, Gallery Coffee House, Diedrich Coffee,** others), which are as plentiful as buffalo used to be. Others worth visiting: **Bump & Grind Cardio**

Cafe, **Java Hut** (just in time for the re-release of the *Star Wars* trilogy), and **Common Grounds.**

The city dips its toe into the alternative scene at the **Ogden Theater,** with new wave rock, neo punk, and more bands, as well as at the **Deadbeat/40th Chapel, 1082 Broadway,** and the **Wreck Room,** where Sunday is gothic night. In a similar vein (so to speak), the **Gallery Coffee House** offers gothic industrial night the first and third Friday of every month.

There's also big band (**Mercury Cafe**) and meringue/salsa (**Maximillian's**). **Grizzly Rose, Urban Cowgirl, Cactus Moon,** and **Stampede** offer mainstream country-western, while **George McKelvey's Comedy Club, Comedy Works, Wit's End,** and **The Denver Buffalo Company Showroom** are good for at least a few laughs. **Macky Auditorium** and **Mammoth Events Center** are stop-offs for traveling chuckle-smiths, too.

This area surely holds the record for beverage factory tours. Aside from breweries (**Anheuser-Busch, Coors, Rockies Brewing Company,** others), there are wineries (**Columbine Cellars, Plum Creek Cellars**) and sake manufacturers (**Hakushika U.S.A.**). You can sober up healthfully at **Celestial Seasonings,** sampling 47 different blends from the tea bar. Denver is also noted for its beer festivals, with its own "Super Bowl" (stein?) being the **Great American Beer Festival,** where 325 large and small American brewers hop, er, hope to win various medals. Here, too, are more free samples, but if you taste all 1,300 entries, you will have imbibed the equivalent of 108 bottles. Other brewski bashes include the **LoDo Brewfest** (August) and **Oktoberfest** (September), with German bands, dancing, food, and you-know-what.

Of course, not all of Denver's annual events are alcohol-based. January boasts the **National Western Stock Show and Rodeo,** the nation's largest moo-ving experience for cattle, sheep, horses, and rodeo riders; while September is the time for the **Colorado State Fair.** There are lots of ethnic festivals as well: the **Denver Pow-Wow** (March) has over 700 dancers and musicians from 70 tribes; **Cinco de Mayo,** the state's largest Latino event (May); **International Heritage Festival** (June), which highlights several countries; **Juneteenth,** which celebrates the end of slavery in Texas; **Denver Black Arts Festival** (July), which honors African-American endeavors and not witchcraft; and the **Colorado Scottish Festival** (August) and **Long's Peak Scottish-Irish Festival** (September), which appeal to more than just members of the clan,

Where It's At

(continued)

Denver Black Arts Festival, City Park, 293-2559

Denver Buffalo Company Showroom, 1109 Lincoln, 832-0880

Denver International Film Festival, 321-FILM

Denver Pow-Wow, 455-4575

Diedrich Coffee, 1224 15th St., 534-4460, other locations

Edge, 2975 Fox, 292-6600

El Chapultepec, 1962 Market St., 294-9126

El Grito, Santa Fe Dr., 534-8342

Enoteca, 1730 Wynkoop, 293-2887

Fiesta! Fiesta!, Larimer Square, 297-0155

Flat Pennies, 1701 Wynkoop St., 534-1881

Gallery Coffee House, 6035 W. Alameda, Lakewood, 202-2024

Gallery Coffee House, 4035 W. Alameda, Lakewood, 399-GOOB

George McKelvey's Comedy Club, 10015 E. Hampden Ave., 368-8900

Great American Beer Festival, 447-0816

Grizzly Rose, 5450 N. Valley Highway, 295-1941

Hakushika U.S.A., 4414 Table Mountain Dr., Golden, 279-SAKE

Herman's Hideaway, 1578 S. Broadway, 777-5840

I-Beam, 1427 Larimer, 534-2355

International Heritage Festival, 979-9095

Java Hut, 6603 Leetsdale Dr., 333-0655

Juneteenth, Five Points, 399-7138

LoDo Brewfest, LoDo, 964-8997

Long's Peak Scottish-Irish Festival, Rocky Mountain National Park, 586-6308

Macky Auditorium, University of Colorado, Boulder, 830-TIXS

Mammoth Events Center, 1510 Clarkson, 860-1333

Maximillian's, 2151 Lawrence, 291-0015

Mercury Cafe, 2199 California, 294-9258 or 294-9281

Modeans, 1410 Market, 632-3532

National Western Stock Show and Rodeo, 4655 Humbolt St., 297-1166

Ogden Theater, 935 E. Colfax, 830-2525

Oktoberfest, Larimer Square, 534-2357

Parade of Lights, downtown, 534-6161

Where It's At

(continued)

Plum Creek Cellars, 1588 S. Pearl St., 399-7586

Proof of the Pudding, 7800 E. Hampden Ave., 694-4898

Purple Martini, 1336 S. Fifth, 820-0575

Rock Bottom Brewery, 1001 16th St., 534-7616

Rockies Brewing Company, 2880 Wilderness Place, Boulder, 444-8448

Rocky Mountain Book Festival, Currigan Exhibition Hall, 273-5933

Sandlot, Coors Stadium

Sluggers, 2229 Blake St., 298-8006

Soapy Smith's, 1317 14th, 534-1111

Stampede, 2430 S. Havana, 696-7686

Tattered Cover Bookstore, 1628 16th St., 436-1070, other locations

Tommy Sunami's, 1432 Market St., 534-5050

Top Hat Tavern, 1512 Larimer, 575-0007

Urban Cowgirl, 9575 W. 57th, 420-4444

Vartan Jazz, 231 Milwaukee, Cherry Creek N., 399-1111

Wild Lights, Denver Zoo, 331-4110

Wit's End, 8861 Harlan St., Westminster, 430-HAHA

Wreck Room, 1080 Broadway, 831-WRECK

Wynkoop, 1634 18th St., 297-1700

Yardie Lounge, 1434 Blake, 899-4936 or 575-0022

Ziggie's, 4923 W. 38th Ave., 455-9930

Zone, 6647 W. Ottawa Ave., 904-2692

Where It's At

 Unless otherwise noted, all area codes are 303.

16th Street Mall, 16th St., between Market and Broadway

Andre's, 370 S. Garfield St., 322-8871

Barolo Grill, 3030 E. 6th Ave., 393-1040

Bella Ristorante, 1920 Market St., 297-8400

although Ku Kluxers can go elsewhere. September offers two more Hispanic celebrations: **Fiesta! Fiesta!** and **El Grito,** which commemorates Mexico's independence from Spain. October brings on another kind of culture: The **Colorado Performing Arts Festival,** the **Denver International Film Festival,** and the **Rocky Mountain Book Festival.** Various holiday celebrations illuminate the last month of the year—the **Parade of Lights, Wild Lights,** and **Blossoms of Light.**

 ## CULINARY AND SHOPPING HAUNTS

Much of what's offered in Denver's restaurants is tasty and healthful as well as inexpensive, with many entrees being in the $7 or under or $8–$11 bracket. "I think I've cooked dinner at home maybe once in six months," laughs Salih. Local specialties include Rocky Mountain trout, fresh Colorado beef, and, for non-sheepish carnivores, lamb, one of the state's primary exports. Buffalo is another popular dish, with places like the **Denver Buffalo Company** and **Bents Fort Inn** serving up the big fellows in a variety of ways. You also can view the stuffed heads of 500 of their friends and relatives at the **Buckhorn Exchange,** the oldest restaurant in the city. Not recommended for members of PETA.

Many neighborhoods have cuisine from around the world: Spots such as Five Points offer up barbecue and soul food; Sakura Square is the center of the Japanese community; while Federal Boulevard near Alameda has proven to be a magnet for Chinese, Thai, and Vietnamese restaurants, groceries, and shops.

Downtown, and particularly LoDo, are loaded with elegant eateries. Others, such as **Bella Ristorante** (Italian), are located in renovated warehouses. Atmosphere and people-watching are as important as victuals: places such as **City Spirit Cafe** (eclectic), **Le Bonne Soup** (French), **Fettoush** (Middle Eastern), **Moondance** (American), and the more expensive **Josephina's** (Italian) and **LoDo's Bar and Grill** (steak) offer ambiance, patios and/or great views. **Paris on the Platte** (Deli/Vegetarian) and **Croc's Cafe** (Mexican) are considered hot spots for those flying solo. Others wanting to chow down with a minimum of fanfare might check in at the **Punch Bowl** (bar food), the **Rocky Mountain Diner** (American), and the **Wazee Supper Club** (Pizza).

Downtown is full of places that Denverites consider pricier: In the $12 to $16 (give or take a dollar or so) range are **Cadillac Ranch** (steak), **Delhi Darbar** (Indian), **Denver ChopHouse** (contemporary), **Le Gourmand**

(French), and the **Little Russian Cafe** (guess what). Those willing to dig deeper ($17+) will find taste titillation at the **Palace Arms** (continental), which actually has a dress code; the **Palm,** the Denver outpost of the famous New York steak/wall sketch landmark; and, a bit farther away from the city center, **Cliff Young's** (contemporary), **Morton's** (steak), the oh-so-romantic French **Tante Louise, California Bar and Grill** (multi-ethnic), the **Briarwood Inn** (contemporary), and others. Pull some **Strings** (contemporary) or stop at **Michael's** (American) and you might find some so-called beautiful people.

Cherry Creek is another pulse point in the local culinary scene. The **Barolo Grill** (Italian) specializes in fine wines; you can make new friends at a community table at the **Chinook Tavern** (contemporary); or not lack for things to read at the Fourth Story, which is on the top floor of the **Tattered Cover** bookstore (American). (Magazine lovers will appreciate the **Newstand,** in central Denver: healthy fare sandwiched among a broad selection of publications.) Food is the primary attraction at **Bistro Adde Brewster** (contemporary), **Starfish** (seafood), **Cafe Paradiso** (seafood/Italian), **Salmagundi** (American), and **Sfuzzi** (although the food isn't) (Italian). You can also find Swiss dishes at **Andre's;** oodles of noodles at **Noodles & Company** (eclectic) and **Piatti** (Italian); and potato latkes at **Zaidy's Deli.** The **Rattlesnake Grill** (contemporary) serves much more than its namesake.

Given Denver's ethnic heritage, the plenitude of Mexican eateries should come as no surprise. Places such as **Benny's, La Casa de Manual, La Fogata,** and the **Riviera** were around long before chilis became chic. Others have sprouted in more than one location, including **Chevys, Chipotle,** and **Las Margaritas.** Authentic food is served on plastic plates with mismatched silver at the 15-seat **El Taco de Mexico.** South America weighs in with **Cafe Brazil** and **Rodzio Grill,** while **Canyon Cafe** and **Zolo Grill** serve Southwestern.

The continent of Asia is well represented, with places such as **Kokoro** having several locations, and three other spots prefaced by the word "Sushi"—**Boat, Den** and **Heights.** More traditional Chinese fare can be found in South Denver: the **Hong Kong Cafe, Imperial Chinese, Red Coral,** and others. There's Moroccan at **Mataam Fez,** Ethiopian at **Meskerem,** and Korean at **Seoul Food** (really!). Breakfast and brunch buffaloes stampede to **Dozens,** the **Egg Shell, Hot Cakes,** and others.

Where It's At

(continued)

Benny's, 301 E. 7th Ave., 894-0788

Bents Fort Inn, 10950 U.S. Hwy. 50, Las Animas, 719/456-0011

Bistro Adde Brewster, 250 Steele St., 338-1900

Briarwood Inn, 1630 8th St., Golden, 279-3121

Buckhorn Exchange, 1000 Osage St., 534-9505

Cadillac Ranch, 1400 Larimer St., 820-2288

Cafe Brazil, 3611 Navajo St., 480-1877

Cafe Paradiso, 2355 E. 3rd Ave., 321-2066

California Bar and Grill, 8505 Park Meadows Center Dr., Littleton, 649-1111

Canyon Cafe, 2500 E. 1st Ave., Cherry Creek, 321-2700

Castle Rock, Castle Rock Factory Shops, Meadows Parkway and I 25, 688-4494

Cherry Creek North, 3003 E. 3rd Ave., 394-2903

Cherry Creek Shopping Center, 3000 E. 1st Ave., Cherry Creek, 388-3900

Chevys, 3000 E. 1st Ave., 388-6633, other locations

Chinook Tavern, 256 Detroit St., 394-0044

Chipotle, 1644 E. Evans Ave., 722-4121, other locations

City Spirit Cafe, 1434 Blake St., 575-0022

Cliff Young's, 700 E. 17th Ave., 831-8900

Croc's Cafe, 1630 Market St., 436-1144

Delhi Darbar, 1514 Blake St., 595-0680

Denver Buffalo Company, 1109 Lincoln St., 832-0880

Denver ChopHouse, 1735 19th St., 296-0800

Denver Entertainment and Fashion Pavilion, 16th St., between Welton and Glenarm, 892-6662

Dozens, 236 W. 13th Ave., 572-0066

Egg Shell, 300 Josephine St., Cherry Creek, 322-1601

Where It's At

(continued)

El Taco de Mexico, 714 Santa Fe Dr., 623-3926

Fettoush, 1448 Market St., 820-2554

Gart Brothers Sport Castle, 351 W. 104th Ave., 452-6241, other locations

Hong Kong Cafe, 2401 S. University Blvd., 733-8250

Hot Cakes, 1400 E. 18th Ave., 830-1909

Imperial Chinese, 431 S. Broadway, 698-2800

Josephina's, 1433 Larimer St., 623-0166

Kokoro, 2390 S. Colorado Blvd., 692-8752, other locations

La Casa de Manual, 2010 Larimer St., 295-1752

La Fogata, 5670 E. Evans Ave., 753-9458

Larimer Square, 1400 block of Larimer St., 534-2367

Las Margaritas, 1066 S. Gaylord St., 777-0194, other locations

Le Bonne Soup, 1512 Larimer St., 595-9169

Le Gourmand, 1401 17th St., 297-8663

Little Russian Cafe, 1424 Larimer St., 595-8600

LoDo's Bar and Grill, 1946 Market St., 293-8555

Loveland, Loveland Discount Center, 360 S. Lincoln Ave., 970/667-3590

Mataam Fez, 4609 E. Colfax Ave., 399-9282

Meskerem, 1501 E. Colfax Ave., 860-0591

Michael Garman's, 1512 Larimer, 572-1600

Michael's, 2710 E. 3rd Ave., Cherry Creek, 321-2324

Mile High Flea Market, 7007 E. 88th Ave., 289-4656

Moondance, 1626 Market St., 893-1626

Morton's, 1710 Wynkoop, 825-3353

Newstand, 630 E. 6th Ave., 777-6060

Noodles & Company, 2360 E. 3rd Ave., 331-6600

Old South Pearl St., 1200–1800 S. Pearl

Palace Arms, 321 17th St., 297-3111

Palm, 1201 16th St., 825-7256

Paris on the Platte, 1553 Platte St., 455-2451

Although Denver touts itself as the shopping capital of the Rocky Mountain West, until recently, it was mall-impaired. Its major claim to consumer fame was the **Gart Brothers Sport Castle,** allegedly the largest store of its kind in the world. "Things have greatly improved," notes Fleming, thanks primarily to three new and in-progress projects: **Park Meadows,** a 120-shop complex, set in a ski lodge motif; **Stadium Walk** in LoDo, which adds 190,000 square feet of retail space (and that Planet Hollywood) to the already bustling district; and the **Denver Entertainment and Fashion Pavilion,** with more than 360,000 square feet of retail, dining, and other diversions.

These complement the reigning mall, the **Cherry Creek Shopping Center,** which has 140 stores of the Nieman-Marcus, Saks, and Lord & Taylor ilk surrounded by sculptures, skylights, and airy public spaces. Even the public restrooms have gold-plated fixtures. Smaller (but equally enjoyable and in some ways more unique) arrays include **Larimer Square,** a restored section of Denver's oldest area; **Michael Garman's,** a miniature city complete with holograms and other special effects along with works of art; the **16th Street Mall,** a chair-lined, mile-long promenade with boutiques, department stores, and cafes (and ideal for people watching); and nearby **Tabor Center,** three levels of shops and restaurants in a glass-enclosed atrium. Antique lovers will find over 100 stores along South Broadway.

Those willing to travel a bit farther can visit **Cherry Creek North,** an eclectic mix of emporiums, clothing designers, and cafes; or **Old South Pearl St.,** South Denver's contribution to the restaurant, gallery, and boutique scene. This is not to be confused with the **Pearl Street Mall** in Boulder, which, along with providing conventional fare, also caters to the grunge/aging hippie set. Bargain hunting can be found at the **Mile High Flea Market,** 80 acres of brand-name, closeout and seasonal merchandise, as well as factory outlet centers in **Loveland, Castle Rock,** and **Silverthorne.** That is, if you can tear yourself away from the slopes.

 ## ETHNIC AND RELIGIOUS PROSPECTS

Denver has more than 2,000 houses of worship, "although it's much more casual and New Age than many other places," observes Michelle Snyder. In some congregations, "people wear jeans to services." Along with several branches of the **Church of Jesus Christ Latter Day**

Saints, **Church of Christ,** and **Church of Christ Scientist,** Denver has a **Presbytery, Episcopal Diocese,** and **Lutheran Family Services.** The **Mother Cabrini Shrine** serves as a spiritual center for more than Catholics, who can contact the **Archdiocese of Denver** for information on houses of worship in their vicinity. The Jewish population is serviced by several synagogues as well as a **Jewish Community Center;** other persuasions can hook up through the **Colorado Council of Churches** for more information.

Although a few years ago Colorado received a lot of flak over Amendment 2, which reversed prior legislation in Aspen, Boulder, and Denver protecting homosexuals against discrimination, "the controversy's pretty much died down," notes one man. "The law wasn't so much against gays, just that they not be given special treatment. They're very conscious of individual rights around here."

That aside, denizens seem very proud of Denver's racial attitudes, or lack thereof. The fact that Mayor Wellington Webb is an African-American is only made obvious when you see his picture; Denver was also rated as one of the top 10 cities for Latinos by *Hispanic* magazine. "By and large, people around here are excited about working together with people of any race," Chamber of Commerce official Steven Velazquez told *Hispanic* magazine. It's a human thing.

CRIB SHEET

Home buyers, take note: There's gold in them thar hills. The Denver real estate market has been flagged as one of the best places for investment in more than one survey, "and prices are going crazy like they did in California a few years ago," adds Tessmer. In particular, Douglas County has enjoyed explosive growth, with such master planned locales as the Stroh Ranch, which offers an outstanding community and recreational center.

Rent can be high, though, with fierce competition for apartments, particularly in popular neighborhoods such as LoDo, Cheesman Park, Southeast Denver, and Cherry Creek. So if you like it, grab it, because it might not be around in a few hours. Apartment finders such as AdvantEdge (1660 S. Albian, 753-1313), Anne Dresser's Apartment Store (6446 E. Hampden Ave., 989-3733 or 758-8888), the Apartment Connection (760 S. Colorado Blvd., 691-5100), and more can help alleviate aggravation from the chase. Selective Network (4155 E. Jewell Ave., 759-8670) matches up compatible roommates, while Corporate Executive Housing (1658 Grant St., 863-7002), InterOffice/Denver (7900 E. Union Ave., 694-5300), and others provide temporary shelter (for a price, of course).

Where It's At

(continued)

Park Meadows, 8401 Park Meadows Center Dr., Littleton, 792-2999

Pearl Street Mall, 3300 28th St., 444-9571

Piatti, 190 St. Paul St., 321-1919

Punch Bowl, 2052 Stout St., 295-7974

Rattlesnake Grill, 3000 E. 1st St., 377-8000

Red Coral, 1591 S. Colorado Blvd., 758-7610

Riviera, 4301 E. Kentucky, 757-8621

Rocky Mountain Diner, 1800 18th St., 293-8383

Rodzio Grill, 7900 W. Quincy, Littleton, 972-0806

Salmagundi, 3000 E. 1st Ave, 322-2200

Seoul Food, 701 E. 6th Ave., 837-1460

Sfuzzi, 3000 E. 1st Ave, 321-4700

Silverthorne, Silverthorne Factory Stores, 145 Stephens Way, 970/468-9440

Stadium Walk, 1616 17th St., 628-5428

Starfish, 300 Fillmore St., 333-1133

Strings, 1700 Humbolt St., 831-7310

Sushi Boat, 3460 S. Locust St., 757-3181

Sushi Den, 1487 S. Pearl St., 777-0826

Sushi Heights, 2301 E. Colfax, 355-2777

Tabor Center, Lawrence St., 572-6868

Tante Louise, 4900 E. Colfax Ave., 355-4489

Tattered Cover bookstore, 2955 E. 1st Ave., 322-1824

Wazee Supper Club, 1600 15th St., 623-9518

Zaidy's Deli, 121 Adams St., 333-5336

Zolo Grill, 2525 Arapahoe, Boulder, 449-0444

Where It's At

Unless otherwise noted, all area codes are 303.

Archdiocese of Denver, 3101 W. Hillside Place, 934-1777

Church of Christ, 1100 Dahlia St., 377-3677

Church of Christ Scientist, 3101 W. 31st Ave., 455-2976

Church of Jesus Christ Latter Day Saints, 9227 W. Dartmouth Pl., 987-8882

Colorado Association of Black Engineers and Scientists, 4301 E. Colfax Ave., 329-6251

Colorado Black Round Table, 1520 York St., 329-3513

Colorado Council of Churches, 1234 Bannock St., 825-4910

Denver Urban League, 1525 Josephine St., 388-5861

Episcopal Diocese, 1300 Washington St., 837-1173

Jewish Community Center, 350 S. Dahlia St., 399-2660

Hispanic League, 660 Sherman St., 863-8483

Lutheran Family Services, 1660 Ogden St., 832-8603

Mother Cabrini Shrine, 20189 Cabrini Blvd., Golden, 526-0758

Presbytery, 1710 S. Grant St., 777-2453

Lodo's prices in particular have escalated, with some ultra-modern lofts reaching into the seven-figure stratosphere. Less costly but equally charming (and perhaps quieter) choices include the older University Park, Park Hill, Washington Park, and Capitol Hill, while Cheesman Park draws the artsy set. The Queen Anne homes in nearby Curtis and Clements Park went through extensive renovation in the late '70s and are considered desirable as well. Just minutes south of downtown is the Denver Country Club neighborhood, with its spectacular old mansions and homes. Nearby Cherry Creek is being transformed from an area of unassuming bungalows to blocks of architecturally striking townhouses.

The suburbs are equally popular: Not only can you get a good deal for your money, but many complexes and planned communities offer on-site health clubs and swimming pools.

East of Denver lies Aurora (average home price: $97,500), one of the region's largest and fastest-growing cities. Somewhat higher in elevation than the rest of Denver, Aurora has less pollution and offers great mountain views. Greenwood Village ($350,000) is another hot spot that's benefitted from the influx of new businesses and a great location while retaining its country aura. With big houses on a little prairie, Highlands Ranch ($280,000) south of Denver is especially popular with Volvo-driving, gold-card-toting yupsters.

Close to the Rockies and Boulder are the charming cities of Wheat Ridge ($170,000), Golden ($187,500), and Arvada ($191,000), small-town life only a few minutes' (non-rush hour) drive from the city center. Urbanesque Lakewood ($91,400) has a hip, funky feel. Folks who work in the nearby metro area and business parks will find lots of good stuff in Englewood ($140,000), Littleton ($140,000) and Castle Rock ($160,000). To the north are the diverse Thornton ($150,000) and Northglenn ($275,000), which have everything from gang activity on certain streets to working class, residential neighborhoods to high-end homes.

Boulder ($252,000) is a choice for techies, outdoor enthusiasts, and those who prefer the life of the mind. "You'll find a lot of higher-thinking alternative-type people here," observes Kyle Snyder. "There's a lot of culture and political involvement." Those not quite ready for the scene can opt for nearby Westminster ($160,000), a progressive place that's won awards for local government, parks, and buildings, or the still primarily residential Broomfield ($151,500), recently liberated from its farm town roots to become a high-tech center.

Unlike some bigger (and older) cities, "the public education system here is excellent," remarks Kyle Snyder. The Denver system is broken down into smaller, more individualized districts (contact Denver Public Schools, 764-3414, for more information), while other suburban schools enjoy good reputations as well. Nearly 80 percent of the students earn a high school diploma (that's well above the national average); most pursue some form of postsecondary education. Several independent and parochial schools offer numerous programs (Association of Colorado Independent Schools, 442-5252).

College tuition is generally lower than the national average. The metro area's two big colleges, the University of Denver (871-2000) and University of Colorado in Boulder (492-6301) are supplemented by several community-based institutions such as the Colorado School of Mines (273-3000), the state's preeminent engineering academy, and Colorado Free University (it isn't) (399-5446).

NAVIGATING DENVER

Compared to places like Atlanta, "which at last count had 58 Peachtree Streets… Denver is a dream to get around in," notes the Denver Survival Guide, an on-line resource for newcomers (www.interealm.com). The city is divided into four quadrants marked by the intersection of I-25 and I-70, and the Rockies are to the west. "You can never get too lost remembering these basics." Major highways include the east-west spine, I-70; I-25 (north-south); Sixth Avenue, which changes from a surface street to a crosstown freeway; U.S. Highway 36 to Boulder and the northwest mountains; I-225 (southeast belt); C-470 (southwest belt); and the area's only toll road, E-470 (north and east), which hooks up to several of the highways. Drivers need to have an emissions test ("Envirotest") on their cars. Based on type and age of vehicle, county of residence, and other mysterious Motor Vehicle Division formulas, tag fees can range from $28 to a budget- (and heart-) stopping $400.

Getting around Denver can be PDQ, what with paired one-way streets, minimal and synchronized traffic lights, "and all those fast, crazy drivers from California," remarks one man. Traffic, however has become a problem in recent years, especially during rush hour. Snow can bring highways to a skidding halt.

The Regional Transportation District (299-6700) provides safe, clean, and extensive bus and light rail service, including "Park and Ride" facilities where you can drop off your car. In addition to the popular light rail, which carries folks around the city, Union Station offers ski trains, and Amtrak (800/872-7245) has several daily runs. Greyhound (293-6560) has regular service as well.

But the big transportation news (and, until recently, an object of skepticism) is the Denver International Airport (342-2200). Although it got off to a "Rocky" start with an automated baggage system more inefficient than any human could possibly be, the delays due to crowding or weather slowdowns have practically dropped to zero. Encompassing 53 square miles and with the tallest control tower in the world, it has widely spaced (and therefore safer) runways; an efficient underground train system; extensive, line-eliminating ticket counters; and an interior that includes art, tree-lined walkways, restaurants, and shopping. Plus "they ditched the computerized baggage system," adds Tessmer.

Or you can also opt for the smaller but still new Colorado Springs Airport (800/GO-COSPG), which is about an hour and fifteen minutes away.

Houston at a Glance

Birthdate and Present Size: 1836.
Metropolitan Statistical Area—1980:
2,735,766; 1990: 3,301,937.
1/1/95 (estimate): 3,688,700.
Percent change, 1980–1990: +20.7%.
Percent change, 1990–1995: +11.7%.

Weather Report: *Average annual
temperature*—66° F. In January:
61/40° F. In July: 90/71° F.
Average annual precipitation—44.76".
Average annual snowfall—None.

Money Matters: *Unemployment rate*—
6.2%.
Per capita income—$14,261 (city),
$15,091 (MSA).
Average household income—$37,296 (city),
$41,650 (MSA).
Average cost of a home—$108,754.
Average rent for an apartment—
$620/month.
ACCRA cost of living indexes (based on
100)—Composite Index: 95.2; Utilities
Index: 96.4; Housing Index: 85.8.
Sales and use tax—6.25% (state); + 2.0%
(local).
Personal income tax—None.

People Profile: *Crime rate* (Per 100,000
population)—7,285.4 (city), 4,135.2
(suburbs), 5,644.0 (MSA).
Racial and ethnic characteristics—
White: 52.8%; Black: 28.1%;
American Indian/Eskimo/Aleut: 0.3%;

Asian/Pacific Islander: 4.0%;
Hispanic Origin: 27.2%; Other: 14.9%.
Gender ratio—98.4 males per 100 females
(all ages); 96.3 males per 100 females
(18 years old+).
Age characteristics—18–24 (11.6%); 25–44
(36.9%). Median age: 30.4.
Educational attainment—percent having
completed high school: 70.5%; percent
having completed college: 25.1%.

Major Players: Services, retail/wholesale
trade, government, manufacturing
(particularly the manufacturing and
distribution of petroleum equipment).
Largest employers—Brown & Root
Holdings (engineering), Compaq
Computer Corp., Hermann Hospital, KCI
Constructors, Methodist Hospital, MW
Kellogg (construction), St. Luke's
Episcopal Hospital, Texas Children's
Hospital, Texas Commerce Bancshares,
Texas Commerce Bank, University of
Texas M.D. Anderson Cancer Center.

Community Services: *Average
hospital cost*—$390.27/day.
Average doctor visit—$44.80.
Average dentist visit—$57.92.
Newspapers—*Houston Chronicle,
Houston Business Journal, Houston
Defender* (black), *Jewish Herald-Voice,
La Informacion* (Spanish language),
La Subasta (Hispanic), *Texas Catholic
Herald, Houston Press* (alternative).

HOUSTON: SPACED OUT

Photo courtesy of the Greater Houston Convention & Visitors Bureau

Although you can't get a rental car with steer horns in Houston, there's still an annual rodeo for livestock and trail riders who set up camp in Memorial Park downtown. Also, keeping cattle on vacant land provides a tax exemption, so it's possible to see beef on the hoof silhouetted against massive skyscrapers. All this and more from the fourth largest—and arguably most ethnically diverse and cohesive—city in the nation, whose name was the first word heard on the moon in 1969 (as in, "Houston, Tranquillity base here. The Eagle has landed.").

Founded by Augustus and John Allen in 1836 and named after Texas hero and general Sam Houston, the city began as a muddy crossroads on the Buffalo Bayou. Things got off to a rather slow start: Yellow fever decimated the population, and, after a couple of years, Texas' capital was moved to Austin. Some local businessmen also decided they wanted to turn the narrow bayou into a full-fledged shipping channel. This took almost 75 years, until 1914.

But with the discovery of oil and the linkage to railways and other ports, the city began to prosper and grow. By the 1960s and '70s Houston was a genuine boomtown: Oil money flowed into real estate, banking, and the service sector. The establishment of the Manned Spacecraft Center (later known as the Johnson Space Center) in 1962 in nearby Clear Lake City guaranteed the take-off of aerospace and related industries.

But the truly striking developments have been more recent. By the 1980s, the decline of the energy industry caused an economic downturn. Less than a decade later, however, the city rebounded, having widened its business base to include banking and finance, electronics, wholesale and retail trade, health care, and other specialties.

Demographics have also transformed. Since 1982, the white population expanded by only 1 percent, although the region grew by close to a fifth. The number of African-Americans increased by 12 percent, Hispanics by 75 percent, and Asians by a whopping 129 percent. Many newcomers from the latter two groups are first-generation immigrants.

"During times of conflict, Houstonians tend to pick up the phone instead of a stone," remarks sociology professor Stephen L. Klineberg, who has conducted a local attitudinal survey over the past several years. Rather than rioting or engaging in acts of destruction, "there's a willingness to work together." Houston appears to have kept in touch with the elements that made America great.

Quality of Life

Everything here is Texas-sized: population, geographic area, even the amount of electricity used (Houston is known as the "air-conditioning capital of the world."). With close to 4 million people (not counting the proliferation of termites, cockroaches, ticks, and other buggy banes), the seven-county area is 10th largest in the United States. Although the climate can be sweltering, the average temperature during August, the hottest month, is 86, while in January it's an enviable 53. Unlike other parts of the state, there's an abundance of greenery.

Another jumbo selling point: cost of living is well below the average for cities of its size. Even better, there are no city or state income taxes. Housing, utilities, groceries, and miscellaneous expenses are also cheaper.

To say there's lots to do is an understatement. The theater and museum districts encompass nearly all the performing arts. Sports enthusiasts have the Astrodome and several professional teams to root for. The climate allows for year-round activity, including water recreation at a number of lakes and the Gulf Coast. The selection of restaurants covers about every type of cuisine, and shoppers can go for two solid weeks without hitting the same group of stores twice.

What the city lacks in architectural homeyness, it makes up for in friendliness. "Houston is a big city with a small-town atmosphere," observes native JoAnn Zuniga, a newspaper reporter. "There will always be a cowboy element, but it's become so international that racial prejudice and intolerance are not acceptable."

Houstonians can be opinionated—just ask for some observations about Dallas—but they'll respect and in many cases solicit your thoughts on various subjects as well. If you could cross-breed the intellectual liveliness of Manhattan with the hi-ya'll amiability of Nashville, you might come up with something very much like Houston.

General Opportunities

With more than 225,000 students enrolled in various local higher institutions of learning, Houston has the largest number of bilingual individuals with college degrees in the U.S. Because of its international flavor, and especially because the passage of NAFTA has further stimulated trade, it has also been cited several times as an excellent place for doing business by *Fortune* magazine.

Education and training, rather than race, are the qualifiers here. "The job opportunities are wonderful," comments Robert Frelow, an African-American who works in local politics. "The economic base has expanded to include plenty of entry and mid-level management positions."

Even the elected officials mirror the city's sense of equality and represent the population distribution. But instead of looking only at the interests of their particular group, "they're more concerned with the larger issues and the overall welfare of the city," adds Frelow.

Although salaries are lower than in, say, New York or Los Angeles, the cost of living makes them comparable. Instead of pistol-wielding Texans (although it is legal to carry a weapon around these parts), transplants find that the "bang" they usually get is for their buck, especially with regard to office space and housing.

MAJOR BREADWINNING

Home to over fifteen Fortune 500 companies, this town employs more than 1.6 million people, a number approximately equal to the population of the city proper (although Houston has *lots* of commuters, which cause the inevitable Texas-sized traffic jams). Fifty-nine consular offices and 27 trade bureaus represent 550 foreign-owned firms. Another 3,300 local enterprises have overseas business connections.

"I've lived in other cities and it takes a while to find a good job," states communications specialist Michelle Dugan. Not so in Houston, where she signed on as a public relations liaison for the Museum of Fine Art. "Houston is the place to be if you want to get ahead."

As the city's largest employer and as the biggest complex of its kind in the world, the Texas Medical Center utilizes nearly 54,000 doctors, nurses, and medical personnel. Physicians and patients come from all over to participate in the development of groundbreaking techniques, such as open-heart surgery, pioneered by Drs. Michael DeBakey and Denton Cooley.

The University of Texas M.D. Anderson Medical Hospital is equally respected as a cancer treatment facility. Dozens of other institutions (there are a whopping 105 in the surrounding 15-county area) focus on specialties ranging from pediatrics to AIDS to family care.

Hospitals as well as nearly 60 local companies (over half of all those in Texas) employ about 5,000 people in biotechnology. Researchers and others create medical devices, surgical instruments, therapeutic drugs, nutritional products, and diagnostic tests.

Although the Johnson Space Center has had close encounters of the federal budgetary kind, it still launches nearly $1.3 billion a year into the economy. More than 3,600 federal workers and nearly 12,000 contractor employees develop space shuttle flights, design the space station projects, and train astronauts.

More than 100 aerospace companies, including Boeing, Rockwell International, Lockheed, and McDonnell Douglas have a presence in Houston. Technical support specialists, including engineers and computer experts, concentrate on aerospace medicine, lunar sample research, orbital debris, and life support systems.

Practically every major U.S. energy company and many foreign enterprises have their headquarters and/or operations here, a total of about 5,000. So it's no surprise that this industry accounts for about 60 percent of the region's economic job base for exported goods and services as well as 45 percent of the nation's basic chemical manufacturing capacity.

> "The job opportunities are wonderful," comments a local. "The economic base has expanded to include plenty of entry and mid-level management positions." Another agrees: "Houston is the place to be if you want to get ahead."

Many positions require technical skills and educational background in research and development, chemical and petrochemical processing and refining, transmission of resources, and oil field service and supply. Companies such as Texaco, Amoco, Shell, and Exxon refine innovations like 3-D seismic imaging and horizontal drilling.

Second in total tonnage in imports/exports in the U.S., the Port of Houston provides the crux of Houston's international business infrastructure. Although the main thrust is petroleum products and grain, the surrounding 25-mile business complex offers a diversity of enterprises and jobs in the transportation, engineering, and legal arenas. In recent years, more than $15 billion has been invested in upgrading and adding to existing buildings and services, assuring the Port's continued growth.

Opportunities in other fields are too numerous to be listed here. Areas of concentration include, but are hardly limited to, accounting, advertising and public relations, banking and finance, design, agribusiness, real estate, computers, professional services, and retail.

SOCIAL AND RECREATIONAL SCENE

How Houston Plays

Between charity balls and association and interest group gatherings, area code 713 might well be considered a networking mecca. "You can attend a different function every night and still not honor all your commitments," comments marketing director Susan Ward. She also finds Houston geared toward young professionals, not only in terms of atmosphere but also in everyday goods and services. "You can go into a restaurant alone and feel comfortable. Places are open later to accommodate longer hours."

Those wanting to increase their social output might do well to become involved with interest groups and/or their church of choice. Popular among the former are the Greater Houston Preservation Alliance (712 Main St., 216-5000), the Houston Area Women's Center (1010 Waugh Dr., 528-2121 or 528-6798), and specialized organizations like the Houston Association of Hispanic Medical Professionals (427 W. 20th St., 864-4755). "There are so many newcomers that everyone's friendly," adds therapist Mary Fitzgerald. "It's rare to meet a native."

Although Houston has its share of formal shindigs and dress-for-success, "people don't judge you by your car or clothes," points out Zuniga. Houstonians "take the time to see what's beneath the surface, unlike Dallas, where money and appearances seem to be all-important."

"An advantage to this city is not running into the same people all the time," remarks one woman. "It's easy to start fresh with someone new."

Such a wide choice can in fact be overwhelming, particularly to the newcomer who's trying to find a niche. Houstonians advise focusing on your area of interest. "Sometimes you just need to kick back and prioritize," adds administrator Susan Pack.

ARTS AND SCIENCES

More than 200 institutions are dedicated to promoting the city's artistic and cultural diversity. Located only a few minutes from downtown and anchored by the state's first municipal art museum (**Museum of Fine Arts**), the Museum District is just the tip of the steer horn for culture lovers.

As one of the most visited attractions of its kind in the U.S., the **Houston Museum of Natural Science** boasts a $6 million assembly of more than 600 mineral specimens, along with your basic 70-foot dinosaur skeleton, Native American artifacts, seashells, and astronaut memorabilia. The Cockrell Butterfly Center allows visitors to (very gingerly) wander among 2,000 live butterflies in a rain-forest setting as well as view a color-filled cornucopia of their deceased brethren under glass.

Houston also has an **Arboretum and Nature Center** and **Zoo and Zoological Gardens.** Kids of all ages can explore a TV studio and exhibits in archaeology, agriculture, and the environment at the **Children's Museum of Houston,** and take a walk through the esophagus at the newly opened **Museum of Health and Medical Science.**

At the other end of the spectrum (sort of) is the **Contemporary Art Museum,** which is housed (really) in what looks like a corrugated metal parallelogram. Here you'll find constantly changing exhibits sharing space with such well-known artists as Calder and Miro. For a dose of tradition, there's the aforementioned Museum of Fine Arts, whose 27,000 items range from Renaissance paintings to African

Where It's At

 Unless otherwise noted, all area codes are 713.

A.D. Players, 2710 W. Alabama, 526-2721

Alley Theatre, 615 Texas, 228-8241

American Funeral Service Museum, 415 Barren Springs, 876-3063

Arboretum and Nature Center, 4501 Woodway, 681-8433

Beer Can House, 222 Malone

Children's Museum of Houston, 1500 Binz, 522-1138

Contemporary Art Museum, 5216 Montrose, 526-3129

Cynthia Woods Mitchell Pavilion, 2005 Lake Robbins Dr., Woodlands, 363-3300

Da Camera Society, 3920 Mandell, 524-5050

Diverseworks, 1117 E. Freeway, 223-8346

Ensemble Theatre, 4212 Main St., 520-0055

Holocaust Museum, 5401 Caroline, 789-9898

Houston Ballet, 1921 W. Bell, 523-6300

Where It's At

(continued)

Houston Grand Opera, 510 Preston, 227-ARTS

Houston Museum of Natural Science, 1 Hermann Circle Dr., 639-4600

Houston Symphony, 614 Louisiana, 227-ARTS

Jesse H. Jones Hall for the Performing Arts, 500 Texas Ave., 853-8000

Kennedy Bakery, 813 Commerce Ave.

Kuumba House, 3412 La Branch, 524-1079

Menil Collection, 1515 Sul Ross, 525-9400

Miller Outdoor Theatre, 100 Concert Dr., 520-3292

Museum of Fine Arts, 1001 Bissonnet, 639-7300

Museum of Health and Medical Science, 1515 Hermann Dr., 790-1838

Orange Show, 2401 Munger, 926-6368

Pigdom, 4208 Crawford

Rice Hotel, 903 Texas St., 222-0132

Sam Houston Park, 1100 Bagby, 655-1912

Texas Mime Theatre, 3100 Richmond Ave., 655-7145

Theatre Under the Stars, 4235 San Felipe, 622-1626

Wortham Theatre Space, 500 Texas Ave., 853-8000

Zoo and Zoological Gardens, Hermann Park, 525-3300

gold. On a much more serious note is the recently constructed **Holocaust Museum,** which re-creates the tragedy of Hitler's concentration camps through movies, photos, and videotaped testimonies.

Lone stars outside the district include the appropriately named **Diverseworks,** which covers alternative art, performance, and publications; the **Menil Collection,** which highlights such eclectic contemporary artists as Cy Twombly; and **Kuumba House,** a gallery space and multicultural arts center.

Houston has a buffalo's share of eccentric collections and folk art. Those wanting a hands-on view might do well to get involved with the **Orange Show.** In addition to encouraging the creative process through various community events, the affiliated foundation maintains a bright orange, whirligig-laden house that celebrates one man's quest for the perfect juicer, among other things. You can further quench your thirst for the unusual by drinking in the self-descriptive **Beer Can House;** visiting **Pigdom,** a purple bungalow with a "pigup" truck in the driveway; and touring the **American Funeral Service Museum,** operated by the huge Service (as in funeral) Corporation International.

Houston has the distinction of being one of the few U.S. cities with resident professional companies in opera (**Houston Grand Opera**), symphony (**Houston Symphony**), theater (**Alley Theatre**), and ballet (**Houston Ballet**). Located in the center of the theater district, they perform at the **Wortham Theatre Space** (opera and ballet), **Jesse H. Jones Hall for the Performing Arts** (symphony), and the aforementioned **Alley Theatre.** The **Theatre Under the Stars,** a local group, mounts Broadway-style productions.

Outside the district, performance spaces include the **Cynthia Woods Mitchell Pavilion,** an outdoor concert facility, and the **Miller Outdoor Theatre,** which offers free shows in Hermann Park. The **Ensemble Theatre** is the largest African-American troupe in the Southwest, and there's even something for chamber music lovers (**Da Camera Society**), Christians (**A.D. Players**), and mime enthusiasts (**Texas Mime Theatre**).

Lots of architecture and history lurk amid the skyscrapers. Located in the city's original central business district, Market Square offers **Kennedy Bakery,** the oldest commercial building in the city, and the venerable **Rice Hotel,** where JFK spent his last night before going to Dallas. As the city's earliest intact neighborhood, the Sixth Ward has hundreds of original Victorian and Greek Revival–style abodes. **Sam Houston Park** includes Houston's oldest home and the first residence built by a freed slave, among other highlights.

THE SPORTING LIFE

Between the clement weather and hundreds of parks and nature centers, you'd be hard-pressed *not* to find an excuse to go out and exercise. "People here are very much into fitness and good health," comments Ward. "I see the same faces every morning when I run." Participants encompass more than just so-called hardbodies. "They're all shapes, sizes, ages, and levels of fitness."

The major city parks include the Texas-sized (10,532 acres) **Cullen Park; Memorial Park,** a favorite jogging spot of former President Bush; and the aforementioned Hermann and Sam Houston parks. There are numerous county preserves as well. Depending upon the facility, activities range from tennis to fishing to golfing to organized teams.

The **Houston Sport and Social Club** offers baseball, softball, volleyball, and other leagues geared towards young professionals. "It's an easy and fun way to meet people," adds coordinator Candy Clardy. Other associations are dedicated to everything ranging from archery to yoga. The **City of Houston Parks & Recreation Department** can provide specifics.

Texas summer heat can be intense, hence the popularity of spots such as Lake Conroe (adjoining Sam Houston Park), Clear Lake (near the Space Center), and Galveston Island, about 50 miles southeast of Houston. With their casual, relaxed lifestyle, floating restaurants, and convenience store marinas, these places are "like a different world," observes therapist Mary Fitzgerald. Those interested in obtaining licenses and regulatory information on hunting, fishing, and boating can contact the **Texas Parks & Wildlife Department.**

Completed in the mid-1960s, the **Astrodome,** the world's first indoor domed stadium, has been renovated and includes some nifty innovations such as the capability to automatically convert from a baseball field to a football facility (it takes about 8 hours and is extremely boring to watch). Daily tours provide an entertaining and useful introduction to the Houston sports scene.

"Houstonians are sort of on the fence about their teams," admits one resident. "People don't tear out their hair when one decides to leave town." Still, there's enough enthusiasm to support (as of this writing) five professional teams. The Astrodome is home to the **Houston Astros** National League baseball team and numerous rodeos, tractor pulls, and other entertainments. The **Summit** hosts the **Houston Rockets** (basketball), the **Houston Aeros** (hockey), and the **Houston Hot Shots** (soccer).

AFTER-HOURS DIVERSIONS

Houstonians know how to party, as is evidenced by the burgeoning Richmond Avenue district. Bars include **Billy Blue's,** a restaurant that serves up blues 'n' ribs in a uniquely Texas atmosphere of hubcaps and auto parts; the **Blue Planet,** a Top 40 dance club that purports to

Where It's At

Unless otherwise noted, all area codes are 713.

Billy Blue's, 6025 Richmond, 266-9294

Blue Planet, 6367 Richmond, 987-5913

Cinco De Mayo Celebration, Miller Outdoor Theatre, Hermann Park, 520-3290

City Streets, Richmond at Post Oak, 840-8555

Easyriders, 5803 Richmond, 266-5400

Fumducks Too, 5706 Richmond, 784-1212

Hou-Dah Parade, Richmond Ave., 296-6150 or 974-4686

Houston Livestock Show and Rodeo, Astrodome, 791-9000

International Festival, downtown, 654-8808

Juneteenth, Miller Outdoor Theatre, Hermann Park, 667-8000

LaBare, 6447 Richmond, 780-0930

Party on the Plaza, Jones Plaza, 439-5786

Rick's Cafe, 3113 Bering, 785-0444

Water Wall at Transco Tower, 2800 S. Post Oak Blvd.

"rock your world"; and **Fumducks Too,** "the best little sports bar in Texas." **City Streets** offers one-stop club-hopping—the cover price includes country-western, comedy, '70s and '80s hits, and game-room venues. Novelty-seekers of both sexes will find entertainment at **Rick's Cafe** (motto: "Room with a View") as well as **LaBare,** which bills itself as Houston's only ladies' club with "the Hottest Bodies From Around the World." This area's so durn trendy, it even has a full-service Harley-Davidson dealer (**Easyriders**).

Another neighborhood, Shepherd's Plaza, "caters to a younger, more see-and-be-seen crowd," observes Susan Pack. Clubs change almost as quickly as patrons' clothing styles. Parking is difficult and "it's more of a pick-up place." However, suits, skates, and bikers (of both the motor and pedal persuasion) do show up for free concerts of rock, reggae, and blues at 10 p.m. on Thursday nights for the **Party on the Plaza** from March through November.

Along with being Houston's most photographed site, the **Water Wall at Transco Tower** is also a favorite hang-out place, attracting Frisbee players and picnickers as well as office workers looking to take a break.

Festivals are a popular pastime and just about every weekend offers up one or more. They range from the **Hou-Dah Parade,** a spoof of local corporations and Mardi Gras traditions, to the **Houston Livestock Show and Rodeo,** in which farmers and trail riders strut their steers and other lively stock. And that's only in February. April showers Houston with the **International Festival,** a creative, multicultural bouillabaisse, including an "art car" parade; May flowers bring the **Cinco De Mayo Celebration,** held in honor of Mexico's independence. **Juneteenth** commemorates June 19, 1865, the day African-American emancipation became official in Texas. The Italians, Greeks, Asians, and Egyptians hold festivals too, and other jubilees center around jazz, azaleas, art, and hot-air ballooning, to mention a few.

Where It's At

Unless otherwise noted, all area codes are 713.

Annapurna, 5827 Hillcroft, 780-4453

Brownstone, 2736 Virginia, 520-5666

Cavatore Italian Restaurant, 2120 Ella Blvd., 869-5622

Cavender's Boot City, 2505 S. Loop W., 664-8999

CULINARY AND SHOPPING HAUNTS

Young marrieds Michelle Dugan and Doug Shoemaker belong to a dinner club that meets every other week. "Each time, we pick a new restaurant," explains Shoemaker. "We have yet to go back to the same spot twice." Not only does Houston offer something for every palate, but "it has to be good, or it won't last long."

With more than 6,000 eateries and a rating as the 10th best restaurant town in America by *Money* magazine, Houston is a dream come true for those who hate to cook. Another bonus: You can usually get a decent meal for between $10–15 per person.

Few discussions of local victuals take place without mention of the Pappas family, creators of the immensely popular **Pappacito's Cantinas,** a chain (to use the word very loosely) of reasonably priced Tex-Mex cuisine. The dining out dynasty has expanded to fish (**Pappas Seafood House**) and beef (**Pappas Bros. Steak House, Pappas Brisket House**) as well.

You can go from one end of the cow to the other by chowing down on USDA beef and wearing out your dancin' shoes at the **Trail Dust Steak House.** A signature menu item is the Bull Shipper, a 50 oz. porterhouse. The **Texas Longhorn Saloon** promises the "most fun you can have with your boots on" along with a buffet.

Other novelty diners include **Dave and Buster's,** which also features a full menu of electronic, skill, and card games, and brew pubs with excellent fare (the **Houston Brewery, Rock Bottom Brewery**). Seafood houses include the moderately priced **Landry's** and the cheaper **Joe's Crab Shack: An Embarrassment to Any Neighborhood.** Only in Houston can you eat at Joe's and get crabs at the same time.

The areas of Upper Kirby, Montrose, and Westheimer Road are particularly restaurant-intensive; the pricey ($20 and over) **Brownstone** and **Palm** are located in the latter. Downtown offers a selection as well, including the DeVille at the **Four Seasons Hotel.** The **DeVille Trolley** will ferry you to the nearby theatre district at no extra cost.

Houstonians are rightfully proud of their ethnic foodstuffs. Along with the usual French (**La Tour d'Argent**), Italian (**Cavatore Italian Restaurant**), and Tex-Mex (**Molina's, Ninfa's**), there's Irish (**McGonigel's Mucky Duck**) and Lebanese (**Sammy's**). The entire Asian spectrum is well-represented: Chinese (**Fung's Kitchen**); Indian (**Annapurna**), Japanese (**Tokyo Garden**), Thai (the **Golden Room**), and Vietnamese (**Kim Son Restaurant**). The **Family Cafe** and **This Is It** dish up soul food.

If shopping were an Olympic sport, Houston would be a great place to go for the gold. Offerings vary from the high-end Neiman-Marcus, Gucci, Tiffany, and dozens of other stores at the **Galleria** to a half-dozen or so major-league flea markets (**Houston Flea Market, Traders Village-Houston**) and include all gradations in between. The more than 20 regional malls include the **Pavilion at Post Oak,** a la-ti-da first cousin to the Galleria, which offers Saks, Ungaro, Hermès, David Webb Jewelers, and others; **Greenspoint Mall,** with the more real-world Foley's, Sears, and Dillard's; and the **Park Shops,** a downtown warren of 75 stores with everything from Texas art and souvenirs to clothing enterprises.

Where It's At

(continued)

Conroe Outlet Center, 1111 League Line Rd., Conroe, 409/856-0214

Dave and Buster's, 6010 Richmond Ave., 952-2233

DeVille Trolley, 652-6250

Don's Western Wear, several locations

Factory Stores of America, 1101 Delray Rd., La Marque, 800/SHOP-USA

Family Cafe, 2712 Blodgett, 520-8444

Four Seasons Hotel, 1300 Lamar St., 650-1300

Fung's Kitchen, 7320 Southwest Frwy., 779-2288

Galleria, 5075 Westheimer, 621-1907

Golden Room, 1209 Montrose, 524-9614

Greenspoint Mall, I-45 North at the Sam Houston Tollway, 875-MALL

Houston Brewery, 6224 Richmond Ave., 953-0101

Houston Flea Market, 6116 Southwest Frwy., 781-2912

Joe's Crab Shack: An Embarrassment to Any Neighborhood, several locations

Kim Son Restaurant, 2001 Jefferson, 222-2461

La Tour d'Argent, 2011 Ella Blvd., 864-9864

Landry's, several locations

McGonigel's Mucky Duck, 2425 Norfolk, 528-5999

Molina's, several locations

Montrose, bounded by Main, Sunset, Shepherd, and West Gray Streets

Ninfa's, several locations

Palm, 6100 Westheimer, 977-2544

Pappacito's Cantinas, several locations

Pappas Brisket House, several locations

Pappas Bros. Steak House, 5839 Westheimer, 780-7352

Pappas Seafood House, several locations

Park Shops, 1200 McKinney, 759-1442

Pavilion at Post Oak, 1800 Post Oak Blvd., 622-7979

Rice Village, just west of Rice University, 526-4799

Rick's Ranchwear, 5085 Westheimer, 623-8222

Where It's At

(continued)

River Oaks, Shepherd at W. Gray,
866-6923

Rock Bottom Brewery, 6111 Richmond
Ave., 974-BREW

Sammy's, 5825 Richmond, 780-0065

Texas Longhorn Saloon, 800 Northwest
Mall, 956-8097

This Is It, 207 Gray, 659-1608

Tokyo Garden, 4701 Westheimer,
622-7886

Traders Village-Houston, 7979
N. Eldridge Pkwy., 890-5500

Trail Dust Steak House, 6100 Richmond
Ave., 266-0656

Upper Kirby, between Southwest Frwy.
and San Felipe, 524-8000

VF Factory Mall, 440 U.S. 59 Loop S.,
Livingston, 409/327-7881

Where It's At

 **Unless otherwise noted,
all area codes are 713.**

Antioch Baptist Church, 5902 Beall
St., 692-5333

Brentwood Baptist Church,
13033 Landmark St., 729-5933

First Baptist Church, 10701 Wiggins
St., 672-2802

Houston Metropolitan Ministries,
3217 Montrose, 520-4603

Second Baptist Church, 10501
Muscatine St., 674-8463

Each area has a particular cachet. The formerly oyster-shell–lined streets of **Rice Village** have more than 325 stores including five-and-dimes, bead shops, and fashionable boutiques. **Upper Kirby** boasts Gallery Row, which showcases Houston artists as well as more famous names. The 23,000-square-foot Antique Pavilion serves up a full spectrum of collectibles under one roof. The Art Deco–inspired **River Oaks** vaunts the yuppified Events (kitchen accessories, gifts), Wilderness Equipment (outdoor supplies at non-Army surplus prices), and the upscale casual Cotton Club, among other stores. Artsy **Montrose** has such interest-provoking emporiums as Texas Junk, Dream Merchant, and Wear It Again, Sam. And these are just the basics.

An essential part of the Houston shopping experience is cowpoke gear. You can saddle up at **Cavender's Boot City, Rick's Ranchwear,** and **Don's Western Wear.** Those willing to mosey a little bit farther will find happy (bargain) hunting at **Conroe Outlet Center,** the **Factory Stores of America,** the **VF Factory Mall,** and others. The quaint burgs of Galveston, Old Town Spring, and Humble offer hand-crafted art, antiques, and eclectic gifts.

 ### ETHNIC AND RELIGIOUS PROSPECTS

Houstonians are so politically enlightened they even refer to whites as "Anglos." "Although there are a few so-called white, black, and Hispanic areas, many neighborhoods are racially mixed," remarks Zuniga.

Workplaces are integrated as well, with more than 90 languages spoken. "There used to be a time when construction workers would make ethnic jokes," states designer Frank Berntsen. "Now the subject never even comes up."

Houston also has a reputation for not asking too many questions of its so-called aliens (those from outer space might be shuttled rather quickly to NASA, however). "There seems to be a willingness to work with immigration, rather than fight it," observes professor Klineberg. "This bodes well for us because we've become a prominent trade gateway to Latin America." The term "Hispanic" can refer to origin in Mexico, Guatemala, El Salvador, Puerto Rico, and other countries.

Zuniga is proud of the fact that she has an Anglo stepfather, African-American sister-in-law, and Korean uncle in her Hispanic-based family. "Interracial dating and marriage are a growing trend. With so many different kinds of people in close contact, it's inevitable."

Still, African-Americans, Latinos, Asians, and Native Americans have their own chambers of commerce, and many Houstonians consider church a great way to meet people. The largest evangelical "meet markets" in town include the **First** and **Second Baptist Churches,** the **Antioch Baptist Church,** and **Brentwood Baptist Church.**

And that's only one denomination: The phone book lists 17 pages of other Protestant and Catholic churches, synagogues, mosques, and temples. Houston also has strong Jewish, Buddhist, and Hindu communities (contact **Houston Metropolitan Ministries**).

CRIB SHEET

Why make a hasty real estate decision when there's so much to choose from? Should your dream house or condo be snapped up by another buyer, there will likely be another one on the market tomorrow. An important factor to consider, however, would be the distance and route of your daily commute. Locals compare rush-hour to riding a bronco (the bucking kind, not the sport-utility vehicle).

Those who prefer city living will find great variety in the zone within Highway 610 known as the "Inner Loop." "This area has become a magnet for young professionals, especially over the last few years," points out communications manager and resident Danni Sabota. "We've become urban pioneers, fighting to preserve and maintain the city's oldest neighborhoods."

Offerings range from the Victorian-era fixer-uppers of the Heights (average price: $72,000; more if the home's been renovated) to the charming yet pricey ($125,000–350,000) bungalows of verdant Montrose. Specialties abound: River Oaks ($400,000 and up) for the elite; South Main (various prices) near the Texas Medical Center for students and health care professionals; Harrisburg-Navigation (various prices), a historic Hispanic locale; and MacGregor-Riverside (various prices), primarily African-American professionals. Bellaire (average price: $132,000) provides everything from 1950s-style ranches to new Georgian mansions, while West University ($244,000) offers much-in-demand estates.

> **What Houston lacks in architectural homeyness, it makes up for in friendliness. If you could crossbreed the intellectual liveliness of Manhattan with the hi-ya'll amiability of Nashville, you might come up with something very much like Houston.**

Outlying areas are loosely divided into the North, Northeast, East, Southeast, South, Southwest, West, and Northwest. Once you leave the city, "there really are no 'hot spots,'" observes Zuniga. "It's all a matter of personal preference." Highlights include the Woodlands (North, average price: $105,000), a uniquely Houston mix of forest habitat and research complex that accommodates a variety of multi-dwelling and housing budgets; Conroe (North, various prices), which has the double bonus of large plots and its namesake lake; and Humble (Northeast, various prices), which better describes the purchase costs than the homes themselves. What it lacks in apartments and condos, Deer Park (Southeast, $71,000) makes up in schools and affordability.

Bustling Clear Lake City (South, $116,000) not only has the NASA/Johnson Space Center but the third-largest boating hub in the U.S. (Rentals are in high demand, however.) Only an hour's ride from Houston and full of quaint Western charm, Galveston (South, various prices) is also popular. The best deal around may be Richmond/Rosenberg/Missouri City (West, $40,000–80,000), small-town living against the backdrop of a historical ranching community.

With the Galleria and loads of fine restaurants, chi-chi "uptown" (Tanglewood/Broadoaks, West, $70,000 and up) is particularly attractive to young marrieds and single professionals. And other 'burbs—Kingswood (Northeast), Pasadena (Southeast), Alief/Sharpstown (Southwest), Bearcreek/The Champions (Northwest)—offer the full range, from apartments to starter homes to planned country-club communities.

Compared to real estate, schools are as simple as A-B-C. The Houston Independent School District (892-6300) has a student-to-teacher ratio of 18:1, multilingual programs, vocational and enrichment classes, and magnet (specialized) schools. More than 300 private and religious institutions cater to parochial tastes (Northwest Academy, 688-0391; St. Anne Catholic School, 526-3279). Many suburbs also have highly rated public systems. Houston's 26 establishments of higher learning include Rice University, Texas A&M, the University of Houston, several community and junior colleges, and medical and science schools such as Baylor College of Medicine and the Albert B. Alkek Institute of Biosciences.

NAVIGATING HOUSTON

Okay, so Houston's the only large city that has experienced a decline in traffic congestion since 1984 (things must have been *really* bad). And engineers have improved roads and are linking over 100 miles of transitways/High Occupation Vehicle (HOV) lanes for carpools, making it the largest such system in the country. Even so, all forms of correctness, political and otherwise, are forgotten on the freeways. When you see a single-driver pickup zooming down that HOV lane, get out of the way. (During these times, remember it's still legal to carry weapons in Texas.) Weenies and those with short fuses might want to look into the extensive METRO (739-4000) bus service.

Still, the highways are fairly navigable, once you get used to entrance and exit ramps that seem to drop suddenly into an apparently unbroken line of speeding cars. Corridors are logically laid out and run north to south (I-45), east to west (I-10), southwest to northeast (Hwy. 59), northwest to southeast (Hwy. 290), and so on. But the pet names for certain stretches of road (e.g., I-10 W is the "Katy Freeway") may take a while to master, and perpetual road construction may make you wonder whether you'll ever arrive at your destination.

But other modes of ground transportation are a snap. METRO rides offer express service to most of the city. Cabs are inexpensive and plentiful. And the downtown tunnel system allows for easy access to above-ground businesses during all types of weather.

Houston's two major airports, Houston Intercontinental (230-3100) and William P. Hobby (643-4597), offer 1,800 flights per day. Located on opposite ends of the city, they're less than half an hour from the central business district. Although Intercontinental is the biggest, newly renovated Hobby is favored by businesspeople.

Alternate ways of getting into town are provided by the Port of Houston and the economical and sociologically interesting Greyhound bus (several locations).

A Brief Glance

Size and Growth: 443,878 (city), 1.6 million (MSA).
Percent change, 1980–1990: –0.6% (city), +7.0% (MSA).
Percent change, 1990–1995: –2.9% (city), +9.3% (MSA).

Money Matters: *Unemployment rate—* 4.4%.
Per capita income—$13,799.
Average cost of a home—$115,953.
Average rent for an apartment— $636/month.
ACCRA Cost of Living Index (based on 100)—95.2.
*ACCRA Housing Index—*92.3.

People Profile: *Crime rate* (per 100,000 population)—12,551.4 (city).

*Racial and ethnic characteristics—*White: 66.9% (city), 84.4% (MSA); Black: 29.6% (city), 12.8% (MSA); American Indian/Eskimo/Aleut: 0.5% (city), 0.5% (MSA); Asian/Pacific Islander: 1.1% (city), 1.3% (MSA); Hispanic Origin: 3.9% (city), 2.9%; Other: 1.9% (city), 1.3% (MSA).
*Gender ratio—*90.3 males per 100 females (all ages); 86.6 males per 100 females (18 years old+).
*Age characteristics—*18–24 (9.8%); 25–44 (32.4%). Median age: 32.7.

Major Players: Services, retail/ wholesale trade, government, manufacturing. Major industries are wheat and cattle.

KANSAS CITY:
THE BUCKS STOP HERE

It's got more boulevards than Paris and more fountains than any city but Rome. It's first in inland foreign trade and underground storage space, second in rail center size, and fourth in number of consulting engineers. It's been touted as one of the best cities for running a home-based or small business (*Home Office Computing, Entrepreneur*), along with being the most affordable housing market (National Association of Home Builders) and having one of the world's most attractive commercial centers (*Fortune*). It's bigger than Connecticut (well, almost), has more freeway miles per capita than any major metro area, and is within 1,900 miles of either coast. We're not in Kansas, Dorothy, but Missouri, that Mecca of Middle America, the hayseed capital of the world (or at least the U.S.), a leader in hard winter wheat marketing, wheat flour production, grain elevator storage capacity, and frozen food accumulation and distribution.

But before you dismiss Kansas Citians as a gaggle of golly-gees, consider that it's the home of Hallmark Cards, U.S. Sprint, AMC Theaters, H&R Block, Hoescht Marion Roussel Pharmaceuticals, and many other business giants.

Along with being a jazz, blues, and barbecue mecca, the city spends 1 percent of its budget on a thriving arts community. Plus, it's the birthplace of the shopping center (Country Club Plaza, known as the Plaza to locals) and has a full complement of professional sports (including football, baseball, and ice hockey). KC also boasts a cool combo Art Deco/skyscraper cityscape that's topped off by four massive steel sculptures perched above the newly expanded convention center. A place with the latest in music, art, and fashion and with regularly scheduled jazz and gallery crawls can hardly be considered a backwater.

True, Kansas City gave the world Teflon, Eskimo Pies, the Rival crock pot, Wishbone Salad Dressing, the McDonald's Happy Meal, and that bane to cinema purists everywhere, the multiplex movie. But KC has also spawned the Crown Center, a mixed-use redevelopment project that revived the flagging inner city; the Linda Hall Library, the largest privately owned science and technology collection in the U.S.; such American unforgettables as Walt Disney and Mickey Mouse, who was first drawn here; former president Harry S. ("The buck stops here") Truman; jazz great Charlie Parker; baseball player Satchel Paige; columnist Calvin Trillin—and a list that goes on and on.

That's a lot of stuff from a town whose history seems as flat as the surrounding prairie. Founded in the early 1800s (in what is now trendy, renovated Westport) by trappers and traders who stopped here via the Oregon, California, and Santa Fe Trails, the settlers willingly shared the land with the Osage, Kansa, and Wyandotte tribes—a refreshing change of pace. During the Civil War, the settlement became the focus of some skirmishes, although the Union triumphed. Shortly afterward, because of the railroad, the Hannibal Bridge (which was the first to span the Missouri River), and the subsequent onslaught of riverboats, the area became a sort of Ellis Island for pioneers, who passed through the City Market area before moving on. Some stayed, however, attracted by the diversified economy. During the past few decades, the population has declined in both the Missouri and Kansas urban areas, even though there has been growth (and new businesses) in the suburbs.

Just about anything goes in Kansas City; there's legalized riverboat gambling here, yet it's the headquarters for several religious organizations. There are lots of big enterprises, including a new Harley-Davidson plant, although KC was the first major metro area designated as a clean air city by the Environmental Protection Agency. Getting around is easy: With well-regulated traffic, any destination can be reached within 25 minutes, and interstates blanket practically every part of town. Although Kansas City has four seasons, winters tend to be on the mild side, with plenty of year-round sunshine. Tornadoes usually arrive between April and August, but it's been a while since the area has had a big one. Thank goodness the National Weather Service is located here.

But, hey, this is the show-me state: "People have this misconception that there's nothing going on here," resident Tim Steger told *Swing* magazine. "It's a great place for artists and musicians. It's an unjaded scene, a little less self-important. I came back for the wide-open sky and soothing lifestyle."

Adds local painter Davin Watne in *Swing:* "There's a camaraderie going on all over Kansas City now. You go across town and recognize people...and it's all very friendly." To quote Dorothy, there's no place like home.

General Opportunities

KC's low cost of living has other big metropoli beat: Not only is housing extremely reasonable (with a wide selection) but every other expense, from food to transportation to utilities, consistently ranks below the national average. Because dollars go farther, in many cases wages aren't as high. For example, average annual take-home pay for buyers is around $26,000; computer operators, $23,500; programmer analysts, $38,000; customer services representatives, $21,500; and drafters, $25,500. This is an educated population, with the percentage of high school and college graduates higher than the national average. Unemployment has consistently dipped at least one full point below the national rate for the past several years.

This city's central location and time zone, strong communications infrastructure, and excellent air, rail, highway, and river access have made it a transportation hub as well as a manufacturing, warehousing, and distribution center. The region is also home to several research and technology powerhouses, including Midwest Research Institute; Center for Telecomputing Research at University of Missouri-Kansas City (UMKC); and Higuchi Biosciences Center, which provides data to pharmaceutical and biological industries.

Jobs have undergone a steady increase: Growth rate for a recent year was 1.8 percent, or approximately 20,000 new positions. The gross regional product also expanded 2.7 percent in the same time period. Add this to copious office construction, and it's no wonder many small businesses think they've found Valhalla. Plus, organizations like the Kauffman Foundation Center for Entrepreneurial Leadership, the Greater Kansas City Chamber of Commerce, and others provide training and support. Even the Wicked Witch of the West might find gainful employment here.

HOW KANSAS CITY WORKS AND PLAYS

Major Breadwinning

Kansas City's smorgasbord of establishments, employing more than 5,000 workers, includes AT&T; the federal, state, and local governments; Hallmark Cards; Health Midwest; Southwestern Bell; Sprint; the University of Kansas Medical Center; and others. Or you can opt for something smaller (a relative term) at AlliedSignal aerospace, General Motors, J.C. Penney, Trans-World Airlines, Wal-Mart, Boatman's First National Bank, Citicorp Credit Services, Dillard's department store, Shawnee Mission Medical Center, and Payless Cashways.

Although two-thirds of the area workforce is white-collar, not all jobs are citified. Folks with a background in agribusiness management and research might do well at such places as the Kansas City Board of Trade, which deals with wheat and other commodities; Farmland Industries, one of the biggest cooperatives in the U.S.; the Bayer Corporation Agriculture Division; and others.

With 29 and 17 percent of the employment pie, respectively, services and retail trade lead the way in total number of positions. Accounting for 51 percent of the region's employment gain (approximately 10,000 jobs), people can be found in services such as business (around 87,000), medical (79,000), professional (48,000), and nonprofit (34,000), while smaller segments include personal services and repair (28,000), amusement and recreation (10,600), private education (10,100), hotels (10,000), and others. Major growth is expected in the business, medical, professional, and nonprofit sectors, and many new positions are coming from smaller enterprises. KC also leads the country in greeting card publishing, using writers,

artists, and others with graphics and marketing skills. With 50,000 workers, the hospital (as opposed to the overall medical) industry is the region's second-largest employer and includes several nationally recognized institutions like St. Luke's, Children's Mercy, University of Kansas Medical Center, and the Bloch Cancer Foundation.

Although retail trade employs nearly 188,000, its rise isn't quite as dramatic. Still, nearly 5,000 jobs are expected to result from the completion of, and additions to, various shopping developments and stores. Low inflation, strong sales, and high effective buying income will help ensure employment in areas such as marketing, purchasing, and management.

As the largest single employer (with 121,000 people working for local, state, and federal agencies), government comprises a whopping 13 percent of all jobs and includes positions in local public schools as well. The outlook isn't as bright here because federal budget cuts are expected to continue.

> "People have this misconception that there's nothing going on here," reports a local in *Swing* magazine. "It's a great place for artists and musicians. It's an unjaded scene, a little less self-important. I came back for the wide-open sky and soothing lifestyle."

At 11 percent, manufacturing is bucking a national trend by staying fairly steady and using about 114,000 people, some of whom are scientists, engineers, computer specialists, and workers in printing/paper production. The addition of Harley-Davidson and the expansion of AlliedSignal aerospace are expected to add even more jobs.

At 9 percent, those who work in finance, insurance, and real estate (FIRE) are in a buyer's market, with about 2,000 jobs being added yearly to a current total of 95,000. Increased home and commercial building, the growing number of people investing money, and the region's healthy banking industry contribute to this upswing. The other set of initials, TCPU (transportation, communications, and public utilities), stands at 7 percent and is holding steady because of mergers and acquisitions that have consolidated operations. However, the demand for telecommunications and networking products is on the rise and will require the skill of folks qualified in these fields.

The other 7-percenter, wholesale trade, employs slightly fewer people (72,000), although it's coming up as a result of KC's efficiency as a distribution center and its greater buying activity. As previously mentioned, construction (5 percent, 56,500 workers) is in a growth mode and will employ architects, engineers, and others in related fields. "Other" (2 percent) consists of mining and farming.

ARTS AND SCIENCES

Area code 816 has Saks Fifth Avenue entertainment at (almost) K Mart prices. Along with the Kansas City Symphony, the nationally acclaimed Lyric Opera, and the State Ballet of

Missouri, there's a full complement of musical offerings at the Conservatory of Music at the UMKC. Dance is presented by the Kansas City Friends of Alvin Ailey, City in Motion Dance Theater, Westport Ballet Theater, and more. The equity Missouri Repertory Theater performs seven shows a year, while the New Theater Restaurant combines comedy with a buffet. The Crown Center boasts the Coterie, which offers professional performances for youth and families, and the American Heartland Theater, which mounts Broadway plays and musicals, often with a big-name performer.

All the city's a stage with the Folly Theater, a former burlesque emporium renovated and reopened in 1981; the Midland Center for the Performing Arts, a classic rococo 1920s movie palace restored for live productions; the Art Deco Music Hall, which also serves up ballet, opera, and more; and the nation's second largest outdoor amphitheater, the Starlight Theater. Name acts and others can also strut their stuff at the Worlds of Fun Amphitheater and the Sandstone Amphitheater, while Stanford's Comedy House, Comedy Sportz, and Lighten Up Improvisational Company are always good for a few (or more) laughs.

Museums include the Nelson-Adkins Museum of Art, one of the most comprehensive of its kind, with nearly 30,000 items dating from 3,000 B.C., including an outdoor sculpture of four 20-foot shuttlecocks (not a pornographic statement, but the "birdie" used in badminton). The newly opened Jazz Museum honors Charlie Parker, Count Basie, and others. "Save a Connie" is dedicated to the preservation of Lockheed Constellation, Martin 404, and D3 airplanes, complete with stewardess uniforms and other related memorabilia.

In between you'll find the Kansas City Museum, which covers land and space pioneers; the self-explanatory Kemper Museum of Contemporary Art & Design; and the Harry S. Truman Library and Museum in Independence, one of the few Presidential libraries in the United States and an inspiration for underdogs everywhere. African-American history is celebrated at the Black Archives of Mid-America and at the Negro Leagues Baseball Museum. And there are loads of "Westward ho!" collections at the Clay County Historical Museum, Frontier Army Museum, Historic Liberty Jail Center (where Mormon founder Joseph Smith and others were confined), Mahaffie Farmstead and Stagecoach Shop, and many others. The Jesse James Bank Museum and Farm & Museum capture the life and times of that bad boy. The recently expanded Kansas City Zoo showcases over 400 African animals and has captured the first-ever IMAX theater in a zoo, while Worlds of Fun and Oceans of Fun offer rides and attractions, and the latter provides water amusements, although (duh!) there's no ocean.

THE SPORTING LIFE

Professional sports include the NFL Kansas City Chiefs and the major league Kansas City Royals, both of which play at the twin stadiums at the Harry S. Truman Sports Complex. You can go off to see the Wizards (outdoor soccer) at the same complex. The Blades (ice hockey) and the Attack (indoor soccer) can be found not at Oz but at Kemper Arena, whose circular, pillarless design allows for unobstructed views from all seats. KC is also home to the NCAA (with its visit-worthy Hall of Champions) as well as the Fellowship of Christian Athletes, for those who feel the need to pray before a big game.

The crown jewel of the area's parks is Swope Park, one of the nation's largest and home to the Starlight Amphitheater and the zoo, as well as lakes, pools, trails, and golf courses. Many of the region's 24 public bodies of water can be found in the various recreational areas, with Blue Springs and Smithville Lakes offering full-service marinas as well as beaches, boating, and fishing. It's easy to get into the swing of things at nearly 35 public and 22 private (and growing) golf courses. Tennis is also popular—there are over 100 facilities—and KC boasts the Explorers, part of the World Team Tennis League. There's ice skating at Crown Center Terrace, skiing at Snow Creek (on the prairie?), and a combination of horse and greyhound racing (although not at the same time) at Woodlands Race Track.

It's Las Vegas on the Missouri with half a dozen or so riverboat casinos, such as Argosy Riverside, Flamingo Hilton, Harrah's, and Sam's, while the mostly Station(ary) gambling palace (only the casinos are waterbound) includes gaming space, a 200-room hotel, nine restaurants, and a theater. Admission is free, although it's a sure bet you'll leave with either more or (probably) less money than you came with.

AFTER-HOURS DIVERSIONS

Westport is the place for nightlife, although downtown, the Plaza, and City Market can jump as well. Jazz is king (or queen) here, with standbys like Phoenix, Club 427, and Jazz-A Louisiana Kitchen playing to the wee hours of the morning. Clubs like Boulevard, Ivy's, and Elbow Room offer jazz as well. Grand Emporium, Harling's Upstairs, Jardines, the Levee, Papagallo, Starkers, Mardi Gras, Epicurean Lounge, and more trumpet a combination of jazz and blues, while alternative, rock 'n' roll, and whatever can be heard at Blayney's, the Hurricane, and others. Those who can't get enough blues and jazz can attend several festivals, most notably the Kansas City Blues and Jazz Festival.

John's Food & Drink offers triple-decker action in the form of a dance floor, pool tables/darts, and live jazz, while Callahan's, Kelly's, and Quaff provide a pub-like atmosphere and TV sports. Beer aficionados will find handcrafted ales at 75th Street Brewery, Mill Creek, and River Market, while Harry's Bar & Tables has more than 50 varieties of single malt scotches, and all the cigars your lungs can handle. Just don't go for a chest X ray afterward.

A change of pace can be found in area coffee shops, where cappuccino can be combined with music (Broadway Cafe, Westport Coffee House, Cafe Europa, West 39th St. Coffeehouse), computers (Cantina No. 211 C@fe, the Java Daily), or food (Classic Cup Westport, Expressly Annedore's, Latteland, East 51st Coffee House). Festivals provide another break from the routine and range from the classic Heart of American Shakespeare Festival to the American Royal Livestock and Horse Show. There's a Renaissance Festival as well as a number of ethnic and neighborhood gatherings.

CULINARY AND SHOPPING HAUNTS

As home to the American Royal BBQ contest and the Kansas City Barbecue Society, which has 1,400 members from all over the U.S. and abroad, KC is the motherlode for that combination of tomato sauce, brown sugar, and other mystery ingredients. So expect world-class BBQ at Arthur Bryant's, Gates & Sons, K.C. Masterpiece, Rosedale, and Winslow's, among many others. You usually can't go wrong with beef at any restaurant, although the Golden Ox, Hereford House, Plaza III, Stephenson's, Walt Bodine's, and others "steak" their claim on it as their specialty. The area's 3,000 other eateries offer everything from American (EBT, Fedeora, Harry Starker's) to soul food (Madry's Dash of Flavor). You can find contemporary at Grand Street Cafe, Italian at Figilo's, and Japanese at Hibachi and Kabuki, and you can't go too far afield at the 39th St. corridor (between Broadway and Rainbow Boulevard), known locally as Restaurant Row.

Kansas City has 400—count 'em, 400—shopping centers and 14 regional malls, so you could visit one every day of the year and still not see them all. Upscale highlights include the previously mentioned Plaza, a fountain-filled, Spanish-style gem; Crown Center, which houses the Hallmark Visitors Center along with 70 stores and restaurants; and the architecturally stunning Town Center Plaza. There are also standard clusters with loads o' emporiums, such as Oak Park (170 stores), Bannister (130), Metro North (125), Antioch (115), and more. If that's not enough, KC boasts plenty of unique spots, such as the quaint neighborhood of Brookside, a combination produce stand/ethnic bazaar at City Market, and 45th & State Line Antiques, full of guess-whats, as well as more than 20 art galleries throughout the area. And, except for Town Center, we're not even in Kansas yet.

ETHNIC AND RELIGIOUS PROSPECTS

African-Americans were instrumental in the region's development and are honored through festivals, exhibits, and historic sights. But, along with constituting almost a third of the city's population, they have contributed much to its leadership as well, as a visit to the Bruce R. Watkins Cultural Heritage Center will attest. Named after a local political activist, it serves as focal point for cultural and social events. The recently dedicated Buffalo Soldiers Monument salutes African-American soldiers who played a role in the establishment of the West.

The musical and artistic scene is particularly active, with such organizations as the Mutual Musicians Foundation, the Ethnic Art Gallery, and a number of museums and commercial enterprises at 18th and Vine, an area that once extended to 12th Street, where many jazz and blues innovations occurred in the '20s and '30s. The renowned Kansas City Art Institute, UMKC Conservatory of Music, and Jazz Film Archives (the largest collection of its kind) provide training and support to creative folks, regardless of race or color.

Take your pick: Along with numerous houses of worship and denominations, this area has the National Conference of Christians and Jews, the Inter-Tribal Indian Society, the Islamic Center, and the Catholic Chancery Diocese. There's also the Gurdwara Midwest Sikh Association, the Lao-Buddhist Association, the Baha'i Faith Organization, and the Dharma Study Center, while the Church of the Nazarene and Reorganized Church of Jesus Christ of the Latter-Day Saints have their headquarters here. Those searching for religious dialogues might find them at the Christian Jewish Muslim Center, the Kansas City Interfaith Council, and the Worlds Faith Center for Religious Experience. Even Auntie Em might expand her consciousness.

CRIB SHEET

Little house on the prairie it isn't; Kansas City's wide choices range from downtown lofts and renovated apartments on Quality Hill to historic homes and condominiums in the Plaza, Hyde Park, and Westport areas. Those with a bit more dinero can opt for the not-so-humble older abodes near the Nelson-Adkins Museum or the mansions lining Ward Parkway. KC's former garment district and stockyards, which include the hip West Bottoms area, offer inexpensive apartments and lofts as well.

Stable neighborhoods, comfortable older homes, and reasonable prices draw young families to picturesque Brookside and Near Northeast. Linwood's bungalows are in the heart of the historical jazz community, while Hyde Park has become renovation central. Janssen Place, a privately owned cluster, boasts elegant mansions and beautifully manicured grounds. Union Hill offers an eclectic mix of traditional and contemporary dwellings, while homes in Swope Parkway date back to the '20s, and those in the Blue Ridge area date back to the '50s and '60s. Little Blue Valley, one of Blue Ridge's most scenic locales, provides luxurious suburbs, some of which have waterfront views.

Lake Lotawana and Lee's Summit are considered hot properties. The former boasts a beautiful, 600-acre man-made body of water and a short commute from downtown; the latter has a mix of new and established neighborhoods and good schools. Other small-town wonders include Oak Grove, once called Lickskillet (a Civil War thing), and Raytown and Sugar Creek, which have assorted recreational activities and educational opportunities.

Kansas City extends beyond the borders of Jackson County to Clay and Platte Counties, allowing for the advantage of urban life in a suburban setting. Nearby Johnson County in Kansas was chosen one of the best places to live and work in the U.S. by *Fortune* magazine, and is still in major growth mode, although home prices have remained fairly stable. With their wide array of homes, fine schools, and outdoor and shopping amenities, the towns of Overland Park, Olathe, Lenexa, Prairie Village, and Shawnee are popular with families. Located in one of the most exclusive areas in the Midwest, Mission Hill mansions blend in with some of the city's finest golf courses.

> Along with being a jazz, blues, and barbecue mecca, Kansas City has a full complement of professional sports (including football, baseball, and ice hockey). A place with the latest in music, art, and fashion and with regularly scheduled jazz and gallery crawls can hardly be considered a backwater.

With three of the nation's top 25 districts located in the region, public schools seem a safe bet, particularly if you investigate each system beforehand (Johnson and Jackson Counties have some excellent ones). And along with 60 magnet schools, the Kansas City School District serves approximately 40,000 students. About 170 private and parochial institutions include the highly regarded Kansas City Academy, Pembroke High School, and Barstow School among the former, and Queen of the Holy Rosary and St. Paul's Episcopal Day School among the latter.

The selection in higher education consists of 15 colleges and universities, among them UMKC, whose 13 schools and colleges encompass dentistry, pharmacy, computer science, and more; Baker University, which has an evening and weekend Master of Liberal Arts program; and the Midwestern Baptist Theological Seminary, which provides "divine" degrees. A number of community colleges (Johnson County, Kansas City, Kansas) offer general studies and noncredit continuing education curricula.

A Brief Glance

Size and Growth: 3.6 million (city); 14.5 million (MSA). Percent change, 1980–1990: +17.5% (city). Percent change, 1990–95: +0.3% (city).

Money Matters: *Unemployment rate*— 8.6%.
Per capita income—$16,188.
Average cost of a home—$174,600.
Average rent for an apartment— $725/month.
ACCRA Cost of Living Index (based on 100)—117.1.
ACCRA Housing Index—134.6.

People Profile: *Crime rate* (per 100,000 population)—7,840.0 (city), 6,425.1 (MSA).

Racial and ethnic characteristics (MSA)— White: 49.7%; Hispanic: 32.9%; Black: 8.0%; Asian/Pacific Islander: 8.8%; American Indian/Other: 0.6%.
Gender ratio—100.7 males per 100 females (all ages); 99.6 males per 100 females (18 years old +).
Age characteristics—18–24 (12.7%); 25–44 (36.0%) (although they may pretend to be younger). Median age: 30.6.

Major Players: Services, retail/wholesale trade, manufacturing, government.

LOS ANGELES: CITY OF ANGLES

Photo by Los Angeles CVB/Michele & Tom Grimm

It's hard to believe, but this sprawling behemoth of a city was once the Native American village of Yang-na, with a population of 300. Even the few dozen Spaniards who moved here in 1781 and named their outpost El Pueblo de Nuestra Senor la Reina de Los Angeles de Porciuncula (later shortened to L.A.) had no inkling of what lay ahead for the desert basin, surrounded by the San Gabriel Mountain Range and bisected by the Santa Monica Mountains. The Mexicans came next, abdicating their claim to the U.S. in 1847. The rest is a Hollywood success story: the arrival of the railroad in the late 1800s, the creation of a harbor around 1910, and the discovery of oil and increased popularity of movies in the 1920s. By World War II, the area was a hub for aircraft manufacturing and became a primary immigration spot for blacks and aspiring movie stars as well as folks from Mexico, Europe, Latin America, and Asia.

Outsiders often associate L.A. with air pollution, freeway traffic, racial tension, earthquakes, crime, and other cultural disasters, not the least of which include bad movies and trashy TV shows. But the "City of Angels" seems to be on the verge of a comeback: Not only has a Metro Rail system been in effect for the past few years, but its completion in 2001 will link 23 miles of subways with 400 miles of commuter lines. And the MTA buses offer service to just about anywhere, except the streets where the stars live. During the day, the DASH will take you in and around downtown for a measly quarter, although it's always a good idea to have a car in a place where folks seem to enjoy driving long distances.

Smog is half of what it was in the '50s, despite four times the number of autos (one for every two people, the highest ratio in the world) and three times the population. Along with being a leader in environmental technology, the "City of Angels" boasts the most improved air quality of any major metropolis in the world. L.A. also ranks 31st in per capita crime, behind such cities as Albuquerque, Columbus, and Seattle. And it's not nearly as expensive as it's made out to be on "90210": cost of living is less than that of San Francisco, Philly, and San Diego

Culturally, L.A. has made great strides. Along with having the largest Hispanic population in the U.S., the influx of Asians has resulted in two Chinatowns, a Little Tokyo, the nation's biggest Koreatown, and a bevy of other Pacific Rim peoples, adding to the city's ethnic bouillabaisse. And the city's highly educated, skilled African-American workforce keeps it in the top five places for that group to live and work, according to *Black Enterprise* magazine.

Over the past decade, art galleries, museums, and theaters have turned up the volume and quality of offerings, while downtown has been revitalized by a cluster of high-rises known as California Plaza. Add a climate that permits year-round outdoor activities; proximity to the ocean, desert, and mountains; and professional teams like the major league Dodgers, NBA Lakers, and pro hockey Kings (as well as USC/UCLA football action and the Rose Bowl), and it's a sports lover's paradise. Revamped and upgraded beaches allow for all the surfing, bodybuilding, and in-line skating you can handle. Cool, dude.

L.A. is also about enterprise. Although the city experienced a decline in jobs in the early part of the decade, mostly due to defense and aerospace cuts, recent years have seen a recovery to prerecession levels, with more than 186,000 new positions predicted by the millennium. And it's still a leader in business and management services, including advertising, computer programming, law, engineering, tourism, health services, international trade, and motion pictures and television. Plus, this city has more telephone area codes than any place in the known universe. And direct dialing seemed like such a simple concept.

Getting around is pretty easy, once you realize that Los Angeles's 511 miles of freeways can have more than one name. Just act as if you know where you're going and never hesitate, even if it means taking a wrong turn (you can usually get right back on). People are good about giving specific directions; should you have trouble or get in an accident, there's a call box every quarter mile. Also try to avoid the freeways during rush hour, which usually starts around 6 a.m. and after midmorning and afternoon breaks can drag on until 7:30 p.m. or so.

The city is basically laid out in five regions. Downtown offers many ethnic neighborhoods and is home to businesses, shopping, and cultural activities. Hollywood (or Hollyweird, as it's known to the disenchanted) is a real community northwest of downtown, as well as a general expression for the filmmaking community throughout the area. The Valley area is the origin of the mall rat/valley girl concept, with shopping and dining galore in Burbank, along

Ventura Boulevard, and in downtown Glendale; the Valley is also the home of the Rose Bowl in Pasadena. The West Side offers the rich and famous Beverly Hills, Brentwood, and Bel Air, as well as Century City and young, hip Westwood Village, close to UCLA. Beaches range from quiet, almost primitive Malibu; to carnival rides and other family fun at Santa Monica; to Venice and Muscle Beach, where John and Jane Q. Public are the freaks among skaters, gurus, and assorted countercultures; to surfing and fishing off Redondo; to perpetual volleyball and parties at Manhattan and Hermosa.

> **There's much more to workaday Los Angeles than what goes on behind the camera. Heavy industries include business and professional management services, tourism, health services, trade, technology, computer programming, financial services, and agriculture/food production.**

Yeah, L.A. has had its share of earthquakes, riots, mud slides, fires, and bad press. But people keep on coming. To quote Bryce Nelson of *The New York Times,* "If this is hell, why is it so popular?"

General Opportunities

With five major airports and with more than 300 route miles of rail transit, it's no surprise that the value of trade has increased 54 percent since 1990. The ports of Long Beach and L.A. rank number one and two in the nation in terms of container traffic and, like LAX, are undergoing major expansion. The Alameda Corridor project, which will link ports and rails and have truck lanes, is expected to be completed by 2001, providing a boost to communities along the route. Major exports include integrated circuits, air- and spacecraft, computers, and parts for aircraft and office machines. Imports consist of computers (again), cars and trucks, integrated circuits, and other items.

Although unemployment is higher than the national average and even the Chamber of Commerce recommends that you have a job before moving here (or about six months' worth of savings), certain positions are in demand, such as computer and clerical workers, as well as those with an electrical engineering or technician background.

However, with nearly 35 Fortune 500 companies, including ARCO, Rockwell International, Walt Disney, Occidental Petroleum, Dole Foods, Pacificare Health, Mattel (where else would Barbie come from?), Computer Sciences, Litton Industries, and more, the area is rife with diverse opportunities. It's also a hub for the U.S. aerospace industry, food and plant products, petroleum refining and extraction, research and development facilities, financial institutions, and more.

Salaries are comparable with, or in some cases higher than, those of other large cities. For instance, those involved in computer/data processing services pull in an average of $46,214 in

Orange County ($41,254 in Los Angeles), followed by aerospace/hi-tech ($40,229 in Orange County, $45,447 in L.A.), and engineering/management services ($41,599 in Orange County, $35,848 in L.A.). FIRE (finance, insurance, and real estate) workers average $35,069 in Orange County and $37,558 in L.A. Surprisingly, motion picture/TV production personnel garner a paltry $34,628 in L.A., which surely doesn't take into account the paychecks of folks like Steven Spielberg.

HOW LOS ANGELES WORKS AND PLAYS

Major Breadwinning

Obviously, there's much more to workaday Los Angeles than what goes on behind the camera, although you can have the best of both worlds at the Streisand Center, 22.5 acres in Malibu donated by Barbra and turned into an environmental think tank. The majority (215,000) of the region's 350,000 businesses are located in Los Angeles County. The area's "Big 10" industries consist of business and professional management services (about 600,000 workers); tourism (432,000); health services (420,000); wholesale trade/distribution (351,000); international trade (341,000); technology and computer programming (266,000); financial services (182,000); motion picture/TV production (160,000); apparel (147,000); and agriculture/food production (119,000). Emerging industries include design—not only for clothing but for furnishings and even automobiles—and technology, with concentration on biotech, clean fuels, digital information, and multimedia. Advertising, engineering, architecture, law, and management consulting make up business/professional management services.

Conventions, TV shows like "Baywatch" and "Melrose Place," and the O.J. Simpson trial, along with the increased cultural attractions, have added sizzle to tourism, L.A.'s second-highest employer. Although growth has been rather pell-mell, folks with good networking capabilities can find jobs in marketing, public relations, and related fields.

Health services are offered at such varied places as the Doheny Eye Clinic, the House Ear Institute, and the City of Hope, although jobs (particularly in hospitals) have flattened out because of the growth of HMOs. The developing biotech industry has helped take up the slack, and the manufacturing of drugs and medical instruments is also on the rise. So folks with research, pharmaceutical, or engineering (again) backgrounds should have hale and hearty prospects. Wholesale trade/distribution has also enjoyed reasonable gains, particularly in toys, clothing, and furnishings, while booming international trade will continue to require skills in foreign relations, languages, marketing, and transportation. International trade has a strong impact in several areas, with advertising, consulting, and engineering expertise being used by foreign firms.

Although technology and computer programming went through an identity crisis of sorts because of defense cuts, the industry has bounced back with business equipment, medical devices, computer and data processing services, research, and testing. Companies such as Douglas Aircraft, Rockwell, Lockheed-Martin, and others have relocated or expanded here, and there are about 30,000 programmers in Los Angeles County alone and 1,800 technology firms in the region.

Financial services such as banking, savings and loans, securities firms, and money management are undergoing a transition in mergers and delivery of services, although the industry remains strong. L.A.'s most "famous" enterprise, motion picture/TV production, continues to fast-forward. Although everyone knows about the major studios, start-ups and independents with 50 or fewer employees make up 96 percent of the industry—good news for beginners.

A lesser-known industry is apparel design/manufacturing, which pumps billions of dollars annually into the economy. And it's more than bathing suits and surfing duds; those with design and manufacturing skills can sign on with Bugle Boy, Carole Little, Guess, Rampage, and many others. And many of the fruits and nuts emanating from this area are the result of agriculture/food production, which also is responsible for greens, sprouts, vegetables, and nursery and seed crops, as well as tuna, anchovy, and mackerel captured locally and processed in seven canneries.

ARTS AND SCIENCES

Area code whatever is best tackled in compartmentalized doses—a museum here, a beach there, an amusement park at another time. There's so much to see, do, and buy that even the most difficult to amuse can be entertained for at least several months, provided they don't overdose on activities. And California is supposed to be laid-back.

The cultural scene begins with theaters, with more than 1,100 productions and 21 openings each week. Offerings range from the Schubert Theater to the studios (the "Big Three" networks as well as Fox, Paramount, and Warner Bros.) to smaller, more specialized performances (at the Alex Theater, Cerritos Center for the Performing Arts, and others) to movies at Mann's Chinese Theater, with hand- and footprints of celebs embedded forever (or until the next earthquake) on the sidewalk outside. Music and ballet are in the air at the Hollywood Bowl, the Greek Theater, and the Orange County Performing Arts Center, while the Irvine Meadows Amphitheater offers concerts. The Music Center has three stages, including the Dorothy Chandler Pavilion, home of the Los Angeles Philharmonic and that awards show broadcast worldwide every March. There's even an L.A. Opera that's not of the soap variety.

It's no shock that the place that spawned the Simon Rodia (or Watts) Towers, now considered the largest piece of folk art ever created by one individual, would also have an astonishing collection of publicly created murals on storefronts, buildings, and freeways. Drive-by art includes Whaling Wall Number 31, with life-size depictions of the big critters; the Great Wall of Los Angeles, a 13' by 2,435' illustration of the trials and travails of ethnic Angelinos; the Pig Murals, partying porcines on the side of a packing plant; and nearly 80 more. The 405 freeway constitutes the world's longest drive-through art gallery.

Along with 150 contemporary art galleries, a number exceeded only by New York, Los Angeles allegedly has more major museums per capita than any other city. A logical starting place is Museum Row, with the Los Angeles County Museum of Art (LACMA). Although it looks like a thin slice of something a starlet would put on her plate, LACMA consists of five buildings with more than 100 galleries. Architect Arata Isozaki designed the statement-making Museum of Contemporary Art (MOCA)—you get to figure out what it means—while Nazi-hunter Simon Weisenthal was instrumental in creating the Museum of Tolerance, dedicated to exploring injustices and prejudices worldwide. The Carol & Barry Kaye Museum of Miniature Art has the largest collection of Lilliputian reproductions in the world, while, in typical billionaire style (an oxymoron), there's the best of Greek and Roman antiquities and classical paintings at the J. Paul Getty Museum.

UCLA offers the Armand Hammer Museum of Art, Grunwald Center for the Graphic Arts, Film and Television Archives, and Fowler Museum of Cultural History. The William Grant Still Arts Center, Southwest Museum, and Craft and Folk Art Museum celebrate black, Native American, and multi-cultures, respectively, while no explanation's necessary for the Japanese American National Museum, California Afro-America Museum, and Pacific Asia Museum. Oddly enough, the Skirball Cultural Center, which focuses on the Jewish American experience, has the second largest collection of wimples, head coverings for nuns.

You can get back in the saddle again at the Autry Museum of Western Heritage, which surprisingly isn't about that famous cowpoke singer but celebrates the American West. But there's plenty of cheesy La-La land at the Hollywood Studio Museum, Hollywood Wax Museum, Movieland Wax Museum, Hollywood Entertainment Museum, and Hollywood Walk of Fame, which flaunts more than 2,000 "big name" brass and pink terrazzo stars. With few, if any, glaring omissions, the Museum of Neon Art (MONA) chronicles the history of signage.

The California Museum of Science and History, Los Angeles Zoo, Los Angeles Museum of Natural History, and G.C. Page Museum of La Brea Discoveries do wonders for the natural world, but there's nothing quite like viewing the real thing at the La Brea Tar Pits, the largest-ever find of Pleistocene remains. Griffith Observatory displays those "other" stars, as does Mt. Wilson Observatory, located atop its namesake mountain. At the other end of the spectrum are Disneyland, Universal Studios, and Universal Citywalk.

 ## THE SPORTING LIFE

Some of the cheapest (and most fun) pastimes can be found in the area's parks and 72 miles of beaches, where there's plenty of room for hiking, biking, or just hanging out.

At 4,000 acres, Griffith Park boasts golf courses, equestrian facilities, an amphitheater, tennis, soccer, and more. The Huntington Gardens, DeCanso Gardens, and the Los Angeles State & County Arboretum (a mouthful, which should be shortened to LASACA) provide the best in flora and fauna, while everything's coming up roses at Exposition Park, which has 150 varieties, along with a sports arena, coliseum, and several museums. For a really quiet afternoon, try Forest Lawn Memorial Park in Glendale and Hollywood Hills, the final resting place of Clark Gable, Nat King Cole, Jean Harlow, and other luminaries. This is one place you *won't* want to see a famous face.

Those wanting to get away from hard bodies and suntan lotion can explore Elysian Park— 600 acres in the foothills overlooking the city. Santa Catalina's Island is also a short ferry ride away and, along with snorkeling, scuba diving, and other underwater activities, is actually where buffalo roam (okay, so they were brought over for a 1920s film shoot) together with deer, fox, and other wildlife. At the foot of the Santa Monica mountains, the Will Rodgers State Historic Park hasn't met a visitor it doesn't like. Truly hardy souls can explore the untamed San Gabriel Mountains and the Angeles National Forest. But the wildlife is exactly that and doesn't care what deal you've just signed.

For other kinds of wild life, try L.A.'s 100 or so public golf courses and dozens of private country clubs.

 ## AFTER-HOURS DIVERSIONS

Hip hangouts include the Third Street Promenade, Beverly Boulevard, and, for the younger set, Melrose Avenue with its New Wave (or whatever's of the moment) offerings. Sunset Strip and Sunset Boulevard have a plethora of rock 'n' roll clubs, including a new, celebrity-filled House of Blues, and Billboard Live, a $5.5 million showplace with an outdoor video-tron that allows plebeians to drool over the seeming A-listers within.

Other legendary venues: the Roxy Theater, where Neil Young first appeared in '73; the Whisky, no longer a go-go but alternative; the Viper Room, owned by Johnny Depp, where River Phoenix overdosed; Bar Marmont, presided over by Cassandra, a bald transvestite maitre d'; and the Roxbury, a see-and-be-seen spot where anyone with Reagan-era duds will be laughed off the dance floor. Raves (parties that move from spot to spot) attract a young-20s, pierced crowd, while Old Hollywood can be rediscovered at Musso & Frank and Trader Vic's.

Before embarking upon night life, be aware that the more favored spots are often fronted by beefy bouncers whose job it is to keep out obvious Rogaine users or trendies who forget to wear black. Although there seems to be reverence for items over half a century old (such as great hats and certain types of furniture and dishes), this unfortunately does not apply to people or animals who happen to be up there in dog or cat years.

If you're in it for the music, there's jazz at the Catalina Bar & Grill, Jazz Bakery, Marla's Memory Lane, Baked Potato, and 5th Street Dick's, which is also known for its great jam sessions. Salsa has become pretty hot, particularly at El Floridita, the Mayan, Club Mambo, and La Fonda, while there are plenty of laughs at the Comedy Store, owned by Pauly Shore's mom, Mitzi (don't hold it against her—plenty of great acts have been launched here), the Improv, the Groundlings, and Acme Comedy Theatre.

But not everything revolves around clubs. Friday nights at LACMA are a big draw, as are coffee shops (Highland Grounds; CyberJava, for the ultimate cool—computers and latte), bookstores (Midnight Special, Book Soup), and even bowling (Hollywood Star Lanes). Those who are into cars will have lots to rev up about: Not only are hot rods and more honored at the Peterson Automotive Museum, but "Big Daddy" Roth, Von Dutch, and many other speed racers live here. Plus, there's an annual "Blessing of the Cars" in Glendale, during which a priest anoints and prays for the safety of several hundred vehicles and their owners. Hey, whatever calibrates the clunker!

CULINARY AND SHOPPING HAUNTS

Entire forests have been written about dining and shopping in Los Angeles, including pocket guides on both from the Los Angeles Convention and the Visitors Bureau (see Appendix B). Suffice it to say that the area's nearly 20,000—count 'em, 20,000—restaurants cover every kind of cuisine imaginable and then some, such as Mandarin minestrone at Yujean Kang or "ori-yentl" at Genghis Cohen. You can choose from the very expensive Valentino to the head-swiveling Spago to Dive! (shaped like a submarine). Anything with the name Pinot (Pinot Bistro, Cafe Pinot, and the potentially copyright-infringing Pinot Hollywood) is somewhat more reasonably priced (*somewhat* is the key word).

You can go totally L.A. and visit an eatery owned by the star of your choice: Twin Palms, owned by Kevin Costner; Eclipse, owned by Whoopi Goldberg, Steven Seagal, and others; and Georgia, owned by Eddie Murphy, Denzel Washington, and others. But don't expect them to be in the kitchen cooking or waiting tables. And whatever your preferences, be forewarned: Without plastic or the green stuff, you'll never eat lunch in this town again.

Even though L.A. is the place that made malls famous, it has its share of *anti*-malls, including Rodeo Drive, which invented upscale and is best for catching glimpses of the famous making their purchases; Melrose Avenue, where one end is well-heeled and the other is tattooed, pierced, and sometimes X-rated; Santa Monica, with its several blocks of unique (read: expensive) boutiques; Montana Avenue, which draws its share of "beautiful people"; the aforementioned Third Street Promenade; and many more. Malls can be served al fresco (Century City) or enclosed (Beverly Center, Del Amo Fashion Center). There are also bargains in them thar hills at the Rose Bowl Flea Market, California Jewelry Mart, LA Fashion District, Citadel Factory Stores, The Cooper Building, and more.

 ### ETHNIC AND RELIGIOUS PROSPECTS

In these parts, ethnicity is big business. Along with the Asian areas, lively Mexican and Latino culture (as well as some of the area's most historical buildings) can be found at Olvera Street and in Boyle Heights, while Leimert Park Village in the Crenshaw District offers African-American shops, jazz clubs, and restaurants. Those wanting a more Kosher experience can opt for the Farmer's Market near Fairfax Avenue. The region's strong Jewish community is fronted by many Jewish Community Centers, Family Services, and Federations; and there are several Mormon wards, Catholic archdioceses, and black, Spanish-speaking, and Korean denominations. A few dozen generic "Churches" are listed in the Yellow Pages. If you want to take potluck, call one of them.

Cultural festivals are important as well: The region has nearly 165, like Mariachi Festival U.S.A., the largest of its kind in the world, and the African Marketplace, which draws representatives from 70 countries.

A sense of progressiveness translates into much dinero for women and minorities. With nearly 235,000 businesses totaling almost $30 million in sales, females here come out way ahead of the pack in comparison with those in other cities. Blacks have about 35,000 firms, with $3.75 million (L.A. is tops in terms of sales for African-American enterprises); Asians have 95,000, with $18 million; and last, but certainly not least, Hispanics have a whopping 109,000, making this group number one in the nation with earnings of nearly $8 million. The result is a small-business–driven economy that's becoming increasingly healthy, particularly in depressed areas, where folks are going back to their neighborhoods and starting enterprises as well as filling a community's specific needs.

CRIB SHEET

Like the region itself, L.A.'s real estate market is vast. However, certain trends seem to apply across the board: Housing and rentals in California tend to be higher than the national average, although since the early '90s, prices dropped in Los Angeles County, Orange County, Ventura County, the West Side of L.A., and the Southeast area. Bottom line: You can get a good deal on a home if you research the market. *Community Choice,* a publication available through the Los Angeles Chamber of Commerce (see Appendix B) details every neighborhood in the three counties. It costs around $20 but can help you decide among hundred of alternatives.

"Cutting edgers" often opt for the stylish, albeit pricey West Side, with places in Brentwood ranging from $850 for the cheapest one bedroom to $3,000 for a deluxe two bedroom. Even costlier, Westwood goes from $900 to $4,000, quite a spread for a rental that might not look it. Hancock Park and Pasadena provide a more preppy, conservative pace, while Downey, Long Beach, Orange, and South Pasadena are a bit more Midwestern.

As always, location is everything, particularly in relation to traffic patterns. Folks employed in business and financial services who want to live closer to work often choose downtown L.A. (average rental: $950–1,800), Century City ($800–1,600), or Glendale ($700–1,300). Tourism is centered in north L.A. County ($700–1,300), the San Fernando Valley ($700–1,200), central Orange County ($600–2,200), and south Orange County ($700–1,675). Likewise, all of Orange County ($600–2,200), Long Beach ($750–1,300), Palmdale (N/A), the San Fernando Valley, and El Segundo/South Bay (N/A) are the center for aerospace. Wholesale trade and distribution are found downtown and in West Hollywood ($850–1,500), Vernon (N/A), and Ontario ($495–950).

> Outsiders often associate L.A. with air pollution, traffic, racial tension, earthquakes, crime, and other cultural disasters, including bad movies and trashy TV shows. But the "City of Angels" seems on the verge of a comeback: Smog and crime are down, culture and improved transportation are up.

Along with health services and hospitals scattered throughout the city, Beverly Hills ($1,100–2,300), Duarte (N/A), Riverside ($495–900), and Irvine ($700–1,675) have several concentrations. Creative industries (apparel, motion picture and TV) have their hubs downtown and in Hollywood ($850–1300), West L.A., and Burbank ($850–1,200). And there are always the beaches—Long, Marina del Ray ($1,000–2,400), Redondo ($750–1,800), Torrance ($750–1,100) and others—a sure bet for those who can't make up their minds.

Although the Los Angeles Unified School District is the second largest in the nation, with higher teacher salaries and expenditures per pupil than the national average, rapid and diverse population growth has caused problems. The LEARN program is currently being implemented to provide more individualized instruction and specific programs. However, schools in surrounding areas have higher SAT scores and overall ratings, and private or parochial education is always an option. Even though L.A. hardly has a reputation for being an academic hotbed, it boasts over 150 institutions of higher learning, including 31 community colleges, and 114 private and 12 state universities. Plus, community colleges offer training programs in a variety of skills that are locally in demand, such as computer-assisted design, apparel design, and others.

LOUISVILLE, KENTUCKY

A Brief Glance

Size and Growth: 269,274 (city), 1,007,905 (MSA, also includes parts of Indiana). Percent change, 1980–1990: -9.8% (city), -0.4% (MSA). Percent change, 1990–1995: +1.0% (city), +3.3% (MSA).

Money Matters: *Unemployment rate—* 3.9%.
Per capita income—$11,527.
Average cost of a home—$108,300.
Average rent for an apartment—$505/month.
ACCRA Cost of Living Index (based on 100)—90.5.
*ACCRA Housing Index—*82.6.

People Profile: *Crime rate* (per 100,000 population)—6,430.5 (city), 4,885.2 (MSA).

*Racial and ethnic characteristics—*White: 69.2% (city), 85.9% (MSA); Black: 29.7% (city), 13.1% (MSA); American Indian/Eskimo/Aleut: 0.3% (city), 0.2% (MSA); Asian/Pacific Islander: 0.7% (city), 0.6% (MSA); Hispanic Origin: 0.6% (city), 0.5% (MSA); Other: 0.2% (city), 0.2% (MSA).
*Gender ratio—*86.1 males per 100 females (all ages); 81.1 males per 100 females (18 years old+).
*Age characteristics—*18–24 (9.9%); 25–44 (31.9%). Median age: 33.1.

Major Players: Services, retail/wholesale trade, manufacturing, government.

LOUISVILLE: BATTING A THOUSAND

Looavull, Luhvul, Lewisville, Looaville, or Looeyville—no matter what you call it, Louisville is ideal for those who like big small towns. Not only is it easily navigated in terms of traffic—rush hour is minimal—but its cost of living (low), job outlook (sunny), climate (moderate), and housing (plentiful and cheap) consistently position it in the Top Ten list in the *Places Rated Almanac.* Conveniently located within a day's drive of more than half the population—at the crossroads of I-65 (north-south), I-64 (east-west), and I-71 (north-east), with I-264 and I-265 serving as outer belts—what's-its-name has the lowest combined residential rates for gas, water, electricity, and (eeuw) wastewater, according to a study by Memphis (TN) Light, Gas, and Water. Among America's largest cities, Louisville is also the fourth cheapest place to do business, based on a survey by Regional Financial Associates.

Add these advantages to rising income levels, grade-A schools, a lively and varied arts scene, good restaurants, more parklands per capita than any other U.S. city, excellent health care, and—at 120 feet and 68,000 pounds—the tallest free-standing baseball bat in the world (at the Louisville Slugger Museum), and you've hit a home run. As the domicile of the "greatest two minutes" (in sports, not that), the Kentucky Derby, Louisville is known for breeding thoroughbred, American stable, and Morgan horses, as well as for its whiskey and bourbon production.

> Perhaps Louisville's true drawing power lies in the Ohio River, which meanders around the heart of downtown. The Kentucky side has gently rolling terrain, while Indiana offers rocky bluffs and stunning views of the countryside. The city is pretty, clean, and safe, so just about any old excuse to move there will do.

Plus, the people are so genuinely nice that they rank second in the nation in giving to the arts and have one of the top United Way programs in America. A recent Crusade for Children telethon mobilized more than 10,000 firefighters and volunteers to raise money for the disabled. And the city's pilot Kentucky Harvest incentive, which makes surplus food available for the homeless and needy, resulted in the creation of a national USA Harvest program. There's even a newcomer's club, which provides specialized activities ranging from cultural exchanges to tennis to bridge to gourmet dinners.

Nothing, of course, is perfect: State and local taxes are costlier than in many other places, and the percentage of residents who've completed high school and college is lower than the national average. And, aside from the Derby, spectator sports consist of Redbirds baseball (the minor league affiliate for the St. Louis Cardinals) and the Louisville Riverfrogs East Coast ice hockey league (which is two leagues below the National Hockey League)—although the University of Louisville Cardinals did manage to capture the NCAA championship a couple of times. And when it snows, watch out: People act as if they've forgotten how to drive, and you can be socked in for days without cleared streets, water, or electricity. But that's a small trade-off for a town that prides itself on being well-rounded.

Louisville has always been rather low-key. Established in 1778 by George Rogers Clark, it was used as a base against the British during the Revolutionary War and was named after King Louis XVI of France, who supported the Colonies. Soon the small Ohio River town became a transportation center and, thanks to the invention of the steamboat, by 1850 was the nation's 10th largest city. Kentucky sided with the North during the Civil War, making Louisville a major supply point for the Union Army. Later it served as a gateway to the South during Reconstruction and afterward. Like many mature cities, it relied on manufacturing until the mid-20th century. But it made a fairly easy transition to services, particularly transportation, health care, and distribution (although manufacturing still represents almost a fifth of the area's employment).

Considering that this place has nurtured folks ranging from heavyweight boxing champ Muhammad Ali to the late Colonel Harland Sanders (of KFC fame) to actor Tom Cruise to Louis Brandeis, the first Jewish Supreme Court judge, to kindergarten teachers Patty and Mildred Hill, authors of "Happy Birthday to You"—just about anyone can thrive here. Just be aware that the three main areas of town (east, west, and south) are known as "ends" and not "sides," that J-town (Jeffersontown) is in Kentucky and J-ville (Jeffersonville) is in Indiana, and that *the* is often pronounced *thuh* and only *thee* when referring the "The Greatest," Muhammad Ali.

General Opportunities

During the past few years, this region has added more than 65,000 new jobs and has had $3 billion in payroll growth, along with an amazing $1.5+ billion in business investment. New or expanding companies include Ford Motor, which increased its workforce by 1,700; Providian Corp., which moved into a new $165 million headquarters; and the national distribution operations for Stride Rite shoes, Natural Wonders shops, and Amgen, a biopharmaceutical enterprise. With an international cargo hub at Louisville International Airport, United Parcel Service (UPS) has become the area's largest employer.

Served by five railroads and at the crossroads of three interstates, Louisville also has easy overland access to major cities in the East, Midwest, and South. The fourth busiest cargo transporter in the U.S., the airport recently completed a $600 million expansion project, while the Ohio River allows for inexpensive barge deliveries of oil, coal, and timber.

Thanks to contracts, expansions, and mergers, the health care sector has done much to bolster the economy as well, while an active home building market and a brisk convention business have also added to local coffers. Jobs are much easier to come by, as evidenced by a steady drop in unemployment over the past few years.

> Louisville is ideal for those who like big small towns. Not only is it easily navigated in terms of traffic, but it's also got a great cost of living (low), job outlook (sunny), climate (moderate), and housing (plentiful and cheap).

Economic incentives for service and technology enterprises, as well as a gain in international investments, have added to the upswing. Because Louisville is home to nearly 85 companies from Europe, Asia, Canada, and the United Kingdom, the city was chosen as one of the top ten places for international business by *World Trade* magazine.

But perhaps Louisville's true drawing power lies in the Ohio River, which meanders around the heart of downtown. The Kentucky side has gently rolling terrain, while Indiana offers rocky bluffs and stunning views of the countryside. The city is pretty, clean, and safe, so just about any old excuse to move there will do.

HOW LOUISVILLE WORKS AND PLAYS

Major Breadwinning

Things have been really looking UPS for Louisville these days. With about 14,500 workers, United Parcel Service has about 5,000 more than the next largest employer, GE Appliances (9,500). Ford Motor Company comes in third with 8,600. These are followed by Jewish Hospital/Health Care Services (5,400), Columbia/HCA Healthcare (4,400), and Humana (3,800), as well as such diverse enterprises as LG&E energy (2,600), Kroger grocery stores (2,600), Philip Morris tobacco (2,400), the Catholic Archdiocese of Louisville (2,100), Bank One Kentucky (1,900), and more. With approximately 146,300 positions, services make up the bulk of employment, followed by trade (130,000), manufacturing (91,300), government (68,500), transportation and public utilities (37,200), and construction (30,600), with FIRE (finance, insurance, and real estate, 29,700) nipping at its heels.

The real success story is in health care, where Louisville has become a regional center for hospital and outpatient treatment. Accounting for about 11.5 percent of local salaries, this industry hit pay dirt in the 1960s, when two Louisvillians founded Humana, a for-profit nursing home that developed into a network of nearly 100 hospitals and is now a managed-care health insurance provider. Humana's recent multibillion dollar contracts and acquisitions have not only added more administrative and hospital jobs but also dispense health insurance to nearly a million military personnel. Vencor, which provides acute and long-term services for the elderly, is another fast-growing provider.

Other growth industries consist of telecommunications, including the establishment and expansion of such companies as UniDial long-distance service, Sprint, and VideoLan, which produces, distributes, and sells videoconferencing capabilities; printing and publishing; advertising and public relations; and television, where the first African-American–owned station in Kentucky recently started broadcasting.

Those with financial processing skills might find employment at the relatively new Liberty Payment or at National City or AdminaStar, which just finished building an $11.5 million facility. Banks, such as Bank One, have been strengthened by mergers and acquisitions, while the Louisville-based Providian Corp. recently increased its life insurance, consumer credit, and capital management products over 14 percent. Five of the "big six" national accounting firms have branch offices here, with a total of almost 2,000 CPAs in the metro area. And while the computer industry isn't as large as in other cities, several companies, including AdWare, Micro Computer, and EAS Technologies, have stepped up operations.

Folks with an ax to design or sell might consider Louisville. The Greater Louisville Economic Development Partnership has teamed with UPS to attract new businesses to the area, adding jobs and millions of dollars to the economy. Along with the largest enterprise zone in the U.S., Louisville has more than 30 reasonably priced office parks, including Bluegrass Research, the fifth largest in the world.

ARTS AND SCIENCES

Area code 502's Goliath-sized arts scene boasts the prestigious Actors Theater of Louisville, whose annual Humana Festival of New American Plays has spawned such hits as *Crimes of the Heart, Agnes of God,* and *'Night Mother.* With three stages, this successful regional professional theater has garnered Tonys and has a year-round season. A block away is the Kentucky Center for the Performing Arts, which, along with an impressive collection of 20th-century art, is home to the Louisville Ballet, Louisville Orchestra, Kentucky Opera, Stage One: Children's Theater, and the Broadway Series. Other entertainments: Afterimages Dance Company, the alternative Bunbury Theater, the Chamber Society of Louisville, Louisville Bach Society, and Music Theater Louisville. The restored Palace movie theater draws concerts and other touring acts as well.

Along with a couple dozen art galleries, including the Kentucky Art & Craft Gallery, Hadley Pottery, and Louisville Stoneware, the Greek Revival Water Tower now pumps out displays of contemporary works. The J.B. Speed Museum brings visitors up to its last name with works by Rembrandt, Rubens, Monet, and (Thomas) Moore, er, more. There's history at the Portland Museum, Filson Club, and Sons of the American Revolution museum. "Local yokels" are honored at collections dedicated to Colonel Harland Sanders, Muhammad Ali, and baseball bats, which are still being made at the Louisville Slugger Museum. There's a celebration of movement at the Kentucky Derby Museum (which adjoins the famous Churchill Downs racetrack), the Howard Steamboat Museum, and the Louisville Auto Museum.

The scientifically curious can explore their environment at the Falls of the Ohio Interpretive Center, McAlpine Locks & Dam, the Joseph A. Callaway Archaeological Museum, and the Louisville Science Center/IMAX Theater. With 1,600 animals, the Louisville Zoo boasts the third-largest gaggle of wooly monkeys in the world, along with "The Islands," which highlights endangered habitats and species. Other uniquely Louisvillian establishments: The American Printing House for the Blind, devoted solely to creating products for the visually impaired; the Belle of Louisville, the nation's oldest operating Mississippi-style sternwheel steamboat; and the Spirit of Jefferson, the area's newest riverboat, which provides excursions to Ohio River sites. Another favorite of tourists, the Kentucky Kingdom Thrill Park, offers such intimidatingly monikered rides as the Hellevator, T2 Terror to the Second Power, Chang (the world's longest, fastest, tallest roller coaster), and more.

THE SPORTING LIFE

Designed by Frederick Law Olmsted, planner of New York City's Central Park, Louisville's green spaces provide more than 10,000 acres of golf courses, tennis courts, lakes, ball diamonds, and swimming holes. Otter Creek Park is a popular destination for campers, hikers, and mountain bikers, while the E.P. "Tom" Sawyer State Park has tamer diversions such as a pool, BMX cycling track, and gymnasium. The Ohio River and various lakes serve up a multitude of water sports, including fishing, skiing, and sailing, while machines at Paoli Peaks and Ski Butler grind out artificial snow in the event there's not enough of the real stuff. Indoor ice-skating at Iceland and Alpine Ice Arena, as well as guess-what at the Ohio Valley Volleyball Center, are available year-round.

Golf is particularly appreciated: Louisville was recently chosen as the final, possibly permanent stop on the men's PGA Championship tour. This is a big country club town, with many outstanding facilities, like the Jack Nicklaus–designed courses at Valhalla and the venerable Louisville Country Club, the area's oldest, founded in 1905. Those who'd like to spend their bucks elsewhere can opt for off-track wagering at Churchill Downs Sports Spectrum, the only one of its kind in the state.

AFTER-HOURS DIVERSIONS

Louisville may be smaller but its mighty nightlife consists of blues and jazz at Air Devils Inn, Big Heavy's, East End Club, and Stevie Ray's Blues Bar, among others; and rock 'n' roll at Butchertown Pub, Dutch's Tavern, and Jim Porter's. The Brewery taps into cutting-edge bands who perform at the Thunderdome, which is not for the faint of ear. The Cherokee draws a post-college crowd with alternative bands, while the Phoenix Hill Tavern offers different rooms for different folks who like rock, blues, and disco. Cafe Kilamanjaro serves up reggae and other African and Third World beats, and the Connection is L-ville's take on female impersonators, along with having five (!) bars and a restaurant. Another multivenue spot, O'Malley's Corner, is one-stop club hopping. There's country at Colonial Gardens, Do Drop Inn, Village Pub, and Coyote's, where the required dress is urban cowpoke (hey, this isn't Wyoming).

The Rudyard Kipling was bohemian long before it became cool, and Twice Told Coffee House presents poetry, jazz, and anything else offbeat. You can get just desserts along with Brewed Awakenings at the coffee shop of that name. Those looking for laughs may find them at the Comedy Caravan, which brings in national acts as well as local aspirants, or at Squirrely's Magic Tea Room, which features a wisecracking magician.

 CULINARY AND SHOPPING HAUNTS

Although Louisville is the home of such varied comestibles as rolled oysters (which originated at Mazzoni's) and outrageously fattening but heavenly Derby Pie, it's also the birthplace of KFC and Papa John's Pizza, which had the good *Fortune* to be tagged by that magazine as one of America's fastest-growing companies. And if these aren't the hallmarks of a good restaurant town, consider that more Louisvillians eat out per capita than in any other city in the U.S. The city's 2,500 chow stops run the full gamut from African (Cafe Kilamanjaro) to Vietnamese (Cafe Mimosa, Vietnam Kitchen) to cuisine of the world (Ramsey's) to barbecue (Mark's Feed Store, Mister Thompson's, many others), Chinese (August Moon, Jade Palace, others), Mexican (Alameda, Tumbleweed), Middle Eastern (Grape Leaf, Pita Pantry), seafood (Captain's Corners, The Fishery, New Orleans House, a school of others), steaks (Del Frisco's, Dillon's, Pat's), and many more in between.

Only in L-ville: Cunningham's, open since 1870, and before that reputed to be a bordello; Derby Cafe, burgers and more at guess-where; Hasenour's, where the young (and old) guard go for prime rib; Kaelin's, allegedly the origin of the cheeseburger; John E.'s, carnivore cuisine in a renovated log cabin; and Mo Flav's, home of jerked goat—a dish, not an abused animal. And these are just appetizers for this varied and mostly reasonably priced scene. Those wanting to spend more ($30 and up) for that special event can choose from Asiatique (Pacific Rim), Deitrich's (Continental), Lilly's (American), and Vincenzo's (Italian), to mention a very few.

Louisville shopping is a little like the city itself: a bit eccentric, but in tune with the times. Along with 65 stores at the Galleria, the downtown area offers antiques at Joe Ley's and Nanny Goat Strut, a must-see to find out the meaning of the name alone (this city seems to have a goat fixation). It might be worth fighting over a parking space on car-clogged Bardstown Road to visit Grateful Threads, ear X-stacy, Electric Ladyland, Kente International, and more, while Frankfort Avenue is the place to go for artsy boutiques. Along with the usual merchandising giants like Barnes & Noble, Louisville has lots of curl-up-and-read bookstores such as Hawley-Cooke, Carmichael's, and Great Escape. And, of course, malls, with the biggest and local favorites being Mall St. Matthews (140 stores, including Bacon's and Dillard's) and Oxmoor Center (125, Jacobson's, Lazarus), followed by Green Tree (125, Sears, J.C. Penney), Jefferson (100, Lazarus, Dillard's), and others.

ETHNIC AND RELIGIOUS PROSPECTS

As a border city between the North and South, Louisville served as a gateway for slaves seeking freedom via the Underground Railroad, and was later a major destination for African-Americans looking for work in an urban environment. With the city population now almost a third black, Louisville has produced such outstanding folks as jockey and three-time Kentucky Derby winner Isaac Burns Murphy; Whitney M. Young, former director of the National Urban League; and Georgia Davis Powers, the first black woman to be elected to the Kentucky State Senate.

Louisville's many African-American neighborhoods include the historical Parkland and Russell districts. The community also hosts the Corn Island Storytelling Festival and the West Louisville Appreciation Day. There are several well-established churches, such as Brown Memorial C.M.E. and the Quinn Chapel A.M.E., as well as organizations such as the Chestnut Street Y.M.C.A., an inner-city branch with a strong youth program.

With the Catholic Archdiocese and Jewish Hospital being two of the largest employers, these groups wield an influence as well. However, many houses of worship seem to be of the Baptist, Church of Christ, Methodist, and Episcopal variety.

CRIB SHEET

Life in downtown Louisville will undoubtedly be enhanced by the Waterfront Development Project, whose goal is an $85 million marina and residential area with ponds, bridges, walking paths, and plenty of space for community activities. Currently, however, there are a variety of homes and apartments in such historic neighborhoods as Butchertown, founded in 1834 by German immigrants; the Cherokee Triangle, a Victorian-era village close to downtown; spacious, vital Old Louisville and the Highlands; and the quaint riverside community of Portland. You'll find upscale elegance in Indian Hills and Glenview, Craftsman-era bungalows in Crescent Hill and Beechmont, and scores of newer developments and bargains in southern Indiana. You can live on a farm and still be a short drive from the center of town.

Real estate seems to be defined by geography. Southwest is predominately suburban, with low-to-moderate subdivisions ranging from $50,000–90,000. West includes Shawnee and West Louisville, with the "shotgun" houses in Portland and residences generally hovering around $50,000. Central boasts many restored homes in Old Louisville and Germantown, and two-story residences in Audubon Park. Smaller places can go for under $85,000, while larger renovated houses net $130,000–280,000. New developments near Audubon Park are priced at $135,000–200,000. Suburban south offers a range of older communities, such as Highview, Okolona, and Newberg; houses in these areas vary from $50,000–90,000, while new builds fetch $100,000–200,000.

Those wanting to show the money can do so in the east end's Cherokee Triangle, the Highlands, Hikes Point, and St. Matthews, where some places sell for close to a million. Most older neighborhoods average in the low-to-mid hundred-thousands, while custom builds go for $350,000 and up. Northeast is another pricey area, with few homes under one hundred grand. Neighborhoods like Harrods Creek, Anchorage, Middletown, and Eastwood provide a wide selection of upscale new and older homes, in the $300,000–400,000 range. Jeffersontown and Fern Creek in southeast Louisville fit a more limited pocketbook, with established older subdivisions costing $85,000–100,000 and more recent models fetching $150,000–200,000. Mostly rural Floyds Fork in this section of town is considered the fastest-growing area in the county.

Thanks to the 1990 Kentucky Education Reform Act, public schools now include limited magnet programs, all-day kindergarten, and year-round classes. With an extensive computer training program, strong parental support, and an attendance rate of 94 percent, the city's public schools rank among the top ten public systems in SAT scores. Private schools include a highly rated Catholic system, several new Christian schools, and preparatory institutions like Kentucky Country Day School, Louisville Collegiate School, and Walden School.

The region's four universities and 16 community colleges enroll more than 53,000 students, while targeted job training is available through agencies such as the Bluegrass State Skills Corporation, Henry Vogt Center for Computer-Aided Engineering and Factory Automation, and city and county organizations. Along with offering degrees in medicine, engineering, and law, the University of Louisville provides doctoral degrees in nearly 25 arenas, while the Catholic Bellarmine College has classes in 45 undergraduate fields, including social and business administration, nursing, and education. Technical, vocational, and business courses can be found at Ivy Tech State College, Sullivan College, and others.

MILWAUKEE, WISCONSIN

Milwaukee at a Glance

Birthdate and Present Size: Settled in 1818; town established in 1830s; incorporated as a city in 1846. *Metropolitan Statistical Area*—1980: 1,397,143; 1990: 1,432,149. 1/1/95 (estimate): 1,474,800. Percent change, 1980–1990: +2.5%. Percent change, 1990–1995: +3.0%.

Weather Report: *Average annual temperature*—46° F. In January: 26/11° F. In July: 80/61° F. *Average annual precipitation*—31". *Average annual snowfall*—30".

Money Matters: *Unemployment rate*— 3.0%. *Per capita income*—$21,797 (city); $22,786 (MSA). *Average household income*—N/A. *Average cost of a home*—$152,250. *Average rent for an apartment*— $684/month. *ACCRA cost of living indexes* (based on 100)—Composite Index: 104.2; Utilities Index: 92.0; Housing Index: 117.4. *Sales and use tax*—5.0% (state); 0.5% (local). *Personal income tax*—4.9% to 6.93%.

People Profile: *Crime rate* (Per 100,000 population)—8,149.8 (city); 3,260.4 (suburbs); 5,356.6 (MSA). *Racial and ethnic characteristics*—White: 63.3% (city), 82.7% (MSA); Black: 30.5 (city), 13.8% (MSA); Hispanic Origin: 6.0% (city), 3.4% (MSA); Other: 3.3%

(city), 1.7% (MSA); Asian/Pacific Islander: 1.9% (city), 1.3% (MSA); American Indian/Eskimo/Aleut: 1.0% (city), 0.6% (MSA). *Gender ratio*—89.6 males per 100 females (all ages); 84.8 males per 100 females (18 years old+). *Age characteristics*—18–24 (12.0%); 25–44 (32.6%). Median age: 30.3. *Educational attainment*—percent having completed high school: 71.5%; percent having completed college: 14.8%.

Major Players: Services, manufacturing, retail/wholesale trade, government. An important Great Lakes port, the city is one of the country's leading manufacturers of automobile parts, beer, machinery and (peripherally) cheese. *Largest employers*—Allen-Bradley, Briggs & Stratton Corp., Firstar Corp., Harnischfeger Corp., Johnson Controls, Journal-Sentinel, Miller Brewing, Northwestern Mutual Life Insurance Company.

Community Services: *Average hospital cost*—$383.40/day. *Average doctor visit*—$51.00 *Average dentist visit*—$53.20. *Newspapers*—The Milwaukee Journal-Sentinel, The Business Journal, Catholic Herald, Milwaukee Community Journal (black community), *Milwaukee Star* (black community), *The Wisconsin Light* (gay/lesbian community), *Milwaukee Labor Press, Shepherd Express* (alternative).

MILWAUKEE: RED, WHITE, AND BEER

Before you dismiss residents of Milwaukee as a bunch of cheeseheads—people who parade around in foam rubber hats of Swiss, American, or Gruyere during various public events—consider that it has spawned such diverse personalities as Gregory Peck, Carl Sandburg, Golda Meir, Douglas MacArthur, Liberace, and Gene Wilder. It has been ranked by *Entrepreneur* magazine as a top city for small businesses, has one of the lowest crime rates in the U.S., and has terrific job opportunities for those just starting out. No wonder Milwaukee is becoming a haven for refugees from Chicago and other big ponds. Once considered the beer capital of the world and noted for its brats, fried fish, and frozen custard galore, Milwaukee is now attractive even to those with an affinity for fern bars and sun-dried tomatoes (which are available as well).

Milwaukee (from the Native American "Milliocki," meaning "where the waters meet"), located at the mouth of three rivers, was a popular spot for various tribes, French missionaries, and fur trappers. However, by the 1840s, most of the Indians had been driven from their land (not in Winnebagos, although they were a major tribe), and many of their burial mounds and artifacts were destroyed as the city was built. German immigrants flocked here first, followed later by Poles, Irish, Italians, and Scandinavians, making it one of the most "foreign" metropolises of the 19th century. During and shortly after World War I, African-Americans and Hispanics migrated in search of jobs, creating a "melting pot" atmosphere that continues.

Starting with the turn of the century, demands for labor reforms brought such socialists as Emil Seidel, Daniel W. Hoan, and Frank P. Ziedler to the mayor's office. Although Milwaukee was hit hard by the Depression, World War II souped up the armament and other businesses so much that the population increased 59 percent from 1940–1980. Although factories closed in the late '70s and early '80s, the modernization of the harbor, redevelopment of downtown, and encouragement of a diverse financial base helped stabilize the economy. And if the water supply is ever contaminated again (as it was in 1993), you can always pop open a can of Pabst and visit one of the city's 108 bowling alleys.

Quality of Life

Unless you're a member of the Milwaukee chapter of the Polar Bear Club—anyone can join, just go to Lake Michigan on New Year's Day, take off your clothes and jump right in— "Winters suck and they last forever," one woman states bluntly. "People don't really get out like they do in cold-weather cities such as Minneapolis. They stay inside and keep to themselves." Still, the city has colorful falls and lush, temperate summers. Close by are inland lakes, streams, farms, and forests where skiing, snowmobiling, hiking, hunting, fishing, and boating are available. With a wide range of courses, golf is fore-most with many locals.

Transportation in general is hassle-free. Amtrak has several one-hour runs a day between Milwaukee and Chicago, making it ideal for commutes and short trips. "Sometimes I'll meet people for dinner and come back," observes meeting planner Karen Lynch. "You're close to the advantages of the big city," without the crime, traffic, and dirt. And you can get almost anywhere within about 20 minutes.

Overall, life in Milwaukee is as comfortable as an old shoe, although it certainly looks and smells nicer. Grocery, transportation, and health care costs are average, while miscellaneous goods and services are less expensive than in other cities. Housing can be costlier than in some cities, "but salaries are so reasonable that it's affordable, even for people starting out," states Carrie Leum, a self-employed public relations executive. "You have enough left over for furniture."

With a steinful of bars and a six-pack of professional sporting teams including baseball, basketball, hockey, soccer, and others, Milwaukee's a great place to be a typical American male, especially since women outnumber men by about 15 percent. But it's also a nice spot to meet others. According to advertising executive Kevin Brandt, "People are genuine"—a term often used to describe Milwaukeans, their city, and their beer. "When you see the homeless, you actually have a conversation with them, rather than pretending they don't exist," adds Brandt. "There's not the same level of cynicism as in larger places." Milwaukee also has a lively arts scene and lots of shopping, restaurants, and other attractions, including a multimillion-dollar Riverwalk district. And there's always a festival or twenty, even in the frigid months.

General Opportunities

With an employment rate that's remained 30 percent below the national average since 1987, "This is a great place for people starting out," observes comptroller Steve Casey. "As an MBA just out of college, I'd have never been able to advance so rapidly" had he moved to Chicago or L.A.

The reasons are simple: "Along with a strong manufacturing base, Milwaukee has a lot of major corporations," remarks Brandt. The service sector provides a good portion of jobs, with banking, finance, insurance, and agriculture comprising most of the rest. It seems that no matter what your training, there's usually a position available—and not the "Would you like fries with that?" kind, either.

Attrition is another factor. "Folks who are born and raised here tend to leave as soon as they acquire skills," continues Casey. As an African-American who's lived in Washington D.C. and California, he finds the city socially lacking. "There's not much here that caters to blacks, and unless you're into bars, the dating scene can be tough," although he points out that his white friends have a different perspective. "They think there's lots to do."

The Port of Milwaukee—which provides a direct route to the oceans via the St. Lawrence Seaway—and a strong highway, freight service, and railroad system help ensure the city's continued prosperity.

MAJOR BREADWINNING

"Once you get plugged into the network, that's it," states Lynch. "It doesn't take long for people to start helping you find something." The addition of almost 130,000 jobs over a 10-year period certainly hasn't hurt.

Competence is rewarded as well. "If you're good at what you do, your name will get out," adds Casey. "It's not uncommon to be approached" by a competing company or "to get a promotion six months to a year after you've started."

> With its favorable employment rate and booming industry, Milwaukee is "a great place for people starting out," says a local.

More than 94 percent of the almost 40,000 existing enterprises employ fewer than 50 people. Lower-than-average business taxes, a 60 percent capital gains exclusion, and a Minority Business Office make this area conducive to those starting out as well as to blacks, Hispanics, Asians, and others. Milwaukee has its share of big businesses as well, including Aurora Health Care, Briggs & Stratton combustion engines, G.E. Medical Systems, Ameritech, Harnischfeger construction, Allen-Bradley electronic equipment, St. Joseph Hospital, St. Luke's Medical Center, and others.

Other brand names—Miller Brewing, Northwestern Mutual Life Insurance Company, Firstar banking, Harley Davidson, Universal Foods, and the rather anachronistically named Manpower (Human Resource Power? Multicultural Power?) employment service—also make

their home here. Quad/Graphics and Arandell-Schmidt, two of the nation's largest printers, lead the way in graphic arts and commercial lithographics, while the suburbs have pulled in major producers of home care products (S.C. Johnson and Son), farm implements (JI Case), and underwear (Jockey International).

With one of the highest per capita outputs in the nation, Milwaukee is the major contributor to Wisconsin international trade. Firms export more than $8.7 billion worth of goods and services. Along with handling more than 3 million tons annually, the Port of Milwaukee provides service to almost 350 cities worldwide.

> According to one local, Milwaukeans are genuine—a term often used to describe the people, their city, and their beer.

Milwaukee's manufacturing base is the third highest (22 percent of about 800,000 employees) in the country, producing $19 billion worth of goods a year, and is one of the nation's best pools of factory and machine tool workers. (As home to the venerable American Society for Quality Control, can Milwaukee have anything but?) There's also plenty of room for white-collar skills in management, accounting, personnel, marketing, and support functions. It's not just "beers and gears" anymore; this city makes everything from medical diagnostic equipment to iron and steel forgings to robotics to electronic controls. In fact, about 7 percent of the workforce is involved in creating high-tech products. And it follows that the city that first mechanized the assembly of auto frames would be plugged into factory automation systems, circuit boards, and the previously mentioned robotics.

Since 1983, service jobs have increased a whopping 39 percent; they now are close to a third of the total. Coupled with wholesale and retail trade (22 percent), they help contribute nearly $33 billion to the economy, while construction (4 percent) adds $1.1 billion. And although it's a mere 7 percent of the employment pie, finance has buoyed up local stability to the tune of $34 billion in assets for banks and savings and loans. Two of the nation's largest financial institutions and a major life insurance company are headquartered here, while 11 mutual fund companies manage another $14.7 billion.

All of this adds up to a potpourri of positions that cover just about every field of endeavor. But if things ever get tough again, no doubt innovative Milwaukeans will come up with a way to save money, as they did in the 1890s when Schuster's Department Store started issuing trading coupons—later spun off by another company as S & H Green Stamps—to be redeemed for cash.

SOCIAL AND RECREATIONAL SCENE

How Milwaukee Plays

Two facts about area code 414: "The people are friendly and you see more obesity than the rest of the country," observes Leum. "Although I think folks are starting to get a wake-up call," given the renewed enthusiasm for sporting activities that don't involve wedging oneself between equally heavy spectators on a narrow bench. (Still, Milwaukee County Stadium claims the world's largest tailgate party, according to *The Guinness Book of World Records*.)

Although Milwaukee isn't exactly the string bikini capital of the world (and that goes for guys, too), there are viable groups of Hispanic, African-American, and white singles, although the pool for the latter is certainly much larger. "It's a matter of self-confidence," remarks Lynch. "If you go out there and proactively seek others, then you'll make contacts."

"You have time to stop and smell the roses," observes Casey. "People are more thoughtful" and therefore more willing to get to know others, rather than rushing from one relationship to the next.

Also, "Chicago is real close and I know lots of guys who go there every weekend," adds Brandt. But there's certainly enough to choose from on the home front as well.

 ## ARTS AND SCIENCES

The **Milwaukee Repertory Theater** dallies in several forms of plays; the **Stackner Cabaret** is a tasty combination of entertainment and food; and touring symphony, opera, ballet, and Broadway companies perform amid plush Victorian elegance at the **Pabst Theater.** The **Milwaukee Ballet, Milwaukee Symphony Orchestra, Florentine Opera** (Milwaukee has two), and more can be found at the **Marcus Center for the Performing Arts,** while the sparkling new **Broadway Theater Center** boasts the **Skylight Opera, Chamber Theatre,** and the cutting-edge, award-winning **Theatre X.** Those wishing to become involved in the local scene or receive more training might want to contact the **Wisconsin Conservatory of Music** or the **Kohler Arts Center.**

Other venues include the **Marcus Amphitheater,** which can entertain 24,000 in one seating, weather permitting, and **First Stage Milwaukee** for children. The **Handsberry-Sands Company** focuses on African-American history and life, as does another troupe, the **Ko-Thi Dance Company.** Not surprisingly, the area serves up an almost baker's dozen of dinner venues, including the **Apple Holler Restaurant Showplace,** the **Fireside Restaurant and Playhouse, Scene of the Crime Productions, Melanec's Wheelhouse,** and others.

A multitude of museums and historic homes include the architecturally compelling **Milwaukee Art Museum,** which holds more than 20,000 paintings, sculptures, drawings, and decorative works. There's more of the same, including Old Masters, at the **Haggerty Museum of Art at Marquette University;** contemporary works at the **University of Wisconsin-Milwaukee (UWM) Art Museum;** and collections/notable residence combos at **Villa Terrace Museum** and the **Allis Art Museum.** Clowns and other youngsters can cavort at the **Betty Brinn Children's Museum** and the **Circus World Museum,** the original

Where It's At

 Unless otherwise noted, all area codes are 414.

Allis Art Museum, 1801 N. Prospect Ave., 278-8295

Apple Holler Restaurant Showplace, 5006 Sylvania Ave., Sturtevant, 800/279-8687

Betty Brinn Children's Museum, 929 W. Wisconsin Ave., 291-0888

Boerner Botanical Gardens, Hales Corners, 5879 S. 92nd St., 425-1130

Broadway Theater Center, 158 N. Broadway, 291-7800

Chamber Theatre, 158 N. Broadway, 276-8842

Circus World Museum, 426 Water St., 356-0800

Discovery World, 712 Wells St., 765-0777

Fireside Restaurant and Playhouse, Hwy. 26 S., Fort Atkinson, 800/477-9505

First Stage Milwaukee, 929 N. Water St., 273-7206

Florentine Opera, 291-5700

Greene Memorial Museum, 3209 N. Maryland Ave., 229-4561

Haggerty Museum of Art at Marquette University, 13th and Clybourn, 288-7290

Handsberry-Sands Company, 820 E. Knapp St., 272-7529

Ko-Thi Dance Company, 342 N. Water, 273-0676

Kohler Arts Center, 608 New York Ave., Sheboygan, 458-6144

Marcus Amphitheater, Summerfest Grounds on the lakefront, 273-FEST

Marcus Center for the Performing Arts, 929 N. Water St., 273-7206

Ringling property which has live shows along with exhibits.

Civic chronicles can be found at the **Milwaukee County Historical Center, Old World Wisconsin,** and the **Wisconsin Black Historical Society/Museum.** The **Wisconsin Ethnic Settlement Trail** has 24 cultural group tours, the most in the country. Other specialized snapshots of the past include the **Pabst Mansion,** a blue ribbon restoration of the former beer baron's crib; the **St. Josaphat Basilica,** one of the few in the U.S.; the **St. Stephen Catholic Church,** the last remnant of the original German settlers; and the **St. Joan of Arc Chapel,** a 15th-century structure brought over from France.

Local prowess is most evident in scientific sites. Ranked number one in exhibits, the esteemed **Milwaukee Public Museum** boasts a Costa Rican rain forest and the world's biggest dinosaur skull, while the recently completed **Discovery World** features interactive science and technology exhibits, an entrepreneurial village, and, in a touch of genius, a "tour" through Einstein's "brain." You can see more than 2,000 real yo-yos at the **Spinning Top Exploratory Museum,** as well as genuine fossils, minerals, and crystals at **Greene Memorial Museum.** Those wanting to ship out—at least in their imaginations—might opt for the **Wisconsin Maritime Museum** or the **Wisconsin Lake Schooner Education Association.**

Natural wonders include The Domes at **Mitchell Park Horticultural Conservatory,** with arch displays of tropical, arid, and seasonal plants; and the **Milwaukee County Zoo,** a perfect-world fantasy in which predators and their quarry appear to live side by side in an indigenous environment (actually, they're separated by hidden moats). Although **Boerner Botanical Gardens** has the largest flowering crabapple collection in America—something most of us could do without anyway—the 40 acres of flora and fauna also include thousands of roses, perennials, and other plants, while the **Wehr Nature Center** is a living laboratory for woodlands and wetlands. Another form of "native" selection takes place at the **Potawatomi Bingo Casino,** with Las Vegas–style slot machines and potentially big payoffs.

THE SPORTING LIFE

With nearly 140 county parks covering over 14,000 acres, 49 miles of Great Lakes coastline, and 240 miles of designated bikeways, "lakefront cycling and in-line skating are

Where It's At

(continued)

Melanec's Wheelhouse, 2178 N. Riverboat Rd., 264-6060

Milwaukee Art Museum, 750 N. Lincoln Memorial Dr., 224-3200

Milwaukee Ballet, 643-7677

Milwaukee County Historical Center, 910 N. Old World St., 273-8288

Milwaukee County Zoo, 10001 Blue Mound Rd., 771-3040

Milwaukee Public Museum, 800 W. Wells St., 278-2700

Milwaukee Repertory Theater, 108 E. Wells St., 224-9490

Milwaukee Symphony Orchestra, 291-6010

Mitchell Park Horticultural Conservatory, 524 S. Layton Rd., 649-9800

Old World Wisconsin, Hwy. 67, Eagle, 594-6300

Pabst Mansion, 2000 W. Wisconsin Ave., 931-0808

Pabst Theater, 144 E. Wells St., 286-3663

Potawatomi Bingo Casino, 1721 W. Canal St., 645-6888

Scene of the Crime Productions, P.O. Box 796, Hales Corners, 800/647-2362

Skylight Opera, 158 N. Broadway, 291-7800

Spinning Top Exploratory Museum, 533 Milwaukee Ave., Burlington, 763-3946

St. Joan of Arc Chapel, 14th and Wisconsin, 288-6873

St. Josaphat Basilica, 2336 S. 6th St., 645-5623

St. Stephen Catholic Church, 5880 S. Howell Ave., 483-2685

Stackner Cabaret, 108 E. Wells St., 224-9490

Theatre X, 158 N. Broadway, 278-0555

University of Wisconsin-Milwaukee Art Museum, 3253 N. Downer Ave., 229-5070

Villa Terrace Museum, 2220 N. Terrace Ave., 271-3656

Wehr Nature Center, 9701 W. College Ave., Franklin, 425-8550

Wisconsin Black Historical Society/Museum, 2620 W. Center St., 372-7677

really catching on," according to Leum. Spectacular nature walks can be found at **Whitnall Park, Riveredge Nature Center,** and the **Schlitz Audubon Center.** And there's certainly no shortage of groups organized around sports activities ranging from **softball** and **baseball** to **soccer** to **swimming** to **tennis.**

Milwaukee offers no excuses for letting exercise slide during cold months. Dozens of health clubs make sure that at least 15 percent of the population stays fit, while indoor facilities encourage Milwaukeans to hone their skills in volleyball (the **Epicenter**), and baseball, softball, and basketball at **Grand Slam USA.** As home of the International and American Bowling Congresses, this city is right up a kegler's alley (**Bowling Proprietors Association**) while the unique, enclosed **Peitit National Ice Center** hosts hockey, speed, and figure skating during all kinds of weather.

Summertime offers golf, at spots such as **Lawsonia** (rated one of America's best public facilities by *Golf Digest*), and two **Silver Springs Country Clubs,** with the West Course hosting the Governor's Cup championship.

Lake Michigan and many picturesque inland bodies of water make fishing, boating, jet skiing, and windsurfing other favorites. Milwaukee's lakeshore has nine beaches; marinas can be found at **McKinley,** the nonprofit **Milwaukee Community Sailing Center,** and others in Sheboygan (**Harbor Centre**), Kenosha (**Southport**), and Racine (**Reefpoint**). Charter boats are available at **Jack's, Wishin' N Fishin',** and other places.

"We are truly blessed that we have so many professional and semi-pro teams to choose from," enthuses Leum. The Major League Milwaukee Brewers at the **Milwaukee County Stadium,** the NBA Milwaukee Bucks at **Bradley Center,** and the NFL **Green Bay Packers,** about an hour and a half away, should satisfy even the most avid fan. The **Milwaukee Wave** (indoor soccer), the **Milwaukee Admirals** (hockey), the **Milwaukee Mustangs** (arena football), and college basketball action at **Marquette** and **University of Wisconsin-Milwaukee** fill holes in any schedule.

Racing's also big, be it of the auto (**Milwaukee Mile, Great Lakes Dragway,** others) or greyhound (**Dairyland Greyhound Park, Geneva Lakes Kennel Club**) kind. And there's the **Wisconsin Center** and the **Milwaukee County Sports Complex** for traveling exhibitions and shows. But for some, it's still not enough. "We need a bigger stadium," asserts Leum.

AFTER-HOURS DIVERSIONS

Particularly during the cold months, "you have to use your imagination" to have an active social life, admits Lynch. "There are lots of social events, fund raisers, and balls for the zoo and other organizations," to complement those of the snow kind. Not to mention a blizzard of activities; January alone has the **Winterfest, International Snow Sculpturing,** and the **Cure for Cabin Fever Antique Show and Sale,** to mention a few, while February and March boast a **Winter Festival** and **PowWow.** Another way to keep warm (at least in terms of raising blood-alcohol levels) would be to visit breweries: **Miller, Pabst,** and **Sprecher** or the **Cedar Creek Winery.**

And there's nightlife year-round. The Water Street area draws a more preppy, upscale crowd. Although it's considered by Milwaukeans to be in a seedy (a relative term) part of town, Walker's Point has become a hot spot for informal types while Brady Street polarizes the eclectic, coffeehouse group. And the developing Riverwalk district is sprouting restaurants, cultural venues, and clubs.

Serious face time can be spent at **Mannequins,** which attracts more than dummies and plastic people; **Brew City Barbeque,** which offers food combined with informal ambiance; and **Buck Bradley's Saloon and Eatery,** which claims to be the state's biggest bar. Perhaps the widest selection of beers and hot libations can be found at **Von Trier,** while you're never too far from a cold one at the **Chancery.** Those desiring the unique will find it at **Taylor's,** a Eurostyle cocktail lounge. Jazz, blues, and a lively atmosphere can be found at **Boobie's Place** (not to be confused with Hooters), **Christopher's,** and **Cibani's.** And Milwaukee's many sports bars include **Luke's, Major Goolsby's,** and the lounges at just about every hotel. Those wishing for actual participation will find volleyball, basketball, pool, and darts at **Sneakers,** while human foibles are the main game at **ComedySportz** and **Dead Alewives.**

Other favorite holes-in-the-wall: **Derry Hegarty's, Kelly's,** and **Village Pub.** Among others, **Isaac's Lounge, Jazz Estate, Junior's Sports Bar,** and **Red Mill** cater primarily to African-Americans.

Festivals and other special events are a major part of Milwaukee life and range from the **Greater Milwaukee Open** pro golf tournament (August) to the **South Shore Water Frolics** (July) to the **Miller Lite Ride for the Arts** for bicyclers (June). The warm months bring locals and tourists to concerts at **Summerfest** (June/July) and **River Jam** (August) to exhibitions of

Where It's At

(continued)

Milwaukee Community Sailing Center, 1450 N. Lincoln Memorial Dr., 277-9094

Milwaukee County Sports Complex, Franklin, 6000 W. Ryan Rd., 421-9733

Milwaukee County Stadium, 210 S. 46th St., 933-1818

Milwaukee Mile, Wisconsin State Fair Park, 8100 W. Greenfield Ave., West Allis, 266-7000

Milwaukee Mustangs, 6310 N. Port Washington Rd., 962-WAVE

Milwaukee Wave, Bradley Center, 243-4625

Peitit National Ice Center, Wisconsin State Fair Park, I-94 and 84th St., 266-0100

Reefpoint, 2 Christopher Columbus Causeway, 633-7171

Riveredge Nature Center, 4458 W. Hawthorne Dr., Saukville, 675-6888

Schlitz Audubon Center, 1111 E. Brown Deer Rd., 352-2880

Silver Springs Country Clubs, N56 W21318 Silver Spring Dr., Menomonee Falls, 252-4666

Soccer, 645-8228

Softball, 645-8228

Southport, 97 57th St., 657-5565

Swimming, Milwaukee County Recreation Department, 645-4095

Tennis, Milwaukee County Parks Information, 257-6100

University of Wisconsin-Milwaukee (ticket office), 229-5886

Whitnall Park, Milwaukee County Parks System, 257-6100

Wisconsin Center, 500 W. Kilbourn Ave., 271-4000

Wishin' N Fishin', 1244 S. 34th St., 835-6570

Where It's At

Unless otherwise noted, all area codes are 414.

African World Festival, Maier Park, 372-4567

Annunciation Church, 461-9400

Asian Moon Festival, 273-5090

Bastille Days, East Town, 271-1416

Boobie's Place, 502 W. Garfield Ave., 263-3399

Brew City Barbeque, 1114 N. Water, St., 278-7033

Buck Bradley's Saloon and Eatery, 1019 Old World Third St., 224-8500

Cedar Creek Winery, Cedarburg, N70 W6340 Bridge Rd., 800/827-8020

Chancery, several locations

Christmas in the Third Ward, downtown, 273-1173

Christmas Parade, Downtown, 272-1166

Christopher's, 1661 N. Water St., 381-4500

Cibani's, 4704 W. North Ave., 444-2001

ComedySportz, 126 N. Jefferson St., 272-8888

Cure for Cabin Fever Antique Show and Sale, Cedarburg Community Center, 800/237-2874

Dead Alewives, 2430 N. Humbolt, 263-3978

Derry Hegarty's, 5328 W. Bluemound Rd., 463-6088

Festival Italiana, 223-2194

Great Circus Extravaganza, downtown, 273-7877

Greater Milwaukee Open, Brown Deer Park, 365-4466

Holiday Folk Fair, Wisconsin Center, 225-6225

Indian Summer, Maier Park, 774-7119

International Snow Sculpturing, Marcus Center for the Performing Arts, 476-5573

Irish Fest, 476-3378

Isaac's Lounge, 4411 N. 27th St., 447-9261

Jazz Estate, 2423 N. Murray, 964-9923

Junior's Sports Bar, 5409 N. Green Bay, 228-0922

jewelry, sculpture, painting, and more at **Lakefront Festival of the Arts** (June) and to multiple parades at the **Great Circus Extravaganza** (July).

Ethnic gatherings include, but are hardly limited to, **African World Festival** (black culture, August), **Holiday Folk Fair** (more than 50 affiliated ethnic groups, November), **Indian Summer** (Native American traditions, September), and **Oktoberfest** (beer, brats, brass, September). In June, Maier Park is also home to the **Asian Moon Festival** and the **Polish Fest;** in July, the **Festival Italiana;** and in August, the **Irish Fest** and the **Mexican Fiesta.** July also sees a gathering of Greeks and others at **Annunciation Church,** and of French at **Bastille Days.** And don't even ask about the holiday season (**Christmas Parade, Christmas in the Third**—not the mental—**Ward,** although after attending every one of these events, one might need a rest in the latter).

CULINARY AND SHOPPING HAUNTS

With potatoes, brats, and high-calorie frozen custard in a multitude of flavors as well as the beer-battered "Friday Fish Fries" popularized by local Catholics, Milwaukee is the place for those in search of the perfect patty melt. And although Wisconsin has big cheese (as opposed to big hair), the former is mostly found in specialty stores like **West Allis Cheese & Sausage Shoppe,** the **Wisconsin Cheese Mart,** and the **Merkt Outlet,** and not on Milwaukee menus. However, the city does squeal about having the so-called Tiffany of sausage makers (**Usinger's**).

"The food in Milwaukee is wonderful, and covers all kinds of cuisines," observes Casey. "Two people can get a nice meal for under $20."

This town's ethnic heritage carries through in its eateries. Spots like the **Pasta Tree, Joe & Mario's,** and **Edwardo's** carry on the pizza/spaghetti and meatball tradition. Italian takes a more classic form at **Bartolotta's,** acclaimed by many as the best new restaurant in the city; also at **Giovanni's** and **Louise's Trattoria.** Places such as **Albaneses Tavern** and **Demarinis** also draw steady crowds.

German restaurants include the **Bavarian Wurst Haus,** undoubtedly the "best" beer 'n' brats to aficionados; the **John Ernst Cafe,** considered one of the city's top 25; **Karl Ratzsch's Old World Restaurant,** another local favorite; and **Mader's,** which also has a "wunder" bar, museum, and collection of armor. Mexican dishes can be found at **Rudy's, La Fuente,** and others, particularly in the South

Side of town. There's Chinese at **Toy's,** Latin American at **Paloma's,** Serbian at **Balkanian New Star** and **Three Brothers,** Thai with the **King and I,** and Vietnamese at **West Bank Cafe,** to mention a few. You can even take English tea (and more) at **Watts** and the **Lobby Lounge** in the Pfister Hotel.

There are also lots of American specialties. Mass quantities of soul and southern food are available at **African Hut, Mr. Kelly's, Mr. Perkins, QF & H Diner,** and **Crawdaddy's Louisiana Cookin',** while spies and others with something to hide might want to visit the **Safe House,** cheap eats in a James Bond-like decor. Diners abound, with places like **Real Chili,** the **Broadway Bar and Grill,** and **George Webb's.** A step up on the food chain, **Rosie's Water Works,** the **Coffee Trader, Pandl's, Wells Street Station,** and **Third Street Pier** offer casual meals.

Steaks are another local forté at **Coerper's 5 O'Clock Club, Butch's,** the **Clock,** and **Steak House 100,** while spots such as **Boulevard Inn, Cafe Knickerbocker, Grenadier's, Sanford,** and **Elsa's** are noted for their flavorful entrees and elegant ambience. "You may pay more but it's worth it," adds Brandt.

The same may also be true for some of the boutiques downtown. "Milwaukee has lots of neat little places tucked away in corners," observes sales manager Joan Ward. These include **Valentina** for women, **Harley's** for men, and **Goldi** for shoes. Downer Avenue on the East Side is a particular magnet for trendy spots. Those with little time to hunt and pick will find 150 stores at the **Grand Avenue** as well as antique galleries and unique shops in **East Town** and the **Historic Third Ward,** a restored warehouse district. **Old World Third Street** and **Westown** offer more emporiums, buildings, and entertainment options.

A fine assortment of malls can be found in the suburbs, including **Mayfair, Northridge, Southridge,** and **Regency Malls.** The smaller **Bay Shore Shopping Center** boasts a classy array, while other clusters are conveniently scattered throughout the surrounding area.

Still, with all the individual and mall outlets, you may never have to pay retail for anything. Milwaukee proper has sheepskin duds at **Ardney** and condiments at the **Spice House,** while around the town footwear and/or clothing can be found at **Allen Edmonds Shoe Bank, Odd Lot Shoes, Land's End, JH Collectibles,** and others. The town of West Bend has the **West Bend Company Outlet Store** for kitchen appliances and, for those with no fear of fat, discount candy

Where It's At

(continued)

Kelly's, several locations

Lakefront Festival of the Arts, Milwaukee Art Museum, 224-3850

Luke's, 1225 N. Water St., 223-3210

Major Goolsby's, 340 W. Kilbourn Ave., 271-3414

Mannequins, 619 N. Water St., 271-6991

Mexican Fiesta, 383-7066

Miller Lite Ride for the Arts, downtown, 276-RIDE

Miller Brewery, 4521 W. State St., 931-BEER

Oktoberfest, Old Heidelberg Park, 462-9147

Pabst Brewery, 915 W. Juneau Ave., 223-3709

Polish Fest, 529-2140

Pow Wow, State Fair Park, 774-7119

Red Mill, 4034 W. Good Hope Rd., 228-6800

River Jam, downtown, 286-5799

Sneakers, 4200 S. 76th St., 321-1898

South Shore Water Frolics, South Shore Park, 224-2753

Sprecher Brewery, 701 W. Glendale Ave., 964-2739

Summerfest, Henry Maier Park, 273-FEST

Taylor's, 795 N. Jefferson, 271-2855

Village Pub, 4488 N. Oakland Ave., 961-9879

Von Trier, 2235 N. Farwell, 272-1775

Winter Festival, Cedarburg, 377-9620

Winterfest, Cathedral Square Park, 273-3378

Where It's At

 Unless otherwise noted, all area codes are 414.

African Hut, 1107 N. Old World Third St., 765-1110

Albaneses Tavern, 701 E. Keefe Ave., 964-7270

Where It's At

(continued)

Allen Edmonds Shoe Bank, 201 E. Seven Hills Rd., Port Washington, 284-7158

Ardney, 200 S. Water St., 271-6260

Balkanian New Star, 901 Milwaukee Ave., 762-6397

Bartolotta's, 7616 State St., 771-7910

Bavarian Wurst Haus, 8310 Appleton Ave., 464-0060

Bay Shore Shopping Center, 5900 N. Port Washington Rd., 963-8780

Boulevard Inn, 925 E. Wells St., 765-1166

Broadway Bar and Grill, 223 N. Broadway, 272-8440

Burke, 5000 70th Ave., Kenosha, 657-5000

Butch's, 555 N. 7th St., 271-8111

Cafe Knickerbocker, 1028 E. Juneau Ave., 272-0011

Chocolate House, 4121 S. 35th St., 281-7803

Clock, 720 N. Plankinton Ave., 272-1278

Coerper's 5 O'Clock Club, 2416 W. State St., 342-3553

Coffee Trader, 2625 N. Downer Ave., 332-9690

Crawdaddy's Louisiana Cookin', 6501 W. Greenfield, 778-2228

Demarinis, 3931 State Hwy. 42, Fish Creek, 868-3316

East Town, 271-1416

Edwardo's, several locations

Elsa's, 833 N. Jefferson St., 765-0615

George Webb's, several locations

Giovanni's, 1683 N. Van Buren St., 291-5600

Goldi, several locations

Grand Avenue, 275 W. Wisconsin, 224-0655

Grenadier's, 747 N. Broadway, 276-0747

Gurnee Mills, I-94 and Rt. 132, 800/YES-SHOP

Half Nuts, 9617 W. Greenfield, West Allis, 476-6887

and other comestibles at **Half Nuts, Burke,** and the **Chocolate House.** Kenosha offers well over 100 stores each at the **Kenosha Factory Outlet Centre** and **Lakeside Marketplace Outlet Center,** while a short drive to Illinois yields the Midwest's largest outlet mall (**Gurnee Mills**). So many deals, so little time.

ETHNIC AND RELIGIOUS PROSPECTS

Although some blacks find Milwaukee limiting, others regard its possibilities as quite good. "Yes, it's easier to meet people if you're white," admits native Joan Ward. "But those who are willing to go out and network will find a fairly large group of single professionals." Resources include the **Urban League,** the **Milwaukee Enterprise Center, Strive Inc.,** and various work-related associations; written information can be found via a multicultural guide published by the **African-American Tourism Coalition.** "In the summer there are lots of ethnic-type festivals, and these bring out people you might not otherwise encounter," she adds.

Milwaukee has a strong Hispanic community as well, and was, in fact, rated one of the best cities for Latinos by *Hispanic* magazine. "There are opportunities and a willingness here that I have seen from the power brokers of the city to embrace and accept us and what we have to offer," lifelong resident Maria Monreal-Cameron told *Hispanic* magazine.

Church is another outlet. "Milwaukee has a strong community with a variety of different religions," observes Steve Casey. Catholics can become connected via the **Archdiocese,** while Jews can contact the **JCC** or **Jewish Reach.** The city also has an **Islamic Hotline** as well as **Familytime Ministries, Presbytery of Milwaukee, United Church of Christ Association,** the **Missouri and Wisconsin Synods of the Lutheran Church,** and dozens of nondenominational houses of worship, to mention a very few. African-Americans can choose from the **Cavalry Baptist Church,** the **Emmanuel Evangelistic Temple,** and the **Brentwood Church of Christ,** among many others. Although according to Casey, "church is not a major thing here," it's nice to know there's a choice when you need one.

CRIB SHEET

With just about everything a few minutes away, "there's much to choose from, although most single people live in

the city," remarks Ward. Favored areas range from the renovated Third Ward to the bustling East Side to neighborhoods around various universities. Reasonable rents also make for an easy selection.

Apartments and condos vary from the high-rises of Juneau Village and Northridge Lakes to the Polish "flats" of the South Side (separate ground floor dwellings in larger family homes on quiet, tree-lined streets) to deluxe models. From the latter category, Landmark on the Lake offers spectacular views of Lake Michigan, East Pointe Commons has both rental and purchase units, and Yankee Hill has location in the much-in-demand East Side. Many residences have a uniquely Milwaukee flavor: "River House" condos provide boat slips for their owners; beer aficionados can brag about residing in a former (although quite lavish) brewery in the Blatz. Rents are higher in the East Side, Bayside, Brookfield, and Fox Point areas, while less expensive places can be found scattered throughout the city and in the communities of Cudahy, Port Washington, West Allis, West Bend, and others.

Still, the lure of cost-effectiveness is hard to resist, and many professionals find themselves purchasing homes. In the city proper, "you can get a two- or three-bedroom starter for between 50 and 80 grand," points out Casey. Multiple choices on the East Side vary from Victorian mini-mansions on Prospect Avenue to bargain basement (read: cheaper) flats on bustling Brady Street.

From there, it's almost a matter of personal preference. The original home of Milwaukee's German population, the North Side is now largely populated by African-Americans, who have built new subdivisions along with renovating stately older homes. Artists and others are drawn to the ethnically mixed Riverwest area, while Thurston Forest offers pre–World War II classics amid lush greenery. Those looking for something newer will find it in the Northwest Side, which has the largest concentration of single-family homes in the city.

Milwaukee's West Side was home to beer barons and other prominent locals, and has Marquette University and several Catholic churches in addition to lots of activities and sporting events. Story Hill, the area's oldest neighborhood, offers brick, stone, and stucco dwellings; other streets have unique homes in picturesque settings.

Due to the natural barrier of the Menomonee Valley, the South Side is considered almost a separate city. It was

Where It's At

(continued)

Harley's, 4009 N. Oakland Ave., 332-3404

Historic Third Ward, 219 N. Milwaukee St., 273-1173

JH Collectibles, 4950 S. 6th St., 747-7447

Joe & Mario's, 601 N. Jackson, 271-8401

John Ernst Cafe, 600 E. Ogden Ave., 273-1878

Karl Ratzsch's Old World Restaurant, 320 E. Mason St., 276-2720

Kenosha Factory Outlet Centre, I-94 and Hwy. 50, 857-7961

King and I, several locations

La Fuente, 625 S. 5th St., 271-8595

Lakeside Marketplace Outlet Center, 12111 120th Ave., 800/969-3767

Land's End, several locations

Lobby Lounge, Pfister Hotel, 424 E. Wisconsin Ave., 273-8222

Louise's Trattoria, 801 N. Jefferson St., 273-4224

Mader's, 1037-41 Old World St., 271-3377

Mayfair, 2500 N. Mayfair Rd., 771-1300

Merkt outlet, 19241 83rd St., Bristol, 857-2316

Mr. Kelly's, 4200 W. Burleigh, 445-9191

Mr. Perkins, 2001 W. Atkinson Ave., 447-6660

Northridge, 7700 W. Brown Deer Rd., 354-1804

Odd Lot Shoes, 8779 N. Port Washington Rd., Fox Point, 352-2563

Old World Third Street, between W. Wells and Juneau

Paloma's, 611 W. National Ave., 649-2570

Pandl's, 8825 N. Lake Dr., Bayside, 352-7300

Pasta Tree, 1503 N. Farwell, 276-8867

QF & H Diner, 3349 Martin Luther King Jr. Dr., 372-2710

Real Chili, several locations

Regency Malls, 5538 Durand Ave., Racine, 554-7979

Where It's At

(continued)

Rosie's Water Works, 1111 N. Water St., 274-7213

Rudy's, 631 S. 5th St., 291-0296

Safe House, 779 N. Front St., 271-2007

Sanford, 1547 N. Jackson St., 276-9608

Southridge, 5300 S. 76th St., 421-1102

Spice House, 1031 N. Old World St., 272-0977, other locations

Steak House 100, 10725 W. Greenfield Ave., 771-2223

Third Street Pier, 1110 N. Old World Third St., 272-0330

Three Brothers, 2414 S. St. Clair St., 481-7530

Toy's, 830 N. Old World Third St., 271-5166

Usinger's, 1030 N. Old World Third St., 276-9100

Valentina, 2625 Downer Ave., 962-1212

Watts, 761 N. Jefferson St., 291-5120

Wells Street Station, 117 E. Wells St., 276-7575

West Allis Cheese & Sausage Shoppe, 6832 W. Becher St., West Allis, 543-4230

West Bank Cafe, 732 E. Burleigh St., 562-5555

West Bend Company Outlet, 400 Washington St., 334-6951

Westown, 276-6696

Wisconsin Cheese Mart, 215 W. Highland, 272-3544

Where It's At

Unless otherwise noted, all area codes are 414.

African-American Tourism Coalition, 510 W. Kilbourn Ave., 800/231-0903

Archdiocese, 3501 S. Lake Dr., 769-3387 or 769-3356

Brentwood Church of Christ, 6425 N. 60th St., 353-6757

Cavalry Baptist Church, 2529 N. Teutonia Ave., 372-4752

originally settled by Polish and Italian immigrants and still has a strong Catholic population and many churches. In recent years, property values have increased 25 percent in this area. A particular hot spot is South Kinnickinnic Avenue, a bustling strip close to the lake, with nearby Walker's Point being a particular favorite. Bonus: the Allen-Bradley Clock tower, the world's largest non-chiming clock (Big Ben in London retains that honor). Its beacon of light used to be known as the "Polish Moon," a concept not expounded upon here in order to retain political correctness.

A little farther (6–20 minutes) from downtown are the golf-oriented communities of Glendale (average price of a home: about $130,000) and Brown Deer ($110,000), with their blend of newer subdivisions and condos. Mucho real estate dinero can be found in the rather ritzy North Shore, whose homes range from $150,000 to well over $500,000 for lakefront estates. The towns of Whitefish Bay ($165,000) and Shorewood ($152,000) offer quaint shops, restaurants, and a variety of residences. More rural areas include Fox Point ($190,000), Bayside ($200,000), and the extremely monied River Hills ($425,000), where the minimum lot requirement is five acres.

A horse of a different collar (blue) can be found in the working-class South Shore, which combines modestly priced homes ($80,000–$100,000+) with clean streets and quiet neighborhoods, while the Southwest 'burbs of Franklin ($127,000), Greendale ($127,000), and Greenfield ($110,000) are noted for their rural flavor and parkland. Lots of year-round activities make the populous West Allis ($85,000) another favorite with those on a budget, while the even-more-of-a-bargain West Milwaukee ($79,000) has been undergoing extensive residential and commercial building. Upscale Wauwatosa ($121,000) boasts the Mayfair Mall, lots of green space, medical facilities, and varied commercial activity. Outlying counties range from up-to-date Racine with its thriving marina to historic, 19th-century Ozaukee to fast-growing yet unspoiled Waukesha and more.

"Although they've gone through some growing pains, city schools have improved in recent years," observes Ward. Milwaukee public schools (475-8393) have a student-teacher ratio of 16:1, with 56 percent of graduates planning to attend college and about 15 percent of students dropping out; figures in other districts are generally even more favorable.

Parochial and private education remain popular choices. The area offers more than 300 Catholic, Lutheran, Jewish, Baptist and other sectarian schools (see previously mentioned listings for churches) as well as the nondenominational and unrelated University School (352-6000) and University Lake School (367-6011), among many others.

Milwaukee's colleges include the previously mentioned UWM and Marquette, which provide quality public and Jesuit-based education, respectively, as well as small private universities like Alverno (382-6160), Cardinal Stritch (351-7504), and more. (Other specialized academies include the Milwaukee School of Engineering, Medical College of Wisconsin, and Milwaukee Institute of Art & Design.) Along with developing the nation's first (and still one of the strongest) vocational education programs, Wisconsin and Milwaukee provide technical training via several institutions (Milwaukee Technical College; Gateway Technical College, Kenosha; others).

NAVIGATING MILWAUKEE

With a well-organized highway system consisting of I-94, I-43, and I-894 (which loops around downtown), Milwaukee has the shortest commuting time in the nation among major metropolitan areas. "Rush hour is just that, one hour," observes Brandt. "It seems ridiculous that radio stations even have traffic reports." A grid layout makes it fairly easy to figure out; should you get lost, you'll likely run into Lake Michigan, a tip-off that you might need to turn around.

Even the snow fails to hamper mobility. "Most people are good drivers in any weather, and the city's prepared, so they're quick about removal," remarks Leum.

And although many have cars—"You can find a parking spot just about anywhere you go," she continues—the Milwaukee County Transit System (344-6711) places nearly 90 percent of area residents within a quarter mile of a bus stop. According to Leum, the city has also considered a monorail network in addition to the existing, highly utilized Amtrak service (271-0840) to Chicago and other places. Bus service out of town is available through Greyhound (606 N. 7th St.) and throughout the state via Badger Bus (276-7490) and Wisconsin Coach Lines (542-8861).

Located just eight miles from the central business district, Mitchell International Airport (747-5300) offers hundreds of daily departures to more than 90 destinations.

Where It's At

(continued)

Emmanuel Evangelistic Temple, 2498 W. Hopkins St., 447-9718

Familytime Ministries, 2130 N. Mayfair Rd., 476-1250

Islamic Hotline, 3611 W. Villard Ave., 525-9910

JCC, Whitefish Bay, 6255 N. Santa Monica Blvd., 964-4444

Jewish Reach, 3510 N. Oakland Ave., 964-2400

Milwaukee Enterprise Center, several locations

Missouri Synod of the Lutheran Church, 8100 W. Capitol Dr., 464-8100

Presbytery of Milwaukee, 1933 W. Wisconsin Ave., 931-7330

Strive Inc., 1737 N. Palmer, 374-3511

United Church of Christ Association, 7635 W. Bluemound Rd., 771-6111

Urban League, 718 N. Memorial Dr., Racine, 637-8532

Wisconsin Synod of the Lutheran Church, 2929 N. Mayfair, 256-3888

Minneapolis/St. Paul at a Glance

Birthdate and Present Size: In 1848, two towns grew simultaneously, forming the metropolitan area known today as the Twin Cities.
Metropolitan Statistical Area—1980: 2,137,133; 1990: 2,464,124. 1/1/95 (estimate): 2,734,200. Percent change, 1980–1990: +15.3%. Percent change, 1990–1995: +11%.

Weather Report: *Average annual temperature*—45° F. In January: 20/2° F. In July: 83/63° F.
Average annual precipitation—26.36".
Average annual snowfall—49.9".

Money Matters: *Unemployment rate*— 2.2%.
Per capita income—$14,830.
Average household income—$33,245 (city); $43,942 (MSA).
Average cost of a home—$120,550 (Minneapolis), $116,533 (St. Paul).
Average rent for an apartment— $598/month (Minneapolis), $620/month (St. Paul).
ACCRA cost of living indexes (based on 100)—Composite Index: 99.7 (Minneapolis), 102.1 (St. Paul); Utilities Index: 104 (Minneapolis), 93.1 (St. Paul); Housing Index: 93.9 (Minneapolis), 92.4 (St. Paul).
Sales and use tax—6.0% (state); 1.0% (local).
Personal income tax—6.0 to 8.5%.

People Profile: *Crime rate* (per 100,000 population)—11,167.0 (city); 5,215.8 (MSA).
Racial and ethnic characteristics—White: 78.5% (city), 92.2% (MSA); Black: 13.0% (city), 3.6% (MSA); American Indian/ Eskimo/Aleut: 3.3% (city), 0.9% (MSA); Asian/Pacific Islander: 4.3% (city), 2.6% (MSA); Hispanic Origin: 2.0% (city), 1.4% (MSA); Other: 0.8% (city), 0.6% (MSA).
Gender ratio—94.1 males per 100 females (all ages); 92.2 males per 100 females (18 years old+).
Age characteristics—18–24 (13.3%); 25–44 (39.2%). Median age: 31.5.
Educational attainment—percent having completed high school: 82.6%; percent having completed college: 30.3%.

Major Players: Services, retail/wholesale trade, manufacturing, government.
In Minneapolis—American Express Financial Corp., Fairview Hospital & Health Care Services, General Mills, Health System Minnesota, Methodist Hospital, Northern State Power Co., North Memorial Medical Center, Norwest Nova (mortgage bankers), Pillsbury Co.
In St. Paul—Blue Cross/Blue Shield Minnesota, 3M (Minnesota Mining and Manufacturing), Minnesota Mutual Life.

Community Services: *Average hospital cost*—$533.20/day (Minneapolis), 676.86/day (St.Paul).
Average doctor visit—$51.40 (Minneapolis), $50.71 (St. Paul).
Average dentist visit—$66 (Minneapolis), $66.17 (St. Paul).
Newspapers—Minneapolis Star Tribune, St. Paul Pioneer Press, Finance & Commerce, Minneapolis Spokesman (black community), Twin Cities Reader (alternative), others.

Photo by Richard Hamilton Smith/Corbis

Although it's the recipient of practically every snowstorm that comes down the pike, it's hard to resist a place that not only has the largest mall in North America but is also the birthplace of Scotch tape™, Cheerios, Thinsulate™, and HMOs (although the latter might prove not to be such a bonus after all). Along with being ranked as one of the three most livable municipalities in the U.S. and among the ten top spots for doing business, Minneapolis/St. Paul makes even travel guru Arthur Frommer jump up and name it as one of his five favorite places in the world to visit. Plus, no one seems to ever, ever want to leave. Wonder who they got to spread all the noise about the weather?

Originally discovered in 1680 by a Franciscan priest, Father Louis Hennepin (who was way off base in looking for a river leading to the Orient), the land was at first named

St. Anthony. Three cities developed. St. Anthony was the initial settlement. The second city, St. Paul, was rescued from being called "Pig's Eye Landing" when Father Lucien Galtier built a chapel dedicated to St. Paul there in 1841, and asked that the city's moniker be changed accordingly. (A good move, since it's the state capitol.) In 1851, the third city, Minneapolis came about when the local Native American tribe signed a treaty turning over 24 million acres of land to Uncle Sam for a whopping 12.5 cents per acre.

> If you want an idea of what it's like to work in this region, check out reruns of "The Mary Tyler Moore Show." Everyone's smiling and a sense of optimism pervades. . .the concept of "Minnesota nice" rules.

Early industry in St. Paul revolved around logging, while the waterfalls at St. Anthony, the largest power site west of Niagara, provided impetus for saw and flour mills. Once bridges and railroads were built, more people migrated "west" 10 miles or so to populate Minneapolis, which absorbed St. Anthony in 1872. By 1876, flour milling began bringing in most of the dough, and a mere four years later the mills had consolidated into what are known today as Pillsbury and General Mills. Minneapolis became known as "Mill City" and the Pillsbury Doughboy became ingrained (so to speak) in our breadsticks, cookies, and rolls. Woo-hoo!

Like any close siblings, the two growing cities fought over rights and privileges. The location of state institutions and population were a cause of much dissent. Ethnic and religious makeup also varied, with Minneapolis being heavily Scandinavian, German, and Lutheran, while St. Paul drew the French, Irish, and Catholics. Each developed a distinct ambience: St. Paul maintained a European, old-world atmosphere with quaint buildings and winding streets, while Minneapolis concentrated on skyscrapers and the latest trends to the detriment of some of its grander structures.

Although only separated by a few miles, "it's said that St. Paul is the last city in the East, while Minneapolis is the first in the West," observes communications manager Laura McCarthy. They diversified economically as well; Minneapolis became an urban hub, while St. Paul was primarily known for its meat-packing and printing facilities.

Underneath the surface, however, today the cities are more alike than different. Monies from public and private partnerships brought about downtown renewal and renovation; improved highways attracted people and businesses to the suburbs; and both are noted for their quality of life, cultural, and employment opportunities. Okay, so Minneapolis is bigger, trendier, and younger, but still everyone's a winner and there's no evil twin in sight.

Quality of Life

To many, Minneapolis/St. Paul is heaven with snowplows. "My first year I tried to avoid the winter, but now I embrace it," admits lawyer Keith Jackson. "There's skiing, outdoor skating, and a Winter Carnival" to help while away the dark season. Excellent snow removal, a plethora of indoor parking garages, and extensive climate-controlled skyways in both downtowns make it so that you don't have to go out in the snow if you don't want to. Getting lost above street level, however, is common among newcomers; friendly natives will help point you in the right direction.

Locals also take pride in their stoic endurance. While conversation may center around movies in L.A. and politics in Washington, D.C., "people here talk about the weather constantly," points out McCarthy. "And when it's nice outside, they take every opportunity to enjoy it."

"There's something here for everyone," adds Jackson. "You can choose from the arts to fishing, all within an hour's drive." Of the state's more than 15,000 lakes, nearly 1,000 are located within the Twin Cities metropolitan area, and Minneapolis has 170 public parks along with dozens of beaches, pools, tennis courts, trails, and ice rinks. With 28 theaters and 180 troupes, this area is second only to New York City in number of per capita theater seats. And although it's not teeming with minorities, "people are very progressive, and if there's racism, it's much less obvious than in many other places," says Jackson. Several thousand Southeast Asians can't be wrong: The area has had a recent influx of the Hmong population, who until they moved to the Twin Cities, wouldn't know frost until it bit them.

In fact, living here is so darned wholesome that life expectancy is higher than in any other state except Hawaii. Minnesota was one of the first states to restrict smoking in public places, recycling rates in the metro area are three times the national average, and the region hasn't had a bad air day (with a Pollutant Standard Index of more than 100) since 1990. Folks here also vote more than most other places in the U.S. There are lots of blondes, but they're not dumb.

So what's not to like about the Twin Cities? "People here can be very reserved," remarks Altmeyer. "It's hard to break through, especially if you're from someplace else."

"The winters last forever," adds Debra Reutter, a teacher. "They usually start around the end of October, and sometimes last until early May. If you're not a cold weather person, it can be miserable." But an active night life, several professional sports teams, and marathon shopping opportunities can melt a lot of ice. Or, just stand on the heated sidewalks in downtown Minneapolis and think about sailing on Lake Calhoun in August.

General Opportunities

With an unemployment rate way below the national average, and per capita income well above it, "you can live here comfortably and save money, too," continues Reutter. Jobs are plentiful and varied: "You'd have to be a real slacker not to find employment," remarks one native.

Despite its Viking undertones, this has traditionally been a land of opportunity. In 1945, then-mayor of Minneapolis Hubert Humphrey instituted an anti-discrimination policy in hiring city employees. Big employers such as Dayton Hudson, IDS Financial Services, 3M, United Healthcare, and others have several high-level female executives, and several local enterprises have been listed in *100 Best Companies to Work For in America*. The Twin Cities ranks second in percentage of women employed and fifth for those in professional and managerial positions.

And between 1980–1990, the number of Native Americans increased 49 percent; African-Americans 79 percent; and Asians 111 percent. Still, "I never felt so ethnic as when I moved here, and I'm only half-Asian," admits sales manager Jennifer Sagawa. "People are tolerant but there's not a real deep understanding of diversity. And it's hard not being among your own, at least some of the time."

However, "There's a genuine acceptance of gay and alternative lifestyles," she goes on. Interracial couples raise few eyebrows, although those with predilection for fair hair and blue eyes may think they've wandered into a Wagnerian fantasy, particularly outside city limits.

MAJOR BREADWINNING

If you want an idea of what it's like to work in this region, check out reruns of "The Mary Tyler Moore Show." Everyone's smiling and a sense of optimism pervades (even those who toss their hats in the air will likely be greeted with nods of understanding). However, "underneath that pleasant exterior lies a nonconfrontational, passive-aggressive reserve," observes community relations specialist Michael Schilling. Hard-charging, outspoken, type-A personalities will likely find themselves thwarted, wondering exactly where they went wrong.

> With an unemployment rate way below the national average, and per capita income well above it, "you can live here comfortably and save money, too," says a local. Residents of the Twins enjoy some of the highest disposable incomes in the U.S.

According to Jackson, "people here are wary," particularly of newcomers. "They can put you in your place in their own quiet way." Still, as one of the fastest-growing job markets in the Midwest, the Twin Cities has attracted both new and expanding manufacturing, printing, electronics, publishing, financial and software development concerns. Health services, medical instrumentation, and advertising are also strong. Construction, communications, transportation, and utilities experienced the highest level of growth; for instance, in 1994, the region added more than 52,000 positions, many in these fields. No wonder office space in downtown Minneapolis decreases every year.

This place practically invented diversity. Only three other cities—New York, Chicago, and Houston—can claim more Fortune 500 companies. 3M, United Healthcare, First Bank, Honeywell, Best Buy, Northwest Airlines, and Dayton Hudson have made the Twin Cities their home. Food and agribusiness enterprises are also big: General Mills, International Multifoods, Cargill bulk commodities, Supervalu, Land O'Lakes, and (woo-hoo!) Pillsbury are all headquartered here, to mention a few. Rollerblade, Toro lawn mowers, Aveda skin products, K-Tel (they of the tacky album covers), Jostens class rings, and Caribou Coffees also emerged here, making it a hotbed for upstart as well as well-established industries. Small businesses will find such incentives as reduced insurance costs to cover all employees. And the Mall of America serves as an excellent incubator for new ideas.

Many service, manufacturing, and retail positions have enjoyed consistent growth, with commensurate salary increases, resulting in one of the highest per capita and disposable incomes in the U.S. The Mall of America alone created nearly 12,000 jobs when it opened in 1992. Service positions, including personal, supply, and health care jobs, generate almost 25 percent of the state's earned revenue and employ one of every four people. Manufacturing is responsible for another 20 percent of salaries and has climbed almost 15 percent in the last five years, despite the fact that the industry has faltered nationally. Those engaged in the production of computers, medical and transportation equipment, and paper products will find a plethora of opportunities.

With 235 medical research centers and the largest concentration of surgical, medical, and dental instrument manufacturers in the nation, health-related jobs are hale and hearty. Along with doctors, nurses, specialists, and support personnel, engineers and those with insurance backgrounds may find plenty of options. Outstanding facilities, such as the University of Minnesota Hospital in the Twin Cities and the Mayo Clinic (which is about 1 hour away), have pioneered such procedures as open-heart surgery, transplants, and state-of-the-art treatment for many ailments. State and local organizations have pioneered pre-paid HMOs, and, most recently, "managed care," which allows for broader consumer choices.

Even the entertainment industry is enjoying a mini-boom: Since 1990, nearly 40 movies have been filmed or produced in and around the Twin Cities, including *Fargo* and the *Mighty Ducks* and *Grumpy Old Men* series. (Those who seek employment as crew, talent, and extras can contact the Minnesota Motion Picture and Television Board, 401 S. Third St., 612/ 332-6493.) And the artist formerly (and predominantly still) known as Prince created the funky "Minneapolis sound"; acts such as Soul Asylum, The Replacements, and Husker Dü have also been formed in an alternative scene that, according to some, rivals Seattle.

More than 80,000 new jobs are forecast by 1998, with the majority (about 55,000) being white-collar, according to the *Places Rated Almanac.* So it's no surprise that the Twin Cities is cited as one of the top spots for continued growth. Combine tact with technical skills, and your future could be as bright as Mary Richard's smile.

SOCIAL AND RECREATIONAL SCENE

How Minneapolis/St. Paul Plays

With one-fourth of the population being single, area code 612 would seem like a Shangri-la for the dateless (although not always desperate). However, "people around here have a tendency to marry young, as in high-school sweethearts," observes McCarthy. Even as someone in her late 20s, "I'm considered an 'older' single woman. That's not the case with cities like Chicago or New York," where a large portion of the population remains unattached well into their thirties. What she has found refreshing is "that men here are very polite and not always coming on to me."

"People actually go to bars to sit and talk," remarks Jackson. Men, he believes, are expected to take the initiative. "Men need to be patient and take things rather slowly."

A sense of trustworthiness pervades all aspects of life and is borne out by the fact that crime here is 22 percent lower than the national average. "You get a small-town feeling and it's nice," adds Sagawa, who has lived in Washington, D.C. and Los Angeles. "You don't have to lock your car or worry about talking to strangers. People do things out of kindness, without expecting anything in return."

Acclimation is possible, if not easier, than in similar-sized towns. "Most of us naturally gravitate toward people we're comfortable with, whether they be transfers, co-workers, or whatever," points out McCarthy. "The ideal situation would be to cultivate different kinds of friendships." Organizations such as the Twin Cities Transplants (484-8052), First Fridays (P.O. Box 50452, 339-9963, Internet: afton.winternet.com/first-fridays) for African-

Americans, and the Twin Cities Sport and Recreation Club (3315 Colfax South, 822-4413) are places to start finding those of like mind and inclination. And with 66 percent of the population being members of an organized religion, church is another obvious choice.

According to one woman, "you almost have to court people and convince them you're worth knowing," but finding exactly what you want is usually worth it.

Where It's At

Unless otherwise noted, all area codes are 612.

American Swedish Institute, 2600 Park Ave., 871-4907

Bach Society of Minnesota, P.O. Box 39292, 649-4692

Ballet Arts Minnesota, 528 Hennepin Ave., 340-1071

Ballet of the Dolls, 1629 Hennepin Ave. S., 333-2792

Bear-Hawk American Indian Museum, 1207 Franklin Ave. E., 872-9166

Bell Museum of Natural History, SE 17th and University aves., 624-1852

Chanhassen Dinner Theatre, 701 W. 78th St., Chanhassen, 934-1524

Children's Theatre Company, 2400 Third Ave. S., 874-0500

Dudley Riggs Brave New Workshop, 2605 Hennepin Ave. S., 332-6620

Ellington Car Museum, 20950 Rogers Dr., Rogers, 428-7377

Ethnic Dance Theatre, 1940 Hennepin Ave., 872-0024

Ex Machina, 230 Crestway Ln., W. St. Paul, 455-8086

Fitzgerald Theatre, 10 E. Exchange St., 290-1221

Ford Playhouse Theatre, Mall of America, 883-8800

Frederick R. Weisman Art Museum, 333 E. River Rd., 625-9494

Great American History Theatre, 30 E. 10th St., St. Paul, 292-4323

Guthrie, 725 Vineland Pl., 377-2224

Hennepin Center for the Arts, 528 Hennepin Ave., 338-8371 or 332-5206

Hennepin History Museum, 2303 Third Ave. S., 870-1329

Hey City Stage, 824 Hennepin Ave., 989-5151

 ## ARTS AND SCIENCES

The wide array of theaters, museums, galleries, music, and dance groups have given fruit to the regional nickname "Mini-Apple." (Notice, however, that many attractions are tactfully labeled "Minnesota" to avoid any politically incorrect Minneapolis-St. Paul predominance.) The theater district in downtown Minneapolis boasts the historic **Orpheum** and **State Theatres**, two vaudeville houses reincarnated to mount touring Broadway productions. Some of the city's immense selection of comedy seats are filled at the **Hey City Stage**. The largest regional playhouse in the U.S., the Tony Award–winning **Guthrie,** offers a mixture of classic to contemporary plays. Along with serving up satire, **Dudley Riggs Brave New Workshop** is the oldest revue of its kind and has had several famous alumni, including the brothers Belushi. Originally a Masonic temple, the **Hennepin Center for the Arts** is the home of Illusion, Cricket, and Lyric Theatres and nearly 20 other groups. As one of the biggest in the country, the **Children's Theatre Company** dispenses entertainment for all ages.

Variety is the backbone of this lively scene (all of the following sites are in Minneapolis unless otherwise designated). Multiculturalism and the black experience are celebrated at the **Mixed Blood Theatre** and the **Penumbra**, respectively. Flag toters might appreciate the **Great American History Theatre**, while the **Refreshment Committee Theatre Co.** emphasizes Biblical and family values. The **Theatre de la Jeune Lune** takes its roots from the Paris scene, while the **Venetian Playhouse** combines Italian-American cuisine with its offerings. There's a plateful of other dinner theaters: the **Old Log Theatre**, whose opera-style seats make it more comfortable than it sounds; the **Ford Playhouse Theatre**, which has luncheon reviews as well; and the **Chanhassen Dinner Theatre**, the nation's largest. Other "stars" of St. Paul include the **Fitzgerald Theatre**, home of Garrison Keillor's "Prairie Home Companion," while the **Ordway**, the crib of the **Minnesota Opera**, was modeled after the performing halls of Europe and is considered one of the finest venues around.

Only in Minneapolis will you find the **Ballet of the Dolls**, a combination of traditional and contemporary movements, and the self-explanatory **Ethnic Dance Theatre**, along with the more usual **Minnesota Dance Theatre and School** and **Ballet Arts Minnesota.** The **Minnesota Dance Alliance** is en pointe of contact for those wanting to get involved. **Orchestra Hall,** as well as the previously mentioned **Ordway,** serve as a base for the **Minnesota Orchestra** and the **St. Paul Chamber Orchestra.**

Other musical organizations range from Bach (**Bach Society of Minnesota**) to baroque (**Ex Machina**) to bluegrass (**Minnesota Bluegrass Association**), and more. You can "try out" reproductions of instruments, as well as see originals, at the **Schubert Club.** Other venues for thespians, minstrels, and tractor pullers include the **HHH Metrodome**, **Northrup Auditorium**, the **Medina Ballroom**, the **St. Paul Civic Center,** and the **Target Center.**

The **Minneapolis Institute of Art** also entertains the masses with its 85,000 objects spanning 4,000 years, including an Egyptian mummy and a sand mural created by Tibetan monks. Its St. Paul counterpart, the **Minnesota Museum of American Art,** is also home to the Landmark Center, hub of the local art scene, which displays multicultural and regional work. Other main attractions include the **Walker Arts Center,** fronted by the extremely large and conversation-inciting Minneapolis Sculpture Garden—check out the mega-sized "Spoonbridge and Cherry." Minneapolis' contribution to weird architecture is the **Frederick R. Weisman Art Museum,** whose cereal-box exterior houses such prizes as a permanent 20th-century collection and traveling exhibits.

Local to wacky annals can be found at spots ranging from the **Minnesota History Center,** which has everything from a 24-ton boxcar to the ex-Prince's Purple Rain ensemble, to the **Museum of Questionable Medical Devices,** which unearths more quacky "cures" than a flock of ducks. In between you'll find urban chronicles at the **Hennepin History Museum,** the displaced Native American story at the **Bear-Hawk American Indian Museum,** as well as that of the Native American's successors at the **American Swedish Institute,** which also has a record-shattering collection of glasswork. Sorry, but they don't give massages.

Planes, trains, and automobiles bridge the gap between art and science at the **Ellington Car Museum;** the **Minnesota Transportation Museum** (streetcars); the **Stillwater Depot,**

Where It's At

(continued)

HHH Metrodome, 501 Chicago Ave., 335-3370

Medina Ballroom, Hwy. 55, Hamel, 478-6661

Minneapolis Institute of Art, 2400 Third Ave. S., 870-3131

Minneapolis Public Library, 300 Nicollet Mall, 372-6500

Minnesota Air Guard Museum, hwys. 62 and 55S, 725-5609

Minnesota Bluegrass Association, P.O. Box 11419, St. Paul, 870-7432

Minnesota Children's Museum, 1217 N. Bandana Blvd., St. Paul, 644-3818

Minnesota Dance Alliance, 528 Hennepin Ave., 340-1156

Minnesota Dance Theatre and School, 528 Hennepin Ave., 338-0627

Minnesota History Center, 345 W. Kellogg Blvd., St. Paul, 296-6126

Minnesota Museum of American Art, 5th and Market, 292-4355

Minnesota Opera, 224-4222

Minnesota Orchestra, 371-5656

Minnesota Transportation Museum, 4291 Queen Ave., 925-3543

Minnesota Zoo, 13000 Zoo Blvd., Apple Valley, 432-9000

Mixed Blood Theatre, 1501 Fourth St. S., 338-6131

Museum of Questionable Medical Devices, 219 SE Main St., 379-4046

Northrup Auditorium, 84 Church St. SE, 624-2345

Old Log Theatre, 5185 Meadville St., Excelsior, 474-5951

Orchestra Hall, 111 Nicollet Mall, 371-5656

Ordway, 345 Washington St., 292-3000

Orpheum Theatre, 805 Hennepin Ave., 989-5151

Penumbra, 270 N. Kent St., St. Paul, 224-1380

Planes of Fame, 14771 Pioneer Trail, Eden Prairie, 941-2633

Raptor Center, 1920 Fitch Ave., St. Paul, 624-4745

Where It's At

(continued)

Refreshment Committee Theatre Co., 801 Dayton Ave., St. Paul, 227-3157

Schubert Club, 75 W. 5th St., St. Paul, 292-3267

Science Museum of Minnesota, 30 E. 10th St., St. Paul, 221-9488

St. Paul Chamber Orchestra, 224-4222

St. Paul Civic Center, 143 W. 4th St., 224-7361

State Theatre, 805 Hennepin Ave., 989-5151

Stillwater Depot, Logging, and Rail Museum, 610 N. Main St., Stillwater, 430-3000

Target Center, 600 1st Ave. N., 673-9000

Theatre de la Jeune Lune, 105 N. 1st St., 333-6200

Valleyfair Amusement Park, 1 Valleyfair Dr., Shakopee, 445-7600

Venetian Playhouse, 2814 Rice St., St. Paul, 484-7215

Walker Arts Center, 725 Vineland Place, 375-7577

Where It's At

 Unless otherwise noted, all area codes are 612.

Afton Alps, 6600 Peller Ave. S., Hastings, 436-5245

Braemar Golf Dome, 7420 Braemer Blvd., Edina, 944-9490

Buck Hill, 15400 Buck Hill Rd., Burnsville, 435-7187

Bunker Hills, Foley Blvd. and Hwy. 242, Coon Rapids, 757-3920

Chilly Open Tournament, Lake Minnetonka, 473-9595

Como Park, Zoo, and Conservatory, between Hamline and Lexington aves. on Midway, St. Paul, 266-6400

Como Golf Course, 1431 N. Lexington Pkwy., St. Paul, 488-9673

Ft. Snelling State Park, Hwy. 5 and 55, St. Paul, 725-2413

Golf Mountain, 883-8899

Hiawatha Golf Course, 4553 Longfellow Ave., 724-7715

Logging, and Rail Museum; the **Minnesota Air Guard Museum** (aircraft); and the **Planes of Fame,** which also offers cockpit air rides. Other hands-on experiences can be found at the **Minnesota Children's Museum;** the **Science Museum of Minnesota,** where you can walk under a dinosaur, "touch" a tornado, and watch a movie on a 76-foot screen that utilizes the world's largest film projector; and the **Bell Museum of Natural History,** which features a room where you can fondle animal skin and bone displays (no, thank you).

"Live" action in the form of several hundred species of animals can be found at the **Minnesota Zoo,** which, in true practical Nordic fashion, also has ski trails. The **Raptor Center** offers tours and educational programs on wildlife rehabilitation, while Minneapolis likely has the only planetarium in the world housed in a public library (**Minneapolis Public Library**). Those who like to have fun without expending any brain cells might enjoy the **Valleyfair Amusement Park,** with more than 75 rides, shows, and attractions.

 ## THE SPORTING LIFE

Sportswise, "those who can't find anything to do around here have themselves to blame," remarks economic specialist Kelly Altmeyer. "In the summer there's fishing, boating, and the parks," while the winter offers skiing, snowmobiling, ice fishing and skating, and boot hockey, a unique pastime involving an outdoor rink, a broom handle, and whatever type of puck is available. There's at least one pro team to root for during each season: the **Minnesota Twins** for major league baseball as well as the somewhat redundant **St. Paul Saints,** a Northern League team. The NBA **Minnesota Timberwolves** and the NFL **Minnesota Vikings** satisfy the fall/winter fix. The International Hockey League's **Minneapolis Moose** (Mooses? Meece?) and soccer's **Minnesota Thunder,** as well as Big Ten action at the **University of Minnesota,** fill any gaps.

You don't have to join a sponsored league (although the **Minnesota Amateur Sports Commission** can arrange it) to get in the swim of things. This state's 90,000 miles of lake shoreline surpass the combined total of California's, Florida's, and Hawaii's. The greenery's enough to make other cities turn a chlorophyll shade of envy: Minneapolis alone has nearly 170 parks covering more than 6,300 acres of land and water. Four state parks, two state trails, almost 20 wildlife management refuge areas, over 40 regional parks, and about 1,000 locally owned spaces comprise the seven-county metro area. The **Minneapolis State Park and Recreation Board** and **St. Paul Department of Parks and Recreation** can provide details.

The most well-beaten paths include **Ft. Snelling State Park,** which offers hiking, biking, canoeing, and paddle-boating in the region of the historic fort. **Como Park, Zoo, and Conservatory** offers, a three-fer with various recreational and water sport options, a free view of 110 species, and Japanese and floral gardens. Lake Minnetonka allows motorized boats for skiing, while **Lake Harriet** provides a variety of organized activities, including boat and street car rides and concerts. Other popular puddles include the Chain of Lakes (of which Harriet is a part), Medicine Lake, and Prior (as opposed to subsequent) Lake. Those wanting to explore the Mississippi à la Mark Twain have five riverboats to choose from at the **Padelford Packet Boat Company,** as well as other cruising options (**Lady of the Lake**).

In winter, Peavy Plaza (downtown), Lake of the Isles (uptown), and Como Lake are real slick for ice-skating, while in-line skating can be found at the Metrodome. Downhill skiers can tip their poles at **Afton Alps, Buck Hill,** and **Hyland Hills.** Cross-country skiing takes place closer to home at Theodore Wirth Park, **Hiawatha Golf Course,** and various lakes. Incredibly, you can even golf during the frigid months at the **Chilly Open Tournament** on Lake Minnetonka (February), while indoor courses are available at the **Braemar Golf Dome** and **Golf Mountain** at the Mall of America. Okay, so one's a driving range and the other's miniature, but when it's 15 degrees below, who can complain?

Since nearly 20 percent of the population does swing a club—on a golf course, that is—there are over 100 courses to choose from, with more being added yearly. And that's not even counting private greens. **Bunker Hills, Como,** and **Stonebrook** are a few public options.

After-Hours Diversions

Although according to one man, "it takes a lot to get Minnesotans to whoop it up," there are a plethora of places to at least try. Here is where St. Paul falls way short of its twin—most hot spots lie across the river. If you're lucky, you might even run into what's-his-name, formerly known as whomever, and his entourage. Should things get lively, there's a little store in uptown Minneapolis called **Condom Kingdom.** Perhaps a better name would be Condom Nation.

Where It's At

(continued)

Hyland Hills, I-494 and Hwy. 100, Bloomington, 835-5428

Lady of the Lake, 8 Water St., Excelsior, 929-1209

Lake Harriet, 929-1200

Minneapolis State Park and Recreation Board, 310 4th Ave. S., 348-2143

Minneapolis Amateur Sports Commission, 785-5630

Minneapolis Moose, St. Paul Civic Center, 221-0010

Minnesota Thunder, National Sports Center, Blaine, 785-3668

Minnesota Timberwolves, Target Center, 337-DUNK

Minnesota Twins, Metrodome, 338-9467

Minnesota Vikings, Metrodome, 333-8828

Padelford Packet Boat Company, Harriet Island, St. Paul, 227-1100

St. Paul Department of Parks and Recreation, 266-6400

St. Paul Saints, 1771 Energy Park Dr., 644-6659

Stonebrook, 22693 S. Cty. Rd. 79, Shakopee, 496-3171

University of Minnesota, 624-8080

Where It's At

Unless otherwise noted, all area codes are 612.

Acme Comedy Co., 708 N. First St., 338-6393

America's Original Sports Bar, Mall of America, 854-5483

Brit's English Pub, 1110 Nicollet Mall, 332-3908

Bryant Lake Bowl, 810 W. Lake St., 825-3737

Bunker's, 761 N. Washington Ave., 338-8188

Cabooze, 917 Cedar Ave. S., 338-6425

Cafe Luxeford, 1101 LaSalle Ave., 332-6800

Caribou Coffee, several locations

Where It's At

(continued)

Champps, several locations

Comedy Olympix, 1414 W. 28th St., 871-1903

Condom Kingdom, 2748 Hennepin Ave., 871-9044

Festival of Nations, St. Paul, 647-0191

Fine Line Cafe, 318 1st Ave., 338-8100

First Avenue/7th Street Entry, P.O. Box 216, 338-8388

Gay '90s, 410 Hennepin Ave., 333-7755

Grand Casino Hinckley, 777 Lady Luck Dr., Hinckley, 800/GRAND-21

Grand Casino Mille Lacs, Hwy. 169, Onamia, 1/800-626-LUCK

Grandma's, 1810 Washington Ave. S., 340-0516

Heart of the Beast May Day Parade, Powderhorn Park, 721-2535

Holidazzle, Nicollet Mall

Jackpot Junction, R.R. 1, Morton, 800/WIN-CASH

Jitters, 1026 Nicollet Mall, 333-8511

Joe Schmidt's Hangout, Mississippi Riverfront, SE Main St.

Joe's Garage, 1610 Harmon Pl., 904-1163

Juneteenth, Theodore Wirth Park, 337-7000

Kieran's Irish Pub, 330 2nd Ave. S., 339-4499

Knuckleheads, Mall of America, 854-5233

Loft Bookstore, 66 Malcolm Ave. SE, 378-8999

Loon Cafe, 500 First Ave. N., 332-8342

Loring Bar, 1624 Harmon Pl., 332-1617

Lounge, 411 Second Ave. N., 333-8800

Lucia's Wine Bar, 1432 W. 31st St., 825-1572

Minneapolis Aquatennial, downtown and other locations, 331-8371

Minnesota Center for Book Arts, 24 N. Third St., 338-8999

Minnesota Heritage Festival, Nicollet Island, 874-0142

Minnesota Renaissance Festival, 4 miles south of Shakopee, 445-7361

Minnesota State Fair, St. Paul Fairgrounds, 662-2200

Music of note has many habitats. Jazz and blues performances combine with food at the **Times,** an old-fashioned pub; **Cafe Luxeford,** a nifty bistro; and **Sophia,** where patrons are serenaded wherever they sit. R & B and favorite local performers appear regularly at **Bunker's, Uptown Bar,** and **Nikki's Cafe.** The **Fine Line Cafe** serves up a full menu of food, regionally and nationally renowned acts, and a Sunday gospel brunch.

Dance clubs offer all kinds of mixes. Although it attracts a younger crowd, **First Avenue/7th Street Entry** is renowned for its Prince-ly association (*Purple Rain* was filmed here), huge dance floor, and cutting-edge scene. His royal indecipherability was also instrumental in opening **Quest,** a high-energy lair. There's a sea of movement on the floor at the **Tropix Beach Club,** which also has a boat, pinball machines, and pool tables to complete the journey. Although the **Gay '90s** used to attract primarily those (homosexuals, not nonagenarians), it has become more mainstream thanks to a piano bar, drag shows, and a disco. A funky campus spot, the **Cabooze,** draws not only well-knowns but also nurtures up-and-comings, while **Grandma's** dishes up a smorgasbord of pool, volleyball, and tunes.

Bryant Lake Bowl has a restaurant, comedy troupe, music, and one of America's favorite sports (hint: not big-screen TV). Strictly comedy can be found at **Acme Comedy Co.,** which hosts national acts; **Comedy Olympix,** which holds improv competitions; **Knuckleheads,** which serves a buffet along with big names; and others.

Two sports bars owned by rival TV personalities are **Rosen's Bar & Grill** and **Joe Schmidt's Hangout. America's Original Sports Bar** has an indoor basketball court and stadium-sized accommodations for viewing all physical endeavors—except perhaps the "adult entertainment" found at **Shieks Palace Royale.** With several locations in the Twin Cities, **Champps** is another winner with fans.

Brew pubs and wine bars flow freely, with the former consisting of the **Rock Bottom Brewery,** which has five different beers made on the premises as well as portions fit for a giant (or at least a Viking) as well as **Kieran's Irish Pub, Brit's English Pub,** and **Old Chicago,** which serves 110 varieties to go with deep-dish pizza. Wine bars include the **New French Cafe, Lucia's Wine Bar,** and the **Lounge. Joe's Garage** offers the best of both libations, along with a full-service menu, a really cool interior, and a great patio view of the skyline.

Those wanting truly atmospheric experiences will find the **Loring Bar** chock-full of overstuffed chairs, live music, and Bohemian-type trendies, while **Nye's Polonaise Room** has a '60s-style piano lounge and a polka room. The **Loon Cafe** has been laughing all the way to the bank for years, while **Runyon's 3rd Ave.** is considered to have some of the best bar fare and armchair commentaries in town. **Caribou Coffee, Starbucks, Uncommon Grounds, Moose & Sadie's** and **Jitters** are stimulating settings for caffeine and conversation.

The creme of the clubs (and Twin Cities society) can be found at **South Beach,** which, in addition to a restaurant, dance floor, and wine bar, also has a fireside lounge to warm your tootsies and the rest of your body during cold nights. Not that the weather ever stopped anyone in this town from going out.

This is especially true during the **Winter Carnival** (January), which came about in 1885, when a New York reporter labeled the region "the Siberia of America." Today it draws 1.5 million snow lovers from all climes and hosts such events as ice carving, snow sculpting, skating, and even the coronation of "royalty." Spring bears the **Festival of Nations** (April), the state's largest multi-ethnic event; the **Heart of the Beast May Day Parade,** a non-Satanic ritual involving 15-foot puppets; and **Juneteenth,** which celebrates emancipation with a parade and African-American marketplace.

July brings the **Minnesota Heritage Festival,** which highlights the state's history; a **Taste of Minnesota,** where local restaurateurs strut their foodstuffs; and the **Minneapolis Aquatennial,** nearly 100 events honoring water, water, everywhere. The **Uptown Art Fair** (August) unites hundreds of thousands of visitors and artists from all over, while the **Minnesota Renaissance Festival** and **Minnesota State Fair** hustle in September with 16th-century recreations and livestock/carnival rides/junk food kiosks. **Holidazzle** (November/December) does just that with sunset parades during the Christmas season, while the **St. Paul Ice Fishing and Winter Sports Show** (December) gears up consumers for the winter onslaught.

Local Native Americans stake their claim with almost 20 casinos, making the Twin Cities the largest American Indian gaming market and a major gambling mecca. The colossal **Mystic Lake Casino** offers more than 2,600 slot machines, 128 blackjack tables, high stakes bingo, and several restaurants, so you never have to leave the grounds—except when you're out of wampum. The **Grand Casino Mille Lacs** has a

Where It's At

(continued)

Moose & Sadie's, 212 Third Ave. N., 371-0464

Mystic Lake Casino, 2400 Mystic Lake Blvd., Prior Lake, 800/262-7799

New French Cafe, 128 N. 4th St., 338-3790

Nikki's Cafe, 107 3rd Ave., 340-9098

Nye's Polonaise Room, 112 E. Hennpin Ave., 379-2021

Old Chicago, 2841 Hennepin Ave. S., 870-1918

Playwright's Center, 2301 Franklin Ave. S., 332-7481

Quest, 110 N. Fifth St., 338-6169

Rock Bottom Brewery, 825 Hennepin Ave., 332-BREW

Rosen's Bar & Grill, 430 1st Ave., 338-1926

Runyon's 3rd Ave., 222 S. 9th St., 339-1116

Screenwriters' Workshop, 868 19th Ave. SE, 331-3880

Shieks Palace Royale, 115 S. Fourth St., 341-0054

Sophia, 65 E. Main St. SE, 378-1111

South Beach, 325 N. First Ave., 204-0791

St. Paul Ice Fishing and Winter Sports Show, St. Paul Civic Center, 922-9000

Starbucks, several locations

Taste of Minnesota, State Capitol grounds, St. Paul, 228-0018

Times, 1036 Nicollet Mall, 333-2762

Treasure Island Casino and Bingo, 5734 Sturgeon Lake Rd., Welch, 800/222-7077

Tropix Beach Club, 400 N. Third Ave., 333-1006

Uncommon Grounds, 2809 Hennepin Ave. S., 872-4811

Uptown Art Fair, Lake St. and Hennepin Ave. S., 827-8757

Uptown Bar, 3018 Hennepin Ave., 823-4719

Winter Carnival, downtown St. Paul 297-6953

hotel, babysitting services, and video games, along with the usual blackjack, roulette, and craps. You can also take a break and go fishing on Mille Lacs Lake. Except for the walleye, more of the same can be found at the **Grand Casino Hinckley, Jackpot Junction,** and **Treasure Island Casino and Bingo,** which features comedy nights to help laugh away increases or decreases in financial status.

Those preferring to invest in aesthetics might choose the Gallery Crawl, a monthly exploration of more than 30 artistic enterprises in Minneapolis's gallery-laden Warehouse District. Famous and local writers appear regularly at the **Loft Bookstore,** while the **Minnesota Center for Book Arts** provides insight into both book creation and production. Other wordsmiths give readings at the **Playwright's Center** and **Screenwriters' Workshop.**

Culinary and Shopping Haunts

Although it's one of the few cities with scant claims to a particular cuisine, more than 2,000 restaurants offer everything from Sri Lankan (**Sri Lankan Curry House**) to Vietnamese (**White Lily**) to gourmet French (see below). Food here is so reasonable that the most costly places are flagged at $16 and up, which of course gives you more money for shopping.

Downtown Minneapolis serves up such trendy spots as the previously mentioned **Joe's Garage** (American), the award-winning **Goodfellow's** (American regional), the **Ichiban Japanese Steak House, Cafe Un Deux Trois** (French), and **Nikolet's** (Nouveau). More casual diners may find the **8th St. Grill & Tavern** (American), **Buca** (Southern Italian), and **Palomino Euro Bistro** to their liking, while good cheap eats for under $10 can be found in **DuJour's** (breakfast, American), **Lyon's Pub** (sandwiches/salads), and the **Old Spaghetti Factory.**

The moderately priced Warehouse District has **Cafe Brenda,** vegetarian and gourmet fare mostly for ladies who lunch; **Gluek's,** your basic German bier hall; **J.D. Hoyt's** (American), which describes itself as "a roadhouse in the city"; and **Linguini & Bob,** Italian grub served in a Tuscan villa setting. Uptown/south Minneapolis boasts such standouts as **Figlio's** (Italian bistro), **Famous Dave's BBQ & Blues,** and the **French Meadow Bakery and Cafe.** Crayons, toys, and games are supplied at **Hey City Cafe** (American) in the University district, while **Maxwell's** (American) is giving McDonald's a run for its money by counting the number of chicken wings sold.

St. Paul offers up Grand Ave., a Victorian-era confection of restaurants, shops, and other enterprises, including the upscale **W.A. Frost & Company,** American cuisine set in an elegantly restored landmark. Less formal spots include **Tavern on Grand** (American), whose motto is "The people

Where It's At

 Unless otherwise noted, all area codes are 612.

8th St. Grill & Tavern, 800 Marquette Ave., 349-5717

Acropol Inn, Greek, 748 Grand, 298-0151

Anything and Everything, 1208 Grand, 222-7770

Bandana Square, 1021 E. Bandana Blvd., 642-9676 or 642-1509

Bogie's Diner, 853-9800

Brookdale, hwys. 100 and 152, Brooklyn Center, 566-3373

Buca, 2728 Gannon Rd., SPA-GETT

Buca, 1204 Harmon Pl., 638-2225

Burnsville Center, I-35E at County Rd. 42, Burnsville, 435-8181

Cafe Brenda, 300 First Ave. N., 342-9230

Cafe Un Deux Trois, 114 S. Ninth St., 673-0686

Calhoun Square, Hennepin Ave. S. at Lake St., 824-1240

California Cafe, 854-2233

Carousel Restaurant, Radisson Hotel, 11 E. Kellogg Blvd., St. Paul, 292-1900

City Center, 40 S. Seventh St., 372-1200

Dayton's River Room, 6th and Cedar, 292-5174

Doin' the Dishes, 3008 W. 50th St., 924-8980

DuJour's, 89 S. Tenth St., 333-1855

are crazy but the food is good!"; the **Acropol Inn** (Greek), home cooking that's garnered four stars; **Table of Contents** (eclectic), called "Minnesota's best kept secret" by *Money* magazine; **La Cucaracha** (Mexican), whose impeccable atmosphere belies its name; and **Tulips,** country French served in a cozy atmosphere.

Elsewhere in the city are **Buca,** whose phone number (SPA-GETT) says it all; the **St. Paul Grill,** beef and other specialties served with distinguished flair; **Dayton's River Room,** American food in an old-world European atmosphere; **Khyber Pass Cafe,** Afghani-type kebabs, stews, and vegetarian offerings; and the **Great Northern Supper Club,** where jazz is served along with American cuisine.

Some places are destinations in themselves. The **Pickled Parrot** flies in fresh stone crabs in the dead of winter, while the **Minnesota Zephyr** dining train takes passengers back to the World War II era including an authentic five-course dinner, attire, and song. The constantly changing view at the **Carousel Restaurant** (American) at the top of the Radisson Hotel is a truly revolutionary experience.

Along with the usual fast-food places, the **Mall of America's** selection of eateries ranges from jungle shenanigans at the **Rainforest Cafe,** where American fare is served during a thunderstorm or two under the watchful eyes of several tropical birds and a snake; **Napa Valley Grille,** politically balanced "multicultural" (their word) meals and a wine connoisseur's delight; **Bogie's Diner,** which includes a high-calorie '50s menu as well as healthy choices; **California Cafe,** voted "Best New Restaurant" by *Minneapolis/St.Paul* magazine; and **Planet Hollywood** (American), located in the "happening" Upper East Side. This section also boasts a karaoke spot (**Puzzles**), contemporary dance music (**Gators**), a country-western bar (**Gatlin Brothers Music City Grille),** and others.

A shopper's Disneyland, the **Mall of America** is a monument to consumerism and includes nine night clubs, 36 specialty food emporiums, and Knott's Camp Snoopy amusement park. (With an interior big enough for seven Yankee Stadiums, fitting in a full-sized Ferris wheel and roller coaster was no problem.) In addition to several previously mentioned attractions, there's the LEGO Imagination Center for little kiddies; Star Base Omega, an interactive laser game; Tempus Expeditions, which allows you to simulate a jungle expedition; and UnderWater World, which features 15,000 fish in 1.2 million gallons of H_2O.

Where It's At

(continued)

Eden Prairie Center, 1018 Eden Prairie, 941-7650

Famous Dave's BBQ & Blues, 3001 Hennepin Ave. S., 822-9900

Figlio's, 3001 Hennepin Ave. S., 822-1688

French Meadow Bakery and Cafe, 2610 Lyndale Ave. S, 870-4740

Galleria, 3510 Galleria/France Ave., 925-9354

Gatlin Brothers Music City Grille, 858-8000

Gators, 858-8888

Gaviidae Common, 60 S. Sixth St., 372-1222

Gluek's, 16 N. Sixth St., 338-6621

Goodfellow's, 800 Nicollet Mall, 332-4800

Grand Ave., one mile south of I-94

Great Northern Supper Club, 175 E. Fifth St., 224-2720

Hey City Cafe, 1430 Washington Ave. S., 333-9202

Horizon, I-94 and Exit 251, Woodbury, 866-5900

Ichiban Japanese Steak House, 1333 Nicollet Mall, 339-0540

IDS Crystal Court, 80 S. Eighth St.

J.D. Hoyt's, 301 Washington Ave. N., 338-1560

Joe's Garage, 1610 Harmon Pl., 904-1163

Khyber Pass Cafe, 1399 St. Clair Ave., 698-5403

La Cucaracha, 36 Dale St., 221-4682, other locations

Linguini & Bob, 100 N. Sixth St., 332-1600, other locations

Lyon's Pub, 16 S. Sixth St., 333-6612

Mall of America, 60 E. Broadway, Bloomington, 883-8800

Maplewood Mall, Hwy. 694 and White Bear Ave., Maplewood, 770-5020

Maxwell's, 1201 Washington Ave. S., 338-1980

Medford, 315 County Rd. 12SW, Medford, 507/455-4112

Where It's At

(continued)

Minnesota Zephyr dining train, 430-3000

Napa Valley Grille, 858-9934

Nikolet's, 815 Nicollet Mall, 341-4011

Old Spaghetti Factory, 233 Park Ave., 341-0949

Palomino Euro Bistro, 825 Hennepin Ave., 339-3800

Pickled Parrot, 26 N. Fifth St., 332-0673

Planet Hollywood, 854-7827

Puzzles, 854-5483

Quilted Bear Craft Mall, 821 E. Lake St., Wayzata, 476-6276

Rainforest Cafe, 854-7500

Ridgedale, 12401 Wayzata Blvd., Minnetonka, 541-4864

Rosedale, Hwy. 36 at Snelling/Fairview, Roseville, 633-0872

Southdale, 6601 France Ave. S., Edina, 925-7885

Sri Lankan Curry House, 2821 Hennepin Ave., 871-2400

St. Anthony Main, 125 Southeast Main St., 378-1226

St. Paul Grill, St. Paul Hotel, 350 Market St., 224-7455

Stillwater/St. Croix, I-35 to 36 east

Table of Contents, 1648 Grand, 699-6595

Tanager, I-35 to Exit 147, 800/4-TANAGER

Tavern on Grand, 656 Grand Ave., 228-9030

Town Square, 445 Minnesota St., 298-0900

Tulips, 452 Selby Ave. S., 699-6595

W.A. Frost & Company, 374 Selby Ave., 224-5715

Warehouse District, west of Hennepin, between Ninth St. and Washington Ave.

White Lily, 758 Grand Ave., St. Paul, 293-9124

World Trade Center, 30 E. Seventh St., 291-1715

Oh, and the three levels divided into four shopping "streets" have more than 400 stores: Bloomingdale's, Macy's, Nordstrom's, Sears, Marshall's, Service Merchandise, and Filene's Basement as well as just about every other major retail chain in the U.S. Shops found hardly anywhere else include Oshman's Supersports USA, where you can shoot hoops, swing a bat, and skate around; Junkyard, featuring unisex duds fronted by three vehicular rust buckets; BareBones, which offers gifts, toys, books, and other items related to medicine and the human body; Custom Foot, where you can order personally sized shoes from Italy; and Marvelous Magnets, a store whose refrigerator decorations pull in lots of business. There's also the Chapel of Love, the nation's first wedding chapel/retail store in an enclosed shopping center. Could a funeral home be next?

But the MoA has hardly stolen any Twin Cities shopping thunder. Downtown Minneapolis alone has more retail outlets than any other metropolis in the country, and it should come as no surprise that the world's first enclosed shopping center was built in 1956 at **Southdale** in the suburb of Edina. "Many people from around here go to local malls and stores," comments McCarthy.

The several blocks encompassing Nicollet in downtown Minneapolis are home to retailers ranging from Neiman-Marcus to Saks to the mother shop of Dayton's. It also serves as the hub for other clusters: the architecturally stunning **Gaviidae Common,** with its four-story waterfall and hand-painted ceiling; **City Center;** and **IDS Crystal Court.** The **World Trade Center** in St. Paul has Dayton's plus about 50 other stores. Nearby you'll find **Town Square,** with several dozen more. With the skyway system, lousy weather's no excuse not to shop.

Elsewhere in Minneapolis, there's **Calhoun Square** in Uptown, a key site for eclectic places and great people-watching. Turn-of-the-century buildings house galleries, antique stores, and eateries in the **Warehouse District,** with particular standouts being the Wyman and Kicker-knick Buildings. More historic structures (and cute shops/eateries) can be found in the original settlement of **St. Anthony Main.** Along with the previously mentioned **Southdale** and the upscale **Galleria,** the first-ring suburb of Edina has its own downtown cluster, including home decor stores, boutiques, and **Doin' the Dishes**—whose name refers not to restitution for skimping on a restaurant bill, but a spot to design your own plates. What a crock!

St. Paul has **Grand Ave.**, anchored by four spiffed-up, brick mini-malls and lots of other emporiums, including (really!) **Anything and Everything.** Another historic consumer whistle stop is **Bandana Square**, where shops and entertainment centers are set in 1880s railroad buildings. The various 'burbs have the "dales"—**Rosedale, Ridgedale,** and **Brookdale** as well as **Burnsville Center, Eden Prairie Center, Maplewood Mall,** and many more. The outlets—**Horizon, Medford, Tanager,** and others—have even more brand names at discount prices. Those looking for the less conventional may find it at **Stillwater/St. Croix,** which offers antiques and specialty boutiques in a riverfront atmosphere. And with 400 vendors, the **Quilted Bear Craft Mall** is a last stop for folks who feel they've seen it all.

 ### ETHNIC AND RELIGIOUS PROSPECTS

What the region lacks in ethnicity, it makes up for in diversity. The cities themselves have the most variety: "If you sit in downtown Minneapolis, you see a wide mix of people," observes Reutter. The Twin Cities "are becoming more international."

There are plenty of religions to choose from. More Minnesotans are members of an organized faith than the average Midwesterner. "We have everything from the traditional Catholic service to the non-denominational Living Word, which uses electric guitars and allows you to speak out loud," remarks McCarthy.

Still, with a population of about 600,000, Catholics rule, at least in the metro area. The **Archdiocese of St. Paul and Minneapolis** oversees 78 churches in the region. Lutherans come in second (about 425,000) and take top honors with one of the largest congregations in the world, **Mt. Olivet Lutheran Church.** With 12,000 members, it's hard to feel conspicuous if you sneeze or decide to take a nap. The area's 31,000 Jews have over 20 synagogues, including **Mt. Zion,** the oldest in the Midwest. The remainder run the gamut from Buddhists to Black Baptists to Methodists to Episcopalians to Friends (as in Quakers, not the TV show) to Presbyterians and more. There's even **Eckankar,** spiritual exercise focusing on the Temple of Eck in nearby Chanhassen. If somebody builds it, it seems, worshipers will come.

Where It's At

 Unless otherwise noted, all area codes are 612.

Archdiocese of St. Paul and Minneapolis, 328 Kellogg Ave., 291-1750

Eckankar, P.O. Box 27300, 474-0700

Mt. Olivet Lutheran Church, 5025 Knox Ave., 926-7651, other locations

Mt. Zion, 1300 Summit Ave., St. Paul, 698-3881

Brookdale, hwys. 100 and 152, Brooklyn Center, 566-3373

CRIB SHEET

When the National Association of Home Builders names a region one of the top five most affordable places to live, the news has to be good. With an average monthly rent of about $400 for a studio, $500 for a one-bedroom, and $640 for a two-bedroom, you can choose from high-rises with fitness centers and heated parking; smaller, older structures with character (read: lacking some amenities); and restored brownstones and lofts. Homes can range from about $73,000 for a new build in the suburb of Apple Valley to $1.3 million for a mansion in exclusive Edina. Green spaces, self-contained neighborhoods, and lakes can be found in even densely commercial areas, making living attractive in downtown Minneapolis.

Most single professionals prefer the bright lights of the bigger city, while families and those who enjoy historic homes and a small-town atmosphere opt for St. Paul. Whichever twin you select, "find out what sort of parking is available," points out McCarthy. Although they may cost more, enclosed spaces are important, unless of course you enjoy scraping several inches of snow from your car.

Many of Minneapolis' earlier dwellings were made of wood and destroyed by fire or expansion, so much of what you'll see here is between the turn of the century to around 1960. The city alone has 80 neighborhoods, including Loring Park, a trendy area with Victorian mansions, brick and brownstone walk-ups, and some newer apartments and condos. Along with lots of theaters and bars, five of the city's largest churches are located here. Downtown also has a variety of high-rises and smaller buildings. Close to several lakes, restaurants, banks, and stores, Uptown options range from houses to apartment buildings; lofts and brownstones in the Warehouse District are scattered amid nightspots, galleries, and restaurants. Those who don't mind dropping a few more greenbacks can opt for the more residential section of lakefront-landed Kenwood, while the tranquil, tree-shaded Linden Hills has been (favorably) compared with Mr. Roger's neighborhood. Consisting of several residential clusters, the University sector is serviced by Dinkytown, a commercial strip.

Made up of 17 "districts," each largely run by the residents, St. Paul has the added advantage of inexpensive housing—many homes are in the $60,000–$100,000 range—as well as architectural charm. (Apartments are scarce and therefore more costly, however.) Favorite neighborhoods include Lowertown, where residents can choose renovated lofts in a thriving arts community near the river; Summit Hill, the former abode of lumber and railroad barons, whose huge restored dwellings and proximity to Grand Avenue have made it an in-town favorite; Highland Park, where "newer" residences (built after 1939) are near shopping, dining, and professional services; and the West Side, a politically active and culturally mixed area.

Although many area suburbs have plentiful parkland and other recreational opportunities, they offer heterogeneity as well. First-time buyers might choose Maple Grove (average home value: about $102,000; commuting time: 29.1 minutes), which has starter homes and express bus service to downtown Minneapolis, or the "bedroom community" of St. Louis Park ($90,000; 18.4 minutes), with its easy access to the lakes and plenty of condos. Mid-priced areas bustling with activity and growth include Bloomington ($106,000; 18.9 minutes), home of the Mall of America; the "boom town" of Eden Prairie ($135,000; 20.6 minutes), a balance of greenery, good schools, businesses, and shopping centers; Minnetonka ($131,000; 19.9 minutes), close to lakeside recreation, nature preserves, and major highways; and St. Anthony ($95,271; 18 minutes), with lower taxes and a wide mix of residents and residences.

The ritzy reputation of Edina ($164,000; 19 minutes) belies the fact that it also has affordable abodes for under $150,000. More exclusive suburbs include North Oaks ($256,000; 22.1 minutes), the only private city in the U.S., with spectacular homes; the mostly rural Orono ($227,000; 26.1 minutes), whose residents include Pillsburys, Daytons, and other notables; and Wayzata ($221,253; 19.9 minutes), a charming spot with loads of retail and water activities. And that's just in Hennepin County, one of the seven counties surrounding the twins.

Although public schools have low dropout rates, high test scores, and many students who continue on to postsecondary education, "there's not as much parental involvement as there could be," admits one expert. "The schools mean well, but there's almost too much leeway" given to students. Those in Minneapolis can choose from traditional, contemporary, Montessori, magnet, and other options. However, schools in the Twin Cities and suburbs remain among the highest-ranked in the U.S., and "the quality of education is quite good."

The Minnesota Department of Education (296-1261), Minnesota Association of School Administrators (645-6272), and *Schoolhouse Magazine* (227-1519) can provide details.

Tuition for the approximately 250 private and parochial schools ranges from $3,000–$10,000 per year, although many students receive need or merit-based scholarships.

Along with the University of Minnesota (625-5000), the Twin Cities have several four-year colleges, community colleges, and technical and trade schools.

NAVIGATING MINNEAPOLIS/ST. PAUL

Transportationwise, "Minneapolis is definitely user-friendly," observes Reutter. Along with a logical grid layout and street numbering format, "parking is readily available and inexpensive." St. Paul is a different story: With no defined pattern or universal dividing lines between north, south, east, and west, its winding byways are further complicated by a house numbering system that goes by the mile, rather than by the block. Still, "there are many ways to get in and out of a place, even with lots of construction." On-ramp meters, electronic signs informing motorists of accidents and road work, and high-occupancy vehicle (HOV) lanes keep the average commute to 21.1 minutes, with a minimum of congestion. Most drivers are courteous, although a penchant for going a few miles below the speed limit can raise the blood pressure of non-"Minnesota nice" practitioners.

Although it has a fleet of 900 buses as well as suburban connectors, the Metropolitan Council Transit Operations (MCTA, 373-3333) was experiencing a decline until the construction of a $2.5 million station in Burnsville. Child care, shops and services, and a clean, hi-tech waiting area made it a success with commuters. A similar setup is in the works for Eden Prairie. Bicycling is also encouraged, with permanent racks and clearly delineated lanes on many busy streets. Various trails through parks can make for an easy commute (at least when there's no snow or ice).

An extensive system of freeways provide easy access in and out of the area. The two major interstates are I-94 (east and west) and I-35 (north and south), which splits into 35W and 35E running through Minneapolis and St. Paul, respectively. Interstates 494 and 694 form an outerbelt around the metro area, while I-394 connects the western suburbs to downtown Minneapolis.

Located 15 minutes away from each twin, the relatively small (3,000 acre) Minneapolis-St. Paul Airport (726-8100) serves as a hub for Northwest Airlines and has flights from several other carriers as well. Occasional overflow is relieved by regional airports.

There's also Amtrak (644-1127), with limited passenger railroad service, and Greyhound stations (726-5118 or 371-3344). Although a light rail system linking the Twins has been batted about, lack of funds have sent it out of the ballpark.

Nashville at a Glance

Birthdate and Present Size: 1779. *Metropolitan Statistical Area*—1980: 850,505; 1990: 985,026. 1/1/95 (estimate): 1,073,100. Percent change, 1980–1990: +15.8%. Percent change, 1990–1995: +8.9%.

Weather Report: *Average annual temperature*—59° F. In January: 46/28 °F. In July: 90/69 °F.
Average annual precipitation—48".
Average annual snowfall—6".

Money Matters: *Unemployment rate*—3.3%.
Per capita income—$23,655 (city); $21,634 (MSA).
Average household income—N/A (city); $38,512 (MSA).
Average cost of a home—$113,179.
Average rent for an apartment—$546/month.
ACCRA cost of living indexes (based on 100)—Composite Index: 94.3; Utilities Index: 95.8; Housing Index: 87.4.
Sales and use tax—6.0% (state); 2.25% (local).
Personal income tax—6.0% (on interest/dividend income only). Nashville ranked #6 out of the 100 largest U.S. metro areas in terms of the lowest state and local tax burden.

People Profile: *Crime rate* (Per 100,000 population)—10,065.0 (city); 3,829.4 (suburbs); 6,913.6 (MSA).

Racial and ethnic characteristics—White: 73.9%; Black: 24.3%; American Indian/Eskimo/Aleut: 0.3%; Asian/Pacific Islander: 1.3%; Hispanic Origin: 0.8%; Other: 0.3%.
Gender ratio—90.2 males per 100 females (all ages); 86.5 males per 100 females (18 years old+).
Age characteristics—18–24 (11.6%); 25–44 (36.2%). Median age: 32.2.
Educational attainment—percent having completed high school: 75.4%; percent having completed college: 23.6%.

Major Players: Services, retail/wholesale trade, manufacturing, government. Also recording, publishing, distribution, and production of country music as well as printing and publishing bibles.
Largest employers—AGC Life Insurance, Aladdin Industries (hardware), American General Life & Accident, Flagship Airlines, Opryland USA, St. Thomas Hospital, Sunday School Bd./ So. Baptist Convention, Third National Corporation.

Community Services: *Average hospital cost*—$259.80/day.
Average doctor visit—$53.13.
Average dentist visit—$46.80.
Newspapers—Tennessean/Nashville Banner, Nashville Business Journal, Nashville Pride (African-American), Nashville Scene (alternative).

Photo by Robin Hood

NASHVILLE: BEYOND HEE-HAW

Call it "Music City USA," the "Athens of the South," "Third Coast," and the "City of Parks,"—anything but "Nowheresville." The second largest metropolis in Tennessee, Nashville packs a punch in the music, automotive, printing and publishing, education, and health care industries, to mention a few. And as home to stars and others in the entertainment business, it's L.A. without the smog, crime, and endemic weirdness. So what if folks talk with a twang? If someone approaches you with a tire iron, they're probably going to help fix a flat. After all, according to a study by Fresno State University, Nashville was named the friendliest city in the country.

The settlers got down to business in the late 1700s, when they decided to build a fort in the area, much to the chagrin of the Cherokee, Chicasaw, and Shawnee, who prior to that time had gotten along fine with the French traders, thank you very much. By 1784, however, the Indians were defeated and the burg was big enough to be renamed from the original Nashborough to the less Anglicized Nash*ville*. Proximity to the Natchez Trace (a major commercial road), the Cumberland River (which was used for shipping cotton), and a rail center ensured its continued growth; by the mid-1800s, it became the state capital. No wonder the Union army lusted after Nashville during the Civil War, occupying it for three years. ("Yankee" is not a term of endearment here, even today.)

> When Teddy Roosevelt coined the term "Good to the last drop," he was referring to the coffee produced by the local Maxwell House Hotel. However, that might apply to life here as well.

The Battle of Nashville in 1864 signaled the end of the Confederacy, and basically destroyed much of the city. But not for long: Within a few decades, Nashville became a center for trade (particularly in printing, sales, and distribution) as well as education with the establishment of, among several others, Vanderbilt University and Fisk, one of the nation's first private black colleges. In the 1920s, the city also served as a mecca for country-and-western music, and the first "WSM Barn Dance" was held. That's the Grand Ole Opry—radio's longest-running program—to city slickers. The 1930s saw another boon in the form of cheap electricity produced by the Tennessee Valley Authority.

Today Nashville is powered by representatives from every major record label, booking agency, and song publisher. A diverse job base has made it an entrepreneurial hot spot according to both *Inc.* magazine and the Cognetic research group. And an annual 9 million tourists pump over $2 billion into the economy, while the metropolitan/suburban region is seeing an increase in population as well. "People come here and want to stay," observes communications coordinator Elizabeth Ladner. "Transfers are pleasantly surprised." Perhaps not always—Nashville was recently rated a top relocation destination by *Fortune* magazine.

Quality of Life

When Teddy Roosevelt coined the term "Good to the last drop," he was referring to the coffee produced by the local Maxwell House Hotel. However, that might apply to life here as well, particularly for certain socioeconomic groups. "Nashville has a small-town feel but there's lots of big-city stuff happening," Ladner goes on. Between the music scene, the colleges, and the growth and expansion of industries, "it's an exciting time to be here."

Plus, it's a pretty place; bucolic green areas share space with gleaming skyscrapers and historical sites of the National Register kind. The climate's fairly temperate, although those with frizzy hair may have it tough during the humid summers, and the "mere" average six inches of snow doesn't take into account several annual ice storms. But fall and spring are particularly long-lasting and spectacular, and the city gets decked out in holiday finery during the Christmas season. With supposedly more churches per square foot than anywhere else and several Christian-based businesses, what else could you expect?

Although the Golden Rule seems to spill over into everyday life, "there are certain sections of town where you only see white faces," confides one man. "It's not that race relations are bad, but that African-Americans and even Asians have their own places just as we have ours."

Bigotry, at least not the overt kind, doesn't seem to be the issue: "Nashville's very integrated corporate-wise, but socially, this is a conservative town," remarks marketing director Haylee Waddey. "You see a little bit of everything because of the colleges," but outside of that, "it's mainly white-bread." Still, "There are lots of single people, including African-American professionals," states sales manager Crystal Fields.

With the cost of living almost as (comparatively) low as the price tag on Minnie Pearl's hat ($1.98), you can live very cheaply here, "although real estate has escalated since the early '90s, with some homes even doubling in price," comments writer Chris Green. "There's been a real explosion in the economy." Apartments and condos can be scarce in the more happening areas, what with some 80,000 college students scattered around the city. But with a drive-by-the-numbers highway system and minimal traffic, "it's really easy to get around and do things." The urban decay that plagued larger metropolises "never left its mark here."

The arts and sports scenes are flourishing. Nashville's cornucopia of entertainment options range from the traditional to alternative/punk, and there are dozens of venues, with more popping up all the time. And with 6,650 acres of parkland in the city and other lakes and major preserves nearby, one never lacks for a run in the country. Fans are also particularly juiced about the 1999 "transfer" of the former Houston Oilers to Nashville's spanking new 65,000-seat stadium.

General Opportunities

With paid employment actually available in the music industry, Nashville can be a musician's dream come true. Along with 175 studios, there are 40 national ad jingle makers, 26 entertainment publications, and 80 production companies, equipment houses, and film/video service businesses. Although this scene may be Nashville's most, uh, note-able appeal, living here also makes dollars and sense. The early '90s saw a 13.1 percent gain in per capita income, while more than 100,000 new jobs have been created since 1990. Bread-and-butter corporations such as Aladdin Industries, Caterpillar Financial, Columbia/HCA Healthcare, and more have made their home or expanded operations here.

The unemployment rate is much lower than the national average, and because of the wide variety of enterprises, the area is somewhat impervious to financial and economic whims. Nashville has also been ranked among the top U.S. cities for job opportunities for new college graduates by Dow Jones & Co. And in spite of its seeming conventionality, "this is a very cosmopolitan, progressive city," comments Fields. "There's not a lot of crime, and we get many of the same shows and entertainment options as larger places."

MAJOR BREADWINNING

In a sense, Nashville might be considered the ultimate 7-11 convenience stop, especially for production and distribution industries such as the Gap, Roadway Packaging Systems, Hartman Luggage, and Kroger foods. It's the site of an international airport, a primary rail hub, and a navigable harbor. Three major interstates converge here, and an enhanced telecommunications infrastructure supports such services as MCI, AT&T, Sprint, and BellSouth.

Because of the high growth of managerial and administrative personnel at increased income levels, the biggest part of the employment pie belongs to services (29.2 percent), followed by trade (24.2 percent); manufacturing (10.1 percent); government (13.3 percent); transportation, communication, and public utilities (5.8 percent); finance, insurance, and real estate (5.7 percent); and construction (4.6 percent). The largest non-government employers consist of Vanderbilt University and Medical Center, Columbia/HCA Healthcare, Saturn (with nearby Spring Hill being the site of many of those corny commercials), Opryland USA, Nissan Motor, and Kroger. Brand names such as Shoney's, Dollar General, Cracker Barrel, Service Merchandise, and First American National Bank are also headquartered here.

> "Nashville has a small-town feel, but there's lots of big-city stuff happening," says an insider. The music scene, the colleges, and the growth and expansion of industries make it "an exciting time to be here."

In the past few years, the assortment of more than 500 businesses that chose to locate and expand here include MagneTek manufacturing, Primus Automotive Financial Services, EMI Christian Music Group, and Nutro Products. Those with sales, publishing, and production skills might find their notch in the Bible Belt at Sullivan Graphics, Waldenbooks, R.R. Donnelly, and Ingram Industries, or with specialty religious publishers like Thomas Nelson, the world's largest printer of Bibles and related literature. The previously mentioned First American National, NationsBank, and SunTrust Bank provide finance-related jobs, while insurance positions might be secured at American General Life, the Willis Corroon Corporation, and others. The hospitality/tourism industry serves up another 43,000+ jobs, with the Opryland Hotel taking the honors as the largest non-gaming property in the U.S.

With more than 250 enterprises, the region's large concentration of health care management firms includes Columbia/HCA, the biggest for-profit hospital operator in the U.S., HealthWise of America, Coventry Corporation, and PhyCor, a physician group practice owner. Medical and related expertise might also be put to good use at the OrNda Health Corp. and Quorum HealthCorp hospital chains, or at one of Nashville's 17 hospitals (two of which are affiliated with medical schools) and more than 115 clinics.

And then there's the $2.5 billion entertainment and music industry, a class by itself. With more than 1,500 businesses and 25,000 people, including about 8,000 who work for Opryland USA/Gaylord Entertainment, "there's nothing quite like it," observes songwriter Joe Nolan. "You're at the crossroads of art and commerce. So along with being creative, you also need to be organized, persistent, and ready to network. Some people are fantastic songwriters and musicians, but without good business sense, their talent may never come to light."

Many seek assistance and guidance through professional groups such as the American Federation of Musicians (11 Music Circle N., 615/244-9514), American Federation of Television and Radio Artists/Screen Actors Guild (1108 17th Ave. S., 615/327-2944), Country Music Association (1 Music Circle S., 615/244-2840), and others.

Most of the noise can be found on 16th and 17th Avenues South, aka Music Row. Dozens of lesser-knowns and specialty labels join major players like RCA, MCA, Columbia, and

Warner and the three largest performing rights societies, ASCAP, BMI, and SESAC. And there's so much more than country: Labels in pop/rock, folk, gospel/contemporary Christian, black, R&B, jazz, and even classical music can be found here. Four cable channels and several film production groups provide jobs and exposure, while music video companies represent the fastest-growing segment of the entertainment industry. Recording studios, music publishing concerns, booking agencies, record manufacturers, theatrical talent organizations, and promotional enterprises offer related positions in transportation, makeup and set styling, catering, graphic arts, photography, lighting, sound, theatrical supply, management, costuming, public relations, and more.

According to Nolan, the Nashville music industry is "highly competitive, with very little money to be made in Nashville clubs because everybody wants to perform there." But salaries can be quite reasonable, particularly if royalties are involved. And if one place turns you down, another one will open tomorrow.

SOCIAL AND RECREATIONAL SCENE

How Nashville Plays

According to native Haylee Waddey, you'll meet two kinds of folks in area code 615: "those who are thrilled with the prospects that come with a growing city, and the rest, who resent the traffic, building activity, and increased crime" that also result. As far as dating goes, "it's actually easier to meet people if you went to college here." Many remain in Nashville after they graduate, "providing a network of ready-made friends and contacts."

Still, "you don't see as many people getting married in their early '20s as you used to," she continues. "There's a trend towards waiting until you're around 30 or so." Professional transplants may have it tougher, particularly if they're from a different part of the country. Although people are generally courteous, "some old southern families keep to themselves and have their particular traditions," states one relocated Northerner. "It can make you feel like an outcast, especially when you sense they're not necessarily being genuine but putting on an air of refinement."

Still, there are plenty of out-of-towners to meet, particularly if "you get involved in a charity or arts group," comments Waddey. Work and "friends of friends" are other good sources. And what with all the bars and live performances, the night life *rocks*.

There are also more than 800 churches. "These and bars are some of the best places to meet people," adds Ladner. Although this seems like a dichotomy, it makes a Nashvillian sort of sense when you consider the city's driving forces.

ARTS AND SCIENCES

Okay, the driveway at the **Hermitage,** President Andrew Jackson's home, is shaped like a guitar, but this city hardly lacks for culture. (In addition to the Hermitage's Greek Revival mansion and Confederate cemetery, the area honors another native President, **James K. Polk,** at his former abode.) Along with having the **Leonard Bernstein Center for Education through the Arts,** a national training facility, Nashville boasts the **Tennessee Performing Arts Center (TPAC),** which has three cutting-edge theaters in addition to Bravo, its young

Where It's At

Unless otherwise noted, all area codes are 615.

Aaron Douglas Gallery at Fisk, 1000 17th Ave. N., 329-8720

Belle Meade Plantation, 5025 Harding Rd., 356-0501

Belmont Mansion, 1900 Belmont Blvd., 386-4459

Where It's At

(continued)

Bicentennial Capitol Mall, 598 James Robertson Pkwy., 741-5280

Broadway Dinner Train, 108 First Ave. S., 254-8800

Car Collectors Hall of Fame, 1534 Demonbreun St., 255-6804

Centennial Park, West End and 25th Aves., 862-8408

Cheekwood, 1200 Forest Park Dr., 356-8000

Citizens Bank, 401 Charlotte Ave.

Country Music Hall of Fame and Museum, 4 Music Square E., 256-1639

Crown, 2421 Powell Ave., 385-3200

Cumberland Science Museum, 800 Ft. Negley Rd., 862-5160

Fort Donelson National Battlefield, P.O. Box 434, Dover, 232-5706

Fort Nashborough, 170 First Ave.

General Jackson Showboat, Opryland, 889-6611

Grand Old Opry House, 889-6611

Grand Ole Opry Museum, Opryland, 889-6611

Hermitage, 4580 Rachel's Lane, 889-2941

James K. Polk's house, West Seventh St., Columbia, 388-2354

Joe L. Evins Appalachian Center for Crafts, 1560 Craft Center Dr., 597-6801

Leonard Bernstein Center for Education through the Arts, 114 30th Ave., 329-1813

Municipal Auditorium, 417 Fourth Ave. N., 862-8930

Music City Car Museum, 2611 McGavock Pike, 885-7400

Music City Queen, Riverfront Park, 255-0835

Nashville Arena, 501 Broadway, 880-2850

Nashville Ballet, 2976 Sidco Dr., 244-7233

Nashville On Stage, 889-6611

Nashville Opera, 719 Thompson Ln., 292-5710

Nashville Symphony, 209 10th Ave. S., 255-5600

affiliates division. TPAC's offerings include the **Nashville Ballet,** the **Nashville Symphony,** the **Tennessee Dance Theatre,** the **Nashville Opera,** and the **Tennessee Repertory Theatre.** The symphony also plays at **Centennial Park** and **Cheekwood.** Named after the locally prominent Cheek family (not the less-classy part of the anatomy occasionally displayed by plumbers and other repair personnel), this restored 1920s mansion is furnished with permanent and traveling works of art set among 55 acres of botanical gardens.

Performance spaces also include the just-built 20,000-seat **Nashville Arena,** as well as the **Crown, Starwood Amphitheatre, Municipal Auditorium,** and others. And the new **Bicentennial Capitol Mall** not only has an amphitheater in a 19-acre park but also an outdoor history museum. If you're looking for a real out-of-town (as in touristy) experience, there's the historic **Ryman Auditorium** (the "Mother Church of Country Music"), the Opry's original home, and, at **Opryland,** the **Grand Old Opry House, Nashville On Stage,** and additional venues. Youngsters and non-country music fans can also visit the theme park, which has a petting zoo and more than 20 rides, including a Hangman roller coaster. The **General Jackson Showboat,** the *Music City Queen* riverboat, and the **Broadway Dinner Train** can provide even more moving entertainment experiences.

Fine arts can be unearthed at the **Parthenon,** which features the world's only full-scale reproduction of the Greek wonder starring Athena, the tallest indoor statue in the Western world, as well as the city's art museum. The **Tennessee State Museum** traces local history from the prehistoric Indians to the early 1900s, while the **Sankofa-African Heritage Museum** focuses on sculpture, carvings, and artifacts from that continent. The **Aaron Douglas Gallery** at Fisk has more of the same, complemented by works of black American artists. Sharing the identical mailing address is **VanVechten Gallery,** a modernistic melange of O'Keeffe, Picasso, Cezanne, and other, newer talents. Over 40 countries/cultures are represented via constantly changing exhibits at the **Vanderbilt University Fine Arts Gallery.** Closer to home, the **Joe L. Evins Appalachian Center for Crafts** showcases basketry, quilting, woodworking, and other skills.

Not surprisingly, Nashville has a potpourri of music-related sites, including but hardly limited to the **Country Music Hall of Fame and Museum** (with Elvis's gold Cadillac and **RCA Studio B,** a fully equipped recording facility); the **Grand Ole Opry Museum,** which salutes past and present singers; and **TNN: The Nashville Network,** where you can see television shows in production. Individual museums also honor artists such as Barbara Mandrell, Minnie Pearl, Hank Williams Jr., Jim Reeves, Willie Nelson, and Kitty Wells, proving that in Nashville, you don't have to be dead to have your own shrine.

Other excesses can be found at the **Car Collectors Hall of Fame,** which has yet another Elvismobile (as well as one of the Batman kind) and the **Music City Car Museum,** which boasts (yawn!) still another Elvis vehicle (they're as common as King sightings around these parts), as well as autos owned by Dolly Parton and George Jones.

Driving deep into the past is **Fort Nashborough,** a circa late 1700s reconstruction of the original settlement. Easier (for some) life and times are re-created at the ornate and unusual **Belmont Mansion,** home of thrice-wed million-airess Adelicia Acklen, and **Belle Meade Plantation,** a former stud farm and antebellum treasure where U.S. President Taft once got stuck in the bathtub. Confederate sites include the home of **Sam Davis, Fort Donelson National Battlefield,** and others. There's also the original **Citizens Bank,** the first African-American–owned S & L in the U.S., which started out in 1904 as the aptly named One Cent Savings Bank.

Children and others with curious minds might enjoy the **Cumberland Science Museum,** with theme shows; the **Nashville Zoo,** with more than 600 exotic animals; and the **Nashville Toy Museum,** with a collection spanning 150 years. A giant among greenhouses, the **Opryland Hotel, Conservatory, Cascades,** and the **Delta** boasts 10,000 tropical plants, indoor "waterfalls," a "lake," and a new 4.5-acre interiorscape, which includes a "river system" with guided boats. And you never have to worry about bird droppings.

THE SPORTING LIFE

"This is an active sports town, both in terms of watching and participating," observes Nolan. Although the really big bruisers—the former NFL Houston Oilers—are yet to come, in the interim Nashvillians can enjoy gridiron action via the **KATS** (a locally owned Arena Football organization) and through **Vanderbilt, Tennessee State,** and **Middle Tennessee State** universities. Nashville also has the **Nashville Sounds,** the baseball farm team for the Chicago White Sox, and the **Nashville KnightHawks,** which slide into ice hockey at Municipal Auditorium. Drag and stock car racing are also pervasive and can be found at **Highland Rim Speedway, Music City Raceway,** and **Nashville Speedway USA.**

Where It's At

(continued)

Fun Boats, 4001 Bell Rd., Hermitage, 800/550-BOAT

Grand Old Golf Amusement, 2444 Music Valley Dr., 871-4701

Hermitage Golf Course, 3939 Old Hickory Blvd., 847-4001

Hermitage Landing Water Park, 400 Bell Rd., Hermitage, 889-7050

Highland Rim Speedway, 6801 Kelly Willis Rd., Greenbrier, 643-8725

KATS, Nashville Arena, 5th and Broadway, 245-KATS

Legends, 1500 Legends Club Ln., Franklin, 791-8100

McCabe Municipal Golf Park, 46th Ave. N. and Murphy Rd., 862-8491

Metro Board of Parks and Recreation, 862-8400

Middle Tennessee State University, 898-2300

Music City Raceway, 3302 Ivy Point Rd., Goodlettsville, 876-0981

Nashville KnightHawks, 259-7825

Nashville Skydiving & Information, 672-2855

Nashville Sounds, 534 Chestnut St., 242-4371

Nashville Speedway USA, Tennessee State Fairgrounds, 726-1818

Nashville Sports Council, 161 Fourth Ave., 259-4738

Percy Warner, 888/867-2757

Radnor Lake, 1160 Otter Creek Dr., 373-3467

Recreation World, 7115 South Springs Dr., 771-7780

Riverside Golf Center, 640 Old Hickory Blvd., 847-2457

Tennessee State Parks, 888/867-2757

Tennessee Skydiving Center, Tullahoma Regional Airport, Tullahoma, 800/483-DIVE

Tennessee State University, 320-3131

Tennessee Wildlife Resources Agency, Ellington Agricultural Center, 781-6500

Vanderbilt University, 322-7311

Those who like their activities organized have lots to choose from. The **Nashville Sports Council** oversees both amateur and professional events, while the **Metro Board of Parks and Recreation** organizes softball and basketball leagues. **Centennial Sportsplex** offers year-round ice skating and swimming; **Recreation World** has everything from an in-line hockey rink to batting cages. Even square and round dancing can be found through the **Cumberland Valley Western Association.**

More than 30 public, private, and resort golf courses range from the 27-hole **McCabe Municipal Golf Park** to the **Hermitage Golf Course** resort to private clubs, such as **Legends.** **Grand Old Golf Amusement** and **Riverside Golf Center** provide miniature guess-what and other options.

Water activities are big here, although they're a bit farther out of town. There's a wave of boating, fishing, and other sports at Old Hickory and J. Percy Priest lakes (including the **Hermitage Landing Water Park** at the latter) as well as other reserves. For information on hunting/fishing licenses, contact the **Tennessee Wildlife Resources Agency.** Boat rentals (**Fun Boats; Birdsong Resort, Marina, & Campground**) are available, as are skydiving and parachuting (**Nashville Skydiving & Information, Tennessee Skydiving Center**) for the truly bold.

Hikers and nature lovers can enjoy nearby **Radnor Lake,** a 1,000-acre nature preserve, and go camping at **Bledsoe Creek.** Facilities at the numerous state parks vary (contact **Tennessee State Parks** for information), although you don't have to go far for green spaces, as about one-third of the land in Nashville/Davidson County remains undeveloped. The city's largest area, **Percy Warner,** is about three times the size of Central Park and has considerably fewer muggers.

 AFTER-HOURS DIVERSIONS

Nashville offers plenty of nightlife, even for non-country fans. "Many places have alternative, rock, and other kinds of music," observes Green. Another advantage: "A lot of big names live here, and they'll go to itty bitty bars with friends and try out their new stuff." So you never know who you might hear for a minimal (or no) cover charge.

One never lacks for things to do, even in the wee hours. Nashville's newest fave is The District, a revitalized downtown area with loads of hip places in refurbished old buildings. The fairly recent **Opryland river taxi service** provides a shuttle between Opryland and downtown, a boon for tourists and businesses alike. Highlights include the **Planet Hollywood,** the **Hard Rock Cafe,** and the **Wildhorse Saloon,** which has a 3,000-square-foot toe-tappin' dance floor, a 22'-by-15' high-definition TV screen, live concerts, and Nashville Network television show tapings. **Tootsie's,** a longstanding Opry tradition, is located next to the Ryman, while **Robert's Western World** sells boots and showcases up-and-comers. Another favorite hangout of the stars and wanna-bees is **Barbara's,** while rhinestone cowfolks strut their stuff at the **Stock Yard Bull Pen Lounge** and at **Denim and Diamonds.** The District also has blues and jazz (**Bourbon Street Blues and Boogie Bar,** the **Merchants, Mere Bulles**), rock (the **Ace of Clubs, Music City Mix Factory**), and **Dancin' in the District,** a Thursday night event from May through August.

Standouts in the trendy Hillsboro, Elliston Place, and Vanderbilt campus/Belcourt Ave. areas include the **Bluebird Cafe, Exit/Inn,** and **Faison's,** respectively. Not only can you hear some of the best jazz, blues, rock, and country around, but you might find yourself listening to the next Garth Brooks or Bonnie Raitt (who, incidentally, got their starts at the Bluebird).

Nashville is also peppered with "hot" smaller performance spaces like the **Pub of Love** (songwriting incubator), **12th & Porter** (top local musicians), **Douglas Corner** (local and national acts), **Stardust Theatre** (variety shows), and **328 Performance Hall** (anything, including alternative) in addition to country magnets like **Nashville Nightlife, Southfork Saloon,** the Opry venues, and more. There's even live blue-grass and free jam sessions at the **Station Inn.** Those who prefer to drink in silence might choose tours of the **George Dickell** and **Jack Daniels** distilleries or the **Beachaven Vineyards and Winery.** But in general, if you've got a problem with live music, then you're in the wrong place.

Nashville may even have more festivals and special events than bars. May and June bring the **Tennessee Jazz and Blues Concert Series;** the **Summer Lights in the Music City Festival,** which features music and art; and the **International Country Music Fan Fair,** a mob scene dreaded by claustro- and country phobics alike.

Non-musical gatherings (no promises, though) include the **Antiques and Garden Show of Nashville** (February), the **Tennessee Crafts Fair** (May), the **African Street Festival** (September), the **Southern Festival of Books** (October), and the **Native American Indian Association Pow Wow**

Where It's At

 Unless otherwise noted, all area codes are 615.

12th & Porter, 114 12th Ave. N., 254-7236

328 Performance Hall, 328 Fourth Ave. S., 259-3288

Ace of Clubs, 114 Second Ave. S., 254-ACES

African Street Festival, Tennessee State University main campus, 299-0412 or 227-7258

Antiques and Garden Show of Nashville, Nashville Convention Center, 352-1282

Barbara's, 207 Printer's Alley, 259-2272

Beachaven Vineyards and Winery, 1100 Dunlop Lane, Clarksville, 645-8867

Bluebird Cafe, 4104 Hillsboro Rd., 383-1461

Bourbon Street Blues and Boogie Bar, 220 Printer's Alley, 242-5837

Christmas at Belmont, Belmont Mansion, 460-5049

Country Christmas, Opryland Hotel, 889-1000

Dancin' in the District, Riverfront Park, 256-9596 or 242-5600

Denim and Diamonds, 950 Madison Square Shopping Center, 868-1557

Dickens of a Christmas, town of Franklin, 791-9924

Douglas Corner, 2106-A Eighth Ave. S., 298-1688

Exit/Inn, 2208 Elliston Pl., 321-4400

Faison's, 2000 Belcourt, 298-2112

George Dickell, Cascade Rd., Tulahoma, 857-3124

Hard Rock Cafe, 100 Broadway, 742-9900

International Country Music Fan Fair at the Tennessee State Fairgrounds and Opryland, 889-7503

Jack Daniels, Hwy. 55, Lynchburg, 759-6180

Merchants, 401 Broadway, 254-1892

Mere Bulles, 152 Second Ave., 256-1946

Music City Mix Factory, 300 Second Ave. S., 251-8899

Where It's At

(continued)

Nashville Nightlife, 2620 Music Valley Dr., 885-5201

Native American Indian Association Pow Wow, Hermitage Landing, 726-0806

Opryland river taxi service, 2802 Opryland Dr., 889-6611

Planet Hollywood, 322 Broadway, 313-7827

Pub of Love, 123 12th Ave. N., 256-5683

Robert's Western World, 416 Broadway, 256-7937

Southern Festival of Books, Legislative Plaza, 320-7001

Southfork Saloon, 2265 Murfreesboro Rd., 361-9777

Stardust Theatre, 2416 Music Valley Dr., 889-2992

Station Inn, 402 12th Ave. S., 255-3307

Stock Yard Bull Pen Lounge, 901 Second Ave. N., 255-6464

Summer Lights in the Music City Festival, 259-0900

Tennessee Crafts Fair, Centennial Park, 665-0502

Tennessee Jazz and Blues Concert Series, Belle Meade Plantation, 5025 Harding Rd., 356-0501

Tootsie's, 422 Broadway, 726-0463

Trees of Christmas, Cheekwood, 353-2162

Wildhorse Saloon, 120 Second Ave. N., 251-1000

Where It's At

 Unless otherwise noted, all area codes are 615.

4th Ave. Deli, 223 Fourth Ave. N., 726-1835

100 Oaks, 719 Thompson Ln., 383-8350

Alkebu-Lan Images, 2721 Jefferson St., 321-4111

Amerigo, 1920 West End Ave., 320-1740

(October). The holiday season's a really big show, with a **Country Christmas, Christmas at Belmont, Trees of Christmas, Dickens of a Christmas,** and more. It's enough to make even Scrooge think twice.

 ## CULINARY AND SHOPPING HAUNTS

Nashville has its share of fancy joints (**New Orleans Manor, Morton's, Ruth's Chris**). Even the unassumingly monikered **Shack,** which provides free peanuts and a floor for customers to throw shells on, has steak and seafood dinners. But the city's culinary backbone is down-home country cookin' such as ham and redeye gravy, fried chicken and biscuits, and barbecued whatever. And most of these victuals cost between $4–10, give or take a couple of quarters. Locals flock to diners such as **Rotiers, Swett's, Elliston Place Soda Shop,** and **Loveless. John Andretti's Car-B-Cue** promises no fried foods—in these parts, a claim akin to a tax-cut promise during an election year (only this one is true). And Craig Claiborne of *The New York Times* raved about the catfish, another Southern specialty, at **Cock of the Walk.**

A full plate of drive-through and/or sit-down BBQ and more can be found at **Bar-B-Cutie, Calhoun's, Corky's Bar-B-Cue, Country Cabin Bar-B-Cue,** and **Red, Hot & Blue** among others. There's pure soul—turnip greens, pork specialties—at **Little Gray's,** while **Jamaica** and **Calypso Cafe** serve up a side trip to the Caribbean. Numerous cafeterias attest to the Nashvillian fondness for plenitude—**Old Country Buffet, Luby's, Morrison's,** and **Piccadilly,** to mention a few. Breakfast is also a main event at the **Pancake Pantry,** where the rich and famous queue up alongside everybody else.

There are enough trendy American eateries around these parts to satisfy even finicky yuppies. The **Bound'ry** offers updated Southern classics, while the Naomi Judd–owned **Trilogy** focuses on California comestibles. **Jules** and **Cafe 123** provide innovative cuisine; and **Sunset Grill, South Street,** and **TomKats on Broadway** are great places to strap on the old feedbag and be seen doing so. At the **Nashville Country Club** (it isn't) you just might overhear industry mavens discussing various deals, while the rest of Broadway is studded with the highly rated (and costly) **Arthur's, Mario's,** and the **Wild Boar.** And you'll never lack for a good steak at **Jimmy Kelly's, Sperry's,** or the **Prime Cut.** And that's not mentioning chains like **Applebee's, Darryl's, J. Alexander's, O'Charleys,** and the extremely descriptive **Frank & Stein Dogs and Drafts.**

The city's extensive menu of Italian selections ranges from the mid-priced **Amerigo, Finezza,** and **Boscos** to the somewhat ritzier **Antonio's, Valentino's** and **Caesar's.** With **LaPaz, Rio Bravo, Iguana,** and **Texana Grill,** Mexican/Southwestern cuisine is a presence as well. And although they're a long way from home, there's a passel of delis (**4th Ave. Deli, NYB, Noshville Delicatessen, Schlotzsky's,** others) and Asian eateries (**Ichiban, Mikado**). "New kids on the block" consist of microbreweries (**Market Street Public House, Big River Grille, Bohannon Brewing's Public House**) and coffeehouses (**Cafe Milano, Henry's**).

For a town that formerly specialized only in Western bow ties, belt buckles, and boots, shopping "has definitely evolved," points out Waddey. "In the past few years, we've gotten more malls and new stores" including Eddie Bauer, the Nature Company, Barnes & Noble, and CompUSA.

The result: pockets of places, with purchasers reaching into theirs as well. Downtown you'll find the **District,** home of many trendy emporiums, including the **Museum of Maillie,** and Eighth Ave., whose **Downtown Antique Mall** has 13,000 square feet of collectibles. More can be found in Nashville proper (**Antiques of Nashville, Belle Meade Interiors Market, Made in France**), while outstanding accumulations are also available in the historic community of **Franklin** and in the suburb of **Goodlettsville.** Also downtown, the **Nashville Arcade** remains a local perennial and one of the last remaining two-tiered pedestrian malls. The new **Farmer's Market** has more than 200 stalls' worth of foods, plants, and other perishables. The flea market at the **Tennessee State Fairgrounds** draws more than 1,000 traders on the fourth weekend of each month. And the primarily African-American neighborhood of Jefferson Street boasts several black-owned businesses, including **Woodcuts, Alkebu-Lan Images,** and the **Old Negro League Baseball Shop.**

Around the city, a sophisticated and eclectic mix can be found at **Hillsboro Village,** while **Music Row** and **Music Valley** are a kitsch-lover's heaven.

Local malls include **Bellevue Center** (motto: "Nashville's Best Place to Shop") with 125 offerings, including the one and only Tennessee State Museum Store and the local chapters of Abercrombie & Fitch, Godiva Chocolatier, and others. The **Mall at Green Hills** is another upscale spot, while Castner Knott, J.C. Penney's, and Dillard's make **Hickory Hollow** and **Rivergate** more middle-of-the-pocketbook. At the new end of the spectrum is **Cool-Springs Galleria,** with 150 more stores, a giant food court, and cinema. The area's first cluster, **100**

Where It's At

(continued)

Antiques of Nashville, 2921 Nolensville Rd., 831-0720

Antonio's, 7097 Old Harding Rd., 646-9166

Applebee's, several locations

Arthur's, 1001 Broadway, 255-1494

Bar-B-Cutie, several locations

Belle Meade Interiors Market, 5133 Harding Rd., 356-7861

Bellevue Center, 7620 Hwy. 70 S., 646-8690

Big River Grille, 111 Broadway, 251-4677

Bohannon Brewing's Public House, 134 Second Ave. N., 242-8223

Boscos, 1805 21st Ave. S., 385-0050

Bound'ry, 911 20th Ave., 321-3043

Caesar's, 88 White Bridge Rd., 352-3661

Cafe 123, 123 12th Ave., 256-7372

Cafe Milano, 174 3rd Ave. N., 255-0073

Calhoun's, several locations

Calypso Cafe, several locations

Cock of the Walk, 2624 Music Valley Dr., 889-1930

CoolSprings Galleria, 1800 Galleria Blvd., 771-2128

Corky's Bar-B-Cue, 100 Franklin Rd., Brentwood, 373-1020

Country Cabin Bar-B-Cue, 7093 Old Harding Rd., 662-1553

Darryl's, 4319 Sidco Dr., 832-1827

District, Broadway, Second Ave., Printer's Alley

Downtown Antique Mall, 612 Eighth, 256-6616

Elliston Place Soda Shop, 2111 Elliston Pl., 327-1090

Factory Stores of America, 2434 Music Valley Dr., 885-5140

Farmer's Market, 900 Eighth Ave. N.

Finezza, 5404 Harding Rd., 356-9398

Frank & Stein Dogs and Drafts, several locations

Franklin, no central address, 800/356-3445

Goodlettsville, I-65 to Dickerson Rd., no central phone

Where It's At

Oaks, received a recent multimillion-dollar facelift and enlargement with discount stores, including Saks Off Fifth, T.J. Maxx, Luxury Linens, and a nearby Burlington Coat Factory. You can plug into an outlet mall across the street from the Opryland Hotel (**Factory Stores of America**), with over 70 shops. Now that won't drive your feet or your budget crazy.

 ## ETHNIC AND RELIGIOUS PROSPECTS

Although being black in Nashville means being part of almost a quarter of the population, "you are aware of undertones, although it's really not different from anywhere else in the country," remarks Fields.

Still, she's found job opportunities to be good "and there really are a lot of social options." These include the African-American sororities and fraternities, Delta Sigma Theta and Alpha Phi Alpha, respectively, where even non-members are welcome to participate. Organizations such as the **Nashville Urban League,** the local chapter of the **NAACP,** and various professional groups provide networking prospects; more information can be gleaned from the **Metropolitan Black Pages.** "There is some interracial dating," adds Fields. "And although it's more acceptable now than it had been in the past, you still can get a few looks" from both whites and blacks.

According to Nolan, the Asian and Latino communities have grown as well. "In the four years I've lived here, Nashville has become much more cosmopolitan."

Nevertheless, it remains God fearin', with dozens of Protestant denominations, including African Methodist Episcopal, Church of Christ, and Southern Baptist; Roman Catholic; Jewish; Seventh Day Adventist; Jehovah's Witnesses; Baha'i; Buddhist; and others. About 250 African-American churches alone can trace their history to before the Civil War. The various religious colleges—**Belmont University, David Lipscomb University, American Baptist College,** and others—can provide guidance, divine or otherwise.

Church remains an easy way to meet people in a non-threatening environment. "A lot of places have Wednesday night groups where all you need to do is show up," observes Waddey. And they're not necessarily ultrareligious or strict. "More casual Unitarian-type organizations are popping up for people who are looking for something but aren't quite sure exactly what." Those who do find what they're searching for—at least in an earthly being—can partake of conveniently arranged weddings at the **Bridal Path Chapel,** at

Metro Parks, or at **Opryland Hotel**. And you don't even have to join a congregation.

CRIB SHEET

According to Waddey, "Nashville has lots of neat condos and duplexes, although they may be expensive or difficult to find," particularly in certain areas of downtown or in popular spots like Hillsboro, Elliston Place, and around the universities. Cost, however, can be relative: Nashville's housing index is way below the national average, and a two-bedroom, two-bath apartment hovers around $550 a month.

The most expensive rentals are in the West End (average: about $860 a month), while the cheapest are older units in the Briley Parkway area (about $480), in the southeast part of the city. And apartment building in Nashville and environs has been going gangbusters: Nearly 3,000 new complexes have been recently completed and almost twice as many are on the way. This seems to have hardly made a dent in the housing shortage: Occupancy has only dropped from about 99 percent to around 95.

Those looking for an older abode in Nashville proper might do well in Edgefield, East End, and Lockeland Springs. The city's first suburb, the Nationally Registered Edgefield, features Victorian, Italianate, and Queen Anne–style cottages and homes on narrow lots, while East End and Lockeland Springs have similar architecture. The Richland-West End offers 1920s and '30s bungalows along with older and newer homes, while Hillsboro–West End and Belmont-Hillsboro provide a grab bag of styles. Many of the structures in Germantown were built between 1830–1870; they're close to downtown, making it a popular choice.

Still, "many people like to live in the suburbs," remarks Fields. Along with an easy commute, decent schools, and lots of shopping, "there's not what you would really call a bad area." Certain neighborhoods seem to have hit a high note: they include Brentwood and Franklin to the south, Goodlettsville and Hendersonville to the northeast, Green Hills to the east, and Bellevue to the west.

South of town "is where a lot of the money is, both old and new," observes one man. The tony suburb of Brentwood features lots of executive-style homes. Most start at $200,000+, making this the choice of many high-level white-collar workers. With buildings that date back to before the Civil War, the suburb of Franklin has an antebellum look and aura. "The area's somewhat elitist and draws some of the more established families," continues the man.

Where It's At

(continued)

Pancake Pantry, 1796 21st Ave. S., 383-9333

Piccadilly, several locations

Prime Cut, 170 Second Ave. N., 242-3083

Red, Hot & Blue, 2212 Elliston Pl., 321-0350

Rio Bravo, 3015 West End Ave., 329-1745

Rivergate, 1000 Two Mile Pkwy., 859-3456

Rotiers, 2413 Elliston Pl., 327-9892

Ruth's Chris, 2100 West End Ave., 320-0163

Schlotzsky's, several locations

Shack, 2420 N. Gallatin Rd., 859-9777

South Street, 907 20th Ave. S., 320-5555

Sperry's, 5109 Harding Rd., 353-0809

Sunset Grill, 2001-A Belcourt Ave., 386-3663

Swett's, 2725 Clifton Ave., 329-4418

Tennessee State Fairgrounds, 625 Smith St., 862-8980

Texana Grill, 847 Bell Rd., 731-5610

TomKats on Broadway, 408 Broadway

Trilogy, 1911 Broadway, 321-8818

Valentino's, 1907 West End Ave., 327-0148

Wild Boar, 2014 Broadway, 329-1313

Woodcuts, 1613 Jefferson, 321-5357

Where It's At

 Unless otherwise noted, all area codes are 615.

American Baptist College, 1800 Whites Creek Pike, 262-3433

Belmont University, Belmont Blvd., 383-7001

Bridal Path Chapel, 2415 Atrium Way, 889-6200

David Lipscomb University, 3901 Granny White Pike, 329-8500

Metro Parks, Centennial Park Office, 862-8400

Where It's At

(continued)

Metropolitan Black Pages, 106
Ed Temple Blvd., 321-0807
NAACP, 1308 Jefferson St., 329-0999
Nashville Urban League, 1219 9th Ave.
N., 254-0525
Opryland Hotel, Opryland, 871-6855

The community of Goodlettsville draws all ages and incomes, while the lake district of Hendersonville is geared more towards sports and water activities.

The Saab- and Lexus-infused Green Hills is a favorite of yuppies and other upscale creatures. Close to this neighborhood is the silk stocking Belle Meade, where some of the lawns are as big as city parks and $500,000–$1,000,000+ price tags are as common as the white faces. Those who want a glimpse of the Old South might do well to drive through here, although most just keep going, especially those who prefer diversity. A breath of fresh air can be found in the smaller towns of Madison and Antioch, whose reasonably priced residences are a favorite with beginners. There's even more choice in Bellevue, with its new homes and subdivisions. Also preferred by the up-and-coming, this is one of the most rapidly growing areas.

Although some feel Nashville's public schools leave much to be desired, 83 percent of the city's children attend them. Nashville schools were recently flagged by *U.S. News & World Report* as being multifaceted and outstanding. In a recent graduating class, 61.5 percent of the students went on to higher education, while 30 percent entered the workforce, leaving a very narrow margin for slackers (Metropolitan Nashville Public Schools, 259-8400).

Those opting for private/parochial schools have more than 70 to choose from. The parents of this definite minority fork over between $1,300 and $7,500 a year.

College-wise, "the Athens of the South" lives up to its reputation. The city's nearly 20 institutions of higher learning range from Vanderbilt, with its renowned law and business schools, to Meharry Medical College, which claims to have trained more than 40 percent of the nation's black doctors and dentists, to Free Will Baptist Bible College.

NAVIGATING NASHVILLE

Getting around is easy, "and traffic jams last for only about ten minutes," says Fields. The city is laid out on a grid, making it fairly simple to give and receive directions. "And even if people don't like your looks, they are always helpful." Along with three interstates—I-40 (east-west), I-24 (northwest to southeast), and I-65 (north-south), the I-440 and I-265 inner loops simplify crosstown travel, making it relatively congestion-free, while the historic Natchez Trace Parkway provides more of a scenic route. A new outer beltway, I-840, is expected to cut down commute time. One caveat: Many streets change names. So make sure you know the precise location of where you're going so you won't think you're lost when you're actually not.

Other in-town travel options include the aforementioned river taxi, the trolley (Nashville Trolley Co., 862-5950), and bus service (Metropolitan Transit Authority, 862-5950). Greyhound Lines (800/231-2222) is available for those wishing to leave town.

With the addition of several new carriers and flights, the Nashville Airport (275-1662) recently stepped up its volume of operations. Located a convenient eight miles from downtown, it handles more than 7.6 million passengers a year. Fourteen additional airports in the region provide service as well.

New Orleans at a Glance

Birthdate and Present Size: 1718.
Metropolitan Statistical Area—1980: 1,256,256. 1990: 1,238,816. 1/1/95 (estimate): 1,322,400. Percent change, 1980–1990: –1.4%. Percent change, 1990–1995: +6.7%.

Weather Report: *Average annual temperature*—68.2° F. In January: 61/42° F. In July: 91/73° F.
Average annual precipitation—62".
Average annual snowfall—0.2".

Money Matters: *Unemployment rate*—6.5%.
Per capita income—$11,372 (city); $12,108 (MSA).
Average household income—$29,283 (city); $32,569 (MSA).
Average cost of a home—$105,335.
Average rent for an apartment—$538 month.
ACCRA cost of living indexes (based on 100)—Composite Index: 94.2; Utilities Index: 131.4; Housing Index: 82.6.
Sales and use tax—4.0% (state); + 5.0% (local).
Personal income tax—2.0% to 6.0%.

People Profile: *Crime rate* (Per 100,000 population)—10,089.7 (city); 6,807.7 (suburbs); 8,041.6 (MSA).
Racial and ethnic characteristics—White: 34.9% (city), 62.2% (MSA); Black: 62.1% (city), 34.8% (MSA); American Indian/Eskimo/Aleut: 0.2% (city), 0.3%

(MSA); Asian/Pacific Islander: 1.9% (city), 1.7% (MSA); Hispanic origin: 3.2% (city), 4.2% (MSA); Other: 1.0% (city), 1.0% (MSA).
Gender ratio—86.6 males per 100 females (all ages); 81.6 males per 100 females (18 years old+).
Age characteristics—18–24 (11.1%); 25–44 (32.8%). Median age: 31.8.
Educational attainment—percent having completed high school: 68.1%; percent having completed college: 22.4%.

Major Players: Services; retail/wholesale trade; government; manufacturing.
Largest employers: Children's Hospital, Christian Health Ministries, DynMcDermott Petroleum Operations, First Commerce Corp. (banking), New Orleans Public Service, Pendleton Memorial Methodist Hospital, Showboat Star Partnership, Southern Baptist Health Systems, Times Picayune Publishing, Touro Infirmary, Tulane University Medical Center, Whitney Holding Corp. (banking).

Community Services: *Average hospital cost*—$366/day.
Average doctor visit—$36.
Average dentist visit—$41.20.
Newspapers—The Times-Picayune, New Orleans City Business, Louisiana Weekly (black), *Clarion Herald* (Catholic), *Gambit Weekly* (alternative), *Offbeat Publications* (arts).

Photo by Susan Leavines, courtesy of New Orleans Metropolitan Convention & Visitors Bureau

New Orleans' abundance of restaurants, bars, music, beautiful homes, shops, parades, opportunities for sexual escapades, and just about everything else can seduce and captivate. Before you know it, "The Big Easy" may lighten the wallet more than anticipated, result in unwanted pounds, and create guilt feelings about current relationships. So take a deep breath of the jazz and spice-infused air and try to stay on course—as much as possible.

Like many a glamorous individual, New Orleans has a checkered past. Founded in 1718 by Pierre Le Moyne, a.k.a. the Sieur de Bienville, it was touted as a land of fabulous riches. One can only imagine the reaction of settlers when they encountered the shacks, swamps, and 'gators that made up the original colony.

Along with floods, hurricanes, diseases, and Indian attacks, New Orleans has known a potpourri of masters. First the

French, then the Spanish, then the French again, and finally the Americans claimed the area as their own. Creoles, descendants of early French and Spanish settlers, and Cajuns, whose ancestors sprang from the Canadian provinces of Nova Scotia and New Brunswick, left their cultural imprint. African-Americans cleared and built much of the French Quarter and brought over African music and the voodoo religion. Even the British tried to seize control of New Orleans during the War of 1812, although they failed miserably.

These influences forged New Orleans' unique personality. Glass-and-steel skyscrapers sprout behind two-story, pastel-colored Old World buildings; festivals and parades such as Mardi Gras are nearly as commonplace as traffic jams. As the second largest port in the U.S. and as an international tourist attraction, "Nawlins" has managed to flourish and keep its sense of humor at the same time.

> **Multiple influences forged New Orleans' unique personality. Glass-and-steel skyscrapers sprout behind two-story, pastel-colored Old World buildings; festivals and parades are nearly as commonplace as traffic jams.**

Quality of Life

Despite a population of over 1.2 million in nine "parishes" (a Catholic colloquialism for county), "New Orleans is a very nurturing, comfortable place," observes Ann Schnieders, a long-time resident who coordinates YA/YA, an arts program for local youth. "People are kind; there's not as much insensitivity and indifference as in other cities of its size." No one knows a stranger in this town; people who have obviously never met before can be overheard swapping stories and advice in bars and restaurants.

The weather is almost as laid-back as the emotional climate. With an average annual temperature of 68 degrees, the region has mild winters and extended springs and falls. The summer's humidity, however, is enough to curl your hair, although an average annual rainfall of 62 inches can cool things down. The moisture also causes other hair-raising complications: because of the city's high water table and the fact that it's four to six feet below sea level, tombs are above ground. Otherwise, as one writer put it, "Imagine listening to the coffin of a loved one gurgling, gurgling, gurgling, as it [sinks] to its rest."

But although New Orleans has 41 cemeteries, there are over 3,000 bars to help you forget the inevitable. The city has the third largest alcohol consumption in the U.S. (behind Nome, Alaska and Washington, D.C.), a fact which is often credited to (or blamed on) the 9 million annual visitors. But you don't have to be a drinker to savor the ambience: at any hour of the day or night, "you can hear everything from all variations of jazz to zydeco to gospel to rhythm and blues" remarks engineer Jeff Mahu, who recently moved here. "If it's eclectic or funky, it's here."

Still, the unwary can find themselves in the wrong section should they wander too far from the beaten path. New Orleans has less total crime than—surprise!—Minneapolis or San Antonio, but the murder rate is among the highest in the United States, although it has recently declined. Many streets are well-tended and maintained, but "there are pockets of poverty and despair," explains artist Rondell Crier.

The city's rich musical, theatrical, and artistic heritage make it a perpetual jamboree. Year-round professional events and teams, as well as excellent hunting, fishing, golfing, and water resources draw sports enthusiasts. Bars, street fairs, and even hanging out provide a plethora of social opportunities. Only in New Orleans can you spot blue-haired ladies in pearls and heels sharing space in Jackson Square with skinheads and Rastafarians. While jugglers and mimes perform and fortune tellers and artists peddle their wares, tourists of all nationalities mingle freely with natives, whose relaxed demeanor encourages conversation. If it's part of the human condition, it's undoubtedly wandering around the French Quarter.

General Opportunities

Compared with other large cities, the cost of living in New Orleans is relatively low. Housing and industrial space and land are reasonable and plentiful, although at slightly a third above the national average, utilities can take a bite out of the paycheck. Wages are about 20 percent below the national average, while food and entertainment are expensive in this tourist town. So you may have to reduce your lifestyle somewhat.

Still, there are an estimated 654,000 jobs within the nine-parish region, up 5 percent from 1990. Unemployment is now in keeping with the national average, having declined steadily over the past few years. Since the early '90s, tourism, maritime and port-related industries, shipbuilding, oil and gas, aerospace manufacturing, and small businesses have contributed nearly $12 billion in capital investments and infrastructure restorations.

With a rate that's four times the national average and ranking in the top third of all metropolitan areas, economic growth will likely continue. The incoming money has also contributed to the grande dame's facelift: a rediscovered riverfront; the renovation of several city neighborhoods; environmental improvements to Lake Pontchartrain; and the continued upgrade of various attractions.

"New Orleans has cleaned up its act," comments Kelley Smith, a hotel sales manager. Between restoration and marketing efforts, "the city has become increasingly popular." As home of the Superdome and Mardi Gras—Mardi Gras *alone* has an annual economic impact of almost $1 billion—and second only to the D.C. area in number of convention bookings, New Orleans will undoubtedly continue bringing in big bucks with style.

MAJOR BREADWINNING

Let's face it: people don't usually move to New Orleans to get rich (although fame may be another story altogether). They are enticed by the lifestyle or the climate. Those looking for the fast track to corporate success might best search elsewhere.

With a more highly educated workforce, a greater number of white-collar employees than the national average, and lower turnover and absenteeism, the New Orleans job market can be tight. And many positions are blue-collar: approximately 40 percent of employment is divided between oil and gas related industries and maritime enterprises. New Orleans is a primary producer of oil (via offshore drilling), natural gas, and multipurpose chemicals such as fertilizers, synthetic rubber, alkalis, chlorine, and others.

Along with its obvious geographical advantage, the Port's access to the Mississippi River waterway and the Gulf Intracoastal Waterway provides inexpensive barge transportation. This translates into over $50 billion in international trade.

> "The city that care forgot" can be especially treacherous for the inexperienced, impressionable, or easily influenced. "New Orleans is not like other places," points out a former resident. "There's a different set of standards. People don't worry so much about what others think."

Another large and rapidly growing economic sector is health care. With an economic impact of $5 billion, this industry furnishes almost 60,000 jobs, with an estimated 40,000 additional employees by 2005. Thirty-five hospitals provide services ranging from women's health to psychiatry to chemical dependency to children's specializations. Called the "Mayo of the South" (as in medicine, not the sandwich spread), the Ochsner Medical Institutions pioneered heart transplants and established an outpatient facility and neighborhood clinics. But this pond may also be too full for swimming: Tulane and Louisiana State University produce a steady stream of doctors, nurses, and other technicians. New Orleans has six physicians per 1,000, compared to the national average of three.

One good entry point is tourism. Not only has it doubled to more than 70,000 jobs in the past 20 years, but New Orleans' unique program of tax-free shopping has furnished a global boost. "Marketing, hotel, and restaurant management skills are welcome here," points out Smith. "Fluency in foreign languages is also a plus, since we have so many international visitors."

Business and professional services account for another 60,000 positions. Once you find your niche, "the service industry is wide open," continues Smith. Accountants, lawyers, retailers, and other people-oriented entrepreneurs "will discover that a little ambition can go a long way. Folks around here are easygoing, so networking comes naturally."

Other occupations require specialized training or have limited positions. Despite cutbacks, the military, federal, and state government pump hundreds of millions of dollars into the economy, and ship-building and -repair and aerospace manufacturing supply nearly 13 percent of the area's total earnings. New Orleans continues to be a major producer of specialized watercraft and innovations in their repair and productivity. NASA's New Orleans assembly facilities provide parts and support for the space shuttle and future ongoing projects.

Although finding a good (key word here) job may not be simple, it *is* doable in a town where inventiveness and business savvy can count more than age and experience. Sums up Smith, "It's not who you know, but whether you're willing to bend your goals to meet the needs of the marketplace."

SOCIAL AND RECREATIONAL SCENE

How New Orleans Plays

"The city that care forgot" can be especially treacherous for the inexperienced, impressionable, or easily influenced. "New Orleans is not like other places," points out former resident Susan Ward, a hotel marketing director. "There's a different set of standards. People don't worry so much about what others think, making it easy to disappear" in a morass of self-indulgence.

Still, area code 504 has the dual advantage of offering an incredible array of things to do in an open and welcoming environment. "It can knock your socks off," observes Ward.

But in many aspects, it's still a small town. "There are established families who only go to particular places and associate with certain people," says one native. "They have their own set of social mores and definitely wield an influence."

So making friends and getting involved might be trickier than it initially appears. But as with just about everything else around these parts, a little creativity can go a long way.

Where It's At

Unless otherwise noted, all area codes are 504.

Aquarium of the Americas,
1 Canal St., 861-2537

Arts Council of New Orleans,
821 Gravier, 523-1465

Audubon Park and Zoo, 6500
Magazine St., 861-2537

Blaine Kerne's Mardi Gras World,
233 Newton St., 361-7821

Botanical Gardens, 1 Palm Dr.,
488-2896

Contemporary Arts Center, 900 Camp
St., 523-1216

Haunted History Tours, 2814 Robert
St., 897-2030

Jefferson Performing Arts Society,
1118 Clearview Pkwy., 885-2000

Le Petite Theatre de Vieux Carre,
616 Peter, 522-9958

Louisiana Philharmonic Orchestra,
523-6530

Louisiana State Museum, 701 Chartres,
568-6968

Metairie, P.O. Box 58105, 588-9387

New Orleans Ballet Association,
821 Gravier St., 522-0996

*New Orleans Center for the Creative
Arts,* 300 Lafayette St., 523-7708

New Orleans Historic Voodoo Museum,
724 Dumane St., 522-5223

 ARTS AND SCIENCES

Comprising 12 full days, 60 parades, and hundreds of private parties and balls, Mardi Gras seems to be the most obvious way to splash onto the scene. An entire trade has grown around it, including costume creators, float makers, throw manufacturers (the cheap souvenirs tossed from floats), even museums (**Blaine Kerne's Mardi Gras World,** and the **Old U.S. Mint,** which also features a historical exhibit on jazz).

Ironically geared toward the season of Lent, "half the town turns out in costume to watch the other half parade," according to Arthur Hardy, publisher of the *Mardi Gras Guide.* Although opportunities for revelry and romance abound, those wanting to catch more than a medallion, doubloon, or sexually transmitted disease can join a *krewe,* a nonprofit club that stages elaborate parades and balls around the Mardi Gras season.

But not only do krewes traditionally shroud their activities in secrecy—Carnival is supposed to be full of surprises, after all—but membership is by invitation only. The resourceful newcomer can start by asking around and finding out which krewes welcome members. "Each one is different," explains Hardy. "Some are in dire need of people, others have a waiting list, and still others are run by old families and no amount of money will get you in." There are krewes for African-Americans (Zulu, est. 1909), women (Iris, founded 1917) and entertainment lovers (Bacchus and Endymion, who have celebrities head up their parades). Annual dues range from $250 to almost $1,000.

Recently enlarged and with exhibits ranging from the pre-Christian era to the present, the **New Orleans Museum of Art**

(NOMA) is considered one of the largest and most influential institutions of its kind. Traveling presentations of Monet and Faberge attract hundreds of thousands of visitors and millions of dollars. Consisting of several historic properties, the **Louisiana State Museum** chronicles the political and religious development of the region.

Also revitalized, the **Contemporary Arts Center** in the newly chic Warehouse District pushes the envelope on architectural, visual, and performing arts. For those interested in potential paper (or worse) cuts, the **New Orleans Historic Voodoo Museum** illustrates that voodoo is going strong, at least locally.

Other (albeit tamer) arts organizations include the **Arts Council of New Orleans,** the **New Orleans Center for the Creative Arts,** and the **Jefferson Performing Arts Society.** New Orleans has its own opera (**New Orleans Opera Association**), ballet (**New Orleans Ballet Association**), and orchestra (**Louisiana Philharmonic Orchestra**) as well as one of the oldest community venues in the U.S., **Le Petite Theatre de Vieux Carre,** and the art deco **Saenger Performing Arts Center.**

Only in New Orleans can visiting a cemetery become a form of recreation. The 42 "Cities of the Dead" offer a cross-section of architectural styles and designs, with the **Metairie** being the most representative. Tours are recommended (**Haunted History Tours; Save Our Cemeteries, Inc.**). Unless, of course, you relish the idea of wandering alone around above-ground ossuaries where family members' bones have been shoveled aside to make room for new additions....

On a less grave note, the **Audubon Park and Zoo** is a top attraction with more than 1500 animals on 58 acres, abundant gardens and ancient trees. A shuttle bus and streetcar ride away, the **Aquarium of the Americas** boasts 10,000 specimens of fish, birds, and reptiles in their natural habitats. 3-D movies at the adjacent IMAX theatre will likely impress even the most jaded or hung over.

Located in City Park, a 1,500-acre tree-enclosed oasis, the **Botanical Gardens** consist of uniquely designed fountains, ponds, and sculptures, and a vivid array of seasonal flowers. A new pavilion features a library, gift shop, and exhibition room.

 ## THE SPORTING LIFE

Both of the aforementioned **Audubon** and **City parks** offer golf, tennis, team sports, hiking trails, and, in the latter park, a storybook playground, with life-sized exhibits for both big and little kids. The 13 landscaped acres of Woldenberg Park on the riverfront are ideal both for people- and Mississippi-watching.

With about 25 private and public courses, New Orleans is a golfer's utopia. Greens fees range from $6 (civilians) and $4 (military) at the **Colombel Memorial** to $125 (including cart) at the **English Turn Country Club**. Home of several

Where It's At

(continued)

New Orleans Museum of Art (NOMA), #1 Lelong Ave., 488-2631

New Orleans Opera Association, 333 Charles Ave., 524-1018

Old U.S. Mint, 400 Esplanade Ave., 568-6968

Saenger Performing Arts Center, 143 N. Rampart, 525-1052

Save Our Cemeteries, Inc., P.O. Box 58105, 588-9357

Where It's At

 Unless otherwise noted, all area codes are 504.

Audubon Park, 861-2537

City Park, 482-4888

Colombel Memorial, Bldg. 49, NAS, 393-3453

English Turn Country Club, One Clubhouse Dr., 391-8019

Honey Island Swamp Tours, 106 Holly Ridge Dr., Slidell, 641-1769

Where It's At

(continued)

Lakewood Country Club, 4801 General De Gaulle, 393-1010

New Orleans Saints, 1500 Poydras St., 733-0255

Superdome, 1500 Sugar Bowl Dr., 587-3808

Zephyrs, 139 Robert E. Lee Blvd., 282-6777

PGA tournaments, the **Lakewood Country Club** welcomes everyone from duffers to potential pros.

The waterways, bayous, and swamps of nearby Lake Pontchartrain and the Gulf of Mexico provide a plethora of sporting and camping opportunities. Dozens of bayous, swamps, and lakes are ripe for hunting, fishing, boating, and other water diversions. You can explore the delta through river excursions such as **Honey Island Swamp Tours.** Fortunately, the alligators prefer marshmallows to sightseers.

The **Superdome** also offers hourly visitations. Along with being home of the Sugar Bowl, the NFL **New Orleans Saints,** and the site of several Super Bowls, the Louisiana leviathan recently got $20.5 million for much-needed renovations.

The Louisiana State Legislature has put a lot of muscle into the local sports scene. Another $84 million has been allotted to build an arena behind the dome. And the recently resuscitated AAA baseball team, the **Zephyrs,** will catch $20 million for a new stadium in East Jefferson. Seven million has even been piked toward a volleyball training facility at Bayou Segnette State Park.

Where It's At

 Unless otherwise noted, all area codes are 504.

Bally's, One Stars & Stripes Blvd., 800-57BALLY

Black Heritage Festival, P.O. Box 61031, 827-0112

Cafe Brasil, 2100 Chartres, 947-9386

Cajun Queen Riverboat, 27 Poydras St. Wharf, 800/445-4109

Check Point Charlie, 501 Esplanade Ave., 947-0979

Creole Queen Paddlewheeler, 27 Poydras St. Wharf, 524-0814

Flamingo Casino New Orleans, 610 S. Peters, 800-587-LUCK

Grant Street Dance Hall, 113 W. Grant St., Lafayette, 318-237-8513

Greek Festival, Robert E. Lee Blvd., 282-0259

House of Blues, 225 Decatur, 529-BLUE

Maple Leaf, 8316 Oak St., 866-LEAF

Mid-City Lanes, 4133 S. Carrollton, 482-3133

Muddy Water's, 8301 Oak St., 866-7174

 AFTER-HOURS DIVERSIONS

Any attempt to quantify the club scene in New Orleans will be met with either glaring omissions or require a document the size of *Webster's Unabridged.* Because they are full of tourists, conventioneers, and heavy-duty party animals, bars may not be the ideal place to develop meaningful relationships, although sexuality flows as freely as frozen daiquiris (and can have even more dire consequences).

Although New Orleanians won't tell you outright—they love their town and are loathe to say anything negative about it—Bourbon Street should be avoided. Unless, of course, you *like* having strangers throw up on your shoes and spill beer in your purse.

The rest of the city rocks with jazz, blues, and just about everything else. The latter includes bars where both sexes strip and do, to borrow a Southern expression, "Heaven knows what."

Jazz is literally everywhere—at street parades, funerals, festivals, and drifting from the open doors of various establishments. Traditional venues such as **Preservation Hall** and the **Palm Court Cafe** have nurtured artists including Percy Humphrey and Wendell Brunious. Innovators like Red Tyler, Edward "Kidd" Jordan, and the Marsalis family cut their musical teeth at uniquely New Orleans spots such as **Snug Harbor** and **Cafe Brasil.**

New Orleans is also known for its development of rhythm and blues, pioneered by locals "Fats" Domino and the late Professor Longhair. Through R & B, clubs such as **Tipitina's** and the **House of Blues** have risen to national prominence. They feature everything from local to international acts (and charge accordingly) as well as a wide variety of music.

Depending upon the night, many clubs offer outstanding home-grown zydeco/cajun performances—choreographed movements set to a hard beat that make the jitterbug look almost stately—in addition to rock 'n' roll, alternative, Latino, reggae, even gospel. The **Maple Leaf, Mid-City Lanes, Muddy Water's,** and **Check Point Charlie** are but a few. Daring souls searching for immersion in the Cajun/zydeco culture can drive a few hours to **Slims Y Ki Ki, Grant Street Dance Hall,** or **Richard's.**

Festivals are another major form of entertainment, with the most prominent being the **New Orleans Jazz and Heritage Festival,** more commonly referred to as Jazz Fest. Born in 1968, this annual spring rite brings together thousands of local and national musicians, cooks, and craftspeople. If you miss one festival, there's always another: the **Black Heritage Festival** (March), **Greek Festival** (May), **Reggae Festival** (June), and **Swamp Festival** (October), to mention a very few. Each March, the **Tennessee Williams/New Orleans Literary Festival** pays homage to the late playwright and, indirectly, other home-grown authors, including Mark Twain, John Kennedy Toole, Truman Capote, and Anne Rice. Most festivals are accompanied by one or more parades, not to mention the various holidays and special events which in and of themselves generate their own parade (like the organizers need an excuse).

Although it certainly seems like a natural outgrowth, gambling's not the force here that it might be. This may be partially due to the unanticipated closing of the temporary Harrah's Casino and the abrupt halting of construction of the permanent building, which stands like a half-finished monolith on the outskirts of the French Quarter. Harrah's has filed bankruptcy and the fate of the casino is an object of speculation and gossip for locals and visitors alike.

Gambling is relatively new to the area, in fact, and mostly takes place on the Mississippi. Open since 1993, riverboat casinos such as **Bally's** and **Flamingo Casino New Orleans** offer gaming tables, slot machines, and other temptations often accompanied by buffets and jazz. Those who prefer to skip the blackjack et al. can opt for a dinner jazz cruise (**Creole Queen Paddlewheeler, Natchez Steamboat**) or simple runs around the river also offered by the previous two as well as the **Cajun Queen Riverboat.**

CULINARY AND SHOPPING HAUNTS

Food is almost a religion in New Orleans. It has its own god (Chef Paul Prudhomme), language, and houses of worship (restaurants, cooking schools). You'll practically need a crash

---

Where It's At

(continued)

Natchez Steamboat, #2 Canal St., 800/233-BOAT

New Orleans Jazz and Heritage Festival, P.O. Box 53407, 522-4786

Palm Court Cafe, 1204 Decatur St., 525-0300

Preservation Hall, 726 St. Peter, 522-2841

Reggae Festival, City Park, 800-367-1317

Richard's, Lawtell, Hwy. 190, 318-543-8233

Slims Y Ki Ki, Hwy. 167, Opelousas, 318-942-9980

Snug Harbor, 626 Frenchman St., 949-0696

Swamp Festival, October, Audubon Institute, 861-2537, ext. 305

Tennessee Williams/New Orleans Literary Festival, University of New Orleans, 286-6680

Tipitina's, 501 Napoleon Ave., 895-8477

Where It's At

 Unless otherwise noted, all area codes are 504.

Andrea's, 3100 19th St., 834-8583

Antoine's, 713 Louis St., 581-4422

Arnaud's, 813 Bienville, 800/453-1020

Bangkok Thai, 513 S. Carrollton, 861-3932

Belle Promenade, 1701 Baratarian Blvd., 341-8585

Billy Bob's Chinese Laundry, 927 Royal St., 524-5578

Brennan's, 417 Royal St., 525-9713

Bugsy's, 829 Convention Center Blvd., 522-6020

Canal Place, 365 Canal St., 566-7245

Clearview Mall, 4436 Veterans Memorial Blvd., 885-0202

Cookin' Cajun Cooking School, 1 Poydras St., 523-6425

Court of Two Sisters, 613 Royal St., 522-7261

Crozier's, 3216 W. Esplanade N., 833-8108

Esplanade, 1401 W. Esplanade, Kenner, 468-6116

Gumbo Shop, 630 St. Peter St., 800/55-GUMBO

Jackson Brewery, 620 Decatur, 568-0000

Jon Antiques, 4605 Magazine St., 899-4482

Krauss, 1201 Canal St., 523-3311

La Petite Fleur, 534 Royal St., 522-1305

Lakeside Mall, 3301 Veterans Blvd., 8355-8000

Margaritaville Store, 1 French Market Pl., 529-4177

Mike Anderson's Seafood, 215 Bourbon St., 524-3884

Mother's, 401 Poydras, 523-9656

Mr. B's, 201 Royal St., 523-2708

New Orleans Centre, 1400 Poydras

New Orleans School of Cooking, 620 Decatur St., 800/237-4841

O'Henry's, 634 S. Carrollton, 866-0002

course to open a menu and differentiate between andouille (spicy sausage) and boudin (pork mixed with onions, rice, and herbs stuffed into a sausage); or a po-boy (fried oysters or shrimp between crispy French bread) and a muffuletta (an Italian sandwich with meats, cheeses, and olive salad). There's courtboullion (a stew with fish fillets, tomatoes, onions, or other veggies), gumbo (another thick soup, with variations of shrimp, chicken, or okra), jambalaya (basically everything tossed into the pot with a highly seasoned tomato base), and etouffee (another wonderful-tasting tangy tomato sauce).

Just about everything is served with French bread and/or white or "dirty" (pan-fried with green peppers, onion, celery, and giblets) rice. And that's not even mentioning the self-explanatory red beans and rice (it includes sausage also) and the special coffees, weird vegetables, and exotic-sounding spices. Most places serve so much food that towards the end of a meal, even the crawfish (not-so-appetizingly called "mudbugs" by the locals) begin to look like ten-pound lobsters. Those wanting to learn the artery-clogging ingredients of these dishes can attend the **Cookin' Cajun Cooking School** or the **New Orleans School of Cooking.** The rest of us will content ourselves with pants that are suddenly too snug.

It's hard to go wrong in the French Quarter. The most famous, and therefore usually most costly ($20 or more), eateries include **Brennan's, Mr. B's, Antoine's, Arnaud's,** and the **Court of Two Sisters** among many others.

The rest of the city offers variety as well: American and Oriental fare Uptown near the Garden District (**O'Henry's, Bangkok Thai**); Continental in the Warehouse District (**Bugsy's**); French and Italian in Metairie (**Crozier's, Andrea's**); even Indian (**Tandoor**). Prices vary from $8.50 to $20, and like most places in New Orleans, just about any type of dress is acceptable.

You can get by for less than $15 at **Mike Anderson's Seafood,** the **Gumbo Shop,** and **Remoulade.** The best and least pretentious bargain would be **Mother's,** which dishes up dinners between $5–10.

Shopping can also be remarkable as well as expensive. It's not the prices that will get you but the wide and unusual selection of whatever catches your fancy, particularly antiques and jewelry. Along with a farmer's mart, restaurants, kiosks, and souvenir stores, the French Market in the Quarter represents a wide range of cost and quality. Royal Street alone offers everything eclectic from jewelry (**Rumors, La Petite**

Fleur) to fashion (**Billy Bob's Chinese Laundry**) to antiques (about 50 stores). There's even a shop catering to the occult (the **Witches Closet**) and the **Margaritaville Store** to serve all your Jimmy Buffett needs.

In the central business district is **Krauss**, a locally owned department store that oozes Southern charm in an old-fashioned atmosphere of personal service and variety. Specialty shops dot the tony Magazine Street area (**Jon Antiques, RATB Designs**).

The Riverfront and business district areas boast a multi-plicity of the urban malls—**Jackson Brewery, Canal Place,** the **New Orleans Centre,** and the **Riverwalk.** Stores range from Gucci to Lord & Taylor to Sharper Image to home-grown enterprises like the Rhino gallery, which highlights Louisiana artists. And if you *still* haven't spent enough money, the 150 shops at **Esplanade** near the airport and convention center will gladly help you part with more.

The surrounding area has a good share of suburban magnets—**Lakeside** and **Clearview Malls** in Metairie; **Oakwood** and **Belle Promenade** in the West Bank; and the **Plaza** in Eastern New Orleans. Bargain hunters willing to rove further might find plentiful pickins at the **Slidell Factory Stores** and **Tanger Outlet Mall.**

 ## ETHNIC AND RELIGIOUS PROSPECTS

"New Orleans prides itself on being color blind," states Schnieders. The historical mix of cultures has resulted in many of the present descendants being of unknown or at least of blended origin. "People here don't worry about what race you are." Venture too far from the region, however, or talk to some older, entrenched Caucasians and you may find a different attitude.

Still, the two major sectors are African-American and white, and depending on where you reside, one predominates over the other, population-wise. More than 60 percent of the city proper is black. The ratio is reversed in the metropolitan/suburban area. In the latter region there's a fair amount of mixing between the races, while the city has primarily black neighborhoods like historic Treme.

Opportunities are based more on income and education as well as other factors. "It's not so much about whether you're black or Chinese," confides one African-American. "It's about whether your grandfather lived in a certain house or associated with certain people. It can be stifling, if you're trying to make it on your own."

Still, New Orleans has its share of African-American standouts. These include but are hardly limited to Louie Armstrong and dozens of other musicians and performers; inventor Norbert Rilleaux; millionaire Sara Walker; boxer Harry Willis; and former U.S. Ambassador and mayor of Atlanta Andrew Young.

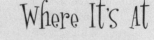

Where It's At

(continued)

Oakwood, 197 Westbank Expy., 362-1900

Plaza, 5700 Read Blvd., 546-1500

RATB Designs, 5509 Magazine St., 800/826-826-7282

Remoulade, 309 Bourbon, 523-0377

Riverwalk, 1 Poydras, 568-8532

Rumors, 513 Royal St., 525-0292

Slidell Factory Stores, 1000 Caruso Blvd., Slidell, 646-0756

Tandoor, 115 University Place, 529-9909

Tanger Outlet Mall, 2200 Tanger Blvd., Gonzales, 647-0521

Witches Closet, 521 St. Philip St., 593-9222

Where It's At

 Unless otherwise noted, all area codes are 504.

Archdiocese, 7887 Walmsley Ave., 861-9521

Corpus Christi, 2022 St. Bernard Ave., 945-8931

Jewish Community Center, 5342 St. Charles, 897-0143

Along with one of the largest African-American Catholic parishes in the country (**Corpus Christi**), there's Xavier University, the only predominately black Catholic college in the U.S. According to figures provided by the **Archdiocese,** the entire region's Catholic population is about 38 percent, largely due to the French and Spanish influence.

The rest of the population consists of a scattershot of other churches as well as a small but tightly knit Jewish community (contact the **Jewish Community Center** for information).

With so many other ways to meet people, church is not the social force it can be in larger or similarly sized cities. Unless, of course, you're a practicing Catholic.

CRIB SHEET

Scratch many neighborhoods in New Orleans and you'll get a medley of people and levels of income. The average price of a dwelling can cover shotgun (where one room follows another), Victorian, Greek Revival, Italianate, California stucco, and Spanish-style homes, converted warehouses, condos, apartments, or Creole cottages, which are usually two rooms wide and two rooms deep. The ultimate recylers, New Orleanians are loathe to tear anything down; hence the hodgepodge of architectural styles and eras. An astounding 82 percent of the buildings in Uptown, the city's largest historical district, were built before 1935.

With 71 neighborhoods within the city proper, it's impossible to tell the players without a program. However, New Orleans real estate has two general axioms: the closer you get to water, the more prices go up, and the more families can (and do) hold onto a house for several generations. Those looking for a 4 bedroom, 2 1/2 bath might have to flee to the newer faubourgs, er, suburbs.

The most obvious starting point would be the French Quarter (also known as the Vieux Carre). With easy access to nightlife and restaurants and the Central Business District—the location of many corporations—it follows that the greatest selection of real estate would be a pricier $150,000 to $350,000+.

The second oldest (but equally desirable) area is the Garden District, which has lush greenery, old trees, and is bisected by the mansion-lined St. Charles Avenue. Exclusive ($200,000–$500,000++) dwellings are mixed in with more modest residences in the $80,000 range. If you like Anne Rice (who owns several blocks of prime property), above-ground cemeteries, and tourists wandering up and down the street, this is the place for you.

Further down St. Charles is Uptown, where an even wider assortment of costs and styles are available, with the largest choice being from $100,000–$375,000. Uptown has the advantage of Tulane and Loyola universities as well as Audubon Zoo and Park, with its attendant sports and recreational opportunities.

The hot spot would be the historic Warehouse District. Located on the Mississippi in the heart of the Central Business District, and having close access to many restaurants and shops, dwellings here consist of converted warehouses. Options range from studios to penthouses, with properties from $80,000–$125,000 or rent from $600 on up. Fortunately, most of the wharf rats have moved elsewhere. Other areas convenient to downtown are Mid City and Algiers as well as smaller communities.

Those looking for a more traditional community might want to consider the planned estates and country-club lifestyle at English Turn ($150,000–$500,000) or the more modern Lakefront and East New Orleans. Closer to Lake Pontchartrain, the older homes at Lakefront

go from $100,000–$275,000; there's a selection of townhouses and condos as well. With homes starting at $60,000, East New Orleans offers a more typical suburban community at a reasonable price. Yet another popular 'bourg is Metairie, a typical New Orleans mix of residences and costs that are about 20 minutes from downtown.

The Catholic influence has translated into a strong parochial school system (see previously mentioned Archdiocese of New Orleans); the city has the largest percentage of private school enrollment of virtually any area of the nation. Private, parochial, and public schools compare favorably with cities such as Houston, Dallas, and Miami (contact the Louisiana State Department of Education, 838-5921). New Orleans also has several colleges, including the University of New Orleans, Tulane, Loyola, and Holy Cross; the latter two are Catholic as well.

NAVIGATING NEW ORLEANS

With ubiquitous (and free) maps, a simple grid layout, and large and frequent signage, getting around the French Quarter can be a breeze, unless you've had too many daiquiris. Cars should be left at home, however, as streets are narrow and parking limited. The Quarter is so condensed that two reasonably healthy feet should suffice.

Parking in the city can be a problem. Rules regarding parade routes, rush hours, driveways, sidewalks, loading zones, neutral grounds (a holdover from when the Americans and Creoles were fighting over land), corners, and crosswalks are heavily enforced, with lots of police wandering around with ticket pads at the ready. The Regional Transit Authority (RTA, 569-2700) offers shuttle service for about a dollar; buses are also available to outlying areas.

A uniquely New Orleans experience is the RTA's St. Charles Avenue Streetcar, which connects the French Quarter with Uptown via the Garden District. Founded in 1835, the original line was once the only form of transportation. Now it's primarily used by tourists and students and is a cheap—albeit slow and bumpy—way of seeing New Orleans for a dollar. You need to know your exact destination, as the rest of the city is rather spread out and things may be farther away than you think.

Once you leave New Orleans, it's rather easy to find your way around. Traffic is typical for a city of its size; unlike some places, drivers seem to actually use their turn signals. Highways are clearly marked and the world's largest bridge, the Lake Pontchartrain Causeway, is an obvious reference point in case you get lost.

Also across the Causeway is Moisant Field (New Orleans International Airport, 464-0831). Named after one of the region's first aviators, the airport is the ninth largest in the nation and offers direct U.S. and international flights. A $650 million capital expansion program is currently underway to accommodate the steadily increasing number of travelers.

Those wanting to leave the city via sea need only go to the Port to catch one of several cruise ships to exotic locales. Or you can exit via 610, which circles the city, onto I-10. There's Amtrak (528-1610) and Greyhound (525-6075) service as well.

NEW YORK, NEW YORK

A Brief Glance

Size and Growth: 1.5 million (Manhattan), 7.3 million (MSA). Percent change, 1980–1990: +3.5% (Manhattan). Percent change, 1990–1995: +0.9% (Manhattan).

Money Matters: *Unemployment rate—* 7.9%.
Per capita income—$16,281.
Average cost of a home—$543,800 (Manhattan).
Average rent for an apartment— $2,820/month (Manhattan).
ACCRA Cost of Living Index (based on 100)—223.8 (Manhattan).
*ACCRA Housing Index—*424.5 (Manhattan).

People Profile: *Crime rate* (per 100,000 population)—7,226.1 (city); 6,648.7 (MSA).

Racial and ethnic characteristics—
White: 52.3% (city), 56.5% (MSA);
Black: 28.8% (city), 26.4% (MSA);
American Indian/Eskimo/Aleut: 0.3% (city), 0.3% (MSA); Asian/Pacific Islander: 7.0% (city), 6.5% (MSA); Hispanic Origin: 23.7% (city), 21.6% (MSA); Other: 11.6% (city), 10.3% (MSA).
*Gender ratio—*88.1 males per 100 females (all ages); 84.5 males per 100 females (18 years old+).
*Age characteristics—*18–24 (10.3%); 25–44 (33.9%). Median age: 33.6.

Major Players: Services, retail/ wholesale trade, government, finance/insurance/real estate.

NEW YORK CITY:
WORLD CAPITAL
OF EVERYTHING

New York: Either you love it or you just don't get it. But there's no avoiding the facts that one in seven Americans can trace their roots back to Brooklyn and that "The Big Apple" is the business capital of the world as well as the center for arts, fashion, finance, and much of the economy. Consisting of the five boroughs of Queens, Brooklyn, Staten Island, the Bronx, and Manhattan, New York is also the most populous city in the United States. But even here, smaller can be mightier.

At only 13.4 miles long and 2.3 miles wide, Manhattan is the Apple of many eyes, packed with more restaurants, arts, major events, and wheeling and dealing per square inch than anywhere else. Just stand on the corner of 42nd and 7th in Times Square—which boasts the highest pedestrian count in the city—and you'll see the full range of the human condition, from millionaires to models to indigents. Some 25.6 million people visit every year, prompting more than one local to remark that they never have to leave because the known universe comes to them.

Practically every square inch of New York has a tale: Wall Street was once a Dutch fortification to keep out the English and Native Americans; Long Island was the scene of several principal battles during the Revolutionary War; the completion of the Erie Canal in 1825 was the seminal event that opened up New York to the rest of the world. And most important (some might say), the hot dog was invented here in 1900 by Nathan Handwerker. Even the term "Big Apple," which had its origins in the '20s and '30s, revitalized the city's flagging image in 1971 to the present tune of $11.9 billion in annual tourist spending.

However, living here isn't always as intimidating as it appears. Although New York seems fueled on hyperbole ("If you can make it there, you can make it anywhere," "The world capital of excitement," yada, yada, yada), the city is manageable. Contrary to rumor, people are basically good-hearted, although they can be pretty blunt at times and want to know what you want in less than 25 words. Even though crime has decreased in recent years, you still have terrorists and crazies, although the odds of encountering those are probably about the same as being in a plane crash; the probability of witnessing smaller (a relative term) felonies and misdemeanors, such as purse snatchings and break-ins, is greater. Being constantly aware, traveling in groups, and installing a set of good door locks are a few ounces of prevention.

And, yeah, the air quality isn't always great and the weather can be really yucky, but more than 1,500 parks and playgrounds, four botanical gardens, and six zoos as well as thousands of annual parades, festivals, and special events can provide a fix for that which is green, living, and smiling. And with nine stadiums and half a dozen professional teams, spectator sports here are hard to top—provided you can get tickets.

Although the prices of co-op apartments and other residences have stabilized or gone down, Manhattan real estate still costs more than four times the national average. But you don't have to live in a postage-stamp-size apartment. Brooklyn, Queens, Staten Island, parts of the Bronx, and outlying areas offer plenty of housing options. With an extensive and cheap public bus and subway system that's used by more than 80 percent of the population, and taxicabs for the adventuresome and multilingual, driving is a headache easily foregone. So what's wrong with an occasional streaker when you have the best in food, entertainment, shopping, and job prospects?

General Opportunities

New York is a 24-7 city, so those looking for 9 to 5 should probably move elsewhere. New York is the number one spot for international business (according to *Fortune* magazine) and the headquarters of more than 2,500 worldwide firms (more than any other U.S. city). Its resources include top accounting, advertising, law, management, and public relations enterprises; a surprisingly large and diverse selection of real estate in the central business district; access to more than $800 billion of the combined assets of 25 banks; the largest and most sophisticated telecommunications system anywhere; and an outstanding transportation network with three airports, the nation's largest railroad hub, and major shipping ports. Certain financial and tax incentives as well as discounts and employee training are available for businesses as well.

> New York is a 24–7 city, so those looking for 9 to 5 should probably move elsewhere. It has been ranked the number one spot for international business; it's the headquarters of more than 2,500 worldwide firms; and its transportation network includes three airports, the nation's largest railroad hub, and major shipping ports.

Although New York's unemployment is somewhat higher than the national average, this city is one of the largest labor markets around, with nearly 200,000 establishments employing 3.2 million people. But you have to be sharp. With a higher than average number of college graduates and a level of productivity that's 48 percent above the U.S. average in the service industry and 54 percent above in wholesale, the Apple is a favorite pick of Fortune 500 companies (some 65 of them are based here).

Along with nearly 300,000 students in more than 120 colleges, the cream of other cities and small towns finds its way here as well. For instance, Columbia University currently has four Nobel laureates on its faculty and both Columbia and New York University (NYU) boast top business, medical, and/or law schools.

This is where creative types go for fame and fortune in the arenas of stage, film, print, broadcast, and design. As the number one media market in the U.S. (18 million TV-viewing households) and with more major television companies, advertising agencies, prominent newspapers, magazine and book publishers, radio stations, and live theaters than just about anywhere else, New York has always been an intellectual magnet. The person working out next to you in the gym may be next year's best-selling author, top clothing designer, or Oscar winner.

The Apple is also home to seven of the world's ten top securities firms and four of the biggest life insurance companies in the U.S. The city also has more banks than London and Tokyo combined. About one-fifth of the nation's economy is transacted here on any given day, through the New York Stock Exchange, the American Stock Exchange, the Commodity Exchange Center, and the New York Mercantile Exchange.

Although New York is expensive, salaries are generally higher than average, with executives and managers as well as technicians averaging $35,000 a year; professionals earning $30,000; and even administrative support and service workers bringing home $19,000 and $18,720, respectively. (Those figures are from a couple of years ago; they're probably higher by now.) Those who want to stay can learn from New York's prolific cockroaches: Keep working when it's dark and never give up.

HOW NEW YORK CITY WORKS AND PLAYS

Major Breadwinning

Like much of life in New York, breaking into the job market can be risky. A few people transfer here; some crackerjack college grads are offered entry-level employment. But many take a chance and wing it on their own, working at anything that pays the bills until the right position opens up. Talent and persistence are almost as much of a commodity as education and experience.

Recent years have seen the influx of companies such as Quaker Oats and Sheffield Labs, and the expansion of industries like Republic National Bank; Capital Cities/ABC; Donaldson, Lufkin, and Jenrette investment bankers; and General Motors. Employment basically mirrors the rest of the U.S. in that the largest group (about 34 percent) is in the service industry. It's followed by government (18 percent), wholesale/retail (16 percent), FIRE (finance, insurance, real estate, 14 percent), manufacturing (9 percent), transportation/utilities (6 percent), and construction (3 percent).

Many jobs can be found in the international arena; bilingualism and a background in global markets are pluses. As a preferred base for worldwide firms and as a gateway to North America, the city attracts thousands of foreign dignitaries, government officials, and businesspeople.

Those with financial expertise might be able to take it to the bank as well. Along with such heavy hitters as Merrill Lynch, Salomon Brothers, Goldman Sachs, Morgan Stanley, and Lehman Brothers securities firms, other major firms include Travelers, American International Group, ITT Corp, Bear Stearns, PaineWebber, and dozens more.

Entertainment and media giants like Time Warner, Viacom, Capital Cities/ABC, Advance Publications, CBS, Hearst, and McGraw-Hill also provide a variety of positions in editing, writing, design, and more. More than 125 consumer magazines include *Newsweek, Time*, and many major women's periodicals; there are also about 60 trade magazines and 80 book publishers. Newspaper opportunities range from the *New York Times* and the *New York Post* to more than 100 ethnic and local dailies/weeklies. Broadcasting and related openings can be found at the "Big Three" networks, several cable stations/companies, and more than 100 radio markets. Hundreds of films, TV movies and series, and commercials provide work for folks in those areas. High-tech companies involved with multimedia, software, and telecommunications are also making inroads, employing filmmakers, musicians, writers, and graphic artists.

New York leads the nation in the manufacturing of printed materials, processed foods, and clothing. The $12 billion fashion industry, most of which is located in the Garment District on Manhattan's West Side, contributes approximately $5 billion to the city payroll. Companies like Bill Blass, Oscar de la Renta, and Donna Karan are headquartered here; dozens more showcase their fall/spring collections to the worldwide press and industry buyers at various New York spots. Other important exports are jewelry; paper, wood, and metal goods; machinery; and textiles. However, several manufacturers have left the area because of high operating costs.

But the service sector has more than taken up the slack. More than 200,000 positions, many associated with cultural activities heavily attended by visitors, can be found in the burgeoning travel/tourism industry. Marketing, public relations, and other skills are needed in New York's 230 hotels and at nearly 400 conventions, as well as at landmarks, theaters, restaurants, and museums. With 91 hospitals and seven medical schools, health care is another evolving field, with facilities combining forces for managed care, research, modernization, and teaching. New York also has the world's largest concentration of charities, cultural organizations, research groups, trade associations, and other nonprofits. Lured by tax incentives as well as security and reasonable rent at Manhattan's Association Center, they're yet another rapidly growing employment segment.

It's all here—the trick is in the taking.

> With more than 400 art galleries, 150 museums, 35 Broadway theaters, 300 Off-Broadway performance spaces, 17,000 restaurants, and 10,000 stores—not to mention the Statue of Liberty and other tourist stuff—you could spend a good portion of your time just figuring out where to go next.

 ## ARTS AND SCIENCES

The question is not what to do in area code 212 but where to begin. With more than 400 art galleries, 150 museums, 35 Broadway theaters, 300 Off-Broadway performance spaces, 17,000 restaurants, and 10,000 stores—not to mention the Statue of Liberty, Staten Island Ferry, Empire State Building, and other tourist stuff—you could probably spend a good portion of your time at home just figuring out where to go next. Better to jump right in and pursue whatever interests you, because no one really cares what you've seen or missed, as many natives who have never even been to the United Nations will attest.

Many newcomers opt to learn about the city through tours like the Big Apple Greeters, where locals serve as guides to points of interest at little or no charge, or Signature Tours, geared to relocators looking for a place to live. Other choices range from conventional motor-coach (Gray Line, Happy Apple, Short Line); to glitzy but expensive limos (Chris Limousines, Romancing Manhattan); to walking with Big Onion, Walk of the Town, and City Walks; to a combo of pied and tush (New York Apple, Marvelous Manhattan Tours Plus).

You can view the Apple from the air (Island Helicopter, Liberty Helicopter) or, if you are financially challenged, take an aerial tram to Roosevelt Island for a mere $1.50. Another sight-seeing alternative is via water (Circle Line, Spirit of New York, Seaport Liberty Cruises, World Yacht), with the best deal around being the Staten Island Ferry at 50¢ round-trip. You can even explore the city through the backseat of a squad car—with the only "charge" being your fee to Manhattan Passport, which offers tours of the boroughs as well.

Architecture, history, and art are highlighted through the New York City Cultural Walking Tours and the 92nd St. Y, while Arts & Events and Arts Horizons International provide an inside look at performers and studios. Ethnic New York can be investigated through Harlem, Your Way!, a variety of sights in the so-called black capital of the world; Liberty View Tours, a close-up of the immigration process at Ellis Island; or the Urban Park Rangers, which explore Native American history as well as—really!— fishing, wildlife, and bird-watching.

A less frenetic method is to familiarize yourself through books. Many of New York's 500+ bookstores have specific sections devoted to their town. Who-when-where fare ranges from the self-descriptive *Mr. Cheap's New York* to the *Best of New York*, a read-it-and-weep upscale guide. The *Encyclopedia of New York City* has everything you need to know and then some. And City & Company publishes local manuals, including the *New York Book of Music*, *New York Book of Dance*, and *New York Book of Coffee & Cake*, which describes local coffeehouses. *How to Meet a Mensch in New York* is the single's guide to zeroing in on a benevolent soulmate.

Like Central Park, Battery Park Esplanade, and other green spaces, the Winter Garden at the World Financial Center offers free concerts, dance performances, and other cultural events, particularly during the warm months. Museums such as the Whitney, the Guggenheim, the Museum of American Folk Art, the Steuben Gallery, and the Metropolitan Museum of Art provide discounts or "pay as you wish" nights. Yet two of the city's biggest attractions, the New York Public Library and the New York Stock Exchange, charge nary a penny (although the latter certainly can tie up money). Tapings of popular TV shows—such as those starring David Letterman, Rosie O'Donnell, Regis and Kathie Lee, Rickki Lake, and others—are another no-cost diversion. And, for the cost of a couple of tokens, you can enjoy the New York Transit Museum, set in a 1930s station and (of course) reachable by subway.

THE SPORTING LIFE

Inexpensive or free activities are a fun way to get acclimated to the city. Central Park has a fishing pond, rowboats, an ice-skating rink, and a wildlife conservation center, while Rockefeller Center boasts summer gardens and more ice skating amid skyscrapers.

Although the Apple itself isn't quite ripe for outdoorsy types (you'll have to go a bit farther afield for skiing, sailing, ice climbing, and bungee jumping), armchair fans have major league excitment in baseball (New York Mets, Shea Stadium; New York Yankees, Yankee Stadium), in NBA basketball (New York Knicks, Madison Square Garden), in NFL football (New York Giants and New York Jets, both at the Meadowlands in New Jersey), in NHL hockey (New York Rangers, Madison Square Garden), and with the U.S. Open Tennis Championships. So many jocks, so little time.

AFTER-HOURS DIVERSIONS

Since Mickey Mouse (that is, the Disney Company) came to Times Square and 42nd Street a few years ago, nightlife hasn't been the same. Peep shows and other tawdry offerings are being replaced by upscale restaurants, renovated theaters, retail outlets, and chic cafes. And the Apple has caught the microbrewery and coffeehouse bug; recent additions to the former include Zip City Brewing Company, while the latter boasts an invasion of Starbucks as well as New World Coffee, Timothy's, Eureka Joe, and Big Cup.

Downtown, Chelsea, the Flatiron district, and artsy neighborhoods such as SoHo, TriBeCa, and (to a limited extent) Greenwich Village are loaded with clubs, although offerings can change as quickly as fashion statements. Neighborhood bars in the boroughs provide a more localized (and hence less up-to-the-minute and more stable) form of night life. According to Andrew Essex of *The New Yorker* and author of *New York's Fifty Best Night Spots*, Sunday is the best night to go out, "when the weekend warriors are in retreat and clubs are empty and accommodating." His recommendations: the glamorous Art-Deco Rainbow

Room; piano music at Bemelmans Bar; Denim & Diamonds, with its dude ranch atmosphere and young professional urban cowpeople (yuckies?); jazz at the Blue Note, Bradley's, and the Village Vanguard; and rock at Mercury Lounge and Wetlands, both of which tend to attract younger Deadhead types.

Other hip-hops: the Fez, Iridium, Visiones, Metropolis, the Knitting Factory, and Webster Hall (a four-story extravaganza featuring acid jazz, reggae, and more). Serious trendies (an oxymoron?) might rave over Soul Kitchen, a roving dance-o-rama that lands at S.O.B's on Tuesdays and Disco 2000/the Limelight on Wednesdays. Make sure you know what they're wearing before you show up.

CULINARY AND SHOPPING HAUNTS

Dining and shopping are best done by the book: Guides include *Access New York Restaurants, Good and Cheap Ethnic Eats Under $10, Born to Shop New York, Marcellino's Restaurant Report,* and dozens more. You can go for the obvious in Manhattan at La Cote Basque and Rainbow Room (both French), Tavern on the Green and Four Seasons (both American/Continental) and the "21" Club. Those with a sense of adventure can travel to Brooklyn and dine at the River Cafe (eclectic), the Heights Cafe (pasta/pizza), or Theresa's (Polish), or visit Queens for Greek food (along Ditmars Boulevard and 31st Avenue) or for Italian (Manducati's). There's more pasta in the Bronx (Pasquale Rigoletto) along with seafood and steak (Emilio's) and shrimp (Ann & Tony's).

As for shopping: Think Bloomingdale's, Macy's, Canal Street, Orchard Street, Fifth Avenue, Trump Towers—not to mention street vendors—and you haven't even scratched the surface.

Bargains galore can be found at the Union Square Green Market, Sixth Avenue Antiques Market, the Lower East Side, Columbus Avenue and W. 76th (on Sundays), and throughout the weekend at Houston Street between Sullivan and Thompson. A bit farther from the central business district are exotic Chinatown and the South Street Seaport, with its living history museum and shopping.

ETHNIC AND RELIGIOUS PROSPECTS

New York is the original melting pot, so just about any race, creed, or color should feel at home here. Even those from another planet (including Hollywood) should find opportunities. Harlem, now mostly black and Hispanic, was the home of the Harlem Renaissance, an African-American literary and artistic movement in the 1920s. The Shomburg Center for Research in Black Culture at the New York Public Library houses the world's largest collection of African-American information, while El Museo del Barrio focuses on Puerto Rico and Latin America. The area is also full of professional and civic groups, such as the Black Leadership Commission and Jack & Jill for African-Americans, and the Hispanic Society of America and many others for Latinos. Other ethnic touchstones include Little Italy and Chinatown.

Although the Apple has its share of WASP male powerhouses, that is changing—nearly 44 percent of the population is Catholic and another 10 percent is Jewish, the largest community of its kind in the U.S. With 7.4 percent, agnostics lord it over Protestants (6.8 percent), and Presbyterians have the smallest number (1.2 percent). The metro area's 6,000 churches, temples, and mosques wield a big schtick. For instance, parts of New York have strong Hasidic and Orthodox Jewish communities, and world-famous houses of worship include St. Patrick's Cathedral, the Cathedral Church of St. John the Divine, Temple Emanu-El, St. Bartholomew's, and Trinity Church.

CRIB SHEET

With a vacancy rate of 3.5–4 percent, finding a place to live around these parts can be difficult. Information about prices, neighborhood characteristics, and availability is not readily obtained: "This is New York; it's not supposed to be easy!" half-jokes one local, when asked about real estate data that is standard issue in most other cities. Although apartments are small, cramped, and overpriced, security is perhaps the most important consideration in choosing where to live. You should investigate this feature thoroughly before making a final decision (there's no guarantee against cockroach invasions, however).

Downtown Manhattan, the oldest part of the city, boasts not only many famous sites but also an incredible variety of living situations, from exotic Chinatown, Little Italy, and the Lower East Side to eclectic SoHo, the East and West Village, and TriBeCa. Chelsea is a favorite of the upwardly mobile, while Gramercy Park offers tree-lined streets and old brownstones. Those who can afford Uptown Manhattan don't need to ask about the price. With four-star restaurants, posh shopping, and major cultural attractions like the Lincoln Center for the Performing Arts, the exclusive Upper West and Upper East Sides are home to celebrities ranging from Ralph Lauren to Woody Allen to Yoko Ono, as well as a host of other wealthy and almost-famous folks. Even the cockroaches have platinum cards. New York's considerable African-American and Hispanic communities reside in historic Harlem and Northern Manhattan, including neighborhoods such as Washington Heights, Morningside Heights, and Inwood.

The boroughs of Brooklyn, Queens, and Staten Island have homes ranging from nineteenth-century manors to suburban-style dwellings to postwar apartment buildings to condos and co-ops. Along with the tree-lined streets and brownstones of Brooklyn Heights, and the historical and recreational area in Prospect Park (another desirable neighborhood), Brooklyn offers everything from Coney Island to Russian nightclubs at Brighton Beach to a cornucopia of cultural activities, many of which spring from the area's 93 racial, ethnic, and religious groups.

The largest borough and the site of John F. Kennedy and LaGuardia Airports, Queens has lots of residences, some of which are in poor neighborhoods. But at least you're close to Shea Stadium, home of the New York Mets, and the USTA National Tennis Center, site of the U.S. Open. Staten Island, on the other hand, boasts a multitude of grand old homes; proximity to the New York Harbor and waterfront dining; Snug Harbor; and Richmondtown Restoration, a complex of colonial-style residences, shops, and public buildings. The Greenbelt, the area's largest natural park, provides 2,500 acres of wildlife and plants as well as 28 miles of hiking trails. Before dismissing the Bronx with that famous cheer (otherwise known as a raspberry), consider that major restoration is taking place in areas such as City Island, Pelham Bay Park, and Orchard Beach. The Bronx is also the location of Riverdale, one of the Apple's most beautiful residential neighborhoods, as well as the New York Yankees and the Wildlife Conservation Society, more popularly known as the Bronx Zoo. However, some streets are still unsafe, even during the daytime.

With approximately 1,110 public schools serving over one million students, it's not surprising that there's a wide variation in the quality of education, particularly in the poorer districts, as about 30 percent of city youngsters are below the poverty level. However, those who rise to the top can qualify for excellent programs at the Bronx High School of Science, Fiorello H. LaGuardia High School of Music and Art and Performing Arts, Brooklyn Tech High School, and others. Folks who can afford it opt for the city's approximately 890 private, preparatory, and parochial institutions, including the exclusive Dalton School as well as the Grace Church School.

ORLANDO, FLORIDA

Orlando at a Glance

Birthdate and Present Size: Settled in 1837; named Orlando in 1857.
Metropolitan Statistical Area—
1980: 700,055; 1990: 1,072,748.
1/1/95 (estimate): 1,385,500.
Percent change, 1980–1990: +53.2%.
Percent change, 1990–1995: +29.2.

Weather Report: *Average annual temperature—*72.4° F. In January: 72/49° F. In July: 92/73° F.
*Average annual precipitation—*47.82".
*Average annual snowfall—*trace.

Money Matters: *Unemployment rate—*4.4%.
Per capita income—$13,879 (city); $14,895 (MSA).
Average household income—$33,136 (city); $39,069 (MSA).
Average cost of a home—$123,138.
Average rent for an apartment—$518/month.
ACCRA cost of living indexes (based on 100)—Composite Index: 98.1; Utilities Index: 110.5; Housing Index: 91.0.
*Sales and use tax—*6.0% (state); 0.0% (local—i.e., none).
*Personal income tax—*None.

People Profile: *Crime rate* (Per 100,000 population)—12,111.7 (city); 6,937.2 (suburbs); 7,628.2 (MSA).
*Racial and ethnic characteristics—*White: 68.6% (city), 82.8% (MSA); Black: 26.9% (city), 12.4% (MSA); American Indian/Eskimo/Aleut: 0.3% (city and

MSA); Asian/Pacific Islander: 1.5% (city), 1.9% (MSA); Hispanic Origin: 8.6% (city), 8.8% (MSA); Other: 2.7% (city), 2.5% (MSA).
*Gender ratio—*101 males per 100 females (all ages); 101 males per 100 females (18 years old+).
*Age characteristics—*18–24 (16.1%); 25–44 (36.4%). Median age: 30.2.
*Educational attainment—*percent having completed high school: 78.1%; percent having completed college: 22.6%.

Major Players: Services; retail/wholesale trade; government. Noted for tourism, fruit-growing, film production site.
*Largest employers—*Walt Disney World; Airport Limousine Services; CPI Church Street (eating places); Harcourt Brace; Martin Marietta (aerospace); Marvista (eating places); Orlando Naval Training Center; Orlando Regional Healthcare System; Page Avjet Corp. (airports); Sea World of Florida; Sentinel Communications; SunTrust; Universal City Florida Partners.

Community Services: *Average hospital cost—*$454.90/day.
Average doctor visit—$48.90.
Average dentist visit—$62.50.
Newspapers—The Orlando Sentinel; Orlando Business Journal; Orlando Weekly (alternative); *The Florida Catholic; Florida Sun Review* (black-oriented); *La Semana* (Spanish community).

ORLANDO: MAGIC KINGDOM

Although it's the home of Disney World and Tupperware, Orlando isn't exactly Mickey Mouse when it comes to commerce, culture, and recreation. "People think that when you move here, you end up living in the attractions," half-jokes Angie Garcia del Busto, who works in public relations. Not only is Disney World et al. a good 15 minutes away from the city, "but Orlando's a great place to start a career and there's lots of diversity in every aspect of life here."

Although Orlando's annual 20 million visitors make it a top tourist attraction, the city also happens to be one of the fastest growing in the country in terms of both population and employment. It has been praised for its large and small business environments (by *Fortune, Business Week*, and *Entrepreneur*), real estate (Baring International Realty Advisers, Ernst & Young, Century 21, others), and youthfulness (rated #1 "magnet city" for those between 25–44 by

American Demographics). Plus, it boasts greater household buying income than any other town in the state, including Miami, and the cost of living is low.

At the outset, Orlando's primary draw was citrus, timber, and sugar cane. Settlers followed soldiers in 1842, after the end of the Seminole War (Indians: 0, Great White Conquerors: several million acres of land). Originally named "Jernigan" after a South Georgia rancher and soldier, it was later changed to Orlando to honor Orlando Reeves, another Native American exterminator. (It's obvious, however, why local boosters were itching to switch the county moniker from Mosquito to Orange in 1845.)

By the late 1800s, steamboats and the railroad had come to Central Florida, along with Northern snowbirds and resorts as well as bumper citrus crops. Cattle ranching and agriculture became another major source of income. Further expansion took place during World War II, when the Army and Air Force established a training center here. During the 1950s, thanks in part to nearby Cape Canaveral (now Cape Kennedy), a major missile parts factory was built (later known as Lockheed Martin) and Tupperware "burped" its way into the international marketplace.

But the real magic began in 1965, when several thousand acres of cattle pasture and swamp were secretly purchased by one Walt Disney. Since opening in 1971, Mickey & Co. have been joined by Epcot, Sea World, Cypress Gardens, Universal Studios, and Kennedy Spaceport USA, along with more than 85 Fortune 500 companies, with more businesses and residents moving in every year. When old Walt declared he was going to build the greatest attraction in the history of Florida, he wasn't being Goofy.

Quality of Life

When asked what keeps people in Orlando, one recurring feature seems to echo: the weather. Particularly in the cold months, "It can't be beat," observes marketing coordinator Aimee Bard. With an average temperature in the low 70s and plenty of rain to keep things lush and green, it's no wonder that the place has become a major mecca for both tourists and transplants. Other leisure-time assets: more than 100 golf courses, 800 tennis courts, a hoopful of professional teams (including the championship NBA Orlando Magic), 2,000 fresh lakes, 3,000 acres of public parks, an active arts scene, dozens of special events and festivals, and tourist-class restaurants and shopping. Beaches on both the East and West coasts of Florida are a short drive away.

Yeah, it can get sticky and muggy between June and August, but almost everything is air-conditioned and extreme temperatures are rare. "And if you want to go outside there are tons of water sports," adds manager Dan Ward.

A wide selection of affordable housing, a tolerant attitude toward ethnic and religious groups, and no state personal income tax keep 'em coming. "Even though it's in the South, this is not what you would call a typical Southern city," points out Ward. "A lot of people are from someplace else." Few speak with an accent—unless it's a foreign one—and the business outlook remains warm and sunny.

General Opportunities

This is one town where enterprises are welcomed with open arms; in the last two years, more than 28,000 ventures were launched (whether they're around a few months later, however, is anybody's guess). Designated as a foreign trade zone, Orlando has initiated commerce with countries such as Great Britain, Mexico, France, Brazil, and others.

Since the early 1990s, Orlando has enjoyed steady growth in services, retail, manufacturing, and health resources. With a civilian labor force of 650,000 and more than 150,000 new positions projected by 1998, "it's easy to get a job," states residential appraiser Stephanie Andrews. Along with the obvious—the tourism industry—positions in business, communications, engineering, and computer science are burgeoning.

With Eatonville, America's oldest incorporated African-American community, and more than 1,000 minority-owned businesses, "being black has never been a challenge, at least as far as employment is concerned," remarks convention services manager Clarence Day. Although African-Americans "do stand out more because the numbers aren't as great, Orlando also has a heavy Latin influence," continues Day. The city is, however, segregated in one aspect: "The tourists go to certain places, while locals hang out others," he adds. "After a while, the theme parks can get old."

MAJOR BREADWINNING

Thanks to two major freezes in the 1980s and competition from Latin America, the citrus industry has all but withered and died. At 36,000 strong, there are three and a half times more Disney workers than remaining acres of trees in Orange County. But scratch the mouse, and you'll find a wealth of other kinds of businesses, including Publix Super Markets, Florida Hospital, Lucent Technology, AT&T, Lockheed Martin, Central Florida Investments, Sprint, and Darden Restaurants.

> With more than 150,000 new positions projected by 1998, "it's easy to get a job," states a local. "There are so many different options here." Along with the obvious—the tourism industry—positions in business, communications, engineering, and computer science are burgeoning.

Major manufacturers include Lockheed Martin Electronics and Missiles (again), Sentinel Communications, Current Semiconductor, Golden Gem Growers, Transpo Electronics, and Florida Crushed Stone Company, as well as a grocery shelf full of brand names: Coca-Cola, T.G. Lee dairy products, Frito-Lay, and Pepsi-Cola. CHEP USA (pallets and containers), Domino's Pizza, BellSouth Mobility, SabreTech (aviation maintenance), and Precision Response (customer service) are new kids in town, while undertakings such as AT&T Microelectronics, Federal Express, Oracle software company, KoJo draperies and bedspreads, and Arcada/Seagate software stores have recently expanded.

The region has more than 4,500 manufacturers and distributors, and its truly weird assortment of corporate headquarters ranges from Tupperware ("Although lately they've put a lid on their operations," cracks one local) to the American Automobile Association to the Campus Crusade for Christ to Ripley Entertainment (believe it or not). The employment pie is somewhat evenly divided, with service taking the largest chunk (36 percent), followed by retail trade (20 percent), manufacturing (8 percent), transportation, communications and utilities (6 percent), and construction (5 percent). More good news: up to 60 percent of newly created positions come from local businesses, rather than companies which have their headquarters elsewhere, thus reducing the chances for transfers or downsizing.

Orlando boasts more than 800 high technology businesses, and is the site of such innovative developments as lasers and the Patriot missile. Those with a cutting intellect and research skills might find employment on "Laser Lane," which houses more than 50 laser/electro-optic companies, along with the University of Central Florida's Center for Research and Education for Optics and Lasers (CREOL). Another 150 enterprises, in addition to the university's Institute for Simulation and Training, are involved in computer simulations that help train military and civilian pilots. Programming skills are also utilized in producing new software applications for still other companies. And engineers, researchers, and others work with high-grade silicon microprocessors and microelectronics. Telecommunications expertise is also needed in producing and marketing that type of equipment.

Orlando's burgeoning manufacturing and distribution industry calls for technical and support jobs also. The seemingly inevitable Lockheed Martin creates and sells defense and aerospace products and is expanding into the commercial market. Orlando's strong transportation system has resulted in the creation of a number of distribution centers including Toys R Us, Behr Processing, Circuit City, and Marriott International.

Recent expansion of two of Florida's biggest hospital groups, Florida Hospital and the Orlando Regional Health Care System, as well as the opening of the first phase of the Walt Disney Memorial Cancer Institute, has given health care a shot in the arm. Doctors, nurses, and others with related skills may find additional employment in the new M.D. Anderson Cancer Center.

Government is another major source of jobs: The Orange County Public Schools are the region's second largest employer (26,000 jobs). Others include the State of Florida (13,300), Orange County (over 9,700), the U.S. Postal Service (8,200), and more, including a Naval training base and U.S. Army simulation center. Other nongovernmental growth sectors consist of mortgage banking, law, accounting, and publishing.

Discounting tourism/recreation as a viable source of professional advancement is like trying to ignore Dumbo in your living room. Jobs in public relations, event planning, marketing, and more can be found in big complexes such as Pleasure Island, Church Street Station, one of Orlando's hundreds of hotels and/or convention centers, and (but of course) Disney World.

Those whose bag is the hospitality industry and communications might find Orlando an excellent starting point. Since 1986, film and television production has grown from a $2.5 million industry to almost $150 million. Movies (*Dead Presidents, Marvin's Room*), TV series (*Star Search, Coach*), animated projects (*Lion King*), as well as commercials, videos and infomercials have provided jobs in production, editing, and acting. Nickelodeon Studios, the Golf Channel, and America's Health Network do their filming here; the area now offers 13 stage production facilities in addition to a large base of vendors and other service providers.

Although on the surface some of Orlando's industries may not seem geared to college graduates, the area has an estimated 200,000 workers with degrees and specialized skills. And by

2005, a projected ten-year growth in employment of 28.8 percent and population of 34.4 percent will likely add even more. "This is a professional, fast-paced business environment," observes Ward. "Even if it's 95 degrees out, people still wear coats and ties." Or power suits and hose, if they happen to be female.

SOCIAL AND RECREATIONAL SCENE

How Orlando Plays

All hands agree that area code 407 is a pretty friendly place. "It's easy for people to meet each other," remarks Garcia del Busto. "Work is a good outlet and there are lots of apartment complexes geared towards singles. Once you find a friend or two, they'll introduce you to others." In clubs and in other places, "you can even strike up a conversation while standing in line outside the bathroom," states Day. "Sometimes you discover you have friends in common and they'll ask you to join their party. That would never happen in Manhattan." For those who'd rather not waste their breath talking to someone who happens to be a tourist, he recommends college alumni organizations. "Orlando has lots of strong groups and you'll make contacts you never would have had a chance to in school."

Good news for women: Orlando has more males than females. (Okay, it's one extra for every 100, but every little bit helps.) "There's a lot of dating," adds Bard. "People who work downtown meet in bars for happy hours or they get involved with professional associations or various charities."

Popular among the latter are New Directions of the American Cancer Society (843-8680), Habitat for Humanity (851-5060), and the March of Dimes (849-0790). The Center for Community Involvement (896-0945) matches personal interests with more than 600 local non-profits. There's plenty of interracial dating as well. "You see mixed groups all the time," notes Day, who goes on to say that biracial relationships are more common in Orlando than in some Northern cities. "Truthfully, anywhere you go, you get stares. But at least around here, it's more accepted."

ARTS AND SCIENCES

Orlando has plenty of culture and history, and we're not talking **Wild Bill's Wild West Dinner Extravaganza** or **Gatorland.** Newcomers wishing to experience at least the first at a discount can send away for the **Orlando Magicard.** Although the card does snag cheaper rates at some restaurants (as well as places like **Ripley's Believe It or Not! Museum, Sea World, Universal Studios,** and more), it's not the cheap key to the Magic Kingdom or **MGM Studios.**

One of the few designated to display the traveling Tombs of Imperial China exhibit, the **Orlando Museum of Art** is home to a *Newsweek*-touted collection of 19th- and 20th-century American, pre-Columbian, and European art. The **Morse Museum of American Art,** which includes the world's largest accumulation of Louis Tiffany glass (among other items), recently expanded and relocated. (Hopefully nothing

---

Where It's At

 Unless otherwise noted, all area codes are 407.

Adventures in Florida, 1250 S. Hwy. 17-92, Longwood, 331-0991

Aloha!, 7007 Sea World Dr., 351-3600

American Gladiators, 5155 W. Hwy. 192, Kissimmee, 390-0000

Arabian Nights, 6225 W. Irlo Bronson Memorial Hwy., Kissimmee, 239-9223

artsMall, Winter Park Mall, Winter Park, 647-3199

Bob Carr Performing Arts Center, 401 W. Livingston St., 849-2001

Where It's At

(continued)

Bok Tower Gardens, 1151 Tower Blvd., Lake Wales, 813/676-1408

Capone's Dinner & Show, 4740 West U.S. Kissimmee, 397-2378

Central Florida Zoological Park, 3755 NW Hwy. 17-92, Sanford, 323-4450

Civic Theatre, 1001 E. Princeton St., 896-7365

Cornell Fine Arts Museum, Rollins College, Winter Park, 646-2526

Cypress Island, 201 E. Monument Ave., Kissimmee, 933-2794

Discovery Island Zoological Park, Lake Buena Vista, 824-4231

Disney World, Lake Buena Vista, 824-4231

Don Garlitz Museum of Drag Racing, 13700 SW 16th Ave., Ocala, 904/245-8661

Dr. Phillips Center, 1111 N. Orange Ave.

Epcot, Lake Buena Vista, 824-4231

Florida Audubon Society, 460 State Rd. 436, Casselberry, 260-8300

Gatorland, 14501 S. Orange Blossom Trail, 800/393-JAWS

Gator Jungle, 26205 E. Hwy. 50, Christmas, 568-1354

Harry P. Leu Gardens, 1730 N. Forest Ave., 246-2620

Hoop-de-do Musical Review, Fort Wilderness Resort, Lake Buena Vista, 824-4321

Jungleland, 4580 W. Irlo Bronson Memorial Hwy., Kissimmee, 396-1012

Kennedy Space Center, State Road 405, 452-2121

King Henry's Feast, 5401 Kirkman Rd., 351-5151

Luau, Lake Buena Vista, 939-3463

Maitland Arts Center, 231 W. Packwood Ave., Maitland, 539-2181

Maitland Historical Museums, 820 Lake Lily Dr., Maitland, 644-2451

Mark Two, 3376 Edgewater Dr., 843-6275

Medieval Times, 4510 W. Irlo Bronson Memorial Hwy., Kissimmee, 396-2900

MGM Studios, Lake Buena Vista, 824-4231

broke during the shuffle.) The **Cornell Fine Arts Museum** has more than 6,000 works, while the **Zora Neale Hurston National Museum of Fine Arts** honors the African-American folklorist through rotating exhibits from blacks around the world. More changing tides are showcased at the **Maitland Arts Center,** which displays contemporary work. Surreal experiences can be found at the **Salvador Dali Museum,** which features the most comprehensive collection of that artist's works; the **U.S. Astronaut Hall of Fame,** home of the U.S. Space Camp; and the **Don Garlitz Museum of Drag Racing,** which "tracks" the sport from its beginnings to today. Those wanting an inside view of local chronicles will find it at the **Orange County Historical Museum,** which has a 1926 firehouse and antique trucks (but is slated to move the bulk of its holdings to the **Old Orange County Courthouse** in the next few months), and the **Maitland Historical Museums,** a restored Victorian home and carpentry shop.

Along with a downtown performing arts complex that is currently in the building/planning stage, the area's passel of (non-dinner) theaters includes the **Bob Carr Performing Arts Center** and the **Dr. Phillips Center,** both of which house the **Southern Ballet Theatre,** the **Orlando Opera Company,** and the **Orlando Philharmonic Orchestra.** Along with performing, the **Orlando City Ballet** offers classes in traditional and modern dance. **Theater Downtown** and the **Orlando Theatre Project** stage a variety of off-Broadway and experimental productions, while the **Sak Theater Comedy Lab** specializes in interactive improvisational performances. New to the area is **artsMall,** which presents music, theater, and dance productions in a haven of consumerism. The **Civic Theatre** features Broadway, family and other productions, while the **Orlando Broadway Series** imports the latest stage hits.

Still, Orlando has to be the world capital of theme dinner theaters. Offerings range from the Equity-mounted Broadway productions at the **Mark Two** to pre-'90s gang bangers at **Capone's Dinner & Show** and **Pirates Dinner Adventure** to an assortment of jousts and myths (**King Henry's Feast, Medieval Times, Arabian Nights**) to **American Gladiators,** which brings physical contact to a whole new level. Disney serves up a variety of options for the innocent-hearted, including the **Hoop-de-do Musical Review** and **Mickey's Tropical Revue** or a **Luau.** Not to be outdone, Sea World has **Aloha!,** it own gen-u-ine South Seas event. Bonus: The **Sleuths Mystery Dinner Theatre** has unlimited beer and wine, which may be a necessity should you attempt to attend too many of these things within a short period of time.

Those wanting a break from the fantasy may find it at the recently completed **Orlando Science Center,** which allows you to peer into a sinkhole (the state's most famous appeared in Winter Park in 1981 and swallowed an entire city block) and create landscapes via computer and other erudite pursuits. Visitors to the **Kennedy Space Center** can have nose-to-nose encounters with shuttles and rockets. A little farther away in Tampa is MOSI (**Museum of Science and Industry**), for those who feel they must have an IMAX theater fix. Although you can supposedly travel the world in a day at Disney's **Epcot, Splendid China** provides an in-depth view of at least one country.

Yeah, you can do the 'gator thing (**Gatorland** and **Gator Jungle**), but the real Florida (or a reasonable facsimile) can perhaps better be found in places like the **Florida Audubon Society,** where you can view eagles, owls, hawks, and vultures and picnic on the grounds. (Hopefully the birds won't make a pit stop while you're eating.) Part of a 109-acre preserve with palms, cypress, and oaks, the **Central Florida Zoological Park** has lions and tigers (and reptiles and birds and primates…), while **Cypress Island** offers 350 exotic critters with the added dividend of Lake Tohopekaliga and boat rides and jet skis.

With the largest artesian limestone spring in the world, **Silver Springs** offers glass-bottomed boat rides, jungle cruises, and animal shows, a jeep safari, a car museum, and concerts. **Jungleland** tours highlight the lifestyles of its more than 500 critters. Those looking for personalized excursions might opt for **Adventures in Florida,** which has everything from river cruises to airboat rides to historic day trips. **Discovery Island Zoological Park** is Walt's version of a scaled-down sanctuary with 120 species of animals and 250 types of plants, including some threatened with extinction. Hey, at least you know what you're getting into.

Central Florida also boasts lots of pretty flowers. The first permanent indoor display of its kind, **World of Orchids** flaunts thousands of the prom accessories in a variety of garden settings and a laboratory. The **Harry P. Leu Gardens** is the place for camellia and rose lovers, with a restored house museum thrown in for good measure. **Bok Tower Gardens** has a Singing Tower with 57 bells, reflecting pools, and 128 acres of greenery. Not recommended for those with allergies or a fear of heights.

Where It's At

(continued)

Mickey's Tropical Revue Polynesian Resort, Lake Buena Vista, 939-3463

Morse Museum of American Art, 133 E. Welbourne Ave., Winter Park, 644-3686

Museum of Science and Industry, 4801 E. Fowler Ave., 800/998-6077

Old Orange County Courthouse, Central and Magnolia aves.

Orange County Historical Museum, 812 E. Rollins St., 987-6350

Orlando Broadway Series, 201 S. Orange Ave., 423-9999

Orlando City Ballet, 1425 Tuskawilla Rd., Winter Springs, 644-3563

Orlando Magicard, P.O. Box 690355, Orlando, FL 32869; www.goflorida.com

Orlando Museum of Art, 2416 N. Mills Ave., 896-4231

Orlando Opera Company, 426-1717

Orlando Philharmonic Orchestra, 647-8285

Orlando Science Center, 810 E. Rollins St., 896-7151

Orlando Theatre Project, 44 E. Church St., 648-0077

Pirates Dinner Adventure, Colossal Studios, 6400 Carrier Dr., 892-7311

Ripley's Believe It or Not! Museum, 8201 International Dr., 363-4418

Sak Theater Comedy Lab, 140 S. Court Ave., 648-0001

Salvador Dali Museum, 100 3rd St. N, St. Petersburg, 800/442-3254

Sea World, 7007 Sea World Dr., 407/351-3600

Silver Springs, 5656 E. Silver Springs Blvd., Silver Springs, 363-2757

Sleuths Mystery Dinner Theatre, 7508 Republic Dr., 363-1985

Southern Ballet Theatre, 426-1733

Splendid China, 3000 Splendid China Rd., Kissimmee, 396-7111

Theater Downtown, 2113 N. Orange Ave., 841-0083

U.S. Astronaut Hall of Fame, 6225 Vectorspace Blvd., Titusville 269-6100

Where It's At

(continued)

Universal Studios, 1000 Universal Studios Plaza, 363-8000

Wild Bill's Wild West Dinner Extravaganza, 5260 Hwy. 192, Kissimmee, 351-5151

World of Orchids, 2501 N. Old Lake Wilson Rd., Kissimmee, 396-1887

Zora Neale Hurston National Museum of Fine Arts, 227 E. Kennedy Blvd., Eatonville, 647-3307

Where It's At

 Unless otherwise noted, all area codes are 407.

A Ragin' Cajun Bass Guide Service, 830 Vermont Woods Lane, 438-2786

A.J. Hackett Bungy, 5782 W. Irlo Bronson Memorial Hwy., Kissimmee, 397-7866

Aerial Adventures, 2754 Michigan Ave., Kissimmee, 944-1070

Air Orlando, 8990 International Dr., 354-1400

Austin-Tindall Sports Complex, 892-2397

Balloons by Renee, 3531 Edgewater Dr., 422-3529

Bass Challenger Guide Service, P.O. Box 679155, 273-8045

Bay Hill Invitational, 876-2429

Blizzard Beach, Lake Buena Vista, 828-3200

Blue Springs State Park, 2100 W. French Ave., Orange City, 904/775-3663

Canaveral National Seashore, 867-2805

Chrysler-Plymouth Tournament of Champions, 800/237-4700

Citrus Bowl, 1610 W. Church St., 849-2500

Congo River, 6312 International Dr., 352-0042

Cypress Creek, 5353 Vineland Rd., 351-3151

Dave's Ski School, 13245 Lake Bryan Dr., 239-6939

 ## THE SPORTING LIFE

Orlando is to sports what it used to be to oranges: there's a bumper crop, especially when the weather's nice. More than 1,500 lakes and rivers provide opportunities for paddling, floating, sailing, powerboating, and personal-watercraft riding. Orlando's bounty of lakes makes it a top water-skiing and bass-fishing venue. Groups such as **A Ragin' Cajun Bass Guide Service, Fishing Connection, Bass Challenger Guide Service,** and many more provide guides, boats, and tours. Those interested in obtaining a hunting and/or fishing license can contact the **Florida Game and Fresh Water Fish Commission.** Scuba divers, water skiers, canoers, and kayakers can hook up with the **Dive Station, Dave's Ski School, Kayaking Touring Adventures,** or others.

An array of parks await those who like their water adventures pre-packaged. Disney has several (**Blizzard Beach, River Country, Typhoon Lagoon**). **Water Mania** and **Wet 'N' Wild** offer speed slides, wave pools, and flumes—and even a toboggan ride (without the snow, of course).

An extensive network of public preserves and recreation areas provide opportunities for bicycling, walking, jogging, in-line skating, hiking, and more. The parks range from the beautiful, primitive **Ocala National Forest** and pristine beaches of the **Canaveral National Seashore** to urban landscapes such as downtown Orlando's **Lake Eola Park** and Kissimmee's **Lakefront Park. Blue Springs State Park** is home to a 72-degree spring that nurtures endangered manatees, while monkeys, raccoons, deer, eagles, and other critters run free at **Hontoon Island State Park.** Those looking for sport and water fun might find it at **Kelly Park** (in Apopka) and **Turkey Lake Park.** A variety of activities can be found at Orlando's **Lake Fairview,** Osceola's **Austin-Tindall Sports Complex,** and the **Seminole County Softball Complex.** Two points of entry for baseball, soccer, tennis and other leagues include the **Orlando Sport and Social Club** and/or the **Orange County Parks and Recreation Department,** where about 30 parks provide leagues, lessons, clinics, and classes for adults.

Not only does Orlando attract golf courses and tournaments, but it's also home to names like Lee Janzen, Corey Pavin, Arnold Palmer, Gary Player, Laura Baugh, and a couple of dozen more. Along with PGA and LPGA events (**Bay Hill Invitational,** March; the **Chrysler-Plymouth Tournament of Champions,** January), it also boasts courses such as **Cypress Creek, Mission Inn,** the **Oaks,** and scores more.

Walt Disney World Resort alone has half a dozen. Or, you can opt for miniature golf at **Pirate's Cove**, **Congo River**, or **Million Dollar Mulligan,** which has the area's only real Bermuda grass putting course with prizes up to $1 million.

Other exotic frolics: **A.J. Hackett Bungy;** bareback bull riding and calf roping at **Kissimmee Sports Arena;** and **Air Orlando** helicopter tours. Also: hot air balloon rides at **Aerial Adventures, Balloons by Renee,** and **Orange Blossom Balloons.** At **Fighter Pilots U.S.A.** the inexperienced can "fly" an F-16 in an air combat mission; and the **Finish Line Racing School** is for folks inspired by the previously mentioned Don Garlitz museum. Orlando does in fact have two speed-racing venues at (but of course) the **Walt Disney Speedway** and **Orlando Speed World.** And less than an hour away is the world-famous **Daytona International Speedway.** Along with grappling with 'gators, a visit to the dog track (**Seminole Greyhound Park, Sanford-Orlando Kennel Club**) or a Jai Alai contest at **Orlando Jai Alai** are truly Floridian experiences.

Although Shaquille O'Neal is no longer with the **Orlando Magic,** big-name professional sports walk pretty tall. There's lots of baseball action with the Orlando Cubs (**Tinker Field**), Class AA affiliate of the Chicago Cubs, and the Kissimmee Cobras (**Osceola County Stadium**), the Houston Astros Class A team. Both the Astros and the Atlanta Braves take their spring training here (the Braves will be at Disney World's new sports complex once that's complete). Although talk of an NFL franchise is in the air, arena football is already afoot (**Orlando Predators**) and the city recently garnered an IHL ice hockey team (the **Orlando Solar Bears**) to go along with its roller hockey team (the **Orlando Rollergaters**). Along with the Magic, all are at the **O-rena,** as the Orlando Arena is called by locals. The **Citrus Bowl** is considered one of the top helmet-crashing events of the New Year.

AFTER-HOURS DIVERSIONS

"Orlando's nightlife is scattered around," observes Andrews. "There are lots of different places to go to, but no real hub." The most obvious are Disney's **Pleasure Island** and **Church Street Station.** The Orlando branch of Planet Hollywood is at the entrance of Pleasure Island, so at least you don't have to pay a fee to get in.

Although Pleasure Island has venues such as Mannequins Dance Palace (dancing for dummies?), Pleasure Island Jazz

Where It's At

(continued)

Daytona International Speedway, 1801 International Speedway Blvd., Daytona Beach, 904/253-7223

Dive Station, 3465 Edgewater Dr., 843-3483

Fighter Pilots U.S.A., 3033 W. Patrick St., Kissimmee, 931-4333

Finish Line Racing School, 3113 S. Ridgewood Ave., Edgewater, 904/427-8522

Fishing Connection, 1016 Emerlda Rd., 296-0083

Florida Game and Fresh Water Fish Commission, 422-6995

Hontoon Island State Park, Deland, 904/736-5309

Kayaking Touring Adventures, 32422 Red Oak Dr., Eustis, 904/589-7978

Kelly Park, Rock Springs Rd. and Kelly Park Rd., Apopka, 889-4179

Kissimmee Sports Arena, 1010 Sulls Ln., Kissimmee, 933-0020

Lakefront Park, Lakeshore Dr., 847-2388

Lake Eola Park, Rosalind Ave., 246-2827

Lake Fairview, Lee Rd. and U.S. Hwy. 441, 246-2288

Million Dollar Mulligan, 2850 Florida Plaza Blvd., Kissimmee, 239-1505

Mission Inn, 104000 County Rd. 48, 800/874-9053

O-rena, 600 W. Amelia St., 849-2001

Oaks, 3232 S. Bermuda Ave., Kissimmee, 933-4055

Ocala National Forest, 10863 E. Highway 40, Silver Springs, 352/625-7470 or 352/625-2520

Orange Blossom Balloons, P.O. Box 22908, Lake Buena Vista, 239-7677

Orange County Parks and Recreation Department, 118 W. Kaley St., 836-4920

Orlando Jai Alai, 6405 U.S. Hwy. 17-92, Fern Park, 339-6221

Orlando Magic, 715 N. Garland Ave., 649-2222

Orlando Predators, 872-7362

Orlando Rollergaters, 843-5181

Where It's At

(continued)

Orlando Solar Bears, 872-PUCK

Orlando Speed World, 19164 E. Colonial Dr., 568-5522 or 568-1367

Orlando Sport and Social Club, 411 E. Jackson St., 839-1622

Osceola County Stadium, 933-5400

Pirate's Cove, 8501 International Dr., 345-0585

River Country, Lake Buena Vista, 824-4321

Sanford-Orlando Kennel Club, 301 Dog Track Rd., Longwood, 831-1600

Seminole County Softball Complex, North St. off Douglas Ave., 788-0609

Seminole Greyhound Park, 2000 Seminola Blvd., Casselberry, 699-4510

Tinker Field, 245-2827

Turkey Lake Park, 3401 S. Hiawassee Rd., 299-5581

Typhoon Lagoon, Lake Buena Vista, 824-4321

Walt Disney Speedway, 3450 N. World Dr., Bay Lake, 363-6158

Walt Disney World Resort, Lake Buena Vista, 824-2270

Water Mania, 6073 W. Irlo Bronson Memorial Hwy., Kissimmee, 396-2626

Wet 'N Wild, 6200 International Dr., 351-1800

Where It's At

 Unless otherwise noted, all area codes are 407.

Bach Festival, Rollins College, 646-2182

Baja Beach Club, 8510 Palm Pkwy., 239-6996

Barbarella, 68 N. Orange Ave., 839-0457

Black History Month, 649-7788

Blazing Pianos, 8445 International Dr., 363-5104

Company, and 8Trax disco, "you rarely see locals there," points out Day. However, the **Baja Beach Club** and the **Laughing Kookaburra** in Lake Buena Vista have DJ mixes and live bands for the general population. Located in a guitar-shaped building and featuring more than 500 items of rock 'n' roll memorabilia, the **Hard Rock Cafe** at Universal Studios may be worth braving the camera-and kiddie-toting masses.

Church Street Station includes well-trod spots like **Rosie O' Grady's,** which features Dixieland jazz and can-can dancing; the **Cheyenne Saloon Country Music Hall,** which offers line dancing and mechanical bull rides (no, thank you); **Orchid Garden Ball Room,** where pop music plays; and **Phineas Phogg's,** a source of contemporary tunes. A few blocks away from the Station's main cluster of renovated historical buildings "are loads of offbeat bars and hangout places," states Ward.

Along with **Sloppy Joe's** and **Chillers,** nearby Orange Avenue serves up coffeehouses, dance clubs, and taverns such as **One-Eyed Jack's, Barbarella, Tanqueray's,** and **Zuma Beach.** At the other end of the musical spectrum are sing-alongs at **Howl at the Moon** or **Blazing Pianos,** which has three—count 'em—three guess-whats. Other places, like **Will's Pub,** the **Renaissance,** and **Sapphire Supper Club,** book local and national alternative and mainstream performers. Larger concerts are held at the **O-Rena** and at the **University of Central Florida.**

According to Day, African-American professionals can meet and mingle at the **Frat House, Downtown Jazz and Blues,** and several bars in Eatonville, such as **Heroes,** which has everything from hip hop to reggae to bass. Sports bar fans will find plenty to cheer for at **Bloopers, Friday's Front Row,** and **Orlando Ale House.** A bygone era can be relived at **Peter Scott's Supper Club,** which features leisurely dining and dancing to big-band music. For the less formal-minded, the **Cocoa Beach Pier** serves up an assortment of restaurants, tropical bars, and other diversions within spitting distance of the Atlantic Ocean.

Orlando's passel of festivals start the year off with the **Boola Bowl Street Party** (New Year's Day), a post-game bash celebrating the Citrus Bowl. January also brings the **Zora Neale Hurston Festival of Arts and Humanities,** a series of theatrical performances, educational programs, and art exhibits honoring her work. February is time for **Black History Month,** the **Central Florida Fair,** and the **Bach**

Festival. A **Bluegrass Festival** (March), an **Irish Festival** (March), and an **Easter Egg Hunt** (April) top off the spring. Summer brings over 100 documentaries, features, and shorts (the movie kind) to the **Florida Film Festival** (June); bull riders, cowboys, and more than 50,000 spectators to the **Silver Spurs Rodeo** (July), along with another occasion worth remembering, **Maude the Elephant's Birthday Party** (August). Halloween has **Horror Nights** at Universal Studios, a **Monster Mash** at Church Street Station, and appropriate (or tasteless, depending upon your viewpoint) celebrations at several other attractions. The holiday season is highlighted by gardening, sculpturing, and other events at **Cypress Gardens** (November) as well as two 45-foot Christmas trees, 204 "singing" human ornaments, a full orchestra, and 320,000 watts of electricity at the **First Baptist Church** (December) and **Christmas in the Park** (December), with Tiffany decorations courtesy of the Morse Museum.

CULINARY AND SHOPPING HAUNTS

With "traditional" foods ranging from citrus items to key lime pie to 'gator tails to barbecue, it's no wonder Orlando has become a test market for restaurant groups. (However, don't expect 'gator quiche with orange-flavored barbecue sauce anytime soon.) Tourism also fuels this town's 3,000 or so eateries and experimental efforts, most of which offer meals priced well under $20.

Those looking for a variety of epicurean adventures will certainly find them here. You can start at the top—in terms of both cost and Mobil/AAA ratings—with places such as **Arthur's 27,** which combines international offerings and a panoramic view; romantic candlelight dining at **Chalet Suzanne**; **Lee's Lakeside,** continental cuisine overlooking downtown Lake Eola; and serenades among the pasta at **Christini's Ristorante Italiano.** However, if you want to be guaranteed a singing waiter, try **Bergamos** (Italian); or for an operetta, call **Pacino's** (not Al, but Italian food). Orlando also boasts the only **Ran Getsu** outside of Tokyo.

Although they tend to be pricier, hotels are a major part of the restaurant scene. Even natives trod the path to **Hemingway's** (Hyatt Regency Grand Cypress) for steak and seafood next to a half-acre swimming pool; **Jack's** (American, Clarion Plaza Hotel), Orlando's take on Sardi's, where celebrity caricatures line the walls; **Dux** (American, Peabody); and **Haifeng** (Chinese, Stouffer Resort). Not all hotel eateries

Where It's At

(continued)

Bloopers, 5715 Major Blvd., 351-3340

Bluegrass Festival, Kissimmee, 363-5871

Boola Bowl Street Party, Church St. Station, 422-2434

Central Florida Fair, 295-FAIR

Cheyenne Saloon Country Music Hall, 129 W. Church St., 422-2434

Chillers, 33 W. Church St., 649-4270

Christmas in the Park, Winter Park, 645-5311

Church Street Station, 129 W. Church St., 422-2434

Cocoa Beach Pier, 401 Meade Ave., Cocoa Beach, 783-7549

Cypress Gardens, 841-9505

Downtown Jazz and Blues, 54 N. Orange Ave., 246-1419

Easter Egg Hunt, Central Florida Zoological Park, 323-4450

First Baptist Church, 425-2555

Florida Film Festival, Enzian Theatre, 629-1088

Frat House, 1159 E. Colonial Dr., 273-9600

Friday's Front Row, 8126 International Dr., 363-1414

Hard Rock Cafe, Universal Studios, 5800 Kirkman Rd., 351-7625

Heroes, 426 E. Kennedy Blvd., Eatonville, 740-0556

Horror Nights, Universal Studios, 363-8000

Howl at the Moon, 55 W. Church St., 841-9118

Irish Festival, Seminole Greyhound Park and Fairplex, 363-5871

Laughing Kookaburra, 1900 Buena Vista Dr., 827-2727

Maude the Elephant's Birthday Party, Central Florida Zoological Park, 323-4450

Monster Mash, Church Street Station, 422-2434

One-Eyed Jack's, 15 N. Orange Ave., 648-2050

O-rena, 600 W. Amelia St., 849-2001

Where It's At

(continued)

Orchid Garden Ball Room, 129 W. Church St., 422-2434

Orlando Ale House, 101 University Park Dr., Winter Park, 671-1011

Peter Scott's Supper Club, 1811 W. State Rd. 434, Longwood, 834-4477

Phineas Phogg's, 129 W. Church St., 422-2434

Pleasure Island, 1500 Lake Buena Vista Dr., Lake Buena Vista, 934-7781

Renaissance, 22 S. Magnolia Ave., 422-3595

Rosie O' Grady's, 129 W. Church, 422-2434

Sapphire Supper Club, 54 N. Orange Ave., 246-1419

Silver Spurs Rodeo, Kissimmee, 363-5871

Sloppy Joe's, 41 W. Church St., 425-6826

Tanqueray's, 100 S. Orange Ave., 649-8540

University of Central Florida, 4000 Central Florida Blvd., 823-2000

Will's Pub, 1850 N. Mills Ave., 898-5070

Zora Neale Hurston Festival of Arts and Humanities, Eatonville, 800/352-3865

Zuma Beach, 46 N. Orange Ave., 648-8363

Where It's At

Unless otherwise noted, all area codes are 407.

Akbar Palace, 4985 W. Hwy. 192, Kissimmee, 396-4836

Altamonte Mall, 451 Altamonte Ave., Altamonte Springs, 830-4400

Amigo's Tex-Mex, 6036 S. Orange Blossom Trail, 857-3144

Antique Alley, Edgewater Dr., College Park

Arthur's 27, Buena Vista Palace Hotel, Lake Buena Vista, 827-3450

B-Line Diner, Peabody, 9801 International Dr., 352-4000

empty the wallet: both the **B-Line Diner** (Peabody) and the **Plaza Diner** (Royal Plaza) have entrees under $9.

Other places have longevity in their favor and are popular among locals. These include **Enzos on the Lake** (Italian), **La Normandie** (French), and **La Scala** (international). Awarded top honors from *Wine Spectator* magazine, **Maison et Jardin** serves continental grub in a Mediterranean villa on five acres, while the reasonably-priced **Le Coq au Vin** (French) has garnered praise from AAA to Zagat, with *The New York Times* in between.

Another kind of "meat market" can be found at steak and seafood houses. Members of the Knife and Fork Club sharpened their cutlery at **Charley's** and found it to be one of their top ten, while **Barney's** has been around since the mid-70s. **Straub's, Del Frisco's,** and the inevitable **Ruth's Chris** are also popular among natives. Since it hardly (if) ever snows, eating outside is as common as warm weather. The **Park Plaza Gardens** serves continental food in a New Orleans–style courtyard, while **Pebbles** made the transition from a five-and-dime to creative cuisine for the masses. Malls, hotels, and even Walt Disney World and the rest of the Kingdom are loaded with chances to dine al fresco.

"Theme" restaurants are big: you can find a safari at **Jungle Jim's** and the **Rainforest Cafe;** fast car memorabilia at **Race Rock;** a (noncannibalistic) aboriginal experience at the **Outback;** and '30s memorabilia and a Tunnel of Love at the **Bubble Room.** You can nibble on Mediterranean appetizers and watch artists work at **Cafe Tu Tu Tango** or take a leisurely afternoon tea at the **Garden View Lounge** or the **Peabody Orlando.** Those who like food-intensive expeditions might want to do Sunday brunch at the **Renaissance Orlando Resort,** the **Metro West Country Club,** or the **Timacuan Country Club.**

Southern cooking varies from soul food at **Shouell's** to barbecue at **Benton's** and **Red's** to po-boys et al. at **Cafe New Orleans.** Cuban offerings can be found at **Numero Uno,** while the **Red Snapper** features Jamaican fare. In another culinary continent is **Ming Court,** which serves up innovative entrees in a glass-enclosed garden. Other Oriental eateries include **Shogun Japanese Steakhouse, Kobe,** and **Mikado.** You can have an Indian repast at a **Passage to India** as well as **Punjab, Akbar Palace,** the **Far Pavilion,** and others. There are plenty of Mexican (**Chevy's, Jose O'Day's, Amigo's Tex-Mex**) and Italian (**Ciao Italia, La Sila, Portobello Yacht Club**) places as well, making it a small world after all.

Take away the "s" and you have "mall," of which Orlando is building and/or planning more than any other city in the U.S. Serious shoppers know discount stores and flea markets can yield terrific bargains, and Orlando has a bunch. Chief among these are the **Beltz Factory Outlet,** with more than 160 stores including Calvin Klein, Bugle Boy, and Bass Shoes; the **International Designer Outlets,** with even more good stuff from Saks Fifth Avenue, Jones New York, and Donna Karan; **Kissimmee Manufacturers Outlet,** with 30 more offerings, such as London Fog, American Tourister (without the gorilla), and Totes; and the **Lake Buena Vista Factory Stores,** with Reebok, Vanity Fair, and others.

It's also a **Flea World** after all, with deals on foods, crafts, and other items in more than 1,700 booths, and the **Osceola Flea & Farmers Market,** which has almost 900 more. Or you can shop for fresh produce, plants, and flowers at the **Farmer's Market** in downtown Orlando or the **Winter Park Farmer's Market.** Speaking of Winter Park, **Park Avenue** there is chock full of chic emporiums and specialty shops ranging from Scott Laurent Galleries to Laura Ashley, as well as cute little restaurants. Unique oldies but goodies might also be unearthed in what's locally known as Antique Row, a string of shops along Orange Ave., while **Antique Alley** has several more, in addition to gently used/resale enterprises.

Attractions ranging from Gatorland to Splendid China have their own line of distinctive, uh, stuff, as does the **Orlando Magic Fanattic.** And it's a **Bargain World** (after all!), which claims to have the cheapest Disneyana in town. Those who like shopping among tourists will find plenty of both at the **Mercado Mediterranean Village** and the **Disney Village Marketplace.** It might be worth having your toes stepped on a few times to experience specialty stores in a Victorian atmosphere at the **Exchange** at Church Street Station, as well as the nearby **Church Street Market.**

It's also a mall world in Orlando, and bigger seems to be better: Among others, a 640,000-square-foot behemoth with 12 anchors is planned at the site of Orlando's first cluster, **Colonial Plaza.** Then there's the **Florida Mall,** which has over 200 shops; **Altamonte Mall,** with 175 emporiums; **Orlando Fashion Square,** with another 165; the new **Seminole Towne Center,** with 120; the enclosed **Osceola Square Mall;** and others. But if you're looking to save money, check the discount stores first.

Where It's At

(continued)

Bargain World, 6454 International Dr., 345-8772; other locations

Barney's, 1615 E. Colonial Dr., 896-6864

Beltz Factory Outlet, 5401 Oakridge Rd., 352-9611

Benton's, 521 Kennedy Blvd., Eatonville, 647-4443

Bergamos, 8445 International Dr., 352-3805

Bubble Room, 1351 S. Orlando Ave., 628-3331

Cafe New Orleans, 1881 W. Fairbanks Ave., Winter Park, 644-2233

Cafe Tu Tu Tango, 8625 International Dr., 248-2222

Chalet Suzanne, U.S. Hwy. 27 and Masterpiece Rd., Lake Wales, 676-6011

Charley's, 6107 S. Orange Blossom Trail, 851-7130; other locations

Chevy's, 1257 State Rd. 535, Lake Buena Vista, 827-1052

Christini's Ristorante Italiano, 7600 Dr. Phillips Blvd., 345-8770

Church Street Market, 55 W. Church St., 872-3500

Ciao Italia, 6149 Westwood Blvd., 354-0770

Colonial Plaza, 2560 E. Colonial Dr., 894-3601

Del Frisco's, 729 Lee Rd., 645-4443

Disney Village Marketplace, Lake Buena Vista Dr., Lake Buena Vista, 828-3800

Dux, Peabody, 9801 International Dr., 352-4000

Enzos on the Lake, 1130 S. Hwy. 17-92, Longwood, 834-9872

Exchange, Church Street Station

Far Pavilion, 5748 International Dr., 351-5522

Farmer's Market, I-4 at Church St., downtown Orlando

Flea World, 4311 N. U.S. Hwy. 17-92, Sanford, 330-1792

Florida Mall, 8001 S. Orange Blossom Trail, 851-7234

Garden View Lounge, Grand Floridian Hotel, Walt Disney World, Lake Buena Vista, 824-4321

Where It's At

(continued)

Haifeng, Stouffer Resort, 6677 Sea Harbor Dr., 351-5555

Hemingway's, Hyatt Regency Grand Cypress, One Grand Cypress Blvd., 239-1234

International Designer Outlets, 5211 International Dr., 352-3632

Jack's, Clarion Plaza Hotel, 9700 International Dr., 352-9700

Jose O'Day's, 8445 International Dr., 363-0613

Jungle Jim's, 55 W. Church St., 872-3111; other locations

Kissimmee Manufacturers Outlet, 4673 W. U.S. 192, Kissimmee, 396-8900

Kobe, 8350 International Dr., 352-1811

La Normandie, 2021 E. Colonial Dr., 896-9976

La Scala, 205 Lorraine Dr., Altamonte Springs, 862-3257

La Sila, 4898 Kirkman Rd., 295-8333

Lake Buena Vista Factory Stores, S.R. 535, Lake Buena Vista, 755-7003

Le Coq au Vin, 4800 S. Orange Ave., 851-6960

Lee's Lakeside, 431 E. Central Blvd., 841-1565

Maison et Jardin, 340 S. Wymore Rd., Altamonte Springs, 862-4410

Mercado Mediterranean Village, 8445 International Dr., 345-9337

Metro West Country Club, 2100 S. Hiawassee Rd., 299-1099

Mikado, One World Center Dr., 239-4200

Ming Court, 9188 International Dr., 351-9988

Numero Uno, 2499 S. Orange Ave., 841-3840

Orlando Fashion Square, 3201 E. Colonial Dr., 896-1131

Orlando Magic Fanattic, 715 N. Garland Ave., 649-3287; several other locations

Osceola Flea & Farmers Market, 2801 E. Irlo Bronson Memorial Highway, Kissimmee, 846-2811

Osceola Square Mall, 3831 W. Vine St., Kissimmee, 847-6941

 ## ETHNIC AND RELIGIOUS PROSPECTS

Geographically, "Orlando's pretty racially divided," observes Andrews. "There are Hispanic sections, black sections, and an Asian section, although race issues seem pretty much the same as anyplace else. But mostly what you see are Caucasians."

Still, "there's less prejudice here than in Miami, particularly against Hispanics," adds Garcia del Busto. "With all the tourism and international visitors, being bilingual is a big advantage."

Day believes genuine efforts have been made to promote equality. "When I worked at Disney, we had a support group of African-American managers who met regularly and discussed various topics." On the job, "it's not an issue of being black or Latino, but of being a well-rounded person."

Although, according to Garcia del Busto, "religion's a not a big deal, and a lot of people don't go to church," there's plenty to choose from, including nearly 550 Protestant houses of worship, 31 Catholic churches, 14 synagogues, and an assortment of Mormon, Buddhist, and Moslem mosques and temples. A few points of contact include the **Greater Orlando Baptist Association** (Southern Baptist), the **First Baptist Church,** the **Trinity Lutheran Church and School,** the **St. Mark African Methodist-Episcopal Church,** the **Life Center Church, St. Nicholas Catholic Church,** and the **Jewish Federation.** In this largely white, Protestant community, "those in a minority may really have to seek out people of the same religion or race," adds Bard.

CRIB SHEET

Such a deal…the average cost of a house in Orlando was almost $47,000 less than the national median. Plus, metro Orlando is considered one of the top U.S. markets by the Mortgage Bankers Association of America. Rent is a bargain as well, with a one-bedroom averaging around $480; a two-bedroom/one bath averaging nearly $530; and a three bedroom/two bath close to $690. Some newcomers opt for apartment living until they're sure they want to stay. "Many times, transfers are reluctant to commit to buying a house because they don't know much about the area," admits one Realtor. Must be all those mouse ears.

Although there are a variety of places, with more being constructed or renovated, occupancy usually exceeds 90 percent. "When you find something you like, grab it," the Realtor advises. Many complexes have year-round swimming pools, tennis courts, health clubs, and parking for boats and RVs, while deluxe places provide running/exercise courses, golf club memberships, even boat ramps and/or docks.

With an average age of 21–30, apartment dwellers are a "friendly and lively bunch," states the Realtor. "It's an easy way to meet people." The largest concentrations of young people can be found close to the various colleges such as the University of Central Florida, near high-employment districts and near attractions.

With easy access to the airport and downtown, the Conway area has several offerings, while older structures are located near the central business district of Orlando. Other suburbs with fairly new clusters include Ocoee, Altamonte Springs, and Longwood. Unlike many other tropical places, Orlando has lots of different terrain, including thickly wooded areas, rolling hills and winding roads, flat streets with palm trees and pastel houses, and beachfront and lakefront properties.

With a growth rate of 12 percent since 1990, Orange County is the choice for those who like living near the city. Young professionals opt for historic areas such as Delaney Park and Eola Heights for their proximity to downtown. Additional older homes can be found in lakes Cherokee, Copeland, and Lawsona, with waterfront land being the most desirable and costly. Other urban communities offering a short commute include College Park, Lancaster Park, and Orwin Manor. Apopka, Pine Hills, and Azalea Park present the best bargains; starter homes here cost around $70,000. One of Orlando's lushest spots, Apopka is also prime horseback-riding country.

Monied areas include lakefront dwellings in Winter Park and Maitland, where prices can escalate from $750,000 to $2 million, although there are less expensive homes here as well.

On a more realistic scale—and a favorite with those who work at Disney and Universal studios because of its convenient location—are the planned communities of MetroWest. Homes here range from $128,000 to the upper $200,000s. Other alternatives include Eatonville, the country's oldest incorporated African-American community, and Ocoee, former citrus land that's now rapidly sprouting subdivisions.

Although it's farther away, Seminole County (growth rate: 13 percent) provides an even wider choice of living situations,

Where It's At

(continued)

Outback, 1900 Buena Vista Dr., Lake Buena Vista, 827-3430

Pacino's, 5795 W. Hwy. 192, Kissimmee, 396-8022

Park Avenue, 150 N. New York Ave., 644-8281

Park Plaza Gardens, 861 W. Morse Blvd., Winter Park, 645-2475

Passage to India, 5532 International Dr., 351-3456

Peabody Orlando, 9801 International Dr., 352-4000

Pebbles, 17 W. Church St., 839-0892; other locations

Plaza Diner, Royal Plaza, 1901 Hotel Plaza Blvd., 828-2828

Portobello Yacht Club, 1650 Buena Vista Dr., Lake Buena Vista, 828-8996

Punjab, 3404 W. Vine St., Kissimmee, 931-2449

Race Rock, 8986 International Dr., 248-9876

Rainforest Cafe, Walt Disney World, Lake Buena Vista, 824-4321

Ran Getsu, 8400 International Dr., 345-0044

Red Snapper, 851 State Rd., 436, Altamonte Springs, 774-0788

Red's, 2516 W. Washington St., 299-0700

Renaissance Orlando Resort, 6677 Sea Harbor Dr., 351-5555

Ruth's Chris, 999 Douglas Ave., Altamonte Springs, 682-6444

Seminole Towne Center, 200 Towne Center Blvd., Sanford, 323-2262

Shogun Japanese Steakhouse, 6327 International Dr., 352-1607

Shouell's, 2700 S. Rio Grande Ave., 425-4411

Straub's, 5101 E. Colonial Dr., 273-9330; other locations

Timacuan Country Club, Lake Mary, 645-4653

Winter Park Farmer's Market, 200 W. New England Ave., 623-3358

Where It's At

Unless otherwise noted, all area codes are 407.

First Baptist Church, 3701 L.B. McLeod Rd., 425-2555

Greater Orlando Baptist Association, 1906 W. Lee Rd., 293-0450

Jewish Federation, P.O. Box 1508, Maitland, 954/645-5933

Life Center Church, 63 E. Kennedy Blvd., 628-3229

St. Mark African Methodist-Episcopal Church, 1968 Bruton Blvd., 422-6941

St. Nicholas Catholic Church, 5135 Sand Lake Rd., 351-1033

Trinity Lutheran Church and School, 23 E. Livingston St., 422-5704

along with excellent schools and shopping. Older neighborhoods such as Casselberry ($70,000 to $140,000) feature small lakes and golf courses. Sanford offers several historic districts and homes ranging from the $70,000s to the $200,000s. Altamonte Springs is a '50s style haven, with densely wooded lots, relatively short commutes to anywhere, and prices to suit different pocketbooks. Newer homes can be found throughout the county as well, particularly in Longwood, Lake Mary, Oveido, and Tuskawilla.

Home to Disney World, the Silver Spurs Rodeo, and the Tupperware Convention Center, Osceola County has certainly become a Magic Kingdom. Although much of the 26 percent increase in population is due to the rapid growth of Kissimmee and St. Cloud, some is the result of the Orwellian-sounding Celebration, a 5,000-acre conglomeration of residences, offices, and shopping centers where home bidders are actually selected by lottery. According to Chamber of Commerce literature, Celebration is "expected…to embody Walt Disney's original dream of Epcot, an Experimental Prototype Community of Tomorrow, with residents who live, work, and spend their leisure time without relying on cars or creating urban sprawl."

With swamps, hills, lakes, and forests, Lake County (growth rate: 16 percent) also serves a diverse community, including farmers, outdoor enthusiasts, young professionals, and retirees. With a town square and quaint shops, New Englandesque Mt. Dora has become popular with those who don't mind the commute; nearby Eustis has several lakefront homes in addition to new developments. First-time home buyers and Magic Kingdom employees appreciate the low-priced Lake County/Clermont district near Walt Disney World.

Although the schools have received mixed reviews, including complaints of overcrowding and mediocrity, "they're trying to catch up with the times," remarks Andrews. Orange County was ranked first in the state by *Expansion Management* magazine; Seminole County has the highest SAT scores and number of National Merit finalists in Florida. (Contact Orange County Public Schools, 849-3200, for more information.) Orlando also has more than 100 private/parochial schools (Page Private School, several locations; Trinity Preparatory School, 671-4140; St. Charles Borromeo & Bishop Moore, 293-7691; many others).

Orlando has quite a few postsecondary alternatives. The publicly funded University of Central Florida (823-2000) boasts several advanced R&D departments in addition to a highly touted engineering school and tourism studies institute. The privately owned liberal arts Rollins College (646-2000) has been ranked among the best in the south by *U.S. News & World Report.* In addition, the area houses nearly 30 community colleges, such as Valencia (299-5000) and the fully accredited Seminole Community College (323-1450), whose graduates are guaranteed admission to Florida's universities.

NAVIGATING ORLANDO

With locals who prefer single-occupant commuting and a lone public system (Lynx, 841-8240) that consists of about 200 buses for a population of more than one million, Orlando's transportation situation looks pretty grim. Although the area is served by several highways—I-4 (east/west), the Bee Line Expressway (S.R. 528), the Greeneway outerbelt (S.R. 417), and the East-West Expressway (S.R. 408)—all but the first are toll roads and "I-4 is like a parking lot during rush hour," states Bard. Another trouble spot is around S.R. 436, the airport's main access road, which jams with incoming and outgoing travelers. A proposed connector between downtown and the airport was recently shelved after years of opposition from the communities that it would have bisected.

> Orlando is to sports what it used to be to oranges: There's a bumper crop, especially when the weather's nice. More than 1,500 lakes and rivers provide opportunities for water sports of all kinds. And although Shaquille O'Neal is no longer with the Orlando Magic, big-name professional sports walk pretty tall.

Still, depending upon where you live, there are other roads, such as U.S. Highways 441, 17-92, 27, and 192 that can get you there, albeit circuitously. "They're not as crowded," adds Bard, even though you may need a map to find your destination, as the outskirts of Orlando are not strictly laid out on a grid. Folks who must regularly use the toll highways can purchase an E-pass, which zips them right through. A proposed light rail/bus system running along I-4 and to the airport provides another glimmer of hope. And along with almost 50 routes, the ever-expanding Lynx service extends though Orange, Seminole, and Osceola counties. Those wanting to get around downtown can consider a FreeBee, gratis bus service to a limited area. Operating out of a 29,000-square-foot facility, Greyhound (292-3422) provides regularly scheduled service out of town as well.

One of the world's busiest, Orlando International Airport (825-2001) serves more than 22 million passengers a year. About 20 minutes south of downtown, it is also a major point of international entry and has more than 30 carriers. Other flight options include Sanford Airport (323-8313) and Executive Airport (894-9831), both of which have charter and private aircraft facilities. Kissimmee Municipal Airport (847-4600) offers tourist flights. Amtrak Intercity Rail (896-0241, 800/272-7245) maintains stations in Orlando, Winter Park, Kissimmee, and Sanford. Amtrak also has frequent connections with other cities in Florida and nationwide.

PHILADELPHIA, PENNSYLVANIA

A Brief Glance

Size and Growth: Approximately 1.9 million (city), approximately 4.9 million (MSA). Percent change, 1980–1990: –6.1% (city); +3.0% (MSA). Percent change, 1990–1995: –1.7% (city); +3.5% (MSA).

Money Matters: *Unemployment rate—* 5.6%.
Per capita income—$12,091.
Average cost of a home—$191,740.
Average rent for an apartment— $723/month.
ACCRA Cost of Living Index (based on 100)—127.2.
*ACCRA Housing Index—*141.4.

People Profile: *Crime rate* (per 100,000 population)—6,434.6 (city), 4,422.3 (MSA).

Racial and ethnic characteristics— White: 53.5% (city), 76.6% (MSA); Black: 39.9% (city), 19.1% (MSA); American Indian/Eskimo/Aleut: 0.2% (city), 0.2% (MSA); Asian/Pacific Islander: 2.7% (city), 2.1% (MSA); Hispanic Origin: 5.3% (city), 3.4% (MSA); Other: 3.6% (city), 2.0% (MSA).
*Gender ratio—*86.8 males per 100 females (all ages); 82.6 males per 100 females (18 years old+).
*Age characteristics—*18–24 (11.4%); 25–44 (30.8%). Median age: 33.1.

Major Players: Services, retail/ wholesale trade, manufacturing, government. (Philadelphia is noted for its new focus on tourism. Education-based institutions are also large employers.)

PHILADELPHIA: AMERICAN BANDWAGON

Founded in 1682 by William Penn as payment for a debt from the King of England, Philadelphia has lots of zip underneath its occasionally stodgy exterior. Along with being known as the City of Brotherly Love (Penn intended that members of all religions live together in harmony), the Cradle of Liberty (Philadelphia is where the U.S. was founded and was the nation's capital before Washington, D.C.), and Birthplace of a Nation (for obvious reasons), it's also the origin of *Rocky* and *American Bandstand*. And it's the home of hoagies, cheesesteaks, soft pretzels, and TastyKakes, a nutritionally questionable dessert item that rivals Twinkies and Ho-Hos but is undoubtedly worth every delicious calorie and gram of fat.

It's also a city of firsts. Philadelphia has the best and second-best restaurants in the country (Le Bec-Fin and the Fountain, respectively), according to *Condé Nast Traveler*, even outdistancing the Big Apple. And Philadelphia offers the highest concentration of colleges and universities in the U.S., with 88 in the region and 25 within the city limits. It has the oldest stock exchange; one of the nation's oldest insurance companies; and the Walnut Street Theatre, allegedly America's most aged (although several metropolises have made the same claim about their local venues).

There's Independence National Historic Park, home of the eminent Independence Hall and the Liberty Bell, as well as dozens of other famed and distinguished sites. Fairmount Park, the largest landscaped city park in the world, is flanked by mansions, a Horticulture Center, and the Philadelphia Zoo—yet another national first. Four major professional sports teams stop here, and this city's ethnic diversity inspires a wide array of shopping and entertainment opportunities. People are friendly, and the crime rate in what folks call Center City (downtown) is the lowest in the nation's metropolitan areas.

In the 1980s, skyscrapers finally arrived, breaking a long-standing gentleperson's agreement that no building be taller than the William Penn statue atop City Hall Tower. Opportunities have been soaring ever since: the opening of a $500 million downtown Convention Center; the start-up of the Avenue of the Arts, a burgeoning cultural district of concert halls, theaters, and other venues; and the transformation of the Delaware waterfront into a happening hub of clubs, dance spots, and entertainment. And in the past five years, the economy has flourished, drawing manufacturing, technology, and banking concerns.

Philadelphia was designed with the pedestrian in mind. Public squares and green spaces dot the gridlike layout of streets; the city appears more European than American. The weather is basic East Coast, although proximity to the Atlantic Ocean and Delaware Bay causes humidity in the summer, while cold air from Canada can wreak havoc with the windchill in winter. But with the excellent subway, trolley, and bus system, getting around is usually a breeze, no matter what the temperature.

But like the Liberty Bell itself, Philly is just a little bit cracked, and nowhere is its sense of lightheartedness more evident than among the natives ("naydivs") who use a sort of slang usually understood by everyone (except, perhaps, when it's coming from Sylvester Stallone). Windas are "the roll-down glass things in the car." Purdy is "the view of the Senda Ciddy skyline out of the windas," and Fiff is "a numbered street between Forf and Sixt." Yo, Adrian, you get da pitcher.

General Opportunities

At the crossroads of the Middle Atlantic States and New England, and only 100 miles south of New York and 55 miles west of the Atlantic Ocean, Philadelphia is easily accessible from all parts of the U.S.—a plus for businesses relying on shipping and import/export. Along with being the hub for CONRAIL freight transportation as well as Amtrak's Northeast Corridor, the Philadelphia International Airport (PHL) is located a mere 8 miles away from downtown. And the Pennsylvania Turnpike (I-76), the New Jersey Turnpike, and the Delaware Expressway (I-95) all ease egress, although traffic can be rough once you reach Center City. Recent improvements include a new terminal for PHL and upgraded facilities in the combined Philadelphia and Camden ports at the mouth of the Delaware River.

Philly is ripe with job possibilities. Manufacturing specialties include chemicals and pharmaceuticals, medical devices, transportation equipment, and printing and publishing, as well as service industries such as health care, insurance, legal, engineering, and architecture. The

Route 202 corridor focuses on information technology. More than 40 advanced research institutions account for nearly 200 million dollars' worth of grants. And local entrepreneurs can take advantage of the banking boom, which has drawn not only financial institutions but investment firms as well. Today more than 25 funds manage close to $3 billion, a figure that continues to grow.

Philadelphia has managed to shift from an industrial-based economy to service and tourism with relative ease for all involved. Although utilities are almost twice the national rate, food is very pricey, and housing is only slightly less than big-ticket areas like D.C. and San Diego, folks keep coming, particularly to the suburbs.

> Philadelphia is a city of firsts. Along with being the first site of the nation's capital, it houses the first and second best restaurants in the country, the highest concentration of colleges and universities in the U.S., the oldest stock exchange, and the nation's first zoo.

But perhaps the best litmus test of a city's durability is its openness to diversity, both on the job and among ethnic groups. Philly passes the latter test as well: Along with the original natives—Germans, Irish, Poles, American Indians, and others—strong black, Jewish, Italian, Asian, and most recently, Russian communities live side-by-side in seeming harmony, bound together perhaps by the "innerestin" sights and positive "addytoods" whenever confronted with civic issues and challenges. Philly was recently rated as one of the best places for African-Americans to live and work by *Black Enterprise* magazine.

HOW PHILADELPHIA WORKS AND PLAYS

Major Breadwinning

In the case of the nine-county metropolitan-suburban area (which also includes portions of New Jersey), the sum is greater than its parts: Projected employment growth by 2020 ranges from 11 percent in Center City itself to a whopping 43 percent in Gloucester, New Jersey; and more moderate rates are expected in Chester, P.A. (38 percent); Burlington, N.J. (28 percent); and Mercer, N.J. (26 percent). The overall average is around 20 percent.

Forecasts for employment growth for the same time period include increases for wholesale trade (28 percent), retail trade (24.3 percent), services (22.4 percent), transportation/utilities (18.7 percent), construction (15.6 percent), government (14.6 percent), and manufacturing (13.5 percent), which seems to bode well for positions in just about any field.

Service-producing industries dominate the economy, with general services providing the most jobs (nearly 700,000), followed by trade, government, FIRE (fire, insurance, real estate), and transportation/public utilities. Although it accounts for a much smaller portion of overall employment, manufacturing consists primarily of goods-producing industries (about 325,000 positions) with nondurable goods creating half that number of jobs. Contract construction and mining come in a weak third.

Although unemployment is still slightly higher than the national rate, scientific minds will find excellent prospects. Philly has a health-care industry that employs 11+ percent of the regional workforce. More than a dozen medical and specialty schools, as well as 10 universities offering advanced degrees in biological sciences, churn out approximately 20 percent of America's physicians, nurses, and related health workers. More than 120 hospitals, such as Children's Hospital, Scheie Eye Institute, and Fox Chase Cancer Center, cover nearly every discipline, engaging more doctors in research than any other metropolitan area.

Research and development establishments include 31 manufacturers of engineering and scientific instruments (for medical, surgical, and dental use) and 250 computer/data processing firms. The pharmaceutical/biotech industry has garnered 11 percent of the job growth since 1991; nearly 100 new biotech firms have been launched over the past decade. As a top ($5.35 billion) revenue producer, pharmaceutical/biotech interests employ more than 865,000 people and encompass branches or home offices of many major pharmaceutical concerns. Not a bad pill for those with the right training.

An increased effort by the city and some corporations to enhance tourism is paying off, particularly in the hospitality and marketing/promotion area. For instance, the recently built Pennsylvania Convention Center drew an additional 700,000+ annual visitors to the city, with a direct economic impact of $140 million. Another ripening industry is food distribution, which not only involves some 148 firms and 5,000 jobs but also has yearly sales of over $2 billion. Transportation and management expertise are used in activities requiring storage, processing, packaging, warehousing, and more. Employment is also boosted by recent area arrivals such as First Union Corp, the nation's sixth-largest commercial bank, and Medical Broadcasting Company, a planning and marketing firm. Expanding economic and printing/publishing institutions also provide a steady font of jobs.

ARTS AND SCIENCES

Area code 215 has lots to do, including plane watching at PHL, where an amazing variety of aircraft take off or land every 90 seconds or so. But before getting to that point, newcomers might want to start out on foot and explore "America's most historic square mile"—Independence National Historical Park. Along with the truly impressive (Independence) Hall 'n' (Liberty) Bell combo, the Park has Congress Hall, where the U.S. Senate and House of Representatives met from 1790 to 1800; City Tavern, where you can hoist a few with the ghosts of Jefferson, Washington, and Franklin; and Carpenters' Hall, where the First Continental Congress meet in '74 (17, that is). Nearby Society Hill's restored cobblestone streets are lined with hundreds of Federal-style townhouses and numerous restaurants.

A few blocks away is Old City, Philly's first commercial area. Although most of the buildings are relatively "new" (dating from the late 1800s), notable exceptions are Elfreth's Alley, the oldest continuously occupied residential street in America; the Betsy Ross House, where the first American flag was created; and Christ Church, where Washington, Franklin, and other Colonial leaders worshiped when they weren't making up rules for democracy. The

Afro-American Historical and Cultural Museum, several Quaker meeting houses, and a thriving arts district with more than 30 galleries are other points of interest.

Penn's Landing, the city's waterfront area, has been transformed into a riverfront park, with many festivals, an ice-skating rink, and historic ships. Notable vessels include the USS *Olympia*, Admiral Dewey's flagship during the Spanish-American War; the *Gazela* of Philadelphia, a fishing boat that's over a century old; and the USS *Becuna*, a World War II submarine. Those wanting to immerse themselves completely can visit the nearby Independence Seaport Museum; the Mummers Museum, which features beaded and sequined costumes celebrating that ancient form of performance art; or the Mario Lanza Museum, which is dedicated to the famous tenor's life and times.

The Benjamin Franklin Parkway contains many of the city's cultural treasures, such as the Philadelphia Museum of Art, whose treasures span 2,000 years and three continents and whose steps are perhaps equally famous from the *Rocky* movies; sculptures at the Rodin Museum; and the Franklin Institute Science Museum, which claims to have pioneered the concept of hands-on exhibits. The Academy of Natural Sciences offers everything from live butterflies to (obviously very) dead dinosaurs, while the Free Library (aren't they all?) has over 6 million holdings. With the largest collection outside Paris (another city that takes itself seriously but which has no sense of humor), Philly makes a strong Impression(ist) with paintings at the Museum of American Art at the Pennsylvania Academy of Fine Arts and The Barnes Foundation in Merion.

More classy entertainment can be found at the grand Academy of Music. As home to the Opera Company of Philadelphia, the Philadelphia Orchestra, Peter Nero and the Philly Pops, and the Pennsylvania Ballet, the Academy gets almost as much of a workout as Sly did. The Forrest Theater and the Merriam Theater at the University of the Arts mount productions on their way to Broadway or on national tour. The Walnut Street Theater, the Philadelphia Drama Guild, the Philadelphia Theater Company, the Philadelphia Festival Theater for New Plays, the American Music Theater Festival, and the Wilma Theater feature more local, regional, and touring efforts. Concerts of all stripes can be found at the Spectrum and, during the summer, at Mann Music Center.

THE SPORTING LIFE

Whereas other cities may have several green spaces, Philly's is all rolled into 8,900-acre Fairmount Park, with creeks, trails, meadows, and 100 miles of jogging and bike paths. Facilities are available for boating, canoeing, golfing, baseball, and just about every other organized activity. Fairmount Park also offers an outstanding collection of Early American homes, a summer outdoor symphony program, and a plethora of other sites. Canoeing and tubing are available at the Bucks River County and in Valley Forge, and there are skiing and summer diversions in the Pocono Mountains.

A full menu of professional sports includes the Phillies (baseball), the Sixers (also known as the 76ers, basketball), the Eagles (football), the Flyers (ice hockey), the Bulldogs (roller hockey), the Wings (lacrosse), and the Kixx (soccer) at the South Philadelphia sports complex, Veterans Stadium, and the Corestates Spectrum. Philly is also home to the Corestates Bicycle Championships, the Army-Navy football game, the Dad Vail rowing regatta, the Comcast U.S. Pro Indoor Tennis Championship, and the Philadelphia Distance Run.

AFTER-HOURS DIVERSIONS

Nightlife centers on the trend magnets of Delaware Avenue and the Delaware River Waterfront; eclectic South Street; and various college campuses, which usually draw a younger, more informal crowd. Spots such as the 70,000-square-foot Dave and Buster entertainment complex, the cutting-edge Milk Bar, and the pyramid- and sphinx-laden Egypt share attention spans with the seasonal KatManDu and Rock Lobster, both located on the pier. Music and/or dancing can be found at Flanigan's, Phoenix, Revival, Trocadero, the Amazon Club, Baci, Barclay Hotel Piano, and North Star Bar. There are jazz vespers and more at the Old Pine Church, Memphis, Zanzibar Blue, and Morgan's Nite Club. Humor's for sale at the Comedy Factory Outlet, Bacchanal, Comedy Works, Going Bananas, and Catch a Rising Star.

CULINARY AND SHOPPING HAUNTS

Philly takes great pride in its *Condé Nast* ranking as the best restaurant city in the nation. Along with the previously mentioned Nos. 1 and 2, other top "contendahs" include La Truffe, Deux Cheminees, Swann Lounge and Cafe, Founders, Grill Room, the Dining Room, the Monte Carlo Living Room, and Restaurant 210. But be prepared to empty your well-tailored pockets: Dinner entrees for many places cost $15 and up, and there's often a dress code. Less intimidating and cheaper feeds can usually be found at places with *pub*, *brew*, or *diner* in their names (Irish Pub, Samuel Adams Brew House, Red Lion Diner), as well as Chinese, Southern-style, deli, and native Philly restaurants. Still, many Italian, French, Continental, and seafood eateries such as Bookbinder's, the Chart House, Striped Bass, and Philadelphia Fish & Company may be worth the additional investment.

Just about anything gourmet, funky, and delectable can be found at Rittenhouse Row in Center City and Main Street in the Manayunk area, and that goes for shopping as well. An eclectic blend of old and new, Philadelphia also has major department stores (Hecht's, Strawbridge's), upscale complexes (The Gallery at Market East, The Shops at Liberty Place) and Old World (Reading Terminal Market, Italian Market). Antique Row and Jewelers' Row are ripe with the possibility of fabulous finds, while Franklin Mills, allegedly the world's largest outlet mall, has been named a bargain hunter's Official Landmark. And you've just begun to shop.

ETHNIC AND RELIGIOUS PROSPECTS

As a city where religious liberty has always been encouraged and practiced—in 1726, for instance, Jews were given equal rights with Christians—Philly's a great place to be a minority. The Coalition of African-American Cultural Services, an alliance between African-American and Latino groups, has given a boost to civic projects like the Avenue of the Arts and the Uptown Cultural District. Newcomers can also get involved with organizations like the Africamericans for Cultural Development, the Martin Luther King, Jr. Association for Non-Violence, and more, while the Asociacion de Musico Latino Americanos and Taller Puertorriqueno support the Latino community. The West Philadelphia Cultural Alliance provides outreach for all groups. Chinatown, the Polish American Cultural Center, American Swedish Museum, German Society, and others serve as points of references for their respective origins. The Balch Institute for Ethnic Studies offers research opportunities as well as changing exhibitions regarding various immigrants.

The only one of its kind, the National Museum of American Jewish History provides an anchor to an already strong community (which boasts the second oldest synagogue in the U.S., Congregation Mikvah Israel). Center City alone has houses of worship ranging from the Old Pine St. Presbyterian Church to Mother Bethel AME Church to First Unitarian Church to Christ Church to Old St. Mary's Church (the First Cathedral of the Diocese of Philadelphia), and many more.

> Perhaps the best litmus test of a city's durability is its openness to diversity. In Philly, the original natives— Germans, Irish, Poles, American Indians, and others—live in harmony with strong black, Jewish, Italian, Asian, and Russian communities, bound together by the "innerestin" sights and positive "addytoods" whenever confronted with civic issues and challenges.

CRIB SHEET

Philadelphia's more than 100 neighborhoods and several counties can make buying decisions either very easy or almost overwhelming. Each area has its own personality, with the architecture, age of dwellings, and ethnic makeup factoring heavily into its appeal to a particular individual. Options include historic homes in Society Hill; contemporary single-family dwellings in Cherry Hill, New Jersey; high-rises on the Benjamin Franklin Parkway; restored Victorians in Mt. Airy and Germantown; row houses in South and West Philly; and a variety of rural and suburban settings in the surrounding counties. Regardless of where folks live, they generally take great pride in their community.

Apartments can vary from around $650–905 for one-bedrooms in Center City to less in most other counties. However, Philadelphia itself has some reasonably priced homes, particularly in the Manayunk, Germantown, Fairmount, and East Falls areas. Society Hill and Mt. Airy tend to be more expensive, and Chestnut Hill is the costliest. Except for the Main Line, which has the lofty suburbs of Radnor, Bryn Mawr, and Gladwyn, many homes in Montgomery and Bucks Counties tend to be in the $125,000–200,000 range, with an even wider variation in Chester and Delaware Counties.

Although Philly's institutions of higher learning spit out tens of thousands of degrees annually (since 1970, 15 Philly faculty members and graduates have received Nobel Prizes), elementary and secondary education can be a bit trickier. In 1995, SAT scores for Philadelphia averaged 740, far below the national median of 910. Surrounding county school statistics are generally higher, and there are also a number of excellent private and parochial schools.

Phoenix at a Glance

Birthdate and Present Size: 1870 (incorporated as a city in 1881). *Metropolitan Statistical Area*— 1980: 1,509,052; 1990: 2,122,101. 1/1/95 (estimate): 2,505,900. Percent change, 1980–1990: +40.6%. Percent change, 1990–1995: +18.1%.

Weather Report: *Average annual temperature*—71° F. In January: 65/39° F. In July: 105/80 °F. *Average annual precipitation*—7.11". *Average annual snowfall*—trace.

Money Matters: *Unemployment rate*— 3.9%. *Per capita income*—$14,096. *Average household income*—$37,159. *Average cost of a home*—$121,017. *Average rent for an apartment*— $618/month. *ACCRA cost of living indexes* (based on 100)—Composite Index: 103.1; Utilities Index: 110.8; Housing Index: 95.3. *Sales and use tax*—5.0% (state); +1.7% (local). *Personal income tax*—3.25% to 6.9%.

People Profile: *Crime rate* (Per 100,000 population)—10,048.3 (city); 6,940.6 (suburbs); 8,290.3 (MSA). *Racial and ethnic characteristics*— White: 81.7%; Black: 5.2%; American Indian/Eskimo/Aleut: 1.9%; Asian/Pacific Islander: 1.6%; Hispanic Origin: 19.7%; Other: 9.6%. *Gender ratio*—98 males per 100 females (all ages); 96 males per 100 females (18 years old+). *Age characteristics*—18–24 (10.5%); 25–44 (35.2%). Median age: 31. *Educational attainment*—percent having completed high school: 78.7%; percent having completed college: 19.9%.

Major Players: Services (particularly tourism activities); retail/wholesale trade; government; manufacturing, including aircraft, aircraft engines and parts, computers, guidance and navigation equipment, and semiconductors. *Largest employers*—Motorola, Samaritan Health System, Allied Signal, Inc., Pinnacle West Capital Corp., Intel Corp., U.S. West Inc., American Express, Bank One, State of Arizona, Maricopa County, City of Phoenix, U.S. Postal Service.

Community Services: *Average hospital cost*—$472.14/day. *Average doctor visit*—$57.20. *Average dentist visit*—$68.37. *Newspapers*—The Arizona Republic, Arizona Business Gazette, Arizona Informant (black), The Catholic Sun, Jewish News of Greater Phoenix, El Sol (Spanish community), Phoenix New Times (entertainment/restaurant weekly), NewDigest (alternative).

PHOENIX: SUN SPOT

What can you say about a place that has sunshine an average of 300 days a year? That it's the "Best Run City in the World" according to the Carl Bertelsmann Foundation? That it's enjoyed consistent growth 27 out of the past 30 years? That it has more Five Diamond/Five Star resorts than any other city in the U.S.? That with 21 tribes and 23 reservations, it has the highest percentage of Native Americans in any state? True, a governor arbitrarily canceled Martin Luther King Day, much to the state's embarrassment and the country's chagrin (it was quickly restored and he was later impeached). And Arizona has the highest rate of skin cancer in the U.S. and, weirdly enough, the largest number of deaths from being struck by lightening (lack of recognition, perhaps?). But you can eat at a different Mexican restaurant once a week for three years and never visit the same location twice. And the golf can't be beat.

A relative latecomer to the American scene, Phoenix, the state capitol of Arizona (also rather affectedly known as the Valley of the Sun), wasn't settled until around 1870. Although it was arid and dry, tribes such as the Maricopa and Pima had lived there for centuries; their predecessors, the Hohokam, developed an irrigation system. Former Confederate officer Jack Swilling and a group of settlers established a canal company based on the Hohokam waterways. They named it after the mythical bird that rose from its own ashes. Soon the area was producing food and clothing for the growing Arizona territory, with a courthouse, schools, and the inevitable saloons and dance halls.

> "When you wake up every day to sunshine, there's no excuse for a bad attitude," remarks one local. Phoenecians are generally friendly, although not too many have established roots here.

Although the population remained at fewer than 30,000 people until 1920, and floods from the Salt River periodically destroyed the canals and surrounding lands, dams were built in the early 1900s, and by World War II Phoenix became a training hub for the armed forces in aviation and desert warfare. Many former soldiers settled here and, thanks to the wonders of air-conditioning and an influx of retirees, the number of inhabitants has increased 500 percent since 1950, making Phoenix the largest business center between Dallas and the West Coast. In the mid-80s the Central Arizona Project began bringing water from the Colorado River, facilitating even more housing developments and artificial lakes.

Willy-nilly expansion has resulted in urban sprawl, traffic, air pollution, crime, homelessness, and an erratic public image, particularly in multicultural arenas. But recent years have been good to Phoenix. A revitalized downtown; a record number of home-based, new, and expanding businesses and jobs; and immediate access to outdoor activities make it desirable for those willing to try life without a snow shovel. Plus, you can wear shorts just about anytime, unless your job has a dress code.

Quality of Life

Topographically, Phoenix is about as different from the typical American city as you can get. With an altitude of 1,110 feet, rocky desert terrain, cacti, and 300 ostrich ranches (which house about 10,000 of the mean-spirited birds), it may take a while to adjust to the lack of forestation—although South Mountain Park is the world's largest, with 20,000 acres of horseback riding, hiking trails, and a panoramic view. Man-made lakes and skiing and summertime hiking in the much-cooler mountains provide a respite. Those willing to take a road run a few hours west will encounter the Pacific Ocean or the glitter of Las Vegas (you can't miss either).

"Everything here is new and clean, with modern architectural designs," observes public relations specialist Molly Caswell. Although you can have your grass and mow it too (year-round), lots of folks opt for the natural but maintenance-free arid look, saving a bucketful on the water bill. Besides, you might be too busy sampling the city's more than 140 golf courses or attending one of the numerous professional sports attractions to care for your lawn. A $5 billion-a-year tourism industry also helps keep restaurants and shops up to par. Even pale, aesthetic types will find museums and coffeehouses, as well as a symphony, opera, ballet, and theater. There are lots of libraries (including a brand new one downtown), art galleries, and more than 1,200 clubs and organizations.

Yeah, it can average 105 degrees in July (record: 122 degrees, on June 26, 1990), "but it's a dry kind of heat, not humid like it gets in New York, where you can't breathe and you sweat," says cultural affairs specialist Karen Frye.

Well, most of the time: "Summers [here] can be almost as bad as the snow" in her home state of Michigan, admits Jennifer Clement, a recent transplant. "The heat can be so intense, you have to stay inside" although she quickly acknowledges that the other nine months more than make up for any major sweltering.

A reasonable cost of living ("You can actually buy a first-time house here," observes accountant Chris Castillo) and slower pace help reduce perspiration. Some of the latter is involuntary, a result of heavy traffic due to a highway system poorly equipped to deal the population influx. Still, roads are being built and even downtown is perking up, what with additions like the Arizona Center restaurant and shopping complex and several cultural and sports attractions (the most notable of which is a new ballpark being readied for the major league baseball Diamondbacks). And with a laid-back Western atmosphere, "there's not as much to fear, although we do have crime, especially in certain areas."

"When you wake up every day to sunshine, there's no excuse for a bad attitude," remarks Frye. Folks are generally friendly, although Phoenix has been accused of having transient-itis, in that not too many have established roots here. In fact, 20-year residents are considered old guard. But those with contacts from college or a willingness to put up with a revolving door of friends will have it made in the shade.

General Opportunities

Yes, there are lots of retirees. But they're friendly and won't run you over with their shopping carts, should you inadvertently cut them off in line at the grocery store. Thanks to Arizona State University (ASU), in nearby Tempe, "there's a large and active pool of young people," observes Caswell. Particularly those who know someone "will find it fairly easy to get a job." In fact, well over a third of the area's newcomers cite employment as their primary reason for moving to Phoenix.

Although people migrate from all over and there is a sizable Hispanic population, "minorities are reluctant to move here because the area's not perceived as being culturally diverse," remarks one recruiter. In some cases, their hesitancy is well-founded. "You still hear racist comments, particularly against Mexicans and Indians, and even about African-Americans." The Martin Luther King Day fiasco didn't help: "There's still a stigma, although the state's made an active effort to introduce multiculturalism and enforce equal opportunity and things have improved in the past few years," the recruiter goes on. And most negative reactions come from "older people and not young professionals." Indeed: Phoenix was recently ranked among the top cities for new Latino entrepreneurs by *Hispanic Business* magazine.

Employers have glommed onto the area as well. An excellent business environment, competitive wages, good public services, local and state economic support and tax breaks, and less restrictive regulations have inspired such companies as Intel to build a $1.3 billion manufacturing plant. With an expected average growth of 4 percent per year, manufacturing, retailing, and business services are closing in on the already strong service, trade, hi-tech, and information markets. "Phoenix is such a new city that you're getting in on the ground floor of what's happening," points out Frye. "There's plenty of room for advancement, regardless of skin color."

MAJOR BREADWINNING

Upon arriving in Phoenix, liberals and Democrats might want to paraphrase the late Jackie Gleason: "How conservative it is." In spite of the expansion and influx of new blood, "basically this is still a gun-toting, Republican kind of state," remarks one woman. "So you need to be careful about how you express your opinions, particularly in the workplace."

But when it comes to employment, Phoenix is so diverse it practically mirrors U.S. composition in services (29.9 percent), government (16.7 percent), manufacturing (13 percent), construction (6.8 percent), transportation/communication/public utilities (5 percent), finance/insurance/real estate (FIRE) (7.2 percent), mining (0.4 percent), and trade (25.2 percent). In the latter, NAFTA has been particularly helpful, stimulating Arizona exports in computers and other high-technology products.

This is one city where just about any skill can be put to use. "Companies are hiring vivaciously. It's the best it's ever been," asserts the recruiter. "There's really no single area that's particularly sought after, unless you count computer programming," which is true of just about anywhere. Along with Motorola and gobs o' government jobs, familiar names with a large presence or headquarters here consist of Bank One, Honeywell, America West airlines, Circle K convenience stores, Safeway groceries, U-Haul, and Southwest Airlines. And most of the state's 148,000 small enterprises are located in Phoenix.

Since Motorola's arrival in the 1950s, manufacturing and high technology have been a mainstay, with a steady increase in hiring. In the former, spin-off and support companies continue to buoy this $32 billion-a-year industry, adding to the nearly 5,000 firms which employ almost 185,000 people. Wage levels are rising along with output of products in both. Along with standbys like Allied Signal and segments of the aforementioned Motorola and Honeywell, new technology enterprises in what is locally known as the Silicon Desert include SGS Thompson Microelectronics, Cycare Systems, and Microchip Technologies, to mention a few. Many of the state's nearly 100,000 hi-tech positions can be found in Phoenix, particularly in the areas of electronic components and computers. With an annual $7.5 billion in exports and with an average salary of nearly $47,000, skilled workers can rake in a bundle.

Health care utilizes another 55,000 souls in administration and as service providers. Centers for behavioral and home health, managed care facilities, and outpatient treatment sites have added diversity to the field. New buildings are popping up everywhere: a $20 million research center for the Barrow Neurological Center, an $11 million osteopathic school for the Illinois-based Midwestern University, and a 132-bed addition for Scottsdale's Mayo clinic, among others.

Training in computers, marketing, and related fields can be utilized in the 40,000-strong telecommunications/information services, a field so fertile that it has spawned an average of one new start-up per month. A solid telecommunications infrastructure makes the area an ideal hookup for existing companies such as Cox Communications.

Recent mergers and acquisitions have strengthened the base of finance and banking. Institutions such as Bank One, Bank of America, Wells Fargo Bank, and Norwest Bank are recent transplants, bringing with them assets in excess of $33 billion and jobs in accounting, credit-card processing, and computers. Added to the already existing First Interstate Bank and smaller organizations, this field employs approximately 11,000 people.

Last but certainly not least, the tourism industry alone accounts for nearly 150,000 positions. And with tens of thousands of annual housing, apartment, and office building starts, construction's always another option for those temporarily out of work. With all those jobs out there, it's no wonder Phoenicians frown upon the homeless and unemployed.

SOCIAL AND RECREATIONAL SCENE

How Phoenix Plays

Area code 602 appears to be a warm and fuzzy place, unless of course you get too close to a cactus. "Phoenix has a real nice mix of people," observes Caswell. "Everyone's so friendly." Those interested in jumping right in might want to contact the 20/30 Club of Scottsdale (948-3680), which organizes fund-raisers and other activities. Or you can participate in one of 600 neighborhood groups that have established associations and block watches (Phoenix Neighborhood Groups, 534-4444).

> Although an alternative/experimental scene is lacking, you can hear a lot of really great bands and there are many singles activities. Phoenix is "a good place to meet people" without the subtle pressure of settling down that often comes with life in a smaller town.

But it may take longer to form meaningful relationships in a spot where almost everybody's from somewhere else, and "native" is usually followed by "American." "It's easier to make close friends if you've gone to college here," admits Castillo. Involvement in the arts or sports, or with a group of people from the state or area you're from, might be easier than, say, trying to hook up in a bar full of cowboys.

Opinions differ on dating, although all hands agree that it's an active scene. "This isn't California, but there's a lot of interracial dating and it's pretty well accepted," continues Castillo. Others are hard-pressed to recall where (or even if) they've seen mixed groups. Native Americans and Hispanics seem to stick to their own areas.

Still, "people live pretty much wherever they want," adds Caswell. And there's a reasonable amount of nightlife that doesn't involve tethering your horse outside the saloon door.

Although an alternative/experimental scene "is lacking, you can hear a lot of really great bands and there are many singles-oriented activities, particularly involving the outdoors," points out Clement. "It's a good place to meet people" without the subtle pressure of settling down that can come from living in a smaller town.

 ## ARTS AND SCIENCES

Those with a particular fondness for Native American and Southwestern art and architecture will think they've died and gone to heaven. A chief source is the world-renowned **Heard Museum,** which also has the nation's largest kachina doll collection. Cowboys as well as grand masters can be found at the **Phoenix Art Museum,** which houses more than 13,000 items, including serious Chinese art and contemporary collections. Even more can be found at the **Scottsdale Center for the Arts,** which also hosts crafts festivals and the Scottsdale Symphony. During the cooler months, Scottsdale galleries open on Thursday evenings for Art Walks, while ASU has the **Fine Arts Center of Tempe** and the **Nelson Fine Arts Center,** which includes a museum with a rotating collection of Mexican crafts along with local works. Modern expression finds a home at the **Fleischer Museum,** which has a collection of American impressionism paintings, and the otherworldy-looking **Taliesin West,** an architectural school established by Frank Lloyd Wright.

Over 20 performing groups include the Arizona Opera, Ballet Arizona, and the Arizona Theatre Company, all of which can be found at the **Herberger Theatre;** the **Phoenix Symphony;** and the **Phoenix Theatre,** one of the longest-running community theaters in the nation. Phoenix is a favorite stop-off for just about every tour to come down the pike—concerts are rarely rained out or uncomfortable due to the weather—and there are plenty of venues, including the recently renovated **Orpheum Theatre;** the **Red River Opry,** home to bluegrass, gospel, and rock 'n' roll; the Frank Lloyd Wright–designed **Gammage Auditorium;** and the 7,000-seat **Sundome,** America's largest single-level theater (not recommended for short people). **America West Arena** and **Blockbuster Desert Sky Pavilion** are two others.

Other forms of "wild" life can be found at the **Phoenix Zoo,** home to 1,300 animals in an imitation natural habitat; the **Wildlife World Zoo,** where you can hand feed the giraffes; the **Desert Botanical Garden,** which includes 20,000 (give or take a few) plants; and **Arcosanti,** an ecological city of the future that's still being developed. The **Arizona Science Center** and **Arizona Museum for Youth** can enthrall children

Where It's At

 Unless otherwise noted, all area codes are 602.

America West Arena, 201 E. Jefferson St., 379-7800

Arcosanti, 6433 E. Doubletree Ranch Rd., Paradise Valley, 948-6145

Arizona Museum for Youth, 35 N. Robson St., Mesa, 644-2567

Arizona Science Center, 147 E. Adams St., 256-9388

Arizona State Capitol and Museum, 1700 W. Washington St.

Blockbuster Desert Sky Pavilion, 2121 N. 83rd Ave., 254-7599

Breck Girl Hall of Fame, 1850 N. Central Ave., 207-2800

Champlin Fighter Museum, Falcon Field Airport, Mesa, 830-4540

Desert Botanical Garden, 1201 N. Galvin Pkwy., 941-1217

Fine Arts Center of Tempe, 54 W. 1st St., 968-0888

Fleischer Museum, 17207 N. Perimeter Dr., 585-3108

Gammage Auditorium, Apache Blvd. and Mill Ave., Tempe, 965-3434

Hall of Flame Firefighting Museum, 6010 E. Van Buren St., 275-3473

Heard Museum, 22 E. Monte Vista Rd., 252-8848

Herberger Theatre, 222 E. Monroe St., 252-8497

Heritage Square, 6th and Monroe sts., 262-5071

Montezuma's Castle, 5525 E. Beaver Green Rd., Camp Verde, 520/567-4521

Nelson Fine Arts Center, Mill Ave. and 10th St., 965-6447

Orpheum Theatre, 203 W. Adams St., 252-9678

Phoenix Art Museum, 1625 N. Central Ave., 257-1222

of all ages, while the **Hall of Flame Firefighting Museum** might deter would-be arsonists, the **Champlin Fighter Museum** might inspire budding pilots, and the **Breck Girl Hall of Fame** might persuade reluctant youngsters to wash their hair.

Local chronicles are available at the restored **Arizona State Capitol and Museum; Heritage Square** museums, shops and restaurants housed in historical buildings; **Rawhide,** a re-creation of an 1880s Wild West town; and archeological excavations depicting Hohokam and Aztec tribal life at **Pueblo Grande** and **Montezuma's Castle,** respectively. A visit to the ornate **Wrigley** (as in the gum magnate) **Mansion** might also give visitors something to chew on.

Those willing to make the drive will find the time investment worth it at the self-explanatory Petrified Forest, the Painted Desert, and the Grand Canyon. You can't use lousy weather as an excuse to miss the red rocks and multi-channels (as in fortune-tellers and seers, not satellite dishes) of Sedona; the Mongollon Rim, a geological fault that's best driven through sober, since the road often goes within a few feet of the drop-off; and Biosphere 2, a scientific experiment gone awry (that still draws half a million visitors a year) and the subject of a Pauly Shore movie.

 ## THE SPORTING LIFE

Here is where the Valley of the Sun lives up to its name, and not just in the sense of blue skies. It's hard to top this place for golf and tennis. And it's even cheaper in the summer, although the heat can discourage even the most dedicated duffers from their 9 million annual appointed rounds. You can opt to live in an apartment, condo, or house near a resort: "Some communities offer club memberships, room service, and even taxis," points out Frye.

Courses are ubiquitous, ranging from city (**Cave Creek, Encanto,** many more) to "toughies" ranked by the USGA (**Club Terravita, Grayhawk;** others). And these are just the public ones. Perhaps the best way to swing into the scene would be through various instructional and reservation services such as **Access Golf, Inside the Ropes,** and **Sports Solutions,** to mention a few. More games people play can be found at the **Arizona Sport & Social Club, Arizona Outdoors Woman, Arizona Snowbowl, ASCEND ARIZONA Mountain Sports,** and the **Maricopa County Sports Commission.**

Where It's At

(continued)

Phoenix Symphony, Symphony Hall, 225 E. Adams St., 262-7272

Phoenix Theatre, 100 East McDowell, 254-2151

Phoenix Zoo, 455 N. Galvin Pkwy., 273-1341

Pueblo Grande, 4619 E. Washington St., 495-0901

Rawhide, 23023 N. Scottsdale Rd., Scottsdale, 502-1880

Red River Opry, 730 N. Mill Ave., Tempe, 829-OPRY

Scottsdale Center for the Arts, 7383 Scottsdale Mall, 955-ARTS

Sundome, 19403 R.H. Johnson Blvd., Sun City West, 975-1900

Taliesin West, Cactus Rd. and Frank Lloyd Wright Blvd., 860-8810 or 860-2710

Wildlife World Zoo, 16501 W. Northern Ave., Litchfield, 935-WILD

Wrigley Mansion, 2501 E. Telewa Trail, 955-4079

Where It's At

Unless otherwise noted, all area codes are 602.

Access Golf, 1601 W. McNair St., 756-2381

Adobe Dam Recreation Area, 43rd Ave. and Pinnacle Peak Rd., 502-2930

All Western Stables, 10220 S. Central Ave., 276-5862

Arizona Adventures, 4518 W. Continental, Glendale, 800/999-2474

Arizona Cardinals, Sun Devil Stadium, 379-0102

Arizona Diamondbacks, Bank One Ballpark, 514-8400

Arizona Outdoors Woman, P.O. Box 9608, 375-1054 or 279-7622

Arizona Rattlers, 514-8383

Where It's At

Those wanting to chill out can visit resort marinas at lakes Mohave and Meade (**Forever Resorts Marinas**), **Lake Powell Resorts and Marinas, Pleasant Harbor Marina** (found near the **Lake Pleasant Recreational Park**), and others. Other popular wet spots include lakes Saguaro, Canyon, Apache, and Roosevelt. Raft and tubing trips are another watery option (**O.A.R.S. Inc., Salt River Recreation, Sun Country Rafting**), while those looking for more lofty pursuits might be sucked into hot air ballooning (**Hot Air Expeditions, Arizona Adventures,** many more) or reach new heights via **Arizona Soaring** or **Turf Soaring School.**

Those preferring the gamble with two feet on terra firma can visit casinos at **Fort McDowell, Gila River, Harrah's,** and others. Or you can opt for a dog and pony show (**Phoenix Greyhound Park; Turf Paradise,** respectively). Folks choosing to ride (rather than watch) horses race can mosey on down to **All Western Stables, Ponderosa Stables,** and more. And there's always the **Firebird** and the **Phoenix International Raceways** for the four-wheels-and-an-engine crowd.

Picnicking, hiking, biking and many other activities can be found at multitudinous parks. Phoenix maintains 32,000 acres of preserves within the city limits; highlights include the aforementioned **South Mountain Park,** with its very own **Mystery Castle; Squaw Peak,** which boasts a spectacular view of the city; and **Papago Park,** which has rugged terrain and excellent fishing. Downtown, you'll find **Margaret T. Hance Deck Park,** 29 acres of green space that's still being developed, and **Patriots Square Park,** with an outdoor stage and oh-so-conveniently located underground parking garage. A bit farther away is (yet another) 18-hole golf course and **Waterworld Safari Motor Park** at the **Adobe Dam Recreation Area.** Brave visitors can investigate an X-Files–type atmosphere at the **Lost Dutchman State Park** (with a missing gold mine, ghost town, and a mountain called Superstition), and more. And although they're four hours away, the White Mountains offer skiing, a casino, and cultural events.

Those with any time (or energy) left over can attend **Cactus League** games, in which seven major league baseball teams play during spring training. The Fiesta Bowl at **Sun Devil Stadium** offers a New Year's Day break, and fall brings on PAC-10 sports action at **ASU.** Several golf tournaments (the **Phoenix Open,** January; **Standard Register Ping,** spring; the **Tradition,** April; and others) make for excellent pro-watching. Other spectator spectaculars include the sold-out NBA **Phoenix Suns,** the NFL **Arizona Cardinals,** and the new major league **Arizona Diamondbacks** with their retractable dome stadium (in case it rains?) as well as the **Arizona Rattlers** (arena football), the **Arizona Sandsharks** (soccer), and the **Phoenix Roadrunners** (hockey). Eat your heart out, Wile E. Coyote.

AFTER-HOURS DIVERSIONS

Although Phoenix may not be a New York or even a Seattle, according to Frye, "you can hear just about every kind of music and it's on the verge" of becoming a happening place. The slowness to catch up with either coast may partially be due to the Phoenician emphasis on comfort, rather than trendiness. "People around here wear pretty much whatever they please."

However, certain areas are magnets for the hip and almost-there: the Arizona Center and the Biltmore area (downtown) and the suburbs of Scottsdale and Tempe have clusters of clubs, boutiques, and chic restaurants, ranging from the small and seedy with lots of wood and dead animals adorning the walls to the huge and loud with an overload of metallic decor. Built in the early '90s, the **Arizona Center** "has done much to revitalize downtown," continues Frye. Favorite watering spots for happy hour and pre/post stop-offs for athletic events include **Little Ditty's,** which features a sing-along with dueling pianists; **Decades,** which plays favorites from the '70s through the '90s; and **America's Original Sports Bar,** which in addition to the requisite big-screen televisions offers sand volleyball and dancing. Another sports bar, **Players,** has a TV in every booth, making it perfect for that date you're not quite sure about. Around 24th Street and Camelback you'll find what's locally known as the Biltmore area, which has a full spectrum of bars and restaurants ranging from the tony **Christopher's** (which won raves from *Food & Wine* and *The New York Times*) to **Filiberto's,** described by one local as "seedy but great."

With its built-in population of college students, Tempe is as close to the avant-garde as you can get around these parts. The mostly 20s crowd flocks to spots like the **Improv** for comedy and the **Timber Wolfe Pub** for more than 99 different bottles of beer on the wall (actually there are 250 brands, along with 150 types of draft). **Fat Tuesday's** and other rapidly changing bars on Mill Avenue feature up-and-coming bands. Those willing to pay a steeper cover price (read: older crowd

Where It's At

(continued)

Phoenix Greyhound Park, 38th St. and Washington, 273-7181

Phoenix International Raceway, 1313 N. 2nd St., 252-2227

Phoenix Open, 379-7575

Phoenix Roadrunners, 340-0001

Phoenix Suns, America West Arena, 379-SUNS

Pleasant Harbor Marina, I-17 and Carefree Highway, 566-3100

Ponderosa Stables, 10215 S. Central Ave., 268-1261

Salt River Recreation, P.O. Box 6568, Mesa, 984-3305

South Mountain Park, 10919 S. Central Ave., 495-0222

Sports Solutions, 5432 E. Alan Ln., Scottsdale, 483-8543

Squaw Peak, 2701 Squaw Peak Dr., 262-7901

Standard Register Ping, 495-4653

Sun Country Rafting, P.O. Box 9429, 800/2-PADDLE

Sun Devil Stadium, ASU campus, 965-9011

Tradition, 443-1597

Turf Paradise, 1501 W. Bell Rd., 942-1101

Turf Soaring School, 8700 W. Carefree Hwy., 439-3621

Waterworld Safari Motor Park, 581-1947

Where It's At

Unless otherwise noted, all area codes are 602.

America's Original Sports Bar, 455 N. 3rd St., 252-2502

Anderson's Fifth Estate, 6820 E. 5th Ave., 994-4168

Arizona Center, 455 N. 3rd St.

Arizona State Fair, 252-6771

Arizona Stock Show and Rodeo, 258-8568

Where It's At

(continued)

Atomic Cafe Nightclub, 8005 E. Roosevelt St., 970-6433

Blue Note, 8708 E. McDowell Rd., 946-6227

Cafestia, 1940 E. Camelback Rd., 265-5509 or 265-2990

Cazadores, 7575 E. Princess Dr., 585-4848

Chandler Ostrich Festival, 963-4571

Christopher's, 2398 E. Camelback Rd., 957-3214

Club One, 4343 N. Scottsdale Rd., 949-3404

Club Tribeca, 1420 N. Scottsdale Rd., 423-8499

Decades, 455 N. 3rd St., 252-2502

Empire/Kyoto Japanese Restaurant, 4824 N. 24th St., 955-5244

Fat Tuesday's, 680 S. Mill Ave., 967-3917

Fiesta Bowl, 350-0900

Fiestas Patrias, 261-8069

Filiberto's, 3433 W. Camelback Rd., 973-3390, many other locations

Gold Bar Expresso, 1707 E. Southern Ave., Tempe, 839-3082

Improv, 930 E. University Dr., 921-9877

Le Girls Cabaret, 5151 E. Washington St., 224-8000

Little Ditty's, 455 N. 3rd St., 252-2502

Maloney's, 7318 E. Stetson Dr., 947-8188

Mingles, 7018 E. Main St., 946-0363

Mr. Lucky's, 3660 NW Grand Ave., 246-0686

New Year Indian American Pow Wow, 622-4900

Parada del Sol Rodeo, 990-3179

Players, 455 N. 3rd St., 252-6222

Rockin' Horse, 7316 E. Stetson Dr., 949-0992

Stixx, 7077 E. Camelback Rd., 481-0970

Tiffany's Cabaret, 44 N. 32nd St., 275-3095

Timber Wolfe Pub, 740 E. Apache Blvd., 517-9383

Toolie's, 4231 W. Thomas Rd., 272-3100

World Villages Coffee Company, 7349 Elbow Bend, Carefree, 800/903-2999

Yesterday's, 9035 N. 8th St., 861-9080

with better jobs) will segue over to the more upscale Scottsdale. Clubs there include **Anderson's Fifth Estate, Atomic Cafe Nightclub, Blue Note, Cazadores, Club One, Club Tribeca, Maloney's, Mingles,** and **Stixx.** "There's jazz, blues, even reggae and African music," adds Frye.

Other not-so-cheap thrills include so-called "Vegas-style" nightspots, including **Tiffany's Cabaret, Le Girls Cabaret,** and others. More tasteful amusements can be found at **Empire/Kyoto Japanese Restaurant,** which features billiards and live music; the country-and-western **Mr. Lucky's, Rockin' Horse,** and **Toolie's;** and **Yesterday's,** a cabaret-type revue. Coffeehouses thrive even in sunny climates, with **Cafestia, World Villages Coffee Company,** and **Gold Bar Expresso,** among others.

Those who enjoy ethnic gatherings will find plenty in Phoenix. There are Native American powwows, mariachi competitions, and arts festivals highlighting the works of various ethnic groups year-round. Top U.S. singers and dancers compete at the **New Year Indian American Pow Wow,** while the **Fiestas Patrias** celebrates Mexican independence. With more than 60 sporting and cultural events, just about everyone gets involved with the **Fiesta Bowl.** The **Arizona Stock Show and Rodeo,** the **Parada del Sol Rodeo,** and the **Arizona State Fair** provide even more local color. And with over 200,000 attendees, few put their heads in the ground over the **Chandler Ostrich Festival.**

 ## CULINARY AND SHOPPING HAUNTS

Food is another local bright spot; much of the wildly popular Southwestern and Tex-Mex cuisine originated from this area. A burrito in Phoenix is not the same as in Columbus, and when someone says a salsa's hot, believe them or risk your sinuses. Specialties range from (almost anything) grilled over mesquite to a "cowboy steak" cooked under an open fire to judgment-impairing margaritas. Most places are reasonably priced, and "there are some really great restaurants," according to Molly Caswell. Best of all, many entrees are easy on the waistline, so too-tight tennis clothes won't be an excuse to avoid going out on the court.

Eateries can be subdivided into Mexican, Southwestern, and Western, although the lines between the three often fuse. Phoenix proper has dozens of Mexican places, such as **Carolina's,** winner of many local awards, and the antediluvian (for Phoenix, that's over 30 years) **Garcia's, Jordan's,** and **Macayo's.** Other local favorites include **Andale, Nola's,** and **Old Town Tortilla Factory.** Southwestern is almost as ubiquitous: the **Arizona Cafe & Grill** prides itself on a brew to match every entree; **Vincent Guerithault** serves up cuisine in a country French setting; **Windows on the Green** offers a view of a championship golf course; while Southwestern meets the rest of the world's fare at relative newcomers **Brio** and **La Tache.** No Phoenix experience would be complete without exposure to Western grub—not beans 'n' franks whipped up by Cookie, but aged and hand-cut slabs of beef at the **Stockyards, T-Bone Steakhouse, Pinnacle Peak Patio, Hunter Steakhouse,** the **Rockin' Horse,** and many more.

The Asian influence (and influx) has also had an impact, "and generally you can't go wrong with Oriental food around here," adds Clement. Along with a highly regarded menu, **P.F. Chang's** in Scottsdale is a see-and-be-seen spot, while Thai food at the **Pink Pepper** has been garnering awards for years. More Thai awaits at the **Bamboo Garden,** and there's dim sum at **C-Fu,** noodles at **New Tokyo,** Vietnamese at **Spring,** and sushi at **Sushi Ko** and **Sushi on Shea.** In fact, in recent years, Phoenix has gone downright exotic with **Al Amir** (Lebanese), **India Palace, Lalibela** (Ethiopian), and Philippine at the **Oriental Gourmet.**

Rounding out a global perspective is Spanish fare at **Andramari, Marquesa,** and **Pepin,** and lots of Italian: **Bianco's Pizza, Focaccia Fiorentina, Franco's, Pronto Ristorante,** and, in Scottsdale, **La Locanda, Mancuso's,** and **Ristorante Sandolo,** which offers complementary gondola rides. In the desert? Well, okay.

A uniquely Phoenician experience can be found at **Eddie's Grill,** whose menu is best described as "eclectic"; **Goldie's 1895 House Restaurant,** which serves up a murder mystery and gourmet food in a Victorian home; **Bobby McGee's Conglomeration,** which offers costumed servers and a salad bar in a bathtub; and crabs and oysters at **Steamed Blues.** Cajun meets poetic justice at **Justin's Ragin Cajun** and **Baby Kay's,** and there's soul in them thar hills at **Willie J.'s.** And that's not even mentioning the rack o' barbecue places, including **El Paso Bar-B-Cue Company, Memphis Blues & Barbecue, Bill Johnson's Big Apple,** and others.

Those wanting a more upscale experience might opt for **Morton's,** the **Chart House,** or **Ruth's Chris,** as well as the kudo-garnering **8700 at the Citadel, Durant's,** and **Tarbell's.** However, you might actually have to lose the jeans or shorts and don actual dress-up clothes.

Where It's At

Unless otherwise noted, all area codes are 602.

8700 at the Citadel, 8700 E. Pinnacle Peak Rd., Scottsdale, 994-8700

Al Amir, 8989 Via Linda, Scottsdale, 661-1137

Andale, 1812 E. Camelback Rd., 265-9112

Andramari, 9393 N. 90th Ave., Scottsdale, 661-6499

Arizona Cafe & Grill, 3113 E. Lincoln, 957-0777

Arizona Center, 3rd and Van Buren sts., 271-4000

Arizona Factory Shops, 4250 W. Honda Bow Rd., 465-9500

Baby Kay's, 2119 E. Camelback Rd., 955-0011, other locations

Bamboo Garden, 9201 N. 29th Ave., 944-2388

Bianco's Pizza, 4709 N. 20th St., 381-1779

Bill Johnson's Big Apple, 3110 N. Arizona Ave., Chandler, 892-2542

Biltmore Fashion Park, 24th St. and Camelback, 955-8400

Bobby McGee's Conglomeration, 7000 E. Shea Blvd., Scottsdale, 998-5591

Borgata, 6166 N. Scottsdale Rd., 998-1822

Brio, 7243 E. Camelback Rd., Scottsdale, 947-0795

C-Fu, 2051 Warner Rd., Chandler, 899-3888

Camelback and Indian School roads, 800/737-0008

Camelview Plaza, 944-3111

Carolina's, 1202 E. Mohave, 252-1503

Chart House, 7255 McCormick Pl., 951-2550

Chris Town Mall, 1703 W. Bethany Home Rd., 242-5042

Durant's, 2611 N. Central Ave., 264-5967

Eddie's Grill, 4747 N. 7th St., 241-1188

El Paso Bar-B-Cue Company, 4303 W. Peoria Ave., Glendale, 931-3218

El Pedregal, Scottsdale Rd. and Carefree Hwy., 488-1072

Where It's At

(continued)

Focaccia Fiorentina, 123 N. Central Ave., 252-0007

Franco's, 8120 N. Hayden Rd., 946-6655

Garcia's, 5509 N. 7th St., 274-1176

Glendale, Glendale and 56th

Goldie's 1895 House Restaurant, 362 N. 2nd Ave., 944-5504

Hunter Steakhouse, several locations

India Palace, 16842 N. 7th St., 942-4224

Jordan's, 2633 N. Central Ave., 266-1213

Justin's Ragin Cajun, 13416 Cave Creek Rd., 404-2900

La Locanda, 10201 N. Scottsdale Rd., 998-2822

La Tache, 4175 Goldwater Blvd., Scottsdale, 946-0150

Lalibela, 8946 N. 19th Ave., 870-4555

Los Arcos, 1315 N. Scottsdale Rd., 945-6376

Macayo's, 4001 N. Central Ave., 264-6141

Mancuso's, 6166 N. Scottsdale Rd., 948-9988

Marquesa, 7575 E. Princess Dr., Scottsdale, 585-4848

Memphis Blues & Barbecue, 1264 W. University Dr., Mesa, 668-9334

Mesa's Fiesta Mall, 1445 W. Southern Ave., 833-4121

Metrocenter, 9617 Metro Pkwy., 997-2641

Morton's, 2501 Camelback Rd., 955-9577

New Tokyo, 3535 W. Northern Ave., 841-0255

Nola's, 2590 E. Camelback Rd., 957-8393

Oak Creek, 6601 S. Hwy. 179, Sedona, 520/284-2150

Old Town Tempe, Mill and Rural rds.

Old Town Tortilla Factory, 6910 E. Main St., Scottsdale, 945-4567

Oriental Gourmet, 3222 E. Camelback Rd., 650-1640

P.F. Chang's, E. Camelback and Scottsdale Rds., 949-2610

You can find dozens of neat little boutiques scattered around the Valley. As a rule, Phoenicians are hardly fashion victims: Stores are loaded with Southwestern items, unique designs from individual artists, American Indian handiwork, antiques, and imported items. The previously mentioned Biltmore area downtown, the Fifth Avenue shops of Scottsdale, **Camelback and Indian School roads,** the antique district in **Glendale,** and **Old Town Tempe** all present a major threat to the line of credit. Those willing to wander a bit farther will find saloons, gifts, and more in Prescott Courthouse Square in downtown Prescott; galleries, T-shirt shops, and other out-of-this-world stuff in the Art District in Sedona; and Bohemian items on North Fourth Avenue in Tucson.

Downtown, the **Arizona Center** offers up specialty shops and marketplace carts, and the **Biltmore Fashion Park** has budget-busting temptations like Polo/Ralph Lauren and Saks. But serious mallmeisters head for Scottsdale. Here you'll find an array as distinctive as the architecture: the **Borgata** consists of stores and eateries in an Old World Italian setting. **El Pedregal** utilizes a desert motif to help sell apparel, luggage, and gifts. Serious money is dropped at the large and luxurious **Scottsdale Fashion Square,** which has many of the above-mentioned stores, along with restaurants and cinemas. Although it has about half the shops, the **Scottsdale Pavilions** have attracted major magnets like Service Merchandise, Home Depot, Sports Authority, and more. Others include **Los Arcos, Papago Plaza,** and **Camelview Plaza.**

The surrounding area has quite a smattering as well. Along with 150 of the usual suspects, **Mesa's Fiesta Mall** has a Disney Store, Phoenix Suns Team Shop, and Exclusively Arizona, while the **Superstition Springs Center** provides a botanical walk and canyon trails along with 130 emporiums. The 200-store **Metrocenter** bills itself as the Southwest's largest, and has the selection (Dillard's, Robinson-May, Sears) to prove it. And both the **Park Central Mall** and **Phoenix Mercado** provide leisurely spending opportunities in an open-air atmosphere, while the **Chris Town Mall** and **Paradise Valley Mall** both offer a Dillard's, J.C. Penney's, Macy's, and more.

Outlet stores, another recent phenomenon, have arrived with a vengeance. You can save both money and driving time at the nearby **Arizona Factory Shops** and **Wigwam Outlet Stores,** which each have more than 60 shops. Those willing to make a day of it can visit the **Tanger Factory Outlet Center,** or a smaller cluster at **Oak Creek,** and, as a bonus, pick up some New Age crystals in town.

ETHNIC AND RELIGIOUS PROSPECTS

"People are finally beginning to realize that cultures need to combine and work together," observes Frye, who assists the various groups through her job. Although strides have been made in the past few years, she hopes to see minority visibility increase in the future.

Those wanting to acquaint themselves with the community can join such organizations as the **Urban League, 100 Black Men** ("Believe me, there are more than that!" adds Frye emphatically), and various African-American professional groups (check out the **Black Commerce Directory**). A larger population may make it easier for Hispanics; organizations like **Friendly House** can be initial points of contact. And with 1,700 houses of worship in the Valley, there's certainly a large selection of churches.

Although Phoenix doesn't have the homogenous religious community of Nashville, its spiritual strength can be found in its diversity. Offerings include the **Arizona Buddhist Church,** the state's largest and oldest Buddhist congregation, which draws from a variety of faiths and nationalities; the traditional **Roman Catholic Church;** and synagogues from Orthodox to the liberal branch of the Jewish Renewal Movement (contact the **Jewish Community Center** or **Jewish Association Singles Service** for more information). A recent poll conducted by the *Arizona Republic* and *Phoenix Gazette* found that more than 75 percent of the residents believed religion to be at least fairly important; many attend services at least once a month.

No single faith seems to predominate in Phoenix, although about 20 percent of the population are Roman Catholics, followed by "mainline" Protestants (Lutherans, Methodists, Episcopalians, etc.) at 17 percent, Baptists at 9 percent, Church of Jesus Christ of Latter Day Saints at 7 percent, and Jews at 2 percent. There's an openness found in even the most conventional churches that's surprising to Easterners, according to an article in *Living in Arizona.* "People coming here are looking for a more spiritual bent," Rabbi Ayla Grafstein told the paper. "Things like Jewish mysticism are popular because it helps people go to a deeper level in their spiritual path." Contact the **Arizona Ecumenical Council** for more information on various groups.

Where It's At

(continued)

Papago Plaza, Scottsdale and McDowell rds., 423-1414

Paradise Valley Mall, 4568 E. Cactus Rd.

Park Central Mall, 3121 N. 3rd Ave., 264-5575

Pepin, 7363 Scottsdale Mall, 990-9026

Phoenix Mercado, 542 E. Monroe St., 256-6322

Pink Pepper, 245 E. Bell Rd., 548-1333

Pinnacle Peak Patio, 10426 E. Jomax Rd., Scottsdale, 585-1599

Pronto Ristorante, 3950 E. Campbell, 956-4049

Ristorante Sandolo, 7500 E. Doubletree Branch Rd., 991-3388

Rockin' Horse, 7316 Stetson Dr., Scottsdale, 949-0992

Ruth's Chris, several locations

Scottsdale Fashion Square, 7000 E. Camelback Rd., 941-2140

Scottsdale Pavilions, Pima and Indian Bend rds., 993-1626

Spring, 5850 N. 43rd Ave., 937-2195

Steamed Blues, 4843 N. 8th Pl., 966-2722

Stockyards, 5001 E. Washington St., 273-7378

Superstition Springs Center, 6555 E. Southern Ave., 832-0212

Sushi Ko, 9301 Shea Blvd., Scottsdale, 860-2960

Sushi on Shea, 7000 Shea Blvd., Scottsdale, 483-7799

T-Bone Steakhouse, 10037 S. 19th Ave., 276-0945

Tanger Factory Outlet Center, 2300 E. Tanger Dr., Casa Grande, 520/836-0897

Tarbell's, 3213 E. Camelback Rd., 955-8100

Vincent Guerithault, 3930 E. Camelback Rd., 224-0225

Wigwam Outlet Stores, I-10 and Litchfield Rd., 935-9733

Willie J.'s, 4621 S. Central Ave., 243-2788

Windows on the Green, 6000 E. Camelback Rd., Scottsdale, 423-2530

Where It's At

Unless otherwise noted, all area codes are 602.

100 Black Men, 404/525-7111

Arizona Buddhist Church, 4142 W. Claredon Ave., 278-0036

Arizona Ecumenical Council, 4423 N. 24th St., 468-3818

Black Commerce Directory, P.O. Box 63701, 420-5226

Friendly House, 1350 S. 11th St., 354-3665, other locations

Jewish Association Singles Service, 1718 W. Maryland Ave., 242-5277

Jewish Community Center, 1718 Maryland Ave., 249-1832

Roman Catholic Church, Diocese, 400 E. Monroe, 257-0030

Urban League, 5644 S. 16th St., 243-4169, several other locations

CRIB SHEET

With a homicide rate that has tripled over the past two decades and a homeless problem exacerbated by a warm climate, "it's best to know what you're getting into residence-wise, particularly if you decide to live downtown," remarks Clement. Apartments and condos are scattered everywhere; a gated community is often the best choice in the city proper. "Some areas simply aren't safe, although certain offshoots can be."

Still, it's amazing what varieties can grow in the desert. An assortment of styles at mostly reasonable prices can be found in Phoenix. The community is fairly spread out, although the Ahwatukee section of Phoenix and the suburbs of Scottsdale, Chandler, Gilbert, and Tempe seem to be the most popular. Initial builds range from $90,000 to around $200,000. Luxury apartment, condo, and home communities often feature classic Southwestern architecture and green spaces with exclusive use of pools, tennis courts, lakes, and even golf courses.

Those looking for a mountain view will find it in well-maintained districts close to Squaw Peak and the Arizona Biltmore, several streets surrounding the Paradise Valley Mall, and in the North Mountain and Moon Valley areas, which also offer easy freeway access, a major bonus around these parts. Camelback Mountain—so named because it resembles a sleeping camel from a distance—has the desirable Arcadia, a citrus orchard turned 1960s-style development. South Mountain cradles Ahwatukee, which provides everything from apartments to golf-course lots in master-planned communities. Along with an explosion of attendant retail development, this area has the added cachet of being served by a suburban school district while still being located in Phoenix. Folks on a budget might want to consider homes a little farther west of I-17 near the Metro Center and farther south and west in areas like Maryvale.

In the East Valley are the communities of Tempe and Mesa. One of the top ten college towns (according to *The New York Times)* and the home of Arizona State and the Fiesta Bowl, Tempe is loaded with restaurants, coffeehouses, and nightlife, as well as being the site of a major crafts festival and other outdoor events. Several hi-tech businesses are located in this young, happening area where homes are slightly more expensive.

Mesa is now the state's third-largest city and boasts such industries as Motorola, McDonnell Douglas, and TRW vehicle safety systems. A strong school system and influx of tourist dollars have encouraged an active cultural scene as well as the growth of malls, golf courses, and parks. About 20 miles away you'll find Chandler, one of the nation's first master-planned communities, and Gilbert, a small-town atmosphere with good schools and a mix of housing. According to Castillo, both are economical and nice, always an attractive combination.

Less than 10 miles from the center of Phoenix, Scottsdale evolved from a Wild West burg in the late 1800s to an exclusive working, living, and shopping area with really classy architecture. Resorts, an active arts scene, and thousands of acres of parks make it appealing to lovers of the good life. More moderately priced homes in the south end draw young professionals.

Unlike Scottsdale, which has an airport and several businesses, Paradise Valley refuses to allow commercial developments within its limits. Homes on large, natural desert lots in a mountain setting attract CEOs, celebrities, and others with mucho dinero. Although they're 30 miles away, Carefree/Cave Creek and Fountain Hills may be worth the commute. Cave Creek has retained its Western flavor, while Carefree was a planned community built in the '50s and has such streets as Easy (really!), and Ho and Hum roads. Fountain Hills claims the world's tallest fountain (at 560 feet high, it produces an explosion of water for 15 minutes of every hour) as well as a secluded locale with spectacular mountain views.

West of Phoenix are Glendale (population: about 185,000), which has a major air force base; Sun City/Sun City West (population: about 60,000), which has a minimum age requirement of 55 and allows no children under 18; and Surprise (population: 11,275, and it isn't), a major snowbird magnet with two big RV parks.

According to Frye, public schools in Phoenix proper "have a ways to go, although they're working on some of the problems," in the classroom and curriculum. Although there are nearly 60 districts in Maricopa County, "you need to be careful where you send your kids and look into each program." For descriptions, contact the Arizona Department of Education (542-4361). Information on the dozens of local parochial and private schools can also be obtained through the Department of Education.

The fifth-largest college in the U.S., Arizona State (965-9011) has branch campuses throughout the Valley and is known for its excellent business and engineering programs. Two-year community colleges in Maricopia County have also been praised by *Reader's Digest* and *U.S. News & World Report.* Larger campuses include Mesa Community (461-7000), Glendale Community (435-3000), and Phoenix College (285-7432). There are also private schools (University of Phoenix) and technical colleges and trade schools (DeVry Institute, High-Tech Institute) as well.

NAVIGATING PHOENIX

Phoenix has a history of transportation glitches. An early settler tried to introduce camels as beasts of burden; it didn't take, so herds were let go to roam the desert. In 1985, a comprehensive freeway expansion project was reduced because of an economic downturn. But people kept coming and now Phoenix is about the same size as San Diego, "with half the expressway system," observes Caswell. "And Scottsdale has nothing at all."

Another bummer: "People around here drive like idiots," gripes another resident. "There's a lot of congestion, but they barrel on ahead anyway. No wonder there are so many accidents."

The average commuting time is 24.6 minutes to cover 12.7 miles, about 30 miles an hour, and the Valley roads are typically clogged for around five hours each workday. And with no subway system, and erratic buses that stop running shortly after 6 p.m. and limited service on Sunday (Valley Metro/DASH, 253-5000), you either drive or hang around the desert hoping to encounter a misplaced camel.

Still, not all the news is bad. Today, construction is going gangbusters. And taxpayers have voted for a beefed-up and improved bus service, with preliminary studies being made for a light rail. Plus, Phoenix's layout is fairly easy to figure out. Central Avenue divides it between east and west; numbered streets run parallel to Central on the east, while numbered avenues do the same on the west. This system continues through Scottsdale (it doesn't apply to the other suburbs, however). And ingress/egress is no problem, with I-17 (the Black Canyon Freeway) heading north to Flagstaff and I-10 (Maricopa Freeway) running east-west from Tucson to Los Angeles. Both form a loop around the city, with U.S. 60 (Superstition Freeway) hooking up on the outskirts. Other major roads include State Highway 51 (north-south), Highway 143 (Hohokam Freeway, north-south), and 202 (Red Mountain Freeway), an airport connector that's part of an ongoing outer loop project. You can always try to remember which one doesn't have a nickname while you're sitting in traffic.

The busiest two-runway airport in the world, Sky Harbor International (273-2231), is expected to open a third runway by 1999. With 27.8 million passengers annually and 1,000 flights a day, Sky Harbor provided relief to the teeming masses in 1990 through the addition of the 2.3 million-square-foot Barry M. Goldwater terminal. Those wanting a less frantic mode of transportation can do the Greyhound thing (271-7430) or Amtrak (253-0121).

PITTSBURGH, PENNSYLVANIA

Pittsburgh at a Glance

Birthdate and Present Size: 1758 (incorporated as a city in 1816). *Metropolitan Statistical Area—* 1980: 2,218,870; 1990: 2,056,705. 1/1/95 (estimate): 2,390,200. Percent change, 1980–1990: –7.3%. Percent change, 1990–1995: +16.2%.

Weather Report: *Average annual temperature—*50.3° F. In January: 34/19° F. In July: 83/61° F. *Average annual precipitation—*36.3". *Average annual snowfall—*44.7".

Money Matters: *Unemployment rate—* 5.6%. *Per capita income—*$12,580 (city); $14,052 (MSA). *Average household income—*$29,587 (city); $34,902 (MSA). *Median cost of a home—*$80,000. *Average rent for an apartment—* $528/month. *ACCRA cost of living indexes* (based on 100)—Composite Index: 113.3; Utilities Index: 158.2; Housing Index: 107.3. *Sales and use tax—*6.0% (state); 1.0% (local). *Personal income tax—*2.8%.

People Profile: *Crime rate* (Per 100,000 population)—7,148.8 (city); 2,256.9 (suburbs); 3,000.6 (MSA). *Racial and ethnic characteristics—*White: 72.1% (city), 90.8% (MSA); Black: 25.9% (city), 8.2% (MSA); American Indian/Eskimo/Aleut: 0.2% (city), 0.1% (MSA); Asian/Pacific Islander: 1.6% (city), 0.7% (MSA); Hispanic Origin: 0.9% (city), 0.5% (MSA); Other: 0.3% (city), 0.2% (MSA). *Gender ratio—*86.8 males per 100 females (all ages); 82.9 males per 100 females (18 years old+). *Age characteristics—*18–24 (13.7%); 25–44 (30.3%). Median age: 34.5 (city), 36.9 (MSA). *Educational attainment—*percent having completed high school: 72.4% (city), 77.4% (MSA); percent having completed college: 20.1% (city), 19.5% (MSA).

Major Players: Services, retail/wholesale trade, manufacturing, government. *Largest employers—*Allegheny General Hospital, Children's Hospital of Pittsburgh, Laurel Run Mining, Magee–Women's Health Corp., Mellon Bank, Mercy Hospital of Pittsburgh, PNC Bank Corp., Presbyterian–University Hospital, St. Francis Medical Center, Western Pennsylvania Healthcare System.

Community Services: *Average hospital cost—*$504.20/day. *Average doctor visit—*$42.40. *Average dentist visit—*$40.80. (Reflects latest available figures, 1994.) *Newspapers—*Pittsburgh Post-Gazette, *Pittsburgh Business Times-Journal, Byzantine Catholic World, New Pittsburgh Courier* (black), *American Srbobran* (Serbian/English), *In Pittsburgh News Weekly* (alternative), *City Paper* (alternative).

PITTSBURGH:
NO MORE HEAVY METAL

The first syllable of "Pittsburgh" is a misnomer. Not only has it been described by no less than *The New York Times* as "the only city in America with an entrance," a dramatic approach through the Fort Pitt tunnel that provides a sweeping view, but it has also been touted as the most livable city and as one of the safest cities, along with having one of the best housing markets, schools, and health-care programs. In recent years, it has also given us a state-of-the art airport that actually charges fair prices, the movie *Night of the Living Dead* (among many others), Mr. Rogers' Neighborhood (in nearby

Oakland), and the Andy Warhol museum, the world's largest collection of the works of a single artist. There's something for every taste.

Even back in 1753, the area surrounding the confluence of the Allegheny, Monongahela, and Ohio rivers attracted notice. George Washington himself recommended that local militia construct a fort at what is now known as the "Golden Triangle." None too happy, the current tenants, the Iroquois, joined forces with the French—who'd built a fortress there and had their own trading agenda—and tried to get their land bank. No such luck: Five years later, the only standing structure was British and named after then-secretary of war William Pitt.

Soon the hills began yielding rich resources of bituminous coal, and the conveniently located river was utilized for distribution of finished goods. The arrival of the Pennsylvania Canal and Portage Railroad in 1834 resulted in additional linkage with Philadelphia and other cities, further increasing commerce. Iron, rope, glass, and boat manufacturing were soon followed by steel and aluminum. By financing museums, parks, and libraries, local steel and iron barons Andrew Carnegie, Henry Clay Frick, and Charles Schwab greatly enhanced the community that made them rich. Still, industry produced an incredible amount of smoke and foul air that was dealt with in typical Pittsburgh style by introducing anti-pollution laws in the 1940s, even before many legislators had heard of such a thing.

Pittsburgh always seems to be one step ahead of the pack. In the early '50s, the city began an urban redevelopment program, cleaning up and renovating the Golden Triangle. By the late '70s, diversification (a buzzword in the '90s) began to take hold in the form of research laboratories, banking and finance, education and training, high technology, and tourism. No wonder corporate headquarters as well as home-based businesses struggling to make their first dollar like it here. Where there once was smoke is now a minimum of firing.

Quality of Life

Although Pittsburghers are inclined to believe differently, their city does have its flaws. "We lack a decent outer belt and our public transportation system's not extensive enough," admits one native, when pressed. "And there aren't a lot of good Indian or Chinese restaurants, and compared to places like Houston, the shopping falls way short."

Perhaps more seriously, there's also a dearth of young people. "The demographics here are much older," observes writer Michelle Fanzo, organizer of PUMP, a group of young professionals working for a stronger presence in city affairs. "Although Pittsburgh's a Democratic city, it can be very conservative because of the labor unions. Sometimes people forget to consider different viewpoints."

But the times they've been a-changin'. "A lot of people are moving back," remarks banker Pete Tsudis, who never even left. "The pace of life is appealing and the job opportunities are terrific." Although salaries are pretty much in line with the national average, housing is a bargain (over $25,000 *below* the U.S. median) and most other commodities are comparably priced. "You can live ten minutes from downtown in a nice home and be close to everything." Neighborhoods are friendly, safe, and well cared for. Folks "have a sense of community and take pride in the city." No kidding.

And while on par with the rest of the Northeast corridor, winters are milder than, say, Cleveland or Chicago, and offer up the added bonus of skiing in the nearby Allegheny Mountains. Avid couch potatoes can chain themselves to their remotes to watch the championship NFL Steelers, one of more than half-a-dozen professional teams. "People aren't real active in the cold months, but they are crazy about their sports teams," comments one woman.

Arts include "world class" (Visitors Bureauese) opera, symphony, theater, and jazz as well as community groups and galleries. Plus, the town has "more festivals than you could visit in a year," adds financial officer Andy Hannah. "It seems like every community and church is advertising one every other weekend." A center for organ transplants, Pittsburgh has two "world class" (those words again!) teaching hospitals. But the location is definitely hard to top: Pittsburgh's about midway between New York and Chicago. And it's the safest city with more than one million residents in the U.S.

Yet despite all the hype and hullabaloo, "you get a small-town feeling," remarks marketing specialist Marla Meyer. "You can go out to eat or to a concert and see someone you know." People talk to strangers on the street, and even stop for pedestrians.

General Opportunities

Pittsburgh has gone global (as opposed to "world class"). The city draws tourists from England, Germany, and Japan; these and many other countries have invested in the region, establishing headquarters or branch offices here. "We get students from all over the world," comments Hannah. "The closer you get into the city, the more the cultures mix. There's no sense of one being better than the other."

Even though the tax base tends to be business-friendly, Pittsburgh does have a stiff state and local tariff. Unemployment is on par with the national average, but jobs are plentiful. Most of the 1.2 million–strong labor force is employed in service industries such as accounting, communications, engineering, and consulting.

And as a rule, Pittsburghers are deeply committed to the work ethic, so turnover is low, while productivity remains high. And they're happy to give beginners a hand. "If you're willing to put forth the effort, the opportunities are there, no matter who you are," observes communications manager Jacob Brody.

MAJOR BREADWINNING

These days, "heavy metal" usually refers to a visiting rock group and "57 varieties" better describes what keeps the nation's largest inland port afloat. With waterfront facilities and commercial navigation channels for three rivers, Pittsburgh processes the greatest amount of waterborne tonnage in the United States. Add this to the triple threat of the airport, railways, and roads, and you've got a major transportation hub.

Pittsburgh's Fortune 500 mix consists of USX, Westinghouse, Alcoa, H.J. Heinz, and others. Top employers include the federal and state government (over 30,000 employees), Westinghouse (16,000), and USAirways (almost 12,000). The University of Pittsburgh, Mellon Bank, and Giant Eagle food retail also add to the blend.

With about 250 international corporations, 110 U.S. headquarters, and thousands of other branch offices and smaller enterprises, Pittsburgh has made the transition from manufacturing to technology, trade, and research without seeming to miss a beat. Nearly 800 firms employ about 80,000 workers in the latter fields, one of the highest concentrations of engineers, scientists, and technicians in the U.S. "It's an exciting time to be living here," remarks Tsudis. "We're going through a lot of changes."

But with companies like PPG (glass) and Allegheny Ludlum (steel) that traditionally translated new developments into practical applications, Pittsburgh has always had an edge. And past research at Carnegie-Mellon University (CMU), the University of Pittsburgh ("Pitt," not to be confused with Brad), and others helped find a cure for polio and refine organ transplants. These forces have resulted in advances in specialties ranging from broadcasting to environmental science to synthetic fuels to microelectronics. Heavy hitters like NASA, IBM, and Motorola have utilized robotics developed in Pittsburgh to gather data on the moon, the Arctic Circle, and underwater.

> Unlike other cities, which have tended to become homogenous as they've grown, Pittsburgh has "held on to its heritage," points out a local.

Pittsburgh's software field—the fifth largest in America—consists of 9,800 workers (a mere 200 fewer than Seattle), making Pittsburgh ideal nerd bait. Over 300 businesses have fostered growth in networking (Transarc, Computerm), client-server systems (Carnegie Group, Enterprise Technologies), and engineering tools (Swanson Analysis Systems, Algor) as well as applications for banking, health care, sales, and other markets. CMU's advances in computer science, engineering, and robotics not only attracted the Department of Defense's Software Engineering Institute but, in conjunction with Pitt and Westinghouse, spawned the Pittsburgh Supercomputing Center. Pittsburgh is also home to Lycos, one of the most utilized Web browsers in existence. The Pennsylvania Department of Labor and Industry estimates that jobs in telecommunications will expand as well.

The Department also projects a 6.7 percent increase in all positions by the year 2000, with health care leading the way. According to *U.S. News & World Report*, Pittsburgh has four of America's best hospitals (Presbyterian Western and Montefiore, both affiliated with Pitt; Children's Hospital of Pittsburgh; and Western Pennsylvania Hospital) bringing the county total to an astounding 50 or so. Pitt's Center for Biotechnology and Bioengineering and smaller companies utilize scientists, analysts, and others with specialized skills for research in AIDS, geriatrics, cancer, multiple organ transplants, and other fields.

The international presence varies from Sony to Bayer, in addition to microcomputers (PEP Modular Computers) and high-speed steel rods (Hitachi/Hi Specialty America).

Other booming areas include banking, tourism, and the Pittsburgh International Airport, which is the third largest in the nation. Assets in the top financial institutions of PNC and Mellon have resulted in the expansion of services and offices. Even the labor movement has been a mixed blessing by providing highly skilled tradespeople who will occasionally agree not to strike so they can, for example, finish the airport on time and under budget.

"Pittsburgh takes care of its own," adds Fanzo. So while some might see such an attitude as insular, it may do wonders for you once you get here.

SOCIAL AND RECREATIONAL SCENE

How Pittsburgh Plays

With most bars closing around 2 a.m., area code 412 "is a pretty married town," observes Meyer. The best way to get into the dating scene is "to be introduced by someone else," a relative, friend, or co-worker.

People also enter the wedded state at a younger age, according to Fanzo. "Many are starting families by their late 20s." Because people tend to make Pittsburgh a permanent home, rather than regarding it as a one- or two-year stint before moving on to bigger things, "They're looking for the spouse, the house, and the car."

Although there is a smaller pool of singles, "and the pickings aren't quite as fruitful, men seem to want to settle down more than women," she continues. Interestingly, many professional women aspire to a larger city, while "men are looking for a steady partner." Females in search of a permanent relationship might want to hang around for a while.

And, even though many residents have also grown up here, "they're searching for new ways to meet people, particularly on a professional level," points out Hannah. Even those just moving in can immediately get involved in neighborhood activities or whatever organization interests them. "It's easy to be accepted."

 ### ARTS AND SCIENCES

With a long and distinguished history and involvement in the arts, the Pittsburgh scene is on par with its much bigger cousins. Practically everywhere you go there's at least one theater, art museum, or historical center.

With four major venues encompassing music, film, dance, and stage, downtown offers the most options. Formerly the Stanley Theatre, the **Benedum Center for the Performing Arts** reopened in 1987 after a $42 million renovation. Not only is the 2,800-seat auditorium comparable in size to the New York Metropolitan Opera, but it's on the National Register of Historic Places and has been rated #1 by *Billboard* magazine. Home to the **Pittsburgh Opera, Pittsburgh Ballet,** and **Civic Light Opera,** it's also a popular venue for Broadway shows.

With 2,847 seats, the **Heinz Hall for the Performing Arts** is another biggie. Built in 1928 by motion picture mogul Marcus Loew, the palatial opal and marble interior has been restored at least twice. Today it serves as the springboard for the **Pittsburgh Symphony** (that of Andre Previn and Lorin Maazel) as well as **Broadway Series** performances. Smaller (1,300 seats) but just as mighty in its own way is the **Fulton,** the area's oldest stage. Now it accommodates touring companies, local productions, and children's theater, as well as concerts and films. And although the **Pittsburgh Filmmakers** don't actually produce movies, they do offer classes and screenings. Pittsburgh has been the site of an impressive number and array of TV shows and movies, more than half of which were shot after 1988.

Where It's At

 Unless otherwise noted, all area codes are 412.

Andy Warhol Museum, 117 Sandusky St., 237-8300

Benedum Center for the Performing Arts, 719 Liberty Ave., 256-2000

Broadway Series, 392-2889

Carnegie, 440 Forbes Ave., 622-3360

Carnegie Museum of Art, 440 Forbes Ave., 622-3131

Carnegie Museum of Natural History, 440 Forbes Ave., 622-3131

Carnegie Science Center, One Allegheny Ave., 237-3400

Children's Museum, Landmark Square, 322-5058

City Theatre, 57 S. 13th St., 431-CITY

Civic Light Opera, 281-5339

Duquesne, 1220 Grandview Ave., 381-1665

Frick Art and Historical Center, 7227 Reynolds St., 371-0606

Fulton, 101 Sixth St., 465-1350

Heinz Hall for the Performing Arts, 600 Penn Ave., 382-4900

Nearby Oakland boasts another cultural powerhouse. Formerly known as the Carnegie Institute, the **Carnegie** includes the Carnegie Library, with its extensive music and art collections and (of course) books; and the Carnegie Music Hall, yet another stage for concerts, operas, and "distinguished" (as opposed to insignificant) lectures. The **Carnegie Museum of Art** highlights French and post-Impressionist and 19th-century work, and the **Carnegie Museum of Natural History** boasts over five million natural history/anthropological specimens as well as an impressive collection of dinosaur skeletons. (What was that guy's name again?)

This area is also home to several other theaters as well as the **Pittsburgh Center for the Arts.** With classes for all levels of artists, exhibits, and openings, the latter offers a friendly entree into the local scene. The **Frick Art and Historical Center** not only includes a tour of Clayton, the magnificent mansion of magnate Henry Clay Frick, but a museum featuring Italian Renaissance paintings and traveling exhibits. What a twofer!

Go north and you'll find the regional troupe, the **Pittsburgh Public Theatre,** as well as the **Manchester Craftsman's Guild,** which also features a jazz series. Two more museums that define eclectic can also be found here. The **Andy Warhol Museum** has much more than 15 minutes worth of his paintings (900), drawings (1,500), prints (500), and photographs (400). And the **Mattress Factory** offers definitely different on-site installations from artists-in-residence from around the world. To the south is the **City Theatre,** another resident group.

Pittsburgh also has unique native attractions as well. More than just a mouthful of words, the **Senator John Heinz Regional History Center** keeps extensive historical society records and artifacts "cool" in a newly restored ice house. You might be inclined, so to speak, toward one of two operating funiculars (a cable railway on a steep slope, with ascending and descending cars balancing each other): the **Monongahela** and the **Duquesne.** Part of the Cathedral of Learning, the world's tallest educational building, the **University of Pittsburgh Nationality Classrooms** consists of 23 rooms designed by various local ethnic groups.

Other scientific and not so erudite pursuits include the **Carnegie** (him again!) **Science Center,** with more than 250 exhibits including a unique interactive planetarium and a World War II submarine; the **Children's Museum,** a "please touch" must for fans of mazes, puppets, and Mister Rogers' Neighborhood (don't forget the cardigan!); and the **Pittsburgh Zoo,** which houses more than 4,000 animals on 77 acres. Plants under glass, seasonal exhibitions, and a Japanese garden can be found at **Phipps Conservatory.** For a one-note stand, there's the **National Aviary,** a colorful (and noisy) indoor collection of live birds. Speaking of no-brainers, **Kennywood Park** lays claim to being the roller coaster capital of the world and includes the Steel Phantom, the highest and fastest. Another global record (for the biggest

Where It's At

(continued)

Kennywood Park, 4800 Kennywood Blvd., W. Mifflin, 461-0500

Manchester Craftsman's Guild, 1815 Metropolitan St., 322-1773

Mattress Factory, 500 Sampsonia Way, 231-3169

Monongahela, 2235 Beaver Ave., 442-2000

National Aviary, Allegheny Commons W., 323-7235

Phipps Conservatory, Schenley Park, 622-6914

Pittsburgh Ballet, 281-0360

Pittsburgh Center for the Arts, 6300 Fifth Ave., 361-0873

Pittsburgh Filmmakers, 809 Liberty Ave., 471-9700

Pittsburgh Opera, 281-0912

Pittsburgh Public Theatre, Allegheny Square, 323-8200

Pittsburgh Symphony, 392-2887

Pittsburgh Zoo, One Hill Rd., 665-3460

Sandcastle Waterpark, 1000 Sandcastle Dr., W. Homestead, 462-6666

Senator John Heinz Regional History Center, 1234 Smallman St., 281-2465

University of Pittsburgh Nationality Classrooms, 5th and Bigelow, 624-6000

hot tub) has been set at **Sandcastle Waterpark,** which also features wet rides and a boardwalk. Not recommended for those who've just had their hair done.

Where It's At

Unless otherwise noted, all area codes are 412.

A.J. Palumbo Center, 1304 Forbes Ave., 396-6058

Allegheny County Department of Parks, 350-2480

Citiparks, 255-2360

Civic Arena, 300 Auditorium Pl., 642-1800

Fitzgerald Fieldhouse, 648-8359

Hidden Valley, 814/443-6454

Laurel Highlands River Tours, 800/472-3846

Oakmont Country Club, 1233 Hulton Rd., Oakmont, 828-8000

Pitt Stadium, 648-8300

Pittsburgh Marathon, Point State Park, 647-7866

Pittsburgh Pirates, 323-5000

Pittsburgh Steelers, 323-1200

Quicksilver Golf Club, 2000 Quicksilver Rd., 800/926-8376

Seven Springs, 800/452-2223

Three Rivers Regatta, Point State Park, 261-7055

Three Rivers Stadium, 400 Stadium Circle

Thrift Drug Classic International Bike Race, Downtown, 621-7223

Whitewater Adventurers, 800/992-7238

THE SPORTING LIFE

Although Pittsburgh lacks NBA basketball, this city has the third highest concentration of athletic facilities per 100,000 population. "People really turn out for games, from high school through professional," observes Hannah. With so many superstars emerging from the region (Johnny Unitas, Joe Montana, Roberto Clemente, to mention a few) "there's an incredible amount of interest" in various pursuits. Locals can brag even more about the impressive number of "firsts"—first professional football contest (1892), first professional hockey game (1894), first African-American baseball team (circa 1900), first World Series (1903), and more. A real capper—the invention of the retractable steel dome. Now that's hard to top.

An example of the latter can be found at the **Civic Arena,** home of the Penguins (ice hockey), Phantoms (roller hockey), and Stingers (indoor soccer). Downtown also has the **A.J. Palumbo Center,** used mostly for basketball. **Three Rivers Stadium** on the north side doubles the excitement with the major-league **Pittsburgh Pirates** and NFL **Pittsburgh Steelers.** Oakland/University of Pittsburgh has **Pitt Stadium** (football) and **Fitzgerald Fieldhouse** (basketball). "Even when the team's on a losing streak, people show up," remarks one native. "Many times they'd rather go to an exhibition game than pursue their own activities."

In May, the **Pittsburgh Marathon** and the **Thrift Drug Classic International Bike Race** are two more major draws.

Pittsburgh has a large amount of public land, as well as more than 70 miles of riverfront. Although there are only a few big city parks like Schenley and Clemente (contact **Citiparks** for more information), the streets are peppered with commons and trees, flowers, and grassy areas. And the county itself boasts about 15,000 acres for biking, hiking, and other recreational activities (**Allegheny County Department of Parks**). Plentiful and excellent golf facilities include the **Oakmont Country Club,** seven-time host to the U.S. Open, and the **Quicksilver Golf Club,** reputedly the best public course in the state.

Sailing, hunting, and fishing (over a dozen species of freshwater game fish) are also big during warmer months. The **Three Rivers Regatta** (July/August) is the largest inland event of its kind. Those wanting to log more even water can opt for white-water rafting (**Whitewater Adventurers, Laurel Highlands River Tours**) an hour-or-so drive from the city. Resorts such as **Seven Springs** and **Hidden Valley** offer excellent skiing in the winter, eliminating any excuses for avoiding year-round exercise.

AFTER-HOURS DIVERSIONS

For a town that's supposedly sedate, there's lots of action once the sun sets, although much of it is good, clean fun (darn it). "Each neighborhood has its own flavor," points out Tsudis. "So each draws very different kinds of bars and people."

"Suits" and others might want to gloat over missing five o'clock traffic while enjoying the view at the **Top of the Triangle** or otherwise savoring happy hour at **Froggy's** downtown. Sports fans will also find lots to celebrate pre- (or post-) game at the **Pub at the Hilton** and **Pietro's** in the Hyatt Regency. The **Terrace Room at the Westin** offers dinner and dancing accompanied by classy Big Band sounds.

Close by but a world away in theme are the Boardwalk/ Strip District. A floating entertainment complex, the former is highlighted by **Donzi's,** a sophisticated nightclub. Two figurative and literal alternatives include **Metropol,** which features moshing and other experimental choreography, and **Rosebud,** an open-air coffeehouse and live venue. Farther north at the other end of the spectrum is the **Penn Brewery,** a traditional German beer hall cum microbrewery.

South Side/Mt. Washington set a more conventional pace with Station Square, an ex-train terminal turned 40-acre megamall. Claustrophobics may feel railroaded at the **Gandy Dancer Saloon,** which is somewhat wider than a private rail car. But Happy Hour bargain drinks, piano music, and free munchies may alleviate any discomfort. Other raucous (but not raunchy) alternatives consist of **Chauncy's,** which takes liveliness to new heights; the **Funny Bone** comedy club; and **Jellyrolls,** whose motto could be "Ve haf vays to make you sing." (Those who don't are in the minority.) **Mario's** and **Blue Lou's** are bars (as opposed to clubs) combining down-to-earth food and music. Walk around the Carson Street area if you want to hear jazz or blues; owners change frequently, although the music doesn't.

Clubs (as opposed to bars) can be found at Shadyside, which attracts a more "upscale" clientele (possibly many of the same people, only dressed better). The **Balcony,** a local jazz institution, is a particularly beloved outdoor venue. **Graffiti** features touring musical groups, while Ellsworth Avenue has coffeehouses and poetry readings. In fact, coffeehouses have saturated the entire city and include **Tuscany, La Prima Expresso,** the **Coffee Tree,** and the inevitable **Starbucks,** which can be found in local Barnes & Noble bookstores. The

Where It's At

 Unless otherwise noted, all area codes are 412.

Balcony, 5520 Walnut St., 687-0110

Blue Lou's, 1514 E. Carson St., 381-5610

Carnegie International Art Exposition, Carnegie Museum, 622-3131

Chauncy's, One Commerce Ct., 232-0604

Coffee Tree, several locations

Donzi's, 1501 Smallman St., 281-1515

Foster's, 100 Lytton Ave., 682-6200

Friday Summer Concert Series in South Park, 835-4810

Froggy's, 100 Market St., 471-3764

Funny Bone, Station Sq., 281-3130

Gandy Dancer Saloon, One Station Square, 261-1717

Gateway Clipper Fleet, Station Square Dock, 355-7980

Graffiti, 4615 Baum Blvd., 682-4210

IC Light Tent/Amphitheatre, Station Sq., 562-9900

Jellyrolls, Station Sq., 391-7464

La Prima Expresso, several locations

Light-up Weekend, 566-4190

Mario's, 1514 E. Carson St., 381-5610

Mellon Jazz Festival, Downtown, 281-3311

Metropol, 1650 Smallman St., 261-2232

Penn Brewery, Troy Hill Rd. and Vinial St., 237-9402

Phipps Conservatory, 622-6915

Pietro's, 112 Washington Pl., 288-9326

Pittsburgh Children's Festival, Allegheny Center, 321-5520

Pittsburgh Folk Festival, Convention Center 281-4882

Pub at the Hilton, 600 Commonwealth Pl., 391-4600

Recreational Vehicle Show, David Lawrence Convention Center, 565-6000

Rosebud, 1650 Smallman St., 261-2232

Smoky City Festival, Schenley Park, 687-8800

Where It's At

(continued)

Starbucks, several locations

Star Lake Amphitheatre, rts. 18 and 22, 947-7400

Steel City Motor Jam—Monster Truck and Thrill Show, Three Rivers Stadium, 635-8480

Terrace Room at the Westin, 530 William Penn Pl., 553-5235

Three Rivers Arts Festival, Downtown, 481-7040

Top of the Triangle, 600 Grant St., 471-4100

Tuscany, several locations

Oakland area offers bars and dance clubs for the academic and medical set, including **Foster's** at the Holiday Inn.

All ages can enjoy rock and other acts year-round at the previously mentioned Palumbo Center and Civic Arena and outdoors in the warmer months at the **IC Light Tent/ Amphitheatre** and **Star Lake Amphitheatre.** And with a million passengers a year, the brunch, luncheon review, and dinner dance cruises on the **Gateway Clipper Fleet** are crowd-pleasers.

There's a whole boatload of festivals as well. January alone has everything from the **Carnegie International Art Exposition** to the **Recreational Vehicle Show.** Spring brings out flowers at the **Phipps Conservatory** (March/April), antiques at the **Carnegie** (April), and various ethnic groups at the **Pittsburgh Folk Festival** (May). Other highly touted arts celebrations include the **Pittsburgh Children's Festival** (May), the **Three Rivers Arts Festival** (June), and the **Mellon Jazz Festival** (June).

Summer consists of the folky and mostly non- **Smoky City Festival;** three days of square dancing at Schenley Park in June; the **Steel City Motor Jam—Monster Truck and Thrill Show** in June (need one add more?); and the free **Friday Summer Concert Series in South Park.** Although by then the weather's usually frightful, the holiday season is also jam-packed with November's **Light-up Weekend** (downtown buildings, not cigarettes or illegal substances) and holidays at the previously mentioned Carnegie and National Classrooms in December. And these are but a drop in the Three Rivers.

 ## CULINARY AND SHOPPING HAUNTS

Meat and potatoes fans will love Pittsburgh, which, like Cleveland, takes pride in the excellence of its pirogies. But there's no question about the origin of the Primanti. Named after inventive brothers who stuffed Italian bread with tomatoes, coleslaw, a deli meat, and fries, this sandwich is a one-stop mouthful of just about every artery-clogging food group. Other places to "steak" a claim would be the **City Grill, Tessaro's, Hotlicks, Ruth's Chris Steak House,** and the seemingly ubiquitous **Morton's.** Unless you like the cow to swim, ask for butter and sauces on the side.

But culinary offerings are hardly limited to those dedicated to maintaining their (Iron City) beer gut. "For a town its size, there are many unique restaurants with spectacular views, beautiful interiors, and great food," remarks Hannah. The Mt. Washington setting of **Christopher's, Tin Angel, Cliffside,** and others is hard to top, so to speak. The **Boardwalk Down by the River** and the previously mentioned Balcony combine American cuisine and people-watching against a pretty

Where It's At

 Unless otherwise noted, all area codes are 412.

Airmall, Pittsburgh International, 472-5180

Banana Republic, 5534 Walnut, 681-2220

Baum Vivant, 5102 Baum Blvd., 682-2620

Boardwalk Down by the River, 1501 Smallman, 281-3900

Cafe Allegro, 51 S. 12th St., 481-7788

Century III Mall, 3075 Clairton Rd., 653-1220

China Palace, several locations

Choices, 5416 Walnut, 687-7600

Christopher's, 1411 Grandview Ave., 381-4500

backdrop. And **Victoria Hall** features Sunday brunch and banquets amid circa 1865 grandeur and antiques.

Only in Pittsburgh will you find **Davio** (Italian), **Mario's** (pasta), **Kaya** (Caribbean), **Kasbah** (Mediterranean/North African), and **Mad Mex** (self-descriptive). And the elegant wood-and-stained-glass **Grand Concourse,** a passenger waiting area in another life, is a must for every wannabe Pittsburgher. And these are just moderately priced (meals cost from $8 to $20). Those willing to spend a sawbuck or two more can indulge in **Le Pommier** (French), and **Cafe Allegro** and **Baum Vivant** (Continental).

Pittsburgh is also noted for the high quality of its Italian offerings. "You can get everything from $5 to $30 meals in Bloomfield, and it's all good," observes Fanzo. Around the city, **Louis Tambellini's** and **Lombardozzi's** attract droves of locals, and excellent pizza can be found at **Mineos, Minutello's,** and **Palio.** There are several popular Asian-style places—**China Palace, Kiku, Sesame Inn,** and others. Those searching for cheaper eats and local chains may find **DeLucas, Kings Restaurants,** and **Eat 'N Park** (in the restaurant, not the car these days) to their liking. The area has multitudinous brand names with Bruegger's Bagels, Ponderosa Steakhouse, Damon's ribs, and others having a presence in many areas.

Shopping can begin practically the moment you step off the plane at the **Airmall,** which offers competitive prices and selections on everything from shampoo at the Body Shop to signed baseball cards at the Upper Deck. A short drive away is the **Robinson Towne Centre,** a cluster of discount emporiums.

A logical leap from planes to trains would be the 60-some Freight House Shops under a soaring roof, and Bessemer Court Shops in antique railcars at the previously mentioned Station Square. Elsewhere, the Golden Triangle boasts the tony **Fifth Ave. Place** and **One Oxford Centre;** the more down-to-earth **PPG Place** and **Warner Centre;** and the venerable **Kaufman's, Saks Fifth Avenue,** and **Lazarus.** The South and North Hills are alive with the sound of cash registers and malls—**Galleria, Century III Mall, Ross Park Mall,** and others. Those who like everything in one place may find **Monroeville Mall** and a bushel of assorted shopping plazas in the east end of town to their liking. The wide selection of crafts, fresh produce, and prepared foods in the **Strip** add a Pittsburgh flavor to the experience.

Where It's At

(continued)

City Grill, 2019 E. Carson St., 481-6868

Cliffside, 1208 Grandview Ave., 431-6996

Davio, 2100 Broadway Ave., 531-7422

DeLucas, 2015 Penn Ave., 566-2195

Eat 'N Park, 7671 McKnight Rd., 364-1211

Fifth Ave. Place, 120 Fifth Ave., 392-4654

Four Winds Gallery, 5512 Walnut, 682-5092

Galleria, 1500 Washington Rd., 561-4000

Grand Concourse, One Station Square, 261-1717

Grove City Factory Shops, I-79 at Exit 61, 748-4770

Horizon Outlet Center, PA Turnpike Exit 10/Somerset on Rt. 601, 800/866-5900

Hotlicks, several locations

Kasbah, 229 S. Highland, 661-5656

Kaufman's, 400 Fifth Ave., 232-2320

Kaya, 20th and Smallman, 261-6565

Kiku, Station Sq., 765-3200

Kings Restaurants, several locations

Lazarus, 501 Penn Ave., 553-8150

Le Pommier, 2104 E. Carson St., 431-1901

Lombardozzi's, 4786 Liberty Ave., 682-5785

Louis Tambellini's, 2302 E. Carson St. 431-6790

Mad Mex, several locations

Mario's, 1514 E. Carson St., 381-5610

Mineos, several locations

Minutello's, 226 Shady Ave., 361-9311

Monroeville Mall, 200 Monroeville Blvd., Monroeville, 243-8511

Morton's, 625 Liberty Ave., 261-7141

One Oxford Centre, Grant and Fourth Ave., 391-5300

Palio, 2056 Broadway Ave., 531-8211

PPG Place, Two PPG Pl., 434-1900

Robinson Towne Centre, Park Manor Blvd., 391-7887

Where It's At

(continued)

Ross Park Mall, 1000 Ross Park Mall Dr., 369-4400

Ruth's Chris Steak House, Six PPG Pl., 391-4800

Saks Fifth Avenue, 513 Smithfield St., 263-4800

Sesame Inn, 711 Browns Ln., 366-1838

Strip, 1600–2500 Penn Ave.

Tessaro's, 4601 Liberty Ave., 682-6809

Tin Angel, 1200 Grandview Ave., 481-4424

Victoria Hall, 201 S Winebiddle St., 363-8030

Warner Centre, 332 Fifth, 281-9000

Where It's At

 Unless otherwise noted, all area codes are 412.

Catholic Diocese, 723 E. Pittsburgh St., 456-3000

Episcopal Diocese, 325 Oliver Ave., 281-6131

Greater Pittsburgh Baptist Association, 5305 Perrysville Rd., 931-6040

Peace Institute, 361-5900

Pitt's Kintu Repertory Theatre, 1617 Cathedral of Learning, 624-6338

Pittsburgh Baptist Association, 1620 Allegheny Bldg., 261-4005

United Jewish Federation, 234 McKee Pl., 681-8000

Neighborhoods can also yield some neat finds. The South Side offers up a variety of antique stores and local crafts; once again, Carson Street's the place. South Craig Street in the Oakland area (between Forbes and Fifth) provides an excellent selection of galleries and imports. Chains such as **Banana Republic** share space with the home-grown **Choices** and **Four Winds Gallery** in Shadyside's Walnut Street area. And an hour or more away, discount malls proliferate—the **Horizon Outlet Center, Grove City Factory Shops,** and others. An added bonus: There's no tax on clothing, groceries, or specialty foods.

 ## ETHNIC AND RELIGIOUS PROSPECTS

With 88 different neighborhoods, Pittsburgh has about as many ethnic districts as Heinz has foods. Unlike other cities, which have tended to become homogenous as they've grown, "we've held on to our heritage," points out Meyer. This is evidenced by the architecture, cuisine, and ambiance of the German North Side, the Eastern European South Side, the African-American Hill district, the Jewish Squirrel Hill, and Italian Bloomfield. Lawrenceville and Polish Hill also have Italian, Irish, and (you guessed it) Polish communities.

Still, everyone mingles freely, and it's not uncommon for the terminally young and hip "in dyed black hair and clothes to be living next to an old Polish lady in row houses," observes Fanzo. The common denominator (and great leveler) is cheap rent.

And although the city and surrounding area have 3,000 churches, synagogues, and temples as well as a large Catholic population, people seem to emphasize the values in their families and churches, rather than the disparity in their backgrounds. "I'm Greek and my wife's Italian, and we chose to stay here because of our friends and relatives," remarks Tsudis. The previously mentioned Nationality Rooms at Pitt are an obvious statement of unity.

"People really are involved in their churches," adds Hannah. Depending upon their religious persuasion, newcomers might want to contact the **Greater Pittsburgh Baptist Association** (Southern Baptist), **Pittsburgh Baptist Association** (American Baptist), the **Catholic Diocese,** the **Episcopal Diocese,** the **United Jewish Federation,** and others.

Pittsburgh's hefty (in numbers, not physical size) African-American population lives mostly within the city, and not just in one section, either. "People here are very friendly," comments Brody, who is black. "But they also respect each others' space and differences."

The area has been supportive of African-Americans since 1750, when several free blacks migrated here. Both they and whites operated "safe houses" to smuggle escaped slaves during the Civil War. Around the turn of the century, many blacks moved North to find job opportunities and start businesses. Beginning in the 1920s, the Hill District was a mecca for jazz, nurturing such notables as Earl Hines and Lena Horne, as well as local playwright August

Wilson, whose hugely successful productions were set in Pittsburgh. Organizations such as the **Peace Institute, Pitt's Kintu Repertory Theatre,** and the previously mentioned Manchester Craftsman's guild are a good way to connect with the current scene.

CRIB SHEET

Not only does Pittsburgh offer everything from expansive estates to traditional colonials to wood-framed homes to ultracontemporary condos, but costs are so reasonable you may feel like you've actually pulled a fast one on the Realtor, instead of the other way around. Average cost for a home in the city is around $80,000; in the surrounding area, about $20,000 more. And "you really get a sense of neighborhood" anywhere you live, according to Hannah.

Apartments are always an option for newcomers. Complexes such as Allegheny Center (near Three Rivers Stadium) are close to city parks and all the action downtown. Rent starts at around $450 a month for an empty studio. Those wanting to live near university and medical facilities might want to consider (among many other choices) high-rises like Bates Hill in Oakland (about $700 for a one-bedroom) or, for approximately the same price, the Highland Plaza in Shadyside. Victorian restorations are a "steal" ($350 or so for an efficiency) in the city neighborhood of Manchester. Other popular rental and condo areas include Squirrel Hill and the North and South Sides.

Many fixer-uppers have retained their ethnic flavor and have the added enticements of reduced closing costs and down payments as well as tax abatements. Crawford Square in the Hill District provides urban living in updated townhouses and single-family homes. More of the latter can be found in Fineview Crest (North Side), while the neighborhoods of Polish Hill, Lawrenceville, and the South Side offer bushels of the former.

The riverfront is another ripe spot, especially since it extends past popular communities. "For years, it remained undeveloped because of all the industry," explains Fanzo. Now that it's been cleaned up, single-family unit ventures (around $100,000 each) are underway in the Allegheny River island oasis, the South Side, and along the shores of the Monongahela.

Areas like Brookline, Manchester, and Beechview have blossomed in recent years, with sales increasing more than 50 percent. More established evergreens have also expanded and include Carrick, Brighton Heights, and the pricier Highland Park and Squirrel Hill. Those wishing to drop a few hundred thousand or so can invest in Shadyside, where large homes sit amidst plentiful acreage and greenery.

Two relatively easy commutes are North and South Hills. With its large selection of new builds, restaurants, and shopping areas, the first is popular with folks starting out. North Park, a nearby recreational area, adds to the appeal. The older and more established south offers spacious landscaping as well as exclusive Mt. Lebanon and its attendant boutiques. Another spot for the horsey/country club set is Fox Chapel, where "verdant" describes not only the neighborhood but the state of locals' pocketbooks.

A bit farther from town is Monroeville. Its well-planned housing communities and the "Miracle Mile" of shopping, eating, and entertainment make it almost worth the migraine-inducing ride through the Squirrel Hill tunnel. Go west and you'll find not only the airport but the quaint burg of Carnegie, where the post office and most stores can be found on a single street and farms and fields replace city lights.

Pittsburgh public schools are another find. Although classes in the city proper tend toward the crowded (up to 30 per class in middle school), the graduation rate is over 80 percent, with nearly three-fourths of the students going on to higher studies (Pittsburgh Public Schools,

622-3615). And the figures get better in many of the outlying areas. There are also more than 100 private/parochial schools (contact the Allegheny Intermediate Unit, 394-5705, for more information).

> **Pittsburgh always seems to be one step ahead of the pack. No wonder corporate headquarters as well as home-based businesses struggling to make their first dollar like it here.**

The region offers a half-dozen vo-tech schools and twice as many colleges, which range from the internationally respected Carnegie-Mellon to the 18,000 strong University of Pittsburgh to the tiny Pittsburgh Theological Seminary. Specialty schools cover everything from art (Art Institute of Pittsburgh) to business (ICM School of Business, Sawyer School, others) to technology (Triangle Tech, Electronics Institute, Gateway Technical Institute, many others). Those not getting training have only themselves to blame.

NAVIGATING PITTSBURGH

"Because Pittsburgh was built around the river and not on a grid, it can be geographically tricky," Meyer understates. An ideal (but not always feasible) way to become oriented would be to go to Point State Park at the edge of downtown. The Park provides a panorama of Pittsburgh's four corners (North and South Side, East and West End) as well as its lowlands and hillsides. And—with interstates 70, 76, and 80 (east-west) and 79 (north-south) entering the city and more than 720 bridges connecting the weaving and bobbing streets, which are partially linked by routes 579, 376, and 279—anything helps.

"Rush-hour traffic can be difficult," adds Hannah. And in some cases, unavoidable: "Pittsburgh is primarily a driving city, with public transportation only available in certain areas."

Still, things have improved somewhat. Through color-coded signs, the recently instituted Wayfinder System organizes the area into five regions, including a "Purple Belt" that assists pedestrians and drivers in navigating the periphery of downtown. And maps are plentiful.

The 50-acre Golden Triangle district is also easily managed on foot, and the "T," Pittsburgh's clean, safe, and aesthetically correct (classical music, objets d' art) subway system, offers free rides to certain sections and can take you across the river to Station Square for a slight charge. It is part of the Port Authority Transit (442-2000), a countywide network of buses, trolleys, and light rail vehicles currently undergoing expansion of routes and improved services.

Fifteen miles west of downtown, the 3.2 million square foot Pittsburgh International Airport (778-2500) makes up for a lot. Rated as one of the top five in the U.S. by *Condé Nast Traveler,* it efficiently processes more than 20 million passengers a year. Along with being a hub for USAirways/British Airways, the airport is serviced by all major U.S. airlines. Humbler modes include Amtrak (325-1524) and Greyhound (392-6513).

PORTLAND, OREGON

A Brief Glance

Size and Growth: 495,000 (city), 1.6 million (MSA). Percent change, 1980–1990: +19.4% (city). Percent change, 1990–1995: +4.8% (city).

Money Matters: *Unemployment rate—* 3.6%.
Per capita income—$14,478.
Average household income—$38,729.
Average cost for a home—$146,630.
Average rent for an apartment— $645/month.
ACCRA Cost of Living Index (based on 100)—107.4.
ACCRA Housing Index—119.5.

People Profile: *Crime rate* (per 100,000 population)—11,815.7 (city), 6,539.9 (MSA).

Racial and ethnic characteristics—
White: 84.8% (city), 90.9% (MSA); Black: 7.6% (city), 3.1% (MSA); American Indian/Eskimo/Aleut: 1.3% (city), 1.0% (MSA); Asian/Pacific Islander: 5.2% (city), 3.6% (MSA); Hispanic Origin: 3.0% (city), 3.5% (MSA); Other: 1.0% (city), 1.4% (MSA).
*Gender ratio—*93.9 males per 100 females (all ages); 91.4 males per 100 females (18 years old+).
*Age characteristics—*18–24 (10%); 25–44 (37%). Median age: 34.5.

Major Players: Services, retail/wholesale trade, manufacturing, government.

PORTLAND:
A PEAK EXPERIENCE

While other cities bask in raves from *Fortune, American Demographics, U.S. News & World Report,* and *Entrepreneur,* Portland revels in its Church of Elvis, where four quarters will buy you a wedding ceremony with all the trimmings; Mill's End, at 24 inches the world's smallest dedicated park; and the fact that more chimpanzees live here and more Asian elephants are born here than in any other North American city (don't ask). Its sidewalks are lined with famous quotes; a 25-foot-tall weather machine in Pioneer Courthouse Square announces the day's predictions amid a fanfare of trumpets; and Portlandia, the nation's second largest hammered copper statue (after Lady Liberty in New York City), greets people from her landlocked perch atop the Portland Building. Along with the International Rose Test Garden, with its 400 different types of blooms, Portland's Oregon Museum of

Science and Industry boasts an "earthquake" that's 5.5 on the Richter scale, which is no big deal considering that the big state to the south has the real thing.

Although the "City of Roses" was purchased for twenty-five cents back in 1843 and has been home to the likes of Joseph "Bunco" Kelly (who in the late 19th century kidnapped young men and sold them to ship captains) as well as hippy-dippy crunchy granola types in more recent years, Portland has been listing toward an establishment-type business base for the last couple of decades. Located at the confluence of the Columbia and Willamette rivers, its sheer beauty, fresh air, plentiful water supply, and pollution-free electricity have attracted people and enterprises alike.

Lush rolling hills, tall trees, and snow-capped mountains present tableaux unrivaled by human hands. With an average rainfall of 37 inches per year, humidity is at a minimum, reducing the percentage of bad hair days, even though late fall and winter can be characterized by fog and murkiness. Portland's 17 bridges, 37,000 acres of parks, and Mount Tabor (its hopefully still-extinct volcano) provide additional dollops of singularity to the trendy shops, plentiful microbreweries (like Denver, Portland claims to have the most anywhere), thriving arts community, and movie theaters and restaurants (of which Portland allegedly has more per capita than any other place in the U.S.).

> Located at the confluence of the Columbia and Willamette Rivers, Portland's sheer beauty, fresh air, plentiful water supply, and pollution-free electricity have attracted people and enterprises alike.

And yes, there is that sense of save-the-environment. Bicycle riders and joggers are given the right of way over vehicles: With nearly 10,000 pedaling commuters, the city provides bike racks on public streets and requires that bike parking spaces be made available in all new and remodeled buildings (re-cycling?). Fareless Square, a 300-block downtown area, is just that. You can ride a Tri-Met bus or MAX light rail car for free, and there's plentiful public transportation to the outlying areas. Carpools are given reduced parking rates, although downtown parking is abundant and cheap. With approximately one block of green space for each 10 city blocks, and with protection of urban growth boundaries, traffic and architectural sprawl have been kept under control. True, homelessness, crime, and drug addiction have increased as the city has prospered. But some Portlanders would prefer that the rest of the country not be clued in on their good thing. "Tell them it really sucks here," writer Jeff Wallach told *Swing* magazine. "Send them to Phoenix."

General Opportunities

A strong youth culture, more than two dozen colleges and universities, and a prolific music/creative scene have invited comparisons to Seattle. Indeed, many budding musicians and artists have made Portland their base before moving on to bigger ponds. But nearly 60 percent of the population has attended or graduated from college, and a variety of institutions provide training in professional fields. Along with being home to nine Fortune 500 companies ranging from Willamette lumber to NIKE to Oregon Steel Mills to U.S. Bankcorp, Portland has also been attracting herds of electronic and high-tech industries. Two advantages—no state sales tax and low-cost land zoned for business—have drawn a wide range of enterprises and kept unemployment well below the national average.

Although the cost of living is slightly higher than in the rest of the U.S., prices for groceries and miscellaneous items are reasonable, as are utility rates, which are almost 20 percent less than the national average (another big plus for manufacturing concerns). Pay is also reasonable. Approximate monthly earnings for computer programmers are about $2,750; accountants, $2,800; public relations specialists, $3,000; computer systems analysts and lawyers, $3,700. But the almighty dollar doesn't seem to be the reason for living: "Five o'clock rolls around . . . and people actually leave work to go out and hike, bike, fish, or just enjoy themselves outdoors," says Wallach in *Swing*.

HOW PORTLAND WORKS AND PLAYS

Major Breadwinning

Portland's economy is nothing if not diverse, with a pool of jobs in high tech and computers, retail, health care, manufacturing, marketing, transportation management, and banking. Major private employers run the full spectrum: Fred Meyer retail has 8,900 jobs; Intel microcomputer, 8,000; Kaiser Permanente health care, 7,700; U.S. Bankcorp holding company, 6,250; Freightliner Trucks, 4,600; Tektronix equipment, 4,500; NIKE, 3,900; and U.S. West Communications, 3,440.

Although Portland was originally named after the city in Maine—it missed being called Boston by the flip of a coin—today it could take on a different meaning. The redundant-sounding Port of Portland consists of a network of ocean shipping, transcontinental railways and highways, river barging, and the rapidly growing Portland International Airport.

The Columbia and Snake rivers comprise the second largest waterway in the nation; and the inland transportation operation, consists of comprehensive barge, rail, and truck service. The latter is supported by a far-reaching web of highways: I-5 (north–south), which runs through the heart of downtown; I-84 (east); U.S. 26 (west); I-405, which loops around downtown and connects with U.S. 30; and I-205, which partially circles the southeast part of the city. No wonder major U.S. companies such as Columbia Sportswear, Nordstrom, Roadway Package Systems, and Albertsons Food Centers have established distribution centers here. Add a Pacific Rim location, and you have major import/export activity. The City of Roses has begun to attract international companies and was tagged as a great place for global commerce by *World Trade* magazine.

While manufacturing is one of the largest sectors (15.8 percent of total employment) and includes machinery, electronics, metals, transportation equipment, and lumber/wood, the real boom is in high technology. Employment in this realm increased 19 percent between 1990 and 1995, with more than 1,100 companies employing some 50,000 people. More impressive perhaps is the amount of money and jobs that continue to flow into Oregon and particularly

Portland. Recently announced investments and expansions include $1.3 billion from Integrated Device Technology, $1.03 billion from Fujitsu Microelectronics, $2.9 billion (and an additional 1,755 jobs) from Intel Corp, and $4 billion (and 2,000 jobs) from LSI Logic. And that's not even mentioning multi-million-dollar financiers such as Wacker Siltronic, SEH America, Komatsu, and others.

Contributing a total of 25.2 percent of all local jobs, retail trade and wholesale trade are booming. Stores and malls are popping up everywhere, and tourism continues to expand to the tune of $3 billion per year, providing more openings in marketing, sales, and management. Even the film industry has filtered in, as word of Oregon's scenic diversity spreads to out-of-state companies. Feature movies, music videos, and TV movies, series, and commercials provide employment within the creative community and in support positions.

> A strong youth culture, more than two dozen colleges and universities, and a prolific music/creative scene have invited comparisons to Seattle. ... Portland has also been attracting herds of electronic and high-tech industries and a wide range of enterprises.

As in the rest of the U.S., most of Portland's jobs (27 percent) are in the service sector. Health care is a major segment and includes companies such as Blue Cross and Blue Shield, Legacy, Kaiser Permanente, Providence, and PACC Health Plans. The Oregon Health Sciences University (OHSU), the state's center for medical research, offers four clinical-care units and training. Areas of expertise include nonsurgical medical treatments and occupational and environmental toxicology. The Vollum Institute for Advanced Biomedical Research studies molecular brain functions, not exactly mind candy. Folks are also receptive to naturopathic medicine and acupuncture, providing an outlet for those skills.

Government (13.2 percent); finance, insurance, and real estate (7.6 percent); transportation, communication, and utilities (5.7 percent); and construction and mining (5.5 percent) make up the rest of the employment pie. In Portland, it seems as if there's a slice for everyone.

ARTS AND SCIENCES

More people are drawn to area code 503 because of its natural beauty and outdoor opportunities than for just about any other reason. But the arts are hardly left to flounder: Portland's 200 arts organizations draw more attendees than local sporting events, adding some $84 million to the economy. With four stages, the Portland Center for the Performing Arts is home to the Oregon Symphony, the Portland Opera Association, the Oregon Ballet Company, the Oregon Children's Theater, and the Portland Center Stage (a resident company). The Portland Repertory Theater performs contemporary classics in a variety of venues. The Northwest Afrikan American Ballet, the Miracle Theater/Teatro Milagro, the Interstate Firehouse

Cultural Center, and the Jewish Community Center serve up a variety of ethnic performances and exhibits. The Oregon School of Arts and Crafts, the Portland Art Museum School, the Multnomah Art Center, and the Training Ground for actors offer classes and provide networking opportunities.

Gallery exhibits, particularly the "First Thursdays" of every month in the newly chic and eclectic Pearl District, have become a hot ticket; and the Portland Art Museum, the oldest of its kind in the Pacific, boasts a collection that spans 25 centuries and contains more than 24,000 objects. The Oregon Historical Society covers local culture, and the Cowboys Then and Now Museum traces their history through exhibits and photographs. On the other side of the social and political fence, the Museum at Warm Springs celebrates the Warm Springs, Paiute, and Wasco tribes. Opened in 1993, it prides itself on being Oregon's first Native American museum (an oddity, considering that the Indians were around long before the settlers).

Another attempt at righting injustices can be found at the Japanese-American Historical Plaza, a monument to those folks who were interred during World War II, while the Oregon Vietnam Veterans Living Memorial honors a different kind of draftee. The first of its kind in the U.S., the American Advertising Museum has artifacts dating from 1612, a depressing thought. Other points of interest: the previously mentioned Oregon Museum of Science and Industry, a 50,000-square-foot structure with an OMNIMAX theater, planetarium, and the USS *Blueback* submarine; and the Oregon Maritime Center and Museum, with more ship paraphernalia from the USS *Oregon*.

THE SPORTING LIFE

Truly great works can be found outdoors and include snow and water skiing, golfing, sailing, wind surfing, camping, hiking, mountain climbing, and just about anything else that requires physical exertion. With 5,000 acres and 35 miles of hiking trails, Forest Park claims to be the largest treed wilderness in a U.S. city, although other green spaces, such as Fairmount Park in Philadelphia, have far more land. A short distance from downtown, Washington Park boasts the famous International Rose Garden and Metro Zoo, along with a Japanese Garden. A few blocks away is more greenery at the World Forestry Center and the Hoyt Arboretum with its miles of nature trails.

To get to the really peak stuff, you need to travel beyond Portland. A few miles east is Columbia Gorge, whose 620-foot Multnomah Falls, trails, and stunning views have earned it the dubious honor of "wind-surfing capital." More of God's country can be found at nearby Mt. Hood, with its extensive cliffs and trail network, and at beaches along the Columbia River. The Oregon Coast Aquarium has both indoor and outdoor displays (as well as Keiko, of *Free Willy* fame, if he hasn't been released into the wild). Enticingly set among 2.5 acres of cliffs, caves, and rocky pools are seals, sea lions, otters, and a giant Pacific octopus. Check out the rest of the coast while you're there: Offerings include Astoria, the first American settlement west of the Rockies; Depoe Bay, a prime whale-watching site; and Tillamook Cheese Factory, which must be pretty good because it draws 800,000 visitors a year.

Oregon itself has 13 national forests covering over 15.6 million acres, 225 state parks totaling more than 91,000 acres, beaches along the Coast Mountain range and the Pacific Ocean, skiing at Mt. Hood, and fishing in more than 62,000 streams and 1,600 lakes. You can camp just about anywhere, as long as you don't mind doing without a plug for your blow-dryer.

Portland is a big spectator city, supporting the annual Rose Festival (June), an à la carte food and local wine sampling called The Bite (August), the city's largest bicultural gala known as Cinco de Mayo (May), and others. Professional sports teams include the NBA Trailblazers, who play at the Rose Garden (not an actual one, but a 21,000-seat multipurpose arena); the Winter Hawks (hockey) and the Pride (indoor soccer), both of whom gear up at the Memorial Coliseum; and the Portland Rockies (Civic Stadium), a farm team for the Denver baseball club by the same name. Collegiate and high school sports enjoy a high level of participation, as do the Portland Marathon, the Fred Meyer Challenge and PING-Cellular One golf tournaments, and events at the Portland International Raceway.

 ## AFTER-HOURS DIVERSIONS

For a town its size, Portland has a divergent and populous club scene. Along with breweries/pubs like Blitz-Weinhard, BridgePort, McMenamins, Nor'Wester, and Widmer Gasthaus, alternative spots such as Satryicon, Laluna, Hi-Hat, Laurelthirst, and E.J.'s provide a variety of music. You can hear acoustic at Rich's; blues at Lacy's and Key Largo; jazz at Atwater's and Jazz de Opus; reggae at Shawdon's; and rock at many of the previously mentioned places as well as the Grateful Burger, Egyptian Room, and Moosehead. Dancing can be found at Da Bomb, Berbati's, Metropolis, UpFront F/X, and others. As in that other Pacific Northwest city, coffeehouses abound and include Montage, Pied Cow, Rimsky-Korsakoffe House, Umbra Penumbra, and Cafe Lena (which, as a bonus, features poetry readings). Bibliophiles will think they've died and gone to heaven at Powell's City of Books. Occupying an entire block, it's arguably the country's largest bookstore.

 ## CULINARY AND SHOPPING HAUNTS

Portland's cuisine is varied and relatively cheap. Restaurants of the moment, such as Bistro Montage (Creole), offer tattooed waiters and shared tables; ask around for other current favorites, as the scene can change quickly. Local standbys consist of American at Waterfront Cafe, Jaimie's, and O'Connor's; barbecue at Doris's Cafe and Jackie's; Asian at Kojo, Bush Garden, August Moon, and Republic Cafe; Greek at Alexis; Italian at Cucina! Cucina! and Genoa; and Mexican at Azteca. Northwest regional reigns with eateries like Black Rabbit, L'Auberge, Tribeca, Salty's, and Huber's Cafe, to mention a few. You can also chow down healthily at Macheezmo Mouse (really!) and Old Wive's Tales.

Along with downtown shopping at Pioneer Place and Pioneer Center (which boast the ever-popular Saks and Nordstrom's, the regional Meier & Frank, and dozens of others), the Galleria several blocks west offers loads of specialty boutiques. One not-to-miss experience is the Portland Saturday Market, the largest weekend bazaar of its kind. More than 300 artisans sell gifts and food and provide a variety of entertainment. In the northwest section of downtown is Nob Hill, a recently revitalized area that features innovative bakeries, restaurants, and emporiums.

Not to worry—neither rugged terrain nor environmental dedication has stopped the malls. Lloyd Center, Clackamas Town Center, Washington Square, and Vancouver Mall have all the old familiars and then some. Lots of neighborhood clusters (Mall 205, Eastport Plaza, Gresham Town Fair) and factory stores (Columbia Gorge, Current Factory Outlet) dot the landscape as well. No shopping expedition would be complete without paying homage, cash, or credit to Nike Town or the Nike Portland Factory Store.

ETHNIC AND RELIGIOUS PROSPECTS

Portland has a local branch of the Urban League and NAACP as well as a Hispanic Metropolitan Chamber of Commerce and several Spanish-language media outlets. Ethnically, everything seems to be coming up roses, despite an occasional discrimination complaint by African-Americans in the local paper. At least for Latinos, the laid-back approach may be partially due to the fact that over a third of the population consists of migrant workers who live here only eight months of the year, while many others are recent transplants from California who regard clean, safe Portland as a sort of modern Valhalla. However, the gay community is very much in evidence, with several insider's guides on the World Wide Web and even a bowling league. Racial tension seems like a vague concept around here, as almost everyone is seemingly liberal and well educated.

Portland has an interesting assortment of religions and denominations, ranging from the traditional Archdiocese of Portland, Jewish Federation, Church of Christ, and Grace Presbyterian Church to the Atma Institute ("Dedicated to the exploration of consciousness, especially answering the question, Who am I?"), the East Portland Universal Life Church ("Counseling in person, via phone, and by e-mail"), and the Strand by Strand Collective ("Feminist witches offering classes and public rituals"). Although there are a lot of white people, you can see that they're definitely not cut from the same loaf.

CRIB SHEET

Divided by Burnside Street north to south and the Willamette River east to west, the City of Roses is pretty easy to get around in, easing house and apartment hunting. (However, make sure you have the full address, as those with street numbers, such as 16th Avenue, might be followed by 16th Place, which can become confusing.) Apartments range from large complexes with security and health clubs to smaller efficiencies. Rent is costliest in downtown and NW Portland, with a one-bedroom flat averaging about $785 and a two-bedroom going for over $1,300. The SW, NE, and SE quadrants are much cheaper, with one-bedrooms costing $560, $520, and $460, respectively.

Many of the 'burbs are comparatively priced, with Gresham, Oregon City, and Beaverton being on the lower end, and with Tualatin, Lake Oswego, Aloha, and Hillboro somewhat higher.

Portland's neighborhoods run the gamut from trendy, busy shopping districts to isolated countryside, bound by a similarity of wood construction (so much lumber, so little conservation back then) with native rock and brick trim. Victorians, English Tudors, bungalows, and others can be found on streets lined with 100-year-old trees that didn't make the cut.

Like everything else, home prices are on an upward swing, particularly in the North and the NE and SE quadrants. A mixture of many neighborhoods, North Portland (average home price: $85,000) is close to the Port, the active community of Jantzen Beach, the University of Portland, and several new stores. Northeast Portland ($118,000) has lots of large, restored older homes, Laurelhurst Park, plenty of shopping, and easy access to public transportation. Southeast Portland ($112,000) has Mt. Tabor Park, a variety of modest to large homes, and great views. Northwest (no available figure) most closely resembles an East Coast neighborhood with its mixture of old and new single-family dwellings, apartments, lofts, shopping, and light industrial activities. The location of Forest Park (NW) appeals to young professionals, artists, and senior citizens alike.

Beyond Portland is the city of Gresham ($135,000), a fast-growing, populous area in full view of the Columbia River Gorge and Mt. Hood. Expanding suburbs in nearby counties with excellent schools and other amenities include Milwaukie ($148,000), Oregon City ($148,000), and Hillsboro ($137,000), as well as the more exclusive areas of Lake Oswego/West Linn ($250,000), West Portland ($214,000), and NW Washington County ($199,000).

With high test scores and relatively small classes, public schools are one of the best bargains around. Some private and several parochial schools are also available. Higher education options include Portland State University, the area's largest four-year institution; the previously mentioned OHSU, with its international research programs; Mt. Hood Community in Gresham, with technical training; and Marylhurst, which offers a wide variety of innovative adult-education courses.

SALT LAKE CITY, UTAH

A Brief Glance

Size and Growth: 1980: 910,222; 1990: 1,072,227. 1/1/95 (estimate): 1,196,300. Percent change, 1980–1990: +17.8%. Percent change, 1990–1995: +11.6%.

Money Matters: *Unemployment rate*—3.4%.
Per capita income—$13,482.
Average household income—$33,648 (Salt Lake County), $26,967 (Salt Lake City).
Average cost of a home—$125,430.
Average rent for an apartment—$527/month.
ACCRA Cost of Living Index (based on 100)—99.6.
ACCRA Housing Index—99.3.

People Profile: *Crime rate* (per 100,000 population)—10,863.3 (city), 6,174.6 (MSA).

Racial and ethnic characteristics—White: 87.2%; Black: 1.6%; American Indian/Eskimo/Aleut: 1.7%; Asian/Pacific Islander: 4.7%; Hispanic Origin: 9.5%; Other: 4.8%.
Gender ratio—96.8 males per 100 females (all ages); 94.8 males per 100 females (18 years old+).
Age characteristics—18–24 (12.3%); 25–44 (33.7%). Median age: 31.

Major Players: Services, retail/wholesale trade, government, manufacturing.
(Salt Lake City is noted for construction, trade, communications, finance, insurance, real estate.)

Photo by Alan Yorgason/Salt Lake City Convention & Visitors Bureau

SALT LAKE CITY: S'NO(W) ANGEL

Salt Lake City has always had religion. Founded in 1847 by a group of Mormon pioneers led by Brigham Young—the man with 20-some wives—the city's first big structure was the Salt Lake LDS (Latter Day Saints) Temple, a spired (some say inspiring) Gothic behemoth that took 47 years to build. Working from what was called the Plat of the City of Zion, Young laid out his vision with city blocks of 10 acres each and broad streets with 120-foot sidewalks. Although this design worked well for turning around with a covered wagon and team of oxen, hiking from one corner to the next during snow-laden winters and scorching summers can be somewhat more of a challenge. Plentiful sunshine and the lack of humidity, however, make for the world's greatest powder—for skiing, that is.

Salt Lake's avenues are arranged according to their distance and direction from Temple Square. "Stand at the Brigham Young Monument at Main and South Temple streets…and you feel you've arrived at the center of the universe," notes writer Peter Fish in *Sunset* magazine. "This was, perhaps, the point." Situated between the Wasatch and Oquirrhs mountains, Salt Lake City is seemingly isolated from the rest of the world, breathtakingly ensconced in a "valley" that's 4,300 feet above sea level. "The greatest snow on earth" has resulted in seven major resorts (with a statewide total of 14), three cross-country areas, and the nation's only recreational ski jumping complex, less than 40 minutes from the airport. Snow lovers (but perhaps not the rest of us) will delight in the fact that the white stuff can reach an annual total of 50 feet and that it's possible to schuss, snowboard, and cross-country ski from November to July.

> Situated between the Wasatch and Oquirrhs mountains, Salt Lake City is breathtakingly ensconced in a "valley" that's 4,300 feet above sea level. "Stand at the Brigham Young Monument at Main and South Temple Streets...and you feel you've arrived at the center of the universe," notes one writer. "This was, perhaps, the point."

But before dismissing Salt Lake as a bastion for religious zealots and white gentiles (non-Mormons), some of whom might bask in the lack of diversity, consider that it has a thriving gay and lesbian community as well as a reasonable population of Hispanics and Pacific Islanders. Some youngsters in the latter group have created a gang problem by joining the Tongan Crips and Sons of Samoa (think of Sumo wrestlers with bandannas).

Still, most of the crime is of the robbery and property-damage kind. And Salt Lake City really has the makings of a promised land. Not only has it been tapped for the 2002 Winter Olympics (after trying and failing four times since 1965), but since 1990, the Salt Lake International Airport has undergone a multi-million-dollar expansion, a light rail system has been added, and the Salt Palace Convention Center is undergoing 70 million dollars' worth of improvements. Construction is underway for a downtown courts complex and the headquarters for American Stores, a 24-story skyscraper. Public spaces, such as the Gallivan Utah Center and City Creek Park, showcase work by local artists; and the western part of downtown, formerly a run-down (for Salt Lake) industrial district, is rapidly being converted to microbreweries, galleries, and boutiques as well as loft apartments and condos.

Although the valley's major freeway, Interstate 15 (north-south), is said to resemble an accordion thanks to fender-benders when someone has a flat tire, the state has been able to finagle mass transit funds for car-pool lanes during these budget-cutting times. Denizens also have the options of I-80 (east-west) and I-215 (an outer belt that partially circles the city). However, traffic can be a problem, as highways are overcrowded and rapid growth has resulted in poor urban planning in some areas.

Lots of accolades are buzzing around the Beehive state and particularly its capital: *Town and Country* and *Fortune* have praised Salt Lake City's aesthetics and business opportunities;

and *Kiplinger's* touts Salt Lake as the best place to start a new firm. Utah has been tapped by *Financial World* as the country's best financially managed state, while *American Demographics* has praised it as having one of the top three economies in the nation. Adds Fish, "The West seems to shift favored cities every decade or so: Denver in the '80s, Seattle in the early '90s. Now Salt Lake wonders whether its turn has come." Or, at the very least, its 15 minutes.

General Opportunities

Utah is practically a fountain of youth—only 9 percent of the citizenry is over 65 years old, and it has the highest proportion of folks under 18 in the U.S. It's also the healthiest: Folks here enjoy lower rates in everything from infant mortality to work-related and automobile deaths to decreased incidences of heart disease, cancer, obesity, tuberculosis, and other ailments. (As a result, people spend 26 percent less than the national average on doctors, medicine, and hospital visits.)

Since 1980, the population has increased 17.9 percent, making Utah one of the fastest-growing states in the U.S. Although some is due to migration, much is related to that most basic of instincts, resulting in a relatively high birth rate. The workforce will likely expand at twice the national level in the next decade, although a steady upswing in jobs, between 5 and 6 percent a year (since 1993), will probably take up the slack. Unemployment is about one-half the national average, even though wages are slightly below normal (as is the cost of living).

With Salt Lake City's high literacy rate and number of high school graduates (for which the city ranks second in the U.S.), the clean-living, healthy-as-a-horse workforce continues to attract companies. Industries cite increased productivity of 25–30 percent in their Salt Lake/Utah facilities, with low absenteeism and union membership in less than 5 percent of manufacturing plants. Along with the old standbys of construction, services, health care, and government, the computer and biotech industries are expanding, as is tourism.

Even those having difficulties or without a specific background can receive assistance. Computer science programs affiliated with Brigham Young University and the University of Utah can offer an entree into local corporations. And new, expanding, and existing companies can take advantage of the state's "custom fit" program, which provides employees with site-specific and on-the-job training through various participating institutions.

The millennium will bring not only the Olympics but more Texans, Californians, and other transplants from the outside world. And for a city that has been pretty self-contained (and, some feel, with one foot in the 19th century), the resulting mix should be very interesting indeed.

HOW SALT LAKE CITY WORKS AND PLAYS

Major Breadwinning

Private enterprises include Intermountain Health Care (17,000), Brigham Young University (15,000), Smith's Food and Drug (5,500), Morton International equipment (5,500), Matrixx Marketing (5,500), Wal-Mart (4,400), Delta Air Lines (4,000), and Thiokol technology (4,000). All contribute to Salt Lake City's multifaceted economy. The public sector is a major player as well, with the State of Utah being the largest employer (19,000), followed by the

University of Utah (15,000, including the hospital), Granite School District (7,500), Hill Air Force Base (7,500), and other school/government operations.

The area's major job growth has been primarily in the private arena, particularly in service, retail, and construction, which provided respective annual gains of 13,700, 6,500, and 5,700 new positions. Manufacturing, government (despite federal layoffs), wholesale trade, and transportation also netted several thousand additional workers. As with most places, service takes the largest portion of the employment pie (26 percent), although it actually falls slightly short of the national rate. Retail and government represent 18 percent each, while at 12.6 percent, manufacturing also lags behind the U.S. average, with wholesale (5.9 percent) and construction (5.7 percent) bringing up the rear.

> Salt Lake City really does have the makings of a promised land. It has been tapped for the 2002 Winter Olympics; construction is underway for a downtown courts complex; and the western part of downtown is rapidly being converted to microbreweries, galleries, and boutiques, as well as loft apartments and condos.

Those searching for wide-open spaces will likely find them in computers and biotechnology. The former employs over 30,000 workers statewide and includes equipment and peripheral manufacturing as well as software development. Companies such as Corel (WordPerfect), Novell, and Iomega are expanding; and Packard Bell recently moved its technical support operations from California, adding even more jobs. The biomedical sector has been germinating at a rate of 10 percent a year. Many new biomed companies and health care facilities are concentrated along what's known as the Wasatch Front, an 85-mile-long urban oasis stretching from Ogden to Provo (with Salt Lake City in the center). More than 8,000 employees are engaged in drug and pharmaceutical manufacturing in addition to biological, genetic, and medical research and testing.

Utah's institutions of higher learning share information with companies, resulting in more than 65 new enterprises with more than 1,250 jobs. As one of the nation's most highly rated public research facilities, the University of Utah has a "technology transfer" program that helps facilitate the latest developments for practical application into the business world. The state is also among the top ten centers of National Information Technology activity and is in the top five for software development.

And don't overlook the Olympic Winter Games as a potential source of employment in fields from marketing to engineering to development. During the next few years, the Wasatch Front (again) will be developed as a winter sports training and competition hub. A ski jump and speed-skating oval are already under construction, and 2002 will yield bobsled runs, a state-of-the-art ice rink, and a 10,000-seat sports arena for ice hockey, among other things—not to mention dozens of promotional and private sector projects associated with the Olympics. Closely related to this activity is a steady increase in tourism, whose 7-million-person, $2-billion contribution to the economy has resulted in a hotel room occupancy rate topped only by Honolulu (what a contrast!).

Such rapid expansion is not without the drawbacks of building constraints, health care restructuring, slower export growth, and an improved business climate in rival Western states. But Salt Lake City has always operated on faith.

ARTS AND SCIENCES

Temple Square is like an elephant in your living room: You can't get around it, so you might as well try to understand why it's there. Although non-Mormons are denied access to the Temple itself, you can admire its architecture (topped by a 1,500-pound gold-leaf statue of the Angel Moroni) as well as visit the Mormon Tabernacle, with its massive organ (11,623 pipes!) and world-famous choir. The Museum of Church History and Art chronicles the Mormon movement, while the Joseph Smith Memorial Building houses LDS administrative offices and provides more information about the Church. Those curious about polygamy might also want to visit the interestingly monikered Lion House, a "supplementary residence" (Convention and Visitors Bureauese) for Brigham Young and his "large family."

Nearby is the official Young residence, also appropriately titled Beehive House. Temple Square tours run from 9 a.m. to 9 p.m. seven days a week; most are free, and no one will try to convert you. Honest. (Bonus: Along with unique buildings, restaurants, and emporiums, Gardener Historic Village in West Jordan has a polygamist museum.)

Area code 801 has lots of secular stuff as well. The Family History Library is the largest genealogical research facility in the world, the Hansen Planetarium's two free floors of exhibits include a rock brought back from the moon, and the Pioneer Museum has 38 rooms of displays plus historic vehicles and farm machinery (no oxen, though). Other points of interest: the Great Salt Lake, Hogle Zoo, The Children's Museum of Utah, and This Is the Place State Park.

Salt Lake City's active scene includes an Arts Council that serves more than 400 non-profit organizations and an Arts Center that features contemporary works. With 2,800 and 2,000 seats, respectively, the Abravanel Hall/Art Center Complex and Capitol Theatre showcase various performances. Abravanel is said to have among the finest acoustics in the world. The Utah Symphony and the Gina Bachauer International Piano Foundation, with its prestigious competition, have helped buff the local image. Ballet West, the modern Ririe-Woodbury Dance Company, the Repertory Dance Company, the Utah Opera Company, the Pioneer Memorial Theatre, and other local troupes round out offerings. Some of those groups perform in the historic Italian Renaissance Capitol Theatre, while the former Orpheum is now the Church's Promised Valley Playhouse.

Nearby Park City—Salt Lake's ritzy, worldly neighbor—has a burgeoning community of its own, with a Writers at Work Conference; an Arts Festival; and the Kimball Art Center, which hooks into local galleries and other groups. (Park City's Silver Mine Adventure, a Disneyesque expedition through underground tunnels, is perhaps for the more easily amused.) Thanks to gatherings such as Robert Redford's Sundance Film Festival and lower production costs, Utah has become the scene of numerous feature films, movies of the week, commercials, and TV series, such as (but, of course) "Touched By an Angel." How saintly.

THE SPORTING LIFE

In addition to the much-touted skiing, Utah boasts seven national forests and five national parks. These include the breathtaking Arches, the largest concentration of natural stone arches in the world; Bryce Canyon, a series of "breaks" plunging 1,000 feet in 13 natural amphitheaters; and Flaming Gorge, famous for its giant trout and red rock mountains. More than 45 state parks and 400 campgrounds set the stage for a plethora of other activities. You can enjoy white-water rafting on the Green, Colorado, and San Juan rivers, and wildlife watching of more than 630 species of critters. Also available are inexpensive golf, cycling, fly-fishing, rock climbing, and boating opportunities. (Although Utah is considered a desert, it has several inland bodies of water.) Spectator sports are rather limited: They include the American Basketball Association (ABA) Stars, the NBA Jazz, and the AAA baseball Buzz. That might change as the Olympics approach and set things in motion.

Only in Salt Lake can you go on dinosaur and rock art history tours, covered wagon treks, or archaeological digs—and later toss down a few at the Holy Cow or Dead Goat Saloon.

 AFTER-HOURS DIVERSIONS

The previously mentioned industrial district between the blocks of 200 and 400 West Street has sprouted microbreweries such as the Fuggles and the Red Rock, cultivating a rather bohemian atmosphere. And rock, hardcore and otherwise, can be heard at Bricks, City Limits, Club 90, Club DV8, Liquid Joe's, and Zephyr, while jazz and blues can be found at Juniors and Sojourners. There's karaoke at Bojangles and Peppermill; country and western at the Old Bottling House, Rocky's, and the Redwood Lounge; and comedy at the Comedy Circuit. Salt Lake even has—gasp!—clubs with exotic dancers: the Gold Bar Saloon, the Office Lounge, State Street Sociables, and Shakers (not the religious group). The Northern X-posure Show Club and Sports Bar offers a bit of everything.

 CULINARY AND SHOPPING HAUNTS

Salt Lake is typically American in its restaurant and shopping options, although with only about 300 eateries in the city proper, less may be more. Culinary standouts include the exclusive and expensive Metropolitan (Continental), the more moderately priced Market Street Grill (seafood) and Fresco Italian Cafe, and the even more economical Care Trang (Vietnamese) and Bubba's (Cajun). Chains like T.G.I. Friday's, Tony Roma's, and Chili's join unique offerings like Baba (Afghan), Star of India, and St. Petersburg Cafe (Russian).

Another kind of religious experience can be found at the local Snelgrove Ice Cream Parlor; urban legend has it that folks in Salt Lake consume more of the stuff than anywhere else in the U.S. But even more bizarre are statewide restrictions on liquor in restaurants and private clubs. In many restaurants, you can't purchase alcohol unless you order food, and you can't get a second drink until you finish the first (the adult equivalent of polishing off your peas before getting dessert). Several private clubs allow for purchase of "temporary" memberships (like cover charges in other cities), which remove many of these constraints, including, in some instances, the sale of only 3.2 beer.

And there are plenty of shopping malls, including Crossroads Plaza (more than 140 mostly upscale stores across from Temple Square), Fashion Place Mall, Valley Fair Mall, and

ZCMI Center Mall. Salt Lake City also features discount outlets like the Factory Stores @ Park City, Factory Stores of America, Zion Factory Stores, and the Sundance Catalogue Outlet Store (established by none other than Bob Redford himself).

Honest John's and State Street Antique Mall peddle antiques galore, and those who don't mind losing a filling or two can sample the wares at the Trolley Taffy Station.

ETHNIC AND RELIGIOUS PROSPECTS

With a population that's 64 percent Mormon, followed by Roman Catholics, Southern Baptists, Episcopalians, and Methodists (as well as nearly 60 other groups including Jews, Quakers, and Muslims), Salt Lake City prides itself on religious freedom and tolerance. And with less than 2 percent being African-American, most ethnic issues revolve around the Mormon Church or dustups within the gay community (such as when a Salt Lake high school banned all nonacademic clubs to exclude a homosexual group). Perhaps more insidious—or advantageous, depending on your point of view—is the fact that the Mormon Church owns a large portion of downtown and therefore has a strong say in the structure of the cityscape.

Yet Salt Lake has been working at shedding its theocratic image. The current mayor is a non-LDS Democrat and a woman (in a largely Republican state), and Utah Center was built to help bridge the physical and social gap between the center of Mormonism and a commercial district formerly built by gentiles. Urban planning and tax breaks are aimed toward attracting new businesses. And, aside from opposing legalized gambling and supporting the restrictive drinking laws, the LDS Church stays out of most civic issues that don't directly involve its holdings. But it still carries a big stick, such as when a spokesman discouraged the idea of a proposed freeway that would increase traffic past Temple Square. And like that proverbial elephant, the Church is definitely there.

CRIB SHEET

Real estate offers a good news/bad news scenario: Although house prices are still relatively low, making ownership affordable for many, Salt Lake City has one of the tightest markets across all home categories in the U.S. Apartment availability has dropped to the low single digits, particularly in downtown areas like Rose Park. However, suburbs such as Jordan and places a bit farther away have more options. And around downtown, construction of new units and conversion of existing buildings into multiple dwellings have begun to ease the situation.

Many newcomers settle along the Wasatch Front; suburbs in and around this area, such as West Valley City and Draper, either didn't exist or were small only a few years ago. Districts like South and West Jordan, Draper (again), and Sandy have experienced pell-mell growth, occasionally resulting in streets that go nowhere and communities that are jammed together.

Those with money and no compunction about worldly goods can opt for Park City, with its plenitude of gold cards and $700,000 homes.

With Salt Lake City having the nation's highest birth rate, it's no surprise that there are special programs for pre- and postnatal care as well as an emphasis on schools. Nearly half the state's budget is spent on public education, although class sizes tend to be bigger. More than 80 private and parochial offerings are also available—a large number considering the size of the city.

San Antonio at a Glance

Birthdate and Present Size: 1718.
Metropolitan Suburban Area—
1980: 1,072,125; 1990: 1,302,099.
1/1/95 (estimate): 1,461,200.
Percent change, 1980–1990: +21.5%.
Percent change, 1990–1995: +12.2%.

Weather Report: *Average annual temperature—*68°F. In January: 62/39° F.
In July: 95/74° F.
*Average annual precipitation—*28".
*Average annual snowfall—*infrequent
(0.5").

Money Matters: *Unemployment rate—*
5.2%.
Per capita income—$11,865.
Average household income—$33,646.
Average cost of a home—$122,500.
Average rent for an apartment—
$555/month.
ACCRA cost of living indexes (based on
100)—Composite Index: 94.5; Utilities
Index: 88.5; Housing Index: 92.4.
*Sales and use tax—*6.25% (state);
1.50% (local).
*Personal income tax—*None.

People Profile: *Crime rate* (Per 100,000
population)—8,768.8.
Racial and ethnic characteristics—
White: 72.3%; Hispanic: 55.3%; Black:

7.0%; American Indian/Eskimo/Aleut:
0.4%; Asian/Pacific Islander: 1.1%;
Other: 19.2%. (Hispanic origin can be of
any race, hence the numbers total greater
than 100%.)
*Gender ratio—*93 males per 100 females
(all ages); 88.7 males per 100 females
(18 years old+).
*Age characteristics—*18–24 (11.5%);
25–44 group (32.4%). Median age: 29.8.
*Educational attainment—*percent having
completed high school: 69.1%; percent
having completed college: 17.8%.

Major Players: Services, retail/wholesale
trade, government, manufacturing.
*Largest employers—*Kelly Air Force Base,
Fort Sam Houston, Lackland Air Force
Base, City of San Antonio, United States
Automobile Association, H.E. Butt
Grocery Company, Baptist Memorial
Hospital System, Fiesta Texas.

Community Services: *Average hospital
cost—*$348.60/day.
Average doctor visit—$39.60.
Average dentist visit—$49.40.
*Newspapers—San Antonio Express-News,
The San Antonio Business Journal, Westside
and Southside Sun* (Hispanic), *San Antonio
Register* (black), *Today's Catholic, San
Antonio Current* (alternative).

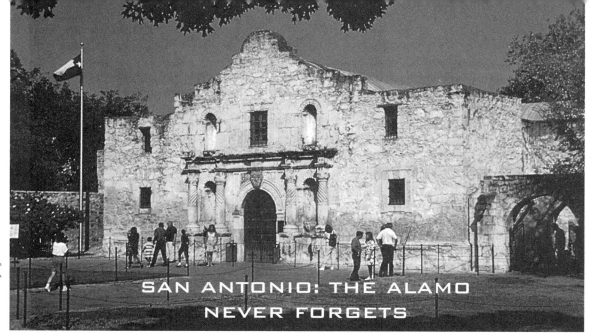

SAN ANTONIO: THE ALAMO
NEVER FORGETS

San Antonio is a jewel box of history, entertainment, and architecture surrounded by a plain brown wrapper of housing tracts and mini-malls. Founded by the Spaniards in the 16th century as a mission to initiate Native Americans into Christianity, it grew into a thriving magnet for several cultures. Along the way, one of its five local missions, the Alamo, became a flash point for the Texas revolution against Mexico. Although all 189 defenders perished in that fateful 1836 battle, their story can be relived daily in the real thing on Alamo Plaza as well as at several local memorials and museums, which range from cheesy to authentic.

The San Antonio (a.k.a. Yanaguana) River played a big part in the city's development from the time of the Coahuilecan Indians (about 100 A.D.), whose descendants helped build irrigation ditches, to today, when it is drained every January for the purpose of retrieving chairs, place settings, and other previously submerged items for the upcoming tourist season.

During the 1800s, San Antonio became a major stop on the perpetual cattle drive that helped steer Texas toward its present prosperity. The establishment of Fort Sam Houston in 1876 and the Southern Pacific Railroad a year later ensured increasing affluence thanks to the military and the transportation industry. By 1920, San Antonio was the largest city in Texas. Although it can no longer claim that distinction, it remains one of the ten biggest cities in the U.S., even though it doesn't act like it.

Quality of Life

With a mild subtropical climate that provides more than 300 days of sunshine and only an occasional sudden, unpredictable downpour, the sky always seems bright in San Antonio. Combined with lots of greenery and clean air—the environment was ranked No. 1 by the World Resources Institute—and an extensive and well-mannered traffic system, the area invariably lures workers and companies. Tourists also love it; more than seven million flock to the Alamo and a myriad of other attractions each year, from the four other faultlessly maintained Spanish missions to the meandering, enterprise- and tree-lined River Walk (Paseo del Rio) to the Mexican-flavored Market Square to the consistently amusing Six Flags Fiesta Texas. With museums, performing arts groups, dance and theater companies, and Tejano music (Mexican ballads accompanied by an accordion), there's something for every cultural preference and taste. Although the primary influence has been Hispanic, nine flags have flown over the Alamo city at one time or another, and each has left an imprint.

> **"San Antonio is a laid-back place,"** observes a longtime resident. **"Although it's growing, the culture remains old-fashioned, so it's retained much of its small-town flavor."**

"This is a laid-back place," observes legislative assistant Vicky Ford, a longtime resident. "Although it's growing, the culture remains old-fashioned, so it's retained much of its small-town flavor."

With nearby lakes, beaches, pools, golf courses, public parks, and the legendary Hill Country to explore, there's always something to do when you're not attending festivals, or sports events at the brand-new Alamodome. Add below-average cost of living and housing expenses, and excellent health care facilities and schools, and you might have to remind yourself that the 21st century is just around the bend.

General Opportunities

Since the mid-'80s, San Antonio's employment has grown more than twice as fast as the rest of the state's. Employment opportunities have diversified in services, trade, and government. Medical research, biotechnology, and distribution of goods between the U.S. and Mexico have also added to the upswing. The increasing popularity of the city as a convention destination has allowed for the expansion of the Henry B. Gonzalez Center and the $3.1-billion-a-year tourism industry. Since 1982, the job market has experienced a phenomenally consistent "above 3 percent" growth rate.

Despite all the activity, an emphasis on tradition permeates every aspect of life. "If a building can be reused, we'll find a way to restore it," points out Anita Uribe of the Hispanic Chamber of Commerce. An example is La Villita, one of the city's original settlements, now a well-traveled agglomeration of artisan workshops, restaurants, and historic homes.

The Hispanic presence is felt in business as well. "It's hard to discriminate against half of the population, particularly when your boss and many of your co-workers have Mexican roots," adds Ford.

MAJOR BREADWINNING

San Antonio's workforce now consists of nearly 700,000 employees in a variety of fields. Although wages are lower than in other large cities, decreases in cost of living more than make up the slack. "I like being a bigger fish in a smaller pond," comments marketing specialist Suzanne Satagaj, who lived in Boston prior to relocating. "There's a slower, friendlier pace to doing business and your dollar goes a lot further." For instance, "in Boston, I had to get a second job just to afford my expenses. Now I have time to meet new people and attend the various activities I enjoy."

Although the majority of jobs are in services (182,000), trade (152,000), and government (128,000), San Antonio has attracted major players in light manufacturing (Bausch & Lomb, GW Plastics), textiles (Reyes Industries), electronics (Sony, VLSI Technology), and food processing (Mission Mexican Foods). Communications has become another star: Because the Alamo city has an exceptional fiber-optics network, it has drawn such telemarketing giants as QVC home shopping network, Citicorp banking, American Airlines customer service, and about 25 other companies. The proximity to Mexico also provides incentive: Both Southwestern Bell and QVC plan to expand their services across the border.

The military has also been an influence. Although cutbacks are occurring elsewhere in the U.S., funding for Lackland and Randolph Air Force Bases has increased, bringing the annual total budgets to $4.1 billion. As a national training center for Air Force personnel and U.S. Army Health Services, the four Air Force bases and Fort Sam Houston employ tens of thousands of civilian workers in technical support, health care, training, and research. Both state and local governments have also grown in the areas of education as well as social work, health, business, and other services.

The word "hub" is becoming synonymous with biotechnology, health care, and research in San Antonio. Private positions alone total over 50,000 and are growing, and biotech is predicted to become a $2-billion-a-year industry around the turn of the century. Not only does San Antonio have the Texas Research and Technology Foundation, but the University of Texas Health Science Center is one of the state's top research/training facilities, and the University of Texas Institute of Biotechnology's work on the genetics of cancer has drawn attention and funding. The nonprofit Southwest Research Institute, the third largest in the U.S., provides scientific and engineering services to industries and governments worldwide. And the 3,000 baboons at the Southwest Foundation for Biomedical Research have helped with advances in studies on human heart disease, AIDS, hardening of the arteries, and other illnesses. (Folks with a soft spot for critters might want to look elsewhere.)

Another 56,000 positions are directly related to the tourism industry. Additional jobs are available in finance, insurance, and real estate, with approximately 43,000 more being added yearly. Even photographers are in demand.

Many who've moved to San Antonio find that it grows on them. "It's not nearly as competitive or pretentious as, say, Austin," points out advertising executive Doug Stratton. "People here keep their jobs and family lives in perspective. They focus on schools and the environment, rather than climbing the corporate ladder."

Those who make the effort can usually find employment. "We newcomers gravitate towards each other and help each other out," adds Satagaj. "Although San Antonio is rather conservative, there's a great tolerance for individual differences."

SOCIAL AND RECREATIONAL SCENE

How San Antonio Plays

The willy-nilly growth of the outskirts is only part of area code 210's transformation. "Traditionally, most people who stayed in town married by the time they were in their early 20s," explains Ford. "College graduates who wanted better opportunities moved elsewhere."

But the influx of business has brought a slew of young professionals. "It still may take a while to feel comfortable," observes attorney Keith Martin. "But once people warm up to you, they remain your friend."

Although there appear to be few barriers between various groups, socially San Antonio can be tough to figure out. "This is a rather conservative place," observes a longtime resident. "We like to have a good time, but there are definite boundaries regarding certain types of behavior." So while partying 'till you drop is acceptable, promiscuity and wild conduct are generally frowned upon. "People here have strong moral and ethical codes."

Since San Antonians take their adaptive re-use seriously, restoration groups are a logical point of entry (San Antonio Conservation Society, 224-6163). "We were recycling before it became fashionable," remarks Uribe. "People around here really care about the old buildings, whether they're a public place or a residence."

Where It's At

 Unless otherwise noted, all area codes are 210.

Alamo, Alamo Plaza, 225-1391

Antonio Botanical Center, 555 Funston Pl., 821-5115

Arneson River Theatre, 418 La Villita, 207-8610

Arts! San Antonio, 222 E. Houston, 226-2891

Blue Star, 116 Blue Star, 227-6960

Carver Community Cultural Center, 226 N. Hackenberry, 225-6516

Children's Museum, 305 E. Houston St., 212-4453

Coppini Academy of Fine Arts, 115 Melrose, 824-8502

 ### ARTS AND SCIENCES

They say everything's bigger in Texas, and the San Antonio arts scene is no exception. **Arts! San Antonio** concentrates on bringing outstanding artists and entertainers to town. **Carver Community Cultural Center** zooms in on contemporary and multicultural performances. The **Guadalupe Cultural Arts Center** showcases primarily Hispanic music, literature, dance, and film. And the **Mexican Cultural Institute** offers exhibitions, lectures, and performances.

San Antonio also has several music, theater, and dance companies, in addition to its own brand-new opera (**San Antonio Opera Company**). Venues vary from the historic **Villita Assembly Hall** to the **Arneson River Theatre** to the larger **Lila Cockrell Theatre** and **Municipal Auditorium** to the **Majestic Performing Arts Center,** a restored movie house, and others.

Texas history is a local obsession, and what better way to ingratiate yourself than by becoming an instant expert? Most of what's available can be found within walking distance of the genuine enchilada, the Mission San Antonio de Valero, a.k.a. the **Alamo.** Located in the center of town, this picturesque, well-maintained 1718 chapel is all that remains of the original fort. Admission is free and you can stay as long as you like. A couple of nearby places dish out more nitty-gritty on the bloody battle and the Wild West experience. The **Cowboy Museum** serves up gen-u-ine gunfighter, Injun (no politically correct references here), and trail drive memorabilia. The **Texas Adventure** is a multimedia re-enactment of the historic battle. The **Plaza Theatre of Wax/Ripley's Believe It or Not!** not only has reproductions of favorite and almost forgotten movie stars but of Texas historical figures as well.

Museums cover a wide spectrum, from the "Big Top" of the **Hertzberg Circus Collection** to the **Institute of Texas Cultures,** which provides a detailed look at how different ethnic groups settled what was once (and may still be to some) the Republic of Texas. The recently completed **Children's Museum** centers on local history and ecology. Everything from Central American ceramics to bronzes by Rodin can be found at the **San Antonio Museum of Art** and **McNay Art Museum.** The **Witte Memorial Museum** complex features Texas history, natural sciences, and anthropology.

The gallery scene is blooming as well. "Artists are moving from places like Santa Fe," points out Satagaj. "They're attracted to San Antonio because it's fresh with a new perspective." Among the creative hot spots are the **Blue Star,** which not only offers a contemporary museum featuring local to international work, but is also a district with studios, lofts, and commercial galleries. The **Southwest Craft Center** has a nationally renowned art school and workshops as well as display spaces. And the **Coppini Academy of Fine Arts** provides exhibits and demonstrations.

Brackenridge Park boasts the **San Antonio Zoo** and **Japanese Tea Gardens.** With the world's largest naturalistic exhibits, this 3,700-animal, 700-species zoo was among the first to successfully reproduce the white rhino in addition to certain types of flamingoes, whooping cranes, snakes, and snow leopards (it must be that clean air!). The Japanese gardens provide tranquil walkways and bridges along with Texas-sized goldfish whose origins are actually Oriental. A bit farther from town, the **San Antonio Botanical Center** is a mini-compendium of the diverse local landscapes, as well as a Biblical garden, a religious experience involving trees and other flora mentioned in the Scriptures.

Where It's At

(continued)

Cowboy Museum, 209 Alamo Plaza, 229-1257

Guadalupe Cultural Arts Center, 1300 Guadalupe, 271-3151

Hertzberg Circus Collection, 210 Market, 207-7810

Institute of Texas Cultures, 801 S. Bowie St., 558-2300

Japanese Tea Gardens, 801 S. Bowie St., 734-3551

Lila Cockrell Theatre, 200 E. Market, 207-8500

Majestic Performing Arts Center, 230 E. Houston, 226-5700

McNay Art Museum, 6000 N. Braunfels, 824-5386

Mexican Cultural Institute, 600 HemisFair Park, 227-0123

Municipal Auditorium, 100 Auditorium Circle, 207-8511

Plaza Theatre of Wax/Ripley's Believe It or Not!, 301 Alamo Plaza, 224-9299

San Antonio Museum of Art, 200 W. Jones, 829-7262

San Antonio Opera Company, 115 E. Travis, 227-6863

San Antonio Zoo, 3903 St. Mary's, 734-7183

Southwest Craft Center, 300 Augusta St., 224-1848

Texas Adventure, 307 Alamo Plaza, 227-8224

Villita Assembly Hall, 401 Villita, 978-3296

Witte Memorial Museum complex, 3801 Broadway, 820-2111

Where It's At

Unless otherwise noted, all area codes are 210.

Alamo Dragway, 15000 Watson Rd., 923-8801

Alamodome, 100 Montana, 207-3663

Brackenridge Park, 950 E. Hildebrand, 821-1300

Choke Canyon State Park, 512/786-3868

Cibolo Wilderness Trail, 249-8000

Friedrich Wilderness Park, 21395 Milsa Rd., 698-1057

Guadalupe River State Park, 249-8000

HemisFair Park, 200 S. Alamo, 207-8572

International Raceway, Hwy. 16, 628-1522

Kicker's Korner, 11224 Atkins, 622-9107

Pear Apple County Fair, 5820 NW Loop 410, 521-9500

Retama Park, Loop 1604, off IH-35, 651-7000

San Antonio Iguanas, 3202 E. Houston St., 227-4449

San Antonio Missions, 5757 Hwy. 90 West, 675-PARK

San Antonio Parks and Recreation Department, 207-8480

San Antonio Rose Palace, 25665 Boerne Stage Rd., 698-3300

San Antonio Sport & Social Club, 1528 Contour Dr., 821-6595

Sea World, Intersection of Ellison Dr. and Westover Hills, 523-3611

Six Flags Fiesta Texas, I-10W to La Cantera Parkway, 800/473-4378

 ## THE SPORTING LIFE

Brackenridge Park is a 343-acre playground with a carousel, railroad, skyride, paddle boats, and stables. Another popular spot is **HemisFair Park,** a politically correct melange with water sculptures and a German Heritage Park, the aforementioned Institute of Texan Cultures and Mexican Cultural Institute, and the Tower of the Americas, a 750-foot colossus that provides an awesome view.

These are but two of the city's 143 parks (for more information, contact the **San Antonio Parks and Recreation Department**). The Parks and Recreation Department organizes sports ranging from basketball to track. The **San Antonio Sport & Social Club** is another popular alternative, especially for newcomers. Golf is also big in the Alamo city. The more than 25 courses host numerous PGA tours and were designed by such notables as A.W. Tillinghast and Tom Weiskopf. Numerous ponds, woods, and sand traps keep things challenging.

A bit farther out are **Friedrich Wilderness Park,** located in the heart of Texas hill country. Bird watchers, hikers, and others with a naturalistic bent will enjoy the reservoir and wildlife at **Choke Canyon State Park,** the **Cibolo Wilderness Trail,** and the **Guadalupe River State Park,** to mention a few. Nearby bodies of water for fishing, boating, and general recreation include Lake McQueeney, Canyon Lake, and Medina Lake (all about an hour away), as well as the Texas Gulf Coast. Here, the numerous beaches and sailing opportunities in the port town of Corpus Christi provide excellent fishing and other pleasures.

Those looking for another kind of lark will find it at **Six Flags Fiesta Texas** and **Sea World.** A local spin on the former includes German-, Southwest-, and Hispanic-themed areas as well as '50s rock 'n' roll and a bone-rattling assortment of roller coasters. Along with Shamu and friends (who make a whale of an appearance), Sea World offers a water park and their less scantily clad take on "Baywatch" as well as other amusements. The **Pear Apple County Fair** is an old-fashioned amusement park with a Ferris wheel, bumper cars, and loads of quarter-eating games.

Completed in 1993 and costing a mere $186 million, the **Alamodome** is the latest notch in the town's belt. One of the few new buildings that blends in with the architecture, it has the added bonus of a cable-suspended roof and can accommodate gatherings ranging from religious revivals to trade shows to the NCAA Final Four, which is scheduled for 1998. Home of the popular (thanks in part to effervescent ex-member Dennis Rodman) San Antonio Spurs basketball team as well as the Texans, a recently transplanted branch of the Canadian Football League, it can also adapt to ice skating, soccer, and other sports.

The town has the **San Antonio Missions,** the farm team for the L.A. Dodgers, and the **San Antonio Iguanas** serve up hockey at Freeman Coliseum. The **Alamo Dragway, International Raceway,** and track at **Retama Park** have lots of madcap auto and horse racing action. A selection of rodeos (**Kicker's Korner, San Antonio Rose Palace,** others) are reminders that in Texas, men are men and livestock had better behave.

 ## AFTER-HOURS DIVERSIONS

San Antonio has several bars, the most famous of which is the **Menger,** where Teddy Roosevelt recruited his Rough Riders, allegedly galloping through the lobby on horseback and shooting at the chandelier. The **Lone Star Brewing Company** features the Buckhorn Bar, the Hall of Horns, Fins, and Feathers, and more than 3,500 game animals who were in the wrong place at the wrong time and ended up mounted on the walls. A real Texas treat.

The River Walk is another exuberant spot—quiet and park-like in some stretches, and full of shops, restaurants, and clubs in others. "You can go from place to place and hear all kinds of music, from country to Tejano to blues to soul," remarks Stratton. Venues range from the jazz bar at the classy **Hyatt Regency** to the wild and zany (**Howl at the Moon, Mad Dogs, Naked Iguana**). Two recently linked developments, South Bank and the Presidio, have the **Hard Rock Cafe** and **Planet Hollywood** as respective anchors. "It's a unique setup; there's nothing like it anywhere else." Quite a turnaround for a site which was almost turned into a sewer after a tragic 1921 flood.

The River Walk's ominous reputation lingered until 1968, when San Antonians began beautification and commercialization in anticipation of the HemisFair (World's Fair). Another romantic and fun means of exploring the area is via a barge. **Yanaguana Cruises** offers everything from 40-minute tours to candlelight dinners replete with linen tablecloths and crystal.

One of the best ways to meet people in this "big small town" is through festivals and other civic events. Such gatherings provide a comfortable way to get to know both natives and transplants. The largest, **Fiesta San Antonio,** is a ten-day extravaganza in April with elaborate parades, ethnic music and food, and arts and shopping fairs. "Each day brings out more people, so by the end it builds to quite a crescendo," adds Uribe.

January gets down and dirty with the **River Bottom Festival and Mud Parade,** which makes the most of the annual river drainage by crowning a Mud King/Queen and in general having a (Mud Pie) Ball. The river is subject to further ignominy and dyed green during the

Where It's At

 Unless otherwise noted, all area codes are 210.

Alamo Irish Festival, 497-8435

Carver Jazz Festival, 225-6516

Dozynki, 225-5551

Fiesta San Antonio, 227-5171

Greek Funstival, 735-5051

Hard Rock Cafe, 111 W. Crockett St., 224-7625

Howl at the Moon, 111 W. Crockett St., 212-4695

Hyatt Regency, River Walk, 222-1234

Lone Star Brewing Company, 600 Lone Star Boulevard, 270-9467

Mad Dogs, 123 Losoya, 222-0220

Menger, 204 Alamo Plaza, 223-4361

Naked Iguana, 521 E. Commerce, 226-8462

Oktoberfest, 222-1521

Planet Hollywood, 245 E. Commerce St., 212-7827

River Bottom Festival and Mud Parade, 227-4262

River Walk Holiday Arts Fair, 227-4262

Tejano Conjunto Festival, 271-3151

Texas Folklife Festival, 558-2300

Wurstfest, New Braunfels, 625-9167

Yanaguana Cruises, 315 E. Commerce, 244-5700

Alamo Irish Festival (March 15–17), although the Alamo city's heritage is not nearly as Irish as Chicago's, another metropolis that follows the same tradition.

Celebrations often have an ethnic slant. May brings the **Tejano Conjunto Festival,** which attracts the premier artists in this musical form. Another melodic offering is the **Carver Jazz Festival** (June), which honors new and established artists as well as African-American emancipation. The Institute of Texan Cultures coordinates the **Texas Folklife Festival,** representing 30 different ethnic groups. The Germans have **Oktoberfest** and **Wurstfest** (November). October also brings **Dozynki** (Polish harvest festival) and the **Greek Funstival.** The **River Walk Holiday Arts Fair** (December) rounds out the year.

 ## CULINARY AND SHOPPING HAUNTS

Don't even think about becoming a vegetarian if you move to this town. San Antonio certainly has had some, uh, interesting cuisine—barbacoa, the pit-cooked head of a cow or pig; menudo, not the singing group but a stew of tripe, pig's foot, and hominy; and chicharron, greasy slabs of pig skin formerly sold on street corners.

But some pretty good eats have also emanated from the Alamo city: the perpetual refinement of chili, which is still the subject of many a cook-off, and fajitas, which have come a long way from meat scraps that were directly thrown on the fire and loaded onto tortillas. And then there are margaritas and German beer, the preparation of which have been elevated to a local art form. Have a few of those and you'll forget all about trying to keep kosher.

Although William Gebhart's "Original Mexican" pre-TV–type dinners branded San Antonio with the moniker "Tamaleville" in the 1920s, local cuisine is not only varied but reasonably priced. Even more expensive eateries such as **Bistro Time**, **La Scala**, and the **Old San Francisco Steakhouse** start at $10–$15 per person. (If you insist on spending more money, **Morton's of Chicago** and **Chez Ardid** will gladly relieve you of a couple of Ben Franklins.) Along with the aforementioned Hard Rock/Planet Hollywood/Morton's pod, you'll find Greek (**Demo's**), Indian (**Simi's**), and Oriental (**Beijing, Thai Kitchen**) as well as "deli"cacies at **Nadler's** and **Charlotte's**.

Although there's a wide range of American and Continental possibilities, the Mexican (**Rosario's, La Margarita,** and **Garcia's**) and barbecue (**Bill Miller's, Bob's Smokehouse**) are hard to beat, drawing tourists and residents alike. Those not wanting to leave the River Walk area also have a huge selection: **La Fonda** and **La Paloma** (Mexican), **Boudro's** (American), **Michelino's** (Italian), **Bayou's Riverside** (seafood) and the inevitable **Hooter's** and **Olive Garden.** Another local favorite is the **Guenther House,** a uniquely San Antonio combination of a

Where It's At

 Unless otherwise noted, all area codes are 210.

Antiques Downtown Mall, 515 E. Houston, 224-8845

Bayou's Riverside, 517 N. Presa, 223-6403

Beijing, 23113 NW Military Hwy., 340-0921

Bill Miller's, several locations

Bistro Time, 5137 Fredricksburg Rd., 344-6626

Bob's Smokehouse, several locations

Boudro's, 421 E. Commerce, 224-8484

Cavender's Boot City, multiple locations

Charlotte's, 6989 Blanco Rd., 377-3354

Chez Ardid, 1919 San Pedro, 732-3203

Crossroads of San Antonio, 4522 Fredericksburg Rd., 735-9137

Demo's, 7115 Blanco Rd., 342-3772

Garcia's, 842 Fredericksburg, 735-4245

Guenther House, 205 E. Guenther St., 227-1061

Hooter's, 849 E. Commerce, 229-9464

Kallison's Western Wear, multiple locations

La Fonda, 849 E. Commerce, 227-3698

La Margarita, 120 Produce Row, 227-7140

museum, restaurant, and store. You can walk off your meal by touring the nearby historic King William district.

Even shopping is flavored with legacy. **La Villita** has 26 stores featuring the work of weavers, potters, glass blowers, and other artisans. Settled in the latter part of the 18th century, the "little town" contains old brick buildings and streets paved with tile. An added bonus: A local psychic can help predict whether you'll be able to meet your charge card payments.

Those who enjoy bartering will find "steals" in crafts, clothing, jewelry, and assorted items in **Market Square.** Although it's patterned after a Mexican plaza, the square also includes imported and Native American products. Nearby, a newly renovated farmer's market offers produce, comestibles, and other commodities. The sound of cash registers is often accompanied by a mariachi band, colorful dancers, or some other sort of celebration.

Those seeking comfort in the old standbys will find plenty of "regular" malls. The most visible is **Rivercenter.** This $200 million River Walk centerpiece boasts 135 name-brand emporiums and specialty boutiques. The **North Star Mall** has even more, including a Marshall Field's and a Saks Fifth Avenue. Antique enthusiasts can zone in on the **Antiques Downtown Mall** as well as antique stores in the nearby burgs of Comfort, Boerne, Castroville, and others. The **Crossroads of San Antonio** and **Loehmann's Plaza** cater to more limited checkbooks, while the truly budget-minded can ferret out bargains at the **New Braunfels Factory Stores, San Marcos Factory Shops,** and **Tanger Outlet Center.** Although a bit farther from town, they're fairly close together so you can save money on gas, too.

Those loading up on peppers and piñatas might want to "compleat" the picture by visiting **Kallison's Western Wear** and **Cavender's Boot City.** The dude duds can be topped off at **Paris Hatters.**

ETHNIC AND RELIGIOUS PROSPECTS

San Antonio is a great place to be Catholic. Not only does it have five historical missions, but one, the **Mission San Jose,** holds a weekly mariachi mass, a unique and lively experience. Except for the Alamo, the missions are strung like rosary beads along a nine-mile stretch of the San Antonio River. Constructed by Spanish conquistadors in the 1700s, **Mission Conception** focuses on religion; **Mission San Francisco de la Espada** emphasizes vocational education; **Mission San**

Where It's At

(continued)

La Paloma, 215 Losoya, 223-3818

La Scala, 2177 NW Military Hwy., 366-1515

La Villita, 418 Villita, 207-8610

Loehmann's Plaza, 4937 NW Loop 410, 648-1557

Market Square, 514 W. Commerce, 207-8600

Michelino's, 521 River Walk, 223-2939

Morton's of Chicago, 849 E. Commerce, 228-0700

Nadler's, several locations

New Braunfels Factory Stores, I-35N at exit 188, 620-6806

North Star Mall, 7400 San Pedro, 340-6627

Old San Francisco Steakhouse, 10223 Sahara, 342-2321

Olive Garden, 849 Commerce, 224-5956, and several other sites

Paris Hatters, 119 Broadway, 223-3453

Rivercenter, 849 E. Commerce, 225-0000

Rosario's, 1014 S. Alamo, 223-1806

San Marcos Factory Shops, I-35N at exit 200, 512/396-2200

Simi's, 4535 Fredricksburg Rd., 737-3166

Tanger Outlet Center, I-35N at exit 200, 512/396-7444

Thai Kitchen, 445 McCarty, 344-8366

Where It's At

 Unless otherwise noted, all area codes are 210.

Jewish Community Center, 103 W. Rampart, 344-3453

Mission Conception, 807 Mission Rd., 229-5732

Mission San Francisco de la Espada, 10040 Espada Rd., 627-2064

Where It's At

(continued)

Mission San Jose, 6539 San Jose Dr., 922-0523

Mission San Juan Capistrano, 9102 Graf, 534-3161

Our Lady of Czestochowa, 138 Beethoven, 333-4582

San Antonio Community Churches, 1101 W. Woodlawn Ave., 733-9159

San Fernando Cathedral, 115 Main Plaza, 227-1297

St. Sophia's Greek Orthodox Church, 2504 N. St. Mary's. 735-5051

Juan Capistrano concentrates on economic endeavors; and the aforementioned Mission San Jose is among the most beautiful and centers on social activity.

San Antonio has more than 700 churches, and although many are geared toward Hispanic Catholics, other nationalities are represented. Canary Islanders built **San Fernando Cathedral; St. Sophia's Greek Orthodox Church** is known for its icons; and an unusual statue of a Black Madonna is an attraction at the predominately Polish **Our Lady of Czestochowa.**

Southern Baptists have a strong presence as well. And even though the Jewish population isn't particularly large, it supports synagogues and a **Jewish Community Center.** For more information on specific houses of worship, contact **San Antonio Community Churches.**

"Affiliated groups are still a great way to meet people," observes Vicki Ford. "They draw more of a younger crowd than even bars."

Ethnic groups are treated with equal regard: Although African-Americans represent only 7 percent of the population, St. Paul's Square, famous for its jazz nightclubs at the turn of the century, is a favorite gathering place, as is the aforementioned Carver Community Center. Germans can claim the King William Historic district and its fully restored mansions, bus tours, and desirability as a residential area. The contributions of Poles, Spaniards, Italians, Native Americans, Orientals, Jews, the English and Irish are honored through both ethnic centers and the population at large. "People respect each others' culture," remarks Ford. Those who think otherwise can just turn around and go home.

CRIB SHEET

Although the hottest area for new homes has traditionally been in the Northwest, "Southtown and Downtown have come into their own, particularly with young professionals," points out Uribe. In 1990, a group of residents banded together to preserve Southtown, an area of several blocks that has recently attracted businesses as well as residents of all income groups, ethnicities, and lifestyles. Although some properties may need renovation, "you get a lot for your money" and the proximity to medical centers, universities, and the River Walk area make them even more attractive. "Downtown in particular has a lot of apartments."

The Alamo city's wide selection of rental units ranges from studios to townhouses to condominiums to duplexes. Apartments begin at about $450 a month for a one-bedroom and bath up to $750 for approximately 1,150 square feet (three bedrooms), and are an amenable option for those unsure about staying or investing in real estate. Condos weigh in at about $100 more a month.

As with many booming areas, the 'burbs are evergreens. Subdivisions in the North Central, North West, and North East have blossomed in the past few years; many homes here top the $200,000 mark. The west side of town can be even tonier. An equally large assortment of modest but nicely developed neighborhoods can be found in the east end of town, where prices average $100,000–$200,000. Pre-owned homes cost about $25,000 less than new builds.

Schools seem to have a major impact on the decision of where to move. Although each district is independent, and San Antonio proper has highly regarded "magnet" high schools, factors such as student-teacher ratio, expenditure per student, and overall size of the district enter into buying decisions (San Antonio Independent School District, 299-5500).

> Many who've moved to San Antonio find that it grows on them. "People here keep their jobs and family lives in perspective," points out a recent transplant. "They focus on schools and the environment, rather than climbing the corporate ladder."

There are also about 150 parochial and private schools, a healthy number for a city this size (Keystone School, 735-4022—private; St. Mary's School, 223-8581—Catholic; and many more).

More than a dozen colleges and universities have a total enrollment of almost 75,000 students. Eleven local institutions offer health care degrees and include the University of Texas Health Center, which has four professional schools—medical, dental, nursing, and allied health sciences—as well as teaching hospitals at the University Cooperative Research Center.

NAVIGATING SAN ANTONIO

Except for flash floods, which can occur in low water crossings, driving around San Antonio can be similar to driving through smaller cities in the Midwest. Traffic is manageable, even during busy times, and people actually use their turn signals. A hub-and-spoke design provides a sort of "directions for dummies," linking major highways I-35 (north to south), I-10 (east to west), I-37 (south), Loop 410 (around the city), Loop 1604 (around the county), as well as US 90, US 281, and others. Most parts of town have easy access to the freeway, so if you get lost, it's your own fault.

Those who'd rather not drive can hop aboard the VIA streetcar system, which will take you to various downtown locations and is a deal at $.50. The VIA Metropolitan Transit (227-2020) provides extensive regular bus service throughout San Antonio and most outlying areas. Other modes of transportation include the Greyhound bus terminal (270-5800) and Amtrak (223-3226).

Although the Alamo city has two airports, most commercial flights emanate from San Antonio International (821-3411), which is served by major airlines. It's a mere 13 miles from the River Walk and is linked by expressway, making for quick entry and exit.

SAN DIEGO, CALIFORNIA

San Diego at a Glance

Birthdate and Present Size: Founded in 1769; incorporated as a city in 1850. *Metropolitan Statistical Area*—1980: 1,861,846; 1990: 2,498,016. 1/1/95 (estimate): 2,690,400. Percent change, 1980–1990: +34.2%. Percent change, 1990–1995: +7.7%.

Weather Report: *Average annual temperature*—63.8° F. In January: 65/48° F. In July: 71/61° F. *Average annual precipitation*—9.32". *Average annual snowfall*—trace. There is sunshine approximately 70 percent of the time.

Money Matters: *Unemployment rate*—5.6%. *Per capita income*—$16,401. *Average household income*—$43,627. *Average cost of a home*—$203,800. *Average rent for an apartment*—$679/month. *ACCRA cost of living indexes* (based on 100)—Composite Index: 121.7; Utilities Index: 99.7; Housing Index: 152.5. *Sales and use tax*—6.0% (state); +1.0% (local). *Personal income tax*—1.0% to 11.0%.

People Profile: *Crime rate* (Per 100,000 population)—6,564.5 (city); 5,147.8 (suburbs; 5,773.6 (MSA). *Racial and ethnic characteristics*—White: 67.2% (city), 75.1% (MSA); Black: 9.3% (city), 6.3% (MSA); American Indian/Eskimo/Aleut: 0.7% (city), 0.9% (MSA); Asian/Pacific Islander: 11.8% (city), 8.0% (MSA); Hispanic Origin: 20.1% (city), 20.0% (MSA); Other:

11.0% (city), 9.8% (MSA). *Gender Ratio*—104.2 males per 100 females (all ages); 103.7 males per 100 females (18 years old+). *Age characteristics*—18–24 (14.4%); 25–44 (36.6%). Median Age: 30.5. *Educational Attainment*—percent having completed high school: 82.3%; percent having completed college: 29.8%.

Major Players: Services, retail/wholesale trade, government, manufacturing, particularly missiles and commercial and military airplanes. *Largest Employers*—City of San Diego, County of San Diego, San Diego Unified School District, Sharp Healthcare, United States Government/Civilian, University of California San Diego, Scripps Institutions of Medicines and Science, State of California, Cubic Corporation (electronics), National Steel and Shipbuilding Co. (NASSCO), Rohr Industries (aerospace), Science Applications International (research and development).

Community Services: *Average hospital cost*—$588.76/day. *Average doctor visit*—$46.50. *Average dentist visit*—$75.50. *Newspapers*—San Diego Union-Tribune; San Diego Daily Transcript; San Diego Business Journal; San Diego Commerce (real estate/legal); San Diego Review (alternative); San Diego Reader (arts/entertainment); Ahora Now and La Prensaz San Diego (both Hispanic); San Diego Jewish Press-Heritage; The San Diego Voice & Viewpoint (black); Update (gay).

Photo by James Blank

San Diego. Shimmering beaches and bays, spectacular sunsets, a climate that's as awe-inspiring and consistent as Michael Jordan's hoop shots. "When people come to visit, they almost always want to move here," observes marketing coordinator Heather Milne. With the ocean, the desert, and the mountains at your fingertips, and with job opportunities ranging from agriculture to aerospace to electronics to oceanics to machinery to biotechnology to tourism, it's no wonder this city—which ranked 43rd in U.S. population in 1940— had jumped to No. 6 by 1990. But although it can be a wonderful life, even paradise has some glitches.

Discovered in 1592 by Juan Rodriguez Cabrillo, San Diego is the oldest town in California. The Spaniards didn't really gain a toehold until 1769, when Father Junipero Serra established the first mission in the new teritory. The local Indians expressed their irritation with the white usurpers by burning down the mission and martyring the padre in charge. But the

Franciscans constructed another church, rebuilding it yet again after an 1812 earthquake. The Mexicans took over in 1821, and for the next few years, the city became a pawn as Mexico and America struggled for supremacy. Guess who won in 1846. California became a state four years later, although a strong Spanish-Mexican imprint remains today.

In the early 1800s, the small mission began exporting cattle hides to New England, and from 1850 to 1870 it became an important whaling center. The coming of the railroad brought entrepreneurs. Shortly after the turn of the century, another San Diego institution came into being with the quarantine of animals imported for the Panama-California exposition. Today, with 3,900 creatures representing 800 species, the San Diego Zoo is one of the most visited attractions of its kind in the world.

Uncle Sam, however, provided much of the impetus for growth. In 1901, the U.S. Navy made San Diego its headquarters. Defense-related industries furnished fertile ground for the research and technology boom of the '90s, despite government cutbacks. Recent development of Horton Plaza, a shopping and entertainment facility, and renovation of the historic Gaslamp Quarter continue to draw tourists and locals. Even proximity to the border of Mexico (and particularly Tijuana), with its problems of illegal immigration and crime, have begun to turn into lemonade, thanks to the North American Free Trade Agreement (NAFTA) and efforts by the U.S. and Mexican governments.

Quality of Life

San Diego is a Teflon sort of town: The living is easy, but finding a niche can be slippery. "It took me about a year to really get used to it," observes public relations manager Kim Land. With a job market that can be tight and folks who are into doing their own thing, "You really have to seek out opportunities and friends. Even when you go to the grocery you sometimes have to work at making eye contact" with the surfer dude who's bagging your order.

However, "There are an incredible amount of things to get involved in," she continues. "People are very concerned about the community; there's a growing arts scene; and we have this amazing outdoors and wonderful weather." Although San Diego also offers professional baseball, football, and indoor soccer teams, "people don't live and die by them, mostly because there's so much else to do," including hanging out at more than 25 beaches.

Cost of living is a major bugaboo: Not only is housing extremely pricey, making it out of reach of most beginner budgets, "but everything else is expensive, too," adds computer specialist Kacey Craig Lovelace. Aside from the "big three" industries—biomedical, high tech, and telecommunications—"this is not the place for those who hope to make lots of money," although generous salaries help compensate for at least the basics. And the traffic patterns are actually normal—for California. Plus, earthquakes are fewer and less intense than in other places around the state, a comforting thought when your knickknacks start shaking.

Yeah, San Diego has Sea World and Balboa Park, but you'll also find academic and research institutions like University of California at San Diego (UCSD), the Salk Institute, and Scripps Institute of Oceanography.

"There's a balance of work and quality of life," remarks Milne. "People put a lot into their jobs, but they are family oriented. San Diego is almost Midwestern in terms of morals, attitude, and atmosphere. And it's easy to meet people," although lasting friendships aren't as easily forged on the beaches and the Gaslamp Quarter as they might be through work or various community organizations.

Being so close to Mexico "gives San Diego an international flavor not found in other cities," she goes on. Not to mention potentially exciting encounters with the policia on the other side of the border.

General Opportunities

In this town, being bilingual is a definite plus. Fluency in Spanish "is like having computer skills," notes political manager Ralph Inzuza. "The economy is extremely diverse, and getting more so as big corporations like Sanyo locate near Mexico to take advantage of NAFTA and the international labor force."

With financial resources that rank 37th in the world, San Diego is not only rated as one of the top areas for projected employment growth through 2005 but is considered one of the best cities for business by *Fortune* magazine. A major agricultural producer, it also has nearly 4,000 manufacturing companies. With even more technology, telecommunications, and computer undertakings popping up, it's a small-business incubator as well.

Yet despite all the cutting-edge stuff, ethnically San Diego is "still somewhat segregated," notes government manager Mitch Mitchell. "People of different races live in their own section of town. There still seems to be a slight feeling of distrust from all populations, even though it's much less than most major cities." Illegal immigration provides tension as well. But when the surf's up and the sun's shining, it's hard not to smile.

Major Breadwinning

Although the working population of San Diego has actually decreased, the number of jobs is on the rise, making it about on par with the national unemployment rate. "The market can be very tight," observes Mitchell. "Sometimes you have to live on free happy-hour buffalo wings and take part-time work until a position in your field opens up." But, like anything else, persistence pays off.

"If you know people, it's easier to find employment," adds Lovelace. "Although in some areas, such as engineering, they're having a tough time recruiting because the cost of living here is higher than many other places."

> "There are an incredible amount of things to get involved in," says a local. "People are very concerned about the community; there's a growing arts scene; and we have this amazing outdoors."

Still, San Diego's fiscal outlook is about as sunny as the weather, despite the fact that some sectors have downsized. According to the UCLA Business Forecasting Project, the state's economy will lead the nation in job growth and wage increases over the next three years.

The government remains one of San Diego's biggest employers. City, county, state, and federal agencies as well as publicly funded universities and school systems provide tens of thousands of jobs. Although reductions in the military have eliminated some positions, San Diego has been designated the principal location for the Navy's West Coast operations, which will result in a continued annual contribution of nearly $10 million (or more) to the economy. Along with three nuclear-powered aircraft carriers and beefed-up Marine Corps operations, the ominous-sounding U.S. Space and Naval Warfare Systems Command will be relocated here, making San Diego an ideal target for ayatollahs, terrorists, and assorted wackos.

> San Diego's fiscal outlook is about as sunny as the weather.
> NAFTA has energized its trade, and the city is cited as one
> of the best global cities for business.

Other high-technology industries are prospering as well, in some degree because of the efforts of laid-off aerospace and defense workers. Positions in telecommunications, computer software and hardware, biotechnology, and electronics can be found in the city's multitudinous small-business startups. As one of the top regions for biotechnology and medical research, San Diego's more than 100 enterprises in this area include the Salk Institute for Biological Studies (where the polio vaccine was developed in 1955), the Scripps Clinic, the La Jolla Cancer Research Foundation, and others.

NAFTA has energized international trade, particularly between San Diego and Tijuana. Mexico remains San Diego's primary export market, especially in electronics and industrial equipment. Canada and Japan rank second and third, while proximity to the Pacific Rim facilitates commerce in the Far Eastern countries. Cited as one of the best global cities for business by both *World Trade* and *Forbes* magazines, San Diego has nearly 850 enterprises involved in import/export. Things can only get better for folks with expertise in these areas.

Manufacturing is San Diego's largest revenue generator in terms of total dollars earned, with international trade accounting for about one-third of this. Electronic equipment; industrial machinery; paper, printing, and publishing; aerospace; shipbuilding; and more provide more than 110,000 positions. As one of the primary agricultural counties in the U.S., this $1 billion-plus industry primarily produces fruits and nuts (no California jokes, please), vegetables, nursery products, and market flowers.

Service, the area's biggest employment sector, encompasses almost a third of all San Diego jobs and includes the $3.8 billion visitor industry, which was only enhanced by the 1996 Republican National Convention. People with marketing, public relations, and communications skills can do well here.

Retail trade comprises another 187,000 jobs, and is flourishing with the addition of shops and growth in specific product areas. So if everything else fails, there's always Nordstrom's, Price Costco, Target Stores, and Lucky grocery stores, all of which have at least 2,000 employees. Or you can do the metal detector thing at the beach and stumble upon enough lost valuables to at least pay some bills.

SOCIAL AND RECREATIONAL SCENE

How San Diego Plays

For unattached women, area code 619 has a major benefit: Males of all ages outnumber females. However, "dating can be difficult," remarks Land. "People here are very much into their own thing." Must be those beach boys with their eyes on the waves instead of the curves.

But that's cool, because "it's really easy to meet people through friends, organizations, or personal interests," states Milne. "You have a real variety of groups" with interests ranging from in-line skating to the arts.

Race seems to have little impact on where you hang out. "Everyone mixes together," adds Mitchell. "Age is more of a factor, with the younger college crowd opting for the Pacific Beach area, while Gastown caters to a more upscale group."

"Most people who really want to become acquainted get involved with committees and various boards," he continues. Or, you can opt for that former last-ditch effort for the desperate and dateless: a matchmaking service. "It's become a respectable option for people in their 30s, at least in California." Places like Young Executive Singles (272-1600) and J. Wingo International (558-6934) might improve the social life, although Beach Bunnies Unlimited, All Ways San Diego, San Diego Hot Bods, and Swingers Hotline might be hazardous to the health.

ARTS AND SCIENCES

Although many feel that culture here isn't as deep as in more entrenched cities—due to financial difficulties, the symphony recently disbanded, although the **San Diego Opera** remains strong—options seem to be increasing with every new season.

The city has set up the **San Diego Commission for Arts and Culture** and has allocated $5.6 million to support associations, activities, and art in public places. And by bringing together 92 theater, music, and dance companies, the **San Diego Performing Arts League** has not only promoted local events. "The scene here is really growing," adds Land. "It's exciting to be part of a core group that's making important decisions."

And there's no shortage of live performances. Lushly landscaped Balboa Park, the city's cultural center, has three outstanding venues at the **Simon Edison Centre for the Performing Arts:** the Tony-award winning Old Globe Theater, one of the nation's leading regional repertory groups; the 225-seat Cassius Carter Centre Stage; and the outdoor Lowell Davis Festival Theater. Other regional standouts include the

Where It's At

Unless otherwise noted, all area codes are 619.

4th and B, 345 B. St., 231-4343

African-American Museum of Fine Arts, 3025 1st St., 696-7799

Balboa Park, 239-0512

California Ballet Company, California Center for the Arts, 560-6741

California Center for the Arts, 340 N. Escondido Dr., Escondido, 800/98-TICKETS

California Surf Museum, 308 N. Pacific St., Oceanside, 721-6876

Centro Cultural de la Raza, 2004 Park Blvd., 235-6135

Children's Museum, 200 W. Island Ave., 233-KIDS

Christian Community Theater, 210 E. Main, El Cajon, 588-0206

Diversionary, 4545 Park Blvd., 220-0097

East County Performing Arts Center, 210 E. Main St., El Cajon

Fern St. Circus, P.O. Box 92162, 235-9756

Fritz, 420 Third Ave., 233-7505

George White and Anna Gunn Marston House, 3525 Seventh Ave., 238-3142

Isaacs/McCaleb and Dancers, UCSD, 550-1010

Japanese Friendship Garden, 2215 Pan American Rd. E., 232-2780

Junipero Serra Museum, 2727 Presidio Dr., 297-3258

La Jolla Chamber Music Festival, 459-3728

La Jolla Playhouse, 2910 La Jolla Village Dr., La Jolla, 534-6760

Where It's At

La Jolla Playhouse, which opened its Tony Award–winning smash hit, the Who's *Tommy,* on Broadway; the **San Diego Repertory Theater,** with its emphasis on ethnically diverse plays; and the summertime **Starlight Musical Theater,** which has been wowing 'em since 1946. Still more: the emerging **Fritz, iversionary,** and experimental **Sledgehammer** companies; the **Southeast Community Theater** and **San Diego Black Ensemble Theater,** which showcase African-American directors and actors; and **Teatro Mascara Magica** and **Sushi Performance Art Space,** which feature the multi-cultural works of ethnic artists.

The new **California Center for the Arts** consists of a 12-acre complex highlighting dance, music, theater and more, while the 1,200-seat **East County Performing Arts Center** also hosts a variety of media. The **Poway Center for the Performing Arts** is the San Diego home of California's Pasadena Playhouse. Those on the lookout for wholesome entertainment will find it at the **Christian Community Theater, Theater in Old Town,** and the **Welk** (as in Lawrence) **Resort Center,** which features Broadway musicals without the late performer's trademark bubbles. Additional eclectics: the **Fern St. Circus,** one ring of theatrical and magical amusements, and the **Spreckels Organ Society,** for free outdoor concerts with a 4,445-pipe organ.

Although San Diegans mourned the day their symphony died, other classical options include the **San Diego Chamber Orchestra,** the Mainly Mozart Festival at the baroque **Spreckels Theater** (June) and the **La Jolla Chamber Music Festival.** There's light opera in the Starlight Bowl, while concerts in all genres are sponsored by places such as Spreckels and **4th and B.** Dancewise, there's the **California Ballet Company** and two modern offerings: **Isaacs/ McCaleb and Dancers,** and **Malashock Dance and Company.** Filipino troupes **Samahan** and **Pasacat,** the **Nations of San Diego** dance festival (January), and other assorted groups round out the scene.

Those looking for visuals will find plenty in San Diego's more than 90 museums. The **Mingei International Museum of World Folk Art,** the **Museum of Photographic Arts,** and the **San Diego Museum of Art,** all clustered together at Balboa Park, enjoy excellent reputations. The **African-American Museum of Fine Arts** and **Japanese Friendship Garden** are relatively recent chronicles of those groups' contributions. The **Stuart Collection** scattered throughout the UCSD campus is an internationally renowned accumulation of contemporary sculpture. The **Museum of Contemporary Art, San Diego** offers homegrown works about the Mexico/United States border experience, while **Centro Cultural de la Raza** focuses on creating native North and Central American art.

Others range from the bodacious **California Surf Museum** to the 's wonnerful **Lawrence Welk Museum** to the **Marine Corps Recruit Depot,** which highlights the military's role in the city's development and is worth at least a few proud grunts of approval. The city's early years are brought to life at **Old Town,** the first European settlement in California and the place where San Diego began; the **Junipero Serra Museum;** the **Villa Montezuma;** and the **George White and Anna Gunn Marston House.** All modes of transportation are covered at **San Diego Maritime Museum, San Diego Aerospace Museum,** the **San Diego Automotive Museum,** and the **San Diego Model Railroad Museum. Balboa Park** alone has 14 cultural and scientific collections.

Although the **San Diego Zoo** represents the premier wildlife experience, about 30 miles from downtown is the **San Diego Wild Animal Park,** a sort of turn-about's-fair-play experience where gorillas, elephants, cheetahs, and more roam free while humans stay in enclosed spaces. It's Shamu time at **Sea World,** where you can see killer whales as well as pet dolphins, star fish, and bat rays (no, thank you). Less threatening (at least to homo sapiens) are the 1,500 fish at the **Stephen Birch Aquarium-Museum,** the public education facility for the Scripps Institution of Oceanography. Other scientific insights can be found through America's largest telescope at the **Palomar Observatory;** at the interactive **Reuben H. Fleet Space Theater and Science Center;** the humanistic **San Diego Museum of Man;** and the **San Diego Natural History Museum,** one of the oldest in the western U.S. The **Children's Museum** encourages creative expression through an arts studio and performance space, while **Virtual World** claims to be the world's first digital theme park with interactive virtual reality adventures.

THE SPORTING LIFE

With a near-perfect climate and a varied terrain, it's no wonder San Diego has been tapped to host several America's Cups sailing matches and 1998's Super Bowl XXXII (at **Jack Murphy Stadium**). San Diego was also selected as the site of the nation's first warm weather, year-round, multi-sport Olympic training complex (**ARCO Training Center**). Although just about every sport can be found here, in-line skating (**Aquarium Surf 'n Skate, Hamel's Action Sports**

Where It's At

(continued)

San Diego Performing Arts League, 710 B St., 238-0700

San Diego Repertory Theater, Lyceum Space, Horton Plaza, 544-1000

San Diego Wild Animal Park, 15500 San Pasqual Valley Rd., Escondido, 747-8702

San Diego Zoo, 2920 Zoo Dr., 234-3153

Sea World, 1720 S. Shores Rd., 226-3901

Simon Edison Centre for the Performing Arts, P.O. Box 2171, 239-2255

Sledgehammer, 964 5th Ave., 544-1484

Southeast Community Theater, 1549 El Prado, 233-4913

Spreckels Organ Society, Balboa Park, P.O. Box 6726, 226-0819

Spreckels Theater, 121 Broadway, 534-TIXS

Starlight Musical Theater, Starlight Bowl, Balboa Park, 239-0512

Stephen Birch Aquarium-Museum, 2300 Expedition Way, La Jolla, 534-FISH

Stuart Collection, 9500 Gilman Dr., 534-2117

Sushi Performance Art Space, 320 11th Ave., 235-2266

Teatro Mascara Magica, 444 4th Ave., 234-9583

Theater in Old Town, 4040 Twiggs St., 688-2494

Villa Montezuma, 1925 K St., 239-2211

Virtual World, 7510 Hazard Center Dr., 294-9200

Welk Resort Center, 8860 Lawrence Welk Dr., Escondido, 749-3448

Where It's At

 Unless otherwise noted, all area codes are 619.

A Balloon Tour, 3443 Tripp Ct., 481-9122

Aquarium Surf 'n Skate, 747 Pacific Beach Dr., 488-9733

Where It's At

(continued)

ARCO Training Center, 1750 Wueste Rd., Chula Vista, 656-1500

Barona Casino, 1000 Wildcat Canyon Rd., Lakeside, 800/227-8238

Baywatch Cruises, 2051 Shelter Island, 222-9999

Bike Tours San Diego, 360 7th Ave., 238-2444

Caliente Jai Alai Fronton Palicio, 7th St. & Revolucion Ave., Tijuana, 231-1910

Caliente Race Track, Blvd. Agua Caliente, Tijuana, 231-1910

California Department of Fish and Game, 525-4215

California Water Sports, 4215 Harrison St., Carlsbad, 434-3089

Carmel Mountain Ranch Country Club, 14050 Carmel Ridge Rd., 451-8353

City Lakes Information Line, 465-3474

De Anza Harbor Resort, 2727 De Anza Rd., 273-3214

Del Mar Thoroughbred Club, 2260 Jimmy Durante Blvd., Del Mar, 755-1141

Del Sol Aquatic Adventures, P.O. Box 2691, La Jolla, 459-4883

Five-Star Tours, 232-5049

Gravity Activated Sports, 16220 Hwy. 76, Pauma Valley, 742-2294

Hamel's Action Sports Center, 704 Ventura, Mission Beach, 488-5050

Harborside Golf Center, 801 W. Ash St., 239-4653

Jack Murphy Stadium, 9449 Friars Blvd., 280-2111

Lake Cuymaca Recreation and Park District, 15027 California Hwy. 79, Julian, 447-8123

Mar Tar Awa, 25 Browns Rd., Alpine, 445-3275

Pala Mesa Resort, 2001 Old Hwy. 395, Fallbrook, 728-5881

Plymouth Holiday Bowl, P.O. Box 601400, 283-5808

San Diego Air Sports Center, 13531 Otay Lakes Rd., Jamul, 421-0968

San Diego Chargers, Jack Murphy Stadium, 280-2111

San Diego County Parks Society, P.O. Box 957, Bonita, 267-7323

Center) is particularly popular among locals, and there are plenty of beaches as well as bike and mountain trails (**Bike Tours San Diego, Solid Rock Gym**). **Gravity Activated Sports** offers the Palomar Plunge, a 16-mile, 5000-foot guided bicycle descent, with lunch thrown in—provided you can keep it down.

The region's many parks include the previously mentioned Balboa, 1,200 acres just north of downtown, and Mission Bay, the largest facility of its kind devoted to water sports and public recreation. Its 27 miles of beaches encompass six designated swimming areas as well as expanses for picnics, hiking, and bicycling. San Diego Bay is another popular spot. As the home port for Navy ships, it is also a major sailing and cruising mecca (**San Diego Harbor Excursions, Baywatch Cruises,** others) and contains waterfront parks such as Shelter Island, Harbor Island, Coronado Tidelands, National City, and more. Publications such as the *Guide to San Diego County Parks* (**San Diego County Parks Society**) and the *Park and Recreation Facilities Guide* (**San Diego Parks and Recreation Department**) have more information.

Whatever your sport, it's likely to be found here, and it's almost always a good way to meet others. Options begin up in the air with barnstorming (**Taildragger Adventures**), skydiving (**San Diego Air Sports Center**), ballooning (**A Balloon Tour**), and sailplaning (**Sky Sailing**). Closer to terra firma are fishing in 18 fresh water lakes (**City Lakes Information Line; California Department of Fish and Game; Lake Cuymaca Recreation and Park District**), water sports (**California Water Sports; Del Sol Aquatic Adventures;** (egad!) **San Diego Shark Diving**), and camping (**De Anza Harbor Resort; Mar Tar Awa**). More than 80 golf courses (**Harborside Golf Center; Carmel Mountain Ranch Country Club; Pala Mesa Resort**) as well as 1,200 tennis courts (**San Diego District Tennis Association; San Diego Tennis Patrons; United States Professional Tennis Association**) complete the cycle of year-round events.

Those wanting a break from all the activity can live vicariously through the NFL **San Diego Chargers** and the **San Diego Padres** baseball team, both at Jack Murphy Stadium, or the **San Diego Sockers** soccer team. The **Plymouth Holiday Bowl** offers college football clashes each December. There's horse racing at Del Mar Fairgrounds (**Del Mar Thoroughbred Club**), polo at the **San Diego Polo Club,** Jai Alai at **Caliente**

Jai Alai Fronton Palicio, and greyhounds at the **Caliente Race Track,** with bullfights being held on Sundays in Tijuana from May through October (contact **Five-Star Tours** for more information). The **Barona Casino, Sycuan Gaming Center,** and **Viejas Casino and Turf Club** provide other ways to while away time and money with a minimum of sweat—unless, of course, you're losing.

AFTER-HOURS DIVERSIONS

With redevelopment in the form of striking mirror-like skyscrapers, a $165 million convention center, Horton Plaza shopping center, several new hotels, and a $2.8 million Children's Park, downtown is the place to be. "There's so much going on in the Gaslamp Quarter that some nights you can barely navigate the sidewalk," observes Lovelace. "It's a lot of fun," with bars, restaurants, and shops crammed from Fifth Avenue at Harbor Drive and spreading 16 blocks to the north and west. Finding a space for your car in this area can be a real killer, so wear comfortable shoes and expect to do lots of walking. Or pray that the parking gods are smiling.

Although Gaslamp is "dressier than the rest of the city," this is a relative term in a place where tank tops show up just about anywhere outside of the office. Additional upscale action can be found in clubs and neighborhood pubs in Mission Valley, La Jolla, and North County, while the community of Hillcrest has a number of gay and alternative bars.

Along with boardwalks and breweries, the beaches—Ocean, Pacific, Mission, and others—are so laid-back you might get away with wearing a bathing suit or reasonable facsimile. **Imperial Beach** in Chula Vista is home to the world's longest-running sand castle competition (July), while **Garnet Avenue** on Pacific Beach is a guaranteed people-watching spot, inside or out.

Those looking for cheap margaritas and loud discos will find these and more at Avenida Revolucion and the new Rio Tijuana area in Tijuana. It's best to take the San Diego Trolley when partying there, however, as U.S. laws don't necessarily work in Mexico and U.S. Customs can be a real buzzkill when it comes to alcohol consumption. (Make sure you know when the last trolley leaves for San Diego). Although it can be a great time, "in many ways, Tijuana is similar to New York City," cautions Inzuza. "You have to know where to go" in order to remain safe.

San Diego District Tennis Association, 2221 Morley Field Dr., 299-8647

San Diego Harbor Excursions, 1050 Harbor Dr., 234-4111

San Diego Padres, Jack Murphy Stadium, 283-7294

San Diego Parks and Recreation Department, 525-8285

San Diego Polo Club, 14555 El Camino Real, Rancho Santa Fe, 481-9217

San Diego Shark Diving, P.O. Box 8881037, 299-8560

San Diego Sockers, San Diego Sports Arena, 224-4625

San Diego Tennis Patrons, 6275 Lusk Blvd., 452-9910

Sky Sailing, 31930 California Hwy. 79, Warner Springs, 782-0404

Solid Rock Gym, 2074 Hancock St., 299-1124

Sycuan Gaming Center, 5469 Dehesa Rd., El Cajon, 800/27-BINGO

Taildragger Adventures, 4855 Cole St., 272-8273

United States Professional Tennis Association, San Diego Tennis & Racquet Club, 4848 Tecolote Rd., 275-3270

Viejas Casino and Turf Club, 5000 Willows Rd., Alpine, 800/84-POKER

Where It's At

Unless otherwise noted, all area codes are 619.

Annual Poinsettia Street Festival, Main Street, Encinitas, 943-1950

Barona PowWow, 443-6612

Belly up Tavern, 143 S. Cedros Ave., Solana Beach, 481-9022

Blind Melons, 710 Garnet Ave., 483-7844

Cabrillo National Monument, 557-5450

Cafe Crema, 1001 Garnet Ave., 273-3558

California Coffee Works, 202 C St., 722-7160

Characters, 4240 La Jolla Village Dr., La Jolla, 587-1414

Where It's At

Trendy clubs serving up a potpourri of live music, local bands, and DJ mixes include **E Street Alley, Blind Melons,** and **Belly up Tavern,** while **D.W.'s Pub** and **Grant Grill** specialize in jazz and blues. More conservative hangouts can be found in the various hotels, such as **Club 950** and **Club Max,** to mention a very few.

Themed venues revolve around sports (**Horton's; Characters; Padres Pub; Tournament of Champions Lounge**), comedy (**Comedy Isle;** the **Comedy Store;** the **Improv**) and dinner-dance cruises (**Hornblower Dining Yachts, Invader Cruises,** others). With music, poetry, and readings, coffeehouses brew a quieter atmosphere. The highest concentration is near Garnet Avenue and in and around the Gaslamp Quarter (**Cafe Crema, California Coffee Works, Pannikin Coffee and Tea**). Those interested in reading their work aloud might try Friday evenings at the **Writing Center.**

Like the Energizer Bunny, San Diego's annual events keep on going, thanks to the clement weather. In January and February, folks can participate in the **San Diego Marathon,** whale watching (**Cabrillo National Monument**), the Mission Mardi Gras (**Mission San Luis Rey**), and the Buick Invitational golf tournament (**Torrey Pines Golf Course**). Spring brings out everyone's Irish at the **St. Patrick's Day Parade and Festival** (March); environmental concerns during **Earth Fair** (April); and the Hispanic community at **Cinco de Mayo** (May).

Edibles, art, and/or agriculture are celebrated at the **Del Mar Fair** (June), **La Jolla Festival** (June), **Julian Apple Harvest Festival** (October), and **Ocean Beach Restaurant Walk** (November), while ethnic groups show their pride at the **Latin American Festival** (August), **Barona PowWow** (September), and **International Friendship Festival** (September). Budding architects who find the previously mentioned sand castle competition too ephemeral might participate in the **LEGO Construction Zone** contest (October). The year ends with sleigh bells (but no snow) at **Christmas on the Farm** (November), the **Annual Poinsettia Street Festival** (December), the **Ocean Beach Parade and Tree Festival** (December), and many more.

 ## CULINARY AND SHOPPING HAUNTS

Although some have accused San Diego of being food-impaired and overly health conscious, area specialties such as fish tacos (found at just about any local fast-food stand), fresh seafood, and anything Mexican are hard to top. Nearly half of this town's 5,200 eating and drinking establishments consist of full-service restaurants; offerings range from British (**Elephant & Castle**) to shark, emu, and other "down under" delicacies at **Sydney's Australian Grill,** with dozens of other countries in between. Like everything else, meals cost a bit more here, although it's possible to dine relatively cheaply, if you know where to go (Mexican, pasta houses, and Oriental restaurants are generally a good bet).

Restaurant row at the Gaslamp Quarter offers an abundant selection, from buffalo and ostrich (as well as ribs) at **Buffalo Joe's** to Cajun (**Bayou Bar & Grill**) to Spanish (**Ole Madrid Cafe; Cafe Sevilla; La Gran Tapa**) to natural/vegetarian at **Kung Food.** Italian is the most well-represented cuisine here; popular spots include **Asti, Bella Luna,** and **Fio's,** while **Salvatore's, John Tarantino's, Sante Restaurant,** and more can be found elsewhere in the region. American/California cuisine figures prominently in the Quarter, with **Croce's,** established by Ingrid Croce in honor of her late husband Jim, **Dakota Grill & Spirits, Dick's Last Resort** (which sells commemorative g-strings along with barbecue), and **RJ's Riptide Brewery.**

Mexican (**Baja Brewery; Cervecerias La Cruda**), Oriental (**China Camp; Taca Sushi; Royal Thai**), and Greek (**Athens Market Taverna; Greek Islands Cafe**) complete the mini-world tour. Old Town is noted for its Mexican fare: **Acapulco, Cafe Coyote, El Fandango,** and others can be found there.

American food seems to predominate elsewhere, particularly downtown, at places such as **Planet Hollywood, Sunsets American Bar & Grill,** and **Chino's. Charley Brown's** is set in a replica of a circa 1880s riverboat. Seafood can be netted at **Brigantine, Red Sails Inn,** and **Anthony's,** which has been around for about half a century. And it's possible to have a good beef at the **Chart House, Ruth's Chris,** and **Rainwater's.**

You can do the '50s thing with burgers, fries, shakes, and other comfort food at **Corvette Diner** or **City Delicatessen** or go for fancy French at **Marius** or **Chez Loma.** This being California, it's natural that many places serve the healthful, namesake cuisine of pizza, pasta, and salads: **Sammy's, Ida Bailey's, Cafe San Diego, California Cuisine,** and **Crocodile Cafe. Mr. A's, Dobson's, Lael's, Molly's,** and **Top O' the Cove** dish out Continental grub, while those preferring Indian can opt for **Ashoka** and **Star of India.**

San Diego's shopping opportunities are tough to duplicate. You can swap till you drop or attend farmer's markets galore, not to mention the bizarre, uh, bazaar-like

Where It's At

(continued)

St. Patrick's Day Parade and Festival, Balboa Park, 299-7812

Torrey Pines Golf Course, La Jolla, 281-4653

Tournament of Champions Lounge, La Costa Resort, Costa del Mar Rd., Carlsbad, 438-9111

Writing Center, 416 3rd Ave., 230-0670

Where It's At

 Unless otherwise noted, all area codes are 619.

Acapulco, 2467 San Juan St., 260-8124

Anthony's, 5232 Lovelock St., 291-7254

Ashoka, 8008 Girard Ave., La Jolla, 454-6263

Asti, 728 5th Ave., 232-8844

Athens Market Taverna, 119 W. F St., 234-1955

Baja Brewery, 203 5th Ave., 231-9279

Bayou Bar & Grill, 329 Market St., 696-8747

Bazaar del Mundo, 2754 Calhoun St., 298-1141

Bella Luna, 748 5th Ave., 239-3222

Belmont Park, 3146 Mission Blvd., 491-2988

Brigantine, 7889 Ostrow St., 268-1030

Buffalo Joe's, 600 5th Ave., 233-2672

Cafe Coyote, 2461 San Diego Ave., 291-4695

Cafe San Diego, 910 Broadway Cir., 239-2200

Cafe Sevilla, 555 4th Ave., 233-5979

California Cuisine, 1027 University Ave, 543-0790

Cervecerias La Cruda, 500 4th Ave., 554-1895

Charley Brown's, 880 E. Harbor St., 291-1870

Chart House, 1701 Strand Way, Coronado, 435-0155

Chez Loma, 1132 Loma Ave., Coronado, 435-0661

Where It's At

(continued)

China Camp, 2137 Pacific Hwy., 232-0686

Chino's, 919 4th Ave., 231-9240

Chula Vista Center, 555 Broadway, 422-7500

City Delicatessen, 535 University Ave., 295-2747

Coast Walk/Green Dragon Colony, 1298 Prospect St., 454-3031

Coronado, Corner of 1st and B sts., 741-3763

Corvette Diner, 3946 5th Ave., 542-1001

Costa Verde Shopping Center, 8650 Genesee Ave., 458-9270

Croce's, 802 5th Ave., 232-4338

Crocodile Cafe, 394 Fashion Valley, 692-0116

Dakota Grill & Spirits, 901 5th Ave., 265-5554

Del Mar, 1050 Camino Del Mar, 727-1471

Del Mar Plaza, 1555 Camino Del Mar, 792-1555

Dick's Last Resort, 345 4th Ave., 231-9100

Dobson's, 956 Broadway Circle, 231-6771

El Cajon, El Cajon at Marlborough, 440-5027

El Fandango, 2734 Calhoun St., 298-2860

Elephant & Castle, 1355 N. Harbor Dr., 234-9777

Encinitas, I St. between 1st and 2nd, 943-1950

Escondido, 635 W. Mission Ave., 745-3100

Fashion Valley, 452 Fashion Valley, 297-3381 or 688-9100

Ferry Landing Marketplace, 1201 First St., 435-8895

Fio's, 801 5th Ave., 234-3467

Greek Islands Cafe, Seaport Village, 239-5216

Grossmont Center, 5500 Grossmont Center Dr., La Mesa, 465-2900

Hazard Center, 7676 Hazard Center Dr., 497-2674

atmosphere of Tijuana, where vendors vigorously peddle clothing, pottery, jewelry, leather, and tequila, although all but the last should be examined carefully before handing over your money. Although you can get good buys, shoddy workmanship and overcharging do occur.

Swap meets can be found in San Diego proper (**Kobey's; South Bay**) as well as in **Escondido, National City, Oceanside,** and elsewhere, while every day but Monday yields up a farmer's market including **Coronado** (Tuesday), **North County** (Wednesday), **Oceanside** (Thursday), **Encinitas** (Friday), **Del Mar** (Saturday), and **El Cajon** (Sunday).

Shoppers who appreciate unique architecture and lots of steps will find downtown's **Horton Plaza,** with 150-some stores tucked into several pastel-colored levels, an experience. Anchored by three major department chains, Horton also has custom dress shirt shops as well as emporiums owned by PBS and the Discovery Channel. "Locals either love it or hate it," admits Lovelace. "Parking's really expensive and for the most part you can find the same thing at suburban malls." Plus you have to try to remember which store is on which floor.

Across from Horton Plaza, the **Paladion** has only three levels and a nifty open atrium with an Art Deco–inspired facade, along with sticker shockers like Gucci, Cartier, et al. Those looking for something quainter will find it at **Seaport Village,** also located downtown. With 60 specialty boutiques, nearly 20 restaurants, and an antique carousel, it recreates a California harbor setting of a century ago.

The surrounding area has lots of goodies as well. Across San Diego Bay on Coronado is the **Ferry Landing Marketplace,** the original dock now redeveloped as a $6.5 million retail and specialty/entertainment complex, including waterfront dining and one-of-a-kind shops. Within Old Town State Park, **Bazaar del Mundo** is a colorful complex with Mexican gifts minus the border hassles and haggling as well as an array of ethnic clothing, jewelry, pottery, furnishings, and other items. The **Old Town Esplanade** has more specialty shops, restaurants, galleries, and a southwestern marketplace. In Mission Valley, the **Hazard Center** features centrally located stores, restaurants, cinema, and the previously mentioned Virtual World, while Mission Beach offers browsing with a roller coaster and more at **Belmont Park.** Still more ocean views can be found at the shops in the **Coast Walk/Green Dragon Colony.**

La Jolla boasts Prospect Street, the "Rodeo Drive" of San Diego, which brims with designer clothing, jewelry, and fine art, while the **Costa Verde Shopping Center** in the nearby Golden Triangle offers a unique mix of specialty stores and services in an open-air setting. The European-style retail village of **Del Mar Plaza** nestles into a hillside with winding walkways and piazzas.

San Diego's major malls, many of which are outdoors, provide even more options. Both **Fashion Valley** and **Mission Valley Center** have many big-name emporiums as well the usual restaurant/cinema combos. Other players include **Chula Vista Center, Grossmont Center, North County Fair, Parkway Plaza, Plaza Bonita,** and more. Outlet shoppers will find the deal of the millennium at the **San Diego Factory Outlet Center,** the **San Diego North County Factory Outlet Center,** and, a bit farther north, at the **Lake Elsinore Outlet Center.**

 ## ETHNIC AND RELIGIOUS PROSPECTS

Immigration issues—from highway traffic signs depicting fleeing families to news reports about deportation to elimination of social services for children of illegals born in the U.S.—color life in San Diego. "It's a terrible situation," admits Land. "Many of these people are hard workers who want a better life. You see them crossing the border in droves and you know some are going to get hurt or killed."

Economic development is one good solution, according to Inzuza. "A middle class is beginning to emerge in Mexico. The country has a lot of potential."

It's a good time to be Hispanic in San Diego, he believes. "Things are really beginning to open up." Plus, "there's a large pool of single Latinos." The **South County Economic Development Council** and local churches (**Hispanic Presbyterian Church; 1st Hispanic Church; Catholic Diocese of San Diego;** many others) are ways to get connected.

Blacks, however, have a different situation. Comprising less than 10 percent of the population, "we're definitely a minority," notes Mitchell. The **Black Economic Development Task Force** or the **African Community Services** might provide a springboard to meeting others. Although some might disagree, "the county is very religious, particularly the Hispanic and African-American communities."

San Diego houses of worship encompass the full spectrum, ranging from **Church of Today** to the **1st Unitarian Universalist** to **Clairemont Covenant Church** to the **Chinese Community Church** as well as dozens of Churches of Jesus Christ of the Latter Day Saints, Churches of Christ, Episcopal Churches, and more. Jews can contact the **United Jewish Federation** for information.

Where It's At

(continued)

Horton Plaza, 324 Horton Plaza, 238-1596

Ida Bailey's, 311 Island Ave., 544-1886

John Tarantino's, 5150 Harbor Dr., 224-3555

Kobey's, 3500 Sports Arena Dr., 226-0650

Kung Food, 2949 5th Ave., 298-7302

La Gran Tapa, 611 B St., 234-8272

Lael's, 1 Market Pl., 232-1234

Lake Elsinore Outlet Center, 17600 Collier Ave., Lake Elsinore, 909/245-4989

Marius, 2000 2nd St., Coronado, 435-3000

Mission Valley Center, 1640 Camino del Rio N., 296-6375

Molly's, 333 W. Harbor Dr., 234-1500

Mr. A's, 2550 5th Ave., 239-1377

National City, 3201 D Ave., 477-2203

North County, 12679 Sunset Dr., 967-9120

North County Fair, 272 E. Via Rancho Pkwy., Escondido, 489-2332

Oceanside, 3480 Mission Ave., 757-5286

Oceanside, 500 block of 3rd St., 440-5027

Old Town Esplanade, 291-1019

Ole Madrid Cafe, 751 5th Ave., 557-0146

Paladion, 777 Front St., 232-1627

Parkway Plaza, 415 Parkway Plaza, El Cajon, 579-9932

Planet Hollywood, 197 Horton Ave., 702-7827

Plaza Bonita, 3030 Plaza Bonita Rd., National City, 267-2850

Rainwater's, 1201 Kettner Blvd., 233-5757

Red Sails Inn, 2614 Shelter Island Dr., 223-3030

RJ's Riptide Brewery, 301 5th Ave., 231-7700

Royal Thai, 467 5th Ave., 231-1990

Ruth's Chris, 1355 N. Harbor Dr., 233-1422

Salvatore's, 750 Front St., 544-1865

Sammy's, 702 Pearl St., 456-8018

Where It's At

(continued)

San Diego Factory Outlet Center, 4495 B Camino de la Plaza, San Ysidro, 690-4492

San Diego North County Factory Outlet Center, 1050 Los Vallecitos Blvd., San Marcos, 595-5222

Sante Restaurant, 7811 Herschel Ave., La Jolla, 454-1315

Seaport Village, W. Harbor Dr. at Kettner Blvd., 235-4014

South Bay, 2170 Coronado, 423-9676

Star of India, 423 F St., 544-9891, other locations

Sunsets American Bar & Grill, 1617 1st Ave., 239-6171

Sydney's Australian Grill, 11915 El Camino Real, 481-6200

Taca Sushi, 555 5th Ave., 238-0555

Top O' the Cove, 1216 Prospect St., La Jolla, 454-7779

Where It's At

 Unless otherwise noted, all area codes are 619.

1st Hispanic Church, 970 Los Vallecitos Blvd., San Marcos, 591-3670

1st Unitarian Universalist, 4190 Front St., 298-9978

African Community Services, 4629 Market St., 527-1075

Black Economic Development Task Force, 720 Gateway Center Dr., 266-7272

Catholic Diocese of San Diego, 3888 Paducah Dr., 490-8200

Chinese Community Church, 1750 47th St., 262-5433

Church of Today, 8999 Activity Rd. 689-6500

Clairemont Covenant Church, 5255 Mount Ararat Dr., 279-6130

Hispanic Presbyterian Church, 320 Date St., 232-7518

South County Economic Development Council, 1200 A Ave., National City, 336-2474

United Jewish Federation, 16236 San Dieguito Dr., Rancho Santa Fe, 759-0600

CRIB SHEET

According to the National Association of Home Builders, 40 percent of the homes sold in San Diego in 1995 were affordable to a middle-income household, compared to 17 percent in 1989, although the area still remains one the most expensive in the U.S.

Many newcomers opt for apartments, although rents have risen as vacancy rates plummet. "Lots of condos and lofts are being built or renovated downtown," notes Inzuza. "Little Italy, Uptown, Golden Hill, and Center City East" are other places with a selection of units as well as lively surrounding communities.

For a two-bedroom, rents range from $529 a month in southeast San Diego and $537 in the rural community of Ramona to $1,375 in Coronado, $1,353 in Rancho Santa Fe, and $1,002 in Downtown. Other desirable spots include LaJolla ($965), Pacific Beach ($955), Encinitas ($796), Hillcrest ($761), Old Town ($760), Imperial Beach ($657), Ocean Beach ($650), and Escondido ($633). Access Apartment Referrals (800/217-3272), Apartment Finders (800/700-3463), Tenant Finders (574-8035), and others can provide leads.

Residences in San Diego proper fit into a variety of price ranges, with condos starting at $59,000 to mansions upwards of $2,500,000. There are planned communities, such as Carmel Mountain Ranch, as well as the apartment, condo, and refurbished-home intensive Crown Point. Those looking for the inexpensive will find it in East San Diego, while houses in the College area, located near San Diego State University, are also reasonably priced. Golden Hill is a beginner's bargain.

A bit farther from the city center is the Golden Triangle, a self-contained community with hotels, homes, apartments, and stores. Hillcrest/Uptown is another happening place: Within walking distance of Balboa Park, it features bookstores, art movie houses, and more. With a median income of over $35,000, young professionals flock to the ravines and valleys of Kearny Mesa and Serra Mesa, while the oceanside community of La Jolla ("the jewel") has thriving, upscale business and fashion districts, with homes priced accordingly. Rancho Bernardo is another ritzy magnet, with outstanding residences, shops, schools, and recreational facilities. In contrast, Linda Vista is loaded with 1940s-style dwellings at a (relatively) reasonable cost, while Mid-City offers small single-family places and student apartments.

Those not minding even older homes (1920s) can opt for trendy North Park. The youthful neighborhoods surrounding Mission, Ocean, and Pacific Beaches provide lots of beach houses and condos, while the amenities of Mission Valley (malls, golf courses, Jack Murphy Stadium), make it popular with starter couples and singles. Those looking for ethnic diversity will find it in Paradise Hills, while Point Loma near the San Diego Bay has great views and a median age of about 25.

Many communities in East County have retained their rural flavor while undergoing redevelopment and a resurgence of popularity. North Inland San Diego still has lots of horses and roadside vegetable stands. Proximity to U.S. military centers has resulted in a boom for South San Diego, where the median age of most residents is well under 30 and housing costs are much cheaper.

Okay, so San Diego schools were one of the lowest ranked on recent SATs (partially because of students for whom English is a second language), and class sizes in California tend to be on the large side (25 to 35 students per class). Still, the public system is flexible: Not only can parents send their kids to any school they wish as long as space is available, but the district's 45 magnet programs offer specialized courses and there are options for children with exceptional needs as well. Kids can even go year-round (180 days of staggered instruction) in some areas (San Diego County Office of Education, 292-3500). "The schools really are working on improving programs," adds Lovelace. "And the private schools are great" and consist of several parochial and preparatory choices (San Diego Family Press, 685-6970).

UCSD, the University of San Diego, and National University were ranked among America's best colleges by *U.S. News & World Report*. They are among the dozens of area universities, community, and vocational/technical specialty schools, which offer everything from health, liberal arts, and sciences (San Diego City College) to advertising (Advertising Arts College) to English and other languages (College of English Language).

NAVIGATING SAN DIEGO

Particularly to folks from Los Angeles, San Diego traffic is a walk in the park. Not only are highways and streets clearly delineated and laid out on a logical pattern, but traffic is actually orderly. "It's blissfully easy to get around in," observes Lovelace. But watch out when it rains: "People act like they've forgotten how to drive. There can be 250 accidents in an hour." About 2 1/2 hours from L.A. on Interstate 5 (which stretches from Canada to the Mexican border), San Diego is served from the east by I-8 and California Highway 52 and from the north by I-15, which runs from Nevada and the intermountain West.

"You don't fear for your life when you get on the freeway, although traffic can get pretty heavy in certain spots," remarks Mitchell. The addition of High Occupancy Vehicle (HOV) lanes and a commuter train (the Coaster, 800/262-7837 or 233-3004) have helped eliminate the dreaded gridlock, "although people still like to use their own cars." A color-coded curb marking system tells you where you can and cannot park; if your vehicle is missing, call 531-2844 before contacting the police. The San Diego Transit Corporation (233-3004) and the San Diego Trolley (595-4949 or 231-8549) provide extensive service.

A few minutes' drive from downtown, the San Diego International Airport/Lindbergh Field (574-1234 or 231-2100) serves more than 13 million passengers and recently underwent a multimillion dollar upgrade and expansion. The Port of San Diego has also become a popular leisure time destination, with cruise ships departing regularly as well as a ferry to Coronado Island (San Diego Coronado Ferry, 234-4111). You can also leave town via conventional means such as Amtrak (239-9021) or Greyhound bus (234-8301; others).

SAN FRANCISCO, CALIFORNIA

A Brief Glance

Size and Growth: 759,300 (city); 6,504,600 (MSA). Percent change: 1980–1990: +6.6% (city). Percent change, 1990–1995: +1.7% (city).

Money Matters: *Unemployment rate—* 5.5%.
Per capita income—$19,695.
Average household income—$45,664.
Average cost of a home—$393,027.
Average rent for an apartment— $1,162/month.
*ACCRA Cost of Living Index (based on 100)—*167.5.
*ACCRA Housing Index—*288.1.

People Profile: *Crime rate* (per 100,000 population)—8,341,8 (city), 5,998.8 (MSA).

*Racial and ethnic characteristics—*White: 53.6% (city), 66.2% (MSA); Black: 10.9% (city), 7.6% (MSA); American Indian/ Eskimo/Aleut: 0.5% (city), 0.5% (MSA); Asian/Pacific Islander: 29.1% (city), 20.5% (MSA); Hispanic Origin: 13.3% (city), 14.1% (MSA); Other: 5.8% (city), 5.3% (MSA).
*Gender ratio—*N/A.
*Age characteristics—*18–24 (9.8%); 25–44 (38.2%). Median age: 35.7.

Major Players: Services, retail/ wholesale trade, government, finance/ insurance/real estate.

SAN FRANCISCO: WHAT A RUSH

Getting a fix on San Francisco is almost like trying to bottle its trademark fog: Just when you think you've grasped it, it disappears and reveals something else entirely. San Francisco—known as simply "The City" to locals and never as Frisco—is unlike any other American town. With cable cars (whose continuance rallied a $60 million renovation effort), and the architecturally astounding Golden Gate Bridge (actually, it's orange-red), San Francisco is a gateway to the Pacific Rim, Mexico, and Latin America. Its citizenry is truly diverse. No ethnic group seems to dominate, and equal opportunity abounds. One of the most scenic metropoli around, San Francisco is also the most compact—a peninsula (about 46 square miles) surrounded by the Pacific Ocean, Golden Gate Strait, and landlocked San Francisco Bay.

And the weather is nice but weird. Naturally air-conditioned, the city has average temperatures from 54° to 65° in summer and 45° to 59° in winter, with lots of sunshine and fog during June, July, and August.

Neighborhoods range from colorful, crammed Chinatown (the largest Chinese community outside Asia); to Japantown, home of the Japan Center, five acres of hotels, shops, theaters, and restaurants; to the mostly Italian North Beach; to the largely Latino Mission District. Other communities include Nob Hill, with its palatial mansions, hotels, and hoity-toity organizations; and the Haight-Asbury district, the greenhouse of flower power, fertilized by sex, drugs, and rock 'n' roll. Yet people dress up to go to the opera and other social functions. Donning resort wear (and referring to cable cars as "trolleys") can separate the 16 million or so folks who visit the city each year from those who at least pretend that they've been here for a while.

Highlighted by the 853-foot TransAmerica Pyramid—whose white steeple was once mistaken for a very tall church by yet another itinerant tourist—San Francisco's 70 high-rises are scattered among its 43 hills, with the most notable being Russian, Rincon, Telegraph, Twin Peaks, Lone Mountain, Mount Davidson, and the aforementioned Nob.

The terrain can make driving in the city—instead of relying on the very extensive and dependable BART (Bay Area Rapid Transit) or MUNI (San Francisco Municipal Railway)—fraught with hazards. Tires on wet cable car tracks can cause your vehicle to go down instead of up a hill or result in a sudden about-face into oncoming traffic. Should you park on any incline, remember to turn your wheels into the curb, set your emergency brake, and for God's sakes, set your gear on *P.* When a sign says *Grade,* it's not referring to a rating system but a hill that's pretty steep. Try to avoid Lombardi street, allegedly the most crooked in the world, unless you actually enjoy turning at a 40-degree angle.

This city is enough to make any newcomer's head spin. The Marina, Pier 39, and Fisherman's Wharf are jam-packed with seafood restaurants, fishing boats, shops, street performers, and artists. Once a fearful federal penitentiary, Alcatraz is now a major tourist attraction, while 1,107-acre Golden Gate Park is loaded with museums, lakes, and trails for golf, tennis, boating, hiking, biking, and more. A monument to the firefighters who battled the flames from the 1906 earthquake, the 210-foot Coit Tower is supposedly designed after the shape of a hose nozzle, or perhaps something more suggestive. And the only tipping you'll do in Cow Hollow (formerly a dairy district) is in the various chic restaurants and shops. Smack-dab in the middle of one of the world's busiest commerce and financial centers is Union Square, a 2.6-acre plot manicured with palms, Irish yews, flowers, and couture boutiques. And that's only part of the hodgepodge.

Yet unconventionality has always been a San Francisco trademark. Originally a Spanish outpost, it was still a part of Mexico as late as 1834. By the time the sleepy town had been incorporated into the state of California, gold was discovered nearby, and the whole place went crazy, sort of like when the namesake 49ers win the Super Bowl (as they've done five times) or the National League Giants capture yet another pennant. Along with drawing folks from all over the world, gold (and, later, silver) mining helped make San Francisco the merchandising and financial hub of the West.

Although the city was decimated by earthquakes in 1906 and (to a much lesser extent) in 1989, it made a quick recovery both times. Unfortunately, the same can't be said for its significant gay population. As the center of gay civil rights activism since the 1970s, and with the highest percentage of HIV cases in the U.S., San Francisco has had its numbers greatly reduced by the AIDS epidemic.

Local boosters dub San Francisco "everyone's favorite city," and many, such as the late Soviet premier Nikita Kruschchev (who threatened to bury America during the height of the Cold War) agree. Still others "prefer a wet San Francisco to a dry Manhattan," according to one wag.

> In San Francisco, being a straight WASP male might almost be a disadvantage. Neighborhoods range from colorful, crammed Chinatown (the largest Chinese community outside Asia) to Japantown to the mostly Italian North Beach to the largely Latino Mission District to Castro Street, center of San Francisco's politically strong gay community.

General Opportunities

With 35 colleges and universities, including the University of California at Berkeley, Stanford University, and San Francisco State, the population is well educated, with 50 percent more college graduates than the national average. Thanks to mostly higher salaries, particularly in engineering and at the professional and executive levels, San Francisco is affluent as well, despite a cost of living that's almost as steep as some of the hills. For instance, computer systems analysts have an average annual income of about $43,000 (programmers make $37,000), while drafters and engineering technicians earn $36,000 and $34,500, respectively. Even word processors ($28,500), secretaries ($26,000), and maintenance electricians ($50,000) pull in good bucks.

A powerhouse financial center as well as a favorite of corporations, San Francisco also provides a supportive environment for entrepreneurs. Minority- and women-owned enterprises thrive here; females alone own nearly 65,000 companies, followed by Asian-Americans (about 20,000), blacks (about 9,500), and Latinos (about 8,000).

With the city's unemployment consistently below state levels but pretty much mirroring the U.S., area jobs have increased in recent years. Growth industries consist of software development, networking and biotechnology, finance, apparel and product design, architecture, and multimedia. Overseas markets have expanded greatly for many of these industries, particularly with regard to knowledge and information technologies. And foreign trade volume has blossomed at a remarkable 25 percent a year.

The only proverbial fly is housing, with the city proper dominated by apartments and a vacancy rate for all residences at under 5 percent. But there's plenty to choose from in outlying areas, and, as an added bonus, the temperature goes up one degree for every mile you travel away from the city. So, if it's 65 in San Francisco, it will be in the 80s in Marin County across the Golden Gate bridge. Far out.

HOW SAN FRANCISCO WORKS AND PLAYS

Major Breadwinning

Along with Fortune 500 companies like Airtouch Communications, Bank America, Chevron oil, the Gap, and Wells Fargo Bank, San Francisco's other big employers include Pacific Telesis telecommunications, Hewlett-Packard, Safeway groceries, and Southern Pacific railroads. Privately owned enterprises consist of Bechtel engineering, Levi Strauss & Co., New United Motor Manufacturing (automobiles), and G.F. Industries (snack foods). Women and minorities are behind such famous area-based businesses as Jessica McClintock clothing and fragrances, Discovery Toys, and Act I Personnel Service. San Francisco's largest foreign-owned companies include Fireman's Fund Insurance, Genetech biotechnology, Roche Bioscience pharmaceuticals, and the Bank of California, as well as the smaller Miller Friedman publishing, Sega interactive entertainment, Nestle Beverage, and ANA Hotels.

A cornerstone of the area economy since the Gold Rush days, finance and banking account for 8 percent of the city's total employment. People with these skills can take them to the Federal Reserve Bank, United States Mint, Federal Home Loan Bank, and numerous private institutions. San Francisco's banks actually walk on the wild side, having pioneered such innovations as suburban branches, interstate banking, discount brokerages, and more. Who knows what these crazy folks will think of next!

Worldwide business and trade are booming, thanks to the Port of San Francisco and the San Francisco International Airport, which is expanding to accommodate increased Pacific Rim travel, as well as a network of highways and bridges (State Route 101, the Golden Gate Bridge; I-80, the Oakland Bridge; the San Mateo Bridge; and I-280 around the outskirts of the city). A strong communications infrastructure has also made international commerce the fastest-growing sector of the economy. With more than 90,000 related jobs and over 170 Pacific Rim companies in San Francisco alone, a background in foreign relations and languages is particularly desirable.

Professional services—accounting, law, recruitment, architecture, and engineering—make up over one-third of San Francisco jobs and usually attract highly skilled employees. Accountants can choose from huge international firms to one-person consultation offices; and, with more than 30,000 attorneys, San Francisco has the dubious honor of having the second largest legal community in the U.S. Management consulting thrives in Silicon Valley and in various corporate headquarters, while executive search firms focus on the financial, high-technology, and telecommunications industries.

Creative services, particularly advertising and public relations, fill a need for graphics, video, and written materials among both big and small businesses, while the apparel industry generates more than 14,000 jobs. Nearly 25,000 health care employees serve at prestigious institutions like UC Medical Center, St. Mary's Medical Center, and Stanford University Hospital. Public health facilities, private institutions, and laboratories are other options. However, people with medical experience might find greater prospects in biotechnology, which includes such big names as Bio-Rad, Chiron, and Genetech.

High technology accounts for more than half of all manufacturing in the Bay Area and encompasses computers, software, semiconductors, electronics, lasers, robotics, and more. Computer programming alone skyrocketed 123 percent between 1980 and 1990. Multimedia is growing so fast that statistics can't keep up, although the most recent estimates suggest that this $4.9 billion industry will quadruple by the year 2000. Those interested in joining the

62,000 souls in this field will find a concentration of companies in "Multimedia Gulch" south of Market Street.

Tourism is San Francisco's number-one industry, generating nearly 300,000 positions (although many jobs do not require degrees). Hotels, restaurants, and attractions employ people with marketing and other professional-level training. So many opportunities, so little time.

> With its cable cars, the 853-foot Transamerica Pyramid, 43 hills, and the architecturally astounding Golden Gate Bridge, this city is enough to make any newcomer's head spin.

ARTS AND SCIENCES

Area code 415's mother lode of cultural offerings consists of some 200 arts organizations, including the San Francisco Opera, which teams up with international stars at the War Memorial Opera House. (The Opera House is also a venue for visiting companies like the Joffrey Ballet.) The San Francisco Symphony performs in the majestic Louis M. Davies Symphony Hall, and the San Francisco Ballet appears at various places. With "sound sculptures" that immerse listeners in euphonies, the Audium is a one-of-a-kind experience, which claims to offer exploration in space through music. Trippy.

Professional theater is concentrated on Geary Street, location of the well-established repertory American Conservatory Theatre and the recently completed Yerba Buena Gardens, with stage and art areas. The "Best of Broadway" series, the experimental Exit Theatre, the intimate 450 Geary Studio Theatre, and the Magic Theatre (offering new plays) are also located there, while long-running amusements run the gamut from the zany *Beach Blanket Babylon* and *Beyond Therapy* (about crazy psychiatrists) to *Forever Tango*, which spotlights Spanish dancing and music. Performance spaces for concerts and other special events include the Golden Gate, Orpheum, Curran, and Marine's Memorial Theatres, among others.

Festivals are a frequent occurrence, often revolving around an ethnic/interest group (Chinese New Year, Lesbian/Gay Pride Freedom Day and Parade), entertainment (Spike and Mike's Festival of Animation, San Francisco Shakespeare Festival, San Francisco International Accordion Festival—monkeys optional), or art (Pacific Fine Art Festival, North Beach Festival, which features a 69-foot salami, ranking it right up there, so to speak, with Coit Tower).

This city's collection of museums includes such obscuriana as the Cartoon Art Museum, the Cable Car Barn & Museum, the Wells Fargo Bank History Museum, and Patti McClain's Museum of Vintage Fashion. The Golden Gate Park alone boasts the California Academy of Sciences, the Asian Art Museum, and the M.H. de Young Memorial Museum, as well as the Japanese Tea Garden and Conservatory of Flowers (which has an incredible accumulation of cherry blossoms in the spring). Along with your basic contemporary works in the new San Francisco Museum of Modern Art and photos in the Ansel Adams Center, there are lots of ethnic archives, such as the African-American Historical & Cultural Society Gallery, the Asian Art Museum, the Chinese Historical Society Museum, the Jewish Museum of San Francisco, and the Museo Italo Americano, to mention a few.

War is a big topic here. Besides visiting the California Historical Society, the Museum of the City of San Francisco, and the Pacific Heritage Museum, you can see the Presidio military fort, the Treasure Island Museum, and the USS *Pampanito* World War II submarine, another excuse to buy flowers from one of the ubiquitous street corner vendors and stick it in a gun barrel. The Maritime Museum in the Maritime National Historical Park is nautical but nice, while the Tech Museum of Innovation, the Exploratorium, the San Francisco Zoo, and many more aptly cover computers, the natural world, and other scientific ground.

 ## THE SPORTING LIFE

Although the highlight of the city's 120 parks and the Golden Gate National Recreation Area (GGNRA) is Golden Gate Park, another popular spot is Ocean Beach, with wildlife and its unusual topography known as Seal Rocks. Swimming can be found at China Beach and Sea Cliff, while hikers and fishing buffs can opt for Baker Beach. Treasure Island, Angel Island, Alcatraz, and others make favorite day trips. A bit farther afield are the Redwood Empire recreational area, with hiking, camping, and other sporting opportunities; the chaparral-covered headlands of Marin County, with lagoons, marshes, and rugged promontories; and the wine country of Napa and Sonoma Counties.

Across the San Francisco Bay in Oakland, the A's American League baseball team and the NBA Golden State Warriors (a transplant from Philadelphia) join the previously mentioned NFL 49ers and the National League Giants. The National Hockey League is represented by the Sharks, located in San Jose.

 ## AFTER-HOURS DIVERSIONS

It's hard to imagine finding spare hours for the various clubs, but nightlife rules. As a touchstone for the fashion industry, San Francisco is particularly style-conscious, and revelers dress accordingly. Live music and/or DJs can be heard at such spots as DV8, Cafe Du Nord, Elbo Room, DNA Lounge, Bimbos 365 Club, Transmission Theatre, and Sound Factory. The Palladium is a perennial favorite of trendsetters. Disco/funk at Holy Cow draws a steady crowd of tourists and regulars, while Club Oz is the spot for the elite see-and-be-seen. Lou's offers a varied menu of food and music; Pearl's, New Orleans Room, and Storyville serve up jazz; and there's blues at the Saloon. Or you can sit down and enjoy a quiet drink at Nick's Lounge or Tosca. San Francisco has its share of female impersonators (Finocchio's) and the genuine article unclothed (Gold Club, Roaring '20s, and others), as well as males au natural at Nob Hill Adult Theatre Arcade. The latter also features first-run gay videos for those who'd rather see the movie.

 ## CULINARY AND SHOPPING HAUNTS

With local specialties ranging from sourdough bread to chocolate (although the Ghiradelli family stopped producing their trademark candy here in the early 1960s) to Dungeness crab, Chinook salmon, and Pacific herring, San Francisco's restaurant scene is almost as wide as the waistlines of those who overindulge in it. Folks here enjoy eating out: City residents are among the biggest restaurant spenders in the U.S.

There's seafood in Fisherman's Wharf, authentic ethnic (including fish with heads and beady eyes) in Chinatown and Japantown; Italian and other cafes on North Beach; taquerias and Mexican bakeries in the Mission District; and Vietnamese, Laotian, and Cambodian places in the Tenderloin. Union Street, Maiden Lane South of Market, and parts of Grant Avenue are ripe with informal to trendy eateries. Nationally acclaimed chefs can be found at Stars, Square One, Kuleto's, One Market, Boulevard, Postrio, and Rubicon. But just about every spot is good—it has to be, in order to survive in this shark tank. This is one town where you're never too far from a decent meal.

Neighborhoods are also loaded with eclectic shopping opportunities, from bargains rarely found elsewhere to exquisite, unique works of art. Atmosphere seems almost as important as selection: The waterfront alone has the Anchorage, an open-air complex "anchored" by hundreds of signal flags and a 27-foot guess-what; the Cannery, which no longer puts out peaches but has three keen levels of walkways, boundaries, and bridges wrapped around a courtyard; Ghirardelli Square, with more than 70 emporiums and restaurants in a historically significant area; and Pier 39, whose 100 or so stores are flanked by a Cyberstation arcade, two-tiered carousel, sea lions, and UnderWater World attraction.

Those who take their sprees seriously would do well at Embarcadero Center (125 stores), three levels of upscale boutiques and more spanning eight city blocks; Crocker Galleria (more than 40), modeled after Milan's vast Galleria Vittorio Emmanuelle; San Francisco Shopping Centre (more than 90), a potentially dizzying experience in a nine-story mall with spiral (!) escalators and the world's largest Nordstrom's; and Stonestown Galleria (more than 120), lots of neat brand names set amid vaulted glass skylights and Italian Renaissance marble. Union Square, the center of the San Francisco shopping universe, has been compared to Fifth Avenue and Rodeo Drive and indeed does have top goods (and prices) in jewelry, luggage, and clothing. Those looking for art can also strike it rich (or poor, depending on your point of view): Dozens of galleries offer everything from American Indian work to contemporary to folk to big names.

ETHNIC AND RELIGIOUS PROSPECTS

In a city like San Francisco, being a straight WASP male might almost be a disadvantage, or at least might not provide the edge that it would in other places. Not only is the city ethnically diverse, but it has a vocal and politically strong gay population, many of whom live in the Castro Street area. However, no minority need worry—African-American, Latino, and other celebrations as well as the Chinese New Year, Hanukkah, and Christmas are given equal play.

Churches seem more open as well. Many, such as Parkside Gospel, Glide Memorial United Methodist, and Providence Christian Center, focus on the poor and homeless, while the City of Refuge Community Church welcomes those of any origin and sexual orientation. A strong Buddhist movement's afoot at the Diamond Way Buddhist Center, Kagyu Droden Kunchab, and San Francisco Buddhist Center, and there's a San Francisco Zen Center as well. The area's many ethnic institutions include the historic black Macedonia Missionary Baptist Church, the San Francisco Korean United Methodist Church, the First Samoan Congregation, and others. The Archdiocese of San Francisco and the Jewish Community Center serve their respective populations also.

CRIB SHEET

It's easy to get into a fog about where to live around here: The average rent for a one-bedroom apartment ($900–1,200) is bound to take a major bite out of the paycheck, if you can find a place at all. Homes are on the increase, although they're mostly in the $500,000+ range.

Still, just about any spot in the city's 15 residential areas offers well-developed educational, shopping, and recreational opportunities and easy access to downtown. Single-family dwellings dominate the western section, while high-rise and large apartment complexes mix with expensive single and semidetached houses northeast. Semidetached row houses and low-rise apartment buildings are scattered everywhere.

Although the most sought-after neighborhoods seem to be the Marina, Pacific Heights, and Upper Market, homes are also desirable in Sunset, South of Market, Potero Hill, and Bernal Heights. Each district has its particular charm. The winding roads of middle-class Richmond/Sea Cliff boast inexpensive shops, restaurants, and lots of the hazy stuff. Pacific Heights/Marina/Presidio Heights is chock-full of elegant mansions, boarding schools, and foreign consulates, while the colorful Nob Hill/Russian Hill/Telegraph Hill attracts artsy types, former flower children, and the wealthy (although the latter two are sometimes mutually exclusive). Along with clanging cable car bells and crooked streets, this area encompasses Chinatown and North Beach.

Revitalized since the 1960s, Buena Vista/Haight Ashbury offers multicultural dining, wooded areas, and a variety of home styles. Central has the primarily gay Castro area, while South of Market (known locally as SOMA) appeals mostly to the moderate checkbook and is up-and-coming. Recognized for its great views and prices, the fixer-upper Queen Annes and Victorians of Bernal Heights are particularly attractive to young professionals. With lots of single-family dwellings, good schools, and a pleasant environment, Inner and Outer Sunset appeal to young marrieds and those with kids.

Other options include South Bay in Santa Clara County, home of the famous Silicon Valley; the Peninsula (San Mateo County), with its high concentration of bioscience, industrial, and business parks; and North Bay/Marin County, a populous area almost totally surrounded by water. East Bay has Alameda County, with its rolling hills, recreational parks, and the University of California at Berkeley; and Contra Costa County, a former bedroom community that's rapidly developing into a business and commercial region.

About one-fourth of the local student population attends private and parochial schools, which speaks volumes about the public school system. With an average class size of 26.8 and standardized achievement tests slightly below the national average, the San Francisco Unified School system has a dropout rate of 16–18 percent, although that is starting to decline. As nearly 60 percent of the children come from homes in which English is not the dominant language, many classes are geared toward the bilingual student, with alternative, special needs, and technical/vocational programs available also.

Private institutions encompass the Bentley School, French-American International School, Convent of the Sacred Heart, and many more. Colleges include the University of California at San Francisco, with its cutting-edge biotechnology program; the outstanding graduate courses of study at Berkeley; and Stanford, with its scientific orientation and top-notch computer school.

SEATTLE, WASHINGTON

Seattle at a Glance

Birthdate and Present Size: Incorporated: 1869.
Metropolitan Statistical Area—1980: 1,607,469; 1990: 1,972,961. Percent change, 1980–1990: +22.7%. 1/1/95 (estimate): 2,216,400. Percent change, 1990–1995: +12.3%.

Weather Report: *Average annual temperature*—51° F. In January: 44/34° F. In July: 75/54° F.
Average annual precipitation—36.2".
Average annual snowfall—13".

Money Matters: *Unemployment rate*—4.9%.
Per capita income—$18,308.
Average household income—$38,895. (Note: $44,338 in the MSA.)
Average cost of a home—$184,950.
Average rent for an apartment—$649/month.
ACCRA cost of living indexes (based on 100)—Composite Index: 120.3; Utilities Index: 68.5. Housing Index: 141.5.
Sales and use tax—6.5% (state); 1.75% (local).
Personal income tax—None.

People Profile: *Crime rate* (Per 100,000 population)—10,717 (city); 6,397.8 (MSA).
Racial and ethnic characteristics—White: 75.4%; Asian/Pacific Islander: 11.9%;

Black: 10.0%; Hispanic Origin: 3.3%; American Indian/Eskimo/Aleut: 1.4%; Other: 1.3%.
Gender ratio—95.1 males per 100 females (all ages); 94 males per 100 females (18 years old+).
Age characteristics—18–24 (11.9%); 25–44 (37.7%). Median age: 34.9.
Educational attainment—percent having completed high school: 86.4%; percent having completed college: 37.9%.

Major Players: Services, retail/wholesale trade, manufacturing, government. Noted for commercial aircraft production and missile research, international trade, high technology, research and development, tourism.
Largest employers—Airborne Freight Corp., Alaska Air Group, Boeing Company, Children's Hospital & Medical Center, Coh-Care, King County Medical Blue Shield, Safeco Corp. (insurance), Seafirst Corp. (banking).

Community Services: *Average hospital cost*—$540.40/day.
Average doctor visit—$57.75.
Average dentist visit—$95.60.
Newspapers—The Seattle Times, Seattle Post-Intelligencer, Puget Sound Business Journal, North American Post (Japanese/American), Seattle Weekly (alternative), The Stranger (alternative).

Photo by Nick Gunderson/Seattle-King County News Bureau

Guess what, Dorothy, there really is an Emerald City. Its name is Seattle, and it even has its very own wizards—Microsoft, Boeing, Starbucks, and Pearl Jam, to mention a few. Seattle was settled in the early 1850s by a group of Illinois pioneers who initially planned on naming it after New York; they changed their minds and decided to honor Squamish Chief Sealth instead, and quickly began to divest the thickly forested countryside of its lumber.

Although the arrival of the railroad in nearby Tacoma and development as a port sped things up in the 19th century, the Alaskan gold rush of the 1890s sealed Seattle's fate as a major player in the Pacific Northwest. Sure, there have been a couple of setbacks—anti-Chinese riots during the peak immigration periods and a major fire that leveled downtown, both in the

1880s—but the city has sailed smoothly towards prosperity and progress. Four transcontinental railroads and the Panama and Lake Washington Canals unlocked accessibility even more, particularly with Russia (via Alaska) and the Pacific Rim countries. The economy was additionally shored up by shipbuilding and fishing

But there's nothing suspicious about Seattle's endurance. Variety has been this city's spice and includes a unique cultural mix of Scandinavians, Japanese, Chinese, and other nationalities. The original "skid road," where logs jostled past brothels and saloons to the waterfront, co-existed with the respectable north side of town. Strikes and labor unrest were juxtaposed alongside several World's Fairs, most notably the 1962 exposition which gave the city the Seattle Center/Space Needle. After World War II, the Boeing Company moved to the forefront, where it transferred the technology developed for heavy bombers to the first passenger jet in 1959. Soon Boeing and its suppliers not only accounted for nearly half of the local jobs, but emerged as (and remain) the world's leading manufacturers of commercial and jet aircraft.

Recent decades have given "logging on" a new meaning. Computer software, biomedical research, and aerospace industries have gradually superseded forestry, agriculture, and fishing. And along with being the undisputed coffee and grunge music capital of America (and possibly the world), this city has the highest percentage of people biking to work, the most active public library in the nation, and is as good a place as any to have a heart attack because so many of its citizens are trained in CPR. Plus, the water is pure and the people are genuinely kind. So you don't have to worry about being gunned down should you cut someone off in traffic. Here are the ruby slippers, Toto, you can go home by yourself.

Quality of Life

Seattlites like to point out—accurately—that their city is behind Atlanta, Houston, Boston, and New York in annual yearly amount of rainfall. As if to prove their point, they purchase more sunglasses than anywhere else in the nation. But the sad truth is that more than 200 days out of the year are overcast "and the gloom can make you a little loopy," observes lawyer Kumi Yamamoto, who recently moved from Boston. Add that to "some really weird but beautiful architecture" and Seattle can provide a unique living experience.

Even when things are dankest, "you can always find things to do," observes activities coordinator Lisa Murray. Shopping, theater, and other cultural options, bookstores, and coffeehouses as well as professional sports provide indoor distractions. "And when the weather's good you feel like you have to go outside" along with the rest of the city.

"Everyone's so nice, at first you wonder if they really mean it," Yamamoto continues. This is in part due to the fact that no one dresses up for anything: the guy sitting next to you at the symphony in holey jeans and Birkenstock sandals may be a millionaire. So you never know who you're insulting if you're rude.

Although this apparent lack of barriers "can make some people crazy," according to one native, it's also Seattle's strength. The city's widely touted racial tolerance has resulted in an increased Asian population and has stimulated trade with the Pacific Rim. And despite a proportionately small black population, the populace elected an African-American mayor. In a place where "our mothers warned us to stay away from those scary garage bands"—which later became Nirvana and Alice in Chains—anything and everything is possible.

General Opportunities

Although minimum wage positions may be easy to obtain, the high cost of living and housing can make things tight. But expenses have leveled off in recent years and utilities, food, and taxes are at or below the national average, while per capita earnings remain generous. And since Seattle has the highest level of people aged 25 and over with a high school education in the nation and nearly one-third of working professionals have a college degree, "training has become increasingly important," remarks native Janet Bayne, a marketing director. "The city has become more technology and service oriented."

> In Seattle, you can put in 60-hour weeks or make a decent living working part-time. This is why folks who've become disinterested in the fast track find the city so appealing.

Still, Seattle has its shticks. Unless you're in Pike's Place Market, jaywalking is illegal and the police *do* hand out tickets. Recycling is next to godliness: over 89 percent of the citizens segregate paper, metal, and plastics. And nearly every social endeavor is somehow linked to charity. "It's like a nonprofit Mafia," confides one resident. A small price for living in a spot where even gas stations sell lattes and the only one making an ash of itself is Mt. Saint Helens.

MAJOR BREADWINNING

"Seattle is a great place for artists and computer whizzes," remarks Payne. Writers, musicians, painters, and other struggling types can live the relatively cheap life in Belltown and Capitol Hill, waiting tables to help pay the rent, peddling their wares to dozens of galleries, restaurants, and clubs. Those with hardware/software skills earn much larger salaries, but "usually don't focus" on conspicuous consumption.

You can put in 60-hour weeks or make a decent living selling cellular phones part-time. This is perhaps why folks who've become disinterested in the fast track find Seattle so appealing. "Bosses are open to flex-time and family and maternity leave," adds Bayne. "There seems to be an emphasis on getting the job done" rather than putting in the allotted 9-to-5.

A glance at the employment pie over the past decade shows a decrease in manufacturing and government and an increase and/or relative stability in services and trade, although Boeing continues to have a major impact. Along with being the number one exporter in the U.S., the aerospace colossus employs 82,000, including engineers for building airplanes and contracts experts for dealings with the government and suppliers. "When they have cutbacks, many people feel the pinch," observes one Seattlite.

But not as much, thanks to economic diversity. Along with Starbucks and Microsoft, companies such as Recreational Equipment Inc. (REI), Paccar truck manufacturing, Nintendo of America, and AT&T Wireless Service have made Seattle their home. Others, like Price Costco discount warehouses, Weyerhaeuser pulp/paper products, Nordstrom Department Stores, and Safeco insurance and financial services, provide thousands of jobs and pump millions of

dollars into the economy. Seattle's approximately 200 foreign-owned firms utilize about 3 percent of the workers, more than 10,000 people.

A recent Harris poll cited Seattle as the second best city in which to locate a company. Compelling factors included a skilled work force, manufacturing capability, and international and domestic transportation and access, as well as a global perspective and cultural heterogeneity. Commercial and industrial real estate are reasonably priced and available.

Much of the optimistic buzz centers around the Port and its increased trade with countries such as Japan, China, Taiwan, and South Korea, as well as European nations and Canada. The fourth largest in the U.S., the rapidly growing harbor moves more than one million containers a year, requiring the services of those with international trade, technical, and electronics skills. The rather chauvinistically named Fisherman's Terminal services the U.S. North Pacific Fishing Fleet and provides most of the U.S. harvest of bottom fish. The Defense Department also supplies approximately 60,000 jobs, many in support of Naval efforts.

Biotechnology also generates $500 million a year, accounting for almost 5,000 jobs in more than 60 enterprises. Areas of concentration include recombinant DNA and cell fusion, immunology, and cancer research in places such as the University of Washington Medical Center, the Fred Hutchinson Cancer Research Center, and Immunex. By 2003, this field is projected to expand to 12,000 positions and earn $3–4 billion a year.

There are approximately 1,500 computer development companies in addition to Microsoft, which not only provide excellent opportunities for what one resident jokingly calls "buckets o' nerds" but also help make Seattle a top spot for running a home-based business. The city offers an excellent breeding ground for smaller undertakings in general: Of Seattle's approximately 76,000 enterprises, 75,000 have fewer than 100 employees.

Tourism, the state's fourth largest industry, is responsible for nearly 39,000 positions and $15 million in Seattle/King County alone. Top rankings from publications (*Money, Condé Nast, Fortune, Savvy,* others) and publicity from TV and movies (*Sleepless in Seattle,* "Northern Exposure," "Twin Peaks"), help stimulate the building and expansion of new hotels, stores, and restaurants, ensuring a steady influx of jobs.

Still, most people would rather go tell it to the mountains. "Seattle is a laid-back place," remarks Jennifer Acres, who sells catering services. "No one really cares where you work. If you know what you want, you can always find something."

SOCIAL AND RECREATIONAL SCENE

How Seattle Plays

Emigres expecting a sort of grunge Welcome Wagon in logging shirts, army boots, and knit caps should think again. "Unless you know someone, it's hard to meet people," admits Yamamoto. Despite its outward affability, "Seattle can be a very closed society."

But the determined individualism of area code 206 shouldn't be mistaken for snobbery or elitism. "People are very much into their own thing here," adds Bayne. "You really have to make an effort."

One newcomer remembers calling her mother in tears. "Everyone was always too busy and I was desperate—so I finally joined the Junior League" (324-3638). She made several contacts and subsequently became involved in local charity functions.

Still, it's not necessary to go bourgeois. "The personals are big here, particularly those on the Internet," remarks Lucinda Payne.

It also depends on what you're searching for. "Those who prefer the casual lifestyle and enjoy sports and just hanging out will have an easier time of it," observes Jennifer Acres, who has found that Seattle has "a very large group of cute guys." But "if you're looking for high-powered types who patronize the trendiest restaurants," well, it could be a long haul. Even if you're unsure of where to start socially, there's lots to keep you busy.

 ## ARTS AND SCIENCES

Seattle is one of a handful of American cities to have a major symphony, opera, and ballet. It also ranks up there with New York and Chicago in terms of equity theaters and number of live shows. The **Seattle Center** not only is the home for most of the above, but its 74-acre complex also has a Children's Museum, Northwest Craft Center, Fun Forest Amusement Park, and a monorail that whisks back and forth from the downtown Westlake mall (arguably the fastest trip between two food courts in the known universe). Oh, and there's the Space Needle—a 605-foot monolith topped by a revolving restaurant with a panoramic view that's especially fantastic at night. Hopefully, you won't get stuck in an unairconditioned elevator full of tourists on your way down.

The **University of Washington School of Drama** and **Langston Hughes Cultural Arts Center** also offer semi-professional and multicultural performances. The restored **Paramount Theatre,** the **Fifth Avenue Theatre, Key Arena,** and **Mercer Arena** host everything from touring musicals to Broadway shows to big-name groups and performers.

Seattle is no slouch in the museum department, either. The new and modernistic-looking **Seattle Art Museum** is fronted by a huge, perpetual-motion "Hammering Man," which stands guard over its outstanding Asian, African, Pacific Northwest, and contemporary American holdings. The same admission ticket will also get you into the **Seattle Asian Art Museum** and its extensive Japanese, Chinese, Thai, and other collections. Housed in the original Boeing Airplane factory, the **Museum of Flight** offers a panorama of planes. And although it's definitely not a gallery, the graves of film stars Bruce and Brandon Lee (**Lake View Cemetery**) pay tribute to the martial arts.

Dozens of "real" galleries (**Foster/White, Semantics, Wild Wings**) line downtown streets and redeveloped areas. Clubs, restaurants, and coffee shops also display museum-quality stuff next to whatever strikes the owner's fancy. Salvation Army meets circus sideshow at **Moe's Mo'Roc'N Cafe;** the **Lava Lounge** offers Tiki chainsaw sculpture amid a South Pacific shipwreck. The **Crocodile Cafe,** the reputed birthplace of

Where It's At

 Unless otherwise noted, all area codes are 206.

Argosy Cruises, 623-1445

Blake's Island Tillicum Village, Pier 55–56, 443-1244

Chittenden Locks, Washington Ship Canal, 783-7059

Crocodile Cafe, 2200 Second Ave., 448-2114

Fifth Avenue Theatre, 1308 5th, 625-1418

Foster/White, 311 1/2 Occidental Ave. S., 622-2833

Key Arena, Seattle Center

Klondike Gold Rush Historic Park, 117 S. Main St. 553-7220

Lake View Cemetery, Capitol Hill

Langston Hughes Cultural Arts Center, 104 17th Ave. S., 684-4757

Lava Lounge, 2226 Second Ave., 441-5660

Mercer Arena, 1001 4th Ave., 382-6667

Moe's Mo'Roc'N Cafe, 925 E. Pike St., 323-2373

Museum of Flight, 9404 E. Marginal Way, 764-5720

Pacific Science Center, 200 2nd Ave. N., 443-2001

Paramount Theatre, 911 Pine St., 682-1414

Seattle Aquarium, Pier 59 on the waterfront, 386-4320

Seattle Art Museum, 100 University St., 654-3100

Seattle Asian Art Museum, 1400 E. Prospect, 654-3100

Seattle Center, 305 Harrison, 684-7200

Semantics, 116 S. Washington St., 624-7370

grunge, flaunts idiosyncratic (read: strange) paintings, while the **Two Bells Tavern** and **Virginia Inn** have been displaying art since the early '80s, way before it was chi-chi. Only in Seattle.

On a more terrestrial level and built in 1851 by the original settlers, Pioneer Square has an entire "underground" section that consists of sidewalks one story down from storefronts. It's best (at least most humorously) explored by the **Underground Tour.** While there, you can unearth the Seattle unit of the **Klondike Gold Rush Historic Park,** which chronicles July 17, 1897, the day the good ship Portland arrived in Elliott Bay with more than a ton of the valuable stuff aboard. Those wanting to see the other half of the park will have to go to Skagway, Alaska.

But you don't have to travel far to see robotic dinosaurs, laser shows, and virtual reality basketball at the **Pacific Science Center.** The **Washington Park Arboretum** celebrates the flora/fauna angle through 200 acres and 4,500 different kinds of trees and shrubs. Nationally noted for its minimum-barrier environment and natural habitats, the **Woodland Park Zoo** has 50 or so endangered species, an African savannah exhibit, and the largest group of liontail macaque monkeys in the world. The **Seattle Aquarium** spotlights Puget Sound via a 400,000-gallon tank with 1,000 sea creatures; a "fish-eye" Omnidome projection screen; and the world's only aquarium-based salmon ladder and hatchery.

Each September, the Aquarium also celebrates a Salmon Homecoming (sans football game and king/queen, since they all look alike anyway). Also, an underwater viewing room in the **Chittenden Locks** provides visitors an unencumbered view of the fight up the fish ladder (a sort of aquatic Super Bowl). Those with a fascination for watching vessels being lifted from the saltwater of Puget Sound to freshwater levels can opt for one of several harbor tours (**Argosy Cruises, Spirit of Puget Sound, Waterway Cruises**) departing daily from Piers 55, 57, and 70. You can choose from options ranging from dinner and jazz to a brief educational spin around Elliott Bay/Lake Washington to overnight trips via the speedy **Victoria Clipper.** Palefaces taking the four-hour tour of **Blake's Island Tillicum Village** view costumed tribal dancing and dinner in a North Coast Indian long house where salmon (again) is cooked over an open-pit fire. And we humans think life is tough!

THE SPORTING LIFE

One way to make buddies in Seattle is to get a boat. The salt waters of Puget Sound, fresh waters of Lake Washington, and Lake Union, which runs throughout the city, provide year-round diversion. Seattle has more floating vessels than anywhere else in the nation: you can choose from canoeing, kayaking, river rafting, or just plain cruising. Conveyances range from parasailing (**Pier 57**) to giant Washington State ferries (**Pier 52**) for the macho-impaired and others with cars.

Where It's At

Kingdome, 201 S. King St., 296-DOME

Marymoor Park, 6046 West Lake Sammamish Pkwy. NE, 296-2966

National Park and Forest Service, 220-7450

Pier 52, 464-6400

Pier 57, 622-5757

Red Tide Hotline, 800/362-5632

Seattle Department of Parks and Recreation, 684-4075

Seattle Mariners, 628-3555

Seattle Seahawks, 827-9777

Seattle Sport and Social Club, 200 2nd Ave. W., 284-7279

Seattle SuperSonics, 283-DUNK

Seattle Thunderbirds, 448-PUCK

Stevens Pass, U.S. Hwy. 2, 306/973-2441

Trade and Economic Development, 306/753-5600

University of Washington, 543-2200

Washington Department of Fish and Wildlife, Olympia, 306/902-2464

Washington State Department of Parks and Recreation, Olympia, 306/902-8563

Ferries depart every hour for Bainbridge Island, with its hiking and biking opportunities and cute little downtown. While crossing the water, look for bald eagles, sea lions, and even whales in certain months.

It goes without saying that the fishing is superb, with plentiful trout, oysters, clams, bottom fish, even Dungeness crab (salmon fishing is allowed only at certain times). The **Washington Department of Fish and Wildlife, Red Tide Hotline,** and nearby sporting goods stores can provide details and information about locations and permits. Those wishing to supplement the experience with camping can contact the **Washington State Department of Parks and Recreation** in Olympia, the **National Park and Forest Service,** and the state's **Trade and Economic Development** program, which respectively cover state, national, and privately owned grounds.

The mountains offer skiing in winter. Resorts in the Cascades include **Alpental/Ski Acres/Snoqualmie Summit, Crystal Mountain,** and **Stevens Pass,** among others. Some have innertubing and sledding as well.

Seattle is a great place to bike, a rarity in the U.S. More than 100 miles of trails, marked routes, and specially designated lanes are utilized by commuters, locals, and tourists. With more than 4,500 members, Seattle's **Cascade Bicycle Club** is the nation's largest and most active. The velodrome at **Marymoor Park** in Redmond provides the uncommon experience of indoor riding and hosts a number of national races as well.

The Burke-Gilman Trail, Sammamish River Trail, Green Lake, Alki Beach Park, Volunteer Park, and Seward Park are also big with walkers and joggers, while those willing to venture a bit farther can explore the back roads of the Olympic Peninsula, Skagit Valley, the San Juan Islands, and the Cascades. The **Seattle Department of Parks and Recreation** can provide a detailed map, along with information on a variety of organized sports.

Perhaps the easiest (and certainly a user-friendly) way to hook up with various endeavors is through the **Seattle Sport and Social Club.** Unlike some city leagues, which require that an entire team sign up in order to play, individuals are welcome. "We gets lots of people who are new to town," remarks director Lisa Murray.

The **Kingdome** bestows its multipurpose favors upon its grateful subjects via the NFL **Seattle Seahawks,** the major league baseball **Seattle Mariners,** and a variety of amateur sports, concerts, and consumer shows. Key Arena hosts the NBA Western Division champion **Seattle SuperSonics** and hockey's **Seattle Thunderbirds.** College football and other women's and men's sports are well-represented through an extensive program at the **University of Washington.** Whatever your pleasure or pain, be it active or armchair, "this city has something for everyone," adds Murray.

 AFTER-HOURS DIVERSIONS

Those starting out in their early 20s will find the Seattle scene different than individuals who have established a career. Although places like the University of Washington supply a perpetual crop of singles, "lots of men here are gay while others don't take kindly to commitment," admits a thirtysomething publicist. "You get disaffected musician and artist types who are hanging out until they make it big."

Although this can be frustrating for those looking for steady relationships, "once you find a compatible group, it's easy to meet others," observes tennis coach Ken Chaffeur. "People are friendly and everyone comes out to hear the bands."

And what music! Any given night on Pioneer Square offers up jazz, funk, reggae, techno, disco, oldies, and that distinctive Seattle sound that's somewhere between grunge, alternative, and way out in left field. Bars such as **Colourbox, New Orleans, Fenix/Fenix Underground, Bohemian,** and others teem with over-21s (state law, strictly enforced). Belltown (also known as the Denny Regrade) and Capitol Hill have their share of trendy fixtures, including the **Art Bar, Belltown Billiards, DV8** (as in "deviate"—get it?), **Paragon, Vogue,** and many more. And that's not even mentioning the north, east, and south parts of town.

Fashion victims and others can wallow in the latest fads, such as "glam" (tailored clothes for both sexes, hats and high heels for women), martinis ("shaken, not stirred"), and the lounge music once favored by hipsters in the '50s and '60s. The aforementioned Art Bar, Moe's, Crocodile Cafe, Lava Lounge, and **Cafe Paradisio** feature acts or special nights. One can attain total immersion (so to speak) in cocktail culture by attending scotch tastings at **Wine and Spirits** and **Hopscotch.** Sounds like a Bond-ing experience.

Those with more pedestrian preferences might prefer to sample the excellent fruits of the local vine and/or hops. The **Hart Brewing Co., Rainier Brewing Co., Redhook Ale Brewery** and wineries in nearby Woodinville (**Chateau Ste. Michelle, Columbia Winery**) offer tastings and tours. Cigar aficionados will appreciate **F.X. McRory's,** a popular bar and eatery that caters to sports fans and allows all forms of (legal) puffery. Gas masks optional.

Not all entertainment takes place in smoke-filled clubs. Spots such as the **Speakeasy Cafe,** the **Online Internet Cafe,**

Where It's At

Unless Otherwise noted, all area codes are 206.

17th of May, Ballard, 784-7894

Art Bar, 1516 Second Ave., 622-4344

Belltown Billiards, 90 Blanchard St., 448-6779

Bohemian, 111 Yesler Way, 447-1514

Bumbershoot, Seattle Center, 682-4386

Cafe Paradisio, 1005 E. Pike St., 322-6960

Chateau Ste. Michelle, 14111 NE 145th, 488-3300

Cherry Blossom/Japanese Cultural Festival, Seattle Center, 684-7200

Chinese New Year, International District, 323-2700

Colourbox, 113 First Ave., 340-4101

Columbia Winery, 14030 NE 145th, 428-2776

DV8, 131 Taylor Ave. N., 448-0888

Elliot Bay Book Company, First Ave. S. and S. Main St., 624-6600

F.X. McRory's, 419 Occidental S., 623-4800

Fenix/Fenix Underground, 323 Second Ave., 467-1111

Folklife Festival, Seattle Center, 684-7300

Hart Brewing Co., First Ave. S and S. Royal Brougham, 68-BEERS

Hopscotch, 332 15th E., 322-4191

New Orleans, 114 First Ave., 622-2563

Online Internet Cafe, 219 Broadway, 860-6858

Paragon, 2125 Queen Ave. N., 283-4548

Rainier Brewing Co., 3100 Way S., 622-6606

Redhook Ale Brewery, several locations

Seafair, 728-0123

Seafair Indian Days Pow-Wow, Discovery Park, 285-4425

Seattle Center, 232-2982

Speakeasy Cafe, 2304 Second Ave., 728-9770

Sundiata, Seattle Center, 684-7200

Where It's At

(continued)

Virtual Commons, 200 Roy, 281-7339

Vogue, 2018 First Ave., 443-0673

Western Washington Fair, Pullyap, 845-5045 or 845-1771

Wine and Spirits, Sixth and University, 389-2564

and **Virtual Commons** not only offer e-mail access but a chance to hook up with some real time mugs. Having an excellent selection of reading material and a coffee shop, the **Elliot Bay Book Company** has been rated by locals as a great place to encounter other intelligent life forms.

Summer brings a slew of festivals. You can take a "Bite of Seattle" at a mass culinary sampling at the **Seattle Center** (July); rediscover what state fairs were really like (cows, cultivation, crafts) at the **Western Washington Fair** (August); and check out the arts scene at **Bumbershoot** (Labor Day Weekend), which offers talent in music, dance, theater, comedy, and literature. Ethnicity is taken to its highest level of correctness at the **Folklife Festival** (Memorial Day Weekend), where artists, craftspeople, and cooks of all nations strut their stuff. Naturally, most groups have their own fests—**Sundiata** (African-American, February), **Chinese New Year** (various dates), Norwegian **17th of May**, **Cherry Blossom/Japanese Cultural Festival** (April), **Seafair Indian Days Pow-Wow** (July), which is part of the hugely successful and long-standing **Seafair** (July), and many more.

 ## CULINARY AND SHOPPING HAUNTS

Seattle is the proud home of "Pacific Rim," a.k.a. fusion or hybrid cuisine. Call it what you will, it's a generally delicious (and healthful) blend of traditional dishes with a touch or two of unusual Asian spices, chilies, and pasta; salmon meets black bean vinaigrette and rice, for example. Some entrees can sound pretty bizarre, such as chilled octopus with green papaya and fried ginger (warning to the uninitiated: smaller calamari can resemble fried spiders).

Although Seattle has an abundance of restaurants, a few favorites keep appearing on various "hot" lists. Many are the pioneers of the fusion movement—**Wild Ginger, Dahlia Lounge, Etta's Seafood, Flying Fish, Painted Table, Bombore,** the previously mentioned Paragon Bar and Grill, and **Lampreia.** Although they're mostly moderately priced ($7.95–19.95, tops) and good, Seattle has lots of great places where you don't need a reservation or have to wait in line for an hour and a half.

These include Northwest/Asian (**Janny's Curry House,** the **Garlic Tree, Shiro's,** many more), Mexican (**Casa U Betcha, Mama's Mexican Kitchen**), and seafood (**Brooklyn Seafood, McCormick's** restaurants, and just about any place on the Waterfront area). Italian and beef houses and pubs are hardly limited to **Italia, Tucci Benucch,** and **Leo Melina,** and for suds 'n'/or steak there's **Metropolitan Grill, Ruth's Chris Steak House, 2 Bells Tavern,** and **Blue Star Cafe.**

Where It's At

 Unless otherwise noted, all area codes are 206.

2 Bells Tavern, 2313 4th Ave, 441-3050

Bellevue Square, NE 8th St. and Bellevue Way, 454-8096

Blue Star Cafe, 4512 Stone Way N., 548-0345

Bombore, 89 University St., 624-8233

Bon Marche, 3rd and Pine, 506-6049

Brooklyn Seafood, 1212 2nd Ave., 224-7000

Cap'n Seattle, 447-2628

Casa U Betcha, 2212 1st Ave, 441-6920

City Centre, 1420 Fifth Ave., 223-8999

Cockpit, 1800 4th Ave., 442-WING

Dahlia Lounge, 1904 Fourth Ave., 682-4142

Dick's Drive-In, several locations

Etta's Seafood, 2020 Western Ave., 443-6000

Flying Fish, 2234 First Ave., 728-8595

Garlic Tree, 94 Stewart St., 441-5681

Ambience can range from the noisy "cheap eats" of **Trattoria Mitchelli** to the French-accented elegance of **Un Deux Trois** to the post-apocalyptic vegetarianism of the **Gravity Bar.** You can choose from Seattle standbys like the **Space Needle Restaurant/Emerald Suite** and **Dick's Drive-In** or the comforting familiarity of the **Old Spaghetti Factory** or **Subway.** And **Starbucks** or some reasonable facsimile are on just about every corner for those needing a cappuccino or biscotti fix.

Consistent with the rest of the city, shopping in Seattle can be an eclectic experience, with lots of reasonably priced bargains, particularly at **Pike's Place Market.** Here, farmers peddle fresh produce and craftspeople hawk silver, totem poles, and other Northwestern-style goodies. (Dickering can work with vendors in the stalls but not in the regular stores.) Merchants in the newly renovated Sanitary Public Market (so proclaimed by a neon sign) and in the various levels leading to the Waterfront sell everything from animal memorabilia (**Merry Tails**) to kitchen supplies (**Kitchen Basics**) to quilts (**Undercover Quilts**). The **Waterfront** offers an 1890s Gold Rush pier with a vintage carousel and seafaring shops like **Cap'n Seattle.** There's even a psychic reader to help predict how much money you're going to spend.

From there, you can walk downtown, which has additional weird and wonderful delights, like **Sub-Pop Mega Mart,** record shop extraordinare and home of the Seattle sound, and the **Cockpit,** a novel (bomber jackets, jeans, aviation memorabilia) enterprise in an even more strangely shaped triangular building. No trip downtown would be complete without a visit to **Nordstrom** and **Bon Marche.** The former was founded in Seattle and has expanded throughout the U.S., while in the latter, traditional offerings share space with coin and stamp collecting and model railroad departments. Both specialize in service and quality.

With a wide assortment of bookstores, boutiques, specialty foods, and imports, street grazers will appreciate Belltown, Pioneer Square, the International and University Districts, and Capitol Hill. Offerings include the **Uwajimaya Market,** the largest Asian superstore in the Northwest that has, among other things, a sushi bar and cooking school. Seattle's "baker's dozen" of traditional malls includes **City Centre, Westlake Center, Northgate, Sea-Tac Mall, Bellevue Square,** and others in and around the various suburbs. About an hour's drive north (Burlington) and west (North Bend) are clusters of discount stores.

Where It's At

(continued)

Gravity Bar, 113 Virginia, 448-8826

Italia, 1010 Western Ave., 623-1917

Janny's Curry House, 1411 N. 45th St.

Kitchen Basics, 622-2014

Lampreia, 2400 First Avenue, 443-3301

Leo Melina, 96 Union St., 623-3783

Mama's Mexican Kitchen, 2234 2nd St., 728-6262

McCormick's, 772 4th Ave., 682-3900 and 1103 First Ave., 623-5500

Merry Tails, 623-4142

Metropolitan Grill, 2nd and Marion, 624-3287

Nordstrom, 5th and Pike, 628-2111; several other locations

Northgate, I-5 E. and Northgate Way, 362-4777

Old Spaghetti Factory, 3801 Elliot Ave., 441-7724

Painted Table, 92 Madison St., 624-3646

Pike's Place Market, Pike St., 587-0351

Ruth's Chris Steak House, 800 Fifth Ave., 624-8254

Sea-Tac Mall, S. 320th St. and Pacific Hwy., 839-6151

Shiro's, 2401 Second Ave., 443-9644; other locations

Space Needle Restaurant/Emerald Suite, Space Needle, 443-2100

Sub-Pop Mega Mart, 1928 Second Ave., 443-0322

Starbucks, several locations

Subway, several locations

Trattoria Mitchelli, 84 Yesler, 623-3883

Tucci Benucch, 400 Pine St., 624-9000

Un Deux Trois, 1329 First Ave., 233-0123

Undercover Quilts, 622-6382

Uwajimaya Market, International District, 519 Sixth Ave., 624-6248

Waterfront, 1301 Alaskan Way, 623-8600

Westlake Center, 400 Pine St., 467-1600

Wild Ginger, 1400 Western Ave., 623-4450

Where It's At

Unless otherwise noted, all area codes are 206.

Church Council of Greater Seattle, 525-1213

Jewish Community Center, 8606 35th Ave. NE, 526-8073

Luke Wing Asian Museum, 407 7th Ave. S., 623-5124

Martin Luther King Jr. Park, 2200 Martin Luther King Jr. Way, 684-4075

Mount Zion Baptist Church, 1634 19th Ave., 322-6500

Nippon Kan Theatre, 628 S. Washington St., 224-0181

Temple De Hirsch Sinai, 1511 E. Pike St., 323-8486

 ## ETHNIC AND RELIGIOUS PROSPECTS

For a town that's three-fourths Caucasian, Seattle is a pretty hip place. "No one thinks twice about who you spend time with," observes Yamamoto. "You see lots of interracial couples."

It wasn't always so, though. "Things have changed over the past 15 years as Seattle has become more sophisticated and cosmopolitan," adds Bayne. The roots of its large and well-established Asian population can be found in the International District (formerly Chinatown), where multilingual signs direct visitors to shops, restaurants, and parks. Landmarks include **Nippon Kan Theatre** and **Luke Wing Asian Museum,** a unique recounting of Asian American history. It's also a neighborhood with storefront apartments.

Although they're relative latecomers, African-Americans are well-represented, particularly in the central and southern part of Seattle. Along with having a respected jazz and blues scene, luminaries such as Ray Charles, Quincy Jones, and Jimi Hendrix have resided in the area. Places like the memorial at **Martin Luther King Jr. Park,** the **Mount Zion Baptist Church,** and several green spaces honoring local notables provide touchstones for the small but cohesive community. Seattle has even fewer Hispanics and American Indians, although the influence of the latter is apparent in crafts and names of places.

A number of churches, synagogues, and temples are geared to a multiplicity of faiths (**Church Council of Greater Seattle**). The Jewish community in particular "is very tightly knit," remarks Payne. "Seattle has a lot of prominent families who contribute heavily to the various charities. And young people are extremely active." Favorite meeting grounds include the **Jewish Community Center** and **Temple De Hirsch Sinai,** which draws many young professionals and their families. "The beautiful thing about Seattle is that people don't judge a book by its cover." Vive la difference.

CRIB SHEET

Homes in Seattle have one thing in common: They're way more expensive than the national average. Architectural styles range from the houseboats depicted in *Sleepless* to apartments and condos in elegant high-rises best described as "neotraditional" and "funky" to New England–style cottages to estate-like layouts featuring the latest gadgets and gizmos.

An apartment or condo is a more economical alternative. Although rent averages about $650 a month, places such as Belltown, Capitol Hill, and the University District are a little less costly. Although they're not as trendy, the south and west part of town and environs have even cheaper rents. Even though the median asking ticket for condos hovers around $115,000, there's a wide variation in styles and size. The majority are in areas around downtown—Capitol Hill, Queen Anne, and Lake Union—as well as some suburbs like East Bellevue and North Redmond.

Still another solution would be to get one or more roommates. Many of the homes are spacious and allow for privacy. "Three of us share a three-bedroom place with a three-car garage for about $300 a month," points out Acres. "It's a bit of a drive and traffic can be bad, but it's affordable."

> "Those who prefer the casual lifestyle and enjoy sports and just hanging out will have an easier time" of meeting like-minded Seattlites, says a local. But "if you're looking for high-powered types who patronize the trendiest restaurants," well, it could be a long haul.

Those opting to sleep in Seattle have plenty to choose from. The Queen Anne/Magnolia district is known for its proximity to downtown, magnificent views, and Discovery Park, a large natural area. Homes vary from $150,000–285,000. The mansions, elegant homes, and classic apartments draw renters and singles of all races and all sexual and fashion persuasions to Capitol Hill/Central. The range is $120,000–245,000, up to $500,000 for waterfront properties, negating the term "cheap chic." Ballard/Lake Union present a bit more of a bargain. Ballard's strong Scandinavian heritage is combined with a relatively thrifty average price of $163,000 (apartments are $507). This area is also home to the burgeoning Belltown/Denny Regrade which has mostly condos and some new residences.

Highlights of North/Northeast/Northwest include Northgate and Haller Lake, which are close to I-5 and Green Lake. Along with parts that have excellent bus service to downtown, certain locales are heavily wooded and reasonably priced (Northgate, $129,000; Haller Lake, $167,000). Greenwood offers homes (for about $133,000), condos, and rentals. The northeastern areas, consisting of the University District and several others, are pricier ($159,000–298,000), with costs escalating as you get nearer to Lake Washington and farther from the student population.

Small, diverse, and unified communities comprise the 12-square-mile area of Southeast Seattle ($97,000–127,000). Access to Lake Washington and city parks keep occupancy rates high. The Southwest boasts the ever-popular Alki, where life's a beach and old cottages intermingle with new apartments and high-toned manors, the latter of which can be quite costly. Homes south of the beach start at $107,000 (to more than $210,000), while homes in neighborhoods a bit farther away average a more economical $116,000 and are closer to major employment sites and recreational outlets.

Seattle's rapid growth in all directions is illustrated by a prodigious array of suburbs, many of which are more than 45 minutes away and are as or more expensive than city neighborhoods. Residents have the benefits of smaller communities, custom builds, and green spaces. Many prefer smaller districts, which have lower student/teacher ratios and specialized programs. Still, "Seattle has excellent schools," remarks Bayne. Even in the city proper, test scores are in line with Washington State and national averages (Seattle School District No. 1, 298-7000).

Another option is the more than 100 private/parochial schools (Private Education, 360/753-2562; Pacific Northwest Association of Independent Schools, 323-6137). And, although it's dominated by the University of Washington (543-2100), Seattle has several small and community colleges that cater to part-time and non-traditional students.

NAVIGATING SEATTLE

For a first-timer, getting around Seattle can be frustrating. Interstates loop crazily over bridges, hills, and waterways; a wrong turn (on Aurora Avenue, for instance), can lead to a 20-minute detour with no way to circle back. Even maps don't always help—not all streets connect as depicted and some are one-way. And the traffic! Drivers weave in and out of congested roads and most ignore the speed limit. Although Seattlites are tolerant about most things, don't try going solo in a HOV (High Occupancy Vehicle) lane designated for car pools. Someone may report your license number to the police.

The cautious-minded might want to become familiar with the ins and outs of the main arteries (1st Avenue, Stewart Street), before attempting I-5 and I-405, which roughly parallel each other and run north to south; State Route 520, east-west; and I-90, which crosses Lake Washington between 5 and 405. Otherwise, you might find yourself in British Columbia (see "Vancouver"). And those leery of bridges should think twice about moving here. It's almost impossible to get from Point A to B without crossing one. Drawbridges, high-span connectors, even floating models interlink Puget Sound, Lake Washington and the ship canal, and Lake Union. When traffic gets heavy, motorists sit awhile, particularly over Lake Washington.

Other forms of transportation are less imposing. Voted #1 in the U.S., Seattle's METRO Transit system (553-3000) offers express routes and free Park 'n' Ride options during certain hours. Their exclusive access to a 1.3 mile underground roadway beneath downtown not only relieves congestion but can reduce commuting times by 50 percent. Community Transit (353-RIDE) has service in and around the city and suburbs. Those living across the Sound can hop aboard the inexpensive and ubiquitous Washington State ferries (Pier 52, 464-6400). The largest such system in the U.S., it "ships" 23 million passengers a year on nine routes.

Along with being smack dab between its two namesakes, the Seattle-Tacoma (Sea-Tac) airport (431-4444) is an easy 20 minutes from downtown, and was recently remodeled. Sea-Tac has steadily increased to more than 20 million passengers a year. Amtrak (800/USA-RAIL) and buses (Trailways, 728-5955; Greyhound, 800/231-2222) are other ways of getting out of town. Those wanting to negotiate the mountains by car should contact the local office of the Washington State Department of Transportation (call 455-7900) for the best routes and road conditions, especially during winter months.

TORONTO, ONTARIO, CANADA

A Brief Glance

Size and Growth: 635,395 (City of Toronto), 4,262,199 (Greater Toronto CMA). Percent change, 1986–1996: +24.0% (CMA).

Money Matters (all in Canadian dollars): *Unemployment rate*—8.5%.
Average household income—$65,000.
Average cost of a home—$199,000.
Average rent for an apartment—$641/month.
Cost of living—$87,392 (for a family of four, compared to the Canadian average of $75,000).

People Profile: *Crime rate*—rated by *Fortune* magazine as the safest city in North America.
Racial and ethnic characteristics (based on "mother tongue" in city of Toronto population)—English, 384,505; Portuguese, 44,955; Chinese, 40,740; Italian, 19,425; Spanish, 12,065; Polish, 11,785; French, 10,595; Greek, 8,320; many others.
Gender ratio—There are slightly more males than females in the 20–24 age group; the ratio is about 50–50 in the 25–29 group and reverses in the 30–34 group, with an even larger number of females in the 35–39 group.
Age characteristics (based on Toronto CMA)—20–24, 279,983; 25–29, 342,872; 30–34, 384,386; 35–39, 379,729. Median age: N/A.

Major Players: Services; retail/wholesale trade; government; manufacturing, especially transportation, equipment, and textiles. With more than 400 business periodicals, 65 ethnic publications, and 300 consumer magazines, Toronto is Canada's publishing and production center.

TORONTO:
DRAFT DODGING

The Huron word for "meeting place," Toronto certainly is that. A region of about 3 million people representing more than 80 ethnic groups and speaking 100 different languages (usually English and something else), Toronto has been tagged by the United Nations as the world's most ethnically diverse city. True, in 1788 the Mississagua Indians sold it to the English for a couple of thousand pounds, some flannels, and axes; and during the War of 1812 the Americans actually took it over for four days (in retaliation, the Brits tried to burn down the White House).

But this city has a time-honored reputation for welcoming refugees, including a 350,000-strong Asian population, some 80,000 Polish expatriates, and another 300,000 West Indians (representing all 25 Caribbean Islands) as well as Vietnam-era draft dodger Yanks. And that's not even mentioning the 400,000 Canadians of Italian descent; the 100,000 Greeks; and strong Portuguese, Jewish, and Korean communities.

With a strong economy, a minimum of crime, and relatively new, sparkly clean skyscrapers interspersed among charming Victorian structures, the huddled-masses approach seems to have paid off in a big way. Toronto's vibrant cultural menu includes theater, art, and filmmaking. Although Toronto's cost of living is on the level with the more expensive American cities, people with work visas, residence permits, and the proper immigration clearance will likely find it an opportune choice.

With a market that has dropped 28 percent since 1989, housing is cheaper and more plentiful than in Vancouver—that other Canadian city known as a politically diverse filmmaking mecca. In the past few years, the rental market has been opening up as well. Folks opting to drive a car will find Toronto's geography mostly manageable, with streets forming a gridlike pattern and motoring on the right (American) side of the road. Those going down Yonge Street had better know the address; as the longest thoroughfare in the world, it extends all the way to Rainy River, Ontario, nearly 1,200 miles away. And traffic, particularly along Highway 401, which skirts the northern edge of the city, is dense. Public transportation consists of a comprehensive network of trains and buses for the frustration-impaired.

Don't be fooled by the talk about Toronto being on the same latitude as Northern California: This place gets cold in the winter. It's no accident that you can purchase and wear great fur and leather coats around these parts without a second glance. Toronto is the site of the world's largest artificial ice-skating rink (at York Quay near the harbor); Nathan Phillips Square in front of City Hall is another well-attended slick spot. You can always find out the forecast by looking at the beacon tower at the Canada Life Building. Lights indicate the trends in temperature, with red for rain and green for clear. Nor is it surprising that, along with lots of unique restaurant and shopping neighborhoods, downtown Toronto's Under-ground City runs for seven miles under 50 buildings. Overlook the Anglicized spelling in some words and it's almost like the USA, eh?

GENERAL OPPORTUNITIES

As one of the world's newest major megalopoli, Toronto is "hip, sophisticated, smart, with lots of character," according to Stephen Williams of *New York Newsday.* "The streets are not lined with gold but with flowers." Toronto's biggest strength is perhaps that much of its business core is situated in several "downtowns"—the city centers in North York, Etobicoke, and Mississagua—as well as growing burgs to the north and east of "Metro," what many locals call the city center.

Although the average household income is higher than in any other Canadian city (and in some cities in the United States), jobs can be scarce, particularly for newcomers without contacts (see the chapter on Vancouver). As a noncitizen on a limited visa, you might have stiff competition from folks already approved by immigration. However, those with jobs or solid leads can prosper from burgeoning tourism, manufacturing, communications, and other fields. Not bad for a city previously nicknamed "Muddy York" because of the condition of its streets and "Hogtown" because of its bacon factory.

HOW TORONTO WORKS AND PLAYS

Major Breadwinning

In downtown Toronto, Bay Street (the Due North version of Wall Street) has the largest concentration of banks and financial institutions in the country and basically dominates the economy. Those with financial and accounting skills may indeed find Metro's office buildings embedded with gold, such as several million dollars' worth of flakes in the tinted windows of the Royal Bank Plaza (fiberglass doesn't quite make the same statement). The Canadian Imperial Bank of Commerce, Royal Bank, the Toronto Dominion Bank, and the Bank of Nova Scotia are among the city's biggest employers, which provide a total of 166,000 of the metropolitan area's close to 2 million jobs.

Folks with a public relations, hospitality, or marketing background may stumble upon a niche in the area's $5.4 billion (Canadian) visitor industry.

Manufacturing is another major player. As part of the world's seventh-largest economy, Toronto businesses construct, design, sell, and service everything from chemicals and local natural resources to aerospace and computer products, supplying about 450,000 positions. The automotive industry is strong, with General Motors of Canada alone employing over 20,000 workers. With Chrysler and Ford represented too, Toronto is like a mini-Detroit on the other side of the Great Lakes. Oshawa Foods, Shoppers Drug Mart, Maple Leaf Foods/ Miracle Mart, and others provide thousands more jobs in food processing and sales.

> With a strong economy, a minimum of crime, and relatively new, sparkly clean skyscrapers interspersed among charming Victorian structures, the huddled-masses approach seems to have paid off in a big way. Toronto's vibrant cultural menu includes theater, art, and filmmaking.

Toronto is a hotbed for the creative. The booming fashion industry even has its own district (Spadina Avenue along Front Street to College Street). And the city boasts nearly 20,000 jobs in film production, which injects about $1 billion a year into the economy and includes work in television series, movies, and commercials. Hey, they invented the wide-screen IMAX process here, eh? The September Festival of Festivals has become at least the second-largest film jamboree around. The CBC Broadcast Centre, one of the most modern facilities in the world, is home to the country's English and French media and television services.

The area has close to 80,000 small businesses, many of which can be found in Metro or North York. More than 95,000 more jobs are tied up with the state, local, and city governments, as well as public education. These jobs may be difficult for noncitizens and newcomers to obtain. But even those whose skills don't exactly fit can always find relatively inexpensive training (or honing) at a variety of institutions, including the University of Toronto, the country's largest; York University; Ryerson Polytechnic University; the Ontario College of Art, Canada's most prestigious; and several community colleges.

ARTS AND SCIENCES

Area code 416 is a genial place, although Canada has its own particular set of social codes and mores (see the chapter on Vancouver). Perhaps the best way to get acquainted with Metro and the smaller downtowns is simply to walk around; should you get lost or even look confused, natives and transplants will likely come to your rescue and tell you what you need to know (although it might not be in English).

Culture vultures and others can flock to a veritable herd of offerings. There are dozens of art collections; the Art Gallery of Ontario, with 15,000 paintings, is the city's biggest. For music and dance, you can visit the Toronto Symphony in spectacular Roy Thomson Hall; the ever-popular Canadian Opera and Toronto Ballet; and the Premiere Dance Theatre at Harbourfront, the only venue of its kind in Canada. Museums include the Royal Ontario Museum, with a dinosaur gallery, ethnic exhibits, and a "bat cave" (no, thank you); the Bata Shoe Museum, a must for fetishists, with 10,000 pairs spanning 4,000 years; the Ontario Science Centre; and the Black Creek Pioneer Museum.

But the city's edge lies in its dynamic theater scene: More than 140 professional companies (up from two in 1962) perform an average of 50 different productions each month. Toronto has the third largest entertainment industry in the English-speaking world (after London and New York), and Torontonians love their movies (the city has the third-largest per capita movie-going population), live plays, musicals, and concerts. Venues vary from the restored Royal Alexandria (circa 1900); to the Pantages, another rescue from multicinema obscurity; to the Elgin and Winter Garden complex, one the world's few remaining "stacked" theaters, where one stage is on top of the other. The lively experimental scene offers the Fringe Festival (50 new plays in a two-week period), Queer Culture (gay and lesbian works), and others.

THE SPORTING LIFE

During the warmer months, about 375 parks (nearly 10,000 acres) provide walking, jogging, and bicycle paths as well as beaches that border Lake Ontario. Popular play spaces include the interconnected Toronto Islands in the harbor; the Martin Goodman Trail for hiking and biking; Allen Gardens, a pretty place in the city center with a large greenhouse; and High Park, Toronto's answer to Central Park with trails, a menagerie, outdoor theater, and Grenadier Pond, to mention a few. Toronto and environs also offer public swimming, skating, tennis, and fitness facilities and instructions. The city has a full complement of professional sports as well: there are the Argonauts football team, the World Series–winning Blue Jays, the National Hockey League Maple Leafs, and the newly formed NBA Raptors.

AFTER-HOURS DIVERSIONS

Dinner theater and comedy usually live up to their hype. Venues such as Second City, Yuk Yuk's Comedy Cabaret, Laugh Resort, The New La Cage Dinner Theatre/Rock 'n' Roll Heaven, and more have spawned major talents such as Jim Carrey, Martin Short, and Howie Mandel. Toronto's ever-changing and fickle nightlife seesaws from jazz bars to rock clubs to alternative/experimental. The warehouse district of Richmond, Adelade, and John Streets packs in trendies and "X"ers at Syn, Atlas, Whiskey Saigon, and Fluid Lounge. Major spots include Crocodile Rock, where Creole culture meets Elvis; glitzy, glamorous RPM/Warehouse, which hosts "A" rock groups including the Rolling Stones; the Joker, four floors of court-and-jester decor and 'Net access too; Studebakers, with its '50s through '70s hits; and the Saloon, offering an authentic Western atmosphere for homesick cowpokes. On the other side of the atmospheric Atlantic are British pubs such as Duke of Westminster, Elephant and Castle, and more. Other areas of note: Yorkville, a groovy haven for the '60s counterculture turned yuppie; Queen Street West (between University and Spadina), which is full of offbeat clubs; and the Underground, where the party continues, no matter what the weather.

CULINARY AND SHOPPING HAUNTS

With more than 5,500 offerings, *extensive* can only begin to describe Toronto's restaurant scene (for an overview, try DineNet: www.dine.net). You can sample more than 80 varieties of food from around the globe at Acme Bar and Grill and Zazu (both Canadian-American cuisine), Amalfi (Italian), Bangkok Garden (Thai), Chez Max (French), Filet of Sole (seafood), Penelope (Greek), and Shopsy's (deli). An easy way to explore culinary Toronto is to go to the various ethnic neighborhoods and stop at whatever looks appetizing.

Shopping began in Toronto's early days as a trading post and has grown exponentially ever since. Metro alone has Bloor-Yorkville, a small upscale enclave of boutiques and galleries, including Hazelton Lanes (not a bowling alley, but a très chic home decor and fashion development); Harbourfront Centre, where you'll find artisans along with standard stores; Spadina Avenue, fashion and fur central and also close to several factory outlet stores; and Queen Street West, avant-garde designers and shops galore. Thousands flock to Eaton Centre, with its 350 stores. Modeled after Milan's Galleria, this underground mall is Toronto's largest.

Other biggies: Scarsborough Town Centre, with 325 shops; Square One, with 280; and Sherway Gardens, with 265. And the Underground City connects to other collections of stores, including First Canadian Place and Royal Bank Plaza. Only in Toronto: Honest Ed's Famous Bargain Centre, with 160,000 square feet of deals and arguably the world's most electrifying sign (with more than 22,000 light bulbs) and Barbie on Bay, for the doll that has everything.

ETHNIC AND RELIGIOUS PROSPECTS

Unlike some American cities, which consider *alien* a dirty word (especially when prefaced by *illegal*), Toronto prides itself on being Canada's number-one destination for immigrants, from both inside and outside the country. Scratch a major global disturbance, and you'll likely find a community in Toronto; a number of Jews relocated here before and after the Holocaust, and since 1980, several thousand Poles have made it their home.

Although the city is often cited as an example of racial integration, its distinct neighborhoods have preserved each country's identity. You can go home again (sort of) and work and live in a particular community, such as Little Italy (Corso Italia); three Chinatowns (which represent Metro's fastest-growing group); Greektown at Danforth Avenue; a Jewish community in Kensington Market and North York; the mostly Eastern European and Catholic Roncesvalles Avenue; Koreatown (Bloor St. W. between Bathurst and Christie); and a West Indian community in the suburbs north of highway 401. The city's considerable gay population is concentrated in the Church and Wellesley area. Even White Anglo-Saxon Protestants can feel comfortable here, as folks of British extraction still make up the city's largest ethnic group. (However, serious Francophiles should try Quebec.)

Although Toronto lost its reputation for Puritanism in the 1800s, it's still the location of a large number of churches. The only difference now is that just about every denomination is covered.

CRIB SHEET

You don't have to be English Canadian to live in the exclusive communities of Rosedale and Forest Hill, although coming from an established family and having lots of the green stuff helps. Rent in Rosedale bottoms out at about $1,900 (Canadian dollars) per month, while condos go for around $269,000, with your basic mansion starting in the low seven figures.

> Toronto has a time-honored reputation for welcoming refugees, including a 350,000-strong Asian population, some 80,000 Polish expatriates, and another 300,000 West Indians. . . And that's not even mentioning the 400,000 Italian-Canadians; the 100,000 Greeks; and the Portuguese, Jewish, and Korean communities.

Still, prices have been dropping citywide, resulting in some really great buys. More in line with beginners' pocketbooks is North Toronto, where places like Yonge-Eglinton cater to the unattached. Yonge-Eglinton offers a variety of residences, from one-bedroom apartments ($550/month) to new townhouses ($275,000) to homes in exclusive Lawrence Park with prices topping $1 million. Other hip neighborhoods include Cabbagetown, where renovation has brought new life as well as escalated costs ($750+ for a one-bedroom apartment; $275,000+ for a home); the Beaches, which has a board-walk and is popular with artists ($500 for a basement apartment; homes for $235,000 to nearly $500,000); and Riverdale, a multi-cultural community, with a wide variety of housing ($600 for an unrestored one-bedroom apartment; $350,000 for a completely updated home). Other spots, such as St. Lawrence Market, High Park, and Parkdale, have a large selection of rentals and condos, while Bloor West Village offers excellent grocery shopping and neighborhoods for young families.

Toronto taxpayers support two school systems: one that's nondenominational and another for Roman Catholics. Schools also offer programs for children with special needs, including the gifted; adult and alternative options; French immersion classes; and other courses of study where the primary language is French. Many private schools are available as well.

VANCOUVER, BRITISH COLUMBIA, CANADA

Vancouver at a Glance

Birthdate and Present Size: 1865.
Metropolitan area population, 1986 census:
1,380,729. 1991 census: 1,602,502.
Percent change, 1986–1991: +16.06%.

Weather Report: *Average annual temperature—*57° F. In January: 41/32° F.
In July: 74/54° F.
Average annual precipitation—57"
*Average annual snowfall—*23.8".

Money Matters: *Unemployment rate—*
8.6%.
Per capita income: $27,476 (all figures in
Canadian dollars)
Average household income—$50,573
(MSA); $45,180 (city).
Average cost of a home—East side:
$311,000; West side: $620,000.
Average rent for an apartment—
$850–$1,250/month.
Taxes—The provincial sales tax is 6%
(excludes food, restaurant meals, and children's clothing). Most goods and services
are subject to a 7% Canadian Federal
Goods and Services Tax (GST).
Cost of living—N/A.

People Profile: *Crime rate—*
Approximately 9,500 criminal acts per
month (all crimes, including traffic
violations). Vancouver has less than 20
homicides per every 6-month period.
Racial and ethnic characteristics—No
specific figures available. Approximately

one-fourth of the population is Asian,
with the remainder being Canadian,
American, French, German, Italian and
other (East Indian, Hispanic, First Nation,
etc.). (Various nationalities can include a
small percentage of blacks.)
Gender ratio—49.2 males to 50.8 females.
Age characteristics—18–24 (N/A);
25–44 (35.7%). Median age: N/A.
Educational attainment—percent having
completed non-university schooling, 28.5
(MSA), 66.0 (city); percent having completed university, 40.7 (MSA), 34.0 (city).

Major Players: Wholesale/retail trade,
manufacturing, banking, forestry, agriculture, mining, fishing, tourism.
Largest employers—Vancouver International
Airport, Vancouver Hospital, City of
Vancouver, B.C. Teachers' Federation,
MacMillan Bloedel Ltd.

Community Services: *Medical care—*
Qualified British Columbia residents can
participate in the Medical Services Plan,
which covers physicians, surgeons, specialized treatment and dental surgery.
Monthly premiums: $36 for one person,
$64 for two or more (Canadian dollars).
*Newspapers—Vancouver Sun, The Province,
The Financial Times of Canada, Globe and
Mail, Oriental Star, Indo-Canadian Voice,
Jewish Western Daily, Terminal City* (alternative), *Georgia Straight* (arts), others.

VANCOUVER: POLITE OASIS

Although it's only about 25 miles from the U.S. border, Vancouver is in another world. Canada 99 weaves through neighborhoods and stoplights, providing a less-than-spectacular entrance into a city that's renowned for its natural allure. Not to worry. Although building is taking place pell-mell, and most streets look like an architectural hodgepodge, Vancouver is in a jewel of a setting. Framed by the snowcapped Coast Mountains, the indigo harbor bustles with ships, freighters, and smaller craft. Unlike some U.S. cities whose ports are hidden behind a grim facade of warehouses, railroad tracks and rubble, Vancouver's is out there in all its natural glory.

Of course, Vancouver wasn't always the fastest-growing city in North America. Discovered in 1791 by the Spanish explorer Don Jose Marie Narvaez, this former rainforest was home to the Salish Indians. British navigator James Cook, the first European to actually land there, decided to name it after

George Vancouver, a member of his expedition who sailed around the island in 1792. Good thing, too—the place could have been called Gastown, after John "Gassy Jack" Deighton, a talkative tavern owner who helped build the first saloon, or perhaps "Cow Crossing," the Dutch translation of the original Vancouver family name. Neither would look good on the cover of a *Frommer's* guide.

> Vancouver may seem quaint and provincial to those used to the centralized bustle of a major American city. But walk around on a midsummer's day, and it seems like everyone but the tourists is fit, tanned, and smiling.

During the early 1800s, the Americans claimed the platelet-shaped island and surrounding territories. They gave it back to the Brits in 1846, and what is now Stanley Park was established to guard the harbor entrance from pugnacious Yanks. The military even put in a cannon, although its main use has been to let the populace know when it's 9 p.m., a sort of Canadian alarm clock. The community prospered, and by the turn of the century it became the largest commercial hub in western Canada.

In the 1960s and '70s, the building boom began as trade with Asia increased. Expo '86, the Canadian World's Fair, accelerated the process. Today tourists and expatriates alike are getting more bang for their buck in both business and recreational opportunities. This bodes especially well for Americans who get another 33 cents or so for their dollar, depending on the rate of exchange.

Quality of Life

Vancouver may seem quaint and provincial to those used to the centralized bustle of a major American metropolis. But walk around on a midsummer's day, and it seems like everyone but the tourists is fit, tanned, and smiling. "Vancouver's a paradise if you're a jock," half-jokes travel writer Isabel Nanton. "It really is true—you can go skiing and sailing in the same day."

Although locals spend more money on sports equipment than anywhere else, they also consume more wine and a heck of a lot of coffee, the latte(r) being a Pacific Northwest thing (see Seattle). Perhaps that comes from sitting around in outdoor cafes—because of the mountains and warm Pacific breezes, Vancouver is exempt from the Nanook of the North whims of the Canadian climate. Even natives, though, have a tough time dealing with the three-month gloom that comes with winter's rainy season. "Those of us who can try to go to Mexico for three weeks," adds communications manager Doti Niedermayer.

Still, the Geneva-based Corporate Resources group gave kudos to Vancouver in terms of quality of life, social and natural environments, culture, health, education, public services, recreation, and housing. Plus, "It's very safe here," Neidermayer continues. "You can leave your purse on a chair and not worry about having it stolen. I can go for a walk in the city at 1 a.m. and not be disturbed. People are very unaggressive and nonthreatening" (still another Canadian thing).

The city is hardly homogeneous. Consisting of more than 60 cultural groups, nearly one-fourth of the population is Asian, with plenty of Americans, Europeans and Indians (the non-Native American kind) thrown in for good measure. "It's large and multicultural enough that you can be yourself and feel comfortable," adds Niedermayer. Official languages are French and English, although the tongues most often heard are English and Chinese, followed by Punjabi, German, French, Italian, Tagalog (Filipino), and Spanish.

With a laid-back lifestyle, funky shops and chic eateries, certain parts of Vancouver resemble the U.S. West Coast. But appearances can be deceiving. People are uniformly courteous, even skateboard-toting high school students. "And no one would think of carrying a gun," adds Niedermayer. There are also lots of small disparities—the metric system, rainbow-colored money, and even the design of candy and chewing gum packages is different. But like the U.S., Vancouver can be a land of opportunity.

General Opportunities

"Vancouver is a magnet for creative people," observes theater director Jay Ono. Movie studios and film crews abound. Because its varied landscape can pass for Africa, China, France, and many American cities, Vancouver has become a premier film-making spot after Los Angeles and New York, and is often dubbed "Hollywood north." With a scene packed with theater, dance, music, literature, and festivals, Vancouver has always been a greenhouse for the arts.

The city has gone construction crazy, and huge cranes seem like a permanent part of the landscape. There's plenty in the works: an expanded airport and rail service; countless housing starts, hotels, and restaurants; a science/space center; and Pacific Place, a mix of high-rise apartments, stores, and parks along the False Creek waterfront.

The downside (and it's a biggie) are housing costs and taxes. The former "has virtually zoomed into outer space," observes one longtime resident. City vacancy rates are usually less than one percent and the average price of a home hovers around $400,000. Even with the U.S. discount of 33 percent, that's still a budget-busting $264,000. "People have started taking in lodgers to just pay their mortgages. It's not strictly legal, but it's either do that or move an hour away." Although food, entertainment, clothing and related expenses are pretty much in line with the average American cost of living, a 7 percent Canadian Goods and Services Tax (GST) is tacked onto just about everything. This is in *addition* to the 6 percent provincial sales tax for most items. Ouch!

Still, growing pains are to be expected. "This is not an old city that's already been built," comments Niedermayer. "We're experiencing unparalleled change." Still, in a country where dollars are referred to as "loonies" any revolution is sure to be civil.

MAJOR BREADWINNING

Obtaining a work permit in Vancouver is done on a case-by-case basis. If a company can justify the need for a certain position, a visa will likely be granted.

Like other nationalities, Americans can do well here. One-third of the approximately 65,000 annual migrants are foreigners. "Canada is a racially tolerant place," comments newspaper editor Malcolm Kirk.

Although the local economy is headquarters for more than 160 major corporations with a total revenue of about $60 billion, Vancouver retains a leisurely charm. Employees may find themselves succumbing to *mañana* (tomorrow) disease: With spring in full bloom by early March and continuing until October, the place isn't exactly conducive to sitting in a windowless office.

The city's connection with Hong Kong has brought much of the prosperity. As a result of the 1997 changeover from the British government to the Chinese government, "People are leaving and bringing their money with them to Vancouver," points out Ono. The combined East/West knowledge of the second-generation Japanese and Chinese population provides even more of an advantage. Vancouver has become a link for trade with Asia. As a gateway to the Pacific and a main hub for foreign-made goods destined for North America (as well as Canadian exports), the port is the country's largest.

The 1995 "open skies" agreement between the U.S. and Canada has also bolstered assets. Along with providing better access to markets across the border, it's made passage easier for tourists of both countries. Travel itself is on the increase: More than 7 million visitors a year translate into $2.2 billion and about 66,000 jobs. The last is only a part of the burgeoning service industry, which encompasses approximately two-thirds of the workforce.

Still, much of the economy depends on forestry (13 percent), food distribution such as fishing (8.1 percent), and mining (6.2 percent). Construction and retail provide a combined 11 percent. And, given the free flow of money, it's not surprising that one of the biggest growth areas has been in finance and banking (5.6 percent). Most Canadian banks and nearly 50 foreign/international institutions can be found in Vancouver.

Diverse, eh? Industry-wise, "Vancouver's a real mixed bag," adds Kirk. And likely to become more so: By 2011, it's estimated that the number of employees will balloon from 750,000 to over 1,200,000.

And while getting ahead is important, "we're not about being No. 1," remarks Niedermayer. In this neck of the Canadian woods, pushy work habits will likely create a negative effect. For those willing to put ruthlessness in the rumble seat, Vancouver can be ideal.

SOCIAL AND RECREATIONAL SCENE

How Vancouver Plays

Unlike other cities "where everyone is focused intently on what they're doing, people in Vancouver take the time to look from side to side," remarks Ono. This can be good or bad news—single-minded individuals might find themselves frustrated, while those with varied interests have lots of resources to start from.

Although perpetually nice and helpful, many Canadians have a reticent side. "We're not like the Brits, who are veddy, veddy proper, but neither are we like Americans, who tend to tell you everything about themselves, often more than you want to know," explains one local.

But even Canadians can have a difficult time in area code 604. "Vancouver doesn't have much of a nightlife," admits Kirk. "It's improved somewhat in the few years I've lived here, but it still has a long way to go."

And the dating scene can be grim, "particularly for those of us who want a committed relationship and have high standards," adds Niedermayer. "People who are looking for something casual will have a better time of it." Things may change as Vancouver enters the megalopolis stage. But until then, newcomers may have to roll up their sleeves and dig. "Ultimately you have your own interests, so the trick is to start from there."

ARTS AND SCIENCES

Those with a creative flair may find it easier to make connections in Vancouver than, say, accountants or computer programmers. With all the artists in Vancouver, it's quite a community of kindred souls.

With an opera house that rivaled the local saloon in attendance, the first arts council in North America, and the first children's festival anywhere (**Vancouver International Children's Festival**), the arts in Vancouver have always been lively. Today the choices are almost overwhelming. More than 3,200 annual events range from men's choirs to baroque orchestra, avant garde theater to Broadway productions, ballet to traditional Japanese dances, and just about everything in between. Those experiencing an overdose of options (or just wanting more information) can call the **Arts Hotline.**

The theater alone has over a month's worth of professional groups (32), 21 venues, and two major festivals (**New Play Festival, Fringe Festival**), as well as the **International Comedy Festival** (July). Designed by internationally acclaimed architect Moshe Safdie, Vancouver's biggest and most recent jewel, the **Ford Centre for the Performing Arts** added another 600,000 seats. The **Vancouver Playhouse** is the area's most well-established troupe, with sold-out performances of both contemporary and classical dramas. Thespians also perform in a renovated fire station (**Firehall Arts Centre**), church (**Vancouver East Cultural Center,** a.k.a. the "Cultch"), or converted warehouses. The latter includes the **Arts Club Theatre** on the Granville Island entertainment complex. Summertime brings the **Bard on the Beach** and **Theatre Under the Stars.**

Music and dance are almost as ubiquitous. Along with a symphony orchestra (**Vancouver Symphony**), opera (**Vancouver Opera**) and ballet (**Vancouver Ballet Society**), Vancouver is the only remaining city in the continent with its own radio orchestra (**Vancouver CBC Radio Orchestra**). It is also a hotbed for taiko music, a combination of New Age and Japanese tunes that utilizes drums, flutes and African and Latin percussion. The **Vancouver Cantata Singers** and half-a-dozen other live groups perform everything from Bach to popular Canadian tunes. Along with a **New Music Festival** (June), **Folk Music Festival** (July), and **Chamber Music Festival** (July/ August), Vancouver has the renowned **duMaurier International Jazz Festival** (July) as well as its very own **Jazz Hotline.** Not to be outdone, the **Dancing on the Edge Festival** (biannual, July) is a 10-day marathon featuring 60–80 pieces created by independent choreographers.

Where It's At

 Unless otherwise noted, all area codes are 604.

Annual Vancouver International Film Festival, various theaters, 685-0260

Arts Club Theatre, Granville Island entertainment complex, 1585 Johnson St., 687-1644

Arts Hotline, 684-ARTS

Bard on the Beach, 1101 W. Broadway, 737-0625

Bloedel Floral Conservatory, 33rd and Cambie, 872-5513

Capilano Salmon Hatchery, 4500 Capilano Rd., 666-1790

Chamber Music Festival, Vanier Park, 602-0363

Cineplex Odeon theaters, various locations

Dancing on the Edge Festival, Firehall Arts Centre, 689-0691

Dr. Sun Yat-Sen Classical Chinese Garden, 578 Carrall St., 662-3207

duMaurier International Jazz Festival, Gastown, 873-1914

Firehall Arts Centre, 280 E. Cordova, 689-0926

Folk Music Festival, Jericho Beach Park, 879-2931

Ford Centre for the Performing Arts, 777 Homer St., 844-2808

Fringe Festival, 873-3646

George G. Reifel Bird Sanctuary, 5191 Robertson Rd., Delta, 946-6980

International Comedy Festival, 683-0883

Inuit Gallery of Vancouver, 345 Water St., 688-7323

Jazz Hotline, 682-0706

Marion Scott Gallery, 481 Howe St., 685-1934

Museum of Geology, Geological Science Centre, 822-5586

Museum of Mining, Britannia Beach, 688-8735

Museum of Sugar, 123 Rogers St., 253-1131

New Music Festival, various locations, 280-3311

New Play Festival, 685-6228

Where It's At

(continued)

Pacific Cinematheque, 1311 Howe St., 688-8202

Pacific Space Centre, 1100 Chestnut St., 738-7827

Park, 3440 Cambie St., 876-2747

Ridge, 3131 Arbutus, 738-6311

Science World British Columbia, 1455 Quebec St., 443-7440

Sri Lankan Gem Museum, 150–195 W. Georgia, 662-7768

Theatre Under the Stars, 2250 W. 33rd Ave., 687-0174

U.B.C. Botanical Garden, 6804 SW Marine Dr., 822-3928

U.B.C. Museum of Anthropology, 6393 NW Marine Dr., 882-3825

Uno Langmann, 2117 Granville St., 736-8825

Vancouver Aquarium, Stanley Park, 685-3364

Vancouver Art Gallery, 750 Hornby St., 682-4668

Vancouver Ballet Society, 649 Cambie St., 669-5954

Vancouver Cantata Singers, 5115 Keith Rd., 921-8588

Vancouver CBC Radio Orchestra, 700 Hamilton St., 662-6000

Vancouver East Cultural Center, 1895 Venable St., 251-1363

Vancouver International Children's Festival, Vanier Park, 687-7697

Vancouver International Writers and Readers Festival, Granville Island, 681-6330

Vancouver Museum, 1100 Chestnut St., 736-4431

Vancouver Opera, #500–845 Cambie St., 682-2871

Vancouver Playhouse, 160 W. 1st Ave., 872-6622

Vancouver Police Historical Society, 240 E. Cordova, 665-3346

Vancouver Symphony, 601 Smithe St., 684-9100

VanDusen Botanical Gardens, 5251 Oak St., 257-8670

Video In, 1965 Main St., 872-8337

With such an active moviemaking community, it follows that cinema would be big as well. The **Annual Vancouver International Film Festival** (October) reels in a growing crowd as well as hundreds of movies and industry insiders. With more than 7,000 members and an immense library, **Pacific Cinematheque** collaborates with film, arts, ethnic, and other groups on various projects. "Art houses" such as the **Ridge,** the **Park, Video In** and others feature foreign and alternative flicks (yes, they're still called that in Canada). Those on a budget will appreciate Cheap Tuesdays, where the cost of all tickets is discounted at Theatre Row in the Granville Street area and at Cineplex Odeon theaters.

Last but certainly not least are the literary/visual arts. With both the highest number of books read and the greatest number of authors in Canada, British Columbia is home to Douglas Coupland (*Generation X*), W.P. Kinsella (*Shoeless Joe,* made into the movie *Field of Dreams*), and Nick Bantock (*Griffin & Sabine*). The **Vancouver International Writers and Readers Festival** (October) attracts thousands of bibliophiles and internationally acclaimed writers as well.

Housed in a former courthouse, the **Vancouver Art Gallery** offers traveling exhibits highlighting local, national, and international works as well as the paintings of regional artist Emily Carr. The **Inuit Gallery of Vancouver, Marion Scott Gallery, Uno Langmann** and many others sell Northwestern art and antiques.

Vancouver's museums are abundant and varied. They range from the glittery gaudiness of the **Sri Lankan Gem Museum** to the "Book 'em, Dano" ambience (weapons, counterfeit money, morgue room) of the **Vancouver Police Historical Society** and others. Those with a historical bent will find lots of regional remnants at the **Vancouver Museum.** The **U.B.C. Museum of Anthropology** offers an outstanding display of original Native American (in Canada, called First Nation) works and European ceramics in a stunning architectural setting.

Science buffs have much to put under the microscope as well. The **Museum of Mining, Museum of Sugar,** and **Museum of Geology** provide insight into the region's natural resources. The **Vancouver Aquarium** and **Capilano Salmon Hatchery** examine what goes on beneath the sea. **Science World British Columbia** and the **Pacific Space Centre** analyze the principles behind tornadoes and exploding zucchini as well as stargazing of the astrological kind.

Those who love plants and/or birds will flourish in the **Bloedel Floral Conservatory.** With the second largest geodesic dome in the world, it showcases 500 species of plants and 100 free-flying tropical birds (head coverings recommended). Step into the traditional world of ancient and modern China at **Dr. Sun Yat-Sen Classical Chinese Garden,** the only authentic Ming Dynasty garden built outside that country. The **U.B.C. Botanical Garden** has several specialized plant collections, while the **VanDusen Botanical Gardens** offers a more global approach with 55 acres of more than 6,500 plants from five continents. No fly-by-night operation, the **George G. Reifel Bird Sanctuary** provides a winter home for hundreds of migratory species.

THE SPORTING LIFE

Sports are a big part of life in Vancouver and "a great way to meet people," observes Malcolm Kirk. "Many move here because of the leisure activities." Almost every physical endeavor, ranging from bicycling (**Cycling British Columbia**) to tennis (**Tennis B.C.**) to running (**Running Room**) to swimming (**Vancouver Aquatic Center**) as well as golfing (**B.C. Golf Association**), in-line skating (**Seymour Demonstration Forest**), windsurfing (**Squamish Windsurfing Society**) and boating and fishing (**Federal Department of Fisheries and Oceans; B.C. Ministry of Environment, Lands and Parks**) can be found in abundance. (Boating licenses can be obtained through the **Registrar of Ships.**) The **Canadian International Dragon Boat Festival** (June) attracts competitors from all over the world. There's even a **Polar Bear Swim** (January 1) for those wanting to get the New Year off to a bracing start.

There's also hiking (**Sport B.C.**), kayaking (**Sea Kayaking Association; Whitewater Kayaking Association**), skiing (**B.C. Alpine Ski Association**), snowboarding (**B.C. Snowboarding Association**), diving (**Canadian Amateur Diving Association**) and birding (**Canadian Outback Adventure Company**). Okay, so the last is a bit of a stretch, but Vancouver draws thousands of would-be naturalists to the aforementioned Reifel Sanctuary and other avian hot spots. **Sport B.C.** or the **Outdoor Recreation Council of B.C.** has a line on about every organized activity.

Many of these workouts can be enjoyed in the nearly 175 parks around the city. With 1,000 forested acres, Stanley Park offers beaches, lagoons, and dozens of trails. Another popular spot, Queen Elizabeth Park, has greenery and tennis courts galore (for information, contact **Vancouver Board of Parks**). Urban adventurers can explore the diverse architecture of False Creek (actually a tidal inlet), get "bogged" down at Point Grey or follow their noses (and watch their feet) at the horse-intensive and monied South-lands. The picturesque **Seymour Demonstration Forest** is not only a

Where It's At

Unless otherwise noted, all area codes are 604.

B.C. Alpine Ski Association, 737-3070

B.C. Golf Association, 294-1818

B.C. Lions, 583-7747

B.C. Ministry of Environment, Lands and Parks, 582-5200

B.C. Place, 777 Pacific Blvd., 669-2300

B.C. Ferries, 669-1211 or 277-0277

B.C. Rail, 800/663-8238

B.C. Snowboarding Association, 737-3027

Bailey Stadium, 4601 Ontario, 872-5232

Canadian Amateur Diving Association, 737-3043

Canadian International Dragon Boat Festival, False Creek, 688-2382

Canadian Outback Adventure Company, 688-7206

Cycling British Columbia, 737-3034

Cypress Bowl, 926-6007

Federal Department of Fisheries and Oceans, 666-3545

General Motors Place, 800 Griffiths Way., 899-7400

Greater Vancouver Regional District, 432-6350

Grouse Mountain, 984-0661

Maverick Coach Lines, 662-8051

Molson Indy, 684-4639

Mount Seymour, 986-2261

Outdoor Recreation Council of B.C., 737-3058

Polar Bear Swim, English Bay, 732-2111

Registrar of Ships, 666-3408

testament to ecological logging (an oxymoron?) but also has the massive Seymour Dam, a great place for a picnic, as long as you watch out for bears.

Regional parks are plentiful; the most popular are in North and West Vancouver and at the Capilano River (**Greater Vancouver Regional District**). Skiers, hikers, and others will not complain about the proximity of **Grouse Mountain** (15 minutes from downtown), **Mount Seymour** (25 minutes), and **Cypress Bowl** (20 minutes). Although local ski resorts abound, the most well-known—and pricey—is Whistler, a scary and dangerous (at least according to locals) 75-mile ride up Highway 99. **Maverick Coach Lines** and/or **B.C. Rail** provide less nerve-wracking transportation options.

At the other end of the gamut are the beaches. Kits Beach, in the Kitsilano area, has a great saltwater pool and lots of places to people-watch. Those who want to let it all hang out can go to the clothing-optional Wreck Beach (hopefully not named after the physical attributes of the sunbathers) at the University of British Columbia. **B.C. Ferries** provides service to the Gulf Islands, Horseshoe Bay in West Vancouver, and other places.

If you still haven't had enough, the National Hockey League's **Vancouver Canucks** and the NBA's **Vancouver Grizzlies** can be found at the spanking new 20,000-seat **General Motors Place** arena. The **B.C. Lions,** as part of the Canadian version of the NFL, play at **B.C. Place,** while the **Vancouver Canadians,** the farm team for the California Angels, is headquartered at **Bailey Stadium.** Other spectator sports include soccer (**Vancouver 86ers**), lacrosse (**Surrey Burrards**), race car driving (**Molson Indy**) and roller hockey (**Vancouver Voodoo** [really!]).

 AFTER-HOURS DIVERSIONS

A stopover for most big acts, Vancouver is a great place for concert-goers. With rock icons such as Aerosmith, Bon Jovi, and Jimmy Page recording here, you may run across these (for some) demi-gods jamming at clubs like the **Commodore.** Celebrity watching in general is best done at the **Gerard Lounge.** The **B.C. Film Commission** has a specific list of who's filming what and where.

There's lots of great local music as well: jazz (**Hot Jazz, Alma St. Cafe, Carnegie's**), blues (**Fairview Pub, Yale**) or dance tunes (**New Club Mardi Gras, Bar None**). Trendies and other seekers will find whatever at the aptly monikered **Shark Club** sports bar, the redundant **Richards on Richards,** and the

MARS Restaurant and Nightclub with its robotic lighting and nitrogen fog screen. Far out.

It's less of a jungle in the flora- and fauna-filled **Garden Lounge** and recently chic pool halls (**Commodore Lanes and Billiards, Soho Cafe**). Coffeehouses, those evergreen meet marts, include the smoke- and writer-filled **Ciao Expresso Bar; Dakoda's,** with an oh-so-conveniently located condom shop next door; **Joe's Cafe,** with its unlisted number and weird combination of local hustlers; and about a million Starbucks. You can expand your mind along with your social circle at author readings (**Railway Bookstore, Women In Print, Vancouver Public Library**). Commercial galleries in Yaletown and South Granville (see "Arts and Sciences") have Thursday night shows, another favorite pastime.

Vancouver also offers lots of neat spots just to hang out. With demonstrations for various causes, skateboarders, and running chess games, the courthouse steps at **Robson Square** provide a chance to relive the glorious '60s and then some.

CULINARY AND SHOPPING HAUNTS

Like Seattle, Vancouver prides itself on Pacific Northwest cuisine. With 85 different kinds of shrimp in the waters of British Columbia, various varieties of salmon, trout, and cod as well as char and Dungeness crab, menus are heavy with seafood and fresh spices, sauces, and vegetables.

Fine dining doesn't necessarily translate into "name" restaurants or snooty maitre d's who look down their noses if you don't have a reservation. And you're so well fed that the discount for American dollars seems like a gift.

The city has loads of classy "nouveau" joints, which combine a pleasant atmosphere with varied entrees. The more costly ($21 to $50+ Canadian) and established consist of **Seasons, Star Anise, Chartwell,** and **Bishop's.** Along with periodic "Astro" dinners—named not for the Jetsons' dog, but for the natal chart and star-sign discussion that accompanies the three-course meal—the more moderately priced ($11–20) **Monterey Lounge & Grill** has a menu and service that rivals its more expensive counterparts. Other popular eateries in this same cost range include **Bistro! Bistro!, Milestones,** and **La Pasta Bar.**

Seafood places are anchored in the local constellation and include **Ship of the Seven Seas,** a real vessel at the foot of Lonsdale Ave. in North Vancouver, **Salmon House on the Hill,** and several **Boathouse** restaurants. Asian eateries also

Where It's At

(continued)

MARS Restaurant and Nightclub, 1320 Richards, 662-7707

New Club Mardi Gras, 1015 Burrard St., 687-0575

Railway Bookstore, 579 Dunsmuir, 681-1625

Richards on Richards, 1306 Richards St., 687-6794

Robson Square, 800 Robson St., 661-7373

Shark Club, 180 W. Georgia St., 687-4275

Soho Cafe, 1144 Homer, 682-0040

Vancouver Public Library, 350 W. Georgia St., 331-3602

Women In Print, 3566 W. 4th Ave., 732-4128

Yale, 1300 Granville, 681-9253

Where It's At

Unless otherwise noted, all area codes are 604.

Bishop's, 7128 W. 4th Ave. 738-2025

Bistro! Bistro!, 162 Water St., 682-2162

Boathouse, 1795 Beach Ave., 669-2225; 6695 Nelson Ave., West Vancouver, 921-8188

Bread Garden, several locations

Cartoon Corner Art Gallery, 1140 Robson, 685-2728

Chanel, 755 Burrard, 682-0522

Chartwell, 791 W. Georgia St., 689-9333

Cheena B.C. Limited, 667 Howe St., 684-5374

Circle Co-op, 1666 Johnston St., 669-8021

Cow's Vancouver, 1301 Robson, 682-2622

Eaton's, 701 Granville St., 685-7112

Fish and Oyster Cafe, 20 E. Hastings St., 681-6546

Fogg 'n' Suds, several locations

Granville Island Brewery, 1441 Cartwright St., 687-2739

Granville Street Mall, Granville and Robson

Where It's At

(continued)

Heaven and Earth India Curry House, 1754 W. 4th, 732-5313

Images, 164 Water St., 685-7056

Imperial Chinese Seafood Restaurant, 355 Burrard St., 688-8191

Isadora's, 1540 Bridge St., 681-8816

Japanese Deli House, 381 Powell St., 681-6484

Jetcom Enterprises, 131–7080 River Rd., Richmond, 273-0182

Keg, several locations

Kids Only Market, 1496 Cartwright, 689-8447

Kirin, 1166 Alberni St., 682-8833

La Pasta Bar, 1232 Robson, 688-1288; 2201 W. 1st Ave., 738-6515

Landing, 375 Water St., 687-1144

Lonsdale Quay, North Vancouver

Lansdowne Mall, 5300 No. 3 Rd., 273-4828

Liliget Feast House, 1724 Davie, 681-7044

Metrotown, 4800 Kingsway, 438-3610

Milanoza Leather Fashions, 1091 Robson St., 687-3564

Milestones, several locations

Monterey Lounge and Grill, 1277 Robson St., 684-1277

New Diamond, 555 Gore Ave., 685-0727

Nick's Spaghetti House, 631 Commercial Dr., 254-5633

O-Tooz Energie Bar, 1068 Davie St., 689-0208

Oakridge Shopping Centre, 650 W. 41st Ave., 261-2511

Pacific Centre, 750 W. Georgia St., 688-7236

Park Royal, 2002 Park Royal South, 925-9576

Phnom Penh, 244 E. Georgia, 687-0729

Pita Plus Bakery and Deli, 2967 W. Broadway, 733-9900

Polo/Ralph Lauren, 375 Water St., 682-7656

Robson Public Market, 1610 Robson

Richmond Centre, 6551 No. 3 Rd., 273-4828

abound: try **Kirin, Imperial Chinese Seafood Restaurant, Phnom Penh,** the **New Diamond,** and the **Japanese Deli House.** East Indian offerings include **Rubina Tandoori, Sitar Indian Restaurant,** and **Heaven and Earth India Curry House.** You can munch on First Nation fare (buffalo, venison, salmon) at the **Liliget Feast House.**

Other ethnic "cheap eats" for about $10 and under include **Nick's Spaghetti House, Tio Pepe, Pita Plus Bakery and Deli,** a **Taste of Jamaica,** and many more. Specialty bargains are plentiful at **Isadora's, Fish and Oyster Cafe, O-Tooz Energie Bar,** and others.

Microbreweries (**YaYa's Oyster Bar, Granville Island Brewery,** and others) were around in various forms before they became fashionable across the border. However, the U.S. undoubtedly provided the capitalistic inspiration for local chains like **Fogg 'n' Suds, Bread Garden,** and **Keg.**

Vancouver's multitudinous shopping options range from Canadian-based department stores (**Eaton's**) to the mammoth **Pacific Centre,** with 200 shops on three floors, covering three city blocks. The latter is connected to the fashion and jewelry-intensive **Vancouver Centre** via an underground labyrinth. The **Granville Street Mall** focuses on unusual items and services.

Burrard St. has the **Royal Centre,** with more than 50 browse 'n' buys and a food court. Haute couture from **Chanel** to **Versace** can be found in the area around Burrard and Hornsby streets. With chi-chi hunting grounds such as **Milanoza Leather Fashions** and **Salvatore Ferragamo,** Robson Street is Vancouver's low-key answer to Rodeo Drive. But mostly reasonable prices and amusing options such as **Cow's Vancouver** and **Cartoon Corner Art Gallery** make it appealing to non-fashion-victims as well.

Although it's a bit on the expensive side, Gastown is always a gas, particularly since the steam clock on the main drag (Water St.) is unique in all the world, or so they say. Shoppers can let off their own tension by checking out Northwest Coast and First Nation sweaters, moccasins, and jewelry at **Images.** On the outskirts is the **Sinclair Centre,** four restored historical buildings offering everything from travel necessities to designer clothing. **Polo/Ralph Lauren** and other stores can be found at the **Landing.**

Other areas include Yaletown (home furnishings), Chinatown (robes, jewelry, produce, cooking utensils), and Kitsilano (gourmet foods, specialty books, unique accessories). Granville Island's public market sells baked goods and fresh produce. Similar marts can be found at **Lonsdale**

Quay, **Surrey Public Market,** and, on a smaller scale, at the **Robson Public Market.** Those wanting to purchase fresh seafood practically off the boat can do so at **Cheena B.C. Limited** or **Jetcom Enterprises.**

Granville Island (actually it's in the middle of Vancouver) also has lots of little crafts emporiums (**Circle Co-op**) as well as a **Kids Only Market.** Cross the bridge and you're in South Granville, which has more establishments. A bit farther down 41st Street is **Oakridge Shopping Centre,** another 150-store complex, and **West Boulevard** with designer duds, delicacies, and housewares. Feet tired yet?

But **Metrotown,** located in Burnaby, has more than 400 enterprises *and* underground parking! Other malls include **Richmond Centre, Lansdowne Mall, Park Royal,** and **Surrey Place.** For those who don't want to rest on the seventh day, the **Sunday Flea Market** offers bargains galore.

ETHNIC AND RELIGIOUS PROSPECTS

Although Vancouver is a multicultural city, in many ways it's still a small town. For instance, "Asians keep pretty much to themselves here," remarks one native. Vancouver's Chinatown is third in size after New York's and San Francisco's; it reverberates with ethnicity. It's also home to the world's thinnest office building (6 feet wide by 2 stories).

Opportunities to learn more about the Asian way of life can be found at the **International Buddhist Society** and the nearby **Buddha Supplies Center.** Japanese culture can be found in the much smaller **Japan Town,** at the **Powell Street Festival,** and places such as the **Yaohan Centre.**

Although Vancouver has thousands of Indo-Canadians—with their hub being the **Punjabi strip**—the black population in the city and Canada in general is relatively minuscule. "When I first came here, I got quite a few strange looks," observes Sibel Thrasher, an African-American who's a professional singer. Still, "they weren't hostile, only curious. And it's gotten better as the city's become more cosmopolitan."

Vancouver has the U.S. beat in the preservation and celebration of First Nation (Native American) culture. Along with special events such as the **All Native Day Festival** (June), **Cedar Cottage Pow Wow** (May), and **North American Native Arts and Crafts Show** (various times), the different tribes hold canoe races and pow wows. Palefaces and other nationalities are welcome at the **Sweat Lodge,** where you can participate in a healing/cleansing ceremony. Many

Where It's At

(continued)

Royal Centre, 1055 W. Georgia St., 689-1711

Rubina Tandoori, 1962 Kingsway, 874-3621

Salmon House on the Hill, 2229 Folkstone Way, West Vancouver, 926-3212

Salvatore Ferragamo, 918 Robson, 669-4495

Seasons, 7501 Stanley Park Dr., 874-8008

Ship of the Seven Seas, North Vancouver, 987-3344

Sinclair Centre, 757 Hastings, 666-4483

Sitar Indian Restaurant, 308 Water St., 681-0678

Star Anise, 1485 W. 12th, 737-1485

Sunday Flea Market, East Vancouver, Terminal and Thornton

Surrey Place, 102 Ave. and King George Hwy., 588-6431

Surrey Public Market, corner of 64th and King George Highway

Taste of Jamaica, 941 Davie St., 683-3464

Tio Pepe, 1134 Commercial Dr., 254-8999

Vancouver Centre, 650 W. Georgia, 688-5658

Versace, 757 W. Hastings, 683-1131

West Boulevard, between Maple and Larch

YaYa's Oyster Bar, 6418 Bay St., Horseshoe Bay, 921-8848

Where It's At

Unless otherwise noted, all area codes are 604.

All Native Day Festival, Capilano Reserve, 251-4844

Buddha Supplies Center, 4158 Main St., 873-8169

Burrard Indian Bend, 929-3454

Cedar Cottage Pow Wow, 3550 Victoria Dr., 876-9285

Where It's At

(continued)

Cowichan Indian Knits and Crafts, 424 W. 3rd St., North Vancouver, 988-4735

Gathering Place Cafe, 3010 Sleil-Waututh Rd., North Vancouver, 929-9421

International Buddhist Society, Buddhist Temple, 9160 Steveston Highway, Richmond, 274-2822

Japan Town, Powell St., between Gore and Dunlevy

Khot-La-Cha Coast Salish Handicrafts, Capilano Reserve, 240 Whonoak, 987-3399

Musqueam Band Office, 263-3261

Squamish Nation, 980-4553

North American Native Arts and Crafts Show, 1607 E. Hastings, 251-4844

Powell Street Festival, 682-4335

Punjabi strip, Main St., between E. 49th and 51st aves.

Sweat Lodge, 3100 block of Dollarton Highway, North Vancouver, 929-3454

Yaohan Centre, 3700 No. 3 Rd., Richmond, 231-0601

tribes hold their own bingo games (**Musqueam, Squamish, Burrard**) and you can make (or visit) reservations at Indian-owned enterprises like the **Gathering Place Cafe, Khot-La-Cha Coast Salish Handicrafts, Cowichan Indian Knits and Crafts,** and many others.

Although Vancouver has a wide assortment of churches, "there's more New Age stuff—women's healing circles, inner self workshops—than in most places," observes Niedermayer.

CRIB SHEET

Unless you have relatives and friends who want longtime guests, most of the news on the home front is bad. Not only are vacancy rates for apartments outrageously low, but rents range from $550 a month for a tiny studio to $1,255 for a three-bedroom townhouse in the West End. Other "hot" areas such as Kitsilano and South Granville/Oak are even more pricey and just as hard to get.

"Vancouver is unique in that people actually want to move downtown," points out Kirk. High-rises share space with office buildings, restaurants, shopping complexes, and parks; they're quickly gobbled up by the tens of thousands moving to the area each year.

Still, there are a few glimmers of hope. Yaletown, a former warehouse district that boasted more saloons per acre than anywhere else in the world, is now being renovated. People can locate in suburban areas like Maple Ridge or Coquitlam, where vacancy rates are higher. With a median price of about $165,000, condominiums and town houses are another relatively economical alternative.

"You really have to save up to even purchase a modest home," observes one native. Although prices aren't much different for popular suburbs like North Vancouver (median cost: $347,000; travel time from downtown: 30 minutes by car, 12 minutes by Seabus) and Richmond ($368,000; 35 minutes by car), would-be commuters might find comparative "bargains" in outskirts like Maple Ridge/Pitt Meadows ($214,000; 40 minutes), New Westminster ($254,000; 35 minutes), Port Coquitlam ($239,000; 50 minutes) and Squamish ($193,000; one hour). South of the Fraser River are other little-known "steals," including Abbotsford (about $200,000) and Mission ($173,000).

Vancouver proper offers a wide choice for those who can afford it. Like downtown and West Vancouver, the hippie-ish Kitsilano consists of mostly younger renters and has an active community and beach scene as well. Southeast are Fairview and Mount Pleasant. The former is made attractive by three bridges that allow easy access to downtown, while the latter lives up to its name by being ethnically harmonious and home to many arts organizations.

On the West Side are Dunbar-Southlands, with different sized homes and a popular hiking/biking trail; Arbutus Ridge, an upscale area with outstanding views of English Bay and excellent shopping; the even tonier Shaughnessy (large lots, curving streets); and more compressed South Cambie. Ethnic diversity is the order of the day in the East Side communities of Grandview-Woodland, Kensington-Cedar Cottage, and Sunset.

Although they have a white-bread reputation, the suburbs of Burnaby and Surrey are growing rapidly. With high-quality neighborhoods, excellent schools, lots of greenery and spectacular views, Burnaby has become a city unto itself. Surrey's population may rival Vancouver's in a few years.

> "It's such an exciting and healthy place and there's so much to do," raves a Vancouver resident. "Vancouver is evolving its own identity. And it's terrific to be a part of this development."

Non-citizens enrolled in Canadian elementary and high schools need immigration and other related papers as well as health and school records (Oakridge Reception and Orientation Centre, 266-8376). Those wanting to find out about private/independent schools should contact the Federation of Independent School Associations (684-6023 or 684-7846). The area is also a hotbed of higher education; colleges include the University of British Columbia, B.C. Institute of Technology, Emily Carr Institute of Art and Design and others, as well as several community colleges.

NAVIGATING VANCOUVER

With one way in and out (Highway 99), Vancouver is fairly simple to get around in. Streets flow logically on a grid pattern and drivers, true to their Canadian heritage, are unfailingly courteous. Still, speeders should beware: Although limits are in kilometers per hour (k.p.h.), they're strictly enforced. Saying you're unfamiliar with the metric system won't get you out of a $100 to $150 ticket. (The fine for not using a safety belt is $75!) And, what with all the construction, traffic can get hairy at times, especially on bridges.

After six months, American citizens must apply for a B.C. driver's license, take a vision test and answer some basic road safety questions. In order to qualify for insurance, which is mandatory in B.C., your vehicle will have to pass an emissions test.

It's also possible to get around Vancouver without a car. A comprehensive system of buses, rapid transit, and ferries, B.C. Transit (521-0400) covers the city and many suburbs. The Seabus transports passengers between Vancouver and the North Shore, while the elevated SkyTrain offers service to outlying communities.

B.C. Rail (800/663-8238) offers extended conveyance throughout the province and VIA Rail (800/561-8630) throughout the rest of Canada. Vancouver International Airport (276-6061) added an international terminal in anticipation of an almost 75 percent increase of its passengers by 2005. Should you ever want to leave Vancouver, there are lots of ways to go.

WASHINGTON, D.C. AND ENVIRONS

Washington, D.C. at a Glance

Birthdate and Present Size: 1790.
Metropolitan Statistical Area—
1980: 3,250,822; 1990: 3,923,574.
1/1/95 (estimate): 4,528,900.
Percent change, 1980–1990: +20.7%.
Percent change, 1990–1995: +15.4%.

Weather Report: *Average annual temperature—*57° F. In January: 43/27° F.
In July: 88/70° F.
*Average annual precipitation—*40.35".
*Average annual snowfall—*23.1".

Money Matters: *Unemployment rate—*4.1%.
Per capita income— $18,881 (city);
$21,416 (MSA).
Average household income—$44,413 (city);
$56,799 (MSA).
Average cost of a home—$211,604.
Average rent for an apartment—$968/month.
ACCRA cost of living indexes (based on 100)—Composite Index: 127.4; Utilities Index: 107.4; Housing Index: 166.3.
*Sales and use tax—*6.0%.
*Personal income tax—*6.0 to 9.5%.

People Profile: *Crime rate* (per 100,000 population)—11,077.9 (city); 5,382.9 (MSA).
Racial and ethnic characteristics—
White: 29.6% (city) 65.8% (MSA);
Black: 65.9% (city) 26.6% (MSA);
American Indian/Eskimo/Aleut: 0.3%

(city), 0.3% (MSA); Asian/Pacific Islander:
1.9% (city), 5.1% (MSA); Hispanic: 5.2%
(city), 5.6% (MSA); Other: 2.4% (city),
2.2% (MSA).
*Gender ratio—*87.2 males per 100 females
(all ages); 84 males per 100 females
(18 years old+).
*Age characteristics—*18–24 (13.4%);
25–44 (35.9%). Median age: 33.4.
*Educational attainment—*percent having completed high school: 73.1%; percent having completed college: 33.3%.

Major Players: Federal government, services, retail/wholesale trade, tourism, education, and research & development.
*Largest employers—*U.S. Government, Children's National Medical Center, Federal National Mortgage Assn., GEICO, General Maintenance Services, Group Hospitalization & Medical Services, Inter-American Development Bank.

Community Services: *Average hospital cost—*$386.43/day.
Average doctor visit—$56.30.
Average dentist visit—$58.70.
Newspapers—The Washington Post; The Washington Times; Washington Business Journal; Catholic Standard; El Pregonero; Hispanic Link Weekly Report; The Washington Informer (black); *New Observer* (black community); *Washington Blade* (gay/lesbian); *Washington City Paper* (alternative).

Talk about plugged in. This city has it all: power, money, and lots of youthful ambition, hormone-driven and otherwise. Its synergy is almost like an aphrodisiac: regardless of what you think about it (and politics), it can sweep you off your feet.

Washington D.C.—or The District, as it's known to both transplants and natives—wasn't always a dazzling conglomeration of government buildings, memorials, museums, galleries, neighborhoods, and national and international commerce. It began life in 1800 on the Potomac River along the Virginia-Maryland border. Fourteen years later, after the seat of government was moved to the Capitol Building in what was then the center of town, British soldiers captured Washington during the War of 1812 and burned it to the ground, a move that's been replicated in fiction and in film (such as when the

White House was blown up by aliens—extraterrestrials, not illegal immigrants—in the movie *Independence Day*).

The District has always thrived on crises. During and after the Civil War, the population doubled from 60,000 to 120,000, when large numbers of people flocked there to support the Union effort. By 1917 (World War I), the numbers increased almost threefold, when even more government workers were needed. A real boon came during the Great Depression: While other cities struggled with loss of jobs, the federal government initiated programs to provide employment in the Capital. So by the time World War II rolled around, denizens had reached a half-million, peaking at about 800,000 around 1950.

Washington has been the scene of countless national demonstrations—civil rights in 1963, Vietnam protests in 1969 and 1970, and the Million Man March in 1995, to mention a thimbleful—and the city government has had an intriguing history. In 1871, Congress established a territorial regime with a Presidentially chosen governor to deal with inadequate housing, streets, sewers, and water. Three years later, it set up a local government composed of three commissioners, also appointed by the President, making D.C. the only U.S. city where the populace didn't elect its own officials. The residents were also not allowed to vote in Presidential elections. Democracy at its best.

In 1963, Congress rescinded the last restriction and, a decade later, residents were allowed to choose their legislators. Although the intentions may have been good, by 1995, the city was in such dire straits that President Clinton signed a bill to create a board to oversee financial matters and balance the budget. And then there was the matter of the current mayor's (known as Marion "Barely" to locals) drug conviction, which didn't stop him from getting reelected in 1994. Apparently it really does take an act of Congress to get things done around here.

Still, Washington has managed to forge ahead and prosper, particularly in the areas of international trade, technology and research, and small and large private enterprises. Although Uncle Sam is still the biggest employer, his capitalistic cousins are rapidly catching up.

Quality of Life

Life in this region may not be perfect, but it's close enough for government work. "Actually, we're kind of spoiled," observes communications manager Kristi Berg. "There are so many resources and incredible people that it's easy to take it all for granted." Along with being elegant and exciting, and having a current crime rate on par with apple-cheeked Minneapolis, Washington attracts an educated and diverse labor force from all races, creeds, and colors.

Although some of the District's 21 neighborhoods and certain 'burbs can be outrageously expensive, there's quite a selection of cribs. Housing has always been at a premium, and although the cost of living is high, this is where residents feel the pinch.

Like many cities that draw mondo (as in 20 million annual) visitors, Washington has a great selection of attractions, entertainment, and recreational activities along with restaurants, shopping, and sporting events fit for a king (or at least a President).

The clean and safe underground metro system makes commuting quick and efficient, as long as you don't mind traveling in sardine cans during rush hour. ("The rest of the time, it's not too crowded," comments marketing director Melanie Suggs.) And although the city has its share of snowstorms, temps rarely dip below the 20s and the white stuff usually melts in a day or so. Spring is a particularly captivating period, bringing cherry blossoms and a brief respite from the summer's humidity. Would that the political climate were so predictable.

General Opportunities

The metropolitan region, which includes northern Virginia and Southern Maryland, has one of the highest median incomes in the nation, with generally low unemployment. For example, the average annual earnings for someone in transportation, communications, and public utilities is around $51,000; finance, insurance, and real estate, $45,893; manufacturing, $47,390; and law, a whopping $63,376. Even retail workers make around $16,000.

> Surrounded by a dazzling conglomeration of government buildings, memorials, museums, galleries, and national and international commerce, Washingtonians "are kind of spoiled," admits a local.

This is a land of prosperity for African-Americans as well, whose earnings average $38,900. Almost one-quarter of blacks are in the $50,000 to $75,000 range, and Washington leads the nation in the number of African-American high school and college graduates.

This is one place where you can get your tax and other dollars to work for you. D.C. is home to some of the top commercial and international banks, including the World Bank, International Monetary Fund, Inter-American Development Bank, and Export-Import Bank. No wonder nearly 65 Fortune 500 companies and more than 75 percent of the largest international firms are headquartered here or have "District" offices. Like it or not, Washington is where key decisions on politics, finance, trade, and industry are made. When this city sneezes, the world offers up a handkerchief and waits in anticipation.

MAJOR BREADWINNING

Although traditionally a mecca for idealistic youth hoping to make the world a warmer, fuzzier place, survival in the Washington work world can require a certain Machiavellian sensibility. Major decisions are made in eateries, bars, and even health clubs; and certain types of information can be even more valuable than a pay raise. Conversely, indiscretion is damaging, as in the case of an individual who joked about doing away with a certain political figure and found a passel of Secret Service agents waiting outside his gym locker.

"The biggest mistakes have been made when people have lowered their guard," points out Berg. "You can be sitting in a restaurant thinking you have privacy, and a reporter can be listening at the next table. Personally speaking, the best advice is not to say anything."

Competition for certain jobs is intense, so many take lower-level, secretarial, or clerical positions to gain a toehold. "Particularly in politics, you need to work your way up," observes Aloysius Hogan, a lawyer for the Republican Party. "People change jobs frequently, so a little schmoozing—writing thank-you notes, doing favors—can go a long way."

Still, Uncle Sam provides only about 40 percent of all the city's employment, including over half of all federal civilian positions in the U.S. The other 60 (and growing) percent consists of lobbying and interest groups; government-related contractors; biotech firms; non-profit organizations; entertainment and retail enterprises; business services (including legal, engineering, accounting, research, management, data processing, and information services); and others. The District has become a true service economy.

"It's possible to be in a job totally unrelated to politics and rise very quickly," points out Hogan. Major players in business, such as the Potomac Electric Power, *The Washington Post*, Bell Atlantic, the American Association of Retired Persons, and the Hyatt Regency, as well as universities and affiliated and independent hospitals cut a wide swath across careers in engineering, hospitality, communications, marketing, health care, education, and more. Competence can be rewarded in Washington, "even if you're a nice person," he half-jokes.

Today's cash cows are technology firms. Standing out in the herd of about 1,800 (in D.C. and environs) are information providers such as America Online, UUNet, and PSINet, as well as rather Orwellian-sounding biotech places like Human Genome Sciences and Life Technologies. According to *Forbes* magazine, Washington is nipping at such hi-tech heels as Boston and the Silicon Valley. Not only has employment doubled in these fields in the past decade, but access to the federal government has proved to be a major ace.

The Library of Congress, the National Institutes of Health, the National Academy of Science, the Food and Drug Administration, Environmental Protection Agency, and Department of Health and Human Services can also be found here. A few good hook-ups with regulators of satellite and other communications (Federal Communications Commission, Communications Satellite Corporation) can generate lots of electricity.

Along with a $125 billion economy and an area of 4,000 square miles, the greater Washington region is also centrally located, a boon for businesses as well as hostile nations who would undoubtedly be vaporized should they try anything funny.

In D.C., jobs are like metro trains; there's always another one coming soon. Considering the amount of turnover—people moving, getting promoted or fired, or quitting when the "cycle" (two-year election period) changes—those who watch and wait may find themselves at an advantage. And then there's the ultimate D.C. job search strategy: making that right connection.

SOCIAL AND RECREATIONAL SCENE

How Washington, D.C. Plays

Not everyone who lives in area code 202 worries about being politically correct. "I pretty much say what's on my mind," observes network analyst William Stevens, who feels comfortable talking freely about any subject. Besides, "I don't hang out in places" where decision-makers go (more on that later).

Although living in D.C. has made her more aware of what's happening in the world, Suggs, who recently relocated from L.A., revels in Washington's small-town friendliness. "You can walk down the street and see people you know." Plus, "I expected shoulder pads and big hair and was surprised at how trendy this city actually is."

Still, it's not advisable to strap on a beer-can bowler and cruise the bars searching for karaoke machines, particularly if your job requires a certain amount of visibility. "This city is definitely more conservative," she continues. Although not your corporate buttoned-down environment, "you do have to dress up more" and there are lots of parties, fundraisers, and receptions. This translates into lots of alcohol and Swedish meatballs.

Developing relationships, however, may not be as seamless. Although there are more women than men, "it seems as if there's a fresh crop of pretty faces every time a new Senator comes to town," grumbles one fellow. Influential men might be able to pick and choose, but "it's just as tough as anyplace else for the average guy."

"Although it takes longer to get to know someone here, the end result is more permanent," says Suggs. Getting involved in activities outside the job, such as with charity, arts, and sports organizations are a great way to take advantage of this city's constantly changing array of faces (and have considerably less of an intimidation factor than, say, a political fundraiser).

ARTS AND SCIENCES

There's a whole other Washington beyond the White House, Washington Monument, and Lincoln Memorial. "This city has an amazing arts scene," remarks Suggs. "People are very well versed in culture." Chief among the centers is the **John F. Kennedy Center for the Performing Arts,** home of the National Symphony, Opera, and TV specials in which glitterati parade before soccer moms and tired construction workers via satellite. Its six theaters present drama, dance, music, and commissioned works from around the world.

Other performances can also be found at the **National, Warner,** and **Ford** theatres, all of which are in close proximity to the **FBI Building** in case things get too subversive. Other venues include the **Arena,** a three-stage complex featuring a variety of popular entertainments; **Wooly Mammoth Theatre,** an unconventional venue; the **Shakespeare Theatre;** and others. **Wolf Trap,** the only national park in the U.S. dedicated to the performing arts, features a variety of shows during the warm months. Other—some might say more plebeian—entertainments (rock groups and home improvement exhibitions) can be found at **Lisner Auditorium, RFK Stadium,** and **USAirways Arena.** Dinner theater/Broadway combos also abound: **Burn Brae, Lazy Susan,** and **West End** are but a few.

Washington, D.C. has the mother of all museums—the **Smithsonian.** Its many tentacles include the **Anacosta Museum** and the **National Museum of African Art,** which focus on black history and art, respectively; the **Hirschorn Museum and Sculpture Garden,** which exhibits new modern works; and the **National Museum of American History,**

Where It's At

Unless otherwise noted, all area codes are 202.

Affrica, 2110-1/2 R St. NW, 745-7272

Anacosta Museum, 1901 Fort Pl. SE, 357-2700

Arena, 6th & Main Ave. SW, 488-3300

Bethune Museum and Archives, 1318 Vermont Ave. NW, 332-9201

Bureau of Engraving & Printing, 14th & C sts. SW, 874-3019

Burn Brae, P.O. Box 180, Burtonsville, MD, 800/777-BBDT

Corcoran Gallery of Art, 500 17th St. NW, 638-3211

DAR Museum, 1776 D St. NW, 879-3239

FBI Building, 9th and Pennsylvania NW, 324-3447

Ford Theatre, 511 10th St. NW, 347-4833

Hirschorn Museum and Sculpture Garden, 7th and Independence Ave. SW, 357-2700

Holography Museum of the 3rd Dimension, 2018 R St. NW, 667-6322

Holography World Collection, 800 K St. NW, 408-1833

John F. Kennedy Center for the Performing Arts, 2700 F St. NW, 467-4700

Lazy Susan, Drawer Q, Woodbridge, VA, 703/550-7384

Lisner Auditorium, 730 21st St. NW, 994-6800

Where It's At

(continued)

National Air & Space Museum, 6th & Independence Ave., SW, 357-2700

National Aquarium, 14th & Constitution NW, 482-2826

National Arboretum, 3501 New York Ave. NE, 544-8733

National Geographic Society, 1600 M. St. NW, 857-7588

National Museum of African Art, 950 Independence Ave. SW, 357-2700

National Museum of American History, 14th and Constitution Ave. NW, 357-2700

National Museum of Natural History, 10th & Constitution Ave. NW, 357-2700

National Theatre, 1321 E. St. NW, 628-6161

National Zoo, 3000 Connecticut Ave. NW, 643-4717

Phillips Collection, 1600 21st St. NW, 387-2151

RFK Stadium, 2400 E. Capitol St. SE, 546-2222

Shakespeare Theatre, 450 7th St. NW, 393-2700

Smithsonian, 1000 Jefferson Dr. SW, 357-2700

Smithsonian Associates Resident Program, 1100 Jefferson Dr. SW, 357-3030

Studio Gallery, 2108 R. St. NW, 232-8734

Tartt Gallery, 2017 Q St. NW, 332-5652

U.S. Holocaust Memorial Museum, 100 Raoul Wallenberg Pl. SW, 488-0400

United States Botanic Garden, 100 Maryland Ave. SW, 225-8333

USAirways Arena, 1 Harry S. Truman Dr. Landover, MD, 301/350-3400

Warner Theatre, 1299 Pennsylvania Ave. NW, 628-1818

West End, 4615 Duke St., Alexandria, VA, 703/370-2500

Wolf Trap, 1624 Trap Rd., Vienna, VA, 703/255-1900

Wooly Mammoth Theatre, 1401 Church St. NW, 393-3939

Young Benefactors Program, 1100 Jefferson Dr. SW, 357-3030

which displays the flag that inspired "The Star Spangled Banner" and First Ladies' inaugural gowns.

The **Smithsonian Associates Resident Program,** as well as its **Young Benefactors Program,** offer a variety of special events. "Just about every major art gallery and organization has an affiliated group," points out Suggs, mentioning the Corcoran 1869 Society (**Corcoran Gallery of Art**), and **Phillips Collection** in particular. The former boasts a variety of masterpieces, while the latter is America's first museum of modern art (and hosts Thursday night musical gatherings as well). The DuPont Circle area alone is home to 20 more galleries, including **Affrica, Studio Gallery,** and the **Tartt Gallery.**

Other historical stop-offs include the **U.S. Holocaust Memorial Museum,** arguably the most moving collection in the U.S. The **National Geographic Society** focuses on global issues and remote countries. And the **DAR Museum** offers up an agglomeration of Americana compiled by the Daughters of American Revolution, an organization that excludes at least half the population by virtue of sex and place of birth. The **Bethune Museum and Archives** spotlights the achievements of African-American women.

With more than 3,000 birds, reptiles, and animals, the 160-acre **National Zoo** is also home to upsized panda Hsing-Hsing as well as a re-creation of the world's largest rain forest. Along with the 45.5 carat Hope Diamond (too big for even Elizabeth Taylor), the **National Museum of Natural History** has assembled dinosaur fossils, an insect zoo, and the world's largest (dead) African bush elephant. The extremely popular **National Air & Space Museum** offers everything from the Wright Brothers' 1903 Flyer to the *Apollo 11* lunar command module to the latest in technology, while the **National Aquarium** and **National Arboretum** respectively serve up a variety of marine life and more than 400 types of flora/fauna (including a Bonsai collection). The **United States Botanic Garden** provides tropical, subtropical, and desert varieties.

Appropriately, Washington has two centers that focus on tricks of the eye: the **Holography Museum of the 3rd Dimension** and **Holography World Collection.** And although they don't give out free samples (darn!), you can see currency in the making at the **Bureau of Engraving & Printing.** Those opting for a historical exhibit without the dirt about J. Edgar Hoover at the previously mentioned

FBI Building had better not get too curious—lest they find themselves on a list.

THE SPORTING LIFE

Despite all the distractions, "this is a big sports town," states Berg. "Congressional offices and organizations have ultimate frisbee, volleyball, softball, and touch football." How Kennedyesque. Those feeling out of their league may want to hook up with the **Washington Sport and Social Club.**

Walking is a popular diversion, "even in the evening," remarks Suggs. In the touristy section, "there are always people around, and the area is heavily policed" although the same can't be said for some city neighborhoods, particularly in the southeast section.

Even though the District has lots of green spaces and jogging opportunities—the National Mall, the steps of the Lincoln Memorial—a major recreation spot is the 1800-acre **Rock Creek Park,** which stretches from Georgetown to suburban Maryland. It includes a 4,000-seat amphitheater, grist mill, Art Barn gallery, and nature center, as well as paths, golf, and tennis courts. Although D.C. proper has several public courses (**Rock Creek, Langston Golf,** others), the **Fairways Group** offer a variety of greens in the 'burbs.

Somewhat more remote playgrounds include **C & O National Historic Park,** with its towpath-sized trails; the Mt. Vernon Trail (**Turkey Run Park**), a picturesque, historical route near George's abode; **Theodore Roosevelt Island,** a wildlife and path refuge accessible by a footbridge; and others. Here you may also have close encounters of the equine kind as parts of the area offer horseback riding (**Rock Creek; Marriott Ranch**). Those who like to play the ponies instead of riding them will find action at **Laurel Race Course, Pimlico Race Track,** and **Rosecroft.**

Although the port of Annapolis, which features a plethora of pleasure craft, is a brief drive away, the District itself offers **Tidal Basin Pedal Boats** and canoes, sailboats, and kayaks (**Thompson Boat Center; Washington Sailing Marina**).

Those who enjoy vicarious thrills will find plenty to cheer in the NBA **Washington Bullets,** the NFL **Washington Redskins,** the **Washington Capitals** (ice hockey), **DC United** (outdoor soccer), and the unattractive-sounding but undoubtedly lovable **Washington Warthogs** (indoor soccer). A variety of college sports can be found at **American University, George Washington University, Georgetown University, Howard University,** and others.

Where It's At

Unless otherwise noted, all area codes are 202.

American University, 885-3030

C & O National Historic Park, P.O. Box 4, Sharpsburg, MD, 301/739-4200

DC United, RFK Stadium, 547-9077

Fairways Group, 9540 Center St., Manassas, VA, 800/383-9901

George Washington University, 994-6650

Georgetown University, 687-HOYA

Howard University, 806-7199

Langston Golf, 26th & Benning Rd. NE, 397-8638

Laurel Race Course, P.O. Box 130, Laurel, MD, 800/638-1859

Marriott Ranch, 5305 Marriott Ln., Hume, VA, 540/364-2627

Pimlico Race Track, Hayward and Winner Ave., Baltimore, MD, 410/542-9400

Rock Creek Park, 3545 Williamsburg Lane NW, 282-1063

Rock Creek, golf course, 16th & Rittenhouse sts. NW, 882-7332

Rock Creek, horseback riding, 5100 Glover Rd. NW, 362-0117

Rosecroft, 6336 Rosecroft Dr., Ft. Washington, MD, 301/567-4000

Theodore Roosevelt Island, Potomac Park, 703/285-2598

Thompson Boat Center, 2900 Virginia Ave. NW, 333-9543

Tidal Basin Pedal Boats, Ohio Dr. and Tidal Basin NW, 484-0206

Turkey Run Park, McLean, VA, 703/285-2598

Washington Bullets, USAir Arena, 301/386-7000

Washington Capitals, USAir Arena, 301/336-2277

Washington Redskins, RFK Stadium, 547-9077

Washington Sailing Marina, 1 Marina Dr., Alexandria, 703/548-9027

Washington Sport and Social Club, 2441 18th St. NW, 547-1916

Washington Warthogs, USAir Arena, 301/499-3000

Where It's At

Unless otherwise noted, all area codes are 202.

15 Minutes Club, 1030 15th St. NW, 408-1855

Annabelle's, 480 King St., Alexandria, VA, 800/386-5047

B. Smith's, Union Station, 289-6188

Bardo Rodeo, 2000 Wilson Blvd., Arlington, VA, 703/527-1852

Big Hunt, 1345 Connecticut Ave. NW, 785-2333

Blues Alley, P.O. Box 3616, 337-4141

Buffalo Billiards, 1330 19th St. NW, 331-7665

Capitol Grille, 601 Pennsylvania Ave. NW, 737-6200

Capitol Steps Political Satire, 1505 King St., Alexandria, VA, 703/683-5912

Club Zei, 1415 Zei Alley NW, 842-2445

Coco Loco, 810 7th St. NW, 289-2626

ComedySportz, 3112 Mt. Vernon Ave., Alexandria, VA, 703/684-5212

Dubliner Pub, 520 N. Capitol St. NW, 737-3773

El Bodegon, 1637 R St. NW, 667- 1710

Fun Factory, 3112 Mt. Vernon Ave., Alexandria, VA, 703/684-5212

Garrett's, 3003 M St. NW, 333-1033

Grand Slam, Grand Hyatt, 1000 H St. NW, 582-1234

Gross National Product, 1602 S. Springwood Dr., Silver Spring, MD, 301/587-4821

Hawk & Dove, 329 Pennsylvania Ave. SE, 543-3300

Insect Club, 627 E St. NW, 347-8884

Kinkead's, 2000 Pennsylvania Ave., 296-7700

Kramerbooks & Afterwords Cafe, 1517 Connecticut Ave. NW, 387-1462

Mr. Smith's, 3104 M St. NW, 333-3104

Mrs. Foggybottom and Friends, Omni Shoreham, 2500 Calvert St. NW, 745-1023

Murphy's, 2609 24th St. NW, 462-7171; other locations

Music City Roadhouse, 1050 30th St. NW, 337-4444

 AFTER-HOURS DIVERSIONS

Few can complain about Washington's night life. Something's always going on in the bars on Capitol Hill and downtown or in various "hot" neighborhoods like Adams-Morgan (multicultural/alternative), DuPont Circle (homosexual/artsy), Georgetown (college crowd), or the suburbs of Old Town/Alexandria (postgraduate preps) and Arlington, Virginia and Bethesda and Silver Spring, Maryland (anyone with money). The trick is to find out where your group hangs. But like Cinderella's coach, the metro stops running at midnight "and you really need to find a cab or someone with a car," observes Stevens. "Parts of D.C. can be very dangerous."

This city offers up entertainment even for those without an agenda. Located in a former Oldsmobile showroom, **Bardo Rodeo** provides pool tables, late model cars, surrealistic paintings, and 23 microbrews to eliminate the tacky aftertaste. Another brewpub, **Big Hunt,** has a tropical motif with vines, volcanoes, and fake wild animals that make it seemingly well-suited to the jungles of Washington. At least a bit of the Wild West can be found at **Buffalo Billiards,** which provides 15,000 square feet to pack 'em in and move 'em out. Arachnophobics might want to avoid the **Insect Club,** which is not only decorated with an infestation of crawlies, but actually serves them on the menu (only by request, of course). With black holes, celestial charts, and close-ups of unearthly surfaces, **Planet Fred** is definitely a star trek.

Still, there's no getting around politics, particularly at **Capitol Steps Political Satire, Gross National Product,** and **Mrs. Foggybottom and Friends,** where mincemeat is regularly made of the current regime. A less expensive alternative would be **ComedySportz** and the **Fun Factory,** which provides improvisational amusement. Those wanting to rub shoulders with the real political thing and/or their staffers might want to try various parking garages (remember Deep Throat?) or places like the pricey **Capitol Grille** as well as the less wallet-draining **Hawk & Dove** and **Tune Inn.**

Birds of a feather flock to other watering holes as well. Attorneys can be found at the **Red Sage** along with bars and grilles in the area of 14th and G streets, a magnet for law firms. Washington Redskins football players and other heavy hitters might be unearthed at the **Grand Slam,** while style mavens (or fashion victims, depending upon your viewpoint) gravitate to **Club Zei,** with its skintightly wrapped house dancers. The **15 Minutes** (as in "of fame")

Club and **Kramerbooks & Afterwords Cafe** cater to the coffeehouse and literary set. Those who like vodka and scotch will enjoy 20 varieties of the former at **State of the Union** and a huge collection of malts in the latter at **Washington Grill.** And everyone's Irish at **Dubliner Pub** and **Murphy's.**

Some clubs, however, are simply about good times. Old Town has **Annabelle's,** while **Garrett's** and **River Club** are Georgetown favorites. Dancing and/or live music can be found at **Coco Loco, Republic Gardens, Spy Club,** and **El Bodegon,** which also offers a flamenco show. **Blues Alley, B. Smith's,** and the **Music City Roadhouse** serve up blues, jazz, and a gospel brunch, respectively. The District is also loaded with piano bars (**Kinkead's, Mr. Smith's, West End Cafe,** many others).

CULINARY AND SHOPPING HAUNTS

There's no getting around it. Dining out in The District is expensive, with the average meal (appetizer, entree, dessert, and non-alcoholic drink) costing about $20–25 per person. You can crash various receptions or take advantage of the "Cheap Eats" mentions in *The Washingtonian* magazine. Ethnic and specialty eateries—delis, oriental, vegetarian—can also be more cost-effective, and many museums have cafes with relatively affordable fare.

Although cooking at home might be an alternative, "the grocery stores in the city are horrible, understocked with a poor selection," states Stevens.

Still, "there are some great restaurants, and the variety is amazing," remarks Suggs. "You can get just about every type of cuisine." Some of the more established under-$25 eateries in Adams-Morgan include the **Andalusian Dog,** where Spanish food meets Dada art and architecture; **Roxanne** and the **Peyote Cafe,** award-winning Southwestern spots that share an address and phone; **Red Sea,** Ethiopian cuisine with a vegetarian flair; and **Veneziano,** plentiful Italian with an extensive wine list. Those wanting to spend a sawbuck or so more might opt for **Cities,** which features the decor and menu of a different city each year; **Felix Restaurant,** eclectic American cuisine; and **I Matte Trattoria,** a three-star Italian chow fest. Dupont Circle has the less expensive **Brickskeller Inn** (American), **Skewers/Cafe Luna** (Middle Eastern/Italian), and **LaFonda** (Mexican) as well as the pricier **19th St. Grille** (seafood), **Carmella Kitty's** (Cajun), and **Palm** (surf 'n' turf). The **Golden Palace Restaurant, Hunan Chinatown,** and **Tony Cheng's Mongolian Restaurant**

Where It's At

(continued)

Planet Fred, 1221 Connecticut Ave. NW, 466-2336

Red Sage, 605 14th St. NW, 638-4444

Republic Gardens, 232-2710

River Club, 3223 K St. NW, 333-8118

Spy Club, 805 W. 15th St. NW, 289-1779

State of the Union, 1357 U St. NW, 588-8810

Tune Inn, 331 Pennsylvania Ave. SE, 543-2725

Washington Grill, 1143 N. Hampshire Ave. NW, 775-0800

West End Cafe, 1 Washington Circle NW, 800/424-9671

Where It's At

Unless otherwise noted, all area codes are 202.

19th St. Grille, 1220 19th St. NW, 785-2866

African Eye Collection, 2134 Wisconsin Ave. NW, 625-2552

Andalusian Dog, 1344 U St. NW, 986-6364

Annapolis Mall, 2002 Annapolis Mall, Annapolis, MD, 410/266-5432

B. Smith's, Union Station, 289-6188

Ballston Common Mall, 4328 Wilson Blvd., Arlington, VA, 703/243-5363

Brickskeller Inn, 1523 22nd St. NW, 293-1885

Carmella Kitty's, 1602 17th St. NW, 667-5937

Chadwick's, 3205 K St. NW, 333-2625

Chanel Boutiques, 1455 Pennsylvania Ave. NW, 638-5055

Chevy Chase Pavilion, 5335 Wisconsin Ave. NW, 686-5335

Cities, 2424 18th St. NW, 328-7194

Crystal City Shops, 1664 Crystal Square Arcade, 703/920-3930

Decatur House, 1600 H St. NW, 842-0920

Fashion Centre at Pentagon City, 1100 S. Hayes St., Arlington, VA, 703/415-2400

Where It's At

(continued)

Felix Restaurant, 2406 18th St. NW, 483-3549

Garrett's, 3003 M St. NW, 333-1033

Georgetown Park, 3222 M St. NW, 342-8190

Golden Palace Restaurant, 720 7th St. NW, 783-1225

HMV Record Stores, 1229 Wisconsin Ave. NW, 333-9292

Hunan Chinatown, 624 H St. NW, 783-5858

I Matte Trattoria, 2436 18th St. NW, 462-8844

Jean Louis, Watergate Hotel, 2650 Virginia Ave. NW, 298-4488

LaFonda, 1639 R St. NW, 232-6965

Maison Blanche, 1725 F St. NW, 842-0071

Martin's Tavern, 1264 Wisconsin Ave. NW, 333-7370

Mazza Gallerie, 5300 NW. Wisconsin Ave., 966-6114

Montpelier, 15th and M sts. NW, 862-1600

National Place, 529 14th St. NW, 783-9090

National Shrine of the Immaculate Conception Gift Shop, 4th and Michigan Ave. NW, 800/333-4411

Occidental Grill, 1475 Pennsylvania Ave. NW, 783-1475

Old Glory, 3139 M St. NW, 337-3406

Old Post Office, 1100 Pennsylvania Ave. NW, 289-4224

Palm, 1225 19th St. NW, 293-9091

Peyote Cafe, 2319 18th St. NW, 462-8330

Political Americana, several locations

Potomac Mills Outlet Mall, 2700 Potomac Mills Circle, Prince William, 800/VA-MILLS

Prime Rib, 2020 K St. NW, 466-8811

Promenade, Grand Hotel, 2350 M St. NW, 429-0100

Provence, 2401 Pennsylvania Ave. NW, 296-6466

Red Sea, 2483 18th St. NW, 483-5001

Roxanne, 2319 18th St. NW, 462-8330

Shops at National Place, 529 14th St. NW, 783-9090

are but a few of the economical Oriental restaurants in Chinatown.

Certain spots may be worth the price of entry (or entree, if you will). You might find yourself among the power crowd while dining on American at **B. Smith's,** the **Signature Room, Tiber Creek Pub,** and others on Capitol Hill. Downtown boasts the exclusive **Maison Blanche** (French); **Montpelier** (Mediterranean); and all-American **Occidental Grill**, **Vidalia,** and **Willard,** not to be confused with the 1971 movie of the same name. (The only rats you'll encounter will likely be two-legged.) Exclusive offerings in Foggy Bottom include the **Prime Rib,** a Zagat Survey favorite; **Jean Louis,** which is actually in the Watergate Hotel; the jacket-only **Provence;** and the **Promenade,** with its sweeping grand-entrance staircase and vaulted dining room. These are places where deep-pocketed mentors, paybacks for favors, and parents come in handy.

Georgetown can be less stuffy with neighborhood pubs like **Chadwick's, Garrett's, Martin's Tavern,** and **Old Glory.** A favorite with students, the **Tombs** serves up homemade fare at bargain prices.

Along with a profusion of ethnic and specialty stores in various neighborhoods, shopping in D.C. can be a downfall to your line of credit as well as to your arches. Individual undertakings range from the **African Eye Collection,** with its international fashions, art, and home accessories, to one of the world's largest **Chanel Boutiques,** to **HMV Record Stores,** which features live performances as well.

Political Americana hawks buttons, bumper stickers, and novelty items for every partisan persuasion, while the **Washington National Cathedral** and **National Shrine of the Immaculate Conception Gift Shop** peddle religious and non- (as opposed to il-) legal statutory items. Not to be overlooked are the various museum shops, such as those at **Decatur House** and the **Smithsonian.**

Further economic depletion is a metro ride away to District and suburban malls. The **Chevy Chase Pavilion** has more than 50 stores, while the **Mazza Gallerie** provides 48 more. Government buildings reincarnated as shopping centers include the Pavilion at the **Old Post Office,** and **Union Station,** where architectural splendor mixes with stores, restaurants, movies, and, in the latter, an Amtrak ticket counter. The tri-level **Shops at National Place** are open 361 days a year, while Victorian-accented **Georgetown Park** is four more floors of exclusive boutiques and eateries.

It gets a little less upscale in the 'burbs. The **Annapolis Mall** and the **Ballston Common Mall** both offer more than 100 stores and a food court. Mall moles (as opposed to mall rats—not to be confused with Willard, of course) might want to burrow in the underground **Crystal City Shops.** Also in Arlington, **Fashion Centre** at Pentagon City has a Nordstrom's and about 159 others.

In addition to the usual array of stores, the **White Flint Mall** in Bethesda, Maryland offers a free shuttle from the metro station. A former munitions building, the **Torpedo Factory Art Center** in Alexandria, Virginia now launches the work of more than 150 artists, while nearby McLean has its own dynamic duo—**Tyson's Corner Center** and **Tyson's Galleria.** Also in Virginia is the **Potomac Mills Outlet Mall,** a mega-discount center. Have fun dragging your purchases back on the subway.

 ## ETHNIC AND RELIGIOUS PROSPECTS

Along with the **National Presbyterian Center**, a **Franciscan Monastery,** and several Islamic Centers and Masonic Temples, The District also has the largest Roman Catholic Church in the U.S. (the previously mentioned National Shrine of the Immaculate Conception) and **St. John's Church,** whose convenient location across from the White House has made it the choice of Presidents. The Jewish community is represented by the **Jewish Historical Society of Greater Washington,** a synagogue built in 1876. **St. Augustine Catholic Church** is the oldest black Catholic congregation in the area.

"Religion is big here, particularly among African-Americans," accountant Terri Franklin explains. "Many affluent people attend services; and churches sponsor singles programs, weekend getaways and community service for the homeless, youth, and inner-city schools. For those of us who don't go to bars, it's the best way to meet people."

Race relations are a bit more complicated. Franklin, who is black, has never felt constrained, and regards her race "as even a slight advantage, because there's such a large community here."

Still, "the city is very segregated," points out one man. "Except for a neighborhood like Adams-Morgan, most people hang out with their own kind. You don't see a lot of interracial dating on Capitol Hill, although politically the town's always been Democratic. People joke about Washington being the beginning of the South, but there's some truth to that."

Where It's At

(continued)

Signature Room, 525 New Jersey Ave. NW, 800/321-3010

Skewers/Cafe Luna, 387-7400

Smithsonian, several locations

Tiber Creek Pub, 15 E St. NW, 800/327-6667

Tombs, 1226 36th St. NW, 337-6668

Tony Cheng's Mongolian Restaurant, 619 H St. NW, 842-8669

Torpedo Factory Art Center, 105 N. Union St., Alexandria, VA, 703/838-4199

Tyson's Corner Center, 1961 Chain Bridge Rd., McLean, VA, 703/893-9400

Tyson's Galleria, 2001 International Dr., McLean, VA, 703/827-7700

Union Station, 40 Massachusetts Ave. NE, 800/527-2554

Veneziano, 2305 18th St. NW, 483-3900

Vidalia, 1990 M St. NW, 659-1900

Washington National Cathedral, Massachusetts and Wisconsin Ave. NW, 537-6247 or 537-6267

White Flint Mall, 11301 Rockville Pike, Bethesda, MD, 301/468-5777

Willard, Willard Inter-Continental, 1401 Pennsylvania NW, 637-7440

Where It's At

 Unless otherwise noted, all area codes are 202.

Franciscan Monastery, 1400 Quincy St. NE, 526-6800

Jewish Historical Society of Greater Washington, 701 3rd St. NW, 789-0900

National Presbyterian Center, 4101 Nebraska Ave. NW, 537-0800

St. Augustine Catholic Church, 1419 U St. NW, 265-1470

St. John's Church, 1525 H St. NW, 347-8766

"This is a very international city, so people are naturally accepting," adds Suggs, who does see a lot of interracial dating among the people she encounters. "This is not about just blacks and whites; relationships cut across every culture." Regardless, tolerance counts in a place where you could be gone tomorrow or end up being the President's right hand.

CRIB SHEET

The city proper is where things are happening, while the suburbs are relegated to a mostly older, more established crowd. Homes in the biggest and most desirable Northwest (NW) district run an average of about $104,000 (condos), $536,000 (townhouses), and $714,000 (single-family homes). Prices in the Northeast (NE), Southeast (SE), and Southwest (SW) sections are considerably less—an average of $54,000 (condo), $126,500 (townhouse), and $156,000 (single-family). But the Washington real estate market seems more volatile than others; depending upon the economy and political climate, median costs can go up or down several thousand dollars in a year.

> Survival in the Washington work world requires a certain Machiavellian sensibility. Indiscretion is damaging—as in the case of one individual who joked about doing away with a certain political figure and found a passel of Secret Service agents waiting outside his gym locker.

Although it's only 10 square miles, the District offers a variety of living situations. And given the transient nature of many appointments, it's logical that rentals would be the preferred residence of newcomers. Here again, quadrant dictates rent, with the NW being the priciest (from $500 for the least expensive studio to $1,800 for a two-bedroom) and having the greatest selection, followed by the NE (studio: $408; three-bedroom: $1,090), SW (studio: $350; two-bedroom: $998), then SE (studio: $349; three-bedroom: $700).

Rather than cost, however, the neighborhood itself may help determine your choice (all are NW, unless otherwise noted). The Adams-Morgan area consists of long-time denizens, international transplants, young professionals, and students. Capitol Hill (ground zero for the city's quadrants) provides renovated Federal and Victorian residences while Foggy Bottom offers quaint, colorful row houses and sleek condos.

In addition to a strong gay community, DuPont Circle has a lively nightlife and elegant brownstones in a parklike setting. Although it costs dearly, Georgetown offers architectural variety and a chance to live among the nation's social and political elite.

Also appealing are Cleveland Park, with its Midwestern ambience; Takoma Park, a hub for artists and political activists; Kalorama, where some of the city's real money resides in mansions amid Embassy Row; LeDroit Park, prime real estate for middle-class African-Americans; and Shaw, the black business district, which has recently been revitalized. One of The District's oldest communities, scenic Anacosta (SE) is also undergoing rejuvenation, while those looking for convenience and variety might find it in the Southwest part of town.

Lower cost of living, countrified atmosphere, and slower pace have caused apartments and condos to blossom in the suburban communities of Northern Virginia and in Maryland. Old Town/Alexandria, Crystal City, Rosslyn, and Arlington in Virginia are but a short hop over the Potomac. Chevy Chase, Rockville, Bethesda, and Silver Spring are preferred Maryland suburbs for the great washed.

With more than 80,000 elementary students speaking 90 languages and coming from more than 130 nations, D.C. public schools (724-4289 or 724-4044) are certainly diverse. A high student-teacher ratio, generous expenditure per student, and specialized high schools can provide an excellent education for those who are motivated. Conversely, a "Street Academy" offers aid to dropouts wanting to come back and earn their degrees, and there's even a special academy for youngsters working as pages on Capitol Hill (like everything else in this city, school programs are contingent upon U.S. government approval).

The area also has dozens of private and parochial institutions as well. Affiliated churches, the Association of Independent Schools in Greater Washington (Washington, DC 20016) and the Independent School Guide (301/986-5370) can provide information.

Those who wish to continue their education can attend universities/colleges, trade and technical schools, and adult education and vocational instruction courses. The area's renowned colleges include American and George Washington universities; Gallaudet University for the deaf and hard-of-hearing; Georgetown, the oldest Catholic college in the U.S.; and Howard University, one of the country's finest black colleges, to mention a few. If you lose one job in Washington, you can always train for another.

NAVIGATING WASHINGTON, D.C.

Even if you don't know north from south, the NW, NE, SW, and SE designations are vital to locating places within The District. Otherwise, you might be fending off gangsters by the Anacosta River rather than enjoying the Reflecting Pool near various monuments. Don't even try to figure out the logic behind the streets: those running north-south are numbered, while those going east-west are lettered A to W—with the exclusion of "J" and with "I" sometimes written as "Eye." It's a French thing. Avenues are named after states and circles for famous Americans, and the city is bisected with the Capitol Building at the center. Just get the best route, have a map handy and never, ever forget the address of your destination. In a city where over half the people are tourists and many others are internationals, asking for directions can be an exercise in futility.

Even if they do own a car, most residents take the Metrorail/Metrobus ("Metro," 637-7000) to get around. Parking is often difficult or expensive, and like many big cities, D.C. has its share of crazy drivers and traffic jams.

Even though public transportation also runs to many outlying areas, suburbs and towns are also easily accessible via the Capital Beltway (I-95 and I-495); I-295 and I-395; U.S. Routes 1, 29 and 50; the Baltimore-Washington Parkway; and I-66 and I-270.

Washington's three airports provide easy migration as well. The largest, Baltimore/Washington International (BWI, 301/261-1000) offers the full range of international/domestic flights. Washington/Dulles (703/661-2700) has a variety of flights too. Closer to The District and also accessible by Metrorail is Washington National (703/661-2700), which provides domestic, commuter, and regional service. Amtrak (906-4971) is very much a presence here. And MTA/Marc Train Service (800/325-RAIL) provides inexpensive and convenient service to points around Maryland. Those wanting to leave town with a minimum of fanfare can always opt for Greyhound/Trailways at the downtown bus terminal (371-2111).

CITIES RANKED

Table 1: Cities Ranked by Cost of Living

This table is an estimate utilizing a scale of 100 against which most large American cities are measured. Cities with an overall ACCRA rating below 100 are considered less expensive; those over 100 are more expensive. Source: ACCRA Cost of Living Index.

City	Cost of Living
Toronto	N/A
Vancouver	N/A
Louisville	90.5
New Orleans	94.2
Nashville	94.3
San Antonio	94.5
Houston	95.2
Kansas City	95.2
Charlotte	97.2
Charleston	97.5
Orlando	98.1
Salt Lake City	99.6
Atlanta	100.9
Minneapolis/St. Paul	100.9*
Albuquerque	101.2
Denver	103.1
Phoenix	103.1
Cleveland	103.8
Milwaukee	104.2
Portland	107.4
Los Angeles	117.1
Seattle	120.3
San Diego	121.7
Chicago	123.3
Philadelphia	127.2
Washington, D.C.	127.4
Pittsburgh	133.3
Boston	139.8
San Francisco	167.5
New York	223.8**

Average for two cities (Minneapolis = 99.7; St. Paul = 102.1).

** *Manhattan only.*

Table 2: Cities Ranked by Per Capita Income

The following table estimates the amount of money available (through income, Social Security, government assistance, property and other assets, and other sources) for each individual in a given city. Because it encompasses everyone, such as the unemployed or retired, it's usually a low figure. Sources: *America's Top Rated Cities* and *World Book*.

City	Per Capita Income
Charleston	N/A
Toronto	N/A
Cleveland	$9,258
New Orleans	11,372
Louisville	11,527
San Antonio	11,865
Philadelphia	12,091
Pittsburgh	12,580
Chicago	12,899
Salt Lake City	13,482
Kansas City	13,799
Orlando	13,879
Albuquerque	14,013
Phoenix	14,096
Houston	14,261
Portland	14,478
Minneapolis/St. Paul	14,830
Atlanta	15,279
Boston	15,581
Denver	15,590
Los Angeles	16,188
New York	16,281
San Diego	16,401
Charlotte	16,793
Seattle	18,308
Washington, D.C.	18,881
San Francisco	19,695
Milwaukee	21,797
Nashville	23,655
Vancouver	27,476*

* Canadian dollars

Table 3: Cities Ranked by Percentage of Residents in 25-44 age group

The following table lists the percentage of residents in the 25–44 age group in each city.
Sources: *America's Top Rated Cities* and *World Book.*

City	Percentage of Residents Ages 25-44
Toronto	N/A
Pittsburgh	30.3
Philadelphia	30.8
Cleveland	31.7
Louisville	31.9
Kansas City	32.4
San Antonio	32.4
Milwaukee	32.6
New Orleans	32.8
Chicago	33.3
Salt Lake City	33.7
New York	33.9
Atlanta	34.7
Charleston	34.7
Phoenix	35.2
Albuquerque	35.4
Vancouver	35.7
Washington, D.C.	35.9
Los Angeles	36.0
Nashville	36.2
Orlando	36.4
San Diego	36.6
Boston	36.8
Houston	36.9
Portland	37.0
Charlotte	37.3
Denver	37.6
Seattle	37.7
San Francisco	38.2
Minneapolis/St. Paul	39.2

Table 4: Cities Ranked by Average Apartment Rent

The following table shows the average monthly rent for an apartment in each city. Source: ACCRA Cost of Living Index.

City	Average Monthly Rent
Charlotte	$484
Louisville	505
Orlando	518
Salt Lake City	527
Pittsburgh	528
New Orleans	538
Nashville	546
San Antonio	555
Charleston	557
Atlanta	561
Minneapolis/St. Paul	609*
Phoenix	618
Houston	620
Kansas City	636
Toronto	641**
Portland	645
Cleveland	647
Seattle	649
Albuquerque	656
San Diego	679
Milwaukee	684
Denver	698
Philadelphia	723
Los Angeles	725
Vancouver	777**
Chicago	827
Washington, D.C.	968
Boston	1057
San Francisco	1162
New York	2820

*Average for two cities (Minneapolis = 598; St. Paul = 620).

** Canadian dollars

RESOURCES

ALBUQUERQUE

Albuquerque Convention and Visitors Bureau
121 Tijeras NE, Albuquerque, NM 87102
(505) 842-9919

The Greater Albuquerque Chamber of Commerce
401 Second Street NW, Albuquerque, NM 87125
(505) 764-3700

ATLANTA

Atlanta Convention and Visitors Bureau
233 Peachtree Street, Atlanta, GA 30303
(404) 521-6600

Atlanta Area Chamber of Commerce
235 International Boulevard NW, Atlanta, GA 30303
(404) 880-9000

BOSTON

Greater Boston Convention and Visitors Bureau
Prudential Plaza, Boston, MA 02199
(617) 536-4100

Greater Boston Chamber of Commerce
One Beacon Street, 4th Floor, Boston, MA 02108
(617) 227-4500

CHARLESTON

Charleston Trident Convention and Visitors Bureau
81 Mary Street, Charleston, SC 29402
(803) 853-8000

Charleston Trident Chamber of Commerce
81 Mary Street, Charleston, SC 29402
(803) 577-2510

CHARLOTTE

Charlotte Convention and Visitors Bureau
122 East Stonewall Street, Charlotte, NC 28202
(704) 331-2283

Charlotte Chamber of Commerce
129 West Trade Street, Charlotte, NC 28202
(704) 378-1300

CHICAGO

Chicago Convention and Visitors Bureau
McCormick Place, Chicago, IL 60616
(312) 567-8500

Chicagoland Chamber of Commerce
200 North LaSalle Street, Chicago, IL 60601
(312) 580-6900

CLEVELAND

Cleveland Convention and Visitors Bureau
3100 Terminal Tower, Cleveland, OH 44114
(216) 621-4111

Greater Cleveland Chamber of Commerce
200 Tower City Center, Cleveland, OH 44114
(216) 621-3300

DENVER

Denver Metro Convention and Visitors Bureau
225 West Colfax Avenue, Denver, CO 80202
(303) 892-1113

Greater Denver Chamber of Commerce
1445 Market Street, Denver, CO 80202
(303) 534-8500

HOUSTON

Greater Houston Convention and Visitors Bureau
801 Congress Avenue, Houston, TX 77002
(713) 227-3101

KANSAS CITY

Greater Kansas City Convention and Visitors Bureau
1100 Main Street, Kansas City, MO 64105
(800) 767-7700

Greater Kansas City Chamber of Commerce
2600 Commerce Towers, 911 Main St., Kansas City, MO 64105
(816) 221-2424

LOS ANGELES

Los Angeles Convention and Visitors Bureau
633 West Fifth Street, Los Angeles, CA 90024
(213) 624-7301

Los Angeles Area Chamber of Commerce
404 South Bixel Street, Los Angeles, CA 90051
(213) 629-0602

Economic Development Corporation
515 S. Flower St., 32nd Floor, Los Angeles, CA 90071
(213) 622-4300

LOUISVILLE

Louisville Convention and Visitors Bureau
400 South First Street, Louisville, KY 40202
(800) 626-5646

Louisville Area Chamber of Commerce
600 West Main Street, Louisville, KY 40202
(502) 625-0000

MILWAUKEE

Greater Milwaukee Convention and Visitors Bureau
510 West Kilbourn Avenue, Milwaukee, WI 53203
(414) 273-3950

Metro Milwaukee Association of Commerce
756 North Milwaukee Street, Milwaukee, WI 53202
(414) 287-4100

MINNEAPOLIS/ST. PAUL

Greater Minneapolis Convention and Visitors Bureau
33 South Sixth Street, Minneapolis, MN 55402
(612) 348-4313

Greater Minneapolis Chamber of Commerce
81 South Ninth Street, Minneapolis, MN 55402
(612) 370-9132

St. Paul Area Chamber of Commerce
55 East Fifth Street, St. Paul, MN 55101
(612) 223-5000

St. Paul Convention and Visitors Bureau
55 East Fifth Street, St. Paul, MN 55101
(612) 297-6985

NASHVILLE

Nashville Convention and Visitors Bureau
161 Fourth Avenue N, Nashville, TN 37219
(615) 259-4747

Nashville Chamber of Commerce
161 Fourth Avenue N, Nashville, TN 37219
(615) 259-4700

NEW ORLEANS

Greater New Orleans Convention and Visitors Bureau
1520 Sugar Bowl Drive, New Orleans, LA 70112
(504) 566-5011

The Chamber/New Orleans and the River Region
301 Camp Street, New Orleans, LA 70130
(504) 527-6900

NEW YORK

New York Convention and Visitors Bureau
2 Columbus Circle & 59th Street, New York, NY 10019
(212) 397-8222

New York Chamber of Commerce
1 Battery Park Plaza, New York, NY 10004
(212) 493-7500

New York City Economic Development Program
110 William Street, New York, NY 10038
(212) 619-5000

ORLANDO

Orlando/Orange County Convention and Visitors Bureau
8445 International Drive, Orlando, FL 32819
(407) 363-5892

Greater Orlando Chamber of Commerce
75 East Ivanhoe Boulevard, Orlando, FL 32802
(407) 425-1234

PHILADELPHIA

Philadelphia Convention and Visitors Bureau
1515 Market Street, Philadelphia, PA 19102
(215) 636-1667

Greater Philadelphia Chamber of Commerce
1234 Market Street, Philadelphia, PA 19107
(215) 545-1234

PHOENIX

Phoenix and Valley Convention and Visitors Bureau
1 Arizona Center, Phoenix, AZ 85004
(602) 254-6500

Phoenix Metro Chamber of Commerce
34 West Monroe Street, Phoenix, AZ 85003
(602) 254-5521

PITTSBURGH

Greater Pittsburgh Convention and Visitors Bureau
4 Gateway Center, Pittsburgh, PA 15222
(412) 281-7712

Greater Pittsburgh Chamber of Commerce
3 Gateway Center, Pittsburgh, PA 15222
(412) 392-4500

PORTLAND

Portland Visitors Association
26 SW Salmon Street, Portland, OR 97204
(503) 275-9751

SALT LAKE CITY

Salt Lake Convention and Visitors Bureau
180 S. West Temple Street, Salt Lake City, UT 84101
(801) 521-2822

Salt Lake Area Chamber of Commerce
175 E. 400 South, 6th Floor, Salt Lake City, UT 84111
(801) 364-3631

SAN ANTONIO

San Antonio Convention and Visitors Bureau
121 Alamo Plaza, San Antonio, TX 78298
(210) 270-8701

Greater San Antonio Chamber of Commerce
602 East Commerce, San Antonio, TX 78296
(210) 229-2100

SAN DIEGO

San Diego Convention and Visitors Bureau
401 B Street, San Diego, CA 92101
(619) 232-3101

Greater San Diego Chamber of Commerce
402 W. Broadway, Suite 1000, San Diego, CA 92101
(619) 232-0124

SAN FRANCISCO

San Francisco Convention and Visitors Bureau
201 Third Street, San Francisco, CA 94101
(415) 391-2000

San Francisco Chamber of Commerce
465 California Street, San Francisco, CA 94101
(415) 392-4511

SEATTLE

Seattle–King County Convention and Visitors Bureau
520 Pike Street, Seattle, WA 98101
(206) 461-5840

Greater Seattle Chamber of Commerce
1301 5th Avenue, Seattle, WA 98101
(206) 389-7200

TORONTO

Tourism Toronto/Metropolitan Toronto Convention and Visitors Association
P.O. Box 127, 207 Queens Way West, Toronto, Ontario, Canada M5J 1A7
(800) 363-1990

Community Information Centre
425 Adelaide St. West, 2nd Floor, Toronto, Ontario, Canada M5V 3C1
(416) 392-0505

VANCOUVER

Tourism Vancouver/Greater Vancouver Convention and Visitors Bureau
Suite 210, Waterfront Centre, 200 Burrard St., Vancouver, BC, Canada V6C 3L6
(604) 682-2222

The Vancouver Board of Trade
World Trade Centre, Suite 400, 999 Canada Place, Vancouver, BC, Canada V6C 3C1
(604) 681-2111

WASHINGTON, D.C.

Washington, D.C. Convention and Visitors Bureau
1212 New York Avenue NW, Washington, DC 20004
(202) 789-7000

Washington, D.C. Chamber of Commerce
1301 Pennsylvania Avenue NW, Washington, DC 20004
(202) 638-3222